Cracking the
GED® Test

2019 Edition

The Staff of The Princeton Review

PrincetonReview.com

Penguin
Random
House

The Princeton Review
110 East 42nd Street, 7th Floor
New York, NY 10017
E-mail: editorialsupport@review.com

ISBN: 978-1-5247-5792-2
eBook ISBN: 978-1-5247-5827-1
ISSN: 1076-5352

Editor: Meave Shelton
Production Editors: Jim Melloan and Kathy G. Carter
Production Artist: Deborah Weber

Printed in the United States of America on partially recycled paper.

10 9 8 7 6 5 4 3 2 1

2019 Edition

Editorial
Rob Franek, Editor-in-Chief
Casey Cornelius, Chief Product Officer
Mary Beth Garrick, Executive Director of Production
Craig Patches, Production Design Manager
Selena Coppock, Managing Editor
Meave Shelton, Senior Editor
Colleen Day, Editor
Sarah Litt, Editor
Aaron Riccio, Editor
Orion McBean, Associate Editor

Penguin Random House Publishing Team
Tom Russell, VP, Publisher
Alison Stoltzfus, Publishing Director
Amanda Yee, Associate Managing Editor
Ellen Reed, Production Manager
Suzanne Lee, Designer

Acknowledgments

Many thanks to the following contributors for their hard work and tireless dedication to the ongoing revision of this book: Joshua Nagel, David Stoll, Kimberly Beth Hollingsworth, Chris Chimera, Erik Kolb, Eliz Markowitz, Becky Robinson, Linda Kelley, Andy Olson, Katie Williams, Chris Hinkle, Kevin Kelly, Gina Donegan, Alexandra Wax Henkoff, Lisa Mayo, and Graham Skelhorne-Gross.

Special thanks to Adam Robinson, who conceived of and perfected the Joe Bloggs approach to standardized tests, and many of the other successful techniques used by The Princeton Review.

Finally, a big round of applause to the production team, Jim Melloan, Kathy G. Carter, and Deborah Weber, for their hard work on this edition.

Contents

Get More (Free) Content

1 Go to **PrincetonReview.com/cracking.**

2 Enter the following ISBN for your book: 9781524757922.

3 Answer a few simple questions to set up an exclusive Princeton Review account. (If you already have one, you can just log in.)

4 Click the "Student Tools" button, also found under "My Account" from the top toolbar. You're all set to access your bonus content!

Need to report a potential **content** issue?

Contact **EditorialSupport@review.com.**
Include:
- full title of the book
- ISBN number
- page number

Need to report a **technical** issue?

Contact **TPRStudentTech@review.com** and provide:
- your full name
- email address used to register the book
- full book title and ISBN
- computer OS (Mac/PC) and browser (Firefox, Safari, etc.)

The Princeton Review®

Once you've registered, you can...

- Supplement your GED® test prep with 8 multiple-choice drills organized by subject (350+ questions total)

- Access insider tips on the GED® test and college success

- Download bonus tutorials on reading comprehension and understanding graphics

- Print out custom answer sheets for the full-length practice tests in this book

- Check to see if there have been any corrections or updates to this edition

- Get our take on any recent or pending updates to the GED® test

GED Ready®: The Official Practice Test

- With your purchase of this book, you are entitled to 20% off the price of the GED Testing Service's official GED® practice test.

- Visit **www.gedmarketplace.com/theprincetonreview** for step-by-step instructions on how to receive this discount.

Look For These Icons Throughout The Book

 ONLINE PRACTICE DRILLS

 ONLINE ARTICLES

 MORE GREAT BOOKS

 PROVEN TECHNIQUES

 APPLIED STRATEGIES

 ASK YOURSELF

 WATCH OUT

 TIME-SAVING TIP

Part I
The GED® Test and You

Chapter 1
How to Use This Book to Achieve a Passing (or a College-Ready) Score

In this chapter, you will assess your goals and learn how to most effectively use this book to ensure you perform your best on the GED® test.

CONGRATULATIONS!

You are reading this book because you want to make a better future for yourself, and that future begins with obtaining the equivalent of a high school degree. The doors that will open depend on your personal and professional goals, as the many successful people who earned a GED® test degree—including some famous people listed nearby—can tell you. We admire your motivation and congratulate you on your decision.

We are also delighted that you have chosen to use this book to prepare for the GED® test. We have helped millions of people achieve their goals, and we are honored to have the privilege of helping you. Your road to a passing—or even a College-Ready—score involves a combination of content, reading skills, writing skills, test-taking skills, practice, and self-evaluation.

The chapters in this book address the content and skills you need, and it is your job to learn the content and practice the skills. Most chapters contain drills that will help you assess your mastery. Answers and explanations for these drills can be found in Part VIII. Moreover, there are two full-length practice tests (along with answers and explanations) in Part IX. While the tests are not computer-based like the actual GED® test, they *are* representative of the number and types of questions you will encounter. You should take these tests under simulated testing conditions. In the pages that follow, we suggest when you should take each test.

Of course, we understand that your needs may differ from someone else's, and we want to ensure that you get exactly what you need from this book. To that end, this chapter will guide you on the proper use of this book based upon your particular knowledge, needs, and goals.

Please begin by answering the three questions below and reading the Road Map that follows.

Famous People Who Earned Their GED® Test Credential

Wally Amos, founder of Famous Amos Cookies
Augusten Burroughs, bestselling author
Ben Nighthorse Campbell, former U.S. Senator
Dr. Richard Carmona, former U.S. Surgeon General
Michael Chang, tennis champion
Eminem, rapper, actor, and record producer
Drake, rapper, songwriter, and actor
D. L. Hughley, political commentator and comedian
Bishop T. D. Jakes, pastor, author, and filmmaker
Peter Jennings, journalist and news anchor
Honorable Greg Mathis, U.S. District Court judge
Ruth Ann Minner, former Governor of Delaware
F. Story Musgrave, NASA shuttle astronaut
Danica Patrick, auto racing champion
Mary Lou Retton, Olympic gold medalist
Michelle Rodriguez, actor and screenwriter
Chris Rock, comedian and actor
Hilary Swank, Academy Award–winning actor
Dave Thomas, founder of Wendy's
Mark Wahlberg, actor and producer

SELF-ASSESSMENT: MY FAMILIARITY WITH THE GED® TEST

1. I am familiar with the structure of the GED® test, how it is scored, and how to register for the test. ☐ *Yes* ☐ *No*
2. I am familiar with the look and feel of the GED® test, including various functionalities, such as the calculator and review screens. ☐ *Yes* ☐ *No*
3. I am familiar with the format of the question types that appear on the GED® test. ☐ *Yes* ☐ *No*

Pace Yourself
Doing a little studying each day is much better than trying to cram it all into one week.

Road Map

- If you answered *No* to either of questions 1 or 2, read Chapter 2 (or the relevant parts of Chapter 2) *before* you complete this chapter.
- If you answered *No* to question 3, read Chapter 3. You may do so now or after you complete this chapter.
- Even if you answered *Yes* to all three questions, we encourage you to read the Other Resources section on page 18 of Chapter 2. You may do so now or after you complete this chapter.

Next, proceed through the following steps.

Step One: Answer each group of questions below.
Step Two: Take the first practice test (Chapter 23).
Step Three: Review and, if appropriate, change your answers to the questions below.
Step Four: Read and follow the Road Map that follows each group of questions below.

Custom Answer Sheets!
When taking the Practice Tests, feel free to use the answer sheets at the back of this book. These are also available to print out via your Student Tools when you register your book online (see pages viii–ix for details).

SELF-ASSESSMENT: MY TEST-TAKING ABILITIES

4. I want to learn or to improve my ability to apply relevant test-taking strategies that an effective tester utilizes. ☐ *Yes* ☐ *No*
5. I want to improve my ability to read and analyze charts, graphs, and other data-based figures. ☐ *Yes* ☐ *No*
6. I want to improve my ability to read and understand text, regardless of which one of the four GED® tests I am taking. ☐ *Yes* ☐ *No*

Road Map

- If you answered *Yes* to question 4, complete Chapter 4.
- If you answered *Yes* to question 5, complete the "Understanding Graphics" tutorial, available for download when you register your book online.
- If you answered *Yes* to question 6, complete the "Reading Comprehension" tutorial, also available for download.

SELF-ASSESSMENT: MY LEVEL OF MASTERY—REASONING THROUGH LANGUAGE ARTS

7. I want to improve my mastery of answering reading questions relating to informational passages. ☐ *Yes* ☐ *No*
8. I want to improve my mastery of answering reading questions relating to literary passages. ☐ *Yes* ☐ *No*
9. I want to improve my mastery of answering language questions. ☐ *Yes* ☐ *No*
10. I want to improve my ability to write extended response answers. ☐ *Yes* ☐ *No*

Road Map

- If you answered *Yes* to question 7, complete Chapters 5 and 6.
- If you answered *Yes* to question 8, complete Chapters 5 and 7.
- If you answered *Yes* to question 9, complete Chapters 8 and 9.
- If you answered *Yes* to question 10, complete Chapters 10 and 11.
- Even if you answered *No* to any of questions 7 through 10, we recommend that you complete Chapters 5, 8, and 10, as well as the drills in Chapters 6, 7, 9, and 11.

SELF-ASSESSMENT: MY LEVEL OF MASTERY— MATHEMATICAL REASONING

11. I want to refine my mastery of one or more of the following concepts of basic arithmetic. ☐ *Yes* ☐ *No*
   - The number line
   - Rounding off
   - Multiplying positive and negative numbers
   - Absolute values
   - Order of operations (PEMDAS)
   - Commutative and distributive properties
   - Factors and multiples
   - Fractions
   - Decimals
   - Percents

12. I want to refine my mastery of one or more of the following concepts of applied arithmetic. ☐ *Yes* ☐ *No*
    - Setup problems
    - Mean, median, mode, range, and weighted mean
    - Ratios and proportions
    - Rate problems
    - Scale and unit conversion
    - Charts and graphs
    - Exponents
    - Radicals
    - Scientific notation
    - Probability
    - Combinations and permutations

13. I want to refine my mastery of one or more of the following concepts of algebra. ☐ *Yes* ☐ *No*
    - Simple equations
    - Inequalities
    - Translating English into math
    - Polynomials
    - Quadratic equations
    - Rational expressions
    - Simultaneous equations
    - Functions

14. I would like to learn a test-taking strategy that may, on certain algebra problems, make those problems easier to solve. ☐ *Yes* ☐ *No*

15. I want to refine my mastery of one or more of the following concepts of geometry. ☐ *Yes* ☐ *No*
    - Lines and angles
    - Rectangles and squares
    - Triangles and pyramids
    - Circles, spheres, cylinders, and cones
    - Setup geometry
    - Graphing (the coordinate plane)
    - Equation of a line

Road Map

- If you answered *Yes* to question 11, complete Chapter 12 and all or the relevant parts of Chapter 13.
- If you answered *Yes* to question 12, complete Chapter 12 and all or the relevant parts of Chapter 14.
- If you answered *Yes* to question 13, complete Chapter 12 and all or the relevant parts of Chapter 15.
- If you answered *Yes* to question 14, complete the Backsolving section in Chapter 15.
- If you answered *Yes* to question 15, complete Chapter 12 and all or the relevant parts of Chapter 16.
- Even if you answered *No* to any of questions 11 through 15, we recommend that you complete Chapter 12, as well as the drills in Chapters 13 through 16.

SELF-ASSESSMENT: MY LEVEL OF MASTERY—SOCIAL STUDIES

16. I want to refine my mastery of civics and government. ☐ *Yes* ☐ *No*
17. I want to refine my mastery of United States history. ☐ *Yes* ☐ *No*
18. I want to refine my mastery of economics. ☐ *Yes* ☐ *No*
19. I want to refine my mastery of geography. ☐ *Yes* ☐ *No*

Road Map

- If you answered *Yes* to question 16, complete Chapter 17 and all or the relevant parts of Chapter 18.
- If you answered *Yes* to question 17, complete Chapter 17 and all or the relevant parts of Chapter 18.
- If you answered *Yes* to question 18, complete Chapter 17 and all or the relevant parts of Chapter 19.
- If you answered *Yes* to question 19, complete Chapter 17 and all or the relevant part of Chapter 19.
- Even if you answered *No* to any of questions 16 through 19, we recommend that you complete Chapter 17, as well as the drills in Chapters 18 through 19.

SELF-ASSESSMENT: MY LEVEL OF MASTERY—SCIENCE

21. I want to refine my mastery of one or more of the following concepts of life sciences. ☐ *Yes* ☐ *No*
    - The scientific method
    - Cell theory and the origins of life
    - Genetics
    - Evolution and natural selection
    - Plants
    - Ecosystems and food chains
    - The human body and human health
    - Bacteria and viruses
22. I want to refine my mastery of one or more of the following concepts of physical and earth sciences. ☐ *Yes* ☐ *No*
    - Energy and heat
    - Physical laws, work, and motion
    - Waves and radiation
    - Solids, liquids, and gases
    - Chemical reactions
    - The changing earth
    - Glaciers, erosion, and the ice ages
    - Natural resources and sustainability
    - Fossils
    - Astronomy

Road Map

- If you answered *Yes* to question 21, complete Chapter 20 and all or the relevant parts of Chapter 21.
- If you answered *Yes* to question 22, complete Chapter 20 and all or the relevant parts of Chapter 22.
- Even if you answered *No* to either of questions 21 or 22, we recommend that you complete Chapter 20, as well as the drills in Chapters 21 and 22.

SELF-ASSESSMENT: MY SCORE GOALS

23. My goal is to achieve a *Passing/College-Ready* score.

Road Map

- If you answered *College-Ready*, we recommend that you complete all chapters in this book, without regard to the Road Maps above.

After you have completed the chapters according to your Road Map, you should take the second practice test (Chapter 25). If the test indicates areas on which you should try to further improve, revisit the appropriate chapters.

Also, remember that you have access to other resources as described on page 18.

If you follow the steps outlined above, are diligent in your work, and assess your progress throughout your preparation, by the time you sit for the GED® test, you should find it familiar and manageable, and you should be able to take it with confidence!

Happy studies and best wishes for a successful future!

Chapter 2
All About the
GED® Test

This chapter will summarize the structure, scoring, and look and feel of the GED® test, and provide important information about other available resources.

WHAT IS THE GED® TEST?

G-E-D Spells Success!
Adults who earn a GED® credential can earn the same level of weekly wages as high school graduates, increasing their earning potential by about $115 a week.
(Source: GED Testing Service)

The GED® test is actually four tests that you can take in one day or over a series of days. Many people refer to it as a high school equivalency test because when you pass the test, you earn a credential that most colleges and employers recognize as the equivalent of a high school diploma.

The questions on the test come in several formats, which we'll describe in Chapter 3. The questions are supposed to measure your knowledge of some of the subjects taught in high school. However, the GED® test writers don't expect you to remember specific details. For example, you will *not* be asked what year Columbus came to America or which planet is farthest away from the sun. If the test writers want to ask about Columbus, they will first provide you with a short reading passage about him, and then they will ask questions based on that passage. If the test writers want to ask about the planets, they will first give you a diagram of the solar system and then ask you questions based on that diagram.

The Four GED® Tests

1. **Reasoning Through Language Arts**
   (150 minutes, approximately 51 questions)

   • Section 1 (35 minutes)
   • Section 2: One Extended Response question (45 minutes)
   • Break (10 minutes)
   • Section 3 (60 minutes)

   Sections 1 and 3 will contain a mixture of grammar and reading comprehension questions. There will be six to eight reading passages with approximately six questions each and two language passages with four drop-down questions in each. The questions for the reading passages will be multiple choice or drag and drop. The reading texts will be in this approximate distribution:

   | Informational Texts | 75% |
   | Literature | 25% |

   In Section 2, you'll be asked to write an essay analyzing two passages that present different views on the same subject. You'll be asked to develop an opinion and support that opinion with specific examples from the text.

2. Mathematical Reasoning
(115 minutes, 46 questions)

- Part 1 (first 5 questions): calculator not allowed
- Part 2 (remaining 41 questions): calculator allowed

The Mathematical Reasoning test comes in two parts. In the first, you will not be allowed to use a calculator. In the second, you will have access to the on-screen calculator. The first section will test your ability to do basic calculations. In the second section, you will be asked to answer questions common in many work scenarios.

Many of these will be word problems. About one-half of the questions will be based on diagrams or charts. These questions come in several formats including multiple choice, fill in the blank, drag and drop, hot spot, and drop down. The test will encompass the following mathematical concepts:

Quantitative Problem Solving (arithmetic, averages, ratios, etc.)	45%
Algebraic Problem Solving	55%

3. Social Studies
(70 minutes, approximately 35 questions)

You will find a mixture of passages, charts, graphs, and maps. The questions will be in multiple-choice, hot-spot, drag-and-drop, and fill-in-the-blank formats. The test will cover the following areas of social studies:

Government and Civics	50%
U.S. History	20%
Economics	15%
Geography	15%

Your GED® Credential Can Lead to a College Degree!
About 95 percent of U.S. colleges and universities accept GED® graduates in the same manner as high school graduates.
(Source: GED Testing Service)

4. Science
(90 minutes, 1 section of approximately 34 questions)

The questions will be based on a variety of information ranging from short passages to graphs and charts. The questions will be in multiple-choice, fill-in-the-blank, drop-down, drag-and-drop, and hot-spot formats. You can also expect to see two short-answer questions that will *not* be timed separately. (Note that, according to GED Testing Service, short-answer questions are not expected to appear on the test forms in 2018 but may be included on future Science tests.) The answers to the questions are almost always supplied in the passages or graphic materials. You need only a *general knowledge* of scientific principles. The questions will be about these general areas of science:

Life Science	40%
Physics and Chemistry	40%
Earth and Space Science	20%

Do You Have to Take the Test All at Once?

The GED Testing Service does not require that students take the test all in one sitting. However, each state has its own rules about this. To find out what your state's policies are, visit www.gedtestingservice.com/testers/2014policypages.

How Is the GED® Test Scored?

For each of the four tests, you will receive a score between 100 and 200. Because each test has a different number of available points, the GED Testing Service will standardize your raw scores (or the number of questions you answered correctly for each test) through a scoring metric to yield a score between 100 and 200. It's important to remember that **there is no penalty for wrong answers or questions left blank**, so it is to your advantage to record an answer to every question.

GED® Test Score Levels
145–164:
Pass/High School Equivalency
165–174:
GED® College Ready
175–200:
GED® College Ready + Credit

The minimum score needed to pass any of the four subject tests on the GED® test is 145. In order to get your completion certificate, you must achieve at least this score on each test. A higher score on one test will not make up for a lower score on another. While a passing score is sufficient to obtain your certificate, you may want to strive for a score of at least 165. Such a score entitles you to a GED® College-Ready Score, a distinction that indicates college and career readiness. And if you achieve a score of at least 175, you'll receive the GED® College Ready + Credit designation, which means that in addition to being ready to take college courses, you qualify for up to 10 hours of college credit.

Once you receive a passing score on a test, you do not need to retake that test. If you want to retake the test to receive a higher score, you may do so.

If you do not receive your desired score on a particular test, you can retake that test two more times without any waiting period, subject to scheduling availability. After the third attempt, you will have to wait 60 days to test again. This schedule allows for eight testing opportunities in a year, if you need that many to pass a section.

Registering for the GED® Test

The best ways to register are to call the information number for your state and/or visit the website www.ged.com. Once you have registered on the site, you will be emailed a letter with instructions on how to schedule your exam online. If you've been taking a preparation course, your teacher may take care of registration for you, but check to make sure this is the case. The tests are administered year-round, and the new online format allows for a lot more flexibility in scheduling, but in some of the larger states, it may take a while for you to get a test date. In most states, it now costs money to take the GED® test—the fee could be as little as $10, but in some states it can run as high as $400.

> **Need Information?**
> Call 877-EXAM-GED
> (877-392-6433).

For information on registering to take the GED® test and for classes in your area, call 877-392-6433 (877-EXAM-GED). To reach the individual state programs directly, go online to www.ged.com where you can type in your ZIP code to find the nearest testing centers and programs.

A COMPUTER-BASED TEST

The GED® test is taken on a computer at a testing center.

In some cases, a question will appear on a single screen. In other cases there will be a split screen, with a passage, chart, or other information on one side and the question on the other. At the bottom of each screen, you may click to move to the prior screen or the next screen. At the top, the question number, total number of questions, and time remaining for the test are shown.

> **Experience the Interface**
> You may experience the user interface and practice using the computer functionality by visiting www.gedtestingservice.com/educators/freepracticetest, where you will also find a Computer Skills Tutorial.

You are able to highlight text, change the foreground and background colors, and adjust the font size. You may also flag a question for later review.

For questions that require you to write, you will have access to cut, copy, and paste functions, as well as undo and redo. Where appropriate, an on-screen calculator is provided, as is a mathematical formulas sheet.

The Review Screen

A useful feature to help you keep track is the review screen. This screen is available at any time during the test and indicates which questions you have answered, which you have left blank, and which you have not read. It also indicates which questions you have marked for later review. From the review screen you can quickly jump to any questions that have been marked or left unanswered by clicking on the question number.

Here's an example of what your review screen will look like:

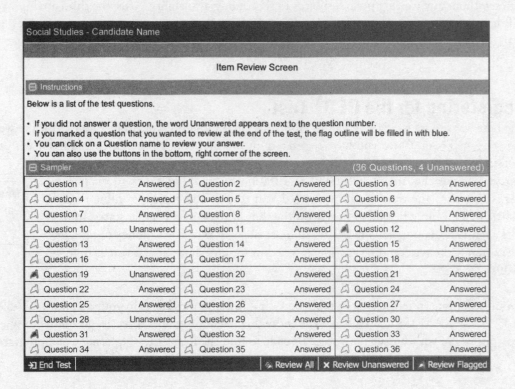

It is good practice to leave a few minutes at the end of each section of each test to check the review screen to make sure you have answered every question or to look up questions that you marked for later review. For any question you need to answer or revisit, you can click on the question number to go directly to the question. Remember that there is no guessing penalty, so do not leave any questions unanswered.

THE ERASABLE NOTE BOARDS

When you take the test, you will not have scratch paper. Rather, you will be provided with three erasable note boards, which are laminated pieces of thick cardboard, each the size of a sheet of legal paper (8.5 by 14 inches)—a little bit larger than a standard piece of notebook paper. You will be given one at the beginning of your test, along with a dry-erase marker. If the marker runs out of ink or dries up, you may ask for a new one.

Using a note board rather than writing directly on a test booklet takes practice. Get into the habit of working with practice scratch paper from the start (assuming that you don't have access to an erasable note board at home).

We recommend that you lay out a note-board strategy as outlined in the different sections of this book. You will have to transfer most of the information on the screen to a note board to work the problems. This is especially true for the Mathematical Reasoning test. Having a consistent way of transferring that information in an organized fashion will help you perform better on the exam.

It is important to note that only three note boards are allowed at a time. While you may use the front and back, you may have to erase work you did earlier once you've covered the entire surface of all three. A good rule of thumb is to always try to completely finish a problem before you move on to the next, to ensure you don't have to restart a problem from, well, scratch.

YOUR TEST RESULTS

One of the great features of a computer-based test is that you will receive your scores very quickly. In most cases you will receive your score within three hours of completion of each of the four tests.

There are a few exceptions to this: Your test center may be late in uploading your test data, or your test may be flagged by the computer for manual scoring. If your test is flagged for manual scoring, it doesn't mean there is anything wrong with your exam, or that you did anything wrong. It simply means that the computer randomly chose your exam to assure accuracy in scoring. If your test is flagged for manual scoring, your score should be available to you in three business days.

In either case, your scores will be available on MyGED™ at www.ged.com.

More Great Books
Thinking about college? Check out our guide books: *The Best 382 Colleges, Paying for College Without Going Broke,* and *Colleges That Create Futures.*

KEY DIFFERENCES BETWEEN THE GED® TEST AND OUR PRACTICE TESTS

While the practice tests in this book are closely modeled on the types of questions you'll see on the GED® test, there are some key differences you should know about.

Our Practice Tests Are Paper-Based

We've slightly adapted the GED® test's computer-based question formats to allow you to answer them without needing a mouse and keyboard. See the general directions at the beginning of Part IX for more information.

Scoring

As we mentioned earlier, GED Testing Service uses a formula to standardize your raw score. Unfortunately, this formula isn't publicly available.

If you want to score your work on the practice tests, you are welcome to tally up your raw score—the number of questions you answered correctly. This should give you a rough idea of how well you did. However, this does not translate into a measure of your readiness to take the GED® test. In other words, we can't promise you that you are likely to pass if you get a certain number of questions right.

GET GED READY®

Fortunately, we *can* point you to the best available indicator of how well you'll do: GED® Ready: The Official Practice Test.

GED Ready® was written by the test creators and gives you the full computer-based experience, as well as an Enhanced Score Report. Although GED Ready® is only half the length of the actual GED® test and doesn't require the same level of endurance, it will give you accurate feedback on your mastery of the content and required skills. You'll be able to access your score report within about an hour of completing the test.

Because you bought this book, you are entitled to a 20% discount off the price of GED Ready®. To access the discount and this feature, visit www.gedmarketplace.com/theprincetonreview.

OTHER RESOURCES

If you are looking for additional support, here are several resources.

PrincetonReview.com—If you register this book at PrincetonReview.com, you will have free access, via your Student Tools, to 350 more questions via eight computer-based multiple-choice drills, organized by subject. For each drill, you will receive an instant, detailed score report.

Exclusive Interview
Register your book online to gain access to these exclusive insider tips on the GED® test and college success! See pages viii–ix for details.

If you're thinking about college, check out our exclusive interview with an admissions counselor, who offers valuable insights on the GED® test credential and college success. In addition, the college section of PrincetonReview.com contains detailed profiles of colleges, ranking lists, and a free dynamic search engine to help you identify your *best fit* college. We also publish several books on colleges that you may find useful.

More Great Books—For more practice, check out our other titles. *5 Practice Exams for the GED® Test* gives you five full-length tests, and *Math Workout for the GED® Test* is chock-full of drills for every type of math question.

GEDTestingService.com—The official website for the GED® test contains a wealth of free useful information, such as test specifications, sample problems, FAQs, a tutorial on how to use the computer interface, and a short free practice test.

Chapter 3
Question Formats

In this chapter, we'll introduce you to the different question formats that you'll encounter on the GED® test.

Because you'll be taking this test on a computer, you will encounter several types of questions that may be unfamiliar to you. In addition to traditional multiple-choice questions, there are enhanced question formats that will require you to use the mouse to perform actions other than clicking the correct bubble.

In the following chapters, we'll give you clear guidance on how to approach these question formats as they apply to each of the four subjects. In this chapter, we'll familiarize you with the look and feel of each type of question and show you how to answer it.

Online Practice Drills

Register your book to gain free access to 350 multiple-choice questions in all 4 GED® test subjects, via your Student Tools. See pages viii-ix for details.

Multiple Choice

You can expect to see this question format on each of the four tests. Multiple-choice questions typically present you with a scenario and ask a question about it. There is one possible answer out of the four choices provided. In order to indicate your answer, use your mouse to click the bubble that corresponds to your answer.

Here is an example.

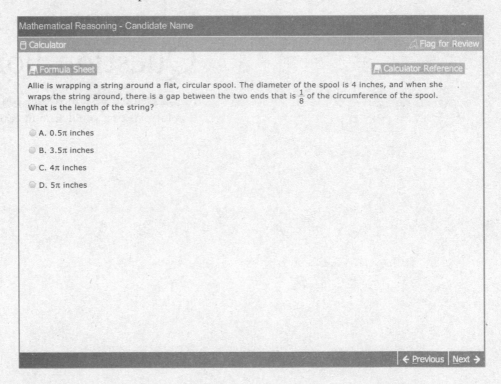

Drag and Drop

Drag-and-drop questions ask you to choose from several options and drag each option to the correct location in the question. Not only must you choose the correct options, you must also make sure to place them in the order requested. This question format appears in each of the four tests.

Your computer screen will look similar to the following set of images. Note that in order to see the complete question, you will need to click on the tab marked "page 2."

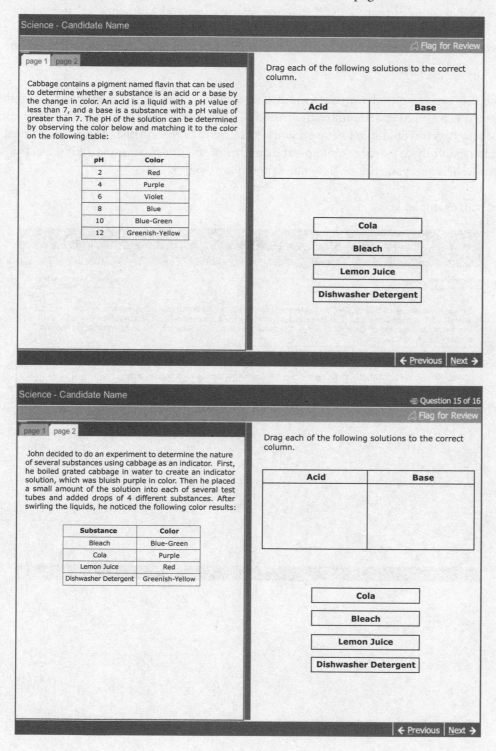

Hot Spot

Hot-spot questions appear in the Social Studies, Science, and Mathematical Reasoning tests. These questions give you a set of information and pose a question. In order to indicate your answer, use your mouse to click on one or several points in a chart or graph that represent possible answers.

While this type of question may seem unusual at first, it's really just a variation on multiple choice. When you have determined the answer, simply mouse over the area for the right answer and click. If you would like to erase a mark, click on it a second time. Make sure to read the question carefully to be sure you know the number of solutions the test is asking for. If it asks for two values and you click on only one, it could hurt your score.

Here is an example.

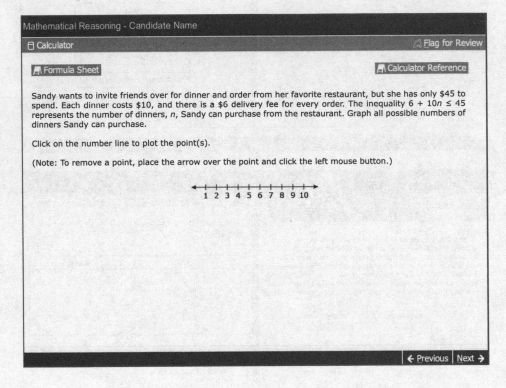

Fill in the Blank

Fill-in-the-blank questions are among the more difficult type of questions, and they appear in each of the four tests. These questions give you a set of information and ask a question. There are no answers provided, and you have to type in your own answer using your keyboard.

Because there are no answers to choose from, these questions are nearly impossible to guess on. Test takers must take care to enter their answer using the correct units and rounded to the correct place. When faced with this type of question, always reread the question to be sure you are correctly following the directions in drafting your answer.

Here is an example.

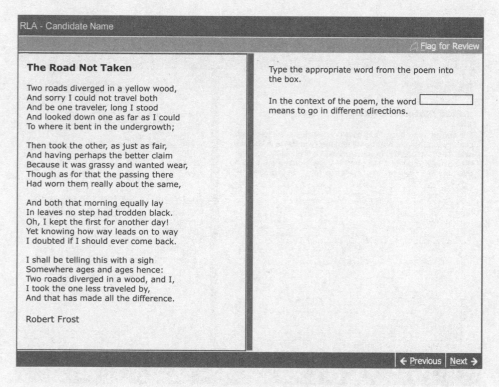

Drop Down

A drop-down question is most similar to a traditional multiple-choice question. It can appear on any of the four tests and is often used to place an answer in the context of a sentence. Use your mouse to click the arrow to the right of the box, and several answers appear in an expanded menu. To select an answer, click on your choice.

Because of their similarity to multiple-choice questions, drop-down questions should feel somewhat familiar. However, it is important to remember to open the box and see the options *before* you try the question. Doing so can greatly reduce the amount of time you spend on the question, as it reduces the number of options to consider.

Here is an example.

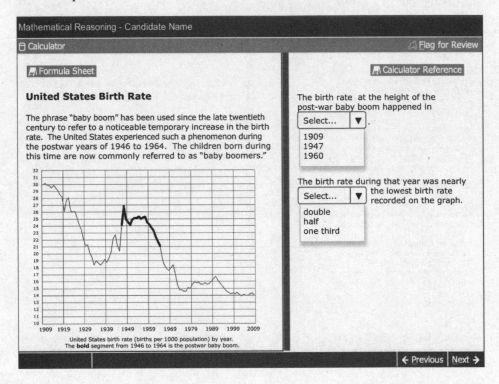

Short Answer and Extended Response

In addition to the types of questions listed above, both the Social Studies and Science tests contain one or more short-answer questions. These visually resemble and have similar functionality to the Extended Response question in the Reasoning Through Language Arts test. The key difference is that an Extended Response question prompt is likely to be longer; you will need to toggle between the page tabs to read it in its entirety. Both short-answer and Extended Response questions require you to type your response in the window provided.

Here is an example of a short-answer question.

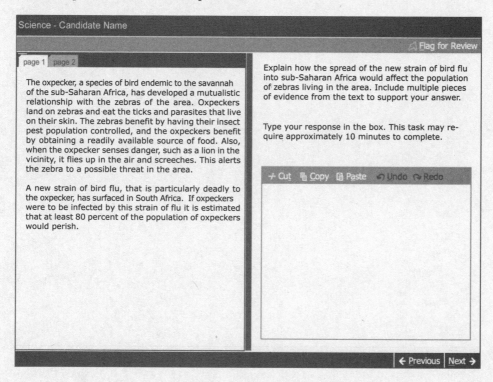

We will show you an example of an Extended Response question, along with more information about it, in Chapter 10.

Please note that while the test does offer some basic word-processing functions (such as cut and paste), the test does not contain many of the options test takers are used to in a word-processing program. Also, the test does not indicate when you have made a possible spelling or grammar mistake, and it does not have an autocorrect feature to fix common typos. Because many test takers are used to using more advanced word-processing programs (such as Microsoft Word), it is important to save some time to proofread your work for typos as well as spelling or grammar mistakes.

As mentioned earlier, please take some time to get comfortable with these question formats. Check out the GED Testing Service's free practice test and computer skills tutorial at www.gedtestingservice.com/educators/freepracticetest for some hands-on practice.

Next, we'll discuss how to use the format of the GED® test to your advantage.

Chapter 4
The Habits
of Effective
Test Takers

In this chapter, we'll show you how to boost your score with key skills designed to maximize your performance.

Taking a standardized test involves more than knowledge. You need to approach the test with strategy and learned skills. Effective test takers adopt certain habits that help to reduce stress and increase points.

1. Answer the Easy Questions First

Depending on your specific skill set and your level of comfort with the range of difficulty on the test, some questions will be easier for you than others. It's important to remember that within each section, all of the questions (besides Extended Response) are worth approximately an equal number of points, which means that getting a difficult question wrong is not going to cost you more than missing an easy question. You also have the freedom to answer the questions in any order you like. So, to maximize your score, first answer all of the questions with which you are comfortable, and come back to the more challenging problems later. If you are running out of time, it is best to have already completed all of the "easy" problems so you can spend your remaining minutes guessing on the difficult ones.

It may feel more natural to do the problems in the order they are presented. However, you want to be able to see all of the questions in a section and know that you have worked through all of the questions you could in the time allotted. With efficient use of the flag button and review screen, discussed below, skipping questions that you consider more difficult is the best use of your time. Remember: **Skip early and skip often**.

2. Use a Note Board to Stay on Task

As we discussed in Chapter 2, you will not be provided with traditional scratch paper but with three erasable note boards and a dry-erase marker. Although you will not be able to save your work and go back to it later, that doesn't mean you shouldn't think about how to use your note boards strategically.

Keeping your hand moving while you focus on the physical task of writing is an essential way to stay focused on the test itself. If your brain has to communicate with your hand, then it is engaged and active and less likely to be distracted, which can force you to reread a question multiple times.

In addition to keeping your brain focused and on task, writing can help you to stay on target with the techniques presented in this book. Having something to write down, such as a summary of a reading passage or a math formula, may be just the push your brain needs to get it moving in the right direction. Using scratch paper, develop a note-board habit for each type of question, and stick to it!

3. Use the Flag Button and Review Screen to Get Unstuck

It is inevitable that at some point during the test, you will encounter a question that you don't understand, or one that you *think* you understand…but the answer you want isn't an option. Often, the problem is that you have misread the question or made a small calculation error. Research shows that once you have misread a question, you are likely to keep reading it in the same way, no matter how many times you try. Meanwhile the clock is ticking, and you aren't getting any closer to an answer. If you get stuck, the best thing to do is to flag the problem for review, and move on. Distracting your brain by doing other problems is often just what you need in order to come back and read the problem with fresh eyes.

At the end of the section, you will be able to use the review screen to quickly jump to any questions you have marked. Once you come back to them, you will have a better understanding of how much time you have left to deal with your marked questions. Then you can decide whether to sit down and work the problem or to simply put in a guess.

4. Pacing

Many wrong answers are the result of simply going too fast and reading too quickly. However, most test takers feel they have to rush through the "easy" problems because they won't have time on the more difficult ones. Try a few questions untimed, and you will make fewer mistakes. You'll also probably work more quickly than you think. The questions don't get harder when you add a timer, but somehow, test takers tend not to score as highly.

The trick is to take the GED® test at an even pace, recognizing when a question is more difficult and should be marked for later. Work for accuracy, because doing all the problems will not get you a higher score unless you do them correctly. Slow down and make sure that you are (a) choosing to do the questions you understand first and (b) giving them enough time, attention, and focus to answer them correctly. If you run into a question that feels like a brick wall, flag it and move on to an easier question.

The only exception to this rule is in the last few minutes of any section. This is the time to use your review screen and marked questions to ensure that you have guessed on all the questions for which that option was available.

5. Guessing and Process of Elimination

The GED® test does not penalize you for an incorrect answer; there is never any deduction for getting a question wrong. So regardless of whether you know the answer to any given problem, it is to your advantage to record an answer to every problem. Thus, guessing on problems that you don't know how to solve, or that you don't have time to work through, can actually *add* points to your score.

Pick a "Guess Letter"

If you had a one-in-four chance to win $10 (and entering didn't cost you anything), you would enter, right? The multiple-choice and drop-down questions on the GED® test are very much like that $10 chance. On any single multiple-choice question, your chance of correctly guessing is 25 percent, and on drop-down questions that chance can increase depending on the number of answer choices available. If you randomly guess a different answer for each question, those odds probably won't add up to as many points as you had hoped. However, if you

Eliminate the Out-of-Scope Answers

Q: What's the capital of Malawi?

A. Paris
B. Dukhan
C. London
D. Lilongwe

Turn the page for the answer.

choose the same answer for every multiple-choice question on which you randomly guess, you are likely to get one in four of the answers correct. Those are pretty good odds, and simply choosing a consistent "guess letter" for drop-down and multiple-choice questions can improve your score.

But what if you could increase your odds even more?

Process of Elimination (POE)

Try the following question:

1.   In what year did Texas become a state?

☐

You don't know? The good news is that the GED® test would never ask such a question. Or rather, if it did, you would be given a reading passage in which the answer could be found. The purpose of this example question is to show what you can do if you have a few extra seconds to add to your guessing.

If this were a fill-in-the-blank question, and you did not have time to read the passage, you would have to guess, but the likelihood of your getting it correct would be very small. However, using a small amount of information to guess could help you if the question was multiple choice or drop down. Now, consider the same question in multiple-choice format.

Test-Taking Tip #1
Use POE to get rid of out-of-scope answers.

1.   In what year did Texas become a state?

A   100 B.C.
B.   25 A.D.
C.   1836
D.   1990

Now the question looks a little easier, right? You know Texas became a state sometime between the 1700s and today. That eliminates (A) and (B). You are also pretty sure that it happened well before 1990, so eliminate (D) too. You didn't know the exact answer, but you did know enough to eliminate wrong answers.

You probably won't be able to narrow down the answer choices to a single one on very many questions, but you may be able to eliminate two answers, which leaves you with a fifty-fifty chance of getting the correct answer. Remember, every choice you eliminate increases your chances of guessing the correct answer.

Try one more.

2. There are 10 students in a class, and their average score on a test is 79 out of 100. If a new student is added to the class, what is the minimum score he would need to achieve in order to bring the class average up to 80 out of 100?

A. 1
B. 79
C. 85
D. 90

This problem may seem fairly complex to figure out. Don't worry if you don't know how to do averages; we will teach you all you need to know in the Mathematical Reasoning chapters. However, you can understand that if a student's score has to bring up the class average, it would have to be higher than the class average to begin with. With this information you could eliminate (A) and (B), and you would have a fifty-fifty chance of guessing the correct number, which is (D).

Test-Taking Tip #2
If you haven't figured out an answer in a minute, skip the problem and come back to it later.

6. Let It Go

No one question is that important to your score. If you read a question and aren't immediately sure how to answer it, flag it and move on. Do not spend any time beating yourself up for not knowing how to do the problem, as everyone is likely to find at least some questions they don't know how to do. If a problem is taking too much time to figure out, fill in a guess and move on. Keeping track of how many questions you think you got correct, or getting upset because you think you aren't doing well, can only impact your score negatively. Know that you have made the right decision for your overall score at every stage, and move forward to deal with the next question with confidence.

Focus on Your Strengths

Sometimes the questions on this test may seem complex and unusual, especially if you have been away from school for a long period of time. It is important to recognize the strengths that you bring to this test; they can help you to achieve the score you are looking for. Implement the six habits to take control of your testing experience. To this foundation, add the preparation and practice from the rest of this book.

By focusing on your strengths, you can maintain the proper perspective. The GED® test is only that—a test. It doesn't measure your worth as a human being. It measures how effectively you have acquired a few skills and how you make use of that knowledge in a timed, stressful situation. Use the test's own limitations to your advantage, and with a little hard work, you can earn your GED® test credential.

Eliminate the Out-of-Scope Answers
A: The capital of Malawi is Lilongwe, but you didn't need to know that to eliminate choices (A) and (C).

Part II
Reasoning Through Language Arts: Reading

Chapter 5
Reading Overview

At 150 minutes, Reasoning Through Language Arts (RLA) is the longest of the four GED® subject tests, combining 95 minutes of Reading and Language, a 10-minute break, and the 45-minute Extended Response (essay) section. We'll talk about the language questions and Extended Response section in upcoming chapters. For now, let's look at Reading, which will take up most of those 95 minutes.

You're more likely to encounter informational (nonfiction) texts than literary passages, which is good news if you've ever had to struggle with complex literary language and ideas while the clock ticks. Only 25 percent of the Reading passages will be literary; 75 percent will be informational material, which tends to be more straightforward, with concrete language and clearer presentation.

Need some extra help with reading comprehension? Register your book online to download our Reading Comprehension supplement from your Student Tools!

RLA AND THE REAL WORLD

The focus on informational material reflects with the GED® test's emphasis on the skills required for a career or college. Employees in every industry and at all levels are expected to respond appropriately to the information they receive, and college students need to work with large volumes of information. That's why the reading passages and questions, with their emphasis on informational material, are considered so important in predicting readiness for a career or for college.

Therefore, the Reading section is all about critical thinking and active reading—analyzing and questioning the passage as you go through it instead of just passively absorbing what it says. You'll see six to eight passages of up to 900 words each, and you will need to show that you not only understand the material, but that you can *do* something with it—summarize it, find reasoning flaws in it, or make inferences from it, for example. (We'll get into that in more detail when we discuss the types of questions you can expect.)

Taking this test gives you a chance to develop and demonstrate critical thinking and analytical skills for potential employers or college admissions officers. The strategies you'll discover as you work through this book will help you prepare, so you'll walk into the testing center knowing what to expect and feeling confident in your abilities.

WHAT KIND OF READING PASSAGES ARE ON THE RLA TEST?

The passages span a range of difficulty (more good news), starting with the type of material that would be appropriate for a student just entering high school. (Some are set at the high school graduation level.) And the topics have been chosen to appeal to the majority of test takers, so there's a good chance you'll find most of the passages interesting to read.

Most of the reading passages are nonfiction texts taken from the real world of the workplace and academia.

What are they about? Well, informational passages could cover a broad range of topics, as long as they're nonfiction. Readings are drawn from both the workplace and the academic worlds; they could be from ads or letters for customers, and from speeches, manuals, or government documents, for example. A literary passage will tell a good story, with vivid characters and a strong narrative line.

WHAT KIND OF QUESTIONS ARE ON THE TEST?

The GED® test is very systematic about the reading skills it assesses, following a detailed set of criteria called the Common Core State Standards (CCSS). So what? So now we know what reading skills the test writers are looking for, which determines the passages they select and the questions they ask.

In fact, there are seven of these reading standards, each with a dizzying array of subsections. Only some subsections will appear on different versions of the test, but you can bet that each of the seven main standards will show up somewhere. And that, in turn, tells us the seven main question tasks you can expect.

The questions will appear in two formats. Most will be multiple choice, with four choices. As always, Process of Elimination is your friend with multiple-choice questions. If you start by looking for what's clearly *wrong*, you should find you can eliminate a couple of the choices, and then look for the *right* answer in the other two—or, worst case, *guess* at which one is right. By using Process of Elimination to get rid of two of the four choices, you've just increased your chances of making a correct guess to 50 percent instead of the original 25 percent.

Where Are the Answers?

They're in the reading passages, although they may not always be obvious. You're expected to use your critical thinking skills, analyze the text, dig beneath the surface, and make inferences. Don't draw on your own knowledge and experience; they could lead you astray. Rely only on the information in the passages.

The computer-based test also presents you with drag-and-drop questions, in which you could be asked to arrange events in the proper order, or sort out which of two authors made which statements. Your options will be mixed up, and you'll need to "drag" them, one at a time, to a chart full of empty boxes and "drop" them into the correct positions on the chart. There will be only one or two drag-and-drop questions per passage, and you might find they're kind of fun to do—a nice break from the multiple-choice questions that predominate. (See Chapter 3 for an illustration of what a drag-and-drop question looks like.)

Most questions are worth one point, but some might be worth two (such as the example mentioned in the previous paragraph, where you need to match statements to one of two different authors), so the number of questions per passage isn't set in stone. You can expect a total of about 48 questions spread across the six to eight passages.

Question Tasks

The seven main reading skills the test writers are assessing lead to seven main question tasks.

> 1. Main Idea or Theme
>
> 2. Development (of Ideas, Events, or Characters)
>
> 3. Language Use
>
> 4. Structure
>
> 5. Purpose (or Point of View)
>
> 6. Evaluation (of the Author's Argument or Reasoning)
>
> 7. Comparison (of Different Passages that Deal with Similar Topics)

You'll notice there's no plain old "comprehension" question task in that list. Comprehension is a given on the GED® test—you need to understand the passage before you can do any of the things the questions will ask you to do with it. Download and read the supplemental tutorial on reading comprehension, if you need to.

A question's format (multiple choice or drag and drop) will NOT tell you what task it's asking you to perform.

One last tip about the questions: Read each one carefully to make sure you understand what it's asking you to do. It's important not to confuse the question's task with its format. Just because the last drag-and-drop question was a development task asking you to arrange events in the proper sequence, for example, doesn't mean the next one is. It could be a comparison question asking you to sort out which of two authors said what, or a purpose question asking you to choose the words that most accurately describe the author's point of view.

Let's take a closer look at what each question task is asking you to do with the passage. In the next two chapters, we'll work through examples of informational and literary passages with the seven question tasks.

Main Idea or Theme

This is what we like to call a "helicopter question," because it asks you to take the 10,000-foot view of the passage (or perhaps of one or more paragraphs in it). This is not about details, or writing techniques, but about the big picture. When you look out the helicopter window and see them all together below, what overall main idea or theme do they convey?

In main idea questions, look at the forest, not the trees.

The question will probably then ask you to *do* something with that big-picture overview you've gained—identify the details that support it, for instance, or draw a conclusion by stitching together the main ideas of a few different paragraphs. Whatever task the question sets, your first step is to get a clear view of that main idea or theme.

Development (of Ideas, Events, or Characters)

The key to development questions is that the passage starts at Point A and ends up at Point B. You need to follow the route the author took to get there.

For some tasks, think of driving to a destination, passing different landmarks along the way. This works for such tasks as arranging events in the proper order (a classic "drag-and-drop" assignment). For other questions, think of a jumble of building blocks (Point A), and piling them carefully on top of each other to construct a tall tower (Point B). This type of task might ask how a particular character contributes to the progression of the plot in a literary passage, or what you can infer about that character from the separate details the author has given. Other development questions might ask you how the author's ideas are connected (cause and effect? problem and solution?), or how the context chosen for an informational passage influences its meaning.

> In **development** questions, follow the author's route from Point A to Point B.

It's all about getting from Point A to Point B, whether that involves encountering things one after another as you travel through the passage, or seeing how one thing builds upon something that came before it, or figuring out how the separate elements connect to create the whole.

Language Use

You'll come across some unfamiliar words in Reading passages, and Language Use questions ask you to figure out an unfamiliar word's meaning from its context. The words won't be obscure technical terms that only a specialist, such as an economist or a master electrician, would know. They'll be words that aren't specific to any particular field of study—words such as "specificity" and "formulate" (in informational material) or "unabashedly" and "faltered" (in literary passages). Look at what the context is telling you, try substituting a word you know for the unfamiliar word, and see if it makes sense. Here's an example.

> In **language use** questions, guess the word's meaning from the context.

> Although the mayor and town council were initially ardent supporters of a new public library building, their position faltered when the cost estimates started coming in.

What does the context tell you about "ardent" and "faltered"? Well, the cost estimates were apparently higher than expected, causing local officials to reconsider. If you guessed from that a meaning of "enthusiastic" or "passionate" for "ardent" and "weakened" for "faltered," you'd be right. You can read more about guessing a word's meaning from its context in the Reading Comprehension supplement.

Language use questions might go further, too, and ask you what impact the author's word choice has on the tone or the meaning of the passage. For example, someone who offers to "assist you in reaching out to a competent attorney" is setting a more formal tone than someone who offers to "help you find a good lawyer."

Structure

In structure questions, ask yourself, "Why is it there"?

Structure questions could ask what a particular part of the passage adds to the author's purpose or to the development of the author's ideas. In other words, why is it there? That's the question to ask yourself with structure questions. Why did the author put a particular description or instruction, sentence or paragraph in the passage, and why does it appear where it does?

Hunting for transitional or signal words will be a big help here. What are those? They're words that indicate a change (or transition)—perhaps from one opinion to another—or that signal a relationship—perhaps between two statements. Consider the following example:

I prefer living in a big city because there are so many things to do. *On the other hand,* (change to the opposite point of view) a small town offers warmth and a sense of community that big cities lack.

Frosty-Man air conditioners are the most energy-efficient units on the market. *In addition,* (signal that the author is going to build upon a previous point), with an average lifespan of 15 years, they are the most reliable.

In the first example above, the transition to the opposite opinion reveals something important about the character making the statements—he or she may be indecisive or confused or perhaps weak. In the second case, the author is strengthening the goal of promoting Frosty-Man air conditioners by building a list of their advantages. Transition and signal words help give the reader a smoother ride through the author's points.

Some Common Transition and Signal Words

Changing course:
- alternatively
- however
- nevertheless
- on the other hand
- otherwise

Adding:
- also
- in addition
- furthermore
- moreover
- not only...but also

Reaching a conclusion:
- accordingly
- as a result
- consequently
- on the whole
- therefore

Purpose (or Point of View)

Here's another helicopter question. From 10,000 feet above the passage, looking at what all of the details and descriptions and sections add up to as a whole, for what purpose did the author write this passage? Did the author want to persuade readers to do something? Educate them? Entertain them? Defend a position against someone who has publicly attacked it?

A related question asks about the author's point of view. Overall, is the author positive about the subject of the passage? Critical? Neutral? Nailing down the point of view can add another dimension to the author's purpose. For instance, if the purpose seems to be to persuade readers to join a local ski club, but the tone seems neutral about the health benefits of skiing and the author strongly cautions readers about the risks of injury, you've got to wonder if promoting the ski club is really the purpose of this piece.

There could even be a deeper, more subtle purpose underlying the obvious surface goal, or perhaps the purpose is not even explicitly stated. That doesn't mean the author's point of view and purpose are difficult to figure out, though, if you just use your critical thinking skills.

Take a look at this brief excerpt, for instance:

Excerpt from *A Narrative of the Life of Frederick Douglass, An American Slave,* by Frederick Douglass, 1845

I was utterly astonished at her goodness. I scarcely knew how to behave towards her. She was entirely unlike any other white woman I had ever seen. I could not approach her as I was accustomed to approach other white ladies. My early instruction was all out of place. The crouching servility, usually so acceptable a quality in a slave, did not answer when manifested toward her. Her favor was not gained by it; she seemed to be disturbed by it.

Even from these few sentences it's pretty clear that the author's purpose, on the surface, is to describe an event in his life, while "crouching servility" gives a clue that his unstated purpose and point of view are critical of slavery.

> In **purpose** questions, ask yourself, "What did the author want to accomplish by writing this"?

Besides simply asking you to identify the author's purpose or point of view, these questions might ask what rhetorical techniques the author uses to achieve his or her purpose more effectively. What are rhetorical techniques? They're simply tools that writers use, like hammers or wrenches, to get the job done better.

One common rhetorical technique is analogy—comparing something to another thing that will be more familiar to readers, in order to help them understand the author's point and increase the chance that they will agree with it. For instance, the passage might explain that "a Hemi engine is more powerful than a flathead engine because the Hemi is designed to minimize heat loss and unburned fuel, in much the same way as a toaster oven is more energy efficient than a full-sized oven."

Another common rhetorical technique is repetition. Think of the last ad you saw for a new car. How many times, in how many different ways, did the ad tell you that you would be powerful, free, safe, and environmentally responsible if only you would buy this car?

If you wanted to be an extremist, you could find ridiculously long lists of obscure rhetorical techniques (paraprosdokian, anyone?). The GED® test, however, is not extremist. The test writers expect you to recognize only a few of the most commonly used rhetorical techniques, and you can often guess a technique's name just by looking at what it does. Try this one:

> **Paraprosdokian,** in case you're curious, is a rhetorical technique in which a familiar phrase gets an unexpected ending—for instance, "Discretion is the better part of making a serious mistake." It can be useful for waking up bored readers.

In your SnoSqual parka, you'll enjoy unmatched protection from the cold, unrivalled flexibility for your gear, and unsurpassed style on the slopes.

Now the question:

Apply the Strategy
You can use Process of
Elimination to answer
this question.

1. The writer creates a positive image and desire for a
    SnoSqual parka through the use of

    A. alliteration.
    B. parallelism.
    C. hyperbole.
    D. repetition.

Remember Process of Elimination, or POE? You can get rid of "repetition"—the sentence doesn't say the same thing over and over. Check out "Some Common Rhetorical Techniques" in the box on the next page, and you'll see that "alliteration" and "hyperbole" are eliminated. So "parallelism" is left, and indeed that's the technique the author uses.

However, you could also have chosen "parallelism" based simply on what the author's description does: It presents the SnoSqual parka's three advantages (warmth, flexibility, and style) in parallel structures (each starting with an "un-" description and ending with a phrase, such as "from the cold," that puts the advantage in context). The end result is a product claim that sounds organized, trustworthy, and appealing, and would advance the author's purpose of making readers want this coat.

Some Common Rhetorical Techniques

Alliteration: creating rhythm through repeating initial consonant sounds. Example: "The *store's spectacular sales season* yielded enormous profits."

Analogy: enhancing readers' understanding by comparing two things that have similar features. Example: "A jet pump *works much like a drinking straw* in a glass of soda."

Hyperbole: exaggerating a statement to make a point. Example: "I've tried *a million* different ways to open the file you sent, but it's broken."

Metaphor: describing something by saying it's the same as an otherwise unrelated thing. Example: "The empty *highway was a ribbon* stretching over the distant mountains."

Parallelism: stringing together phrases or sentences with similar structures. Example: "*First push the power button, then select fan mode, and then select the fan speed.*"

Qualifying Statement: toning down what sounds like an extreme statement. Example: "That's the worst lasagna I've ever eaten—*since I had Aunt Mabel's lasagna last week*, that is."

Repetition: stating the same thing in different ways to emphasize a point. Example: "A snow shovel with a curved handle *puts less strain on your back*. It *makes shovelling easier* and *minimizes the risk of injury*."

Simile: adding impact to a description by comparing one thing to another unrelated thing using the word "like" or "as." Example: "His stare was *as cold as ice*."

Understatement: making something sound less significant than it really is to achieve an effect. Example: "The country has a *minor* trade deficit of $3 trillion."

Evaluation (of the Author's Argument or Reasoning)

Yes, you, the GED® test taker, get to evaluate whether the author has done a thorough, reliable, persuasive job of making his or her case. How's that for giving you power and letting you show off your critical thinking skills?

To begin, of course, you need to travel through the passage to create a map of the argument as the author moves from Point A to Point B to Point C to arrive at a final conclusion. Only then will you be able to do what the questions ask you to do with that argument. For evaluation questions, those tasks generally fall into three categories.

First, you could be asked to evaluate the evidence the author uses to support claims. Is the evidence trustworthy—the opinion of a well-known expert in the field, perhaps, or the results of a professional research study? Is the evidence directly applicable to the claim, or does it sound

> **Evaluation** questions ask you to judge the author's evidence, reasoning, or assumptions.

good but really not have much to do with the author's point? Does the author provide *enough* evidence to support a claim, or perhaps no evidence at all?

Some Common Logical Fallacies

Slippery Slope—In an attempt to persuade people to do (or not to do) something, this technique claims the result of inaction (or action) will be widespread disaster, but doesn't provide evidence to support that conclusion. Wars have been started this way: "If we don't stop this dictator now, he'll take over every country in the whole region."

Straw Man—This technique exaggerates or misstates an opponent's argument so it's easy to knock it down. For instance: "Advocates of compact fluorescent light bulbs want us all to die from mercury poisoning in order to save energy."

Appeal to Emotion—In appealing for donations, a charity often tells heartbreaking stories of the people it has helped. But do these emotional appeals perhaps hide the fact that the organization is paying its executive director a huge salary, or that it uses half of the money it raises to pay for more fundraising campaigns?

Ad Hominem—If you can't refute the opponent's argument, attack the opponent. An ad hominem fallacy might concede that a prominent scientist's latest published theory "seems to sound promising, but don't forget that this is the author who was suspected of plagiarizing other researchers' work a few years ago."

To explore more logical fallacies, take a look at the Purdue University Online Writing Lab (OWL) at owl.english.purdue.edu/owl/resource/659/03/

Second, the question might ask you to evaluate whether the author's reasoning is sound. Here you're looking for what are called logical fallacies—major flaws in reasoning that may not be apparent until you really think about it. Like rhetorical techniques, logical fallacies come in a long list of creatively named types. In this case, the GED® test writers won't expect you to know those names, but they will expect you to recognize faulty reasoning when you see it.

One logical fallacy you might find familiar is called the slippery slope. Politicians often use it to gain support for their positions by generating fear. For example, "If we allow the Bank of Broad River to refuse loans to any company that hasn't been profitable for the past 10 years, pretty soon all of the banks will be refusing those loans and small business in the state will collapse." The first act is the beginning of a snowballing slide down toward destruction. But wait a minute—who said any other banks would adopt the same policy? What evidence does the author provide to support that claim? The chain of reasoning from one bank's change in policy to the annihilation of small business in the entire state is unreliable.

Third, you might need to dig out the assumptions behind the author's argument and judge whether they're valid. For instance, say a candidate for mayor is trying to persuade voters to support her because her top priority is expanding the mass transit system to reduce traffic gridlock. What are the underlying assumptions? She's presuming that most voters use mass transit or that they even care about it enough to fund it with their tax dollars. She's thinking they would choose mass transit as a solution instead of adding traffic lanes or a new by-pass highway. In a large, sprawling city where many businesses and shopping areas are miles away and constructing long rail or subway lines could be very expensive, her assumptions might not be valid. She could just have lost a large group of potential supporters.

Comparison (of Different Passages That Deal with Similar Topics)

> Comparison questions ask about the differences between passages with separate formats, styles, or biases.

In comparison questions, you're looking for what's different and why. Those differences will fall into three broad categories.

First, the two readings could present the same information in different formats. Think, for instance, of a computer blog's feature article about a new tablet and the technical spec sheet for that same product on the manufacturer's website. Both pieces probably include such information as processor speed and memory size, but the two formats will present it in quite different ways. Why? Think about the purposes, audiences, and tone of the two pieces. The article aims to interest a more general audience—readers who are perhaps just investigating tablet brands—and will have a more casual tone. The spec sheet, on the other hand, is designed to give detailed technical information to more knowledgeable readers who are seriously considering a purchase, and will have a neutral, objective tone to inspire confidence in the accuracy of the information.

Second, the two pieces might treat a similar topic differently because they were written in different eras, when writing styles and cultural values differed. Consider, for example, these two quotes about education:

> "I know no safe depository of the ultimate powers of the society but the people themselves; and if we think them not enlightened enough to exercise their control with a wholesome discretion, the remedy is not to take it from them, but to inform their discretion by education."
>
> —Thomas Jefferson

> "What does education often do? It makes a straight-cut ditch of a free, meandering brook."
>
> —Henry David Thoreau

Jefferson, one of the Founding Fathers, writes in the lengthy, complex, formal sentence structure of his era and his status, at a time when the young democracy was defining itself and establishing its legitimacy. In plain language, he's saying that ordinary people are the only safe source of power and if you don't think they'd exercise it wisely, then educate them to do it. Thoreau, on the other hand, writes with the simplicity of a naturalist during the American Romantic era and sees man-made institutions, including education, as threats to nature. Even if you weren't familiar with these two authors or the times in which they wrote, you would be able to see the differences in their writing styles and in the values they consider important. The questions will target those more general differences.

The third and trickiest type of comparison questions will present opposing viewpoints on a topic and ask you to delve down to see how the arguments rely on different interpretations of the same facts, or how they emphasize different evidence that supports their positions. Look for authors with rigid opinions who select evidence to support conclusions they've already reached. For example, fracking (or hydraulic fracturing) is a topic for which there is a lot of information—from the shale gas industry on one side and environmental groups on the other. An author could easily construct a strong pro or con argument just by selecting the right research results or expert statements. The GED® test question could expect you to detect that type of bias.

OUR APPROACH

In the next two chapters, we'll look at informational and literary reading passages in more detail, with examples to help you develop strategies for tackling different question tasks. Then, we'll give you a drill for each kind of passage to try on your own.

Chapter 6
Informational
Passages

In this chapter, we'll look at informational texts and then guide you through active reading strategies to help you crack the questions.

Think about it—what do you spend more time reading and listening to in a typical day? News reports, advertisements, political speeches and similar nonfiction material, or literary stories? Nonfiction, right? Life is filled with informational material that you need to deal with in some way (even if only to decide to tune it out), so that's what the GED® test emphasizes. In fact, 75 percent of the six to eight reading passages are classified as informational.

The critical thinking and active reading skills you'll gain in preparing for the reading passages will help you sort through the informational material that fills your life outside the test, too. With those skills you'll learn to question, identify flaws in reasoning, recognize a legitimate argument when you see it, and in short, become a wiser, more discriminating consumer of information.

> Use critical thinking skills with the information that fills your own life, too.

WHAT KIND OF INFORMATIONAL PASSAGES ARE ON THE TEST?

How about an article explaining how wind turbines work? Or a speech from a company's president outlining the great opportunities for growth—and profit—that lie ahead? Or perhaps the results of a study on which foods are the best choices for good cholesterol?

Since the GED® test aims to measure readiness for career and college, subjects can be drawn from both the workplace and the academic worlds. That's a pretty big target, and indeed, the range of real-world subjects is broad.

From the workplace, you could see letters or ads aimed at customers, corporate policy statements, executive speeches, or community announcements about events the company is sponsoring. From the academic world, subjects focus on science (especially energy, human health, and living systems) and on social studies. Those social studies subjects are built around what's called The Great American Conversation, which includes documents created when the United States was founded as well as later discussions about American citizenship and culture. There, you might see editorials or essays, speeches, biographies, letters written by famous people, government documents, court decisions, or contemporary articles.

> Informational texts come from the real world of the workplace and from the fields of science and social studies.

Readings could be in the public domain, which means they're old enough that any copyright has expired and they sport the long sentences and flowery language characteristic of earlier styles of writing. The older writing style means that you'll have to apply a fair amount of critical thinking in order to get what the author is saying.

Try this Great American Conversation excerpt, for instance:

Excerpt from *A Defense of the Constitution of Government of the United States of America,* by John Adams, 1786

If we should extend our candor so far as to own, that the majority of men are generally under the dominion of benevolence and good intentions, yet, it must be confessed, that a vast majority frequently transgress; and, what is more directly to the point, not only a majority, but almost all, confine their benevolence to their families, relations, personal friends, parish, village, city, county, province, and that very few, indeed, extend it impartially to the whole community.

That's how people wrote back in 1786. Once you break this long sentence into pieces, skip over the parts that don't make a direct statement and substitute simpler words in the parts that do, you end up with a pretty straightforward summary: "Even if we say that most men mean well, we have to admit that almost all of them limit their kindness to the people around them." The context should help you take a good guess at the meaning of words that may not be familiar, such as "candor," "benevolence," and "transgress," as well as the unusual meaning of "own." After you've tossed out the extra words and phrases, though, the only one of these words really needed for your straightforward summary is "benevolence," and the pairing of that word with "good intentions" makes its meaning fairly obvious.

What you won't see among the informational readings are objective, neutral passages that simply describe or explain something, such as you'd find in an encyclopedia or a product instruction manual. The GED® test's informational passages are more complex than that. They will have a "voice"—an author with a specific point of view and purpose. The author might be trying to persuade readers to boycott a particular company, for instance, or the author may be giving a speech criticizing a new government policy. These passages will draw on your analytical and critical thinking skills to discover not only the author's purpose but also what techniques the author uses to support a position, what assumptions the author has made, and whether the argument is logical and sound.

> Informational passages are written by an author who has a specific purpose and point of view.

HOW SHOULD I READ INFORMATIONAL PASSAGES ON THE TEST?

First, keep your mind actively engaged with the passage and second, think critically instead of simply accepting the passage at face value.

While you may not have time for full-blown active reading strategies, you'll still need to use them (and your note boards) to some extent in order to seize control of the passage and make it give you what you need, instead of letting the passage run the show. You're on a mission—you have questions to answer in a limited amount of time—and passively absorbing (or worse, skimming through) the passage will only force you to keep going back and rereading it.

Active Reading
Using your **note boards** can remind you to read actively and help you take control of the passage.

How do you read actively? In a nutshell, keep asking questions and looking for specific things as you go through the passage. Hunt for the flaws and gaps that weaken an argument; recognize the strong support and smooth organization that strengthen it. When you read each section or paragraph, summarize quickly, in your own words, what it's saying.

You'll need to do a lot of this in your head—that's about all you have time for—but you can scribble a couple of words to capture a main idea, or a one-word-per-line list of what happens first, second, and so on. You won't need to get far into the passage before you'll know what's important. For many people, just writing something down helps them remember, even if they don't look at their note board again, and searching for words that would be important enough to jot down can force you into active reading mode. You can try using this technique with the drills and practice tests in this book to see how much it helps you.

Questions to Ask As You Read Informational Passages

- What does the author want readers to do or to think after they read this?
- Who is the intended audience?
- What is the author's main point?
- How, and how well, is the main point supported?
- Does the author have an obvious bias or point of view?
- What assumptions does the author make?
- What is the author's tone?
- Is the author's reasoning logical?
- Is the piece complete, or does it leave unanswered questions?
- Are the language and sentence structure appropriate for the audience and for the time in which the author was writing?

Answering those questions as you read will put you in command of just about any informational piece, whether it's from a workplace or an academic context. Then you can start cracking the questions.

PUTTING IT ALL TOGETHER

Let's go through a couple of examples that will help you practice reading actively and approaching the different question tasks.

1   Even by genre standards, Texas bluesman Sam "Lightnin"
Hopkins released a stupefying amount of material during his
lengthy career. As a guitar player, he was never what one would
call a perfectionist: few of his recordings are free of off-notes or
mis-fretted chords, and he had no compunction about putting out
version after version of the same song, either under the same or
different titles.

2   For such reasons, many fans feel that Hopkins is better served
by "Best of" compilations than by individual albums. But how
is one to choose which tracks to include on a compilation CD,
when there is such a surfeit of material? How can one select
the best, say, "Mojo Hand," when there are 30-odd recordings
of it floating around? Seemingly every time he sat down to
record, he'd do another run through "Mojo Hand." Every time he
recorded the song he played it a little differently: each has its
recommendations, each its shortcomings. And every one of those
takes has been released at some point over the years.

3   Since so many versions of the song were released, none sold
appreciably better than the others—making "popular acclaim" a
moot point. No particular recording can be called a "Greatest
Hit," even though the song itself is probably his best-known
composition.

4   So, when it's time to put out another "Lightnin" Hopkins
compilation CD, that means it's time to decide upon a "Mojo Hand"
to include on it.

5   It would seem that all the intrepid compiler can do is choose
one version of "Mojo Hand" that is just as good as (although
admittedly no better than) many others...and then do the same for
"Katie Mae," and again for "Lightnin's Boogie," and on and on...thus
rendering any purported "Best of" album less representative of
Sam "Lightnin" Hopkins than of the person putting it together.

6   So it is with this most recent album: the song titles are there,
and a fan finds few surprises among them. But do you need
this album? Do you need these particular versions, culled from
various sessions spanning five decades? Do you need yet another
"Lightnin" Hopkins CD titled—you guessed it—MOJO HAND?

Before we tackle some questions, let's look at how to read this passage actively by asking yourself questions as you go through it. To train yourself in the active reading techniques you'll
need for the test, note your answer on some scratch paper (or at least *think* of your answer)
before you read the one below the question.

What does the author want readers to do or to think after they read this? The overall impression, by the time you reach the end of the review, is summed up in the question, "do you need *this* album?" (paragraph 6). The author wants readers to understand that, if they already have a selection of "Lightnin'" Hopkins's huge roster of albums, they probably don't need this one, too.

Who is the intended audience? You can tell by the casual tone, lack of musical terminology (except for "mis-fretted chords" in paragraph 1), and absence of background information on the singer or the songs mentioned, that the reviewer is writing for people who are probably not professional musicians but who are familiar with Hopkins's work.

What is the author's main point? That's in the references to how many versions of a song Hopkins habitually recorded, and in the conclusion that so many versions make "any purported 'Best of' album less representative of Sam 'Lightnin'' Hopkins than of the person putting it together" (paragraph 5).

How, and how well, is the main point supported? The difficulty of compiling a truly representative "Best of" album is well supported. The author says that Hopkins "had no compunction about putting out version after version of the same song" (paragraph 1) and that "each [version] has its recommendations, each its shortcomings" (paragraph 2). There is no objective yardstick for selecting what to include, leading to subjective decisions by the person making the selections.

Does the author have an obvious bias or point of view? The author clearly thinks Hopkins was sloppy in creating his body of work ("few of his recordings are free of off-notes or mis-fretted chords, and he had no compunction about putting out version after version of the same song" (paragraph 1).

What assumptions does the author make? The lack of background information about the artist and the songs mentioned reveals an assumption that readers are already familiar with Hopkins's work.

What is the author's tone? You can tell from opinions such as "never what one would call a perfectionist" (paragraph 1) and "all the intrepid compiler can do is choose one version of 'Mojo Hand' that is just as good as (although admittedly no better than) many others" (paragraph 5) that the author is critical of both the singer's careless approach and the objective of creating a "Best of" compilation.

Is the author's reasoning logical? Yes; the author builds a logical chain of reasoning from too many versions of a song, with none standing out as superior, to a compilation that relies on the subjective opinions of an unknown compiler and is therefore of questionable value in representing the best of an artist's work.

Is the piece complete, or does it leave unanswered questions? Since the author places so much weight on the person selecting which version of each song to include, it would be helpful to know who actually made the compilation. Was it someone who had followed Hopkins's career for a long time? Someone who is well versed in that genre of music?

Are the language and sentence structure appropriate for the audience and for the time in which the author was writing? Yes; the language is appropriate for an educated audience well versed in this genre of music but not professional musicians. The sentence structure is contemporary and varied, making the piece interesting to read.

Now that you've got a good sense of what the author is trying to achieve and how he or she went about reaching that destination, let's look at a few questions. Try to select the answer yourself, using the insight you gained from the active reading questions, before you read the explanation below the choices.

1. The questions in the final paragraph are intended to make the reader

    A. wonder if compilation CDs serve any purpose.
    B. realize that Hopkins was less talented than many listeners believe.
    C. see that this compilation CD may not be a necessary addition to a Hopkins collection.
    D. understand that nobody can predict which version of a song will sell the most copies.

Apply the Strategy
Reading actively can help you to answer this question.

Here's How to Crack It
You got the answer to this structure question (Why is it there?) from the very first active reading question (What does the author want readers to do or to think?) that you asked yourself as you read through the passage. The author wants them to think (C). The last paragraph reinforces the reasons given earlier in the passage: With so many versions of a song, all of about equal value, why would someone need these particular, subjectively chosen versions?

Choice (A) is too broad (the passage is talking only about Hopkins's work); (B) is inaccurate (Hopkins is described as careless, not untalented) and (D) is beside the point (the compilation is being done from an existing body of work, so no prediction is involved, and it is supposed to include the best, not necessarily the best selling).

2. The writer describes the compiler (paragraph 5) as being

    A. misguided.
    B. intelligent.
    C. artistic.
    D. adventurous.

Here's How to Crack It

This language use question is asking you to figure out the meaning of "intrepid" from the context. You've discovered from your active reading that we're not told anything about the compiler's credentials for making selections, and that choosing from a long list of roughly equal versions is, at best, a subjective gamble. Process of Elimination gets rid of (A) (the compiler is not following a wrong path by making a compilation, but just has to make a judgment call when doing so) and of (B) and (C) (intelligence and artistic talent wouldn't help when all of the versions have about the same value). That leaves (D) as the correct answer, and indeed, an adventurous spirit would be useful in taking that subjective gamble with track after track.

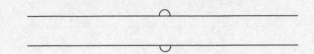

3. The author implies that "Katie Mae"

    A. exists in multiple versions.
    B. is better than "Lightnin's Boogie."
    C. was recorded after "Mojo Hand."
    D. has been overshadowed by Hopkins's other songs.

Here's How to Crack It

At its heart, this is a development question. You know from your active reading that this song isn't the main focus of the passage. So what is the author saying about it and how does that contribute to the development of the main point? The answer, as always, is right in the passage. "Katie Mae" is yet another instance of having to choose one version "that is just as good as (although admittedly no better than) many others" (paragraph 5). It's a building block in constructing the main point about any Hopkins compilation representing the compiler, not the singer. So (A) is the only answer that is supported in the passage.

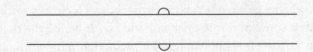

4. The author infers that Lightnin' Hopkins's body of musical works

    A. is larger than that of any other blues musician.
    B. is filled with too many mistakes for any of the recordings to be considered good.
    C. resists easy song selection processes.
    D. cannot be represented on a compilation CD.

Here's How to Crack It

This question takes the main point, which you've already identified in your active reading questions, and then asks you to take it a step further to figure out what it infers about Hopkins's work. For this question, you'd follow the main point to (C): the many and roughly equal versions of the same songs make selection difficult, leading to a compilation that is more representative of the person doing the selecting than it is of the singer's work. The author never says (or infers) (A), (B), or (D); they are all too extreme for the statements made in the passage.

How Do the Seven Question Tasks Look in an Informational Passage?

Now that we've seen how the active reading questions can help you take control of a passage and answer questions about it, let's go through an example in which we can focus on the seven question tasks in action.

Killer Clothing Was All the Rage In the 19th Century

Arsenic dresses, mercury hats, and flammable clothing caused a lot of pain.

by Becky Little, *National Geographic*

1   While sitting at home one afternoon in 1861, poet Henry Wadsworth Longfellow's wife, Fanny, caught fire. Her burns were so severe that she died the next day. According to her obituary, the fire had started when "a match or piece of lighted paper caught her dress."

2   At the time, this wasn't a peculiar way to die. In the days when candles, oil lamps, and fireplaces lit and heated American and European homes, women's wide hoop skirts and flowing cotton and tulle dresses were a fire hazard, unlike men's tighter-fitting wool clothes.

3   It wasn't just dresses: Fashion at this time was riddled with dangers. Socks made with aniline dyes inflamed men's feet and gave garment workers sores and even bladder cancer. Lead makeup damaged women's wrist nerves so that they couldn't raise their hands. Celluloid combs, which some women wore in their hair, exploded if they got too hot. In Pittsburgh, a newspaper reported that a man with a celluloid comb lost his life "While Caring for His Long Gray Beard." In Brooklyn, a comb factory exploded.

4   In fact, some of the most fashionable clothing of the day was made using chemicals that are today considered too toxic to use— and it was the producers of this clothing, rather than the wearers, who suffered most of all.

Mercurial Maladies

5   Many people think that "mad as a hatter" refers to the mental and physical side effects hat-makers endured from using mercury in their craft. Though scholars dispute whether this is actually the origin of the phrase, many hatters did develop mercury poisoning. And even though the phrase has a certain levity to it, and while the Mad Hatter in *Alice's Adventures in Wonderland* was silly and fun, the actual maladies hat-makers suffered were no joke— mercury poisoning was debilitating and deadly.

6   In the 18th and 19th centuries, a lot of men's felt hats were made using hare and rabbit fur. In order to make this fur stick together to form felt, hatters brushed it with mercury.

7   "It was extremely toxic," says Alison Matthews David, author of *Fashion Victims: The Dangers of Dress Past and Present*. "Especially if you inhale it. It goes straight to your brain."

8   One of the first symptoms was neuromotor problems, like trembling. In the hat-making town of Danbury, Connecticut, this was known as the "Danbury shakes."

9   Then there were the psychological problems. "You would become very shy, very paranoid," Matthews David says. When medical examiners visited hatters to document their symptoms, hatters "thought they were being observed, and they would throw down their tools and get angry and have outbursts."

10   Many hatters also developed cardiorespiratory problems, lost their teeth, and died at early ages.

11   Although these effects were documented, many viewed them as the hazards that one had to accept with the job. And besides, the mercury only affected the hatters—not the men who wore the hats, who were protected by the hats' lining.

12   "There was always kind of a bit of a pushback from the hatters themselves," Matthews David says of these dangerous working conditions. "But really, honestly, the only thing that made [mercury hat-making] disappear was the fact that men's hats went out of fashion in the 1960s. That's really when it dies. It was never banned in Britain."

Arsenic and Old Lace

13 Arsenic was everywhere in Victorian Britain. Although it was known to be used as a murder weapon, the cheap, natural element was used in candles, curtains, and wallpaper, writes James C. Whorton in *The Arsenic Century: How Victorian Britain Was Poisoned at Home, Work, and Play.*

14 Because it dyed fabric bright green, arsenic also ended up in dresses, gloves, shoes, and artificial flower wreaths that women used to decorate their hair and clothes.

15 The wreaths in particular could cause rashes for women who wore them. But like mercury hats, arsenic fashions were most dangerous for the people who manufactured them, says Matthews David.

16 For example, in 1861, a 19-year-old artificial flower maker named Matilda Scheurer—whose job involved dusting flowers with green, arsenic-laced powder—died a violent and colorful death. She convulsed, vomited, and foamed at the mouth. Her bile was green, and so were her fingernails and the whites of her eye. An autopsy found arsenic in her stomach, liver, and lungs.

17 Articles about Scheurer's death and the plight of artificial flower makers raised public awareness about arsenic in fashion. The British Medical Journal wrote that the arsenic-wearing woman "carries in her skirts poison enough to slay the whole of the admirers she may meet with in half a dozen ball-rooms." In the mid-to-late 1800s, sensational claims like these began to turn public opinion against this deadly shade of green.

Safety in Fashion

18 Public concern over arsenic helped phase it out of fashion— Scandinavia, France, and Germany banned the pigment (Britain did not).

19 The move away from arsenic was hastened by the invention of synthetic dyes, which made it "easy to let arsenic go," according to Elizabeth Semmelhack, senior curator at the Bata Shoe Museum in Toronto, Canada....

20 This raises interesting questions about fashion today. While arsenic dresses might seem like bizarre relics of a more brutal age, killer fashion is still very much in vogue. In 2009, Turkey banned sandblasting—the practice of spraying denim with sand to give it a fashionable distressed look—because workers were developing silicosis from breathing in sand.

21 "It's not a curable disease," Matthews David says of silicosis. "If you have sand in your lungs it will kill you."

22 Yet when a dangerous production method is banned in one country—and when the demand for the clothing that method produces remains high—then production typically moves somewhere else (or continues despite the ban). Last year, Al Jazeera found that some Chinese factories were sandblasting clothes.

23 In the 1800s, men who wore mercury hats or women who wore arsenic-laced clothing and accessories might have seen the people who produced these items on the streets of London, or read about them in the local paper. But in a globalized economy, many of us don't see the deadly effects that our fashion choices have on others.

Source: "Killer Clothing Was All the Rage in the 19th Century," Becky Little, National Geographic News Online, October 17, 2016. Reproduced by permission of National Geographic Creative.

1. Based on the passage, how would the author likely account for a man who locks his door and checks his windows at night, yet uses the same password for several different online accounts?

   A. He believes there is no security risk involved in online accounts.
   B. He feels responsible for safeguarding his tangible assets (such as his house and its contents), but not for intangible cyber assets (such as his online accounts).
   C. A burglar would be a specific person whom the police might catch; an online attacker could be in any country and would likely remain unknown.
   D. He's not aware that reusing the same password makes all of his accounts vulnerable to attack.

Here's a two-part main idea question. First you need to determine which main idea (for the entire passage? for a section of it?) is relevant to the question. Then you need to do something with that main idea. In this case, the question asks you to speculate about how a main idea would apply to a new situation.

Here's How to Crack It

A good way to approach this type of question is to start by eliminating answer choices that have nothing to do with any of the main ideas in the passage. If you used active reading techniques, you should have identified the main idea of each section of the passage as you were going through it, so you should already have a list (either in your head or else jotted down in a few key words).

The passage discusses health risks, not security risks, and in several cases implies that those health risks were well known, so (A) can be eliminated. Choice (B) can also be eliminated, since the passage doesn't contain a main idea about responsibility for safeguarding an asset. The passage doesn't contain a main idea about lack of awareness making someone vulnerable to an attack, so (D) can also be eliminated.

What about (C)? That's close to the main idea in the last paragraph: concern about a local, identifiable person but lack of concern about someone far away and who can't be seen or identified. So the correct answer is (C).

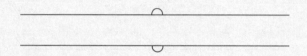

2. One reason the author introduces the present-day fashion industry is to

    A. show that nothing has changed with respect to unsafe manufacturing techniques.
    B. illustrate the effect of globalization.
    C. demonstrate how public concern about the welfare of fashion workers has increased.
    D. explain how fashion manufacturing has changed since the 1800s.

This development question concerns the overall way in which the author connects, develops, and organizes her ideas.

Here's How to Crack It

You need to look at a development question in the context of the overall chain of ideas in the passage. In this case, why does the author move from discussing fashion manufacturing in the 1800s to the modern day? She has described how mercury disappeared when hats went out of fashion, and how synthetic dyes accelerated the end of arsenic. But so what? Does that mean today's fashion industry is safe? Moving on to the present allows her to answer those questions.

She makes an abrupt transition which still skillfully manages to connect the two eras ("This raises interesting questions about fashion today," paragraph 20). Then she goes on to say that at least one unsafe technique (sandblasting) is used today. So her answer is no, the fashion industry still isn't free of danger.

At first glance, it seems that none of these choices hit that mark accurately. In a case like that, the best approach is Process of Elimination (POE)—first get rid of the most clearly wrong answers and see which one (or possibly two) remains.

Choice (A) is too extreme—usually a suspect answer in a GED® question. Some manufacturing techniques have changed; arsenic and mercury are no longer used, for example. Another clearly incorrect answer is (D). The author gives one example (sandblasting) of present-day "killer fashion" which, she says, is "still very much in vogue" (paragraph 20). So the dangerous nature of fashion manufacturing has not changed since the 1800s, even if the specific hazards are now different.

Choice (C) is also incorrect. Public concern has not increased since Matilda's well-publicized death raised an outcry that helped end the use of arsenic. In fact, public concern has declined. Why? "In a globalized economy" (paragraph 23), banned sandblasting simply moved from Turkey to China, and the deadly effects on workers are hidden far away from the consumers who wear the sandblasted products. So the correct answer is (B). The industry still presents dangers to fashion workers today, as it did in the 1800s, and a global economy has made their situation more hopeless.

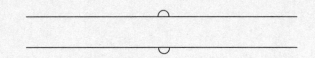

3. In paragraph 3, the author claims that "fashion at this time was riddled with dangers." What connotations (implications or suggestions) does the word "riddled" add to her description of fashion? Drag the most accurate answers into the empty boxes below. (For this example, letters have been added to each answer choice to clarify the explanation that follows.)

(a) It suggests something hidden.
(b) It means "saturated."
(c) It reinforces "dangers."
(d) It implies "deadly."
(e) It indicates hazardous or treacherous.
(f) It concerns weakening or damaging something.

In this language use question, you'll need to consider the context of the passage as a whole to determine why the author chose to use a particular word.

Here's How to Crack It

Think about the main idea the author conveys about Victorian fashion. Some pieces (hats, skirts, combs, even socks) posed health hazards for the wearers and especially for the producers. However, not everyone died as a result. And not every piece of clothing is described as being dangerous. So the extreme choices—(b) and (d)—can be ruled out. Fashion wasn't thoroughly filled with danger (b) and wasn't always deadly (d). The dangers weren't hidden, either—Matilda's death from arsenic was widely publicized, and medical examiners documented the effects of mercury on the hat-makers. That eliminates (a).

So the remaining three answers must be correct (to fill the three boxes) and indeed, they are. The use of "ridded" reinforces the idea of danger (c)—think "riddled with bullets" or "riddled with corruption." It indicates that something is hazardous or treacherous (e), although not always deadly, as the more extreme (d) says. And it portrays fashion as weakened or damaged by the dangers, as a solid material is weakened or damaged by numerous punctures.

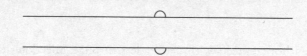

4.   What primary function do the anecdotes about Fanny Longfellow and Matilda Scheurer serve in the passage?

    A.   They introduce humor to the author's tone.
    B.   They add credibility to the passage.
    C.   They help the author connect with her readers.
    D.   They demonstrate how thoroughly the author has researched her topic.

Here's a structure question: Why did the author include these anecdotes? What do they add to achieving her purpose?

Here's How to Crack It

A good way to approach this type of question is to ask yourself what the passage would be like without the structural elements identified in the question (the anecdotes, in this case). If you've practiced active reading techniques (asking yourself about the author's audience, main point, purpose, etc.) as you worked through the passage, you should have a good idea of what the author is trying to achieve. Could she do it as effectively without the anecdotes? Why not?

Right at the beginning of the passage we learn that poor Fanny died after her dress caught fire. This introductory anecdote draws readers in and stimulates their interest in a way that a straightforward opening statement (such as "Clothing was dangerous in Victorian times") never could.

And just before we hear about Matilda's "violent and colorful death" from arsenic, the author gave a detailed account of the adverse health effects suffered by hat-makers because of mercury. In Matilda's case, though, we know the victim's name, her age, the era in which she worked. The vivid focus on one girl's tragic death gives readers a high-impact, memorable example of unsafe work in a way that the broader, generic description of hat-makers doesn't.

So the anecdotes arouse readers' interest and make them understand—through the story of a specific person's fatal experience—how serious the issue of dangerous clothing was to both consumers and workers. Which of the answer choices best reflects that function?

There is an element of probability to each choice, although (A) would point to very dark humor, so it can be eliminated first. Next to go is (B). The question stem asks for the primary function of the anecdotes, and the author's references to experts and books convey credibility more than the two anecdotes do. Choice (D) can be eliminated for a similar reason: there are many other descriptions in the passage that point to thorough research, so that's not the primary function of the anecdotes.

That leaves (C). The author connects with her readers through anecdotes that capture their attention and convince them of the importance of the topic. Both are necessary for the author to achieve her purpose of informing a general audience in an interesting, entertaining way.

This approach of finding the correct answer by first eliminating the incorrect choices is called Process of Elimination. When there is some element of truth to each choice, as there is here, it's usually the fastest, most accurate way of finding the correct answer.

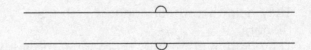

5. What is the relationship between the author's point of view and her purpose?

    A. The point of view is aligned with the author's purpose.
    B. A different point of view would advance her purpose more effectively.
    C. Her point of view changes at different points in the passage.
    D. The purpose and point of view work against each other.

This purpose/point of view question demands a "big picture" analysis of the passage as a whole.

Here's How to Crack It

First you need a firm grasp of what the author's purpose and point of view are. The title tells you that this passage is drawn from *National Geographic*, which attracts a general audience with an interest in learning more about our world. Even if you're not familiar with *National Geographic*, the intriguing topic and the author's explanation of terms (such as "neuromotor problems") suggest a general audience. The author's purpose, then, would be to inform this audience, but in an interesting, entertaining way that would capture and hold the audience's attention. She likely hopes that, after reading the article, some readers might stop to think about whether any fashion worker was put at risk by making the article of clothing they're about to put on.

What about her point of view? As (C) points out, the author's point of view does change. It is at times neutral, at times authoritative (when she cites scholarly books about Victorian fashion, for instance), at times mildly critical, at times humorous. Those are all consistent with her purpose of informing while entertaining and arousing interest. That makes (A) the correct answer —the purpose and point of view are aligned.

Choice (C) is incorrect because it deals with only half of the question. It ignores purpose and how that relates to these changing points of view. Choices (B) and (D) say essentially the same thing: the author's point of view and purpose are not working together, which is not correct.

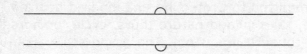

6. As the passage describes the end of dangerous materials and manufacturing techniques, the underlying assumption is that

    A. consumers preferred fashion over their own safety.
    B. the practice was so entrenched that external pressure was required.
    C. consumers valued themselves more than they valued the workers who produced fashion garments.
    D. fashion workers had no power to bring about change.

This evaluation question requires you to identify the assumptions underlying a topic.

Here's How to Crack It

You need to zero in on the specific topic raised in the question—the end of a dangerous practice—and not be distracted by the extensive range of fashion dangers the author covers, from fire-prone dresses to sandblasted jeans. The passage describes only two cases of a dangerous practice actually ending: the mercury hats and the arsenic flowers. To what does the author attribute those two endings? "Men's hats went out of fashion" (paragraph 12) in the former case, and a combination of "public concern" (paragraph 18) and "the invention of synthetic dyes" (paragraph 19) in the latter.

Now you just need to see which answer choice applies to both of those two cases. It's not (A); the author says that mercury didn't pose any danger to the consumers who wore the hats. It's not (D), either; the author implies that the hatters chose not to stop making hats with mercury. Choice (C) is tempting. However, the passage doesn't say whether consumers were even aware of the dangerous effects of mercury on the hat-makers, and Matilda's death from arsenic did raise public concern. That leaves (B) as the correct answer. Hats went out of fashion, public concern about arsenic was aroused, and synthetic dies were invented to replace it. The need for external pressure to stop the use of mercury and arsenic suggests that the practices were so entrenched they would have continued otherwise.

Now, assume that the passage is paired with the following brief excerpt.

Rocky Flats: From Hazard to Haven

1   On the site of what was once a highly contaminated nuclear weapons production facility, the Rocky Flats National Wildlife Refuge is committed to protecting endangered species. Visitors can now hike, take guided nature tours, cycle, or horseback-ride along a year-round trail system. The grand-scale cleanup, initially estimated at $37 billion over 60–70 years, was completed within 10 years for just $7 billion.

2   But just how safe is this former weapons plant site? The debate revolves around the concerns of thousands of nearby homeowners who claim that residual plutonium and other toxins put their health at risk.

7. Drag and drop the concept or theme evident in each passage under the correct passage on the chart. (For this example, letters have been added to each answer choice to clarify the explanation that follows.)

Killer Clothing	Rocky Flats

(a) financial gain chosen over health
(b) one affected group has no choice
(c) advances in materials bring improvements
(d) responsibility cannot be assigned to specific individuals or groups

This comparison question requires you to grasp and analyze the major themes of two works that deal with similar topics.

Here's How to Crack It

Four empty boxes, four answer choices. There are no "extra" alternatives to eliminate as a starting point. In a case like this, the best approach is simply to look at each concept or theme in turn and decide which of the two readings best exhibits that trait. If you're not sure about one choice, skip it and see if there's an empty box left for it at the end.

The concept of choosing financial gain over health is explicitly stated only in the Killer Clothing excerpt. Hat-makers knew the dangers of mercury, but "viewed them as the hazards that one had to accept with the job" (paragraph 11), so (a) falls under Killer Clothing. The Rocky Flats excerpt does not say that developers knew about the potential dangers and deliberately chose to put hikers and homeowners at risk.

Only one group—"endangered species" (paragraph 1) living in the Rocky Flats refuge—has no choice about being exposed to risk. All of the other affected groups in the two excerpts could theoretically educate themselves about the risks and choose not to buy dresses with hoop skirts, for example, or make sandblasted jeans. They could choose not to live or even hike next to a former nuclear weapons plant. So (b) goes in the Rocky Flats column.

Choice (c) goes under Killer Clothing, since the development of synthetic dyes helped eliminate arsenic as a production material. The Rocky Flats piece does not mention any advances in materials that would have made the surprisingly low-cost, speedy remediation effort more effective.

The Rocky Flats excerpt does not provide enough information to assign responsibility, so (d) goes in that column. Did the government or the weapons production company undertake the cleanup? Who decided to build a residential development and trail system next to such a potentially dangerous site? On the other hand, responsibility can be assigned in the Killer Clothing piece—consumers created a market for dangerous clothes, hatters wanted to earn money despite the risks, and employers hid the dangers of arsenic from the flower-makers.

Informational Passage Drill

Over to you now. Ask yourself the active reading questions as you go through this passage, and make sure your critical thinking skills are in gear. Then try the questions, using your knowledge of the seven question tasks. (The order of those tasks is mixed up in this drill, as it will be in the test.) You can check your answers and reasoning in Part VIII: Answer Key to Drills.

Companies use statements of Corporate Social Responsibility (CSR) to explain the values and principles that govern the way they do business, and to make a public commitment to follow them. These documents typically have high-level support from management and the board of directors, and are made available to all stakeholders, from employees to investors, customers to government regulators.

Pine Trail Timber—Statement of Corporate Social Responsibility

1   In carrying out our mission to supply the residential construction industry with the highest quality products from sustainably managed sources, Pine Trail Timber adheres to the following commitments to its stakeholders, to the communities in which it does business, and to the environment.

Responsibility to Stakeholders

2   Our stakeholders place their trust in us, and we work every day to merit that trust by aligning our interests with theirs.

3   All employees deserve a safe, supportive work setting, and the opportunity to achieve their full potential. We stress safety training, prohibit any type of discrimination or harassment, and support employees' efforts to enhance their job-related skills. In return, we expect our employees and officers to devote themselves to fulfilling our commitments to other stakeholders.

4   Investors have a right to expect transparency, sound corporate governance, and a fair return on their investments. We pride ourselves on full disclosure, adherence to the most rigid standards of ethical oversight, and a track record of profitable operations, as our rising stock chart and uninterrupted five-year series of dividend increases show.

5   Our valued customers are entitled to exceptional value and service. Our product innovation and wise management of resources ensure that they receive both.

6   Our suppliers rely on us for fair dealing in specifying our requirements and in meeting our obligations. We consider our suppliers to be our partners—when we succeed, they succeed.

7   We meet the expectations of government and industry regulators by complying with all applicable laws of the countries in which we carry out our business operations, and cooperating in all authorized investigations.

8   We fulfill our duty to the media and the public through providing timely information about any events that might have an impact beyond our operations, and making senior spokespeople available on request.

Support for Local Communities

9   We aim to enhance our host communities. Our presence provides training and jobs, and contributes to the local economy.

10   In the field and in our processing facilities, we recognize the impact our activities may have on local groups. We strive for open communication in order to build relationships, and create opportunities for consultation to foster understanding of our plans.

11   In urban centers where we have administrative operations, we match charitable donations made by our employees and run programs that give employees a block of time off work to volunteer with local organizations. Pine Trail Timber routinely forms one of the largest volunteer groups in the annual Arbor Day activities in several countries, planting trees and teaching other participants how to care for them.

Respect for the Environment

12   We recognize that our current and future success depends on the wise use of renewable resources. We value our reputation as a conscientious steward of the lands that furnish our products.

13   All of our production and processing operations worldwide are certified by the Forest Stewardship Council (FSC) as meeting its rigorous standards for responsible resource management. The FSC certification assures our stakeholders and host communities of independent verification of our operations.

14   Through constant process innovation, we aim to make the least possible use of non-renewable resources in our production.

15   We strive to leave the smallest possible footprint and, where necessary, carry out prompt and thorough remediation. After we finish our operations in an area but before we leave, we ensure that the land is returned to a state where it can produce abundant crops, offer a welcoming home for wildlife, and provide outdoor enjoyment for local residents.

We're Listening

16   If you have any questions or comments about our Corporate Social Responsibility commitments, we invite you to contact Mr. Joseph d'Argill, our Chairman and Chief Executive Officer.

1. The CSR statement specifies that employees are expected to "devote themselves to fulfilling our commitments to other stakeholders" (paragraph 3) because

    A. the authors of the CSR statement are worried that they can't take responsibility themselves for the promises they're making.
    B. the authors know that stakeholders will usually be dealing with lower-level employees instead of with the senior executives and board members who created the CSR statement.
    C. the authors want to exert additional influence on employees through this public statement that stakeholders can expect everyone who works for Pine Trail Timber to fulfill these commitments.
    D. employees work in many different locations and countries, far from the home office where the senior executives and directors behind the statement work.

2. When the company refers to "obligations" (paragraph 6), it means

    A. its responsibilities as a good corporate citizen.
    B. burdens it must bear.
    C. its duties.
    D. money it owes.

Question 3 refers to the following table.

Number of employees	North America	Central America	Africa	Southeast Asia
In production jobs	54,200	17,054	3,214	9,875
In remediation jobs	1,210 [2.2%]	651 [3.8%]	55 [1.7%]	62 [0.6%]
Earned safety certification	11,254 [20.8%]	1,675 [9.8%]	424 [13.2%]	681 [6.9%]
On worker safety committees	325 [0.6%]	153 [0.9%]	107 [3.3%]	31 [0.3%]
Designated as safety representatives	22 [0.04%]	103 [0.6%]	28 [0.9%]	3 [0.03%]
Refused dangerous work	318 [0.59%]	122 [0.72%]	116 [3.6%]	19 [0.02%]

3. Compare the figures in the table above to the overall company image portrayed in the CSR statement. From the answer choices below, identify the *most significant* similarity or difference in topics covered by *both* of the two sources. (Assume the percentages shown in the table are correct; you do not need to calculate them.)

   A. The table suggests the safety and remediation commitments made in the CSR statement apply unevenly to different geographic locations.
   B. The table reinforces the extensive worldwide operations suggested in the text statement.
   C. The table reveals that workers have more control over their safety than the text statement says.
   D. The table confirms the CSR statement's commitment to restoring the land after the company's work there is complete.

4. The authors wrote and published this CSR statement because

   A. government regulations require them to do it.
   B. they want to present a public image of Pine Trail Timber as a responsible, ethical, trustworthy company.
   C. all of their competitors in the forestry industry have one.
   D. they want to explain the company's mission.

5. Decide whether the claims below are supported in Pine Trail Timber's CSR statement or whether the company makes the claim without providing support for it. Drag each claim to the appropriate column in the chart.

(For this drill, write the letter next to each claim in the appropriate column.)

Claim is supported	Claim is not supported

(a) We manage resources responsibly.

(b) We consult with local residents.

(c) We take responsibility for the claims made in this CSR statement.

(d) We put the safety of our employees first.

(e) We provide exceptional customer service.

(f) We run a profitable business.

6. Considering the overall theme of the CSR statement, what conclusion can you draw from the last two paragraphs in the "Responsibility to Stakeholders" section (paragraphs 7–8)?

A. The company sometimes fails in its goals of being a trustworthy steward and improving the areas in which it has operations.

B. Responsibilities to regulators and to the public are considered less important than responsibilities to employees and other stakeholders.

C. The company fosters close relationships with governments and the media.

D. There is a strong sense of responsibility to stakeholders who are not directly involved with the company's business operations.

7. What is the most significant contribution made by the mention of Arbor Day (paragraph 11) to the company image portrayed in the CSR statement?

A. It reinforces the global nature of the company's operations, since Arbor Day is celebrated in many different countries.

B. It supports the company's claim of giving employees time off work to volunteer for charitable activities.

C. It would help attract potential employees who want to preserve the environment.

D. It demonstrates the company's wise use of resources, since participation in Arbor Day would replace some of the trees the company takes in its harvesting operations.

Chapter 7
Literary Passages

In this chapter, we'll move on to fictional texts and how to crack questions about them.

These passages should keep your interest up if you're not the type of person who prefers the real-world grounding of informational passages. The literary selections are more fanciful, imaginative, and for some people, easier to read. On the other hand, though, fictional passages leave a lot more scope for complexity—flashbacks, dream sequences, raving mad narrators, multiple layers of meaning—and can challenge your active reading and critical thinking skills more than informational passages drawn from the real world.

WHAT KIND OF LITERARY PASSAGES ARE ON THE TEST?

From the modern era or from an older time, with lots of dialogue or with paragraphs of lengthy descriptions—you could find it all in the literary selections. These passages don't fall into clear categories as the informational passages do. What the literary selections have in common is good storytelling—a strong plot line and well-developed characters—and the use of literary elements such as imagery and rich language. Beyond that, though, it's the Wild West and you could encounter just about any topic or type of literature.

These passages run between 450 and 900 words, like the informational passages, and make up roughly a quarter of the reading tasks. Like the informational passages, they may represent earlier eras when different styles of writing—such as the long, intricate sentences of Victorian novels—were common. Take a look at this one, for instance:

**Excerpt from *The Pickwick Papers,*
by Charles Dickens, 1837**

They had no sooner arrived at this point, than a most violent and startling knocking was heard at the door; it was not an ordinary double-knock, but a constant and uninterrupted succession of the loudest single raps, as if the knocker were endowed with the perpetual motion, or the person outside had forgotten to leave off.

Yes, that's all one sentence and yes, essentially it just says "someone kept banging on the door." Early Victorian writers were not known for getting straight to the point, though, and this lengthy description adds vivid images of sight and sound that a modern version would lack. So while literary passages can indeed be filled with complex layers, they can also (as in this example) be simple, written in a style that's completely in keeping with the writer's era. The active reading technique of summarizing in your own words will help you see the difference between real complexity and writing styles that may look complex but really aren't.

> Even though literary passages tell interesting stories, you still need to read them actively and think critically about them on the test.

Greater length can also lead to more complexity, though. Now there's room for things like flashbacks, knocking events out of sequence, or for different levels of meaning. (For instance, when is a house a place to live and when does it symbolize a particular culture's claim to a stretch of land?)

Consider this brief excerpt, drawn from a literary source that is classified at a level appropriate for grades 9 and 10:

Excerpt from *Candide, Or The Optimist* by Voltaire

1   The French captain soon saw that the captain of the victorious vessel was a Spaniard, and that the other was a Dutch pirate, and the very same one who had robbed Candide. The immense plunder which this villain had amassed, was buried with him in the sea, and out of the whole only one sheep was saved.

2   "You see," said Candide to Martin, "that crime is sometimes punished. This rogue of a Dutch skipper has met with the fate he deserved."

3   "Yes," said Martin; "but why should the passengers be doomed also to destruction? God has punished the knave, and the devil has drowned the rest."

Excerpt from *Candide, Or The Optimist*, by F.A.M. de Voltaire. Translated by H. Morley. London: George Routledge and Sons, Ltd., 1888 (1759).

Even from this short exchange, you can guess that something more is going on than the simple sinking of a ship in battle. There are indications of much broader concepts of justice, retribution, and good and evil. You can expect layers of meaning like that in many of the literary passages.

HOW SHOULD I READ LITERARY PASSAGES ON THE TEST?

You can't just relax and soak up a story the way you can when you're reading a novel for entertainment. You're taking a test and need to seize control and shake the right answers out of the passage. That means active reading again. The questions to ask yourself as you go through the passage will be different than they were for informational texts, though.

Questions to Ask as You Read Literary Passages

- What's happening?
- Who are the main characters?
- Who is telling the story?
- What is the setting?
- What is the mood?
- Who is the intended audience?

PUTTING IT ALL TOGETHER

Let's work through a couple of examples that will help you practice reading actively and approaching the different question tasks in literary passages.

Excerpt from *The Moonstone*
by William "Wilkie" Collins

1   "I'm afraid Rosanna is sly. It looks as if she had determined to get to that place you and I have just come from, without leaving any marks on the sand to trace her by. Shall we say that she walked through the water from this point till she got to that ledge of rocks behind us, and came back the same way, and then took to the beach again where those two heel marks are still left? Yes, we'll say that. It seems to fit in with my notion that she had something under her cloak, when she left the cottage. No! not something to destroy—for, in that case, where would have been the need of all these precautions to prevent my tracing the place at which her walk ended? Something to hide is, I think, the better guess of the two. Perhaps, if we go on to the cottage, we may find out what that something is?"

2   At this proposal, my detective-fever suddenly cooled. "You don't want me," I said. "What good can I do?"....

3   "If I go alone to the cottage, the people's tongues will be tied at the first question I put to them. If I go with you, I go introduced by a justly respected neighbour, and a flow of conversation is the necessary result. It strikes me in that light; how does it strike you?"

4   Not having an answer of the needful smartness as ready as I could have wished, I tried to gain time by asking him what cottage he wanted to go to....

5   On the Sergeant describing the place, I recognised it as a cottage inhabited by a fisherman named Yolland, with his wife and two grown-up children, a son and a daughter....Rosanna's acquaintance with them had begun by means of the daughter, who was afflicted with a misshapen foot, and who was known in our parts by the name of Limping Lucy. The two deformed girls had, I suppose, a kind of fellow-feeling for each other....The fact of Sergeant Cuff having traced the girl to THEIR cottage, set the matter of my helping his inquiries in quite a new light. Rosanna had merely gone where she was in the habit of going; and to show that she had been in company with the fisherman and his family was as good as to prove that she had been innocently occupied so far, at any rate. It would be doing the girl a service, therefore, instead of an injury, if I allowed myself to be convinced by Sergeant Cuff's logic....

6   Good Mrs. Yolland received us alone in her kitchen. When she heard that Sergeant Cuff was a celebrated character in London, she clapped a bottle of Dutch gin and a couple of clean pipes on the table, and stared as if she could never see enough of him.

7   I sat quiet in a corner, waiting to hear how the Sergeant would find his way to the subject of Rosanna Spearman. His usual roundabout manner of going to work proved, on this occasion, to be more roundabout than ever. How he managed it is more than I could tell at the time, and more than I can tell now. But this is certain, he began with the Royal Family, the Primitive Methodists, and the price of fish; and he got from that (in his dismal, underground way) to the loss of the Moonstone, the spitefulness of our first house-maid, and the hard behaviour of the women-servants generally towards Rosanna Spearman. Having reached his subject in this fashion, he described himself as making his inquiries about the lost Diamond, partly with a view to find it, and partly for the purpose of clearing Rosanna from the unjust suspicions of her enemies in the house. In about a quarter of an hour from the time when we entered the kitchen, good Mrs. Yolland was persuaded that she was talking to Rosanna's best friend, and was pressing Sergeant Cuff to comfort his stomach and revive his spirits out of the Dutch bottle....

8   The great Cuff showed a wonderful patience; trying his luck drearily this way and that way, and firing shot after shot, as it were, at random, on the chance of hitting the mark. Everything to Rosanna's credit, nothing to Rosanna's prejudice—that was how it ended, try as he might; with Mrs. Yolland talking nineteen to the dozen, and placing the most entire confidence in him. His last effort was made, when we had looked at our watches, and had got on our legs previous to taking leave.

9   "I shall now wish you good-night, ma'am," says the Sergeant. "And I shall only say, at parting, that Rosanna Spearman has a sincere well-wisher in myself, your obedient servant. But, oh dear me! she will never get on in her present place; and my advice to her is—leave it."

10   "Bless your heart alive! she is GOING to leave it!" cries Mrs. Yolland....

11   Rosanna Spearman going to leave us! I pricked up my ears at that. It seemed strange, to say the least of it, that she should have given no warning, in the first place, to my lady or to me. A certain doubt came up in my mind whether Sergeant Cuff's last random shot might not have hit the mark. I began to question whether my share in the proceedings was quite as harmless a one as I had thought it. It might be all in the way of the Sergeant's business to mystify an honest woman by wrapping her round in a

network of lies... Beginning to smell mischief in the air, I tried to take Sergeant Cuff out. He sat down again instantly, and asked for a little drop of comfort out of the Dutch bottle. Mrs. Yolland sat down opposite to him, and gave him his nip. I went on to the door, excessively uncomfortable, and said I thought I must bid them good-night—and yet I didn't go.

This passage is complex in its character development, its layers of appearance and reality, and its unstated implications. Did you pick up those characteristics as you were reading through it? Let's explore the active reading questions for literary passages to find some clues to what's going on under the surface. To sharpen your active reading skills, note your answer on some scratch paper (or at least think of your answer) before you read the one below the question.

What's happening? Imagine that you are reading a book, and your friend asks you what the book is about. You wouldn't just start reading aloud to your friend; instead, you'd probably describe the action and characters. In other words, you'd give your friend a summary of the text. If you can summarize a GED® Reading passage in your own words—ideally as you're reading it, not just after—then you're in control.

Summarize in your own words by answering the classic news questions: who, what, when, where, why and how?

How do you summarize? A good place to start is to answer as many as possible of the classic news reporter questions: who, what, when, where, why, and how? In this passage, a detective is tracking a girl. He talks the narrator into accompanying him to the fisherman's cottage where he traced the girl. The detective talks to the fisherman's wife and drinks some Dutch gin. He and the narrator start to leave, then return.

So there's not a lot of action in the passage. However, the excerpt is rich in layers. One person's view of what's going on isn't the same as another's. What appears on the surface differs from the reality beneath, particularly when it comes to motivation. The detective is sure the girl has a stolen diamond, but he tells the narrator that a visit to the cottage could help him discover what the girl might have hidden under her cloak. The narrator sees through Cuff's "round-about manner" (paragraph 7) of trying to get information from Mrs. Yolland, but later wonders whether the sergeant has duped him, too, into doing Rosanna "an injury" instead of "a service" (paragraph 5) by introducing him. Cuff wants to find Rosanna and the diamond, the narrator wants to prove that Rosanna had been "innocently occupied" (paragraph 5), and Mrs. Yolland thinks she is "talking to Rosanna's best friend" (paragraph 7). The answers to some of the classic news questions will differ markedly depending on which character is in focus.

Who are the main characters, and what do we know about them? There are four main characters in this passage, although only three are present.

Mrs. Yolland is a humble fisherman's wife, completely incapable of seeing through Cuff's subtle tactics. A simple and "honest woman" (paragraph 11), she is overwhelmed by the visit from a "celebrated character in London" (paragraph 6) and reassured by the presence of a "respected neighbour" (paragraph 3), so she speaks openly and places "the most entire confidence" (paragraph 8) in the detective. She even reveals to the narrator that Rosanna was planning to leave his house.

The narrator seems more perceptive than Mrs. Yolland, but even he is no match for Cuff. He doesn't want to go to the cottage because his "detective-fever suddenly cooled" (paragraph 2). Then, however, he allows himself to be persuaded when he learns it's Yolland's cottage, where Rosanna was "in the habit of going," proving that she "had been innocently occupied" (paragraph 5). He recognizes the detective's "roundabout manner" in questioning Mrs. Yolland, but admits that "how he managed it is more than I could tell" (paragraph 7). In addition, the narrator had no idea that Rosanna was planning to leave his house, even though she worked there and he presumably saw her every day. He suspects that Cuff might have deceived him: "I began to question whether my share in the proceedings was quite as harmless a one as I had thought it" (paragraph 11). He senses "mischief in the air" (paragraph 11) and tries to get Cuff to leave, but ends up staying with the sergeant and Mrs. Yolland. The narrator seems unaware and not in control when manipulative tactics and subterfuge are directed at him.

Sergeant Cuff is a master at reading the other characters and manipulating them to achieve his own ends. He wins Mrs. Yolland's confidence and convinces her that his aim is "clearing Rosanna from the unjust suspicions of her enemies in the house" (paragraph 7). He enlists the narrator's help by giving him an opportunity to prove that Rosanna "had been innocently occupied" (paragraph 5). He is also a skilled reader of evidence, figuring out how Rosanna had moved on the beach to conceal her path.

We only learn about Rosanna through the statements and actions of other characters, yet she is the force that sets the entire passage in motion. She is described as "deformed" (paragraph 5), a servant in the narrator's house, and persecuted by other women servants. Except for the Yolland family, she is alone. She is also devious, planning to leave without telling her employers. Beyond that, Rosanna is an enigma. Would she be capable of stealing a diamond and outwitting Sergeant Cuff? She may be "sly" (paragraph 1), but couldn't fool him with her attempts to avoid being traced on the beach. Why was she preparing to leave in secret? Where would she be able to go? We can't answer those questions from the information in the passage.

Three other characters are simply mentioned: Yolland, the fisherman, his adult son and adult daughter, Limping Lucy, who seems to be Rosanna's only friend.

Who is telling the story? A story can be told by either a first-person narrator (an "I" narrator who is a character in the story) or a third-person narrator (a narrator who is not a character in the story, using "he/she/they," but not "I"). They could be as objective as an unbiased third-person narrator, or they could be highly biased or just plain crazy, too. You need to pay close attention to what they reveal about themselves in order to judge whether you can take the story they're telling at face value.

> First-person ("I") narrators may not be reliable or objective in telling their stories.

In this case, the narrator can see through Cuff's "usual roundabout manner" (paragraph 7) of questioning someone. However, as we saw in the analysis of his character, he's not particularly reliable or perceptive concerning tactics that are directed at him.

What is the setting? Sometimes the setting (place and time) can add a lot to your grasp of the passage, and sometimes it doesn't reveal much. In this passage, the places—the deserted beach, the fisherman's cottage—reinforce the distance between the celebrated London detective and the other characters. Cuff is in an alien environment, but is still functioning very effectively, revealing his skill. The narrator and Mrs. Yolland are on home ground, but Cuff still manages to get what he wants from both of them.

What is the mood? There is a murky, mysterious mood to this passage that complements the plot line of a clever detective trying to penetrate appearances and discover the truth. Cuff's method of mystifying "an honest woman by wrapping her round in a network of lies" (paragraph 11), and the narrator's suspicion that Cuff has outsmarted him, add a negative tone. Does the detective's goal justify his rather devious methods?

In other passages, the mood could be lighthearted or neutral; it could add a lot to your understanding of the passage or it might not be very helpful. It all depends on the passage.

Who is the intended audience? You might not be able to guess from the passage; it's not as easy with literary texts as it is with informational pieces. If you can get a picture of the intended audience, though, you'll have another layer of insight into the passage. Perhaps it's intended for young readers. That would explain fairly black-and-white characters and straightforward action. Or perhaps it's intended for readers of detective and mystery fiction, as this example is. That's your clue that the undertones you may have sensed in this passage are, in fact, real; these readers would expect and be looking for them.

Now that active reading has given you a firmer grip on the passage, let's tackle a few questions. Try to choose the answer yourself, using the insight gained from the active reading questions, before you read the explanation below the choices.

1. What main function does Limping Lucy serve in the passage?

   A. She increases the reader's sympathy for Mrs. Yolland.
   B. She helps create a picture of a "balanced" family.
   C. She makes the reader feel more negatively toward Sergeant Cuff.
   D. She reinforces the impression that Rosanna is alone and vulnerable.

Here's How to Crack It
Here's a structure question as it applies to a literary passage. Limping Lucy isn't present in the excerpt; she's mentioned only briefly. Why? What main purpose does that brief mention serve?

The narrator explains that Rosanna knew the Yolland family through Limping Lucy. That's not one of the answer choices for Lucy's function, though. The fact that Mrs. Yolland has a daughter with a "misshapen foot" (paragraph 5) might add to the sympathy readers feel because of the way Cuff is manipulating her (A). However, the question asks for the main purpose. Is there a stronger choice?

You can guess that there probably is from the fact that the author concentrates his description of Limping Lucy on Rosanna, not on Mrs. Yolland. Both girls are "deformed" and have "a kind of fellow-feeling for each other" (paragraph 5). Contrast this with "the hard behaviour of the women-servants generally towards Rosanna" (paragraph 7). Lucy is the only one to whom Rosanna feels a connection. Her colleagues reject and persecute her. That leads to (D), reinforcing the impression of Rosanna as alone (except for Lucy) and vulnerable.

Choice (C) is incorrect because it refers to essentially the same thing as (A). If readers feel sympathy for Mrs. Yolland because of Cuff's behavior toward her, then they would also feel negative sentiments toward Cuff. Again, (D) is a stronger choice. Choice (B) is also incorrect. It's too vague. What does a "balanced" family (presumably a son and a daughter) add to the passage?

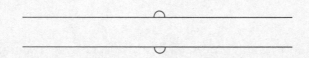

2. Does the narrator's account of Sergeant Cuff's questioning of Mrs. Yolland support Cuff's contention that he is "making his inquiries about the lost Diamond...partly for the purpose of clearing Rosanna" (paragraph 7)?

   A. Yes. While he is talking to Mrs. Yolland, Cuff refers to "the hard behaviour of the women-servants generally towards Rosanna" and to the "unjust suspicions of her [Rosanna's] enemies in the house" (paragraph 7), suggesting he wants to help Rosanna.
   B. No. The narrator says that Cuff is "wrapping her [Mrs. Yolland] round in a network of lies" (paragraph 11), implying that Cuff's stated purpose can't be believed.
   C. Yes. The narrator agrees to accompany Cuff to the Yollands' cottage because that allows Cuff to be "introduced by a justly respected neighbour and a flow of conversation is the necessary result" (paragraph 3). Cuff wants Mrs. Yolland to feel comfortable talking to him.
   D. No. The narrator says Cuff was "firing shot after shot, as it were, at random, on the chance of hitting the mark" (paragraph 8), suggesting that Cuff's questions had a hostile, destructive quality.

Here's How to Crack It

This is an evaluation question as it applies to a literary passage. Here you're evaluating whether the narrator's account of the questioning is consistent with the motive Cuff explains to Mrs. Yolland.

Too much in the narrator's description contradicts the two "yes" choices, so those can be eliminated. The detective's references to Rosanna's enemies (A) are part of his tactic of convincing

Mrs. Yolland that "she was talking to Rosanna's best friend" (paragraph 7). And Cuff could just as easily want Mrs. Yolland to open up to him (C) out of a desire to accuse Rosanna as out of a desire to clear her.

That leaves the two "no" choices. Which one provides a more direct answer to the question? Choice (D) has merit. The narrator's descriptions of "firing shot after shot" and "hitting the mark" do suggest hostility rather than goodwill. However, (B) is a more direct answer, and is therefore the correct choice. The narrator's account describes Cuff's questioning as a "network of lies," and therefore does not support Cuff's stated motive, which would also be a lie.

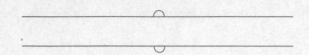

3. When the narrator says Mrs. Yolland was "talking nineteen to the dozen" (paragraph 8), he is referring to her

    A.   refusal to let Cuff get a word in.
    B.   attempts to evade Sergeant Cuff's questions.
    C.   unrealistically positive comments about Rosanna.
    D.   meaningless chatter about irrelevant topics.

Here's How to Crack It

The passages on the GED® test are often in the public domain, which means they have an older style of writing (such as very long sentences) and terms that aren't familiar to modern readers. (*The Moonstone* was written in 1868.) That's true of both the informational and the literary selections. Language use questions such as this one will help you develop skills in using context to guess the meaning of an unfamiliar word or term. These questions force you to delve deeper into the passage and understand it more thoroughly (instead of simply skipping over the part you can't figure out). In some cases, they'll help you expand your vocabulary, too.

Since this is a literary passage, first ask yourself what's going on when that term is used. Sergeant Cuff is getting nowhere in his attempts to wring some information about Rosanna and the diamond from Mrs. Yolland. He needs—and is exercising—"wonderful patience," firing random questions at her "on the chance of hitting the mark," but all he's hearing is "everything to Rosanna's credit, nothing to Rosanna's prejudice" (paragraph 8). Moreover, Mrs. Yolland is "talking nineteen to the dozen" (paragraph 8).

Process of Elimination (looking for clearly wrong answers and eliminating those first) is an efficient approach when you're really not sure. Mrs. Yolland is talking about a relevant topic (Rosanna), which eliminates (D). The narrator says she's an "honest woman," in contrast to Cuff's "network of lies" (paragraph 11), which gets rid of (C). She places her "entire confidence" (paragraph 8) in the detective, and has been persuaded that he is "Rosanna's best friend" (paragraph 7), so she wouldn't be trying to evade his questions, eliminating (B). Now only (A) is left. Does it make sense? Yes. Mrs. Yolland feels safe talking to Cuff, and is excited about the visit from this celebrated man. As the greater weight of nineteen compared to a dozen suggests, she's talking practically nonstop, outweighing his conversation and making it difficult for him to launch even his random-shot questions.

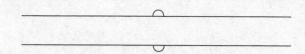

4. Why does the passage begin with Sergeant Cuff's efforts to trace Rosanna's movements on the beach?

A. Cuff needs to find out where Rosanna went before he can find the diamond.

B. The tracking episode shows how clever Rosanna is.

C. It helps Cuff determine whether Rosanna was carrying something to destroy or something to hide.

D. Cuff's reasoning while tracking Rosanna illustrates his ability to understand people.

Here's How to Crack It

You could encounter two types of development questions with a literary passage: plot development and character development. Often the two types overlap, such as when the development of a character also advances the plot, or when a development in the plot also reveals more about a character.

The event described in the question falls into that last category. In terms of the plot, Cuff is able to figure out where Rosanna went and decide to go there, too. That development in the plot also reveals something new about his character. He shows that he can read people well enough to understand what Rosanna did to try to hide her tracks, and why. That same character trait is put to use again later on in the passage, when he convinces the narrator to accompany him to the cottage and when he gets Mrs. Yolland to reveal that Rosanna is planning to leave.

Now you need to decide which answer choice provides the closest match. Choice (A) is incorrect because it deals only with plot development. It ignores the aspect of Cuff's character that is revealed by his reasoning as he follows Rosanna's movements. If Rosanna were that clever, Cuff wouldn't have been able to track her, so (B) is incorrect. Choice (C) is too narrow. Cuff wants to figure out where Rosanna went, too, not simply what she was carrying. That leaves (D) as the correct answer. The part of the plot that occurs on the beach also provides a way to develop Cuff's character as someone with a keen ability to understand people and get what he wants from them.

How Do the Seven Question Tasks Look in a Literary Passage?

Now that we've seen how the active reading questions can help you get a better grip on a literary passage, let's go through an example in which we can focus on the seven question tasks in action.

Excerpt from *Tom Sawyer*, by Mark Twain, 1876

1   Tom did play hookey, and he had a very good time. He got back home barely in season to help Jim saw next-day's wood and split the kindlings before supper—at least he was there in time to tell his adventures to Jim while Jim did three-fourths of the work. Tom's younger brother (or rather half-brother) Sid was already through with his part of the work (picking up chips), for he was a quiet boy, and had no adventurous, troublesome ways.

2   While Tom was eating his supper, and stealing sugar as opportunity offered, Aunt Polly asked him questions that were full of guile, and very deep—for she wanted to trap him into damaging revealments. Like many other simple-hearted souls, it was her pet vanity to believe she was endowed with a talent for dark and mysterious diplomacy, and she loved to contemplate her most transparent devices as marvels of low cunning. Said she:

3   "Tom, it was middling warm in school, warn't it?"

4   "Yes'm."

5   "Powerful warm, warn't it?"

6   "Yes'm."

7   "Didn't you want to go in a-swimming, Tom?"

8   A bit of a scare shot through Tom—a touch of uncomfortable suspicion. He searched Aunt Polly's face, but it told him nothing. So he said:

9   "No'm—well, not very much."

10   The old lady reached out her hand and felt Tom's shirt, and said:

11   "But you ain't too warm now, though." And it flattered her to reflect that she had discovered that the shirt was dry without anybody knowing that that was what she had in her mind. But in spite of her, Tom knew where the wind lay, now. So he forestalled what might be the next move:

12   "Some of us pumped on our heads—mine's damp yet. See?"

13   Aunt Polly was vexed to think she had overlooked that bit of circumstantial evidence, and missed a trick. Then she had a new inspiration:

14   "Tom, you didn't have to undo your shirt collar where I sewed it, to pump on your head, did you? Unbutton your jacket!"

15   The trouble vanished out of Tom's face. He opened his jacket. His shirt collar was securely sewed.

16   "Bother! Well, go 'long with you. I'd made sure you'd played hookey and been a-swimming. But I forgive ye, Tom. I reckon you're a kind of a singed cat, as the saying is—better'n you look. *This* time."

17   She was half sorry her sagacity had miscarried, and half glad that Tom had stumbled into obedient conduct for once.

18   But Sidney said:

19   "Well, now, if I didn't think you sewed his collar with white thread, but it's black."

20   "Why, I did sew it with white! Tom!"

21   But Tom did not wait for the rest. As he went out at the door he said:

22   "Siddy, I'll lick you for that."

23   In a safe place Tom examined two large needles which were thrust into the lapels of his jacket, and had thread bound about them—one needle carried white thread and the other black. He said: "She'd never noticed if it hadn't been for Sid. Confound it! sometimes she sews it with white, and sometimes she sews it with black. I wish to geeminy she'd stick to one or t'other—I can't keep the run of 'em. But I bet you I'll lam Sid for that. I'll learn him!"

1. The main theme of this passage is

   A. the contrast between Tom's personality and Sid's.
   B. the conflict between chores (work) and school on the one hand, and avoiding those duties on the other.
   C. the contrast between the choices Tom can make and the choices Jim has.
   D. the struggle between Tom and Aunt Polly to outwit each other.

Here's How to Crack It

Several subjects run through this passage, but we're looking for the overall big-picture theme to answer this question. Choices (A) and (B) are certainly present, but they're not central to the entire passage. Tom does seem to have more options than Jim—Tom can go to school or go swimming, but Jim has to prepare wood and do most of the work as he listens to Tom talk about his day. Jim isn't at supper with Aunt Polly and the other two boys, either. Again, though, (C) doesn't filter through the entire passage.

After eliminating those sub-themes, (D) emerges as the main theme. It's evident right from the beginning (Tom playing "hookey" [line 1] in defiance of Aunt Polly) to the end (Tom feeling outfoxed by Aunt Polly's habit of switching thread colors).

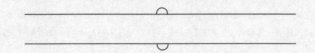

2.   What was Aunt Polly's aim in questioning Tom?

    A.   She hoped to start an argument between Tom and Sid.

    B.   She wanted to practice using the diplomatic skills she believed she possessed.

    C.   She wanted to get Tom to admit that he'd gone swimming instead of going to school.

    D.   She was trying to exert her authority over him.

Here's How to Crack It

This question examines the development of the plot. Let's use Process of Elimination to get rid of the incorrect answers first. Aunt Polly made no attempt to draw Sid into the conversation, so (A) is gone. Her supposed diplomatic skills were a means to an end; simply practicing them was not her objective, so (B) is out, too. Now we're left with (C) and (D): Was Aunt Polly trying to achieve a specific victory (C) or establish her authority in general (D)?

The narrator says that "Aunt Polly asked him [Tom] questions that were full of guile, and very deep—for she wanted to trap him into damaging revealments" (paragraph 2). That pretty well takes us to (C) as the correct answer, but just to make sure, we need to figure out what on earth "revealments" means.

The passage was written almost a century and a half ago, and Aunt Polly is from a particular geographic region and economic class (as indicated by the references to the heat and to family members doing their own sewing and wood-chopping), so her use of language seems unusual to modern readers throughout the dialogue. The narrator's choice of an odd word such as "revealments" isn't too surprising in the context of the way Aunt Polly speaks. Combined with "trap" and "damaging," the word points to its root, "reveal," indicating she is questioning Tom in order to get him to disclose something he wants to hide. We learn later what that is, when she says, "I'd made sure you'd played hookey and been a-swimming." So, (C) is correct.

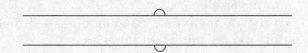

3.   What does Aunt Polly regret when she feels "her sagacity had miscarried" (paragraph 17)?

    A.   that she had wrongly accused Tom
    B.   that she hadn't taken him to school herself, to make sure he went
    C.   that Tom apparently hadn't played hookey after all
    D.   that her cunning had failed her

Here's How to Crack It

Here's a challenging language use question in the context of a passage that displays unusual language throughout. First, look at the context. The next part of that sentence eliminates (C): Aunt Polly says she is "half glad" (paragraph 17) that Tom apparently had gone to school, so that's not what she regrets. If he went to school after all, there would be no need for her to take him there herself, so (B) is out, too.

Now we're left with (A) and (D), which are different in a subtle way. Is Aunt Polly sorry about making this specific false accusation (A), or is she sorry that her cunning (which led her try to make Tom admit the accusation was true) had failed (D)? The description of Aunt Polly in the second paragraph points to (D). She believes she has a "talent for dark and mysterious diplomacy" (paragraph 2) and sees her attempts to display it as "marvels of low cunning" (paragraph 2). She tried using those powers to get Tom to admit he'd played hookey, and when it seemed he'd really been at school, she's troubled by the failure of her talents. That's (D). Her cunning (sagacity) had failed to achieve her intended purpose (it had miscarried).

4.   What main function does the character of Sid serve in the passage?

    A.   He acts as a counterweight to Tom.
    B.   He is an example of the type of boy Aunt Polly prefers to Tom.
    C.   He introduces another source of tension in Tom's life, in addition to Aunt Polly.
    D.   His status in the family suggests that Tom isn't a full member.

Here's How to Crack It

This is a structure question as it applies to a literary passage: Why is Sid there? He doesn't appear very much in the passage, but when he does (with the observation about the thread color), his impact is significant.

The passage doesn't give us enough information to know whether (D) is correct. Sid is Tom's half-brother, and their caregiver is Tom's aunt, but we don't know whether Aunt Polly is Sid's mother. There are suggestions that (B) might not be true. Sid is quiet, with "no adventurous, troublesome ways" (paragraph 1). Aunt Polly seems to enjoy Tom's adventurous spirit in a way, though—it gives her an opportunity to try to outwit him—and Sid's comment about the black thread ends her ability to be "half glad that Tom had stumbled into obedient conduct for once" (paragraph 17). So let's eliminate (B).

Sid does fulfill the functions described in both (A) and (C): He is the opposite of Tom (A) and seems determined to get Tom into trouble (C). Which is the *main* function, though? Choice (A) is too general: Sid could be acting as an opposite balancing force to any aspect(s) of Tom's character. Choice (C) is the correct answer because it reflects the tension between Tom and Aunt Polly. That tension runs throughout the dialogue, and Sid reignites it from left field when he pops up with the thread comment.

5. For what purpose did the author use a dialogue between Aunt Polly and Tom instead of simply describing the conflict over going to school?

    A. so readers could get to know the characters more directly
    B. to convey the type of language used in that time period and geographic area
    C. because he does a better job of writing dialogue than he does of writing narrative descriptions
    D. because the literary style in the author's time favored dialogue

Here's How to Crack It

Here's a purpose question as it applies to a literary passage. In this case, we're trying to discover the author's purpose in choosing to tell the story the way he did.

Again, let's use Process of Elimination to get rid of the wrong answers. Choice (B) is too general. If that were the author's purpose, he could have done the same thing elsewhere besides the dialogue. Indeed, he uses the same type of language in narrative sections. Choice (C) isn't as silly as it might sound. If there were an obvious difference in skill between the narrative and the dialogue sections, it could be true. However, there isn't in this passage. Choice (D) would take you beyond the passage if it were true, and you need to stay within the boundaries of the passage to find the right answer.

So we're left with (A). Instead of having the narrator describe the conflict, which would be one step removed from the characters involved, the author lets the characters speak for themselves, putting readers more directly in touch with them.

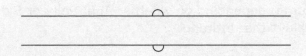

6. Does the author's account of the exchange between Aunt Polly and Tom support the idea that they seem about equally matched?

   A. No. The author describes the talents and cunning Aunt Polly believes she can put to use in dealing with Tom, but Tom is just a disobedient boy with no special abilities.
   B. Yes. Tom senses immediately what Aunt Polly is trying to find out, and "forestalled what might be the next move" (paragraph 11) by explaining his wet hair without being asked.
   C. Yes. Tom gets Jim to do most of the wood splitting, so he would be a match for Aunt Polly's attempts to get him to admit to playing hookey.
   D. No. Until Sid intervenes with his observation about the thread color, Tom is the clear winner.

Here's How to Crack It

This is an evaluation question as it applies to literary passages. The author obviously wants to portray Tom and Aunt Polly as pretty well equally matched in their ongoing contests. (Aunt Polly's concession of defeat *"this* time" [paragraph 16] suggests a series of exchanges like this, where she doesn't always win.) Has the author done a credible job of it, though?

Tom seems to have a natural ability to anticipate Aunt Polly's moves and head them off (when he sewed his shirt collar again after swimming, for instance). That eliminates (A). Tom won only *"this* time" (paragraph 16), not *every* time, which eliminates (D).

That leaves us with two choices that say yes, the author has done a credible job of presenting Aunt Polly and Tom as about equally matched, but for different reasons. The only one that pits Tom directly against Aunt Polly in a contest of wills is (B), which is the correct answer. Just because Tom can outwit Jim, as (C) claims, doesn't make him a match for Aunt Polly.

7. In this passage, both Aunt Polly and Sid are Tom's adversaries. But when it comes to the contest of wills with Tom, their approaches differ. Drag the descriptions of their approaches to the correct column, depending on whether Aunt Polly or Sid displays that attitude.

Aunt Polly	Sid

mystifying

a game

a source of mixed emotions

serious

a test of wills

a risk

Here's How to Crack It

This comparison question asks you to dig deeper into the relationships among the characters, based on what the passage tells us. If you find the descriptions and statements surrounding Aunt Polly's attempt to get Tom to admit to playing hookey (or better yet, if you jotted a word or two down as you were actively reading the passage), you'll see that the second, third, and fifth descriptions apply to her approach to the contest with Tom. She treats it as a bit of a game and as a test of her powers of "dark and mysterious diplomacy" (paragraph 2) against Tom's deceptive ways. It's also a source of conflicting emotions for her, though, since she's half upset that her powers failed and half glad that Tom wasn't deceiving her for once.

There are no "left over" descriptions in this question, so the other three must apply to Sid. Indeed, his deliberate attempt to get Tom into trouble by mentioning the thread color is both mystifying and a risk, since he likely knows from past experience that Tom will make good on his threat to "lick you for that" (paragraph 22). There's a serious quality to his confrontation with Tom, too: He doesn't take part in the game-like contest of wills between Tom and Aunt Polly, but just calmly reignites the dispute when it seems as if Tom has won.

Literary Passage Drill

Now it's your turn. Ask yourself the active reading questions as you go through this passage, and use your critical thinking skills. Then try the questions, using your knowledge of the seven question tasks. (All seven are represented in the questions below, to give you a chance to try each task on your own. However, the order of the tasks is mixed up.) You can check your answers in Part VIII: Answer Key to Drills.

Excerpt from *The Leopard Man's Story*, by Jack London, 1903

1   He was the Leopard Man, but he did not look it. His business in life, whereby he lived, was to appear in a cage of performing leopards before vast audiences, and to thrill those audiences by certain exhibitions of nerve for which his employers rewarded him on a scale commensurate with the thrills he produced.

2   As I say, he did not look it. He was narrow-hipped, narrow-shouldered, and anaemic, while he seemed not so much oppressed by gloom as by a sweet and gentle sadness, the weight of which was as sweetly and gently borne. For an hour I had been trying to get a story out of him, but he appeared to lack imagination. To him there was no romance in his gorgeous career, no deeds of daring, no thrills—nothing but a gray sameness and infinite boredom.

3   Lions? Oh, yes! he had fought with them. It was nothing. All you had to do was to stay sober. Anybody could whip a lion to a standstill with an ordinary stick. He had fought one for half an hour once. Just hit him on the nose every time he rushed, and when he got artful and rushed with his head down, why, the thing to do was to stick out your leg. When he grabbed at the leg you drew it back and hit him on the nose again. That was all.

4   With the far-away look in his eyes and his soft flow of words he showed me his scars. There were many of them, and one recent one where a tigress had reached for his shoulder and gone down to the bone. I could see the neatly mended rents in the coat he had on. His right arm, from the elbow down, looked as though it had gone through a threshing machine, what of the ravage wrought by claws and fangs. But it was nothing, he said, only the old wounds bothered him somewhat when rainy weather came on.

5   Suddenly his face brightened with a recollection, for he was really as anxious to give me a story as I was to get it.

6   "He was a little, thin, sawed-off, sword-swallowing and juggling Frenchman. De Ville, he called himself, and he had a nice wife. She did trapeze work and used to dive from under the roof into a net, turning over once on the way as nice as you please.

7   "De Ville had a quick temper, as quick as his hand, and his hand was as quick as the paw of a tiger. The word went around to watch out for De Ville, and no one dared be more than barely civil to his wife. And she was a sly bit of baggage, too, only all the performers were afraid of De Ville.

8   "But there was one man, Wallace, who was afraid of nothing. He was the lion-tamer, and he had the trick of putting his head into the lion's mouth. He'd put it into the mouths of any of them, though he preferred Augustus, a big, good-natured beast who could always be depended upon.

9   "As I was saying, Wallace—'King' Wallace we called him—was afraid of nothing alive or dead. He was a king and no mistake.

10   "Madame de Ville looked at King Wallace and King Wallace looked at her, while De Ville looked at them darkly. We warned Wallace, but it was no use. He laughed at us, as he laughed at De Ville.

11   "But I saw a glitter in De Ville's eyes which I had seen often in the eyes of wild beasts, and I went out of my way to give Wallace a final warning. He laughed, but he did not look so much in Madame de Ville's direction after that.

12   "Several months passed by. Nothing had happened and I was beginning to think it all a scare over nothing. We were West by that time, showing in 'Frisco. It was during the afternoon performance, and the big tent was filled with women and children.

13   "Passing by one of the dressing tents I glanced in through a hole in the canvas: in front of me was King Wallace, in tights, waiting for his turn to go on with his cage of performing lions. I noticed De Ville staring at Wallace with undisguised hatred. Wallace and the rest were all too busy to notice this or what followed.

14   "But I saw it through the hole in the canvas. De Ville drew his handkerchief from his pocket, made as though to mop the sweat from his face with it (it was a hot day), and at the same time walked past Wallace's back. The look troubled me at the time, for not only did I see hatred in it, but I saw triumph as well.

15   "'De Ville will bear watching,' I said to myself, and I really breathed easier when I saw him go out the entrance to the circus grounds. A few minutes later I was in the big tent. King Wallace was doing his turn and holding the audience spellbound. He was in a particularly vicious mood, and he kept the lions stirred up till they were all snarling, that is, all of them except old Augustus, and he was just too fat and lazy and old to get stirred up over anything.

16   "Finally Wallace cracked the old lion's knees with his whip and
       got him into position. Old Augustus, blinking good-naturedly,
       opened his mouth and in popped Wallace's head. Then the jaws
       came together, *crunch*, just like that."

17   The Leopard Man smiled in a sweetly wistful fashion, and the
       far-away look came into his eyes.

18   "And that was the end of King Wallace," he went on in his sad,
       low voice. "After the excitement cooled down I watched my chance
       and bent over and smelled Wallace's head. Then I sneezed."

19   "It...it was...?" I queried with halting eagerness.

20   "Snuff—that De Ville dropped on his hair in the dressing tent.
       Old Augustus never meant to do it. He only sneezed."

1. The overall structure of this passage most
    closely resembles which of the following
    shapes?

    A.   an inverted pyramid
    B.   a maze
    C.   a frame within a frame
    D.   a spiral

2. Why does the author give such a lengthy
    description of the Leopard Man's attitude
    toward the work he does?

    A.   to show that any profession can get
          boring after a while
    B.   to reveal how aging can affect
          someone's enthusiasm for life
    C.   to highlight the contrast between
          the Leopard Man and Wallace
    D.   to reflect one of the main ideas
          in the story that the Leopard Man
          tells

3. When the narrator speaks of the
    "ravage wrought by claws and fangs"
    (paragraph 4), he is referring to

    A.   the result of performing with
          leopards throughout the Leopard
          Man's career.
    B.   the Leopard Man's advancing age.
    C.   the damage caused by the big cats
          the Leopard Man fights.
    D.   the Leopard Man's lack of
          excitement about his career.

4. Compare the Leopard Man's attitude
    toward De Ville with Wallace's. Which of
    the following statements is true?

    A.   Both the Leopard Man and Wallace
          let their guard down.
    B.   The Leopard Man believed warnings
          were needed; Wallace completely
          ignored warnings.
    C.   Wallace underestimated De Ville;
          the Leopard Man did not.
    D.   Wallace thought his physical
          strength made him invincible; the
          Leopard Man knew that De Ville's
          cleverness was more dangerous
          than physical strength.

5. Drag and drop the events into the chart in the order in which they occur in the passage. Not all of the events below actually take place, so you will have some left over.

    (For this drill, write the event letters in the chart.)

Order of Events

(a) Wallace stops looking at De Ville's wife.

(b) The Leopard Man watches De Ville walk behind Wallace.

(c) Wallace notices the hatred in De Ville's stare.

(d) De Ville's wife looks at Wallace.

(e) Augustus sneezes.

(f) Wallace tries to talk to De Ville to defuse the tension.

(g) Several people in the circus warn Wallace about De Ville.

(h) De Ville tells the Leopard Man that he intends to get revenge on Wallace.

6. Which event in the passage has the *weakest* support from the other descriptions and events in the passage?

    A. the Leopard Man repeatedly warning Wallace about De Ville
    B. De Ville waiting so long for revenge when the cause of his anger had stopped
    C. Wallace not being afraid of De Ville
    D. Augustus biting off Wallace's head

7. The moral of this passage is

    A. brains are better than brawn.
    B. don't try to fight nature.
    C. never underestimate your opponent.
    D. the grass is never greener.

Part II Summary

- There are five main features of the Reading assessment:
  - There are six to eight passages of up to 900 words each.
  - The majority (75 percent) of the passages deal with informational (nonfiction) topics drawn from real-world contexts. The rest are literary (fictional) texts.
  - The questions test critical thinking and analytical skills, not simply comprehension. You will need to practice active reading techniques, summarizing and asking questions as you read.
  - Each question has four answer choices.
  - Most questions will be in the familiar multiple-choice format. The computer-based test also presents you with drag-and-drop questions, where you "drag" alternatives to a chart full of empty boxes and "drop" them into the correct positions on the chart.

- The reading passages might be mixed in with the language passages. You will have 95 minutes to answer all of the reading and language questions.

- There are 48 reading questions spread across the six to eight passages. For both informational and fictional passages, the questions cover seven main tasks:

  1. Main Idea or Theme
  2. Development (of Ideas, Events, or Characters)
  3. Language Use
  4. Structure
  5. Purpose (or Point of View)
  6. Evaluation (of the Author's Argument or Reasoning)
  7. Comparison (of Different Passages that Deal with Similar Topics)

o   Informational passages are drawn from the workplace and academia. Workplace texts could include ads, policy statements, executive speeches, or community announcements. Academic topics cover science (energy, human health, and living systems) and social studies (the Great American Conversation, ranging from the country's founding to modern American culture). They will all have a "voice"—an author with a specific point of view and purpose.

o   Literary passages don't fall into any topic categories. They all feature good storytelling, a strong plot line, and well-developed characters.

Part III
Reasoning Through Language Arts: Language

Chapter 8
Language Overview

What would you think of an employer who posted a job ad full of obvious grammar mistakes? Does that sound like someone who might mess up your paycheck too? Or how about a political candidate who dropped off a "vote for me" flyer filled with spelling errors? Is that someone you would trust to be careful with your tax dollars?

Proper use of the English language isn't just about grammar or punctuation—it's about clarity and credibility. It's about getting your message across and inspiring confidence in the skill and accuracy people can expect from you. If you don't care whether your résumé is written clearly and correctly, why should an employer spend time figuring out what it says? If you don't bother putting proper sentences together on a loan application, why would the lender trust you to make the effort to repay it on time?

Your language use can reveal a lot about yourself; you want it to make the best impression.

> Get your message across and inspire trust by using language correctly.

HOW DOES THE GED® TEST MEASURE LANGUAGE USE?

You're about to explore one of the two ways the GED® test evaluates your language skills: the Language assessment. It consists of two passages, each containing four places where you need to select from four possible ways to complete a sentence correctly. Those two passages could be mixed in with the reading passages or they might appear at the end. Either way, you will have 95 minutes to do the six to eight reading passages and two language passages, before the 10-minute break.

Since the GED® test aims at skills that demonstrate readiness for a career or college, the language passages are drawn from the real world: workplace documents, professional communications, and messages to consumers. You might see business letters or emails, flyers, advertisements, or employee notices. Like the reading texts, these passages reflect different high school levels. They're shorter (350–450 words) and less complex than the reading passages, though, to allow you to focus on the language issues.

Why are there only two language passages? It's because part of your essay score in the Extended Response section is based on language use, too, so your language skills are being tested in both editing tasks (that's this section of the test) and in writing.

WHAT WILL I NEED TO KNOW ABOUT LANGUAGE?

The GED® Language assessment targets eight areas of language use that have been identified as the most important for a career or college. Don't panic when you see the list below, though—in the next chapter, you'll learn how the question format on the GED® test makes it easier to reach the correct answer.

Language Skills on the GED® Test

- **Word choice**: avoiding words that are often confused or used in a nonstandard way
- **Agreement**: of subject and verb, of noun and pronoun
- **Pronoun use:** clear antecedents, correct case
- **Modifiers:** correctly placed
- **Joining thoughts:** proper coordination, subordination, and parallel construction
- **Sentence construction:** avoiding wordiness, run-on sentences, and fragments
- **Logic and clarity:** effective use of words and phrases that mark a clear path for the reader
- **Punctuation and capitalization**

You don't even need to know the names of any of these areas of language use, either. For the Language assessment, you simply need to be able to recognize when something is wrong—for whatever reason—and when it's correct. Looking at the eight target areas simply shows you what kind of errors you can expect to see on the test so you can eliminate them more quickly from the four answer choices.

Of course, you'll also be expected to know how to express your ideas clearly and concisely when you write an essay for the Extended Response section. (See Chapter 11 on page 129.) Reviewing the language skills covered in this chapter can help you improve your Extended Response score, too, because part of the essay is evaluated on how well you demonstrate these skills.

Examples of the Key Areas of Language Use

First let's look at some brief examples of what those eight language targets look like in practice. Then in the next chapter, we'll explain how the GED® question format will help you find the right answer. This chapter isn't a complete grammar review—there are plenty of thorough grammar textbooks and reliable online grammar resources already. Instead, it's a brief refresher to help you recognize if there is a key area in which you know you have difficulty, so you can focus on that aspect of language use when you're preparing for the test.

Word Choice

Some words are commonly confused or easily used in a nonstandard way, especially when you're working under time pressure. Here are some examples:

They're (contraction for "they are") putting *their* (possessive) coats over *there* (location).

The *effects* (noun) of climate change will *affect* (verb, action) us all.

It's (contraction for "it is") amazing how quickly the tree shed *its* (possessive) leaves when *it's* (contraction for "it is") still so warm at night.

That report is due on Friday. If you submit it *then* (a point in time), the boss will be more willing to consider a raise *than* (a comparison) if you hand it in late. If you're even later *than* (a comparison) Steve usually is, *then* ("in that case") you can probably forget about any raise this year.

You should *try to see* ("to see" is the infinitive form of the verb "see") him before he leaves. (not "*try and see...*," which is a nonstandard, incorrect use)

You're the best one to make a list of the words that you sometimes confuse or use incorrectly. Research them in a good grammar book or online resource before the test, so you can choose the correct word with confidence, in spite of the time pressure.

Other Commonly Confused Words

accept/except
allusion/illusion
cite/site
complement/compliment
fewer/less
ensure/insure
principal/principle
stationary/stationery
whose/who's

Other Nonstandard Uses

anyway (not "anyways")
couldn't care less (not "could care less")
a couple of (not just "a couple")
regardless (not "irregardless)
supposed to (not "suppose to")
would have (not "would of")

Agreement

Subject-verb agreement is fairly straightforward: If the subject is singular, so is the verb. Here are some examples:

John *learns* quickly.

Beth and Marc *learn* (plural, now there are two subjects) more slowly.

Neither Sam nor Anita *learns* (singular again, because we're dealing with only one singular subject at a time) much at all.

The entire class, which will be going on a camping trip this weekend, *is learning* (singular because "class" is singular; don't get tripped up by the words stuffed in between the subject and the verb) how to read a compass.

Noun-pronoun agreement is a common difficulty, though. Try this one:

The company released _____ quarterly results before the board members announced _____ intention to raise the dividend.

The first answer is "its" because "company" is singular. The second is a plural pronoun, "their," because we're talking about more than one board member. If the sentence said "...before the board of directors announced...," the pronoun would again be "its" because "board" is singular. "Board" is the subject; "of directors" is simply a phrase that describes it.

Another common error occurs when people try to avoid using "his or her":

> Each student should buy _____ own books.

If you said "their," you're making that common mistake. The answer is actually "his or her own books" because we don't know the gender of the student. The student is singular, though, so the pronoun must be singular, too. If you find "his or her" awkward, you can avoid using it by making the subject plural: *Students* should buy *their* own books.

Pronoun Use

There are a couple of flavors of correct pronoun use on the GED® test. The first is that every pronoun must have a clear antecedent (the noun that the pronoun is replacing). Things can get rather confusing when it's difficult to figure out which noun should be paired with the pronoun. Consider the following example:

> Jorge asked Tony if he had found his wallet yet.

Well, whose wallet is missing? Has Tony been searching for his own wallet, or had he offered to find Jorge's wallet for him? The antecedent of "his" (Jorge or Tony) isn't clear.

The other aspect of pronoun use is correct case. The old comedy line "*Whom* shall I say is calling?" is actually incorrect. Reword the sentence "I shall say whom is calling," and it becomes apparent that the correct version would be "I shall say *who* is calling," because "who" is the subject of the verb "is calling." (Similarly, it would be correct to write, "I should say she is calling," using the subjective "she.") On the other hand, in another phrase—"To *whom* am I speaking?"—the pronoun "whom" is in the objective case, because it is the object of the preposition "to."

Modifiers

A modifier describes a noun, as in "the golf ball *that went into the sand trap*." It's not the golf ball in the caddy's hand or the one at the bottom of the water feature; it's the one in the sand trap. The problem arises if a modifier is misplaced—not clearly beside the noun it's (there's that "it is" contraction again) modifying. That can make things confusing for the reader. Take a look at this example:

> The delivery man left a package at the door *that looked as if it had been used as a football by the night crew.*

Just what was the night crew kicking around here—the door or the package? To fix this confusing sentence, you could either omit "at the door" (after all, where else would he leave it?) or else start a new sentence ("The beaten-up package looked as if...").

That's called a misplaced modifier—it's placed too far away from what it's describing. Just as confusing is the dangling modifier. That occurs when a sentence starts with a modifier but the thing that comes right after it is not, in fact, what the

> Put **modifiers** near the noun they describe in order to avoid confusion.

modifier is describing. The modifier just dangles there at the beginning of the sentence without being attached to anything sensible. Here's an example:

> *Determined to cut the budget, salaries* were lowered by 12 percent after the new governor took office.

So the salaries are determined to cut the budget? No; those words must be describing the new governor, not the salaries:

> *Determined to cut the budget, the new governor* lowered salaries by 12 percent after she took office.

Joining Thoughts

There are two sides to this coin. The first is parallel construction, and you can see it most easily in bulleted lists. To guide the reader smoothly through the list, each bullet point should be built the same way. Try to figure out which bullet point needs to be changed in this example:

When you go on the wilderness survival course, you'll learn

- how to start a camp fire
- how to canoe
- tree climbing
- how to hunt

There are three "how to" bullets and one oddball "…ing," which needs to be changed to "how to climb trees" in order to make the structure of the bullets the same, or parallel.

The second aspect of joining thoughts is coordination and subordination. What's the difference? Well, in coordination, the two thoughts are equally important; in subordination, one is more important than the other. The choice of coordination or subordination—and the choice of which thought is subordinated—can have a profound impact on the meaning.

Build them the same (parallel). Build them equal (coordination). Build them unequal (subordination).

Take a look at two brief statements that someone might be including in a cover letter for a job application:

I have no paid work experience in marketing.

I chaired the volunteer marketing committee for a charity.

Coordinating those two thoughts (using "and") would just plain confuse the employer:

> I have no paid work experience in marketing, and I chaired the volunteer marketing committee for a charity.

What is this applicant trying to tell the employer? By coordinating the two facts, the applicant is presenting them as equal in importance. It seems as if the statements on either side of the "and" are fighting each other, though. Now see what a different impression you can create by subordinating each of those statements:

> Although I chaired the volunteer marketing committee for a charity, I have no paid work experience in marketing.

What does the employer see and remember? "No paid work experience in marketing." Now consider this sentence:

> Although I have no paid work experience in marketing, I chaired the volunteer marketing committee for a charity.

Now what does the employer see and remember? This applicant is being honest about his lack of paid experience, but he's downplaying it by subordinating it (with "although"), and highlighting his volunteer leadership experience instead.

Sentence Construction

Here we're looking at three things: wordiness, run-on sentences, and sentence fragments. All three can torpedo a clear, concise expression of your ideas.

Let's start with wordiness. Here's part of a letter from a cellist who blew her audition for the local symphony orchestra:

> I hope you will reconsider and think again about giving me another chance to audition. I was extremely tired and nervous that day because I hadn't slept much the night before. I was too anxious and excited to sleep. If you'll just give me another chance, I'll show you how well I can play because I won't be as nervous the second time.

Now how's that for saying the same thing several times in slightly different ways? That's wordiness, and it puts readers to sleep. Say it once, say it concisely and move on.

Run-on sentences also make good sleeping potions:

> Ingrid might make a good addition to the volleyball team, I guess, except that she hasn't been playing for very long and she doesn't have a car, so someone else would always have to take her to out-of-town games and besides, she never has any money so she couldn't go out with us after the games, so maybe we shouldn't ask her to join the team after all.

There are several separate sentences in that monster run-on, and that's how they should be presented.

Watch out, too, for separate sentences that are being held together by a comma, like this:

Industries are using less coal, natural gas is often the replacement of choice.

There should be a period after "coal" and a new sentence starting with "Natural" or, if the writer *really* wants to stress the connection between the two ideas, a semicolon after "coal." A comma never connects two separate sentences.

Sentence Sins
Wordiness, Run-ons:
There's too much
stuffed inside.
Fragments: It's not
all there.

Sentence fragments are the opposite of run-ons: Instead of having too much in them, fragments aren't all there. A complete sentence needs a subject and a verb, at minimum, and it must stand on its own. Fragments don't have both a subject and verb (sometimes they don't even have either one), and they need something else added before they can stand alone.

The conductor ran. (That's a complete sentence.) Being cold and wet from the howling storm that threatened the train's very survival. (That's not— there is no subject and no verb.)

Logic and Clarity

Communication that is clear and logical is easy for the reader to follow. It guides the reader with transition and signal words that indicate a change in direction, perhaps, or a more detailed explanation of a point just made. The skilled use of these road signs allows the reader to concentrate on the writer's argument instead of struggling to figure out exactly what that argument is. See how easy you find it to read this example:

Deep water drilling promises to unlock rich sources of untapped energy. There are environmental concerns. A major storm could damage a drilling rig, leading to an oil leak that would threaten the surrounding ecosystem.

Now see how much more sense that example makes if you simply add "however" before the second sentence and "for example" before the third, telling the reader that you're changing direction and then that you're going to elaborate on a point.

For a list of common transition and signal words, see page 40 in Chapter 5.

Punctuation and Capitalization

Every sentence must begin with a capital letter and conclude with end punctuation (a period, question mark, or exclamation point). Capitalize the names of specific people, places, national holidays, months, days of the week, and titles when used with a person's name (Dr. O'Reilly). Read the answer choices carefully, though. Don't let time pressure trick you into missing the lower case "t" on "tuesday." The GED® Language assessment could very well have a question like that because the ability to take in and process information carefully is very much part of readiness for a career or college.

In addition to those general punctuation and capitalization rules, the GED® test focuses on three specific punctuation items. One is the correct use of an apostrophe in possessives. "The banker's bonus" (apostrophe "s" if the noun is singular: the bonus of the banker) and "the boys' skateboards" ("s" apostrophe if the noun is plural and ends in "s": the skateboards of the boys) are fairly straightforward cases. How about "the people's choice," though? Even though there are a lot of individuals in that noun, "people" doesn't end in an "s," therefore the possessive form is apostrophe "s," just as if the noun were singular. Another special case is possessive pronouns (such as hers, theirs, and its) that do not have apostrophes.

A second focus is the use of commas in a series or in apposition (we'll explain that one):

> She stopped off at the grocery store for bread, eggs, milk, and cheese. (That's a series of three or more items separated by commas.)

> Wheeling General, the largest employer in town, is building another new plant next year. (That's apposition: "Wheeling General" and "the largest employer in town" both refer to the same thing and share the same function in the sentence—both work as the subject. "The largest employer in town" is *in apposition* to "Wheeling General" and needs commas around it.)

The third punctuation item the GED® test highlights is punctuation between clauses. An independent clause stands alone (it could be a separate sentence); a dependent clause doesn't (it depends on the independent clause for its existence). You need a comma between two independent clauses that are joined by a word such as "but" or "and" (a coordinating conjunction):

> Fire destroyed six houses on the street, but the corner store suffered only minor damage.

You also need a comma when a dependent clause comes before an independent clause, but not when it comes after:

> Even though fire destroyed six houses on the street (the dependent clause; it needs a comma because it comes first), the corner store suffered only minor damage (the independent clause).

> The corner store suffered only minor damage (the independent clause; no comma because the dependent clause comes after it) even though fire destroyed six houses on the street.

There are other rules for comma use in English, but the ones we've noted are the ones that GED Testing Service prefers to test.

OUR APPROACH

Now that you've learned to recognize the types of language mistakes you could see on the test, you're well on the way to using Process of Elimination to narrow down the choices. Remember that it's often easier to eliminate what's obviously wrong than it is to start by searching for what's right. In the next chapter, we'll see how the question format can help you get even closer to the right answer, and give you some practice with passages and questions.

Chapter 9
Language
Questions

In this chapter, you'll learn how the format of the language questions can help you find the answer more easily.

Sometimes it's easier to figure out what you don't want than what you do. Shopping for a car or a place to live can be like that—you hate the transmission shift or the neighborhood, but couldn't explain exactly why or describe what would make you happier instead.

So it is with the language questions, only in this case, getting rid of what's clearly wrong should, ideally, leave you with what's right. You don't need to know exactly *why* an answer is wrong—perhaps it just sounds odd—but as long as you can find and eliminate at least a couple of those incorrect choices, you're closer to the right answer.

WHAT KIND OF QUESTIONS ARE ON THE TEST?

Now that we've reviewed the key language use skills that are targeted on the test (see Chapter 8 on page 97), let's see how the questions make it easier to find the right answers. The language questions are all drop-down items within a passage. There will be a big gap in a sentence, with the word "Select" in the gap. When you click on it, a menu of four possible answers drops down. Click on an answer from that list and poof!—magically it appears where the gap was. (See page 24 in Chapter 3 for an illustration of a drop-down question.)

Drop-down questions let you see your chosen answer in the context of the passage.

There are two good things about that type of question: One, you get to see your answer within the context of a passage right away, and two, there *has* to be one correct choice within the four options. It's much easier to judge whether an answer seems right in the context of a passage than it is in an isolated sentence.

What Strategies Should I Use to Answer the Questions?

The wrong answers represent common errors in any of the eight language use areas covered in Chapter 8. You don't need to remember the names of the errors or how to fix them, although reviewing the list will help you learn to recognize them more quickly. All you need to do is use Process of Elimination to identify the three wrong choices, click on the fourth one, and verify that it is correct when read in the context of the passage.

You do need to be careful when you're reading the choices, though, because they can be very close to each other in wording, and time pressure can trip you up. Would you notice the difference between these two answer choices on a test?

"...your poor customer service and having high costs. if you..."
"...your poor customer service and high costs. If you..."

The first one lacks parallel structure in the last two items on a list, and is missing a capital letter at the beginning of the next sentence. If you were skimming the answer choices quickly, though, the two seem close. Those are the kinds of tricky differences the test writers can and do throw at you.

Read Carefully. One comma or capital letter can make the difference between a right and a wrong answer.

A good approach is to compare the choices that are left after you've eliminated those that are wrong. Is one answer missing a capital letter where it should have one? Does one have an extra word, such as "although," that turns a complete sentence into a fragment? The difference between a right and a wrong answer can be that small.

After you've made your final choices, check your answers in the context of the passage. Context can be a huge help in showing you whether you've made the right decision.

How Do the Drop-Down Questions Look in a Language Passage?

Here's an example of a typical GED® language passage. It's a flyer that a candidate for mayor is using to introduce herself to voters, and it needs some help. Try to select the correct answer yourself, circling it with a pencil, before you read the explanations that follow the passage. The wording for the passage instructions is the same as the wording you'll see on the test.

> Review the language use errors in Chapter 8 so you can spot wrong answers more quickly.

The passage below is incomplete. Navigate to each "Select..." button and choose the option that correctly completes the sentence.

A Mayor for the Rest of Us!

Sybil Simbalah lives in a neighborhood like yours. She grew up here, and has watched this city change from a family-friendly place into a sprawl of uncontrolled urban development, fueled by your tax dollars and pouring profits into the pockets of corrupt elected officials and their buddies in business and industry.

During four years on the city council and, before that,

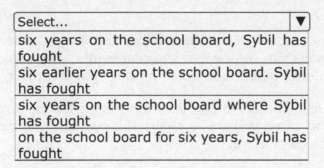

Select... ▼
six years on the school board, Sybil has fought
six earlier years on the school board. Sybil has fought
six years on the school board where Sybil has fought
on the school board for six years, Sybil has fought

tirelessly and courageously for family values. She gathered enough support to defeat the ill-conceived expansion of the freeway through town, and

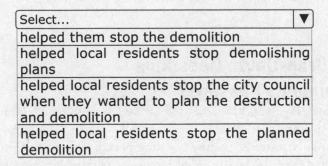

of a beautiful 100-year-old library building. She has fought every proposed rate hike for mass transit and, on the school board, defeated a plan to cut back after-school programs.

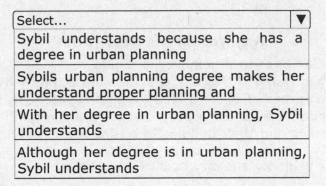

what makes a city welcoming, healthy, and livable. She is always ready to hear from the people she represents, and consults with her constituents before she votes on any major project.

Sybil lives in a century-old house with her husband, three children, and three dogs. She chairs the symphony's community engagement committee,

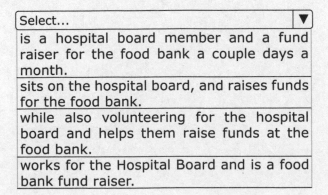

Sybil Simbalah knows what the residents of this city need.

- Reliable electricity

- Safe drinking water

- Affordable mass transit

- Parks and playgrounds

- A new team in charge at city hall

As long as the current city officials run the show, their cronies in industry and big business will continue getting the contracts—and the kickbacks—for massive projects we can't afford and don't need.

You can end corruption in city hall and stop big business and industry from dictating where your tax dollars go.

It's time to capture city hall—for the rest of us!

On November 13, take back control of your city and vote Sybil Simbalah for mayor!

To join Sybil's team of eager volunteers or contribute to Sybil's campaign, contact her campaign office at

- 531-3115
- gosybil@mayor.com
- mayorsybil.com
- 1395 Baker Lane, Unit 43

We'd love to hear from you or meet you!

Now let's go through the process for finding the errors and choosing the correct answers to complete the four sentences.

In the first set of drop-down answers, the first choice is correct. Read on to see how you could have eliminated the other three (which all contain errors in the key language skills) and arrived at this one through Process of Elimination.

> During four years on the city council and, before that, <u>six years on the school board, Sybil has fought</u> tirelessly and courageously for family values.

Apply the Strategy
Use POE on Language questions like the ones in this passage!

The second choice (below) is wordy—"before that" and "earlier" say the same thing. Only one word ("earlier") separates this answer from the correct choice, but that's enough to make this one wrong. That's why you need to read the answer choices very carefully.

> During four years on the city council and, before that, <u>six earlier years on the school board. Sybil has fought</u> tirelessly and courageously for family values.

The addition of "where" in the choice below makes the sentence into a fragment instead of a complete sentence. Again, only one word separates this choice from the correct answer.

> During four years on the city council and, before that, <u>six years on the school board where Sybil has fought</u> tirelessly and courageously for family values.

The fourth choice (below) lacks parallel construction.

> During four years on the city council and, before that, <u>on the school board for six years, Sybil has fought</u> tirelessly and courageously for family values.

In the second set of drop-down answers, the first choice is wrong because it has an unclear antecedent. (See page 101 in Chapter 8.) Who is "them"?

> She gathered enough support to defeat the ill-conceived expansion of the freeway through town, and <u>helped them stop the demolition</u> of a beautiful 100-year-old library building.

The next choice (below) has awkward, unclear wording that would confuse a reader. Is "demolishing" a verb or an adjective here? Are the residents demolishing (a verb) plans, or are they stopping plans that describe demolishing (an adjective)?

> She gathered enough support to defeat the ill-conceived expansion of the freeway through town, and <u>helped local residents stop demolishing plans</u> of a beautiful 100-year-old library building.

Now where do we start listing the problems with the third choice below? There's a noun-pronoun agreement problem ("city council" is singular, so "when *it* wanted..."), it's wordy (what's the difference between the "destruction" and the "demolition" of a building?), and it's just plain longer than it needs to be.

> She gathered enough support to defeat the ill-conceived expansion of the freeway through town, and <u>helped local residents stop the city council when they wanted to plan the destruction and demolition</u> of a beautiful 100-year-old library building.

The one below (the fourth choice) is the one you want. Now it's clear whom (objective case—remember that one from Chapter 8?) Sybil helped and what she helped them do.

> She gathered enough support to defeat the ill-conceived expansion of the freeway through town, and <u>helped local residents stop the planned demolition</u> of a beautiful 100-year-old library building.

In the third drop-down question, the first choice is wrong because it breaks up the independent clause ("Sybil understands what makes...") with a dependent clause ("because she has a degree in urban planning"). The dependent clause should begin this particular sentence, followed by a comma (remember that from Chapter 8?) before the independent clause.

> <u>Sybil understands because she has a degree in urban planning</u> what makes a city welcoming, healthy, and livable.

Aside from the fact that the second choice (below) is wordy (one would hope an urban planning degree would lead to an understanding of proper planning), the lack of an apostrophe on the possessive ("Sybil's") eliminates this version. You can see how carefully you need to read the choices when just one missing apostrophe means a wrong answer.

> <u>Sybils urban planning degree makes her understand proper planning and</u> what makes a city welcoming, healthy, and livable.

After you eliminate the first two choices because of the errors in them, you come to the third choice (below), which is the correct one.

> <u>With her degree in urban planning, Sybil understands</u> what makes a city welcoming, healthy, and livable.

Now why would anyone subordinate the urban planning degree with "although"? The degree *explains* Sybil's understanding of a healthy city. This improper subordination in the fourth choice makes it sound as if her understanding is in spite of the degree, not because of it.

> <u>Although her degree is in urban planning, Sybil understands</u> what makes a city welcoming, healthy, and livable.

In the final set of drop-down answers, the first choice (below) might have been the one you eliminated first. The structure in this list of volunteer activities isn't parallel, and there is a problem with nonstandard word use ("a couple days a month" instead of "a couple *of* days a month"). It's not clear whether the "couple of days" applies only to the food bank or to all three volunteer activities, either. Specifying the small amount of time Sybil devotes to volunteer activities also undercuts the image of extensive community involvement that she's trying to present.

> She chairs the symphony's community engagement committee, <u>is a hospital board member and a fund raiser for the food bank a couple days a month.</u>

Yes, this is the one (the second option). The structure of the three descriptions of Sybil's volunteer activity is parallel (each one begins with a verb) and there are no other errors.

> She chairs the symphony's community engagement committee, <u>sits on the hospital board, and raises funds for the food bank.</u>

This third choice was likely your second throw-away. The structure of the three volunteer activity descriptions isn't even close to parallel, and it's not clear who "them" means.

She chairs the symphony's community engagement committee, <u>while also volunteering for the hospital board and helps them raise funds at the food bank.</u>

In addition to the lack of parallelism in the three volunteer activities, the fourth choice (below) has a capitalization problem. There is no reason to capitalize "Hospital Board" when the symphony committee and the food bank are not capitalized.

She chairs the symphony's community engagement committee, <u>works for the Hospital Board and is a food bank fund raiser.</u>

Language Drill

Now you try a language passage on your own, circling your selections. Review the eight language use areas from Chapter 8 before you start; the errors you see will be in those eight areas. Remember to read the answer choices carefully, too, so you won't miss a small difference between a wrong answer and one that's correct. You can check your answers in Part VIII: Answer Key to Drills.

The passage below is incomplete. Navigate to each "Select..." button and choose the option that correctly completes the sentence.

Subject: Request to restructure loan

Dear Ms. Mertz:

Thank you again for your time during our phone conversation this morning. As requested, I am sending this email to confirm my request for a restructuring of my small business loan.

I would appreciate an additional six months to pay, and a 0.25 percent reduction in the interest rate. If you are unable to approve both requests, then the additional six months would be my priority.

Economic conditions have deteriorated since I first applied for a loan, unfortunately, with the result that I need to request this restructuring. My customers are spending more of their food dollars on groceries and less on restaurant meals. The harsh winter kept people at home more

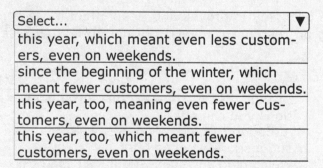

You asked what efforts I've made to increase revenue by attracting new customers. Let me assure you that I have tried a variety of things during the past year. For example, I advertised in the local media, offering a special "new customer" discount.

Select... ▼
Participating in a local trade fair, the recent "Home Grown Goodness" food exhibition. I sponsored
I participated in a local trade fair, the recent "Home Grown Goodness" food exhibition, and sponsored
I participated in a local trade fair the recent "Home Grown Goodness" food exhibition and sponsored
I participated in a local trade fair, the recent "Home Grown Goodness" food exhibition, and we were also sponsoring

a booth for a local charity at the fall fair. Hoping to attract new business from the surrounding communities, I promoted my restaurant through coupons and worked with a well-known insurance company to host special group dinners for its top salespeople in the region.

In spite of my efforts, however, any increase in customers is more than offset by the increase in my costs. Food is getting more and more expensive, and leasing and insurance costs are rising at a rate far greater than inflation. I changed the menu and laid off some staff in an attempt to reduce expenses. I have a small restaurant, though, and I can carry cost-cutting only so far before it starts to have a negative impact on my ability to keep my remaining customers happy.

Until the economy improves and people feel more comfortable spending on restaurant meals, I'm not sure what else I can do.

Select... ▼
I would, of course, welcome any suggestions you can offer.
Although I would, of course, welcome any suggestions you can offer
Welcoming any suggestions you can offer, you may have some other ideas for me.
Since I don't have any other ideas, I would, of course, welcome any suggestions you can offer but I believe I've already tried every possible way to cut costs and raise revenue so I'm not sure you could present any new ideas.

I realize you probably have several customers asking for the same type of loan relief as I am requesting.

Select... ▼
However, I hope that my excellent credit record and their long business relationship with me
I hope that my excellent credit record and my long business relationship of doing business with your bank
However, I hope that my excellent credit record and my long business relationship with your bank
However, I hope that my excellent credit record and I have a long business relationship with your bank which

would make me eligible for special consideration. I look forward to a favorable response after you have a chance to consult your manager.

Kind regards,

J. Enrico Flavino

Part III Summary

- o The Language test consists of two passages, each 350–450 words long and each with four drop-down sentence completion questions. Topics are drawn from the real world of business and professional communication. The language passages might be mixed in with the reading passages. You will have 95 minutes to answer all of the reading and language questions.
- o This section of the GED® test evaluates language use in editing tasks. The Extended Response section tests language use in a writing task.
- o Errors in the answer choices will fall within the eight areas of language use that are considered the most essential for career and college readiness:
  - Word choice: avoiding words that are often confused or used in a nonstandard way
  - Agreement: of subject and verb, of noun and pronoun
  - Pronoun use: clear antecedents, correct case
  - Modifiers: correctly placed
  - Joining thoughts: proper coordination, subordination, and parallel construction
  - Sentence construction: avoiding wordiness, run-on sentences, and fragments
  - Logic and clarity: effective use of words and phrases that mark a clear path for the reader
  - Punctuation and capitalization
- o Strategies for answering the questions include:
  - Using Process of Elimination to discard choices that are clearly wrong
  - Reading the answer choices carefully to spot small differences (such as one word or a punctuation mark) that can make one choice correct and another one wrong
  - Comparing the answer choices to identify the differences among them
  - Reading your chosen answer in the context of the passage to see if it fits with the context

Part IV
Reasoning Through Language Arts: Extended Response

Chapter 10
Extended Response
Overview

If any part of the Reasoning Through Language Arts (RLA) Test could make prospective test takers gasp and rethink their plan, it would be the Extended Response section.

You can relax, though. No, *really*—relax. With the strategies you'll discover in this book, you'll have a process and a plan for tackling the Extended Response, so you won't have to waste time figuring out your approach on test day. You'll know exactly what to write about and where to start, and you'll gain some good tips for improving your writing, too.

WHAT IS THE EXTENDED RESPONSE TASK?

First we're going to look at *what* you're doing for the Extended Response section. Then, in the next chapter, we'll look at some strategies for *how* to do it.

You'll tackle the 45-minute Extended Response question right after the 10-minute break that follows the first reading and language section. The prompt will include two passages arguing opposite sides of a real-world "hot button" issue such as oil pipelines or the minimum wage. The passages could come in different formats (for example, an employee memo and a magazine article). The authors might also be quite different—a professional teacher and a concerned parent, for instance.

Choose the passage on which you feel you could do the best job. There is no "right" or "wrong" passage.

Your task is to explain which passage provides better support for the position it argues. The passages have been chosen so the support they provide is roughly equal. There is no "right" or "wrong" passage. In other words, you could argue effectively that either one of the passages provides better support. As you read through them, you might find that one type of support is more familiar to you, or that you feel more comfortable with one format. Choose the passage for which you feel you could build a stronger argument.

What Is All of That Stuff On the Screen?

The Extended Response screen might seem crowded and confusing at first. It's intended to put everything you need in one place, and it makes sense once you understand the different pieces. It has four main parts.

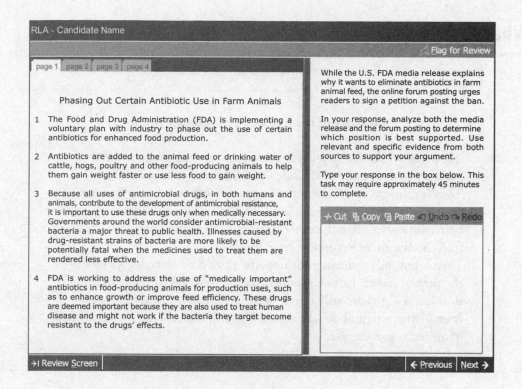

1. The passages appear on the left side, one after the other, spread across several pages. Tabs at the top are labeled with consecutive page numbers. You need to click on, for example, the "page 2" tab to get to the next page and continue reading. Make sure you cycle through all of the tabs and read both passages. Together they will be about 650 words.

    The paragraphs are numbered consecutively so when you're writing, you'll be able to find points that you've already noted more quickly. If the first passage ends with paragraph 5, then the second passage will begin with paragraph 6.

2. At the top of the right side of the screen, you'll find a brief introduction to the two passages. It will mention the topic and might include a description of what each passage is (for example, it might say that one passage is part of a speech and the other is a newspaper letter to the editor).

3. The prompt (which describes your task) is also on the right, just below that introduction. It has four parts, which we'll explain next.

4. The fourth part of the Extended Response screen is a text box where you'll type your essay. It's also on the right, just below the prompt. It looks very small but it keeps growing as you enter more text, and a scroll bar will appear on the right-hand side to let you review your essay.

    There are no spelling or grammar checkers. You can cut, copy, and paste within the text box, but you can't copy text from the passage and paste it into your essay.

What Is the Prompt Telling Me to Do?

The wording of the prompt will vary slightly, depending on the topic of the two passages. It will always have the same four components, though.

Four Parts of the Extended Response Prompt

1. The prompt asks you to analyze the arguments presented in the two passages to determine which side provides stronger support.
2. Then it cautions you to connect your essay to the passages: "In your response, develop an argument in which you explain how one position is better supported than the other. Incorporate relevant and specific evidence from both sources to support your argument."
3. Then it reminds you that your response should be objective and focus on the *support* rather than on the topic itself: "Remember, the better-argued position is not necessarily the position with which you agree."
4. It ends with a note about the time: "The task should take approximately 45 minutes to complete."

Here are some important tips to keep in mind about the task that's described in the prompt.

> Write about which author's argument is better supported, not about the topic of the authors' arguments.

*   **Take a step back from the topic.** Two authors are making opposing cases about an issue. Your mission is to look at *how* they make their cases, not at the cases themselves. Focus on the *support* provided by the two authors, not on the topic they're discussing. If, for example, you think burning coal is a major cause of climate change and air pollution but you feel that the passage promoting clean coal has better support for its position, then your essay will explain how the clean coal passage is better supported. It won't discuss the issue of burning coal. Your grade will be lowered if your essay strays far from support to the topic itself. (We'll explain later on how the essay is graded.)
*   **Stick to the passages**. That's where you'll find the support. If you bring in your own opinions or knowledge about an issue, you run the risk of wandering into an essay about the topic instead of an essay about how the two authors make their cases.
*   **Back up your points with evidence from the passages.** For instance, perhaps you feel that one passage provides stronger support because it mentions specific studies and experts instead of simply making vague claims. Your essay should refer to those specific details.
*   **There are no right or wrong answers.** If you can make a credible case that one side of the argument provides better support, and back that up with evidence from the passages, then your position will not be considered wrong.

What Does the Prompt Mean by "Support"?

Support can take several forms, which we'll outline below. You might also find it helpful to review the section on evaluation questions in the reading part of the test (pages 43–44 in Chapter 5), because that's exactly what you're doing here—evaluating the evidence, reasoning, and assumptions of two authors to argue that one has provided better support for his or her position.

> Evaluate each author's evidence, reasoning, and assumptions, just as you did for evaluation questions in the reading passages.

Support Through Evidence

The most obvious type of support would be evidence—examples or other details that the author provides, or authorities the author cites. Elements such as those can add a lot of weight to an argument. Consider this example:

> The polar bear population is threatened.

> vs.

> A 2006 study revealed that the skull size and body weight of adult male polar bears in the Southern Beaufort Sea population had decreased during the past 20 years. Fewer cubs were surviving, too. Scientists saw both measures as symptoms of stress, and a repeat of the warning signs noticed earlier in the polar bears of Western Hudson Bay. There, the population subsequently fell from about 1,200 in 1987 to about 950 bears 17 years later.

Clearly the second claim provides stronger support for this specific point. It outlines specific research studies, years, symptoms, and numbers; and it builds its case on the findings of scientists, who are the authorities in the field.

Support through evidence can be a bit less clear cut, too. For instance, suppose one side of the argument makes only one major claim, but backs up that claim thoroughly with evidence from professional research studies and the opinions of acknowledged experts in the field. The other side gives four reasons for its position instead of one, but doesn't offer as much support for any of them. Which one is stronger? There are no right or wrong answers, as long as you can build a credible argument and support it from the passages. In this case, you would choose the side for which you can do a better job of explaining why the support for that position is stronger. Another test taker might choose the opposite side and that's fine, as long as he or she can explain what makes that side's support better.

When you're looking at evidence-based support, watch for adequacy and relevance, too. Does the author provide enough credible evidence in comparison to the other passage, and is that evidence relevant to the claim the author is making?

Support Through Reasoning

This support issue is more subtle than evidence-based support. Is the author's chain of reasoning sound and logical? Or do you detect a logical fallacy? (See page 44 in Chapter 5.) Do the author's claims *seem* well supported by evidence, but when you follow the path from claim to conclusion, does it go seriously off course?

Suppose, for example, an author claims that purple loosestrife, an invasive plant species, is harming natural wetlands in the area by discouraging wildlife and beating out native plants in the competition for nourishment and space. Studies done during the past three years show the retreat of native species and the alarming spread of purple loosestrife, backing up this claim. So far, so good. But then the author says that this means that the town authorities should begin a program of spraying toxic chemicals on wetlands in order to eliminate the invasive plant. The author is making a big leap, going from saying that there's a problem (and presenting evidence) to insisting on a drastic solution (without evidence for the solution being a good one). What happens to the remaining native plants if toxic chemicals were sprayed? And what about the wildlife in the area? The claim looks good, the evidence looks good, but the reasoning leading from the claim to the extreme solution is flawed. Due to faulty reasoning, the author's position is not well supported.

Support Through Assumptions

Another subtle support issue involves the author's assumptions. Are they valid, considering the likely audience? All the evidence and logical reasoning in the world doesn't make a well-supported argument if the assumptions on which it's based don't make sense. Consider, for instance, an author who wants to add life to a new suburb filled with young families. The writer argues that $20 should be added to each property tax bill to fund facilities for a Wednesday morning fruit and vegetable market in the local park. The piece includes compelling evidence of the health benefits of eating fresh fruits and vegetables, and the wisdom of buying produce grown "close to home." What's wrong with this argument? The author is assuming that there will be enough customers on a Wednesday morning (the traditional market day) to make the project a good business proposition for vendors. What about the suburban adults who have day jobs and their kids who are in school? The invalid assumption drains support from the author's position.

HOW IS THE EXTENDED RESPONSE GRADED?

The Extended Response task pulls together the critical thinking, active reading, analytical, and language skills you'll also use in the reading and language sections of the RLA Test. As in other sections, the aim is to allow test takers to demonstrate the skills required for college or a career.

The Extended Response task draws on the critical thinking, active reading, analytical, and language skills you needed for the reading and language sections of the test.

In the Extended Response section, you'll be graded on how well you can

- understand and analyze the two source passages
- evaluate the argumentation in those passages
- create a written argument in your own words, supported by evidence drawn from the passages

One bit of good news: Because you have only 45 minutes to plan, write, and edit the essay, it's considered an "on demand draft" and is not expected to be completely free of errors.

Exactly What Traits Should My Essay Demonstrate?

Instead of one overall holistic grade, as on the old Extended Response section, the essay is now scored on three separate rubrics. Each one covers a trait that should be evident in your essay.

Creation of Arguments and Use of Evidence

This trait looks at two aspects of your essay: how well you build an argument for your position about which passage is better supported, and how well you incorporate evidence drawn from the passages. We'll give you some practice Extended Response questions in the next chapter. The following questions will help you evaluate your own practice essays for this trait:

- Did you establish a purpose that's connected to the task in the prompt? In other words, is it clear that your purpose is to explain why one passage is better supported than the other (instead of discussing the topic of the two passages)?
- Did you make clear claims?
- Did you explain why the evidence you're taking from the passages is important (instead of simply plunking it into your essay without any commentary)?
- Have you demonstrated that you can distinguish between supported and unsupported claims in the passages?
- Have you shown that you can evaluate the credibility of the support the authors use?
- Have you spotted any faulty reasoning in an author's argument?
- Are you making reasonable inferences about the assumptions underlying the authors' arguments?

Development of Ideas and Organizational Structure

Now that you've shown you can create a solid argument for your position, we're moving on to how well you develop and organize that argument. Here are some questions to ask yourself about your practice essays:

- Did you explain how your ideas are relevant to the task, or did you just fire off ideas without elaborating on them?
- Is there a logical progression to your ideas, or do they jump around all over the place? (You might find it helpful to review the transition and signal words on page 40 in Chapter 5.)
- Is there a clear connection between your main points and the details that elaborate on them? (In the next chapter, you'll learn more about connecting main points and accompanying details.)
- Do the style and tone of your essay demonstrate an awareness of your audience and purpose? (Do you use complete sentences most of the time, instead of point-form bullet lists? Is the language appropriate, or is it filled with slang and inappropriate short forms?)
- Did your organizational structure contribute to conveying your message and purpose? (We'll talk about organizing your argument in the next chapter.)

Clarity and Command of Standard English Conventions

There's just one question to ask yourself for this trait: Did you follow all eight of the language skills described in Chapter 8? The editing questions in the Language assessment were the first part of testing you on the elements of language use that are considered most important for a career or college. The writing task in the Extended Response section is the second part.

Is There Really a Robo-Grader?

Yes. The essay is graded by computer, so you won't have to wait weeks for your results. In fact, the scoring is done almost immediately. Scoring by computer (instead of tying up a bunch of human graders) also allows for giving you specific feedback on your essay performance as part of the score report.

How can a computer (actually, it's called an automated scoring engine) do an accurate job of assessing your unique, original essay? The test writers spent months teaching it, feeding it the scores awarded by human graders to an extensive range of sample essays so it would learn the characteristics of, say, a high score on the trait of "development of ideas and organizational structure." If the scoring engine doesn't recognize something about an essay (one that's unusually short, for instance, or that uses uncharacteristically sophisticated vocabulary), it kicks the essay out to a human grader. However, the test writers are confident that the engine will score at least 95 percent of the essays accurately.

OUR APPROACH

Now that you understand the Extended Response task and the traits you need to demonstrate in your essay—that's the "what"—we'll move on in the next chapter to the process for building and organizing your argument—the "how." We'll walk you through that process, using some examples and then give you one to try on your own. Along the way, you'll pick up some tips for improving your writing in any type of task, too.

Chapter 11
Extended Response Writing

In this chapter, we'll guide you through the process of assembling and organizing points for your argument and writing the essay. Then we'll give you some practice.

Anyone can learn to write an essay. Yes, anyone. You need a plan to follow (which we'll give you in this chapter) and confidence (which will increase as you get more practice writing and evaluating your own work).

You can use our method to help you analyze the arguments you encounter in everyday life beyond the test, too. Try it the next time you get a message from someone urging you to buy something or do something. Switch into active reading (or active listening) mode right away and start looking for the main arguments and how well they're supported. You'll soon know if you should consider the request or not.

HOW DO I BUILD MY ARGUMENT?

From studying the prompt (the test writers call it "unpacking the prompt"), you know what you need to do:

1. Analyze the arguments in the two passages to decide which author you think provides stronger support.
2. Write your own argument about which one is better supported, using evidence from the passages.
3. Be objective; consider the support, not the topic.
4. Do it in 45 minutes.

First, we'll define each author's argument using our active reading skills. Remember active reading from Chapter 5? That's where you summarize and ask questions as you read, forcing the passage to give you what you need from it. And that's where you'll start assembling the points and evidence for your argument.

Let's try active reading with a brief example. *While you are reading* the excerpt below (not after you're done), determine the author's argument and the support he provides for it, and note them briefly on your scratch paper. You'll likely find it helpful to make a quick chart for yourself, such as this one:

Argument	Support

Excerpt from *The New Freedom*, by Woodrow Wilson

For indeed, if you stop to think about it, nothing could be a greater departure from original Americanism, from faith in the ability of a confident, resourceful, and independent people, than the discouraging doctrine that somebody has got to provide prosperity for the rest of us. And yet that is exactly the doctrine on which the government of the United States has been conducted lately. Who have been consulted when important measures of government, like tariff acts, and currency acts, and railroad acts, were under consideration? The people whom the tariff chiefly affects, the people for whom the currency is supposed to exist, the people who pay the duties and ride on the railroads? Oh, no! What do they know about such matters! The gentlemen whose ideas have been sought are the big manufacturers, the bankers, and the heads of the great railroad combinations. The masters of the government of the United States are the combined capitalists and manufacturers of the United States.

That was published in 1913 so yes, the sentences are a bit long, but we can still define the author's main points. Your chart might look like the one below:

Argument	Support
U.S. government is being run by leaders of business and finance instead of by the people, as originally intended (paragraph 1)	Three examples: tariff, currency, and railroad acts (paragraph 1)

Apply the Strategy
Use active reading and scratch paper (or your note boards on test day) to boil the passage down to the evidence you need for your essay.

On the test, of course, you'll be working with several paragraphs in each passage, so you would also note the number of the paragraph that contains each point so you can find it again quickly. And since you're under a strict time limit, your chart would contain short forms and abbreviations that are meaningful to you. You should note all three of the types of support outlined in Chapter 10, too: evidence, reasoning, and assumptions. (See pages 125–126.)

What's the value of this chart? It boils an article, or a news release, or a letter—any of the different types of documents you might encounter in a passage—down to one common bare-bones list of the arguments and support points you need for your essay. It saves you the time of rereading and flipping from page to page just to find something again. And it gives you a clear picture of the support in each passage, making it easier to decide which one you think provides the best. That's the topic of your essay, after all.

Later on in this chapter, we'll give you some examples that will let you practice active reading and boiling the passages down into argument/support charts.

HOW DO I ORGANIZE MY ARGUMENT?

You've read both passages actively, and now you've got a couple of quick charts listing the authors' arguments and the support for those arguments. You can make a clear case for which author provides better support for his or her position. In other words, you have the main points that you want your essay to hit. Now what?

Let's work through an example of how you would organize and develop your essay. Suppose one of the two passages on the test is a letter to the editor from a local consumers' group complaining about the large, unexplained car insurance rate increase imposed on drivers in that city. The other is a response from a local association of insurance brokers arguing that, after three years of flat rates, an increase was overdue.

The Essay Template
The Beginning

- Introductory paragraph
  - Attention-getter
  - Thesis statement
  - Big picture list of evidence that proves the thesis statement

The Middle

- One paragraph for each piece of evidence that proves the thesis statement
  - Topic sentence
  - Evidence from the passages
  - Explanation of how the evidence supports the thesis statement

The End

- Restatement of the thesis in different words
- Reminder of the pieces of evidence that prove the thesis

The Essay Template

First, let's look at the template—or framework—for the essay. We'll discuss the pieces in more detail later, but first we need a picture of what the whole structure looks like.

In 45 minutes, you won't be able to produce a polished essay. Even the test writers regard this as an "on-demand draft" and expect that it will contain some errors. However, if you have a concept of how an ideal essay would be structured, you'll have a plan for where to start and what to write in the limited time available.

The essay has a beginning, a middle, and an end. Well of course, you may say. However, it isn't quite as simple as it sounds. The essay has a *specific* beginning, middle, and end. You might be familiar with the classic advice given to people who have to make a speech: "Tell them what you're going to tell them, tell them, tell them what you told them." That's a pretty good outline of the beginning, middle, and end of the essay, too.

The Beginning

This is the first paragraph, which sets expectations about what readers will find in the rest of the essay. It has three components.

The Attention-Getter Ideally, the first paragraph begins with an attention-getter—something that would make a human reader want to see what's in the rest of your essay. Although you don't have a human reader for the GED® Extended Response, an attention-getter will still get your essay off to a strong start for the robo-reader. Remember, everything it knows, it learned from human graders.

What would capture a reader's attention?

- You could begin with a question—for example, "Why have car insurance rates gone up so much?"
- You could start with what's called the "startling fact"—for instance, "The average U.S. driver pays about $900 in car insurance premiums." (You can probably find a good startling fact candidate in the two Extended Response passages.)
- You could open with a quotation (if one pops into your head without spending time thinking of one). It doesn't have to be a direct quote, using the exact words of whoever said it. You could paraphrase it instead. For example, a paraphrase such as "Abraham Lincoln claimed that it was impossible to fool everyone all of the time" would avoid trying to remember Lincoln's exact words. In this example, you'd need to add a sentence tying that quote to the passages: "However, in its letter to the editor, the consumers' group complains that car insurers seem to be trying to do just that—fool all of their customers into accepting unexplained rate hikes."

> The essay begins with a three-part paragraph.
>
> - An attention-getter, which makes the reader want to keep going
> - A thesis statement, which outlines what the essay will prove
> - A big picture outline of the arguments that prove the thesis statement

If you can't think of an attention-getter quickly, then you could simply begin with a statement about the two passages: "Rising car insurance premiums are drawing complaints from consumers and forcing the industry to defend itself, as these two passages reveal." This leads readers into the essay rather than hitting them over the head right at the start, and it's a much stronger opening than "This essay will discuss..." or "The subject of this essay is...."

You're not writing about car insurance premiums, though; you're writing about which side (consumers or brokers) makes the stronger case in the passages. The thesis statement, which we'll discuss next, makes the topic of your essay clear.

The Thesis Statement   After the attention-getter comes the thesis statement, which makes the claim that you intend to prove in the rest of your essay. In this case, the claim is that passage X provides the stronger support for its position. The thesis statement might read as follows:

> "In the dispute between drivers and insurance brokers, the consumers' group provides stronger evidence for its position that the steep rise in car insurance premiums is both unfair and unnecessary."

Depending on your attention-getter, you might need to add some type of transition sentence to tie that first sentence to the thesis statement.

Although it's called a statement, the thesis can be more than one sentence long. It should be specific: The example above mentions the two sides, the subject of the dispute, and the stronger side's position. It should also cover *only* what you will support with evidence in your essay.

The Big Picture Arguments   Finally, the first paragraph ends with a high-level list of the evidence that supports your thesis statement and which you'll explain in detail in the middle paragraphs. You've already got a list of this evidence (the authors' arguments in the chart you made up during your active reading of the passages). Sticking with the car insurance topic, let's say you found three pieces of evidence that make the "stronger" side's support better. You would finish the introductory paragraph by listing those three arguments:

> "As the consumers' group points out, insurance companies made record profits last year, while the average driver had to cope with a 10 percent increase in gas prices but only a one percent rise in wages."

The Middle

In the next few paragraphs (likely the same number as the number of points you outlined in the "big picture arguments" part of the first paragraph), you'll provide evidence to support each argument that proves your thesis. Be sure to explain *why* or *how* it proves your thesis. Remember, too, that you need to incorporate some evidence from the less-supported passage, too. Deal with one point per paragraph, and start each paragraph with a topic sentence.

The Topic Sentence The topic sentence is just what it says—a sentence that introduces the topic of the paragraph. Like transition and signal words (see page 40 in Chapter 5), it guides the reader through your essay and demonstrates your skill in organizing and developing your argument, traits on which you'll be graded. It does not give details about the topic (such as dollar amounts or dates or specific examples). Those come later in the paragraph.

Let's take the example of the consumers' first argument in the car insurance case. They say that car insurance companies already made record profits last year. Read the paragraph below and see how you think it flows, not counting the bracketed words, which are just our own notes and would not be in the actual essay. Remember that it would be the next paragraph after the introductory paragraph.

> The consumers' argument that the car insurance industry recorded $10 billion in profits last year, more than any year in the past decade, proves that the insurance companies don't really need extra money. The brokers' position [here we're drawing in some evidence from the less-supported passage, too] is much weaker because it doesn't address the industry's financial success. Three years of flat premiums do not justify raising prices, as the brokers argue, when the insurance companies have already made so much money.

The essay writer just jumped into that first argument. Now see how much more smoothly this writer glides into the argument by using a topic sentence before getting into specific details such as $10 billion in profits.

> The consumer group refutes the brokers' claim about cash-poor insurance companies. The consumers' argument that the car insurance industry recorded $10 billion in profits last year....

The next paragraph (the third one), could then begin with a topic sentence introducing the consumers' second argument and making a smooth transition to the new point.

> On the other hand [this signals a transition], the consumers argue, they are already paying more to drive.

Following that topic sentence, you would provide details about this second argument (the 10 percent increase in gas prices), and point out what makes it stronger (likely the brokers ignored the issue).

The fourth paragraph would repeat this formula with the third argument, which says consumers' wages haven't increased enough to cover the extra driving costs they already face.

The Evidence The rest of each middle paragraph will give details about the "relevant and specific" (as the prompt says) piece of evidence you're explaining in that particular paragraph. Again, this information is in the chart you made during the active reading phase. So, continuing on from the topic sentence, you'll

> Be specific. If the passage says the price of cabbages fell by two percent, use that product and figure. Don't be vague and say the price of vegetables is lower.

- describe the author's argument and the support he or she provides for that argument in the passage; remember to be specific
- explain why that evidence proves your thesis that one passage has the better support (in other words, explain why it's relevant)

Here's the complete paragraph describing the consumer group's first argument, with notes pointing out what function each part of the paragraph performs.

> The consumer group refutes the brokers' claim about cash-poor insurance companies [the topic sentence]. The consumers' argument that the car insurance industry recorded $10 billion in profits last year, more than any year in the past decade, [the argument and support for it] proves that the insurance companies don't really need extra money [how this argument proves the thesis that the consumers' case has better support]. The brokers' position is much weaker because it doesn't address the industry's financial success [evidence brought in from the other passage]. Three years of flat premiums do not justify raising prices, as the brokers argue, when the insurance companies have already made so much money [how this argument is weaker, which again proves the thesis that the consumers' case has better support].

Quoting and Paraphrasing Evidence How you incorporate evidence into your essay is important. You can't quote directly from the passage unless you put the author's words in quotation marks. Without the quotation marks, it's called plagiarism. In many colleges, that earns you a black mark on your record the first time and expulsion the second. Adults well into their careers have lost their jobs when plagiarism from decades earlier was exposed. So it's a good idea to get into the habit of avoiding plagiarism.

How do you include evidence from the passages, then? Most of the time, the answer is paraphrase—rephrase the evidence in your own words. For example, let's say the brokers' passage contains the following argument and support for the argument:

> Insurance companies report little or no increase in average premiums during the past three years. However, claims payouts have risen, on average, by three percent in each of those years.

Try rephrasing that in your own words.

Did you end up with something like "The brokers argue that premium revenue has remained flat for three years, while claims expenses have kept increasing"?

Next, you need to explain *why* that paraphrased piece of evidence is important to your thesis.

> The brokers weaken their own case by mentioning rising claims costs but failing to acknowledge the other side of the story: the record profits that more than cover the insurance companies' higher claims payouts.

When should you use a direct quote (in quotation marks)?

- When the passage author's exact words are important for proving your thesis
- When the author phrases an idea in such a unique way that a paraphrase wouldn't convey its true meaning accurately

Both cases will be rare in the passages you're likely to encounter in the Extended Response section, so you should usually count on paraphrasing your evidence. You would also be sure to mention which side of the debate offered the evidence you're using.

Paraphrasing Exercise Imagine the following statements are made in a passage. Try paraphrasing them so you can use them as evidence in your essay. Some possible paraphrases are below the list of statements.

1. A landmark study conducted in Antarctica found that penguins were thriving despite the evidence of the toll taken by climate change on other facets of the environment.
2. In its report, the commission concluded, "We should all learn from the experiences of First Nations people, who are trying to strike a balance between their traditional customs and the change demanded by industrial development."
3. Although fish farming increases the supply of fish, there is alarming evidence that it lowers the quality.

There is no one "correct" paraphrase. An acceptable paraphrase should be in your own words and should convey the content of the original statement accurately. Below are some possible ways to paraphrase these statements.

1. Penguins in Antarctica are flourishing, according to a pioneering study, even though climate change is causing environmental damage elsewhere on the continent.
2. The commission's report highlighted the lessons to be learned from the conflict between the growth of new industries and the traditional way of life for First Nations.
3. Evidence suggests that fish farms lead to higher production but lower quality.

The End

Ideally, the final paragraph concludes your argument by restating your thesis *in different words,* and reminding readers of the arguments that prove your thesis. Your final paragraph will be stronger if you simply say it and avoid starting with "In conclusion,..."

> Because it considers both consumers and the insurance industry, and backs up its claims with actual figures, the consumer group's letter to the editor provides the better support. (This topic sentence introduces the main arguments and restates the thesis.) The group draws a strong contrast between the industry's record profits on the one hand and, on the other, a 10 percent increase in drivers' fuel costs that must be financed with only a one percent average increase in wages. The brokers' weak argument that a premium increase is overdue, and their failure to consider consumers' financial hardship, make their position the weaker of the two. (These sentences remind readers of the main arguments in the passages.)

The Five-Paragraph Essay

This is the classic template. You might even remember it from earlier years in school. The first paragraph is the introduction (the beginning described above). Along with the attention-getter and the thesis statement, it gives three high-level reasons why the thesis statement is true.

Each of the next three paragraphs provides details about one of those three reasons. The second paragraph begins with a topic sentence covering the first reason you mentioned, and explains details about it. The third paragraph does the same for the second reason, and the fourth paragraph for the third reason. Those paragraphs are the middle described above.

The fifth paragraph is the conclusion (the end). It wraps up the thesis statement and the details from the middle section, and concludes your argument neatly. It doesn't simply restate the introduction, though, because by now you've added details that put meat on the bare bones of the introduction.

Of course, your essay doesn't have to be five paragraphs. You might have four reasons for your thesis statement, or only two. There might be six reasons, but two of them are so weak they're not worth discussing. There is an expectation that the essay will be more than one paragraph, but that's the only guideline the test writers give. The essay can be as long or as short as the time and doing a good job of the prompt task allow.

> There is no set length or number of paragraphs for your essay.

Prewriting

The template above gives you an organizational structure into which you can pour your essay (remember, organization is one of the traits on which you'll be graded) and a plan to follow in developing your argument about which passage has stronger support.

> You'll save time and write a better essay if you spend five minutes planning.

The template also explains why you don't just jump in and start writing. Your essay will sound like you just jumped in and started writing. For a coherent, persuasive essay that responds to the prompt, "hangs together" well, and gets a high score, you first need to plan it. That's where prewriting comes in.

Understanding your task through upfront thinking and planning has a tremendous impact on the quality of the final product (your Extended Response, in this case). As one of the world's great minds said,

> "If I had an hour to solve a problem I'd spend 55 minutes thinking about the problem and 5 minutes thinking about solutions."

—Albert Einstein

We're certainly not advocating that you spend more than 90 percent of the time thinking about the task in the prompt, but do spend five minutes or so thinking about why one passage provides stronger support, and planning the order in which you'll discuss the evidence from the passages. Use a note board to jot down any ideas you have for a strong opening paragraph and conclusion. Write a number beside each point in your argument/support chart to remind yourself which claim you want to cover first, second, and so on. You can cross off each one as you finish discussing it, so you'll see the progress you're making.

Taking a few of your 45 minutes to plan will save you from getting 40 minutes into writing and realizing you're badly off track. It will also leave you a couple of minutes at the end to review your essay so you can improve it and fix errors. (There are no spelling or grammar checkers for the Extended Response section, so you're on your own.)

Your goal with prewriting is to have the whole essay essentially done—in your head, in thin air, on your note boards, wherever. It's just not written down yet, and that's all you need to do with the next 30 or so minutes, leaving yourself a couple of minutes at the end to review and improve what you've written.

HOW CAN I IMPROVE MY WRITING?

You already encountered several ways to improve your writing: the eight areas of language use targeted on the GED® test (see page 99 in Chapter 8) and the use of a topic sentence to begin each paragraph (see page 134 in this chapter).

Here are two more tips to make your writing stronger, more interesting, and easier to read.

Dividing Up Your Time

5 minutes—Actively reading the two passages, noting the main arguments and supporting points on the chart

5 minutes—Prewriting

32 minutes—Writing

3 minutes—Reviewing and improving the essay

_____

45 minutes

Use Active Verbs

As the name implies, with an active verb, the subject is performing the action. With a passive verb, the subject is passive; the action is being done to it. Take a look at these stripped-down examples:

> John closed the door. (That's an active verb. The subject, John, is doing the closing.)

> The door was closed by John. (That's passive. The subject, the door, is getting the action done to it.)

Recognizing active and passive verbs gets a bit more complicated when phrases and clauses enter the picture:

> Tired, cold, and hungry from their frightening adventure in the dark woods, the *three boys began devising a plan* to return home without attracting the attention of anyone in the house. (That's active—the wayward boys are devising the plan.)

> Although the antique mahogany piano weighed a ton and would have sold for a fortune, *it was unloaded* from the moving van quickly and carelessly, in complete defiance of its great value. (Here's a passive verb—the subject, the piano, is getting the action of being unloaded done to it.)

There are a few cases in which you might want to use a passive verb. Let's say the owner of the small company where you work forgot to pay the computer service contract fee last month, leading the service company to cancel its contract. What do you tell Sofia in accounting when she asks why she can't get her computer fixed? Do you say, "Our idiot boss forgot to pay the computer service invoice last month"? (That's an active verb, by the way—the subject is doing the forgetting.) No, not likely. You might say something like, "The bill wasn't paid on time last month." That's passive—the subject is the one getting acted upon (in this case, not being paid). By using a passive verb, you can focus on the action and avoid blaming the one who carried out that action (the boss).

Cases in which a passive verb is a better choice are rare, though. Your writing will be stronger and more interesting to read if you use active verbs most of the time.

Active Verb Exercise

Try turning the passive verbs in the following sentences into active verbs. You'll find answers below. After you've finished, compare the active and passive versions. Notice how much stronger and easier to read the active version is.

1. An umbrella was purchased by Juanita because of the weather forecast for several days of rain.
2. Since it was clearly dying, the tree was felled by city maintenance workers.
3. After receiving a prize for the best children's book of the year, the author was honored at a lavish reception given by the local literary society.
4. The house was renovated during the winter by electricians, plumbers, and painters.

Here are some possible answers:

1. <u>Juanita bought</u> an umbrella because the weather forecast called for several days of rain.
2. <u>City maintenance workers felled</u> the tree because it was clearly dying.
3. <u>The local literary society held</u> a lavish reception to honor the author of the best children's book of the year.
4. <u>Electricians, plumbers, and painters renovated</u> the house during the winter.

Use Variety in Sentence Length and Structure

How many paragraphs like the one below could you read?

> Carrots are a root vegetable. Carrots are healthy. Carrots contain beta-carotene. Beta-carotene is an antioxidant. Carrots have Vitamin A. Vitamin A is good for vision.

Are you tired of those short, choppy sentences yet? They're all the same structure and all about the same length. They soon become boring, and they make the topic they're describing sound boring, too.

Look what happens when you combine these short sentences in different ways, though. Now the subject is interesting and the writing is more engaging.

> Carrots, a root vegetable, are healthy because they contain the antioxidant beta-carotene. They also have Vitamin A, which is good for vision.

> Carrots are loaded with beta-carotene, an antioxidant. This root vegetable is also healthy because it contains Vitamin A, a vision-boosting nutrient.

> Carrots, a member of the root vegetable family, provide the vision and health benefits of Vitamin A and the antioxidant beta-carotene.

> Health and vision benefits come from carrots, a root vegetable, because of the beta-carotene (an antioxidant) and Vitamin A they provide.

As those examples show, you can combine short sentences into more interesting structures in several ways.

- By coordinating or subordinating thoughts from two or more sentences (see pages 102–103 in Chapter 8)
- By using phrases ("Carrots, a member *of the root vegetable family,...*")
- By using a series of words ("...beta-carotene and Vitamin A")
- By using compound subjects or verbs ("*Health and vision benefits* come from carrots...")

Sentence Variety Exercise

Try your hand at combining the following short sentences into more varied structures. See how many different solutions you can create. One possible answer is below the short sentences.

> The house was painted white. The house was old. The paint was faded. The stairs were crooked. The porch floor had a hole. Some windows were broken. The house was empty. The house was not welcoming.

There are many possible ways to combine those sentences into a more interesting description of the house. Here's just one way:

> The old house, with its faded white paint and broken windows, stood empty. Its crooked stairs and unsafe porch floor made it seem unwelcoming.

HOW DO I IMPROVE MY COMPLETED ESSAY?

Because you planned your essay before you started writing, you should have about three minutes left to review it. The test writers don't expect a perfect job in 45 minutes (*they* probably couldn't do a perfect job in 45 minutes, either). However, you should use the extra time to improve your essay as much as you can, revising and editing it as you read through it.

Revising

When you revise your work, you're making changes to the content. No, you won't have much time to do this, but you can check to make sure that you've supported each of your arguments with evidence drawn from the passages, and that you've explained how the evidence proves your thesis (that one passage is better supported than the other). If you notice a statement that seems unclear, see if there's a better way to say what you intended.

Editing

Editing involves simply correcting language and spelling errors, without changing the content of your essay. Watch for the eight language use points explained in Chapter 8. (See page 99.) Remember, too, that you can't rely on spelling or grammar checkers in the test.

> The test has no spelling or grammar checkers.

PUTTING IT ALL TOGETHER

Let's use a fairly straightforward example to work through the process of building and organizing an argument. The first passage is a flyer for a seminar at which modern urban cave dwellers can learn about the Paleo diet, the diet of the hunter-gatherers who roamed the earth before the birth of agriculture and the domestication of livestock. The second is a warning notice on the bulletin board of a sports medicine clinic that has many patients who do CrossFit training, a program that recommends the Paleo diet.

The summary (in the top right-hand corner of the screen) would read as follows:

> While the seminar flyer promotes the benefits of the Paleo diet, the sports medicine clinic warns about its dangers.

The prompt (below the summary) would read as follows:

> In your response, analyze both the flyer and the clinic's warning to determine which position is better supported. Use relevant and specific evidence from both sources to support your argument.
>
> Type your response in the box below. This task may require approximately 45 minutes to complete.

The passages will appear on the left side of the screen, spread across several pages, which are numbered in the tabs across the top.

Use active reading to extract the authors' arguments and support as you read, and note them in the chart. Then plan, write, and review your essay. Use the questions listed in Chapter 10 (see page 127) to assess your own work. Then read the suggestions at the end of this example.

Passage A

Are you living in an unheated, unlit basement cave but still eating like it's the 21st century?

1   Embrace the Paleo diet and harmonize your lifestyle!

What is the Paleo diet?

2   It's a way of eating that's close to that of primitive humans. It means eating the foods that our bodies evolved to consume.

3   The Paleo diet eliminates all foods that were not available in Paleolithic times. It avoids many staples of the modern American diet, such as grains, dairy, high-fat meats, starchy vegetables, legumes, sugars, salty foods, and processed foods. It includes foods that are as similar as possible to foods available to Paleolithic man. That means grass-fed beef and free-range bison instead of the corn-fed meat readily available at most grocery stores.

What makes it good for you?

4   • By eliminating legumes, grains, and processed foods, the Paleo diet results in a healthy weight loss for most people. In a study of 14 participants, those who followed a strict Paleo diet lost an average of five pounds after three weeks on the program.

    • Debilitating diseases such as cancer, arthritis, multiple sclerosis, and diabetes are a modern problem, brought on partly by cultivated crops. These illnesses were unknown in Paleolithic times, when people ate a diet rich in meat and in the berries, fruits, and nuts that grew naturally around them.

    • The Paleo diet is "clean." It doesn't contain additives, preservatives, or chemicals that have been linked to lower energy levels and problems focusing on detailed tasks. The plant nutrients in the Paleo diet have significant anti-inflammatory benefits, and the higher red meat intake leads to an increase in iron. Followers find they can accomplish more in their day.

    • The Paleo diet promotes a natural rotation of nutrients in harmony with the seasons and the landscape. By eating only what would have been available in a particular season and location, people following the Paleo diet avoid overworking their digestive systems with out-of-synch foods, such as fresh oranges in the depths of the Wisconsin winter.

Want to learn more?

5   Join us for a free seminar to

- see the Paleo diet creator, Dr. Loren Cordain, on video as he explains the theory and benefits of eating the Paleolithic way

- hear real-life stories from fans who will never go back to a modern diet

- sample some Paleo staples

Tuesday night at 7:30 p.m.
Charming Gulf District School auditorium
at the corner of Relling & 184th St

Don't just live like our ancestors—eat like them too!

Passage B

6   The medical staff at Sutton Sports Medical Centre cautions patients about the harmful effects of the Paleo diet, which many of you are following.

7   The potential risks include:

8   **Nutritional imbalance**—Even with a very long list of allowed foods, the Paleo diet does not provide guidance on a balanced approach to nutrition. It also does not guarantee that people following the plan get enough of certain nutrients that are necessary to optimal health.

9   **Weight gain**—Because many of the allowed foods (such as nuts) are very high in calories, some people may find that following the Paleo diet actually causes weight gain instead of the rapid weight loss promised by the program. For instance, calorie consumption becomes a problem if a person eats five pounds of nuts in the course of one day.

10   **Suboptimal athletic performance**—The diet is restrictive in carbohydrates, which may be inadequate for athletes who use carbohydrates as a source of energy when exercising. Athletes need between three to six grams of carbs per pound of body weight per day; this is very difficult to achieve when consuming only the foods allowed by the Paleo diet. Thus, athletes may be faced with suboptimal performance.

11 **Bone and heart problems**—Removing all dairy products from your diet can cause a significant decrease in calcium and Vitamin D. A reduction in these essential nutrients can be harmful to bone health. In addition, the diet's focus on red meat can cause heart problems; a 2012 study confirmed that red meat consumption is associated with an increased risk of cardiovascular disease.

12 The clinic's resident nutritionist, Dr. Arpad Geuin, is available to create a diet plan customized to your nutritional needs and athletic goals.

Here's How to Crack It
Follow the steps we've explained.

1. Build your argument, using active reading to extract evidence (the authors' arguments and how they support those arguments), and note them on the chart.
2. Decide on your thesis (which passage is best supported).
3. Plan how you will organize the evidence.
4. Fill in the essay template to write your essay.
5. Review and improve your work.

———————————◯———————————

Building the Argument

This example makes it easy to find the arguments each side uses to make its case. In most of the passages you'll encounter in the Extended Response section, the arguments will be "buried" in text paragraphs instead of clearly laid out in bullet points.

The charts you filled in during your active reading might look like the ones below. (Of course, given the limited time you have on the test, yours would contain a lot of short forms and abbreviations.)

Pro side (flyer):

Argument	Support
weight loss (paragraph 4)	study (paragraph 4)
no modern illnesses (paragraph 4)	unknown in Paleolithic times (paragraph 4)
followers get more done (paragraph 4)	more energy, better focus (paragraph 4)
followers don't overwork digestive systems (paragraph 4)	natural rotation of nutrients (paragraph 4)

Con side (warning):

Argument	Support
nutritional imbalance (paragraph 8)	no guidance on balanced nutrition (paragraph 8)
weight gain (paragraph 9)	nuts example (paragraph 9)
lower athletic performance (paragraph 10)	amount of carbs needed (paragraph 10)
bone and heart problems (paragraph 11)	red meat study (paragraph 11)

Now you have a bare bones list of the evidence you need. Each side presents four arguments, all of them supported. Two of the arguments are contradictory (weight loss/weight gain). Which passage is better supported?

Choosing Your Thesis

Although an effective argument can be created for either passage, for this example let's say you choose the warning. You might choose this one because it cites one study (as the flyer does), but also gives specific figures (the nuts and carbs) for two other arguments. Its author is familiar enough with the diet to know that it doesn't include advice on balanced nutrition. (Showing an understanding of the other side's position boosts credibility.) The warning's support is more specific and credible than the support offered in the flyer, too. In two cases, the flyer supports arguments with only the vague experiences of unidentified "followers" of the diet.

The strongest reason for choosing the warning side, though, could lie in the authors and their purposes. The flyer's author is trying to promote a seminar, and is making the assumption that urban cave dwellers want to eat like the real thing—not necessarily a valid assumption. The promotional tone of the flyer and the benefits offered (free food samples, video) undercut the credibility of the "pro" side's argument. The warning's author, on the other hand, has the credibility of being a medical professional. This author's purpose is to prevent the clinic's patients from damaging their health with a harmful diet, and the underlying assumption that patients are concerned about their health is valid.

Organizing Your Argument

From the chart, you can see that you'll end up with a six-paragraph essay: the introduction (the beginning), one paragraph for each of the four arguments (the middle), and a conclusion (the end).

You have two choices for the order in which you'd discuss the arguments. You could stick with the order in which they're listed in the better-supported passage you've chosen (the warning), or else start with the warning's strongest argument (either the heart issue, which is supported with a specific study, or else the low athletic performance, which would be important to the warning's audience). Here, too, there is no right or wrong answer; choose the order you think you could do the best job of covering in the middle four paragraphs. Remember to start each paragraph with a topic sentence and use transitions (such as "in addition" or "furthermore") to guide readers smoothly through your discussion of the four pieces of evidence.

Writing the Essay

Now you've got everything you need to write your essay. You have your thesis (that the warning provides the best support), the evidence that supports your thesis (the arguments from the chart), and the template to follow in presenting your points. So let's get started on the writing.

The Introduction This example would work well with a question attention-getter:

> Should modern urban cave dwellers and athletes be eating like Paleolithic man?

Then you would tie that question to the topic of your essay, state your thesis, and give the big picture outline of the arguments:

> The promoter of a Paleo diet seminar thinks they should. However, a sports medicine clinic's warning about the diet's nutritional, health, and athletic dangers is better supported than the arguments in favor of eating like our ancient ancestors.

The Middle Here you'd give the evidence from the passage (one argument per paragraph), and explain why it proves your thesis that the case against the Paleo diet is better supported.

For instance, if you're following the order used by the better-supported side, you would begin with the evidence about nutritional imbalance, which is supported by a medical professional's familiarity with the Paleo diet and its lack of guidance about nutrition. You could also point out the weakness of the corresponding argument from the seminar promoter: The vague statements about a natural rotation of nutrients and not overworking the digestive system aren't credible from someone who isn't a professional nutritionist.

The next three paragraphs would deal with the next three arguments, always explaining how each one contributes to proving your thesis that the warning is better supported.

The End Here you would restate your thesis in different words, and remind readers of the main pieces of evidence that prove your thesis. This concluding paragraph might say something like this:

> Based on the credibility of the medical professional who wrote the warning and the specific support for the arguments given, the case against the Paleo diet is better supported. Detailed figures back up the arguments about health dangers (weight gain and cardiovascular problems) as well as the argument about lower athletic performance. This author has also made the effort to learn about the Paleo diet, and has noted its failure to provide nutritional guidance. The seminar promoter, on the other hand, cites only one study and is clearly trying to entice people to attend by mentioning the goodies that will be available.

Reviewing Your Work

Now, while you're practicing, you have time to ask yourself the questions listed in Chapter 10 (see page 127) to assess your own work. During the test, of course, you won't. Then, you'll simply be reviewing your essay to revise it (is something not clear? is there a better way to say it?) and edit it (correcting grammar or spelling errors).

Extended Response Drills

Now *you* try building and organizing your argument and writing an essay on your own. There are two Extended Response tasks below. (Remember, the more practice you get, the better you'll become at doing these essays.)

The first task, about electric vehicles, will give you some experience digging evidence out of the text paragraphs in two very different types of documents. The second, about antibiotics in farm animal feed, provides an example of unequally weighted evidence (one main argument on one side, several on the other). Depending on your opinion about this issue, it might also allow you to exercise the discipline of arguing for a position with which you don't agree.

Use active reading to extract the authors' arguments and support as you read, and note them in a chart. Then plan, write, and review your essay. Use the questions listed in Chapter 10 (see page 127) to assess your own work. Then read the suggestions in Part VIII: Answer Key to Drills.

Electric Vehicles

Below are two passages: a government document about the benefits of electric vehicles and a letter from a father to his daughter, urging her not to buy an electric car because of the dangers.

Passage summary:

> While the U.S. Department of Energy lists the benefits of electric vehicles, the father's letter to his daughter outlines the dangers.

The prompt:

> In your response, analyze both the government document and the letter to determine which position is better supported. Use relevant and specific evidence from both sources to support your argument.
>
> Type your response in the box below. (For this drill, type your response on a computer, if one is available. Otherwise, write your response on paper.) This task may require approximately 45 minutes to complete.

The following document uses these short forms (or acronyms) in discussing different types of vehicles powered by electricity: EV (electric vehicle), HEV (hybrid electric vehicle) and PHEV (plug-in hybrid electric vehicle).

Benefits and Considerations of Electricity as a Vehicle Fuel

1   Hybrid and plug-in electric vehicles can help increase energy security, improve fuel economy, lower fuel costs, and reduce emissions.

Energy Security

2   In 2012, the United States imported about 40% of the petroleum it consumed, and transportation was responsible for nearly three-quarters of total U.S. petroleum consumption. With much of the world's petroleum reserves located in politically volatile countries, the United States is vulnerable to price spikes and supply disruptions.

3   Using hybrid and plug-in electric vehicles instead of conventional vehicles can help reduce U.S. reliance on imported petroleum and increase energy security.

Fuel Economy

4   HEVs typically achieve better fuel economy and have lower fuel costs than similar conventional vehicles.

5   PHEVs and EVs can reduce fuel costs dramatically because of the low cost of electricity relative to conventional fuel. Because they rely in whole or part on electric power, their fuel economy is measured differently than in conventional vehicles. Miles per gallon of gasoline equivalent (mpge) and kilowatt-hours (kWh) per 100 miles are common metrics. Depending on how they're driven, today's light-duty EVs (or PHEVs in electric mode) can exceed 100 mpge and can achieve 30–40 kWh per 100 miles.

Infrastructure Availability

6   PHEVs and EVs have the benefit of flexible fueling: They can charge overnight at a residence (or a fleet facility), at a workplace, or at public charging stations. PHEVs have added flexibility, because they can also refuel with gasoline or diesel.

7   Public charging stations are not as ubiquitous as gas stations, but charging equipment manufacturers, automakers, utilities, Clean Cities coalitions, municipalities, and government agencies are establishing a rapidly expanding network of charging infrastructure. The number of publicly accessible charging units surpassed 7,000 in 2012.

Costs

8   Although fuel costs for hybrid and plug-in electric vehicles are generally lower than for similar conventional vehicles, purchase prices can be significantly higher. However, prices are likely to decrease as production volumes increase. And initial costs can be offset by fuel cost savings, a federal tax credit, and state incentives.

Emissions

9   Hybrid and plug-in electric vehicles can have significant emissions benefits over conventional vehicles. HEV emissions benefits vary by vehicle model and type of hybrid power system. EVs produce zero tailpipe emissions, and PHEVs produce no tailpipe emissions when in all-electric mode.

Source: Office of Energy Efficiency and Renewable Energy (EERE), U.S. Department of Energy (Abridged)

Passage B

10   My dear Melissa:

11   I'm so proud of you for completing your dental technician course and graduating with such exceptional grades!

12   As promised when you first returned to school, I'm transferring enough money to your account to allow you to buy a reasonably priced new car. You deserve this reward for your perseverance and hard work.

13   The choice of car is up to you. However, I know you want to "live green" and I'm concerned you might be thinking of an electric vehicle. If you are, I want to urge you to buy a regular gasoline-powered car instead. Your safety is very important to me, and there are just too many dangers with an electric vehicle.

14   First, you could find yourself stranded on a dark highway in the middle of nowhere. Electric cars have such a limited range (an average of about 80 miles) and even the state with the most public charging stations, California, has only about 5,000. Assuming you can find a public charging post when you need one, a charge can take hours if it's not a rapid-charge station. I have visions of you hanging around some station alone at night for up to eight hours.

15   Second, parts and repairs for electric cars are much more expensive. And the batteries need to be replaced after about five years, at a cost of thousands of dollars. That's on top of the initial price of the car, which can be as much as twice the cost of a gasoline-powered car.

16   Third, with a top speed of about 70 miles per hour, electric cars aren't safe for highway driving. What if you had to pass someone quickly, or speed up suddenly to get away from a dangerous situation? That means you wouldn't be able to drive home to visit your mother and me.

17   And finally, I've been seeing news reports of a few electric vehicles catching on fire while they're just sitting in the owner's garage or driveway. No one seems to know what causes them to ignite, but I don't want to be worrying about you every night asleep in your ground-floor apartment while your car is burning away just outside.

18   I hope you enjoy your well-deserved reward, and that you'll use it wisely and choose a gasoline-powered car.

19   Your loving father.

Antibiotics in Farm Animal Feed

Below are two passages: a government media release about a voluntary ban on antibiotics in farm animal feed, and a posting on a farmers' online forum warning about the negative effects such a ban would have on farmers, consumers, and the economy.

Passage summary:

> While the U.S. FDA media release explains why it wants to eliminate antibiotics in farm animal feed, the online forum posting urges readers to sign a petition against the ban.

The prompt:

> In your response, analyze both the media release and the forum posting to determine which position is better supported. Use relevant and specific evidence from both sources to support your argument.
>
> Type your response in the box below. (For this drill, type your response on a computer, if one is available. Otherwise, write your response on paper.)

Passage A

1   The Food and Drug Administration (FDA) is implementing a voluntary plan with industry to phase out the use of certain antibiotics for enhanced food production.

2   Antibiotics are added to the animal feed or drinking water of cattle, hogs, poultry, and other food-producing animals to help them gain weight faster or use less food to gain weight.

3   Because all uses of antimicrobial drugs, in both humans and animals, contribute to the development of antimicrobial resistance, it is important to use these drugs only when medically necessary. Governments around the world consider antimicrobial-resistant bacteria a major threat to public health. Illnesses caused by drug-resistant strains of bacteria are more likely to be potentially fatal when the medicines used to treat them are rendered less effective.

4   FDA is working to address the use of "medically important" antibiotics in food-producing animals for production uses, such as to enhance growth or improve feed efficiency. These drugs are deemed important because they are also used to treat human disease and might not work if the bacteria they target become resistant to the drugs' effects.

5   "We need to be selective about the drugs we use in animals and when we use them," says William Flynn, DVM, MS, deputy director for science policy at FDA's Center for Veterinary Medicine (CVM). "Antimicrobial resistance may not be completely preventable, but we need to do what we can to slow it down."

6   Once manufacturers voluntarily make these changes, the affected products can then be used only in food-producing animals to treat, prevent, or control disease under the order of or by prescription from a licensed veterinarian.

7   Bacteria evolve to survive threats to their existence. In both humans and animals, even appropriate therapeutic uses of antibiotics can promote the development of drug-resistant bacteria. When such bacteria enter the food supply, they can be transferred to the people who eat food from the treated animal.

Why Voluntary?

8   Flynn explains that the final guidance document made participation voluntary because it is the fastest, most efficient way to make these changes. FDA has been working with associations that include those representing drug companies, the feed industry, producers of beef, pork, and turkey, as well as veterinarians and consumer groups.

Source: U.S. Food and Drug Administration (Abridged)

Passage B

The following posting appeared on the FairToFarmers.org forum.

Ban the FDA's Antibiotic Ban!

9   The FDA is banning the use of antibiotics in animal feed. Food producers will be barred from adding antibiotics to feed or water unless an animal is sick and threatens the health of the rest of the herd or flock. Even then, a veterinarian's order will be required.

10   The FDA fails to realize that the regular use of antibiotics *prevents* disease, and prevention is much cheaper than curing an illness that has taken root on the farm. Antibiotics not only maintain animal health; they also promote faster growth, and therefore faster time to market. In addition, antibiotics lead to more efficient growth, since less feed is required to reach the desired weigh.

11   The FDA's reasoning is that antibiotic use in food animals *might* contribute to the development of antibiotic-resistant "superbugs." Scientific studies have so far been inconclusive, and some point to doctors overprescribing antibiotics for human patients as the cause, together with unsafe food handling practices by consumers. The FDA made the ban voluntary for the present; but if the scientific evidence were clear, the ban would have been mandatory right away.

12   European countries that have banned antibiotics in animal feed have not seen a decline in antibiotic-resistant diseases, but they have seen a significant increase in meat and poultry prices and a reduction in export sales. Food animals take several days longer to reach the desired weight and consume more feed before they do, increasing farmers' costs.

13   Each American farmer today feeds an average of 155 people, *six times* more than in 1960. Advances in agricultural practices, including the regular use of antibiotics in animal feed, have made that possible. Without antibiotics, American farmers will not be able to meet the food needs of a growing population.

14   Do people want enough food? Do they want affordable food? Do politicians want a thriving agricultural economy? Then we must end this voluntary ban on antibiotics in animal feed while we still can, before it becomes mandatory.

15   Add your voice to the petition to ban the FDA's ban on antibiotics in animal feed. Simply click on the button below. The petition will be delivered to the FDA when we have 100,000 signatures.

> Petition to Ban the FDA Ban on Antibiotics in Animal Feed

Part IV Summary

- o The Extended Response section combines the active reading, critical thinking, and language use skills that are required for the Reading and Language assessments.
- o You will have 45 minutes to
  - • analyze two passages (about 650 words total) that present opposing sides of a "hot button" issue
  - • decide which position is better supported
  - • explain your choice in an essay, using evidence drawn from both passages
  - • revise and edit your work
- o The essay is considered an "on demand draft" and is not expected to be completely free of errors.
- o There is no required length or number of paragraphs.
- o There are no spelling or grammar checkers. You can cut, copy, and paste within the text box where you type your essay, but you can't copy text from the passage and paste it into your essay.
- o There is no right or wrong answer, as long as you build a credible case for the best-supported passage and back it up with evidence from the passages.
- o Look for evidence in the authors' arguments for their positions and in the support (such as studies or statistics) they provide for their arguments. Also judge the authors' reasoning and assumptions.
- o The essay is graded by an automated scoring engine that has "learned" how humans graded an extensive range of sample essays. If it doesn't recognize the characteristics of an essay, it assigns the work to a human grader.
- o The essay is assessed on how well you
  - • create your argument and use evidence from the passages
  - • develop and organize your ideas
  - • use language

- Divide your time efficiently.
  - During the first five minutes, use active reading to build your case for which passage is better supported. Note each author's arguments and how the authors support them.
  - Take the next five minutes to plan your essay.
  - Spend about 32 minutes writing what you planned.
  - Allow three minutes at the end to revise and edit your work.
- Use an essay template to organize your ideas.
  - The Beginning
    - —Introductory paragraph
    - —Attention-getter (optional)
    - —Thesis statement (which passage is better supported)
    - —Big picture list of evidence that proves the thesis statement
  - The Middle
    - —One paragraph for each piece of evidence that proves the thesis statement
    - —Topic sentence
    - —Evidence from the passages
    - —Explanation of how the evidence supports the thesis statement
  - The End
    - —Restatement of the thesis in different words
    - —Reminder of the pieces of evidence that prove the thesis
- Improve your writing by
  - reviewing the eight areas of language use explained in Chapter 8
  - starting each paragraph with a topic sentence
  - using active verbs
  - varying the structure and length of your sentences
  - revising and editing your work

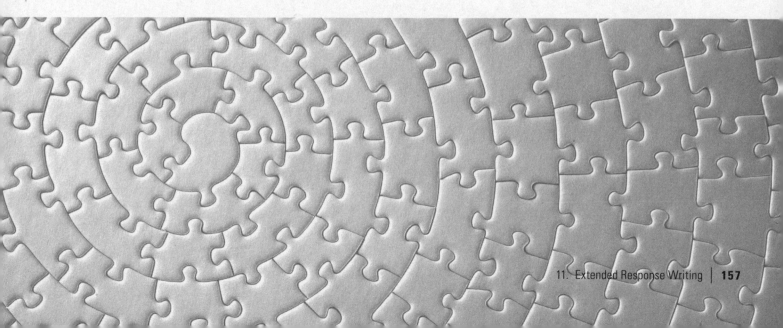

Part V
Mathematical Reasoning

Chapter 12
Mathematical
Reasoning
Overview

If the GED® Mathematical Reasoning test covered all the math topics taught in high school, it would be an overwhelming test. Fortunately, it doesn't, and it isn't. The GED® test writers concentrate on a few areas very heavily, which means that by reading the chapters that follow and doing the exercises we provide, you should be able to score very well—even if you've always hated math.

What's on the Test

The Mathematical Reasoning test contains 46 questions to be answered in 115 minutes, which gives you two and a half minutes for each question. The areas covered in the Mathematical Reasoning test are as follows:

Quantitative Problem Solving with Rational Numbers	25%
Quantitative Problem Solving in Measurement	20%
Algebraic Problem Solving with Expressions and Equations	30%
Algebraic Problem Solving with Graphs and Functions	25%

What Isn't on the Test

There is no calculus or even precalculus. No logs, no proofs, no imaginary numbers. To make things even easier, the Mathematical Reasoning test provides a list of formulas, so that in case you don't remember how to find the volume of a cylinder, for example, you can always just look it up.

To Calculate, or Not to Calculate?

The 46-question Mathematical Reasoning test is broken up into two parts. In the first part, you will have 5 questions and you *will not* be allowed to use a calculator. You MUST submit your answers to these five questions before moving on to the rest of the test. In the second part, you will have 41 questions and you *will* be allowed to use a calculator.

You may think that the second section (in which you can use a calculator) would be easier than the first, but there's one hitch: You can't take your *own* calculator. You must use the on-screen calculator that is automatically available: the Texas Instruments TI-30XS, shown below.

You will be provided on-screen instructions for using the calculator. However, it is vital that you become familiar with this particular model ahead of time. Why spend your valuable test time learning how to use the calculator when that time could be better spent actually solving the questions? We strongly recommend that you buy (or borrow) this specific calculator and practice with it for several weeks before the test. It is available in most office supply stores or online for about $18.

There are two major features of the Texas Instruments TI-30XS that can be pretty confusing. They are the arrow keys and the green "2nd" key.

The arrow keys (located at the top right) can be used to move within a function on the screen or to exit a function and return to the main expression you are calculating. You will use the arrow keys to input fractions, mixed numbers, or numbers in scientific notation.

Pushing the "2nd" key (located at the top left) before another key accesses the function that is written above the key, similarly to the way the "Shift" key works on a computer keyboard. You will use this to input mixed numbers and to calculate roots and percentages.

Let's take a look at how you would input the mixed number $12\frac{1}{2}$:

You can see why we are telling you to get the calculator in advance and become familiar with it.

Will All the Math Questions Be Multiple Choice?

At least fifty percent of the Mathematical Reasoning test is multiple choice. But both Parts 1 and 2 could include question formats such as fill in the blank, drag and drop, hot spot, or drop down. You should have already seen what these look like in Chapter 3 of this book. If not, now would be a good time to review that chapter.

Ballparking

We've already introduced you to the concept of POE in Part I of this book, and we've explained that there's no guessing penalty on the GED® test. On the Mathematical Reasoning test, you can use POE to eliminate any out-of-scope answer choices, leaving just the answers that make sense. This is what we call **Ballparking,** and it is especially useful for answering those difficult questions that you may not know how to solve!

Ballparking is a guessing strategy that can help you eliminate "out of the ballpark" answers.

In school, you may once have encountered a problem on a math test that looked like this:

> This month, 1,500 new members joined a particular health club. The club's goal for this month was 2,000 new members. What percentage of the club's goal was achieved?

If you weren't sure how to solve this fill-in-the-blank problem during that test, you were pretty much out of luck. It certainly wouldn't have made sense to guess, would it? For example, if you had closed your eyes and picked a number at random ("...uh, 14!"), the chances that you would happen to pick the right answer would have been pretty slim. (By the way, if you aren't sure how to do this problem right now, don't worry. We'll cover percentages in Chapter 13.)

But most of the problems on the GED® test are NOT the fill-in-the-blank types. Most questions are in the multiple-choice format. Here's how that question would look on the GED® test:

> This month, 1,500 new members joined a particular health club. The club's goal for this month was 2,000 new members. What percentage of the club's goal was achieved?
>
> A.   75%
> B.   82%
> C.   112%
> D.   150%

You may be saying, "Big deal. Same problem." But, in fact, this is not the same problem at all. If you happened to spot this question on the real GED® test and still didn't know how to do it, you would have an enormous advantage because you no longer have to guess completely at random. In the multiple-choice question format, there are only four possibilities, and *one* of them has to be right. Just by guessing among the four answer choices, you have a 25 percent chance of answering the question correctly.

We can do even better than that. Fortunately, it turns out that many answers to Mathematical Reasoning questions aren't reasonable at all. In fact, some of them are pretty crazy. Let's just think about that problem above. The health club's goal was 2,000 new memberships, but they actually got only 1,500 new memberships. Did they reach their goal? No way. Putting this in the language of percentages, let's restate the question: Did they reach 100 percent of their goal? The answer is still no.

Obviously, the correct answer to this problem must be *less* than 100 percent. Even if you are unsure about how to calculate the exact percentage, there are several answer choices that are simply way out of the ballpark. Look at (D), 150%. This answer implies that not only did the club meet its goal, it exceeded it as well. Forget (D). Look at (C), 112%. Again, this is just crazy. The correct answer must be less than 100%. Both of these answers are way out of the ballpark.

Apply the Strategy
By taking a step back from a problem, you can often eliminate at least one or two answer choices.

We have eliminated two answer choices. This means the correct answer to this question is either (A) or (B). All of a sudden, your odds of getting this question correct are much better. You now have a fifty-fifty chance of being right. Pick one. If you picked (A), you just got the question correct.

Even if you picked (B) and got the question wrong, there are probably more questions that you can ballpark. Let's say you have two questions that you don't know how to solve, but you can ballpark. You probably get both of them narrowed down to two possible answers (as we just did). Thus, in each question, you are down to a fifty-fifty guess. What would be the results if you were to guess on both of them? The odds say you're going to get one of them wrong (maybe you picked (B) for this question). That's a shame, but after all, there's no guessing penalty, and more to the point, you didn't know how to do the question anyway, so you're no worse off than you were before. However, the odds also say that you're going to get the other one *right*! And that's not bad, considering you had no idea how to do that question either.

> Don't know how to "do" a question?
> Try Ballparking and then guess!

Okay, let's say you know exactly how to do a problem. Should you bother to ballpark it first? Definitely. Taking the GED® test does funny things to people. You might be the greatest mathematician in the world ordinarily, but by the time you get to the Mathematical Reasoning test, your brain may be so fried from the other four tests that you just aren't thinking completely straight. Or you may be rushing to finish a question and make a mistake that you would never normally make. You can prevent lots of careless errors by stepping back from a math problem and saying,

> *Wait a minute. Before I even start multiplying or dividing, which answers don't make sense?*

Once you've gotten rid of the crazy answer choices, then you can start solving the problem. And if your calculations happen to lead you, mistakenly, to one of those out-of-scope answer choices—well, you'll know you just made a mistake, and you'll be able to figure out what went wrong.

You'll find that once you start looking at GED® problems in this way, you'll spot many opportunities to ballpark. This is because the test writers construct their incorrect answer choices not to be reasonable but to anticipate common errors that test takers make when they're in a hurry.

> You can ballpark on
> many question types:
> • Multiple choice
> • Drop down
> • Drag and drop

Partial Answers

One of the most common errors that the GED® test knows that test takers make is not reading the math question carefully enough, and therefore solving only some of what the question requires. Such a mistake can lead you to wrongly choose a *partial answer* (even though you may be on the right track). Let's look at another multiple-choice problem.

1. Eric buys a coat from a mail-order catalog. The coat costs $140, plus an $8 shipping charge and a $2 handling fee. If there is a 10% sales tax on the entire amount, what would be the total cost of buying the coat?

   A. $135
   B. $150
   C. $160
   D. $165

Like many problems on the Mathematical Reasoning test, this requires several steps. What is the first thing you would do if you were actually buying this coat? We add up the costs we have so far.

the coat	$140
shipping	$8
handling	+ $2
	$150

We are already up to $150, and we haven't even added in the tax yet. Do you see any answer choices we can cross out? If you said (A) and (B), you are right on the money. The correct answer must be *greater* than $150, which means there are only two possibilities left: (C) and (D). Look at that—we just created another fifty-fifty chance of guessing the correct answer.

Slow Down for "Traps"

GED® test writers love to leave "trap" answers for you—such as an answer that subtracts two numbers instead of adding them. Watch out for these traps by working the problem carefully, which may mean you need to SLOW DOWN. It is better to take your time and answer one question correctly than to hurriedly answer two questions incorrectly.

Why did the test writers choose two answers that didn't make sense? Because they wanted to include some answers that many test takers are likely to pick by mistake. For example, let's say that you were doing this problem, and you got to the point we have already reached: You added up the numbers and got $150. If you were anxious, or in a hurry (as most test takers are), you might look at the answer choices, see (B), $150, figure that you must be done, and click the bubble for (B) on the screen. However, this number is only a *partial* answer to the question.

To find the correct answer to this question—(D), $165—requires you to do three separate calculations. First, add up the cost of the coat and the postage and handling. Check. Second, calculate the tax. To compute this, you find 10 percent of $150, which turns out to be $15 (Don't worry if you weren't sure how to find 10 percent of 150. We'll show you how in a later chapter.) Third, add the tax to the previous total. If a test taker chose (B), $150, it was not because he made a mistake in his calculations. The answer to step one of this problem is $150. And if a test taker chose (A), $135, it was because he accidentally subtracted the tax instead of adding it.

On the GED® test, you will frequently find partial answers lurking in wait for you. To avoid getting taken in by one of these, you have to read the problem very carefully the first time and then read it again just as carefully right before you select your answer.

Because the test writers employ partial answers so often on the Mathematical Reasoning test, you can actually use the partial answers as clues to help you find the final answer. For example, working on a two-step problem, you may find that the answer to the first step of the problem is also one of the answer choices. This is a good sign. It means you are on the right track. If the answer to your first step is *close* to one of the answer choices, but just a little off, you might try redoing the calculation to see if you made a mistake.

Using Graphics to Ballpark

Anywhere from one-third to one-half of the questions on the Mathematical Reasoning test refer to "graphic material": drawings of geometric figures, graphs, and charts. Whenever you see a diagram on the Mathematical Reasoning test, you have the single most efficient way to ballpark that you could possibly imagine: You can just *measure* the diagrams. We know it's bizarre, but it's true.

Here's a typical drag-and-drop geometry problem:

Question 1 refers to the following diagram.

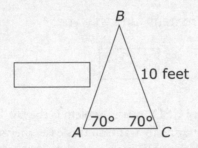

1. If angle *A* and angle *C* both equal 70°, then what is the length of side *AB*? Click on the number you want to select and drag it into the box.

3 feet	7 feet	9 feet
10 feet	12 feet	15 feet

For extra help reading charts and graphs, download our Understanding Graphics supplement from your Student Tools, free when you register your book online!

Don't worry if you don't remember the geometric principle involved in solving this problem (the properties of an isosceles triangle). We'll review geometry in Chapter 16.

The question is, how long is side *AB*? Let's find out. Simply take any straight edge you can find, and carefully measure side *BC*, which the diagram says is 10 feet long. Mark the length of side *BC* along the edge of one of the erasable note boards that is provided to you for the duration of the test. Now all you have to do is compare that length to side *AB*. If it's a lot bigger, you can get rid of any choices less than 10. If it's a lot smaller, you can get rid of any choices greater than 10.

If you measured our diagram correctly, you probably noticed that side *AB* appears to be exactly the same size as side *BC*. So is the correct answer 10 feet? Well, in fact it is. However, because the GED® drawings are drawn only *roughly* to scale, you wouldn't know for sure that the answer is exactly 10 feet unless you knew the geometric reasoning behind the problem. Going by the diagram alone, you could only have gotten the answer down to either 9 feet or 10 feet.

Between these two, it would have been too close to call. However, you could be pretty certain that the answer was *not* 3 feet, 7 feet, 12 feet, or 15 feet.

The Red Herring

On every Mathematical Reasoning test, there will be several problems that give you more information than you actually need. We call this extra information the "red herring." Here's an example of a fill-in-the-blank question type:

Sounds Fishy to Me
A "red herring" is an expression in which a clue or piece of information is intended to be misleading or distracting from the actual question. Distractor answers are common on standardized tests like the GED® test.

1. This year, $\frac{3}{4}$ of the employees at Acme made contributions to a voluntary retirement fund. Last year, only $\frac{2}{3}$ of the employees contributed. If there are now 2,100 employees, how many contributed to the voluntary retirement fund this year?

The most important part of any GED® math problem is the last line, which is where the test writers tell you what they really want. In this case, they want the number of employees who contributed to their retirement fund *this* year. In this problem, the only year you care about is *this* year. To answer the question, you have to find out from the problem what fraction of the total employees contributed this year, and then multiply that fraction by the total number of employees. (If you aren't sure how to find a fractional part of a number, don't worry. We'll show you how in Chapter 13.)

Look at the problem and ask yourself, "Is there any information that is not about this year?" Well, as a matter of fact, there is. The second sentence, "Last year, only $\frac{2}{3}$ of the employees contributed," has nothing to do with what the question asks. The GED® test writers threw that sentence in to see if it would trick you. It was a red herring.

To answer this question, we need to take $\frac{3}{4}$ of 2,100. The correct answer is 1,575.

Taking the Mathematical Reasoning Test

When you click to begin the Mathematical Reasoning test, you will probably begin with Question 1, then do Question 2, and then do Question 3, and so on. This is a fine strategy as long as you are prepared to be flexible. Every year, we hear stories from test takers who got stuck on some early problem—let's say it was Question 3. They just couldn't get it. They read it and read it again. They tried solving it one way and then another. But some people have orderly minds, and *darn it*, they aren't going to go on to Question 4 until they get Question 3. After 10 minutes, when they finally give up and go on to number 4, they are thoroughly rattled, jittery, and very angry at themselves for wasting so much time.

The lesson here?

Don't Get Stubborn

There are always going to be problems that, for whatever reason, you just can't get. It might be a mental block, or maybe you never learned a particular type of problem, or maybe the question was simply written so confusingly that it is impossible to understand. No matter how easy you think the problem ought to be, don't be pigheaded. Even if you can't do the very *first* problem, there are 45 others waiting for you, and you will find that many of them are pretty easy.

First Pass, Second Pass

Of course, it isn't necessary to solve every problem to do very well, and in fact, you will see that by skipping the problems you don't know how to do, you can actually increase your score. Here's how.

The Two-Pass System can help to save you time and lock in those points!

We recommend that you take the Mathematical Reasoning test in two passes. On your first pass, you'll begin at the beginning and do every problem that comes easily to you. If you read a question and know just what to do, then it is a first-pass problem. However, if you read a problem and have no idea of how to solve it, then you should click the "Flag for Review" icon in the upper right corner and move on. You have not skipped this problem forever. You are merely saving it for later, after you've locked in all the easy points.

> First pass: Do the ones you KNOW you can get.

When you finish your first pass, a "Question Review" screen will show you which questions you flagged along the way. Now you can take a second look. Sometimes, when you read the problem again, you'll immediately see what was unclear to you the first time, and you'll know just what to do. Other times you may not be sure, but you'll be able to eliminate several answer choices by Ballparking. And sometimes, of course, you will just say, "Yuck!" and answer with your best guess. Remember, you should NEVER leave a question unanswered on the GED® test. Right before you submit the Mathematical Reasoning test, make sure that the status for every question number (even the flagged ones) is "answered."

> Second pass: Go back over your flagged questions.

Chapter 13
Basic Arithmetic

This chapter reviews basic math terminology and definitions including the number line, positive and negative numbers, digits, rounding off, multiplying and dividing, using the order of operations, fractions, decimals, and percents.

The arithmetic on the Mathematical Reasoning test is not necessarily the arithmetic you learned in school. The folks who write the test are striving to make GED® math more relevant to real life. Consequently, you won't find any questions on the more theoretical aspects of arithmetic—properties of integers, for example. Nor will there be any questions about prime numbers, imaginary numbers, or any of the other terms that generally go under the name "axioms and fundamentals." Instead, the test focuses on practical math. Several of the questions will be word problems that try to evoke situations you might find in everyday life.

In this chapter, we're going to show you all the basic arithmetic topics that come up on the Mathematical Reasoning test. With each topic, we'll first show you the concept behind the topic, then illustrate it with typical examples, and finally give you a small drill so you can practice the concept on your own. At the end of the entire chapter, there will be a big drill in GED® test format, including all the concepts we've shown you. The purpose of this is to give you some practice recognizing the different types of questions when they are all mixed together—as they are on the real GED® test. In the next chapter, we'll cover *applied* arithmetic topics in just the same way.

Here are the basic arithmetic concepts that appear on the GED® test:

- The number line
- Rounding off
- Operations with positive and negative numbers
- Order of operations
- Commutative and distributive properties
- Fractions
- Decimals
- Percents

THE NUMBER LINE

The number line is a visual way of understanding positive and negative numbers in relation to one another.

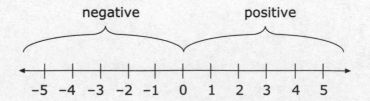

Positive numbers are to the right of zero on the number line above. Negative numbers are to the left of zero on the number line above. Zero itself is neither negative nor positive.

Note that positive numbers get bigger as they move away from zero. Negative numbers get smaller. For example, −3 is smaller than −1. A number line can extend infinitely to the left or right, but the number lines on the GED® test generally look like the example on the previous page, with a fairly small number of position points. Let's try identifying some points on the number line.

Find point X on the number line. What number does point X represent? If you said 4, you were absolutely right. How about points Y and Z? If you said −3 and 1, you were right again. Here's how a number line problem would look on the GED® test:

Question 1 refers to the following number line.

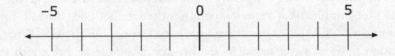

1. Which point represents the number −3?

    Click on the number line to plot a point.

Here's How to Crack It

Generally, the only thing that's difficult in a number line problem is orienting yourself. The best place to begin is to find 0. Did you find it? Now, determine the scale. Count the number of spaces between 0 and 5. There are five. Therefore, each space is represents 1. Now, in which direction do you move for negative numbers? To the left. And how many places to the left do you count from 0? Three. Mark your point there (or click the cursor on the real GED® Mathematical Reasoning test) and you're done!

Here's a slightly more difficult number line problem:

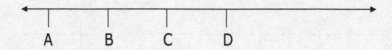

Question 2 refers to the following diagram.

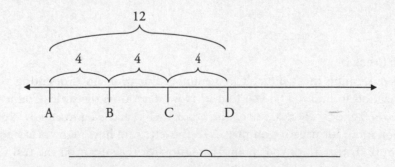

2. On the number line above, AB = BC = CD. If
    AD = 12, then what is the length of AB?

    A. 3
    B. 4
    C. 5
    D. 8

Here's How to Crack It

When a question asks for the *length* or *distance*, the answer MUST be positive.

In this problem, there is no way to orient yourself because neither the diagram nor the problem identifies a specific point on the number line. Instead, this problem is concerned with the *lengths* of segments on the line. On the GED® test, lengths are always positive, never negative. In this case, the only actual length you are given is AD, which equals 12. Let's look at the other information in the problem. If AB = BC = CD, then these segments break up AD into three equal parts. Because the whole is 12, what is the length of a single part? Divide the total length 12 by the 3 equal segments to find that the length of AB is 4, and the answer is (B).

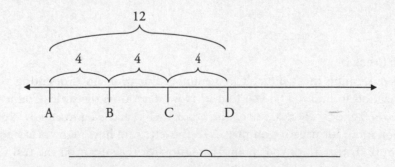

The *absolute value* of a number is the distance from the number to zero on a number line. Since absolute value measures distance (or length), it is always a nonnegative number. To write the absolute value of a number, you place the number in between two vertical lines. For example, you would write the absolute value of –5 as |–5|. How far from zero is –5 on the number line? –5 is five steps from 0, so |–5| = 5. The absolute value of a number will always be positive (or zero).

Sometimes number line problems will ask you about the midpoint of a line segment. A **midpoint** is simply the place halfway between either end of the line segment. A GED® problem might look like this:

Question 3 refers to the following diagram.

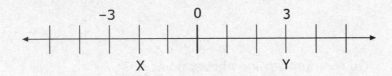

3.   If point X on the line above represents –2 and point Y on the line represents 3, then the midpoint of segment XY would be between which two numbers?

    A.   –2 and –1
    B.   –1 and 0
    C.   0 and 1
    D.   1 and 2

Here's How to Crack It

This time, there are concrete numbers marked on the number line, so take a second to get oriented. Now, the midpoint of XY is the point exactly halfway between point X and point Y. Count how many spaces there are between X and Y. Did you get 5? Good. What is half of 5? Half of 5 is $2\frac{1}{2}$. So all you have to do is count over $2\frac{1}{2}$ to the right of point X or $2\frac{1}{2}$ to the left of point Y. In either case, the midpoint is between 0 and 1, and the correct answer is (C).

Number Line Drill

You can check your answers in Part VIII: Answer Key to Drills.

Questions 1 through 3 refer to the diagram below.

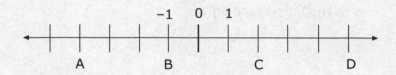

1. On the number line above, point A is

    | Select... ▼ | point B.
    | greater than |
    | equal to |
    | less than |

2. On the number line above, what is the distance from point A to point B?

    A. −4
    B. −3
    C. 3
    D. 4

3. If a new point E was to be added to the number line exactly halfway between points A and D, where would it be located?

    A. between points −3 and −2
    B. at point 0
    C. between points 0 and 1
    D. at point 2

Digits

All numbers are made up of digits. In the number 6,342, there are four digits: 6, 3, 4, and 2. In this case, the 2 is in the ones place. The 4 is in the tens place, the 3 is in the hundreds place, and the 6 is in the thousands place.

In the number 0.57, there are two digits: 5 and 7. In this case, the 5 is in the tenths place. The 7 is in the hundredths place.

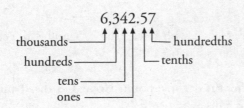

6,342.57

thousands ──┐
hundreds ──┐ │
tens ──┐ │ │
ones ──┐ │ │ │

hundredths
tenths

Digit Quiz
Q: Which of these
numbers has more
digits?
(1)   37.5
(2)   342

Turn the page for the
answer.

ROUNDING OFF TO THE NEAREST WHATEVER

The GED® test writers sometimes ask you to round off a number. The problem might read, "To the nearest thousand, how many..." or "What number to the nearest tenth..."

Whether you round to the nearest thousand or the nearest tenth, the process is exactly the same. Let's begin by rounding to the nearest dollar. If you have up to $1.49, then to the nearest dollar you have $1. If you have $1.50 or more, then to the nearest dollar you have $2.

Exactly the same principles hold true when you round any type of number.

1.   Identify the place you are rounding to.
   • For example, let's round 6,342.57 to the nearest ten.
   • Which digit is in the tens place? The 4 is in the tens place.

   Since we are rounding to the tens place, draw a number line that counts by tens:

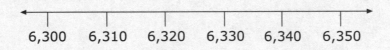

6,300   6,310   6,320   6,330   6,340   6,350

2.   Look at the digit that comes *after* the place you are rounding to.
   In our example, what is the digit after 4? The next digit is 2.
   • If that digit is 0, 1, 2, 3, or 4, you will round the tens place down. (Keep the 4.)
   • If that digit is 5, 6, 7, 8, or 9, you will round the tens place up. (Change the 4 to a 5.)

   Let's look at this on the number line. Make a mark where the original number lies.

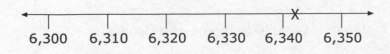

6,300   6,310   6,320   6,330   6,340   6,350

Is it closer to 6,340 or to 6,350? In this case, it is closer to the smaller amount, 6,340.

3. Replace any digits after the rounding place with zeros.
   - Which digits will we replace with zeros? The 2, 5, and 7 all get replaced.
   - So our number now looks like 6,340.00.

Do we need the zeros after the decimal point? Nope. Go ahead and drop those off to get the final answer: 6,340.

Here's how this might look on the GED® test.

1. You buy a loaf of bread for $2.99, deli meat for $3.65, and sliced cheese for $4.49. To the nearest dollar, how much will you owe at checkout?

$

Here's How to Crack It
There are two steps to the problem. The first step is to add up the items you will be purchasing. $2.99 + $3.65 + $4.49 = $11.13. Great—now don't forget about Step 2! The problem asks for the total "to the nearest dollar." So Step 2 is to round. Which is the dollars place? If you aren't sure, try saying the number out loud: "Eleven *dollars* and thirteen cents." So we have 11 dollars plus 13 cents more. Now look at the first digit after the dollars place, which is 1. Since this is less than 5, round down. The correct answer is $11.

Rounding Off Drill
You can check your answers in Part VIII: Answer Key to Drills.

1. To the nearest thousand, what is 3,400?

2. To the nearest tenth, what is 3.46?

3. To the nearest hundred, what is 565?

4. What is $432.70 to the nearest dollar?

5. What is 4.80 to the nearest hundredth?

ADDING AND SUBTRACTING POSITIVE AND NEGATIVE NUMBERS

Let's look at that number line one more time.

Many people have trouble adding and subtracting negative numbers. The number line helps us perform these operations effectively. First, lets look at adding. For example, $(-2) + 6$.

To add any two numbers, begin by locating the first number on the number line.

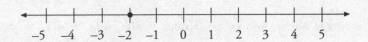

The absolute value of the second number tells us how many steps we'll move. $|6| = 6$, so we'll move six steps.

If that second number is positive, we'll move that many steps to the right. If it's negative, we'll move that many steps to the left. The number 6 is positive, so we'll move six steps to the right from (-2).

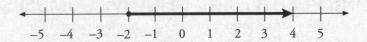

So, we see that $(-2) + 6 = 4$.

This method works whether you are adding two positives, a positive and a negative, or two negative numbers!

Using the same method, we can see that $7 + (-5) = 2$, and $(-3) + (-5) = (-8)$.

Subtracting positive and negative numbers is also pretty straightforward, if we consider one thing: subtracting is the same as adding the opposite. Did you notice, in our example above, that $7 + (-5)$ is the same as $7 - 5$? That's an illustration of this very idea.

Whenever you have a subtraction question, you can change it to an addition (of the opposite) question, and solve it like we did above. This is very helpful when you are subtracting with negative numbers. Here's how it works:

$$4 - 7 =$$

Let's rewrite this, so instead of *subtracting*, we're *adding* the *opposite*.

4 – 7 is the same as 4 + (–7). Now we've got an addition question, so we'll use our addition method, and see that 4 + (–7) = (–3).

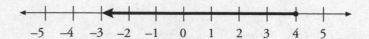

This method works on all subtraction questions, even the kind that most people find the trickiest: subtracting a negative. Consider this example:

$$(-11) - (-7) =$$

This is perplexing at first. So many minuses! But let's rewrite it so we're *adding* the *opposite*. Instead of subtracting –7, we'll add the opposite of –7, which is positive seven. So, (–11) – (–7) = (–11) + 7.

Use your addition steps above, and count 7 steps to the right of –11. Where do you land? On –4.

$$(-11) - (-7) = (-11) + 7 = (-4)$$

It might take a little time and practice to perfect these adding and subtracting processes, but that time and energy is worth it. These processes work no matter what the numbers are.

MULTIPLYING POSITIVE AND NEGATIVE NUMBERS

Multiplication is actually just the process of adding a number several times. For example, to multiply 4 by 3, you are actually just adding 4 three separate times

$$4 \times 3 = 4 + 4 + 4 = 12$$

or adding 3 four separate times

$$3 \times 4 = 3 + 3 + 3 + 3 = 12$$

To multiply 5 by 2, you are actually just adding 5 two separate times

$$5 \times 2 = 5 + 5 = 10$$

or adding 2 five separate times

$$2 \times 5 = 2 + 2 + 2 + 2 + 2 = 10$$

Of course, it's a lot quicker to use the multiplication (times) tables. We just wanted to remind you of the theory behind multiplication. If your times tables are a little rusty, don't worry. You're going to get lots of opportunity to practice over the next three chapters.

There are four rules regarding the multiplication of positive and negative numbers.

positive × positive = positive $2 \times 3 = 6$

positive × negative = negative $2 \times -3 = -6$

negative × positive = negative $-2 \times 3 = -6$

negative × negative = positive $-2 \times -3 = 6$

We have provided the following multiplication table for you to fill in to refresh your memory.

	1	2	3	4	5	6	7	8	9
1									
2									
3									
4									
5									
6									
7									
8									
9									

DIVIDING POSITIVE AND NEGATIVE NUMBERS

Division is actually the opposite of multiplication. If we multiply 2 by 3, we get 6. If we divide 6 by 2, we are actually asking what number times 2 equals 6?

$6 \div 2 = 3$. You can also write this as $\frac{6}{2}$ or $2\overline{)6}$.

The same four rules of multiplication apply to the division of positive and negative numbers.

positive ÷ positive = positive	$6 \div 2 = 3$
positive ÷ negative = negative	$6 \div -2 = -3$
negative ÷ positive = negative	$-6 \div 2 = -3$
negative ÷ negative = positive	$-6 \div -2 = 3$

Adding, Subtracting, Multiplying, and Dividing Positive and Negative Numbers Drill

Do these problems first on your own. Then, on a separate piece of paper, do them again using your calculator.

You can check your answers in Part VIII: Answer Key to Drills.

1. $5 + (-3) =$

2. $(-4) + (-7) =$

3. $(6 \times 3) =$

4. $(-2)(6) =$

5. $(-3) - (2) + (6) =$

6. $10 \div 2 =$

7. $(-5)(-2) =$

8. $-21 \div -7 =$

9. $12 \div -3 =$

10. $-12 \div 3 =$

ABSOLUTE VALUES

Remember the number line from earlier in the chapter.

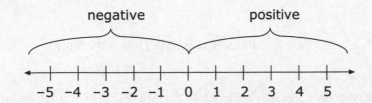

Let's look at the numbers 5 and –5. What do they have in common? Remember that positive and negative numbers are defined based on their relationship to 0. Positive numbers are to the right of 0, and negative numbers are to the left of 0. In particular, the number 5 is five units to the right of 0, and the number –5 is five units to the left of 0. Even though they are in different positions on the number line, both are the same *distance from the number 0. In math, this is said to mean that they have the same absolute value.* Since both 5 and –5 are five away from 0, both have an absolute value of 5. In an equation or an expression, the absolute value is represented by two vertical lines: | |. Therefore, it can be written that $|5| = |-5| = 5$.

Although, by definition, the absolute value refers to distance from 0, it can be used to express the distance from any other number. Consider $|4 - 1|$ and $|-2 - 1|$. One way of thinking about this is by taking the difference and then taking the absolute value of the result like below.

$$|4 - 1| = |3| = 3$$

$$|-2 - 1| = |-3| = 3$$

Another way of thinking about this is by considering the distance on the number line to both 4 and –2 from 1. Both quantities above are equal to three because both 4 and –2 are three units from 1 on the number line: –2 being three units to the left and 4 being three units to the right.

Absolute Values Drill

You can check your answers in Part VIII: Answer Key to Drills.

1. $|4| =$

2. $|-7| =$

3. $|6 - 2| =$

4. $|3 - 5| =$

5. $|x| = 10, x =$

6. $|y - 9| = 5, y =$

ORDER OF OPERATIONS

In a problem that involves several different operations, the operations must be performed in a particular order. There's an easy way to remember the order of operations:

Please Excuse My Dear Aunt Sally

Tip: Remember the acronym PEMDAS for the correct order of operations!

First, you do operations enclosed in **P**arentheses; then you take care of **E**xponents; then you **M**ultiply and **D**ivide; finally you **A**dd and **S**ubtract. We're going to save exponents for the next chapter, but let's try out PEMDAS with a couple of problems.

$$((-5)+4)\left(\frac{8}{2}\right)+4 =$$

How about this one?

$$(3)+\left(\frac{8}{2}\right)(4-5)+1 =$$

If you did these in the correct order, you should have gotten the same answer both times: 0.

Using Your Calculator on Order of Operations

PEMDAS Quiz
Q: 3(7 − [5 − 3]) = ?

Turn the page for the answer.

During Part 2 of the Math test, the Texas Instruments TI-30XS calculator you will be provided on-screen automatically knows the order of operations. As long as you enter the equation correctly, it will give you the correct answer every time. But entering the equation correctly can be painstaking work. For example, in the operation above, you would enter 3, hit the "plus" key, then the "left parentheses" key, then 8, then the "division" key followed by the 2, then the "right parentheses" key, then the "multiplication" key, then the "left parentheses" key, then the 4 followed by the "minus" key, then the 5, then the "right parentheses" key, then the "plus" key, then the 1 key, and finally the "enter" key.

Many students find that they can do this faster on paper.

COMMUTATIVE AND DISTRIBUTIVE PROPERTIES

The Commutative Property: When you add a string of numbers, you can add them in any order you like. The same thing is true when you are multiplying a string of numbers.

$$4 + 5 + 8 \text{ is the same as } 8 + 5 + 4.$$

$$6 \times 7 \times 9 \text{ is the same as } 9 \times 7 \times 6.$$

> The Commutative Property applies ONLY to addition and multiplication. It does NOT pertain to subtraction or division.

The Distributive Property: The GED® test writers will sometimes use an equation that can be written in two different ways. They do this to see if you know about this equation and if you can spot when it is in your interest to change the equation into its other form.

The distributive property states that

$$a(b + c) = ab + ac \text{ and } a(b - c) = ab - ac$$

Example: $3(4 + 2) = 3(4) + 3(2) = 18$
Example: $3(4 - 2) = 3(4) - 3(2) = 6$

If a problem gives you information in "factored" format—$a(b + c)$—you should distribute it immediately. If the information is given in distributed form—$ab + ab$—you should factor it. Take the following example:

$$\frac{1}{2}(5) + \frac{1}{2}(3) =$$

Finding $\frac{1}{2}$ of 5 and $\frac{1}{2}$ of 3 is a bit troublesome because the answers do not work out to be whole numbers. It isn't that you can't find half of an odd number if you have to (or at least you *will* be able to, after our review of fractions later in this chapter), but why do more work than necessary?

Look at what would happen if we changed this distributed equation into its factored form instead:

$$\frac{1}{2}(5+3)=$$

Isn't that a lot easier? One half of 8 equals 4. Always be on the lookout for chances to do less work on the GED® test. It's a long, tiring test, and you need to conserve your strength. Now, try this one.

───────────○───────────

1. If 3X + 3Y = 21, then what is the value of X + Y?

    A.   3
    B.   6
    C.   7
    D.   Not enough information is given.

Here's How to Crack It

Everyone's first impulse on a problem like this is to pick (D), not enough information is given. After all, there are two different variables (X and Y), so unless we know what both variables are, how can we figure out the problem?

A number directly in front of a parenthesis implies multiplication. To enter 2(5 + 3), first enter 2, then the "multiplication" key, then "left parentheses," then 5 "plus" 3, then "right parentheses."

The answer is the distributive property. You may not have noticed that the equation in the problem above was in one of the formats we were just looking at: *ab* + *ac*, otherwise known as the distributive form. Therefore, before we give up hope, let's try putting the equation into its mirror-image format: *a(b + c)*, otherwise known as its factored form.

$$3X + 3Y = 3(X + Y) = 21$$

Hmm. You want to know what (X + Y) equals. Well, three *times* (X + Y) equals 21. Three times what number equals 21? That's right, 7, and the correct answer to this question is (C).

───────────○───────────

Order of Operations and Commutative and Distributive Properties Drill

Do these problems first on your own. Then on a separate piece of paper, do them again using your calculator.

You can check your answers in Part VIII: Answer Key to Drills.

1. $5(3 - 4) + 2 =$

2. $7 \times 2 \times 3 =$

3. $3(3 - 1 - 2) + 6(2 - 4) =$

4. $8[4(3 - 5)] =$

5. $\dfrac{1}{4}(3) + \dfrac{1}{4}(9) =$

FACTORS AND MULTIPLES

Factors are numbers that divide evenly into a given number. For example, what would be the factors of 6?

$$6 \div 1 = 6, 6 \div 2 = 3, 6 \div 3 = 2, \text{ and } 6 \div 6 = 1.$$

When 6 is divided by 1, 2, 3, or 6, the result is a whole number; therefore, the numbers 1, 2, 3, and 6 are factors of 6. However, when 6 is divided by 4 or 5, the result is a decimal. Therefore, 4 and 5 are not factors of 6. Let's look at an example.

---

1. Which of the following is a list of all the factors of 18?

   A. 1 and 18
   B. 1, 3, 6, and 24
   C. 1, 2, 3, 6, 9, and 18
   D. 1, 2, 3, 4, 6, 9, 12, and 18

Here's How to Crack It

To find the factors of a number, start with the two obvious factors. The number 1 is a factor of every number as is the number itself. Therefore, 1 and 18 are factors of 18. Now work upward from 1. Is 2 a factor of 18? Since $18 \div 2 = 9$, 2 is a factor and so is 9. Is 3 a factor of 18? Since $18 \div 3 = 6$, 3 is a factor and so is 6. Is 4 a factor of 18? Since $18 \div 4$ is a decimal, it is not. Is 5 a factor of 18? Since $18 \div 5$ is a decimal, it is not. Is 6 a factor of 18? Remember that 6 is already on the list since $18 \div 3 = 6$. When you get to a number that's already on the list, you have all the factors. Therefore, the complete list is 1, 2, 3, 6, 9, and 18. The correct answer is (C).

One concept that is important to factors is that of the *greatest common factor* (GCF). Consider the numbers 24 and 40. To find the GCF of 24 and 40, find the factors of both numbers. Find the factors of 24 and 40 in pairs as in the problem above. The factors of 24 are 1 and 24, 2 and 12, 3 and 8, and 4 and 6. The factors of 40 are 1 and 40, 2 and 20, 4 and 10, and 5 and 8. The common factors of 24 and 40 are the numbers that are in both lists (regardless of what pairs they're in). The common factors of 24 and 40 are 1, 2, 4, and 8. The GCF is simply the greatest number of the list of common factors. In this case, the GCF is 8. Let's look at another example.

---

2.   What is the greatest common factor of 15 and 28?
      A.   1
      B.   3
      C.   4
      D.   15

Here's How to Crack It

Find the factors of each number. The factors of 15 are 1, 3, 5, and 15. The factors of 28 are 1, 2, 4, 7, 14, and 28. The only number that is a factor of both 15 and 28 is 1. Therefore, the GCF of 15 and 28 is 1. The correct answer is (A).

The concept of a factor goes hand in hand with the concept of a multiple. A multiple is a number for which a given number is a factor. Since 1, 2, 3, and 6 are factors of 6, 6 is a multiple of 1, 2, 3, and 6. To find the multiples of a given number, take the number and multiply it by other whole numbers. For example, $6 \times 1 = 6$, $6 \times 2 = 12$, $6 \times 3 = 18$, $6 \times 4 = 24$, and $6 \times 5 = 30$, so 6, 12, 18, 24, and 30 are all multiples of 6. Notice that 6 is both a factor and a multiple of itself. This is the case for every number. Also, since 1 is a factor of every number, every number is a multiple of 1.

Another way to think of multiples is as "counting by" a number. To "count by 6", start with 6 and keep adding 6. Since $6 + 6 = 12$, 12 is a multiple of 6. Since $12 + 6$ is 18, 18 is a multiple of 6. Since $18 + 6 = 24$, 24 is a multiple of 6. Since there is no limit to the number of times you can add 6, there is no limit to the multiples of 6 or any other number.

An important concept of multiples is *least common multiple* (LCM). For any two numbers, a common multiple is simply a number that is a multiple of both. Consider the numbers 4 and 6. Some of the multiples of 4 are 4, 8, 12, 16, 20, 24, 28, 32, 36, and 40. Some of the multiples of 6 are 6, 12, 18, 24, 30, 36, 42, 48, 54, and 60. Therefore, some of the common multiples of 4 and 6 are 12, 24, 36, and 48. The LCM is the smallest number on the list of common multiples. In this case, the LCM of 4 and 6 is 12. Let's look at another example.

3. What is the least common multiple of 15 and 25?
   A. 1
   B. 5
   C. 75
   D. 150

Here's How to Crack It
To find the LCM of two numbers, list the multiples of one number and stop when one is also a multiple of the other. In this case, find the multiples of 15 by counting by 15 and stopping when one is a multiple of 25. Counting by 15, the multiples of 15 are 15, 30, 45, 60, 75, 90, 105, 120, 135, 150, etc. The numbers 15, 30, 45, and 60 are not multiples of 25, so none of them are the LCM. However, $75 = 25 \times 3$, so 75 is a common multiple. Since none of the lesser multiples of 15 are common multiples, 75 must be the least common multiple. The correct answer is (C).

Factors and Multiples Drill
You can check your answers in Part VIII: Answer Key to Drills.

1. List the factors of 36.

2. List the factors of 43.

3. List the factors of 80.

4. List the first ten positive multiples of 7.

5. List the first ten positive multiples of 9.

6. What is the greatest common factor of 32 and 80?

7. What is the least common multiple of 7 and 9?

8. What is greatest common factor of 24 and 48?

9. What is the least common multiple of 24 and 48?

FRACTIONS

A fraction is part of a whole. We write a fraction as $\frac{(PART)}{(WHOLE)}$, where the top number is the number of parts we are referring to and the bottom number is the total number of parts that make up one whole.

Take a look at the pie below:

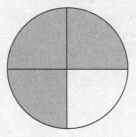

This pie has been divided into four equal pieces. Three of the four pieces are shaded. If we wanted to express the part of the pie that is shaded, we would say that $\frac{3}{4}$ of the pie is shaded. If we wanted to express the part of the pie that is not shaded, we would say that $\frac{1}{4}$ of the pie is not shaded.

A fraction is always a part over a whole.

$$\frac{1}{2} \quad \frac{(PART)}{(WHOLE)}$$

In the fraction $\frac{1}{2}$, we have one part out of a total of two equal parts.

In the fraction $\frac{3}{7}$, we have three parts out of a total of seven equal parts.

Another way to think of a fraction is as just another kind of division. The expression $\frac{1}{2}$ means 1 divided by 2. The fraction $\frac{x}{y}$ is nothing more than x divided by y. A fraction is made up of a numerator and a denominator. The **numerator** is on top; the **denominator** is on the bottom. When a number can be written as a fraction in which both the numerator and denominator are integers (for example, numbers with no fraction or decimal part), then the number is called a **rational number**.

$$\frac{1}{2} \quad \frac{\text{numerator}}{\text{denominator}}$$

In math, a number cannot be divided by 0. Therefore, anytime the denominator of a fraction is 0, the fraction is undefined.

REDUCING (SIMPLIFYING) FRACTIONS

Every fraction can be expressed in many different ways:

$$\frac{1}{2} = \frac{2}{4} = \frac{3}{6} = \frac{4}{8} \dots \text{ and so on.}$$

Each of these fractions means the same thing. To reduce a fraction with large numbers, see if the numerator and the denominator share a number that divides evenly into both of them. For example, both the numerator and the denominator of $\frac{2}{4}$ can be divided by 2, which reduces the fraction to $\frac{1}{2}$. With larger fractions, it may save time to find the largest number that will divide evenly into both numbers, also known as the *greatest common factor* (*GCF*). You can still reduce a fraction using any common (shared) factor, but you will probably have to reduce several times. Using the GCF guarantees that you will have to reduce only once! So how can you find the GCF of your numerator and denominator? Look at the factors of each. Let's take the fraction $\frac{8}{12}$. What are the different ways to make 8? $1 \times 8 = 8$ and $2 \times 4 = 8$.

So the factors of 8 are 1, 2, 4, and 8.

Now, what are the different ways to make 12? $1 \times 12 = 12$, $2 \times 6 = 12$, and $3 \times 4 = 12$.

The factors of 12 are 1, 2, 3, 4, 6, and 12.

To find our GCF, we compare these two lists. What is the largest number that occurs in both? That's right—4 is your GCF. Now divide both your numerator and denominator by 4 and you have the simplest (most reduced) form of your fraction.

$$\frac{8}{12} = \frac{8 \div 4}{12 \div 4} = \frac{2}{3}$$

Whenever your answer to a math question is a fraction, make sure to reduce the fraction to its simplest form. The multiple-choice answers will virtually always be fractions in their simplest (most reduced) form.

Reducing Fractions Drill

Reduce the following fractions to their lowest terms. You can check your answers in Part VIII: Answer Key to Drills.

1. $\dfrac{9}{12}$

2. $\dfrac{11}{33}$

3. $\dfrac{14}{35}$

4. $\dfrac{4}{9}$

5. $\dfrac{15}{8}$

Comparing Fractions

Sometimes a problem will involve deciding which of two fractions is bigger.

Which is bigger, $\dfrac{2}{5}$ or $\dfrac{4}{5}$? Think of these as parts of a pie. Which is bigger, two parts out of five, or four parts out of five? The fraction $\dfrac{4}{5}$ is clearly bigger. In this case, it was easy to tell because both fractions had the same whole, the same denominator.

It's more complicated when the fractions have different denominators. Which is bigger, $\frac{2}{3}$ or $\frac{3}{7}$? To decide, we need to rewrite the two fractions so that they have the same denominator. How do you decide what your new denominator should be? It's called the *least common denominator* (*LCD*), and is the smallest number that all of your denominators can divide into. How do you find the LCD? Start by listing the multiples of each denominator. Let's find the LCD of 3 and 7. What are the multiples of 3?

Count by threes: 3, 6, 9, 12, 15, 18, 21, 24, 27, 30, 33, 36, 39, 42,....

Don't go on forever; just write down a few and if you need to add more later on you can. Now what are the multiples of 7?

Count by sevens: 7, 14, 21, 28, 35, 42, 49,....

Do we have a number that is common to both of these lists? Yes—21 and 42 appear in both lists. But which number is the smaller of the two? The smaller number, 21, is our LCD.

Now we'll rewrite our two original fractions so they have the same denominator. We'll change the denominator of $\frac{2}{3}$ into the number 21. To get 3 to equal 21, we have to multiply it by 7. Because we want an equivalent fraction, anything we do to the denominator, we have to do to the numerator, so we also have to multiply the numerator by 7.

$$\frac{2 \times 7}{3 \times 7} = \frac{14}{21}$$

The fraction $\frac{14}{21}$ still has the same value as $\frac{2}{3}$ (it would reduce to $\frac{2}{3}$) because we multiplied the fraction by $\frac{7}{7}$, or one.

Let's change the denominator of $\frac{3}{7}$ into 21 as well.

$$\frac{3 \times 3}{7 \times 3} = \frac{9}{21}$$

The fraction $\frac{9}{21}$ still has the same value as $\frac{3}{7}$ (it would reduce to $\frac{3}{7}$) because we multiplied the fraction by $\frac{3}{3}$, or one.

Now we can compare the two fractions. Which is bigger, $\frac{14}{21}$ or $\frac{9}{21}$? Clearly $\frac{14}{21}$ (or $\frac{2}{3}$) is bigger than $\frac{9}{21}$ (or $\frac{3}{7}$).

Let's do it again. Which is bigger, $\frac{2}{3}$ or $\frac{3}{5}$?

First we look at the two denominators, 3 and 5.

The multiples of 3 are 3, 6, 9, 12, 15, 18, 21,....

And the multiples of 5 are 5, 10, 15, 20, 25,....

This time, the least common denominator is 15.

$$\frac{2}{3} \qquad\qquad \frac{3}{5}$$

$$\frac{2}{3} \times \frac{5}{5} = \frac{10}{15} \qquad \frac{3}{5} \times \frac{3}{3} = \frac{9}{15}$$

So $\frac{2}{3}$ is bigger than $\frac{3}{5}$.

Using Your Calculator on Fraction Problems

We have found that a calculator is only of limited use on fraction problems. It can make comparing fractions very easy: Simply divide the numerator by the denominator of each fraction and pick the bigger number. If you need your answer in fraction format, the Texas Instruments TI-30XS has a convenient button called the answer toggle. It looks like ◀ ▶ and is located at the bottom right, just above the enter button. Pressing this button will change a decimal answer into a fraction (or root). If you enter an expression as a fraction, using the $\frac{n}{d}$ button, the answer will be automatically given as a fraction. And if you need to change that answer into a decimal, you can press the answer toggle, ◀ ▶, button to do so.

The Bowtie

The Bowtie is a shortcut that finds a common denominator and converts the numerators for you. Let's compare the last two fractions again. First, we get the common denominator by multiplying the two denominators together:

$$\frac{2}{3} \longrightarrow \frac{3}{5} = \frac{}{15}$$

Tip: Save yourself time by using the Bowtie!

Then, we get the new numerators by multiplying using the bowtie-shaped pattern shown below:

$$\textcircled{10}\frac{2}{3} \times \frac{3}{5}\textcircled{9} = \frac{}{15}$$

Finally, compare the fractions. Once again, we see that $\frac{10}{15}$ (or $\frac{2}{3}$) is bigger than $\frac{9}{15}$ (or $\frac{3}{5}$).

ADDING AND SUBTRACTING FRACTIONS

Whenever you add or subtract fractions, you need the fractions to have a common denominator. You can use the LCD method that we looked at to compare fractions, or you can use the Bowtie method, but you must somehow rewrite the fractions in the problem to those with a common denominator before you add or subtract.

Let's use the Bowtie to add $\frac{2}{5}$ and $\frac{1}{4}$.

$$\frac{2}{5} + \frac{1}{4} =$$

$$\textcircled{8}\frac{2}{5} \times \frac{1}{4}\textcircled{5} = \frac{8 + 5}{20} = \frac{13}{20}$$

Fraction Quiz

Q: Which is bigger,

$\frac{8}{9}$ or $\frac{7}{8}$?

Turn the page for the answer.

Let's use the Bowtie to subtract $\frac{2}{3}$ from $\frac{5}{6}$.

$$\frac{5}{6} - \frac{2}{3} =$$

$$\overset{\text{(15)}}{\frac{5}{6}} \diagup\hspace{-0.5em}\diagdown \overset{\text{(12)}}{\frac{2}{3}} = \frac{15-12}{18} = \frac{3}{18} = \frac{1}{6}$$

Adding and Subtracting Fractions Drill

You can check your answers in Part VIII: Answer Key to Drills.

1. Which is bigger, $\frac{4}{5}$ or $\frac{5}{7}$?

2. $\frac{4}{5} + \frac{4}{7} = ?$

3. $\frac{2}{3} - \frac{1}{4} = ?$

4. $\frac{1}{3} + \frac{1}{6} + \frac{1}{18} = ?$

5. $\frac{2}{7} - \frac{1}{3} = ?$

MULTIPLYING FRACTIONS

To multiply fractions, line them up and multiply straight across.

$$\frac{5}{6} \times \frac{4}{5} = \frac{20}{30} = \frac{2}{3}$$

Was there anything we could have canceled or reduced *before* we multiplied? You betcha. We could cancel the 5 on top and the 5 on the bottom. What's left is $\frac{4}{6}$, which reduces to $\frac{2}{3}$.

Sometimes people think they can cancel or reduce in the same fashion *across an equal sign*. Consider this example:

$$\frac{\cancel{5}x}{6} = \frac{4}{\cancel{5}} \quad \text{No!}$$

You *cannot* cancel the 5's in this case or reduce the $\frac{4}{6}$. When there is an equal sign, you have to cross multiply, which we will cover in the chapter on algebra, Chapter 15.

DIVIDING FRACTIONS

To divide one fraction by another, just invert the second fraction and multiply.

$$\frac{2}{3} \div \frac{3}{4} \text{ is the same thing as } \frac{2}{3} \times \frac{4}{3} = \frac{8}{9}.$$

You may see this same operation written like this:

$$\frac{\frac{2}{3}}{\frac{3}{4}}$$

Since every fraction is the numerator divided by the denominator, this is the same as $\frac{2}{3}$ divided by $\frac{3}{4}$. So, just invert and multiply. Try the next example.

$$\frac{6}{\frac{2}{3}}$$

Think of 6 as $\frac{6}{1}$, and so we do the same thing.

$$\frac{6}{1} \div \frac{2}{3} = \frac{6}{1} \times \frac{3}{2} = \frac{18}{2} = 9$$

Fraction Quiz

A: Use the Bowtie! The fraction $\frac{8}{9}$ is bigger than $\frac{7}{8}$.

Reciprocal Fact

Dividing by 6 is the same thing as multiplying by $\frac{1}{6}$.

CONVERTING TO FRACTIONS

A whole number, such as 8, can always be expressed as a fraction by making that number the numerator and one the denominator: $8 = \dfrac{8}{1}$.

Sometimes the GED® test gives you numbers that are mixtures of whole numbers and fractions, for example, $3\dfrac{1}{2}$. These numbers are called mixed fractions (or mixed numbers). It is often easier to work with these numbers by converting them completely into fractions. Here's how you do it: Because the fraction is expressed in halves, let's convert the whole number into halves as well: $3 = \dfrac{6}{2}$. Now just add the $\dfrac{1}{2}$ to the $\dfrac{6}{2}$. You get $\dfrac{7}{2}$.

There is also a shortcut for converting mixed fractions. Multiply the denominator by the whole number, and then add the numerator. This number becomes your new numerator and you keep the original denominator.

$$3\dfrac{1}{2} = \dfrac{3 \times 2 + 1}{2} = \dfrac{7}{2}$$

Fractions like $\dfrac{7}{2}$ are called **improper fractions,** because the numerator is larger than the denominator. Despite the name, though, there is nothing wrong with improper fractions. They are much easier to do any operation with than mixed numbers are, so whenever you have to add, subtract, multiply, or divide with mixed numbers, change them to improper fractions.

Multiplying, Dividing, and Converting Fractions Drill

You can check your answers in Part VIII: Answer Key to Drills.

1. $\dfrac{4}{5} \times \dfrac{3}{8} =$

2. $\dfrac{9}{10} \div \dfrac{3}{5} =$

3. $\dfrac{\frac{2}{9}}{\frac{12}{10}} =$

4. $\dfrac{2}{3} \times \dfrac{3}{4} \times \dfrac{4}{5} =$

5. $1\dfrac{1}{3} \times \dfrac{3}{8} =$

FRACTION WORD PROBLEMS

Now let's try some fraction problems in the GED® test format.

———————○———————

1. If $\frac{1}{2}$ of a group of students say their favorite leisure

    activity is swimming, and $\frac{1}{3}$ of the group say their

    favorite leisure activity is tennis, what fraction

    of the group prefer neither swimming nor tennis?

    A. $\frac{1}{8}$

    B. $\frac{1}{6}$

    C. $\frac{1}{2}$

    D. $\frac{5}{6}$

Here's How to Crack It

Test takers are often intimidated by word problems, but you should realize that beneath all those words there lies a simple math problem.

Before you even read it, there should be one thing you notice right away: There are fractions in the problem. That can mean only one thing. This is a fraction problem.

On the GED® test, the only things you are ever asked to do with fractions is add them, subtract them, multiply them, divide them, or compare them—and you've just learned how to do all those things, if you didn't know them already.

Let's read the problem. Half of the students like swimming. One-third like playing tennis. Basically, the question is, who's left? After we take away the students who like swimming and tennis, what fraction of the students remains?

Before you do any work at all, let's see if we can *ballpark* a little. If we add $\frac{1}{2}$ and $\frac{1}{3}$ together, that's quite a lot. There can't be too much of the whole left over. So do any of the answer choices strike you as unlikely? Choices (C) and (D) are clearly out of the ballpark. Let's eliminate both of them and now actually solve the problem.

First, let's use the Bowtie to add up the parts of the whole that we know about.

$$\frac{1}{2} \diagdown \frac{1}{3} = \frac{3+2}{6} = \frac{5}{6}$$

So $\frac{5}{6}$ of the students like either swimming or tennis. Now the big question: What part of the whole remains? That's right, the answer is $\frac{1}{6}$, and the correct answer is (B). Note that (D), $\frac{5}{6}$, was a *partial* answer. It was there for people who were in a hurry and thought they were done when they finished adding $\frac{1}{2}$ and $\frac{1}{3}$. However, if you read the question carefully and ball-parked this problem first, there was no way you were going to fall for that trap. You already knew it was a crazy answer.

––––––––––––––––––––○––––––––––––––––––––

Here's another example:

––––––––––––––––––––○––––––––––––––––––––

2. It takes $1\frac{1}{4}$ hours for a factory worker to assemble one television set. How many television sets can be assembled in $17\frac{1}{2}$ hours?

[   ]

Here's How to Crack It
Again, at first glance, you may feel intimidated by all the words in this problem, but don't let it fool you. This one's easy.

As we said earlier, whenever you see mixed numbers, you probably should change them into improper fractions before you do any calculations.

$$1\frac{1}{4} = \frac{5}{4}$$

$$17\frac{1}{2} = \frac{35}{2}$$

It takes $\frac{5}{4}$ of an hour to make one TV. How many sets can you make in $\frac{35}{2}$ hours? We want to know how many $\frac{5}{4}$ s go into $\frac{35}{2}$, and that just means division.

$$\frac{35}{2} \div \frac{5}{4} = \frac{35}{2} \times \frac{4}{5}$$

Let's do some canceling.

$$\frac{\cancel{35}}{2} \times \frac{4}{\cancel{5}} = \frac{7}{\cancel{2}} \times \frac{\cancel{4}}{1} = \frac{7}{1} \times \frac{2}{1} = 14$$

The correct answer is 14.

—————————○—————————

Fraction Word Problem Drill

You can check your answers in Part VIII: Answer Key to Drills.

1. In the town of Arkville, a total of 80 people came in to be tested for Lyme disease. Half of them were found to have the disease. Of those who did not have the disease when first tested, one quarter later developed it. What fraction of the original 80 people got Lyme disease?

   A. $\frac{1}{4}$

   B. $\frac{1}{2}$

   C. $\frac{5}{8}$

   D. $\frac{3}{4}$

2. A pie company baked 100 pies in July, as shown in the table below. In August, the company increased production by $\frac{1}{10}$. In September, the pie company again increased production by $\frac{1}{10}$. Determine the number of pies baked in the months of August and September.

   Click on the numbers you want to select and drag them into the table.

Month	Number of Pies
July	100
August	
September	

101	102	110
112	120	121

3. According to a company survey, $\frac{1}{3}$ of the workers take public transportation to get to work, $\frac{2}{5}$ drive cars to work, and the remainder walk to work. What fraction of the workers walk to work?

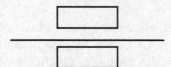

DECIMALS

Fractions can also be expressed as decimals and vice versa. You probably know the decimal equivalent of certain fractions by heart (for example, $\frac{1}{2} = 0.5$), but you may not know how to convert a fraction into a decimal.

As we said earlier, one way to think of a fraction is just as a division problem.

$$\frac{1}{2} = 1 \div 2 = 2\overline{)1.0}^{\,.5}$$

$$\frac{3}{4} = 3 \div 4 = 4\overline{)3.00}^{\,.75}$$

You can also convert any decimal into a fraction. The first digit to the right of the decimal is the tenths place. The second decimal is the hundredths place. Consider this example:

$$0.5 = \frac{5}{10} = \frac{1}{2}$$

$$0.75 = \frac{75}{100} = \frac{3}{4}$$

Adding and Subtracting Decimals

Calculating with decimals, unlike calculating with fractions, is almost always faster on the calculator. However, because you won't have the calculator during the first part of the test, it makes sense to practice these both ways. To add or subtract decimals, all you have to do is line up the decimal points and then add or subtract, just as you would any two normal numbers.

$$
\begin{array}{cccc}
\begin{array}{r} 2.5 \\ +\ 9.3 \\ \hline 11.8 \end{array} &
\begin{array}{r} 10.3 \\ -\ 6.4 \\ \hline 3.9 \end{array} &
\begin{array}{r} 1.423 \\ +\ 2.620 \\ \hline 4.043 \end{array} &
\begin{array}{r} 3.92 \\ +\ 2.61 \\ \hline 6.53 \end{array}
\end{array}
$$

If you're adding or subtracting one number that has fewer digits than another, it helps to add zeros to fill out the decimal places. For example, to subtract 3.26 from 8.4, adding a zero to 8.4 makes the problem easier to see:

$$
\begin{array}{r}
8.40 \\
- 3.26 \\
\hline
5.14
\end{array}
$$

Multiplying Decimals

The best way to multiply decimals is to ignore the decimal points entirely until after you've done the multiplication. For example, let's multiply 4.3 by 0.5. We'll start by multiplying 43 by 5:

$$
\begin{array}{r}
43 \\
\times 5 \\
\hline
215
\end{array}
$$

Now count the total number of digits to the right of the decimal points in the two original numbers you were multiplying. In this case, there were a total of two digits to the right of the decimal points. Therefore, this is how many digits there should be to the right of the decimal point in your final product. The answer is 2.15. Let's do another.

$$
\begin{array}{r}
5.6 \\
\times 0.03 \\
\hline
\end{array}
\qquad
\begin{array}{r}
56 \\
\times\ 3 \\
\hline
168
\end{array}
$$

There are a total of three digits to the right of the decimal points in the original numbers, so after multiplying, we place the decimal so that there are three digits to the right in the answer as well. The answer in this case is 0.168.

Dividing Decimals

The best way to divide decimals is first to convert the number you are dividing *by* (in math terminology, the **divisor**) into a whole number. You do this simply by moving the decimal point to the right as many places as necessary. This works as long as you remember to move the decimal point in the number that you are *dividing* (in math terminology, the **dividend**) the same number of spaces.

For example, to divide 12 by 0.6, set it up the way you would an ordinary division problem:

$$0.6\overline{)12}$$

To make 0.6 (the divisor) a whole number, you simply move the decimal point over one place to the right. You must also move the decimal one place to the right in the dividend. Now the operation looks like this:

$$6\overline{)120} \qquad 6\overline{)120}^{\,20}$$

Decimals Drill

Do these problems first on your own. Then, on a separate piece of paper, do them again using your calculator.

You can check your answers in Part VIII: Answer Key to Drills.

1. $1.34 + 5.72 =$

2. $7.6 - 3.24 =$

3. $3.4 \times 2.41 =$

4. $6.4 \div 0.002 =$

5. $32 \div 0.8 =$

PERCENTS

A percent is really just a fraction whose denominator happens to be 100.

$$25\% = \frac{25}{100} \qquad 50\% = \frac{50}{100} \qquad 32\% = \frac{32}{100}$$

Decimal/Percentage Dictionary

0.01 = 1%
0.1 = 10%
1.0 = 100%

Like any fraction, a percentage can be converted to a decimal and vice versa. Percentage/decimal conversion is even easier than converting a normal fraction because both percentages and decimals are almost invariably *already* being expressed in hundredths.

$$25\% = \frac{25}{100} = 0.25 \qquad 0.50 = \frac{50}{100} = 50\%$$

To convert a regular fraction into a percent, you can first convert the fraction to a decimal, which, as we just said, is very close to a percentage already. Here are a few examples:

$$\frac{2}{5} = 5\overline{)2.0}^{\,0.4} = 0.4 = 0.40 = 40\%$$

$$\frac{12}{20} = 20\overline{)12.0}^{\,0.6} = 0.6 = 0.60 = 60\%$$

$$\frac{2}{3} = 3\overline{)2.000}^{\,0.666} = 0.666666\ldots \approx 66.67\%$$

$$\begin{array}{r} 18 \\ \hline 20 \\ 18 \\ \hline 20 \end{array}$$

In that last example, you'll notice that no matter how many places you carry that division to, you will always get a remainder. The fraction $\frac{2}{3}$ produces a decimal that goes on forever. However, if we are going to round to the nearest percent, then it's 67%.

There are some fractions, decimals, and percentages that come up so often that it's worth memorizing them. We've filled in some for you. Practice your conversions on a separate piece of paper to fill in the remaining boxes. Check your work with a calculator afterward.

Fraction	Decimal	Percent
		1%
$\frac{1}{50}$		
	0.05	
$\frac{1}{10}$		
		11.11%
	.2	
$\frac{2}{9}$		
		25%
$\frac{1}{3}$		
$\frac{2}{5}$		
		44.44%
	.5	
$\frac{5}{9}$		
		60%
$\frac{2}{3}$		
	.75	
$\frac{7}{9}$		
		80%
$\frac{8}{9}$		
	1	

Most percent problems on the Mathematical Reasoning test ask you to find a percentage of a larger number. Here's an example:

1. If 10% of the 3,400 people who enter a sweepstakes won a prize, how many people did <u>not</u> win a prize?

    A.   34
    B.   340
    C.   3,060
    D.   3,366

We'll come back to this problem in a minute. But first, we want to show you...

To find 20 percent of a number, multiply the number by 0.20. To find 35 percent of a number, multiply the number by 0.35. To find 5 percent of a number, multiply the number by 0.05.

Old-Fashioned Percents

Here's the way you probably learned percents: A percentage is just a fraction with 100 in the denominator, and the word *of* always means *multiply* in math. So when the GED® test asks you to find 20 percent of 400, it can be written this way:

$$\frac{20}{100} \times \frac{400}{1} = ?$$

Now you could do some canceling.

$$\frac{20}{\cancel{100}_{1}} \times \frac{\cancel{400}^{4}}{1} = 80$$

While this method will get you the right answer, it can be a long and tedious process when the numbers don't work out as nicely as the ones we chose for this example. But don't worry because you are about to learn a more efficient way to approach these problems.

The Princeton Review Percents

We have a fast, foolproof method for finding percents. This method involves almost no written calculation at all. You can thank us later.

Ballparking Percent Quiz

Q: Roughly speaking, what's 10 percent of 305?

Turn the page for the answer.

To find 10 percent of any number, all you have to do is move the decimal point of that number over one place to the left.

> 10% of 4 = 0.4
> 10% of 30 = 3
> 10% of 520 = 52
> 10% of 21 = 2.1

Now, here's the great part. Ten percent of 30 = 3, right? So how much is 20% of 30? That's easy. It's twice as much as 10 percent, or 6. Here are a few examples:

> What is 20% of 520?
> 10% of 520 = 52, so 20% of 520 = 2 × 52 = 104.

> What is 20% of 4?
> 10% of 4 = .4, so 20% of 4 = 2 × 0.4 = 0.8.

> What is 30% of 600?
> 10% of 600 = 60, so 30% of 600 = 3 × 60 = 180.

> What is 40% of 500?
> 10% of 500 = 50, so 40% of 500 = 4 × 50 = 200.

This takes care of a lot of GED® problems right here, but there are some GED® problems that will ask you to find amounts like 15 percent or 27 percent. How do you do this?

To find 1 percent of any number, all you have to do is move the decimal point of that number over *two* places to the left.

> 1% of 4 = 0.04
> 1% of 30 = 0.3
> 1% of 520 = 5.2
> 1% of 21 = 0.21

In just the same way that we found 20 percent by doubling 10 percent, we can now find 2 percent by doubling 1 percent.

> What is 2% of 500?
> 1% of 500 = 5, so 2% of 500 = 2 × 5 = 10.

> What is 3% of 60?
> 1% of 60 = 0.6, so 3% of 60 = 3 × 0.6 = 1.8.

Now, here's the *really* great part. We can combine these two techniques to find any percentage the test writers can invent.

Let's find 23% of 600.

Well, 10% of 600 = 60.
So 20% of 600 = 2 × 60 = 120.
And 1% of 600 = 6, so 3% of 600 = 18.

So what is 23% of 600?
20% of 600 = 120
3% of 600 = 18
120 + 18 = 138

Ballparking Percent Quiz
A: Roughly speaking, 10 percent of 305 is about 30.

Most students find that with a little practice they can do this process in their heads or with minimal scratch work. Which is faster: using this method or using a calculator? Why don't you try it both ways on the following drill?

Percents Drill

Do these problems on your own. Then, on another piece of paper, do them again using your calculator.

You can check your answers in Part VIII: Answer Key to Drills.

1. Find 20% of 83.

2. Find 30% of 15.

3. Find 40% of 720.

4. Find 3% of 70.

5. Find 5% of 180.

6. Find 23% of 500.

7. Find 15% of 98.

8. What is 35% of 140?

9. What is 50% of 62?

10. What is 25% of 144?

(Hint: On the last two problems, remember that 50% = $\frac{1}{2}$ and 25% = $\frac{1}{4}$.)

PERCENT WORD PROBLEMS

Now, let's go back to the first percentage problem we showed you.

1. If 10% of the 3,400 people who enter a sweepstakes won a prize, how many people did <u>not</u> win a prize?

    A. 34
    B. 340
    C. 3,060
    D. 3,366

Outta Here!
In the following question, find the answers that are out of the ballpark.

Q: Barry Bonds hits three home runs of lengths 375 feet, 380 feet, and 400 feet. What was the average length of his home runs?

A. 385 feet
B. 405 feet
C. 420 feet
D. 1,155 feet

Turn the page for the answer.

Here's How to Crack It

The first thing you see is "10% of 3,400." At this point, figuring out 10 percent of anything should be second nature to you. Using either Old-Fashioned Percents or The Princeton Review Percents method, we find that 10 percent of 3,400 is 340. But are you done?

Reread the last line of the question. It asks you how many people did *not* win a prize. You need to take one more step. The total number of people who entered the sweepstakes was 3,400. You now know that 340 of them won a prize. So how many people didn't? All you have to do is subtract the winners from the entire group. What you're left with is the number of losers: 3,400 − 340 = 3,060. The correct answer is (C).

If you were really thinking, you could have saved yourself a step by realizing that if 10 percent won, then 90 percent didn't. You could simply have multiplied 340 (10 percent) by 9 to get 3,060 in one step.

Could you have ballparked this problem? Sure. A careful reading of the question would have told you that the number of people you were looking for was the number who did not win. Because only 10 percent won, you were looking for a large percentage of the people who entered. Which answers didn't make sense? Choice (A) was ridiculously small. Choice (B) was a partial answer for those who forgot that they were looking for the losers, not the winners. It was easy to pick (B) from a math standpoint, but impossible to pick if you were Ballparking.

Here's another example:

2. A DVD player is on sale for 20% off its normal price of $400. If the sales tax is 5%, what is the cost of the DVD player?

Here's How to Crack It

This question requires two separate operations. First, let's find the sale price of the DVD player.

What is 20% of 400?
      10% of 400 = 40
      20% of 400 = 2 × 40 = 80

So if the DVD player has been marked down by $80, the sale price is $400 − $80 = $320.

Now let's find the sales tax. Here's the tricky part: Is the sales tax on the original $400 or on the sale price of $320? That's right—it is on the sale price.

What is 5% of $320?

      10% of 320 = 32

      5% of 320 = $\frac{1}{2}$ × 32 = 16

So what's the final price?

$$\begin{array}{r} \$320 \\ + \ \$16 \\ \hline \$336 \end{array}$$

Backward Percents

Sometimes the test writers will ask you a percentage problem backward.

─────────────○─────────────

3. If a mailing of 15,000 letters resulted in 3,750 responses, what was the percentage of responses to the mailing?

    A. 20%
    B. 25%
    C. 30%
    D. 35%

Outta Here!

A: Choice (D), 1,155, is WAY out of the ball-park—it's the sum of all three numbers in the question. So are (B) and (C) because the average length can't be bigger than the largest number being averaged. The correct answer is (A).

Here's How to Crack It

Your old teacher from high school, a gleam in her eye, would be telling you to set up an equation—but there's a much simpler way. Let's use POE to get rid of wrong answers.

Start with (A), 20%, and (C), 30%. Both of these are multiple of 10%, and we already know a great trick to find that! Take the 15,000 letters and move the decimal over one place to the left to get 10% = 1,500. Multiply by three to find 30% = 4,500. That's too big! Now multiply 1,500 by two to get 20% = 3,000. This isn't big enough.

Do we need to calculate an exact amount for (B), 25%, and (D), 35%? No! If 20% is too small, and 30% is too big, we know our answer must be somewhere in between. The correct answer must be (B), 25%.

─────────────○─────────────

Percent Word Problems Drill

You can check your answers in Part VIII: Answer Key to Drills.

1. An investor is deciding between two different investments, X and Y. Investment X is a one-year certificate of deposit that pays 8% in interest, into which the investor would deposit $650. Investment Y is a high-yield savings account that pays 3% in interest, into which the investor would deposit $1,500.

   After one year, the amount earned by investment X will be

   | Select... ▼ | the amount earned by investment Y.
   | greater than |
   | less than |
   | the same as |

2. Janice sells household products door to door. If she must pay her supplier 60% of the money that she takes in, how much would she keep for herself if she took in $1,200?

   A. $720.00
   B. $560.50
   C. $480.00
   D. Not enough information is given.

3. A student furnishing his first apartment goes shopping and buys a bed for $120, a sofa for $635, and a lamp for $74. If the sales tax is 9%, how much did the student pay in total for the furniture?

   $

4. Carmen owns a computer store and had $6,750 in sales this May. The year before, she had $8,437.50 in sales in May. If Carmen had a profit of $5,400 this May, what percent of her sales were profits?

   A. 36%
   B. 60%
   C. 64%
   D. 80%

PUTTING IT ALL TOGETHER

Now that you've seen the basics of arithmetic one topic at a time, we're going to give you a drill that mixes up all the different problems we've discussed so far. Often, the toughest part of the Mathematical Reasoning test is recognizing what kind of problem you are facing.

As we said at the beginning of this chapter, the last line of a question is usually the key to understanding the entire question. Read the question carefully—you may need to slow down—to ensure you don't fall for any tricks or traps along the way. And if you are unsure of an answer, flag the question to come back to later with a fresh perspective.

"Standardized" Means Predictable

The nice thing about any standardized test is that each one is very similar to the one before. This means that after you have gone through this book, done our practice tests, and perhaps taken GED Ready®: The Official Practice Test, you will have seen every type of problem and topic that they could possibly throw at you at least three or four times each. The GED® test presents percent problems exactly the same way each time. Number line problems employ the same ideas year after year.

This means that it's important for you to remember the problems you've already done. Math questions that you do in this book should be added to a mental file. Then, when a problem just like one of them surfaces on the real GED® test, instead of staring at it perplexedly, you'll be saying, "Ah, what an interesting variation on that decimal problem I studied last week."

Basic Arithmetic Drill

You can check your answers in Part VIII: Answer Key to Drills.

1. Which of the following have the same value as $\frac{3}{5}$? Click on the numbers you want to select and drag them into the boxes. (For this drill, write the numbers in the boxes.)

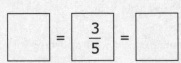

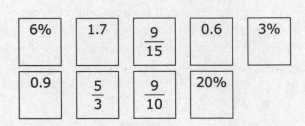

2. Ralph goes out to lunch and receives a bill listing a subtotal of $14.65 and tax of $1.47. Ralph leaves a 20% tip on the total amount. The amount he tips is

Select... ▼	the amount of tax
greater than	charged.
less than	
equal to	

3. If a boat takes 2 hours to travel 30 miles, how long will it take to travel 72 miles?

   A. 1.2 hours
   B. 4.0 hours
   C. 4.8 hours
   D. 6.0 hours

4. Susan did $\frac{1}{4}$ of her homework on Tuesday and $\frac{1}{5}$ of her homework on Wednesday. What fraction of her homework remains to be done?

   A. $\frac{9}{20}$

   B. $\frac{11}{20}$

   C. $\frac{7}{9}$

   D. $\frac{19}{20}$

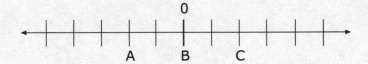

5. In the figure above, point B represents the number 0. If the midpoint of segment AB is at point −2 on the number line and the midpoint of BC is at point 2 on the number line, then which point represents the midpoint of segment AC?

   Click on the number line to plot the point. (For this drill, plot the point by marking an X on the number line.)

6. You are working out a one-year payment plan for a new bicycle. The bicycle costs $275. Tax on the purchase is 11%. You will make 12 equal payments and do not owe any additional interest. How much is each payment, to the nearest dollar?

   A. $20.00
   B. $23.00
   C. $25.00
   D. $30.00

7. If $5R - 5S = 35$, then what is the value of $R - S$?

   A. 5
   B. 6
   C. 7
   D. Not enough information is given.

8. $5(2 - 4 + 1) + \dfrac{2}{3}(7 - 1) = ?$

9. If 30 people in a room of 70 people are smokers, approximately what percent of the people in the room are smokers?

   A. 23%
   B. 30%
   C. 43%
   D. 57%

10. A bankrupt company agrees to pay its creditors 80% of what they are actually owed. If the company pays $9,600, what did they originally owe?

    A. $7,680
    B. $8,000
    C. $11,520
    D. $12,000

11. Click on the numbers below and drag them into the boxes that represent the appropriate places on the number line. (For this drill, simply write the numbers in the boxes.)

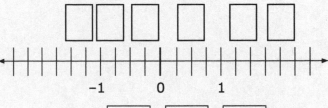

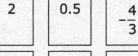

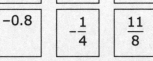

12. On the number line below, click on the X and drag it onto the number line above the tick mark that represents 1.25. (For this drill, simply write the X on the number line.)

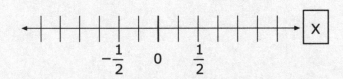

13. Which of the following represents the sum of the factors of 14?

    A. 9
    B. 10
    C. 23
    D. 24

14. Which of the following is NOT a multiple of 4?

    A. 4
    B. 12
    C. 34
    D. 68

Chapter 14
Applied Arithmetic

In this chapter, we go over more arithmetic problems involving setup problems, averages, ratios and proportions, rate problems, charts and graphs, exponents, radicals, scientific notation, probability, and counting.

Now we're going to show you some additional arithmetic concepts that build on the ideas you've already learned in the last chapter. As in that chapter, we'll introduce a concept first and then give you some sample GED® questions followed by a short drill. At the end of the chapter, you'll find a big drill that mixes and matches all the different concepts. These are the subjects we'll cover.

- Setup problems
- Mean, median, mode, range, and weighted mean
- Ratios and proportions
- Rate problems
- Charts and graphs
- Exponents and square roots
- Scientific notation
- Probability
- Counting

SETUP PROBLEMS

Wouldn't it be interesting if a test question asked you to do the entire setup of a problem, but didn't want you to actually solve it? In fact, if you go on to college, you will find that this is often exactly what college math tests are like. College professors are much more interested in seeing *how you think* than how careful you are with your addition and subtraction.

Here's an example:

1. Jim started a business selling mattresses. He sold 12 standard mattresses and 7 deluxe mattresses last week. Which expression below represents how many dollars he took in last week if the standard mattress costs $100 and the deluxe costs $160?

   A. 12(100) + 7(100)
   B. 12(160) + 7(100)
   C. 12(100) + 7(160)
   D. 12(160) + 7(160)

Here's How to Crack It

To find out the total price, you have to multiply the number of standard mattresses by the price of a standard mattress, and the number of deluxe mattresses by the price of a deluxe mattress. There were 12 standards at $100 each, so that's 12(100). There were seven deluxes at $160 each, so that's 7(160). Altogether that's 12(100) + 7(160). The correct answer is (C).

Take Your Time...

Try not to be in too much of a rush on setup problems. The answer choices are all close variations of one another, and it's easy to pick the wrong one if you're in a hurry. In addition, sometimes the GED® test writers may not have written their equation in quite the same way that you did. For example, in this problem, you might have written *your* equation starting with the expensive mattresses—7(160) + 12(100)—in which case, if you looked through the answer choices quickly, you might have thought *your* answer wasn't there. So be prepared to be flexible as you look at the answer choices on a setup problem. You may have to add the numbers in a different order or convert a fraction to a decimal.

...But Not Too Much Time

Some test takers actually *solve* setup problems; they find the correct answer (even though the problem does not require it) and then find the answer choice that adds up to the same number they calculated. We think this generally takes a little too much time. However, if there's one problem that you're really not sure of, you can check the equation you wrote by solving the problem and then making sure that the answer you chose agrees with the number you calculated.

Here's another setup problem, this time about percentages:

2. Mr. James goes into an investment with two partners. Together the three of them put a total of $30,000 into an investment that pays annual interest of 12%. At the end of the year, the three people share the interest evenly. How much did Mr. James receive in interest?

A. $\dfrac{30,000 \times 12}{3}$

B. $\dfrac{30,000 \times 0.12}{3}$

C. $\dfrac{30,000 \times 3}{12}$

D. $\dfrac{30,000 \times 3}{0.12}$

Here's How to Crack It

Mr. James and his two partners share the interest evenly. If this were a normal problem, first you would find 12% of $30,000, and then you would figure out Mr. James's share. If you want to, you can do the problem this way—actually solve it and then figure out the numeric value of each of the answer choices, one by one, until you find the one that matches your solution. Unfortunately, as we said, this can take some time.

Rather than solving this problem, it may be better to set it up as if you were *going* to solve it using a traditional equation. When we first discussed percents in Chapter 13, we said that the word *of* always means *multiply*. If we want to find 12% of $30,000, we could write that in two ways:

$$\frac{12}{100} \times 30{,}000 \quad \text{or} \quad 0.12 \times 30{,}000$$

They both mean the same thing.

Whatever this number is—and remember, in this problem, you don't need to know what it is—it represents the entire amount of interest. The problem is asking for only Mr. James's share. Because all three investors share the interest evenly, you have to divide the entire amount by 3.

$$\frac{0.12 \times 30{,}000}{3}$$

The correct answer is (B).

Setup Quiz

Q: Which two setups below are identical?

(A) 40($1.25) + 25($0.90)

(B) 25($0.90) + 40($1.25)

(C) (40 + 25)($1.25 + $0.90)

Turn the page for the answer.

Setup Drill

You can check your answers in Part VIII: Answer Key to Drills.

1. Sam works 8 hours per day, 6 days a week, delivering flowers. If he earns $5.50 per hour, how much does he make in 4 weeks?

    A. $8 \times 6 \times 4 \times 5.50$
    B. $8 \times 6 \times 5.50$
    C. $[4(8) + 4(6)]5.50$
    D. $5.50 \times 8 + 5.50 \times 4$

2. This year, the price of a particular model of car went up 4% from last year's price of $12,000. Which of the following represents the new price?

A. 0.04($12,000)

B. 0.04($12,000) + $12,000

C. $\dfrac{\$12,000}{0.04}$ + $12,000

D. 0.96($12,000) + $12,000

MEAN, MEDIAN, MODE, RANGE, AND WEIGHTED MEAN

The **mean,** or **average,** is a single number that represents the central value of a set of numbers. In spite of its name, a mean problem is almost always pretty gentle and easy. To find the *mean* of several different numbers, first add them up, and then divide the sum of the numbers by the actual number of items that you added. For example, to find the average of 5, 10, and 15, first add the three numbers:

$$\begin{array}{r} 5 \\ +10 \\ \underline{+15} \\ 30 \end{array}$$

Then, because there are three items being added, divide the sum of the numbers by three:

$$3\overline{)30} = 10$$

That's it. The mean (average) of 5, 10, and 15 is 10. Let's try a problem like some you'll see on the GED® test.

1. A realtor hires a plumber to make x repairs. The plumber bills the realtor $1,450 in total. Which expression determines the average cost of each repair?

   A. $1,450x$

   B. $1,450 + x$

   C. $\dfrac{1,450}{x}$

   D. $\dfrac{x}{1,450}$

Here's How to Crack It

This problem is different from the above example in two ways. First, there is no actual number of repairs. Instead, that number is represented by a variable, x; second, in this problem you don't have to add up the individual elements (i.e., the cost of *each* of the individual repairs) because it has already been done for you.

In spite of these differences, this is still an average problem and we can solve it using the average formula:

$$\frac{\text{sum of all items}}{\text{number of items}} = \text{average}$$

Okay, let's start by adding the elements to get the sum of all the elements—oh, wait, the elements have *already* been added. The total cost of all the repairs is $1,450. All that's left to do is divide the total cost ($1,450) by the number of repair jobs—oh, wait, there is no precise number. Well, you do at least have a variable representing this number, so divide by the variable:

$$\frac{1,450}{x}$$

The correct answer is (C).

The *median* of a set of ordered numbers is the number right in the middle. For example, the median of 3, 16, and 17 is 16. The median of 139, 234, 326, 327, and 328 is 326.

The median is usually different from the mean. Let's take the numbers 2, 3, and 10. The mean of these numbers is $\dfrac{2 + 3 + 10}{3}$, or 5, but the median is simply the middle number, or 3.

If you are asked to find the median of a set of numbers that is not in ascending order, first put the numbers in ascending order, and then take the middle number. For example, the median of 3, 7, and 6 would be 6.

What if there is no middle number? Take the following list of numbers:

4, 8, 10, 20

This time, two numbers are sharing the middle. In cases like this (where there is an even number of items), take the mean of the two middle numbers. This time, the median is 9.

How do median problems look on the Mathematical Reasoning test?

2. Missy played 4 Starmaster games at a video arcade. Her scores were 125, 135, 120, and 140.

    Click on the numbers you want to select and drag them into the boxes.

    What was her mean (average) score? [   ]

    What was her median score? [   ]

| 120 | | 125 | | 128 | | 130 |

| 130 | | 135 | | 140 |

Ballparking Averages
The average of a string of numbers has to be less than the biggest number and more than the smallest number.

Here's How to Crack It

As soon as you see the words *mean* and *average*, you know just what to do: Add the four numbers together, and divide by four.

$$
\begin{array}{r}
120 \\
125 \\
135 \\
+\ 140 \\
\hline
520
\end{array}
$$

$$
4\overline{)520} = 130
$$

The correct answer to the first question is 130.

To find the *median*, you must first order the numbers from least to greatest: 120, 125, 135, 140. What number is in the middle? There are two numbers in the middle, 125 and 135, which means you must take the *mean* of those two. Find the sum, 125 + 135 = 260, and then divide by two, 260 ÷ 2 = 130.

The correct answer to the second question is also 130!

The *mode* of a set of numbers is the number that appears the most often. For example, the mode of 1, 4, 4, 5, 5, 5, 8 is 5. The number 4 occurs twice, but the number 5 occurs three times, so 5 occurs the *most* in this list.

Sometimes there is more than one mode. Let's look at another example set: 2, 5, 9, 2, 4, 1, 8, and 5. First you should order the numbers from least to greatest: 1, 2, 2, 4, 5, 5, 8, 9. Now it is much easier to see which numbers repeat. Both 2 and 5 occur twice, and no number occurs more than twice. So, both 2 and 5 are the modes.

Try it out on this problem:

---

3. If there were 24 traffic summonses issued in September, 45 in October, 24 in November, and 39 in December, what was the mode number of summonses issued over the three months?

    ☐

Here's How to Crack It

First, put the numbers in ascending order: 24, 24, 39, 45. Now, do any numbers appear more than once? That's right—the correct answer is 24.

The *range* of a set of numbers is the distance between the smallest value and the largest value. For example, look at the following set: 2, 5, 6, 8, 99. The largest value is 99 and the smallest value is 2, so the range is $99 - 2 = 97$. As with the mean, median, and mode, be sure your numbers are in ascending order before subtracting!

See if you can solve the following GED® range question.

Jill's Work Week

	Number of Hours Worked	Hourly Pay
Monday	6	$15.00
Tuesday	5	$15.00
Wednesday	8	$12.50
Thursday	7	$12.50
Friday	4	$15.00

4. Jill gets paid different rates for working on different projects. She worked on one project Monday, Tuesday, and Friday of last week, and worked on the second project on Wednesday and Thursday of last week. Her hours spent working and pay rates are shown in the table above. What was the range of Jill's daily earnings last week?

   A. $2.50
   B. $20.00
   C. $37.50
   D. $40.00

Here's How to Crack It

This question asks about Jill's daily earnings. Do you know how much she earned each day? No, but you can find out. Multiply the number of hours worked each day by the hourly rate for that day to find Jill's daily earnings.

On Monday, Jill earned 6 × $15.00 = $90.00.

On Tuesday, Jill earned 5 × $15.00 = $75.00.

On Wednesday, Jill earned 8 × $12.50 = $100.00.

On Thursday, Jill earned 7 × $15.00 = $87.50.

On Friday, Jill earned 4 × $15.00 = $60.00.

Therefore, the greatest daily earnings was $100.00 on Wednesday and the least was $60.00 on Friday.

To calculate the range, we need to find the distance, or difference, between those two values. So we subtract $100.00 − $60.00 = $40.00. The correct answer must be (D).

The *weighted mean* is used when the numbers in a set are not all equally important. Those with more importance are given more *weight* when calculating the mean, or average. Here's how.

Let's say there are 4 tests in total for a certain class: Exam A, the Midterm Exam, Exam B, and the Final Exam. Exams A and B may be worth only 20% each of your final grade, while the Midterm and Final Exams may each be worth 30% of your final grade. You happen to score the following on each:

> Exam A—95
> Midterm Exam—90
> Exam B—92
> Final Exam—87

To calculate your final grade for the class, you can't *just* take the mean (average), since the Midterm and Final exams have more weight than Exams A and B. So you must find the weighted mean. Start by writing the weights next to each corresponding item.

Exam A—95	20%
Midterm Exam—90	30%
Exam B—92	20%
Final Exam—87	30%

Now multiply each score by its weight and write that new value off to the right.

Exam A—95	→	20%	=	1,900
Midterm Exam—90	→	30%	=	2,700
Exam B—92	→	20%	=	1,840
Final Exam—87	→	30%	=	2,610

Add up both the final column and the weights column.

Exam A—95	→	20% =	1,900
Midterm Exam—90	→	30% =	2,700
Exam B—92	→	20% =	1,840
Final Exam—87	→	+ 30% =	+ 2,610
		100%	9,050

Now divide the total value by the total of the weights to get the weighted average:

$$100 \overline{)9050} = 90.5$$

Your final grade in the class would be 90.5.

In summary, you can calculate the weighted mean by following these steps:

1. Multiply your values by their respective weights.

2. Add all your weights together and all your new values together.

3. Divide the total new value by the total weight.

Try another weighted mean problem.

5. Bryce is the best player on his basketball team. During the first 8 weeks of the season, he scored on 65% of his attempts. For the following 4 weeks, Bryce scored on only 32% of his attempts. During the final 4 weeks of playoffs, Bryce practiced more and scored on 74% of his attempts. If Bryce made the same number of attempts each game, then what percent of his attempts during the entire season did he score?

    A. 57%
    B. 59%
    C. 63%
    D. 67%

Here's How to Crack It

This may not seem like a weighted mean problem at first, but look closer. The percentages given throughout the season represent Bryce's *average* scoring over those periods. So in order to find his percentage for the entire season, you must combine the 65 percent, 32 percent, and 74 percent. Notice that if you calculate just the mean (average) of 65, 32, and 74, you get (A), 57 percent. This is a trap!

Each percentage represents a portion of the season—65 percent for 8 weeks, 32 percent for 4 weeks, and 74 percent for 4 weeks. First multiply these percentages by the length of time over which they occurred.

$$65 \times 8 = 520$$
$$32 \times 4 = 128$$
$$74 \times 4 = 296$$

Since the question asks about the entire season, find the total number of weeks and the total of the new weighted values.

$$8 + 4 + 4 = 16$$
$$520 + 128 + 296 = 944$$

Now divide the total weighted value by the total number of weeks.

$$16\overline{)944}^{\,59}$$

The correct answer is (B).

———————————○———————————

Mean, Median, Mode, Range, and Weighted Mean Drill

You can check your answers in Part VIII: Answer Key to Drills.

Do these problems on your own. Then, on another piece of paper, do them again using your calculator.

1. A consumer group buys identical radios at 14 different stores. If the mean (average) price per radio is $23.40, how much did the consumer group spend for all the radios?

$

2. The data below represents the scores students achieved on a test.

92, 85, 86, 92, 86, 89

Complete the line plot to display the data. Click on the red X and drag it onto the graph as many times as necessary. (For this drill, simply mark the X's on the line plot.)

Student Test Scores

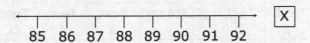

85 86 87 88 89 90 91 92   X

3. What is the range of weekly business expenses of a sewing supply shop over a three-week period if $65.00, $73.23, and $35.77 were the weekly expense totals for the three weeks?

   A. $8.23
   B. $29.23
   C. $37.46
   D. $58.00

Ice Cream Cones Sold at the Store "Cone Central" Over 5 Consecutive Days

Monday	Tuesday	Wednesday	Thursday	Friday
105	80	95	110	205

4. What is the mean (average) number of ice cream cones sold at the store "Cone Central" during the period shown in the graph above?

   A.   95
   B.   105
   C.   110
   D.   119

5. What is the median number of ice cream cones sold at the store "Cone Central" during the period shown in the graph above?

   A. 95
   B. 105
   C. 110
   D. 119

6. Olivia is calculating her grade in math class. Her scores for the class are recorded in the table below.

	Test 1	Test 2	Midterm	Test 3	Test 4	Test 5	Final
Scores	83	95	84	93	84	92	90

   The five in-class tests account for 50% of her final grade, while the midterm and final exams account for the other 50%. What is Olivia's grade in math class, rounded to the nearest percent?

   A. 84%
   B. 87%
   C. 88%
   D. 89%

RATIOS AND PROPORTIONS

As we said earlier, a fraction can be expressed in many different forms. For example, $\frac{1}{2} = \frac{2}{4} = \frac{3}{6}$....

A ratio or proportion problem merely asks you to express a particular fraction in a slightly different form. Here's an example:

---

1. A map uses a scale in which 1 inch = 200 miles. If the distance between two cities measures 5 inches on the map, how many miles separate the two cities?

   A. 1,000
   B. 800
   C. 600
   D. 400

Here's How to Crack It

Let's talk about this problem in terms of inches per mile, which can be expressed as follows:

$$\frac{1 \text{ inch}}{200 \text{ miles}}$$

This is actually a ratio, which is a way of writing a part-to-part comparison. A ratio is very similar to a fraction, and has many of the same properties that a fraction does. Like a fraction, a ratio can be expressed in an infinite number of different equivalent ratios. For example, it could equal a ratio with a numerator of 5:

$$\frac{1 \text{ inch}}{200 \text{ miles}} = \frac{5 \text{ inches}}{?}$$

You have just set up a proportion, which is two equivalent ratios. One inch represents 200 miles, so five inches represents…you don't know yet. Instead of "?" put an x in its place, to represent the number you don't know yet. To find out how many miles are represented by five inches, cross multiply the denominator of the left-hand ratio with the numerator of the right, and then the denominator of the right-hand ratio with the numerator of the left:

$$\frac{1 \text{ inch}}{200 \text{ miles}} \times \frac{5 \text{ inches}}{x \text{ miles}} \qquad 1{,}000 = 1x$$

And $x = 1{,}000$ miles. To check this, you can stick this number into the proportion you just wrote:

$$\frac{1 \text{ inch}}{200 \text{ miles}} = \frac{5 \text{ inches}}{1{,}000 \text{ miles}}$$

Does $\dfrac{5}{1{,}000}$ reduce to $\dfrac{1}{200}$? You bet. The correct answer is (A).

Let's do another:

---○---

2. If Jane can finish her work assignment in half an hour, what part of it can she finish in 20 minutes?

A. $\dfrac{1}{6}$

B. $\dfrac{1}{3}$

C. $\dfrac{2}{3}$

D. $\dfrac{3}{4}$

Here's How to Crack It

First of all, did you notice that this is the same type of problem we just did above? Jane can do one job in 30 minutes, so how much can she do in 20 minutes? To solve this, set up a proportion.

To make our job easier, we should use the same time measurement throughout the problem, so instead of talking about half an hour, permanently convert that to 30 minutes. Now, on to the proportion.

$$\frac{1 \text{ job}}{30 \text{ minutes}} = \frac{x \text{ (part of the job)}}{20 \text{ minutes}}$$

As you did before, cross multiply.

$$\frac{1 \text{ job}}{30 \text{ minutes}} = \frac{x \text{ (part of the job)}}{20 \text{ minutes}} \qquad 30x = 20 \qquad x = \frac{20}{30} \text{ or } \frac{2}{3}$$

The correct answer is (C).

---○---

Could you have done some Ballparking here? Of course! If the whole job takes 30 minutes, obviously 20 minutes is time to do more than half the job. Both (A) and (B) are less than half and can be eliminated right away. In fact, you might even have noticed that 20 minutes out of

30 minutes was $\frac{2}{3}$ without even setting up the proportion. But it's always a good idea to do the work, just to make sure.

Ratios and Proportions Drill

You can check your answers in Part VIII: Answer Key to Drills.

1. If a shrub 5 feet tall casts a 2-foot shadow, how tall is a tree standing next to the shrub that casts a 10-foot shadow at the same moment?

    A. 50 feet
    B. 25 feet
    C. 20 feet
    D. 13 feet

2. Two songwriting collaborators decide that they will share profits in a song in a ratio of 3 parts for the lyric writer to 2 parts for the music writer. If the music writer gets $2,500, how much does the lyric writer receive?

    A. $2,500
    B. $3,750
    C. $5,000
    D. $7,500

3. A particular lawn requires 6 bags of fertilizer. A lawn next door requires 4 bags of fertilizer. How big is the lawn next door?

    A. 10 square feet
    B. 24 square feet
    C. 50 square feet
    D. Not enough information is given.

RATE PROBLEMS

It's easy to spot rate problems: They almost always use the word "per" in the question.

Rate Problem Quiz

Q: How do you spot an $R \times T = D$ problem?

Turn the page for the answer.

You may not think so, but you already know the formula to solve every rate problem. Don't believe us? Let's say you drive in a car for 2 hours at 50 miles per hour. How far have you traveled? That's right: 100 miles. Fifty miles per hour is the *rate* at which you traveled, 2 hours is the *time* it took you to travel, and 100 miles is the *distance* you traveled.

The formula looks like this:

$$\text{Rate} \times \text{Time} = \text{Distance}$$
$$50 \qquad 2 \qquad 100$$

Or like this:

$$\text{Rate} = \frac{\text{Distance}}{\text{Time}}$$

Both equations are the same, as you will see in Chapter 15, Algebra. Memorizing this formula can save you a headache later on when you aren't sure whether to divide or multiply. Let's try two problems.

---

1. A train traveled at a speed of 120 kilometers per hour for $2\frac{1}{2}$ hours. How many kilometers did the train travel?

    A. 300
    B. 280
    C. 240
    D. 200

Here's How to Crack It

As soon as you see the words "kilometers *per* hour" and "hours," you should immediately be writing down $R \times T = D$ on your scratch paper, even before you finish reading the problem. Now all you'll have to do is plug in the numbers they gave you:

$$R \times T = D$$
$$120 \times 2\frac{1}{2} = ?$$

Multiplying $120 \times 2\frac{1}{2}$, you get 300, which is (A).

———————————————○———————————————

Could you have ballparked this question? Sure. If the train is traveling at 120 kilometers per hour, then in one hour it must have traveled 120 kilometers. Since your train has been traveling for more than two hours, it must have traveled more than 240 kilometers. Eliminate (C) and (D).

Here's another example:

———————————————○———————————————

2. Flying at 400 miles per hour, approximately how long will it take for a plane to travel between two cities that are 2,600 miles apart?

   A. between 4 and 5 hours
   B. between 5 and 6 hours
   C. between 6 and 7 hours
   D. between 7 and 8 hours

Here's How to Crack It
Again, after reading the first line, you should have been reaching for your scratch paper to write down $R \times T = D$. Plug in the numbers the problem gives you.

$$R \times T = D$$

$$400 \times \ ? = 2,600$$

Ballpark a little first, before you solve this. The answer choices give you some clues as to what this missing number T should be. Start with (A). If T were 4 hours, given that the rate is 400, what would the distance be? $4 \times 400 = 1,600$. You need a larger T if you want the distance to be 2,600. Now if T were 5 hours, $5 \times 400 = 2,000$. That's still not large enough. Let's try 6 hours: $6 \times 400 = 2,400$. Well, you're getting closer. How about 7 hours? $7 \times 400 = 2,800$. Now this is too big. The correct time must be between 6 and 7 hours.

How do you calculate this problem the traditional way? Solve for the missing T. If $R \times T = D$, then $T = \dfrac{D}{R} = \dfrac{2,600}{400} = 6.5$ hours. The correct answer is (C).

———————————————○———————————————

Rate Problems Drill

You can check your answers in Part VIII: Answer Key to Drills.

1. If a man runs 12 miles in 3 hours, what is his rate in miles per hour?

2. A glacier is moving at a rate of 4 feet per year. At this rate, how long will it take the glacier to travel one mile?
   (1 mile = 5,280 feet)

   A. 920 years
   B. 1,100 years
   C. 1,320 years
   D. 1,540 years

Rate Problem Quiz
A: It will use the word "per" in the question.

3. Marie drives from her home to the supermarket 10 miles away and then drives back home after shopping. If it takes her two hours for the entire trip, including one hour spent shopping in the supermarket, what was her average speed driving to and from the supermarket?

   A. 5 mph
   B. 10 mph
   C. 15 mph
   D. 20 mph

SCALE AND UNIT CONVERSION

Sometimes you will be asked to find the scale on which something is drawn. The easiest way to find the scale is to set up a proportion, which you already know how to do! Let's see how this might be introduced to a problem.

1. Amy builds a toothpick model of a bridge for a school project. The real bridge is 1,650 feet long and 134 feet high. Amy's model bridge is only 8 inches high. Find the scale that Amy uses for her model bridge. Then determine the approximate length of her model bridge shown in the drawing below.

Click on the numbers you want to select and drag them into the boxes.

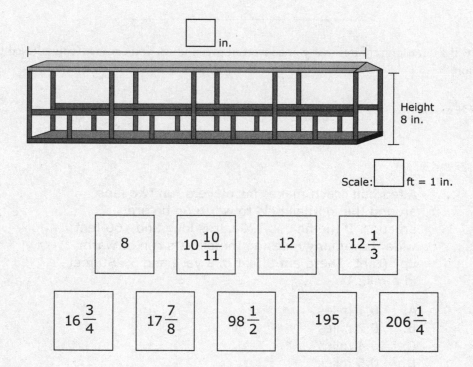

☐ in.

Height
8 in.

Scale: ☐ ft = 1 in.

8	$10\frac{10}{11}$	12	$12\frac{1}{3}$

$16\frac{3}{4}$	$17\frac{7}{8}$	$98\frac{1}{2}$	195	$206\frac{1}{4}$

Here's How to Crack It

Set up a proportion for the measurements of the heights versus the lengths:

Heights   **Lengths**

$$\frac{8 \text{ in.}}{134 \text{ ft.}} = \frac{x}{1{,}650 \text{ ft.}}$$

Now cross multiply to get

$$1{,}650 \times 8 = 134x\,?$$

The length of the model bridge must be approximately 98.5, or $98\frac{1}{2}$ inches.

Now, to determine the scale, set up a similar proportion as before, but to determine the number of feet represented by 1 in:

$$\frac{8\text{ in.}}{134\text{ ft.}} = \frac{1\text{ in.}}{y}$$

Now cross multiply to get

$$134 \times 1 = 8y$$

The scale must be 16.75, or $16\frac{3}{4}$.

───────────○───────────

Similarly, if a question requires that you convert between units, you can use (you guessed it!) a proportion.

Take a look:

───────────○───────────

2. A football coach makes his players run two laps around the football field to warm up before practice. If the field is 120 yards long and 160 feet wide, how many miles do the players run to warm up? (Hint: There are 3 feet in a yard and 5,280 feet in a mile.)

    A. 0.1 miles
    B. 0.2 miles
    C. 0.4 miles
    D. 0.5 miles

Here's How to Crack It

This problem uses three different units of measurement—feet, yards, and miles. Yikes! Before you do any major calculations, try to get all of the numbers in the same unit. You start with 120 *yards* and 160 *feet*. Which one will be easier to work with? Feet. So convert 120 yards:

$$\frac{120\text{ yards}}{x} = \frac{1\text{ yard}}{3\text{ feet}}$$

$$120 \times 3 = 1x$$
$$360 = x$$

Now you know that the football field is 360 feet long, and the width is already in feet. How far is one lap around the field? The 360 feet and 160 feet are only one length and one width, but a lap consists of running two lengths and two widths. You could add all four measurements: 360 + 160 + 360 + 160 = 1,040. Or you can add the single length and single width, and then multiply by two:

$$360 + 160 = 520$$
$$520 \times 2 = 1,040$$

Either way will result in the same answer. You know how far one lap around the field is, but the question asks for two laps. Double the answer: $1,040 \times 2 = 2,080$. You're not done yet! All of the answer choices are in *miles*. Convert 2,080 feet to miles:

$$\frac{2,080 \text{ feet}}{x} = \frac{5,280 \text{ feet}}{1 \text{ mile}}$$

$$2,080 \times 1 = 5,280x$$

Then divide 2,080 by 5,280 to find the answer in miles: $2,080 \div 5,280 = 0.4$ miles, or (C).

You can also use common sense to help in converting units. You have 120 yards and want to convert to feet. There are 3 feet in a yard. Since you are converting to a smaller unit, *multiply* 120 by 3 to find the answer.

Let's look at converting 2,080 feet to miles. There are 5,280 feet in a mile. Are miles a bigger or smaller unit than feet? They are bigger, so you will *divide* 2,080 by 5,280.

Scale and Unit Conversion Drill
You can check your answers in Part VIII: Answer Key to Drills.

1. A man who weighs 200 pounds goes on a diet and loses 16% of his body weight. How much weight, in ounces, did he lose? (Hint: 1 pound = 16 ounces.)

    A.   2
    B.   32
    C.   200
    D.   512

2. A cookie recipe that makes 24 cookies calls for the following ingredients:

$2\frac{3}{4}$ c. flour $1\frac{1}{3}$ c. sugar $\frac{3}{4}$ c. butter

1 egg $3\frac{1}{2}$ t. baking powder $1\frac{1}{2}$ t. vanilla extract

Amy is hosting a party and will have a total of 16 people in attendance, including herself. She wants to make one large batch of cookies to accommodate everyone. If each person will eat three cookies, what are the new amounts that Amy must measure for each ingredient?

Click on the numbers you want to select and drag them into the boxes. (For this drill, write the numbers in the boxes.)

☐ c. flour   ☐ c. sugar   ☐ c. butter

☐ egg   ☐ t. baking powder   ☐ t. vanilla extract

| $1\frac{1}{4}$ | $1\frac{1}{2}$ | 2 | 3 | $2\frac{2}{3}$ | $2\frac{1}{2}$ |

| $4\frac{1}{4}$ | 5 | $5\frac{1}{4}$ | $5\frac{1}{2}$ | 6 | 7 |

CHARTS AND GRAPHS

Some test takers are scared by charts and graphs. If you count yourself among them, we recommend that you review our "Understanding Graphics" supplement, which you can download online once you register your book. Roughly one-third to one-half of the Mathematical Reasoning test questions include a graphic of some sort. This can be a figure, a chart, a graph, or a table. One great thing about the graphics is that they are roughly drawn to scale, so you can always ballpark. Math test graphics review all the concepts included in this book, from the number line and percentages to the slope and equation of a line. Look at the following problems:

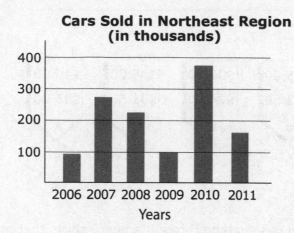

Cars Sold in Northeast Region (in thousands)

1. In the figure above, by approximately how much did sales of cars increase from 2009 to 2010?

   A. 100,000
   B. 200,000
   C. 260,000
   D. 360,000

Here's How to Crack It

If you've read the "Understanding Graphics" supplement, you know that you should always take a moment to read the title of the graph and study the two variables. You are looking at the number of cars sold in a particular region, broken down *by year*. The number of cars is expressed *in thousands*.

In 2009, according to the graph, 100,000 cars were sold. In 2010, more than 300,000 were sold. How many more? It's difficult to say exactly because the scale on the left is marked only every 100,000 cars, but it looks to be a little more than half the distance between the markings, or about 70,000 more. So the total 2010 figure is about 370,000. The question wants to know the increase from 2009 to 2010. How do you get that? Subtract. Roughly 370,000 minus 100,000 is roughly 270,000. Is this close to any of the answers? Yes. The correct answer is (C).

In effect, this was officially sanctioned Ballparking. There was no way to get the precise answer mathematically. The GED® test writers expected you to use your eyes and estimate in order to get the right answer.

Let's try another.

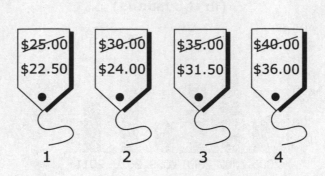

2. A man is searching through a bin of shirts that are on sale, some for 10% off and some for 20% off. Which sales tag above has been reduced by 20%?

   A. 1
   B. 2
   C. 3
   D. 4

Here's How to Crack It

In spite of the fact that there is a graphic that goes with it, this is just a percent problem. The question asks you to identify the tag that has been reduced by 20 percent. Begin with the first tag. It started at $25.00, and has been reduced to $22.50. Take away 20 percent from 25 and see if you get 22.50. If you do, it's the answer. If you don't, you can throw it back in the bin and try another. Twenty percent of $25.00 is $5.00, so the reduced price ought to be $20.00 if this were the correct answer. It isn't, so you can eliminate (A). Go to the next tag: It started at $30.00 and has been reduced to $24.00. What is 20 percent of 30? That's right: 6. If you take away the $6, you are left with $24.00. Bingo! The answer is (B).

Charts and Graphs Drill

You can check your answers in Part VIII: Answer Key to Drills.

Types of Telephones in Use

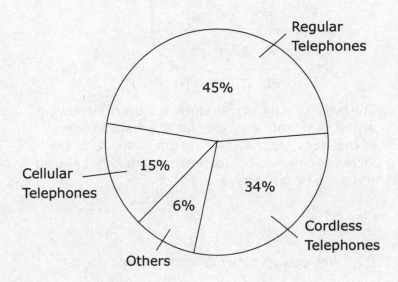

1. In the figure above, the number of regular telephones in use is how many times the number of cellular phones?

   A. 2.5 times
   B. 3 times
   C. 4 times
   D. 7.5 times

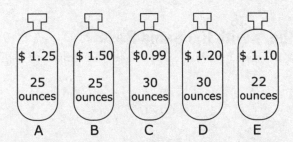

2. Each of the bottles in the figure above contains different amounts of cola at different prices. Which bottle represents the cheapest price per ounce?

Average Stock Prices This Week

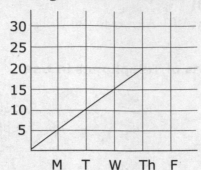

3. The price of a particular stock has been increasing at the same rate each day for the first four days of the week, as shown in the graph above. If the increase continues at its present rate, what should the price be on Friday?

    A.   20
    B.   25
    C.   30
    D.   Not enough information is given.

EXPONENTS

An exponent is shorthand for multiplication. The expression $4 \times 4 \times 4 \times 4 \times 4$ can also be written as 4^5, because the 4 is being multiplied 5 times. This is expressed as "4 to the fifth power." The large number (4) is called the **base,** and the little number (5) is called the **exponent.**

Although there aren't very many exponent questions on the GED® test, there are a few rules that you should remember.

Multiplying Numbers with the Same Base

When you multiply numbers that have the same base, you simply add the exponents.

$$6^2 \times 6^3 = 6^{(2 + 3)} = 6^5$$

Why is this true? Let's write this out in long form:

$$6^2 = 6 \times 6 \qquad 6^3 = 6 \times 6 \times 6$$

$$\text{so, } 6^2 \times 6^3 = 6 \times 6 \times 6 \times 6 \times 6 \text{ or } 6^5$$

Dividing Numbers with the Same Base

When you divide numbers that have the same base, you simply subtract the bottom exponent from the top exponent.

$$\frac{6^3}{6^2} = 6$$

Why is this true? Let's write it out in long form:

$$\frac{6^3}{6^2} = \frac{6 \times 6 \times 6}{6 \times 6} = \frac{6}{1} = 6$$

Raising a Number with an Exponent to Another Exponent

When you raise a number with an exponent to another exponent, multiply the exponents.

$$(6^2)^3 = 6^{2 \times 3} = 6^6$$

Why is this true? Let's write this out in long form:

$$(6^2)^3 = 6^2 \times 6^2 \times 6^2 = (6 \times 6) \times (6 \times 6) \times (6 \times 6) = 6^6$$

The Zero Power

It may seem strange, but any number to the zero power is 1.

$$4^0 = 1 \quad x^0 = 1$$

The First Power

Anything to the first power equals that number.

$$4^1 = 4$$
$$-3^1 = -3$$

But Watch Out For…

There are several operations that seem like they ought to work with exponents but don't.

Does $x^2 + x^3 = x^5$? NO!!
Does $x^4 - x^2 = x^2$? NO!!!

Does $\dfrac{x^2 + y^3 + z^4}{x^2 + y^3} = z^4$? NO!!!!

In fact, none of these three expressions can be reduced.

Exponent Facts
$5^0 = 1$
$5^1 = 5$
$5^2 = 25$
If $x^2 = 25$, then $x = 5$
or -5.

You would expect that raising a number to a power would increase that number, and usually it does, but there are exceptions.

- If you raise a positive fraction of less than 1 to a power, the fraction gets smaller.

$$\left(\frac{1}{2}\right)^2 = \frac{1^2}{2^2} = \frac{1}{4}$$

- If you raise a negative number to an odd power, the number gets smaller.

$$(-3)^3 = (-3)(-3)(-3) = -27$$

(Remember −27 is smaller than −3.)

- If you raise a negative number to an even power, the number becomes positive.

$$(-3)^2 = (-3)(-3) = 9$$

Exponent problems on the GED® test tend to be pretty basic.

---

1. 3^3 equals which of the following values?

   A. 9×9
   B. 3×3
   C. 3×9
   D. 1^{27}

Here's How to Crack It

The expression 3^3 equals 27. All you have to do is find the answer choice that also equals 27. You got it. The correct answer is (C).

RADICALS

The **square root** of a positive number x is the number that, when squared, equals x.

For example:

- The square root of 16 equals 4 because $4 \times 4 = 16$.
- The square root of 9 equals 3 because $3 \times 3 = 9$.
- The square root of 4 equals 2 because $2 \times 2 = 4$.

The symbol for a positive square root is $\sqrt{}$, also called a radical.

$$\sqrt{16} = 4$$

$$\sqrt{9} = 3$$

To find the square root of a number on your TI-30XS, first press the "2nd" key, then the "x^2" key, enter the number, and then press the right arrow key.

Many numbers do not have a whole number square root. For example, there is no whole number whose value is $\sqrt{13}$. But we can say that $\sqrt{13}$ is *between* 3 and 4. Here's an example:

1. The square root of 7 is between which of the following pairs of numbers?

   A. 2 and 3
   B. 3 and 4
   C. 4.5 and 5.5
   D. 9 and 10

Radical Facts

$\sqrt{4} = 2$

$\sqrt{1} = 1$

If $x = 4$, then

$\sqrt{x}$ = positive 2.

Here's How to Crack It

There is no whole number square root of 7, so see what numbers it is between that do have a square root. The expression $\sqrt{9}$ is the next biggest number that comes out evenly: $\sqrt{9} = 3$. The expression $\sqrt{4}$ is the next smallest number that comes out evenly: $\sqrt{4} = 2$. Thus, the square root of 7 is between 2 and 3. The correct answer is (A).

Sometimes a question will ask for the square root of a fraction. To do this, take the square root of the numerator and denominator separately. For example, to determine $\sqrt{\dfrac{9}{4}}$, start with the fact that $\sqrt{\dfrac{9}{4}} = \dfrac{\sqrt{9}}{\sqrt{4}}$. Since $\sqrt{9} = 3$ and $\sqrt{4} = 2$, $\sqrt{\dfrac{9}{4}} = \dfrac{\sqrt{9}}{\sqrt{4}} = \dfrac{3}{2}$. Let's look at another example.

---

2. What is $\sqrt{0.25}$?

    A.   0.005
    B.   0.05
    C.   0.5
    D.   5

Take 0.25 and convert it to a fraction: $0.25 = \dfrac{0.25}{1.00} = \dfrac{25}{100} = \dfrac{1}{4}$. Since $0.25 = \dfrac{1}{4}$, $\sqrt{0.25} = \sqrt{\dfrac{1}{4}} = \dfrac{\sqrt{1}}{\sqrt{4}} = \dfrac{1}{2}$. Since the answer choices are decimals, convert $\dfrac{1}{2}$ into a decimal: $2\overline{)1.0}$ with quotient 0.5. The correct answer is (C).

Exponents and roots are two related concepts. In fact, a root can be expressed as an exponent. For example, how can $\sqrt{2}$ be expressed as a number with an exponent? Note that $\left(\sqrt{2}\right)^2 = 2$, since the square root and the square are inverses. Remember also that this equation can be rewritten as $\left(\sqrt{2}\right)^2 = 2^1$. If we rewrite $\sqrt{2}$ as 2^x, we get $(2^x)^2 = 2^1$. Multiply the exponents on the left side of the equation to get $2^{2x} = 2^1$. Therefore $2x = 1$ and $x = \dfrac{1}{2}$, so $\sqrt{2} = 2^{\frac{1}{2}}$. Let's look at an example.

---

3. What is the value of $9^{\frac{3}{2}}$?

    A.   3
    B.   9
    C.   27
    D.   81

Here's How to Crack It

Rewrite the exponent $\frac{3}{2}$ as $\frac{1}{2} \times 3$ to get $9^{\left(\frac{1}{2} \times 3\right)}$. Multiplication within the exponent is equivalent to raising to an exponent, so $9^{\left(\frac{1}{2} \times 3\right)} = \left(9^{\frac{1}{2}}\right)^3$. Since $9^{\frac{1}{2}} = \sqrt{9} = 3$, $\left(9^{\frac{1}{2}}\right)^3 = 3^3 = 27$. The correct answer is (C).

Exponents and Radicals Drill

You can check your answers in Part VIII: Answer Key to Drills.

1. Which of the following values is equal to 2^3?

    A. $(2 + 2)^2$
    B. $2^2 + 2$
    C. 4^2
    D. $2(2^2)$

2. $3^3 + 2^2 = ?$

3. What is the value of $\sqrt{16} - \sqrt{4}$?

    A. 2^2
    B. $\sqrt{12}$
    C. $16^2 + 4^2$
    D. $\sqrt{4}$

4. Which of the following is equal to $(0.04)^{\frac{5}{2}}$?

    A. 0.00032
    B. 0.0032
    C. 0.032
    D. 0.32

SCIENTIFIC NOTATION

Scientific notation combines your knowledge of decimals and your knowledge of exponents to allow you to express very large numbers without endless strings of zeros. Take the number 3,200,000,000. Numbers like this can be difficult to read and even more difficult to add or subtract. Here is the same number in scientific notation:

$$3.2 \times 10^9$$

How do you expand this out to its full size? Let's start with an easier example.

$$3.2 \times 10^2$$

All you have to do to simplify this expression is move the decimal point over to the right by the same number as the power of ten. In this case, two places.

$$3.2 \times 10^2 = 320$$
$$3.2 \times 10^3 = 3,200$$
$$3.2 \times 10^4 = 32,000$$

How do you contract a big number into scientific notation? Just perform the same process in reverse. Let's take 4,750,000. If you wanted to express this as 4.75 to the nth power of ten, what would the nth power be? On the large number, put your pencil point where you want the decimal to be (in this case, between the digit 4 and the digit 7), and now count the number of places you have to move the pencil to the *right* to get to the end of the number. Did you move your pencil 6 places? You are now a certified scientific notationalist.

$$4,750,000 = 4.75 \times 10^6$$

Let's try a problem.

---

1. Which of the following expresses the number 5.6×10^4?

   A. 0.00056
   B. 5,600
   C. 56,000
   D. 560,000

Here's How to Crack It

On a piece of scratch paper, write down 5.6 with some space to the right of it. Now, take your pencil, and move the tip of the pencil over four times, like this:

5.6 〜〜〜〜

Fill in the 0s. The correct answer is (C).

PROBABILITY

If you flip a coin, what are the odds that it's going to come out tails? If you said anything but "$\frac{1}{2}$," "1 out of 2," or "fifty-fifty," then there's a poker game we'd like to invite you to next Thursday.

To figure out the probability that something is going to happen, you take the number of chances that the thing could happen and compare that to the *total* number of possible outcomes of *all* kinds. For example, let's take that coin we just mentioned. If you toss the coin once, how many chances are there on this *one* toss that it will be heads? One chance. And how many total possible outcomes are there? There are two possible outcomes—heads or tails. Therefore, you have a 1 out of 2, $\frac{1}{2}$, or fifty-fifty chance of seeing tails.

On the GED® test, probabilities are generally expressed as fractions. The number of possibilities that *one* thing could happen is the numerator. The number of *total* possibilities is the denominator.

Probability Quiz

Q: If there is one probability question on your 46-question Mathematical Reasoning test, what's the probability that the first question on the test will be a probability question?

Turn the page for the answer.

Let's try a problem.

_____○_____

1. 9 workers decide to draw straws to see who will be the one to stay late and clean up. If there are 9 straws, 8 long and 1 short, what is the probability that Jim, who goes first, will draw the short straw?

    A. $\dfrac{1}{18}$

    B. $\dfrac{1}{9}$

    C. $\dfrac{1}{8}$

    D. $\dfrac{8}{9}$

Here's How to Crack It

To solve any GED® probability problem, you have to find the number of chances that a particular thing could happen (in this case, there is only one short straw, so Jim has only one chance of picking a short straw). This is your numerator. Then you have to find the total number of outcomes of *any* kind (in this case, the total number of straws is 9). This is your denominator. The correct answer to this question is (B).

_____○_____

Let's try another.

_____○_____

2. If a box of chocolates contains 3 caramels, 3 nut clusters, and 5 raspberry creams, which of the following fractions represents the chance of picking a caramel on the first try?

    A. $\dfrac{1}{11}$

    B. $\dfrac{1}{3}$

    C. $\dfrac{3}{11}$

    D. $\dfrac{5}{11}$

Here's How to Crack It

As before, figure out the number of possible ways to pick a caramel. There are three caramels, so there are three possibilities for picking one. That becomes your numerator.

Probability Quiz
A: 1 out of 46

Now, you need the total number of possibilities of any kind. There are a total of 11 chocolates, so that becomes your denominator. The correct answer is $\frac{3}{11}$ or (C).

Scientific Notation and Probability Drill

You can check your answers in Part VIII: Answer Key to Drills.

1. A painting has three lights illuminating it, each with an output of 2,550 lumens. What is the total amount of light illuminating the painting, in lumens, expressed in scientific notation?

    A. 51.0×10^4
    B. 76.5×10^3
    C. 7.65×10^3
    D. 5.1×10^3

2. Erica's closet has no light. Erica owns 2 blue dresses, 1 green dress, 1 purple dress, and 2 green dresses. What is the probability that she will pick a blue dress?

    A. $\frac{1}{4}$

    B. $\frac{1}{3}$

    C. $\frac{1}{6}$

    D. $\frac{1}{2}$

3. Which of the following is equivalent to
    $(3.4 \times 10^3) + (4.1 \times 10^4)$?

    A. 75,000
    B. 750,000
    C. 444,000
    D. 44,400

COMBINATIONS AND PERMUTATIONS

On some GED® questions, you will have to determine the number of possible choices that you can make in a given situation. If you're choosing what to have for lunch and are offered either a sandwich, soup, or a salad, how many choices would you have? That's right: 3. However, the GED® test is not likely to ask questions like this. The GED® test is more likely to ask questions that require you to determine the total number of options when making multiple choices. Let's look at an example below.

1. The manager of a department store has to hire a new cashier, a new salesperson, and a new shift supervisor. If there are 3 applicants for cashier, 8 applicants for salesperson, and 5 applicants for shift supervisor, and no applicant applies for more than one position, how many different ways can the manager hire one person for each of the three positions?

    A. 17
    B. 20
    C. 60
    D. 120

Here's How to Crack It

The manager needs to hire people to fill three positions. The question tells you that no applicant applies for more than one position. This means that there is a completely different pool of applicants for each position. When there is a different source for each choice, treat each choice independently. Draw a slot for each position as below.

_____   _____   _____

Cashier   Salesperson   Shift Supervisor

Now, for each position, fill in the number of possible applicants as below.

3	8	5
Cashier	Salesperson	Shift Supervisor

Now, multiply each of the three numbers to get $3 \times 8 \times 5 = 120$. The correct answer is (D).

———————○———————

Sometimes, however, you'll be working with the same source of items for each choice that you're making. In some of these examples, the order will matter but not in others. If the order doesn't matter, mathematicians call it a **combination;** if order does matter, it's called a **permutation**. The method you use to solve questions in which there is one source and order matters is actually very similar to that for questions in which there are multiple sources. This is common in questions that ask about arrangements or filling different positions. Let's look at one below.

———————○———————

2. A DJ has enough time to play four more songs at a school dance. If she has seven different songs available to choose from, how many different orderings of songs can she choose?

    A. 22
    B. 35
    C. 840
    D. 2,401

Here's How to Crack It

The DJ needs to choose four songs. Just as before, draw a slot for each position as below.

_____ _____ _____ _____

Now, for each song, fill in the number of possible choices. For the first song, there are seven choices. For the second song, there are six choices remaining (since you already used one song as the first selection). For the third song, there are five choices remaining (since you already used two songs). For the fourth song, there are four choices remaining (since you already used three songs). Fill this in as below.

7	6	5	4

Now, multiply each of the three numbers to get $7 \times 6 \times 5 \times 4 = 840$. The correct answer is (C).

———————○———————

In other cases, though, the order will not matter. This means there will be fewer possibilities than cases in which order does matter. In these cases, you will follow the same method as when order matters but with an extra step to reduce the number of possibilities. This is common when questions ask about teams or committees. Look at an example below.

———————————————————○———————————————————

1. A DJ is choosing four new records to add to his collection. If he is in a store that has seven different records available to choose from, how many different groups of records can he choose?

   A. 22

   B. 35

   C. 840

   D. 2,401

Here's How to Crack It

This looks similar to the previous question, and it is but with a key difference. The DJ needs to choose four records. Just as before, draw a slot for each position as below.

—————————— —————————— —————————— ——————————

Now, for each record, fill in the number of possible choices. For the first song, there are seven choices. For the second song, there are six choices remaining (since you already used one song as the first selection). For the third song, there are five choices remaining (since you already used two songs). For the fourth song, there are four choices remaining (since you already used three songs). Fill this in as below.

_____7_____ _____6_____ _____5_____ _____4_____

So far, it is the same as the previous question. The difference is that since each record will simply either be purchased or not purchased, the order doesn't matter. When this is the case, you want to divide by the number of possible ordering of each set of 4. This is $4 \times 3 \times 2 \times 1$. Divide this by the numbers above to get the following:

$$\frac{7}{4} \times \frac{6}{3} \times \frac{5}{2} \times \frac{4}{1}$$

Reduce these fractions before you multiply them. The 6 in the numerator can cancel with the 3 and 2 in the denominator and the 4 in the numerator can cancel with the 4 in denominator to get the following:

$$\frac{7}{1} \times \frac{1}{1} \times \frac{5}{1} \times \frac{1}{1}$$

Now, multiply what remains to get $7 \times 5 = 35$. The correct answer is (B).

———————————————————○———————————————————

Combinations and Permutations Drill

You can check your answers in Part VIII: Answer Key to Drills.

1. A deli offers a made-to-order sandwich to its customers. Customers can choose one type of bread, one type of meat, one type of cheese, and one type of lettuce. If the deli has four types of bread, five types of meat, eight types of cheeses, and three types of lettuce, how many different types of sandwiches can a customer order?

    A. 20
    B. 120
    C. 240
    D. 480

2. A school president is choosing three cabinet members to appoint: a vice president, a secretary, and a treasurer. If she has eight candidates to choose from, each of whom can serve any cabinet position, how many possible cabinets can the president appoint?

    A. 21
    B. 56
    C. 336
    D. 512

3. A teacher is selecting students for a trivia bowl. If there are nine interested students and a trivia bowl team consists of three players, how many different teams can the teacher select?

    A. 24
    B. 84
    C. 252
    D. 504

PUTTING IT ALL TOGETHER

Now that you've seen the basics of applied arithmetic one topic at a time, we're going to give you a drill that mixes up all the different applied arithmetic concepts we've discussed in this chapter. This drill will help to reveal whether you're having trouble recognizing individual types of problems, as we discussed in the last chapter. Some people are fine once they know that a question is about probabilities or percents, for example, but they have trouble spotting the key words that should tell them what type of problem they're dealing with. As you do this drill, make it a point to identify each question before you start calculating:

"This is an average question."
"That is a rate problem."
"This one is an exponent question."

Applied Arithmetic Drill

You can check your answers in Part VIII: Answer Key to Drills.

1. Darryl puts $5,000 into an insured bank account that pays simple interest of 8%. How much interest will he earn in 2 years?

   A. $2[0.08(5,000)]$

   B. $\dfrac{0.08(5,000)}{2}$

   C. $2[0.92(5,000)]$

   D. $2[1.08(5,000)]$

2. If Laverne walks steadily at a rate of 5 kilometers per hour, how long will it take her to walk 17.5 kilometers?

   A. $1\dfrac{3}{4}$ hours

   B. $3\dfrac{1}{2}$ hours

   C. 52 hours

   D. $87\dfrac{1}{2}$ hours

Computer Preferences

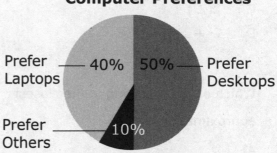

3. The figure above shows the results of a survey of a group of 200 professionals who were asked what type of computer they preferred. How many more people prefer desktop computers than prefer laptop computers?

   A. 5
   B. 10
   C. 15
   D. 20

4. There are a total of four tests in Sara's history class. She earned 94, 88, and 85 on the first three. What score does Sara need on the fourth test to pass the class with an average of 90 (the equivalent of an A)?

   A. 89
   B. 90
   C. 91
   D. 93

5. Which of the following is equal to $5^2 - \sqrt{9}$?

   A. 2^{11}
   B. $3^2 + \sqrt{25}$
   C. $2(2^3) + 6$
   D. $2^3 + 3^2$

6. Which of the following is the closest approximation of $\sqrt{10}$?

   A. 2
   B. 3
   C. 5
   D. 100

7. Michael calls a taxi to pick him up at his house. He knows that the taxi company has 1 limousine, 2 sedans, 3 vans, and 1 compact. What is the probability that he will ride in a sedan?

8. A set contains the following five numbers: 12, 4, 8, 16, 23. What is the median of the set?

9. Sheila works in a factory for $14.50 per hour for any hours up to 40. After 40 hours, she is paid an overtime rate that is one and a half times her regular pay. If Sheila worked 43 hours last week, which expression below shows how much she earned?

   A. 40(14.50) + 3(1.5)
   B. 40(14.50) + 3(1.5)(14.50)
   C. 43(1.5)(14.50)
   D. 43(14.50)

10. If one cell is 2.3×10^4 microns wide and another cell is 3.2×10^4 microns wide, then one cell is how much bigger than the other in microns?

    A. 0.9
    B. 11.0
    C. 110.0
    D. 9,000.0

11. Marie has five television shows recorded on her DVR. She has enough time to watch three of them today, and must decide in what order she will watch them. How many different orderings of the three shows she watches today can Marie choose?

    A. 10
    B. 30
    C. 60
    D. 120

12. Which of the following is the value of

    $$\frac{(2^{12})(2^5)(\sqrt{5})^4}{(2^{16})(5^3)} ?$$

    A. $\dfrac{2}{5}$

    B. 4

    C. 10

    D. 20

Chapter 15
Algebra

In this chapter, we introduce the basics of algebra—plus we'll show you powerful techniques that make certain types of difficult algebra questions really easy.

Algebra accounts for slightly more than half of the GED® Mathematical Reasoning test. Most people just don't like algebra, and they never did. Well, we have some good news for you.

You don't always need to use algebra to solve the algebra problems.

In just a few pages, we'll show you a great technique that will allow you to do some of the tougher algebra problems without writing equations. However, let's begin by going over the basics of the easy "solving for *x*"-type of GED® problems.

SIMPLE EQUATIONS

If you've done the first two math chapters, then you've already been solving simple equations, also known as equalities. Every time you set up a proportion or an average formula, you were using algebra. Here is the most basic type of algebra equation:

1. If $2x - 14 = 10$, then $x = ?$

    A. 5
    B. 12
    C. 15
    D. 22

The GED® test writers use some variation of this problem on practically every test. To find the answer to this question, we must "solve for *x*," which simply means getting *x* all alone on one side of the equation, and everything else on the other side. The *x* is already on the left-hand side of the equals sign in this equation, so let's try to move the *other* numbers on the left side over to the right side.

First, let's tackle the number 14 that is subtracted from $2x$. To make this *subtraction* of 14 disappear, we must *add* 14 to the left side. This is the concept of inverse operations, because adding is the inverse (opposite) of subtracting. Now, we want both sides to remain equal, so we must then add 14 to the *right* side of the equation as well, since that's what we did to the left side.

$$
\begin{array}{r}
2x - 14 = 10 \\
+ \quad 14 \quad 14 \\
\hline
2x - 0 \ = 24
\end{array}
$$

As long as you add or subtract your number to *both* sides of the equation, the equation actually stays the same. So now, the equation looks like this:

$$2x = 24$$

Now, tackle the number 2, which is being multiplied by *x*. To make this *multiplication* of 2 disappear, you must *divide* by 2 on the left side, since dividing is the inverse of multiplying. As before, you want to avoid unbalancing the equation, so also divide by 2 on the right side.

$$\frac{2x}{2} = \frac{24}{2}$$

As long as you multiply or divide your number on *both* sides of the equation, the equation stays proportionately the same. At this point, you can cancel the 2s on the left side and reduce the fraction on the right side as shown:

$$\frac{\cancel{2}x}{\cancel{2}} = \frac{\overset{12}{\cancel{24}}}{\cancel{2}} \quad \text{so} \quad x = 12$$

The correct answer to this question is (B).

> Whatever you do to the left side of an equation, you MUST do to the right side as well.

Another kind of algebraic-equation question that comes up fairly often on the GED® test looks like this:

2. Given the formula $2a = 3b(c - 4)$, find a if $b = 5$ and $c = 6$.

   A.   30
   B.   23
   C.   15
   D.   9

Here's How to Crack It
These problems give you an equation and values for two of the three variables. All you have to do is plug the values for the two variables you know into the equation and then solve for the third.

Start by writing the equation on your scratch paper, substituting 5 for b and 6 for c. It should look like this:

$$2a = (3 \times 5)(6 - 4)$$
$$2a = (15)(2)$$
$$2a = 30$$

If you were in a hurry, you might now pick (A), 30, but the problem asks for the value of a, not $2a$. To solve for a, you must divide both sides by 2. The correct answer is 15, or (C).

Simple Equation Drill

You can check your answers in Part VIII: Answer Key to Drills.

1. If $2x - 5 = 11$, then $x =$

   A. 32
   B. 12
   C. 8
   D. 3

2. If $3x + 6 = 51$, then $x =$

   [ ]

3. Evaluate $3x^2 - 4y$, if $x = 2$ and $y = 3$.

   A. 24
   B. 6
   C. 0
   D. −6

INEQUALITIES

While an equality or an equation allows you to solve for x and get one answer, an inequality has a range of answers. For example, in the inequality $x > 5$, we know that x must be greater than 5, but there is an infinite number of values that x could be. Thus, an inequality defines a range of values for the variable without giving you one specific value. Here are the symbols for inequalities:

>	greater than
<	less than
≥	greater than or equal to
≤	less than or equal to

An inequality is solved in exactly the same way as an equality. Let's use the same example we used at the beginning of the chapter, with one small change.

1. If $2x - 14 > 10$, then which of the following
    expressions gives all the possible values of x?

    A. $x > 5$
    B. $x > 12$
    C. $x < 15$
    D. $x < 22$

Here's How to Crack It

Pretend it's just a normal equality. This is what your work should look like:

$$
\begin{array}{r}
2x - 14 > 10 \\
+\ \ \ 14 \quad 14 \\
\hline
2x - 0\ > 24
\end{array}
$$

$$
\frac{2x}{2} > \frac{24}{2}
$$

So, the correct answer is (B), $x > 12$.

The only difference between an inequality and an equality occurs when you have to multiply or divide by a negative number.

> An inequality is just like an equality EXCEPT when multiplying or dividing by a negative number. In this case, the inequality sign flips!

2. If $-3x + 6 < 18$, then which of the following
    expressions gives all the possible values of x?

    A. $x < 2$
    B. $x < -4$
    C. $x > 2$
    D. $x > -4$

Here's How to Crack It

Until the very last step, this will be just like solving an equality. This is what the work should look like right up until that last step:

$$
\begin{array}{rcr}
-3x + 6 & < & 18 \\
-6 & & -6 \\
\hline
-3x & < & 12
\end{array}
$$

Now, comes the tricky part. When you multiply or divide an inequality by a negative number, the unequal sign flips over (that is, goes from > to <, or vice versa).

In this case, to get x alone on the left side of the equation, you're going to divide both sides by -3.

$$
\frac{-3x}{-3} < \frac{12}{-3}
$$

But the moment you divide by a negative number, the sign flips over.

$$
x > -4
$$

So, the correct answer to this question is (D).

———————○———————

Take a look at a typical GED® inequality below.

———————○———————

3. For which value of x below is the inequality $4x > 3$ true?

    A. -4

    B. 0

    C. $\dfrac{3}{4}$

    D. 1

Here's How to Crack It

You want to isolate x on one side of the equation, so get rid of the 4 by dividing both sides by 4.

$$\frac{4x}{4} > \frac{3}{4}$$

So $x > \frac{3}{4}$. When you look at the answer choices, you may be tempted to choose (C), $\frac{3}{4}$. However, read the question again. "For which value of x below is the inequality...true?" In other words, which of the answer choices is within the range of values expressed by the inequality $x > \frac{3}{4}$? Is -4 greater than $\frac{3}{4}$? No. Is 0 greater than $\frac{3}{4}$? No. Is $\frac{3}{4}$ *greater* than $\frac{3}{4}$? No. Is 1 greater than $\frac{3}{4}$? Yes! The correct answer is (D).

Inequalities Drill

You can check your answers in Part VIII: Answer Key to Drills.

1. Freida is not allowed on the roller coaster because she is under the minimum age of 5. Which of the following inequalities expresses all the ages that *are* allowed on the roller coaster?

   A. $x < 5$
   B. $x > 5$
   C. $x \geq 5$
   D. $x > -5$

2. If $5x + 3 < 28$, then which of the following expressions gives all the possible values of x?

   A. $x < 5$
   B. $x < -5$
   C. $x > 0$
   D. $x > 5$

3. If m is the positive number 4, which of the following inequalities contains the number m?

    A. $x < 3$
    B. $x > 7$
    C. $2x > 6$
    D. $3x \leq -6$

BACKSOLVING

You've seen throughout this book that POE—Process of Elimination—can be a very important tool in answering difficult multiple-choice GED® questions. **Backsolving** is the ultimate extension of POE. Let's look again at the very first example from this chapter.

Work backward from the answer choices to see which one solves the problem.

1. If $2x - 14 = 10$, then $x = ?$

    A.   5
    B.   12
    C.   15
    D.   22

The traditional way to solve this problem is to use algebra to "solve for x." In fact, this problem is pretty easy, and you will probably want to do it the traditional way (which we just showed you above).

However, there is another way to do this problem, and we're going to show it to you because this same way can be used to solve many more difficult algebra problems that appear on the Mathematical Reasoning test.

The correct answer is staring you in the face. The problem asks for the value of x and then presents you with four possible answers. In other words, one of those four possibilities is the number you're looking for.

Well, since one of these four answers is correct, why not try plugging each of them back into the question until we find the one that works?

We'll start with (C). Let's suppose for a moment that 15 is the correct answer and plug it into the question.

$$2(15) - 14 = 10$$

Is this true? No! $30 - 14 = 16$. We've just proven that (C) is wrong.

But we've done something even better than that. Choice (C) is not just wrong—it's too big. Do we need to check (D), 22, which is even bigger than (C)?

Just by trying out (C), we eliminated any answers that were bigger. On the Mathematical Reasoning test, multiple-choice math answers are always listed in ascending or descending order. Therefore, every time you try substituting one of the middle answer choices—(B) or (C)—back into the problem, you will eliminate at least one other answer immediately. If the number you get is too big, you can get rid of any choices that are even bigger. If the number you get is too small, you can get rid of any choices that are even smaller.

The only two possibilities left are (A) and (B). Let's try (B).

$$2(12) - 14 = 10$$

Is this true? When we substitute 12 into the equation, we get exactly the correct answer: $24 - 14 = 10$. Therefore, the answer to this problem is (B).

This technique is called Backsolving, and while it is probably unnecessary on a simple equation such as this, it will save your life on tougher questions. The method is always exactly the same: Start with one of the middle numbers. Plug it into the equation in the problem. If it makes the equation work, then you're done; you have the right answer. If the number is too big, eliminate any choices that are bigger, and zero in on the remaining choices. Try one of them. If it's still too big, then the answer must be the remaining choice. Pick it, and move on.

Let's try this technique on some more difficult problems.

2. The 8 passengers on a small plane have paid a total of $900 for the flight. If an economy ticket costs $100 and a first-class ticket costs $200, how many first-class tickets were bought?

    A.   5
    B.   4
    C.   2
    D.   1

Apply the Strategy
Use Backsolving to answer questions like this one.

Here's How to Crack It

At first glance, this may not seem to resemble the equation problem we just finished. This is a word problem, for one thing, and there doesn't seem to be an equation in the problem at all.

In fact, the words of this problem actually contain an equation. The difficulty is that it's pretty tricky to translate these words into math. The correct equation that will solve this problem is

$$200x + [100(8 - x)] = 900$$

Backsolving Quiz

Q: With which answer choice do you start when you backsolve?

Turn the page for the answer.

But if you don't think you could have come up with this, don't spend any time kicking the ground because you can solve this algebra problem *without* algebra.

Backsolve! One of those four answers must be correct, so try putting one of them into the problem and see what happens. Which choice do you want to start with? Choice (B) works because it's in the middle. If (B) is too big, you can eliminate the choice that is even bigger. If (B) is too small, you can eliminate the choices that are even smaller. If (B) is just right, then you can go on to the next problem because you'll be done.

Choice (B) says that four passengers flew first class. And because there were a total of eight passengers, that means that four passengers flew economy class.

$$4 \times \$200 = \$800$$

$$4 \times \$100 = \$400$$

If this is the correct answer, the total dollar amount should add up to the total given in the problem: $900. Does it? No, it's way too big. Which choices can you then eliminate? That's right: Cross off (A) and (B). The only remaining possibilities are (C) and (D). We'll try (C) next.

Choice (C) says that two passengers flew first class. And because there were a total of eight passengers, that means that six passengers flew economy class.

$$2 \times \$200 = \$400$$

$$6 \times \$100 = \$600$$

If this is the correct answer, the total dollar amount should add up to the total given in the problem: $900. Does it? No, but you're getting warmer; $1,000 is a lot closer to $900 than you were before.

You know the answer is *not* (A), (B), or (C). Can you guess what the correct answer to this problem is?

Just to be sure, check (D). Choice (D) says that one passenger flew first class. And because there were a total of eight passengers, that means that seven passengers flew economy class.

$$1 \times \$200 = \$200$$

$$7 \times \$100 = \$700$$

Does this add up to $900? You bet. The correct answer to this tough algebra word problem is (D).

Can You Use This Technique on *Every* GED® Problem?

No. Many problems on the GED® test cannot be backsolved because their answer choices contain variables or formulas or because the correct answer choice is the final result of a calculation rather than a missing ingredient in an equation. And, of course, it is impossible to work backward from the answer choices when there are no answer choices. Generally, each GED® test contains as many as three or four problems that can be backsolved. These are frequently considered some of the hardest problems on the test because they involve algebra. Of course, if you backsolve, these problems are actually kind of easy.

How Do You Spot a Backsolve Problem?

Problems that can be backsolved have several characteristics. First, they must be multiple choice; the answer choices are invariably made up of simple numbers (such as 16, 27, or 5) rather than formulas or variables. In addition, the last lines of the problems ask straightforward questions (such as "How many of the workers are women?" or "How many tickets were bought originally?").

Most important, the best way to spot a backsolve problem is to recognize that the only other way to solve that particular problem—the *traditional* way—would be to write an algebraic equation. If you need to write an algebraic equation, then you could backsolve instead.

Let's try another:

---○---

3. Forty-two people have signed up for the little league annual dinner. If there are twice as many children as adults signed up, how many children are signed up?

    A. 14
    B. 20
    C. 28
    D. 32

Here's How to Crack It

Is this a Backsolving problem? It certainly has all the earmarks: It is a multiple-choice question, the last line asks a straightforward question, and the answers are simple numbers rather than variables or equations. Most important, the only other way to do this problem would be to write an algebraic equation. And by the way, if you came up with the equation ($x + 2x = 42$), you could *still* get the wrong answer because when you solve for x, you get 14—which happens to be (A). Unfortunately, the variable x in this equation represents the number of *adults*, not the number of children. In this problem, you could have written a perfectly good equation and still have gotten the problem wrong.

> **When to Backsolve**
> You can backsolve if
>
> 1) there are numbers in the answer choices.
> 2) the last line of the question asks a simple question.
> 3) the only other way to solve the problem is to use algebra.

Try Backsolving instead. The question asks how many children have signed up for the dinner. One of the answer choices has to be right. Why not start with (B), 20? The problem tells you that there are twice as many children as adults, so if there are 20 children, how many adults can there be? That's right: 10. If you add the number of children and the number of adults, you are supposed to get the same total number of people as there are in the problem (42 people). Do you? No, you have only 30. Choice (B) is not just the wrong answer—it is too small. So you can eliminate any choices that are smaller than (B), which means (A) bites the dust as well.

The answer is either (C) or (D). Let's try (C), 28. If there are 28 children and there are twice as many children as adults, that means that there are 14 adults. If you add 28 and 14, you are supposed to get 42. Do you? Yes! The correct answer to this difficult algebra question is (C).

Backsolving Drill

You can check your answers in Part VIII: Answer Key to Drills.

1. Two physical therapists have a total of 16 patients to see in one day. Marcie has to see 2 more patients than Lewis. How many patients will Marcie see?

   A. 9
   B. 7
   C. 5
   D. 3

2. Which of the values of m below would make the inequality $3m < 12$ true?

   A. 7
   B. 6
   C. 4
   D. 2

3. If there are 4 times as many women as men employed by the Ace Insurance Company, then how many of the 75 workers are women?

   A. 75
   B. 60
   C. 45
   D. 15

4. If the tax on a $45.00 restaurant check is $4.05, what is the tax rate?

   A. 8%
   B. 9%
   C. 10%
   D. 11%

5. If $2x - 7 = 3$, then $x =$

   A. 2
   B. 3
   C. 4
   D. 5

TRANSLATION

Math itself is a kind of language that can be translated into English. For example, when you see $3 + 4 = 7$, you automatically translate the symbols on the page into English (three plus four equals seven). A small number of Mathematical Reasoning problems will ask you to do the reverse: translate a word problem from English into algebra. These problems are easy to spot, for the answer choices always contain variables. Here's an example:

1. Marjorie makes an investment and doubles her money. If she ends up with $480, which equation below could be used to discover the amount of her original investment of x dollars?

   A. $\dfrac{x}{2} = 480$

   B. $x - 2 = 480$

   C. $x + 2 = 480$

   D. $2x = 480$

To translate a problem from English to math, you need to know what some English terms mean in math. Here are the terms that come up on the GED® test.

GED® Term	What It Means	Example
of	multiply	"$\frac{1}{5}$ of the 30 women" (translated: $\frac{1}{5} \times 30$)
percent	over 100	"40 percent" (translated: $\frac{40}{100}$)
double	times 2	"is double the original amount, x" (translated: $2x$)
triple	times 3	"is triple the original amount, x" (translated: $3x$)
more than	add	"…three more than m" (translated: $m + 3$)
less than	subtract	"…three less than n" (translated: $n - 3$)
is, are	equals	"The number of boys is five more than the number of girls" (translated: $b = g + 5$)

The key to any translation problem is its variable. The variable (x, y, z, or whatever) is always defined for you by the GED® test writers. For example, in the previous problem, the variable represents the original amount of money Marjorie had before the investment. In a translation problem, you have to figure out what to do to this variable to get the final outcome of the problem. Let's look at Marjorie's question again.

Math/English Dictionary
- "is" means "="
- "of" means "×"
- "more than" means "+"
- "less than" means "−"

1. Marjorie makes an investment and doubles her money. If she ends up with $480, which equation below could be used to discover the amount of her original investment of x dollars?

    A. $\frac{x}{2} = 480$

    B. $x - 2 = 480$

    C. $x + 2 = 480$

    D. $2x = 480$

Here's How to Crack It

The gist of the problem is this: Marjorie put her nest egg into an investment that doubled her money.

You need to express this in mathematical terms, and the key, as always, is the variable. In this case, the variable x represents the money Marjorie had *before* she invested. The $480 represents the money she had *after* she invested. Mathematically, what do you have to do to x in order to double it? That's right: $2x$. (If you aren't sure of this or any other translation we talk about in the next couple of problems, just look it up on the chart on the previous page.) And after it was doubled, how much money did she have? That's right: $480. The equation should read:

$$2x = 480$$

The correct answer is (D).

———————○———————

Let's try another one.

———————○———————

2. Sally is three years less than twice the age of her brother Hector. If h represents Hector's age, which expression shows Sally's age?

   A. $h - 3$
   B. $3 - 2h$
   C. $2h - 3$
   D. $3h - 2$

Here's How to Crack It

The variable h represents Hector's age. What can you do to h in order to get Sally's age? Let's translate. She is *three years less than* (which we know from the chart above means "$- 3$") *twice Hector's age* (which we know means "$2h$").

When you see "three years less than," leave some space and put $- 3$ as below.

$$\underline{\qquad} - 3$$

Then fill this space with whatever follows "than": in this case "twice the age of her brother Hector." Since Hector's age is h, "twice" means two times something, this is $2h$. Fill this into the space to get:

$$2h - 3$$

The correct answer is (C).

———————○———————

Sometimes, the GED® test writers will require you to translate information in a word problem into a system of equations. Let's look at an example.

———————○———————

1. A coffee shop sells only large and small lattes. It sells large lattes for $2.50 and small lattes for $1.75. If a group of friends goes into the coffee shop and buys 5 lattes for a total of $10.25, which of the following systems of equations could be used to determine the number of large lattes, L, and the number of small lattes, S, that the group of friends bought.

    A. $L + S = 5$
        $2.50L + 1.75S = 10.25$

    B. $L + S = 5$
        $1.75L + 2.50S = 10.25$

    C. $L + S = 10.25$
        $1.75L + 2.50S = 5$

    D. $L + S = 10.25$
        $2.50L + 1.75S = 5$

Here's How to Crack It

The question tells you that L and S represent the number of large and small lattes bought, respectively. A total of 5 lattes were bought. Total translates to addition, so $L + S = 5$. Eliminate any choice that doesn't include this equation. Eliminate (C) and (D). The total cost is $10.25, so the sum of the cost of the large lattes and the cost of the small lattes is $10.25. Each large latte costs $2.50, so the cost of L large lattes is $2.50L$. Each small latte costs 2.50, so the cost of S large lattes is $1.75S$. Therefore, $2.50S + 1.75S = 10.25$. Eliminate any choice that doesn't include this equation, so eliminate (B). The correct answer is (A).

———————○———————

Translation Drill

You can check your answers in Part VIII: Answer Key to Drills.

1. Sandra weighs 5 pounds more than her younger brother John. If John's weight is represented by x, what is an expression for the *combined* weight of the two children?

   A. $x + 5$
   B. $2(x + 5)$
   C. $2x + 5$
   D. $2(x) + 2(5)$

2. The number of rabbits at a zoo doubled in 2000 and rose to five times the original number by the end of 2001. If the original number of rabbits is represented by m, then how many rabbits did the zoo have by the end of 2001?

   A. $2m$
   B. $5m$
   C. $7m$
   D. $10m$

3. Frank is two years more than three times the age of Sam. If x represents Sam's age, which expression shows Frank's age?

   A. $x + 2$
   B. $2x - 3$
   C. $3x + 2$
   D. $3x - 2$

4. Alexis is playing a game in which blue chips are worth 5 points and red chips are worth 3 points. If Alexis has 9 chips for a total of 21 points and the game has no other color chips, then

A. $B + R = 21$

$5B + 3R = 9$

B. $B + R = 21$

$3B + 5R = 9$

C. $B + R = 9$

$5B + 3R = 21$

D. $B + R = 9$

$3B + 5R = 21$

POLYNOMIALS

A **polynomial** is an expression that has multiple terms. These terms can include combinations of variables, numbers, and exponents. On the GED® test, you may be asked to simplify a polynomial by combining like terms or to rewrite a polynomial by factoring it. We will start with simplifying a polynomial.

$$4a - 2b + 2c + a + 8b - 3c^2 = ?$$

First, identify the terms that share the same variable(s). There are six terms in the above expression; each is separated from the others by a + or a − sign.

$$\boxed{4a} - 2b + 2c + \boxed{a} + 8b - 3c^2$$

The terms $4a$ and a share the same variable, so combine the two to get $5a$.

$$5a - \boxed{2b} + 2c + \boxed{8b} - 3c^2$$

Now let's combine the terms $-2b$ and $8b$ to get $6b$.

$$5a + 6b + 2c - 3c^2$$

The only terms left to combine are $2c$ and $-3c^2$. However, even though both $2c$ and $-3c^2$ have the same variable c, the different exponents mean that these are not like terms, so the two CANNOT be combined. The simplified version of the original polynomial will look like

$$5a + 6b + 2c - 3c^2$$

Here is another example of simplifying a polynomial:

---○---

1. Which expression below is equivalent to $2x^2 + 8y - x + 3y - 13$?

    A. $x^2 + 11y - 13$
    B. $x^2 - 2y$
    C. $2x^3 + 11y - 13$
    D. $2x^2 - x + 11y - 13$

Here's How to Crack It

The first term contains the variable x^2; are there any other terms that also contain an x^2? No. Leave it and move on to the following term, $8y$. There is another term that also contains the y variable, $3y$. Add the two to get the new y term: $11y$.

Looking at the third term, $-x$, are there any other x terms? No. What about the final term, -13? It does not have a variable, so it cannot be combined with any other variable terms. Leave that one as well.

The correct answer is (D).

---○---

Adding and Subtracting Polynomials

Adding and subtracting polynomials simply means combining the like terms.

---○---

2. $(3z^2 - 12z + 7) + (-5z^2 + z + 6) =$

    A. $-2z^2 - 11z + 13$
    B. $8z^2 - 11z + 13$
    C. $-2z^2 - 13z + 13$
    D. $8z^2 - 13z + 13$

Here's How to Crack It

Since the polynomials are being added together, simply ignore the parentheses and rewrite like this: $3z^2 - 12z + 7 - 5z^2 + z + 6$. Remember that adding a negative is the same as subtracting. Now combine like terms. $3z^2 - 5z^2 = -2z^2$. $-12z + z = -11z$. $7 + 6 = 13$. The result is $-2z^2 - 11z + 13$, which is (A).

───────────○───────────

Subtracting polynomials is the same except you have to be careful with the negatives.

───────────○───────────

3. $(-10b^2 + 6b + 2) - (-4b + 1) =$

    A. $-10b^2 + 2b + 1$
    B. $-10b^2 + 10b + 3$
    C. $-10b^2 + 2b + 3$
    D. $-10b^2 + 10b + 1$

Here's How to Crack It

Again rewrite without the parentheses, but this time the negative must be distributed to every term in the second set of parentheses. Remember that two negatives equal a positive. This looks like $-10b^2 + 6b + 2 + 4b - 1$. Now combine like terms to get $-10b^2 + 10b + 1$, which is (D).

───────────○───────────

Multiplying, Factoring, and Dividing Polynomials

Multiplying polynomials relates to the distributive law from Chapter 13. Remember that

$$a(b + c) = ab + bc \text{ and } a(b - c) = ab - ac$$

The same principle applies to polynomials. Consider $(x + 2)(x^2 + 3x - 5)$. The $(x + 2)$ factor distributes to each term of the $(x^2 + 3x - 5)$ factor to get $(x + 2)(x^2) + (x + 2)(3x) - (x + 2)(5)$. Now apply the distributive law again to each of the resulting terms. Distribute (x^2) in $(x + 2)(x^2)$ to get $(x)(x^2) + (2)(x^2) = x^3 + 2x^2$. Distribute $(3x)$ in $(x + 2)(3x)$ to get $(x)(3x) + (2)(3x) = 3x^2 + 6x$. Distribute (5) in $(x + 2)(5)$ to get $(x)(5) + (2)(5) = 5x + 10$. Thus, $(x + 2)(x^2) + (x + 2)(3x) - (x + 2)(5) = (x^3 + 2x^2) + (3x^2 + 6x) - (5x + 10)$. Now the problem becomes one of polynomial addition and subtraction. $(x^3 + 2x^2) + (3x^2 + 6x) - (5x + 10) = x^3 + 2x^2 + 3x^2 + 6x - 5x - 10 = x^3 + 5x^2 + x - 10$. Let's look at an example.

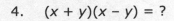

4. $(x + y)(x - y) = $?

    A. $2x - 2y$
    B. $x^2 - y^2$
    C. $x^2 + 2xy + y^2$
    D. $x^2 - 2xy + y^2$

Here's How to Crack It

In the case of multiplying binomials (i.e., polynomials with only two terms), there is a short-cut method. This method is called **FOIL (Firsts, Outers, Inners, Lasts).** Multiply the FIRST term of each factor by each other: $(x)(x) = x^2$. Then multiply the OUTERMOST terms together: $(x)(-y) = -xy$. Next, multiply the INNERMOST terms together: $(y)(x) = xy$. Finally, multiply the LAST terms by each other: $(y)(-y) = -y^2$. Combine the results of these four steps to create the polynomial expression and then simplify: $x^2 - xy + xy - y^2 = x^2 - y^2$.

A polynomial expression can be factored by identifying terms that share factors. For example, let's factor this expression:

$$3x + 15$$

The term $3x$ factors into 3 times x and the term 15 factors into 3 times 5. Do these two terms share a factor? They both can be factored by 3.

$$(3)(x) + (3)(5) =$$
$$3(x + 5)$$

Now let's try a longer polynomial expression:

5. Which of the following is equivalent to the expression $5x - 10 + x^2 - 2x$?

    A. $(5 + x)(x - 2)$
    B. $(5 - x)(x + 2)$
    C. $2(x + 5)$
    D. $5(x^2 - 2)$

Here's How to Crack It

Look at the first two terms, $5x$ and -10. They share the factor 5. The last two terms, x^2 and $-2x$, also share a factor, x. Rewrite these two pairs.

$$5x - 10 + x^2 - 2x =$$
$$(5)(x) - (5)(2) + (x)(x) - (2)(x) =$$
$$5(x - 2) + x(x - 2)$$

Now you see yet another factor appear, $(x - 2)$. Rewrite the expression again.

$$5(x - 2) + x(x - 2) =$$
$$(x - 2)(5 + x)$$

The answer is (A). You can also check your answer by using FOIL to arrive at the original polynomial.

Factoring is the key to dividing polynomials. Look at $\dfrac{x^2 + 5x}{3x + 15}$. Factor x from both terms in the numerator to get $x(x + 5)$, and factor 3 from both terms in the denominator to get $3(x + 5)$. In the resulting fraction, $\dfrac{x(x + 5)}{3(x + 5)}$, cancel $(x + 5)$ to get $\dfrac{x}{3}$.

Now let's look at a more complex example.

---

6. Which of the following expressions is equivalent to

$$\frac{x^2 - 7x - 2x + 14}{x^3 + 2x^2 - 3x - 2x^2 - 4x + 6}?$$

A. $\dfrac{(x + 2)}{(x^2 + 2x + 3)}$

B. $\dfrac{(x - 7)}{(x^2 - 2x + 3)}$

C. $\dfrac{(x - 2)}{(x^2 + 2x - 3)}$

D. $\dfrac{(x - 7)}{(x^2 + 2x - 3)}$

Here's How to Crack It

Start by factoring the numerator. Factor the x from $(x^2 - 7x)$ to get $x(x - 7)$ and -2 from $(-2x + 14)$ to get $-2(x - 7)$, leaving a numerator of $x(x - 7) - 2(x - 7)$. Now factor $(x - 7)$ to get $(x - 2)(x - 7)$. Now factor the denominator. Factor x from $(x^3 + 2x^2 - 3x)$ to get $x(x^2 + 2x - 3)$ and -2 from $-2x^2 - 4x + 6$ to get $-2(x^2 + 2x - 3)$, leaving a denominator of $x(x^2 + 2x - 3) - 2(x^2 + 2x - 3) = (x - 2)(x^2 + 2x - 3)$.

From the resulting fraction, $\dfrac{(x-2)(x-7)}{(x-2)(x^2+2x-3)}$, cancel $(x - 2)$ to get $\dfrac{(x-7)}{(x^2+2x-3)}$. The correct answer is (D).

Remember the Translation lesson from earlier in the chapter? Sometimes the GED® test will include polynomial word problems. The basic rules of translating still apply to polynomials. For example, if a question were to refer to the sum of the cube of x and the square of the difference between x and 3, what would be the result? Remember that *sum* refers to addition. What is added? The first term is *the cube of x*. Since *cube* refers to raising a number to the third power, the first term is x^3. The second term is the *square of the difference between x and 3*. Break this term into pieces. The *difference between x and 3* is $(x - 3)$. The word *square* refers to raising an expression to the second power so the second term is $(x - 3)^2$. Therefore, the entire expression is $x^3 + (x - 3)^2$. Let's look at another example.

---

7. When an object is stationary and begins to move at a constant acceleration, the square of the velocity is twice the product of the acceleration and the distance traveled. If an object travels at a constant acceleration of 10 m/s² for 45 m, what is its velocity, in meters per second?

    A. 30
    B. 90
    C. 450
    D. 900

Here's How to Crack It

First translate the statement: *the square of the velocity is twice the product of the acceleration and the distance traveled.* Let the velocity be represented by v, the acceleration be represented by a, and the distance be represented by d. Translate this one piece at a time. First, *the square of the velocity* translates to v^2. The word *is* translates to =. The word *twice* translates to 2 times whatever follows. What follows is *the product of the acceleration and the distance traveled*. Since *product* translates to multiplication, this translates to $a \times d$. *Twice* this is $2ad$. Therefore, the statement translates to $v^2 = 2ad$. The question states that $a = 10$ and $d = 45$, so plug in these values to get $v^2 = 2(10)(45)$, so $v^2 = 900$. Take the square root of both sides to get $v = 30$. The correct answer is (A).

Polynomial Drill

You can check your answers in Part VIII: Answer Key to Drills.

1. What is the sum of $5x + 2y + x - 3y$?

    A. $6x - y$
    B. $6x + y$
    C. $5x^2 - 6y^2$
    D. $4x - y$

2. Which of the following is a factor of
    $x^2 - 4x + 3x - 12$?

    A. $(x + 4)$
    B. $(x - 4)$
    C. $(x - 3)$
    D. $(x - 2)$

3. Which of the following is equivalent to

    $$\frac{1}{4}x^2 + \frac{2}{4}x - \frac{2}{3}x - \frac{4}{3}?$$

    A. $\left(\frac{1}{4}x + \frac{2}{3}\right)(x + 2)$

    B. $\left(\frac{1}{4}x - \frac{2}{3}\right)(x + 2)$

    C. $\left(\frac{1}{4}x + \frac{2}{3}\right)(x - 2)$

    D. $\left(\frac{1}{4}x - \frac{2}{3}\right)(x - 2)$

4. Which of the following is equivalent to
    $(x^2 + 2x + 8)(x - 4)$?

    A. $x^2 + 2x + 32$
    B. $x^2 + 3x + 4$
    C. $x^3 - 2x^2 - 32$
    D. $x^3 + 6x^2 + 16x + 32$

5. In a certain card game, a deck has cards with integers labeled 1 through 10, and each player has two cards. A player's score is determined by taking the sum of the squares of the numbers on the two cards. If the numbers on Jennifer's two cards have a product of 24 and a sum of 11, what is her score?

    A. 52
    B. 73
    C. 148
    D. Cannot be determined

QUADRATIC EQUATIONS

A quadratic expression is a polynomial in which the highest exponent is 2. Some quadratic equations are fairly simple. For example, look at this equation:

$$x^2 = 36$$

This question can be solved by using the inspection method. The inspection method simply involves taking the square root of both sides. The square root of x^2 is x and the square root of 36 is 6. However, the answer is not as simple as $x = 6$. It is true that $6^2 = 36$, so $x = 6$ is *one of* the solutions to the equation. However, remember the lesson on multiplying negatives. The product of two negatives is positive. Therefore, $(-6)^2 = (-6)(-6) = +36$, so $x = -6$ is also a solution to this equation. Quadratic equations will often have two solutions. When an equation is in the form $x^2 = a$, the inspection method will yield the solutions $x = \pm\sqrt{a}$.

However, other quadratic equations will be more difficult to solve: in particular, ones that have not only an x^2 but also an x term. We already discussed this type of quadratic (although not by name) in the polynomial multiplication lesson. These expressions are often the result of using the FOIL method. Let's look at an example.

---

1. Which of the following is equal to $x^2 + 6x + 8$?

    A. $(x + 2)(x + 1)$
    B. $(x - 3)(x + 4)$
    C. $(x + 1)(x - 3)$
    D. $(x + 4)(x + 2)$

Here's How to Crack It

You now know how to FOIL, so you can use the answer choices and FOIL each one to see which one gets the expression that is given. To save some time, though, notice that the number by itself must be 8. The number by itself is represented in the LAST step of FOIL. By multiplying just the LAST numbers in the parentheses, you can see that the LAST term in (A) is going to be 2, in (B) is –12, in (C) is –3, and in (D) is 8. Since (D) is the only one that is 8, it must be the correct answer. If you use FOIL on (D), you multiply the FIRST terms (x and x) to get x^2, multiply the OUTSIDE terms (x and 2) to get $2x$, multiply the INSIDE terms (4 and x) to get $4x$, and multiply the LAST terms (4 and 2) to get 8. The result is $x^2 + 2x + 4x + 8 = x^2 + 6x + 8$.

Factoring

Another way to get the answer to the previous question is by factoring. Factoring is the opposite of using FOIL. It takes a quadratic like the ones you've just seen, and puts it into the two sets of parentheses. Let's take a look at $x^2 + 6x + 8$ again. To factor it, draw two sets of parentheses:

$$(\quad)(\quad)$$

The first two terms will usually be x and x. You might sometimes have a number before one or both of them, but in this case there isn't a number before the x^2 so they are both just x.

$$(x \quad)(x \quad)$$

Now you need to figure out what the numbers are. The term without a variable in this quadratic is 8. When you FOIL, you get this number by multiplying the "last" terms in the parentheses, so the two numbers in this case must multiply together to equal 8. Think about what has a product of 8: 1 × 8 or 2 × 4. As you saw before, you find the second term in the quadratic, the x, with the "outside" and "inside" terms that are added together after being multiplied. So the two numbers must add or subtract to equal 6 since that is the number before the x in the second term of this quadratic. The numbers 1 and 8 cannot add or subtract to equal 6, but 2 and 4 can if they are added. Thus the parentheses look like this:

$$(x + 2)(x + 4)$$

You can and should always use FOIL to check that your factors multiply together to equal what you started with.

Let's try an example that involves negatives.

$$x^2 - 4x - 12$$

Start with the parentheses and x in each one:

$$(x \quad)(x \quad)$$

Now list the factors of 12: 1 × 12, 2 × 6, and 3 × 4. Ask yourself which one could add or subtract to equal −4. Keep in mind that since they multiply to equal −12, one will be positive and one will be negative because two positives or two negatives multiply together to equal a positive. The only two that could add or subtract to equal −4 are 2 and 6.

$$(x \quad 2)(x \quad 6)$$

Now determine which is positive and which is negative. If it is +6 and −2, the sum will be positive 4. It needs to be −4, so that will be −6 and +2. The quadratic factored is as follows:

$$(x + 2)(x - 6)$$

One type of question you may see involves an equation, not just an expression like the previous examples. You may have to factor a quadratic and also solve for x. Using the same example, the problem might look like this:

---

2. Consider this equation: $x^2 - 4x - 12 = 0$

What is the positive solution in the equation above?

☐

Here's How to Crack It

Finding the solution to an equation that looks like this always requires factoring first. We've already done this above and determined that it was $(x + 2)(x - 6) = 0$. Don't forget to write the "= 0" part at the end. Notice now that we have two binomials multiplied together that equal 0. How could this equal 0? Well, a product equals 0 if either of the two factors equals 0, so if the first or the second binomial equaled 0, the whole thing would equal 0. Set the first binomial equal to 0: $x + 2 = 0$. Now subtract 2 from both sides to get $x = -2$. This is one solution. Now set the second binomial equal to 0: $x - 6 = 0$. Add 6 to both sides to get $x = 6$. The two solutions are $x = -2$ and $x = 6$. It is common for quadratic equations to have two solutions as this one does. In this case, the question asks for the positive solution, so you enter 6. You may also see a multiple-choice question that asks for both solutions or it may even ask for something like the sum or the product of the solutions. Regardless, the method is the same.

Note: If the equation doesn't equal 0 but does involve an x^2 term and an x term like the polynomials we've seen in this section, be sure to subtract everything from the right side so it equals 0 if you use the factor method.

Completing the Square

There are other methods that can be used to solve a quadratic. One is called completing the square. Consider this quadratic equation:

$$x^2 - 6x + 9 = 0$$

Using the factor method, you need to find a pair of numbers with a sum of −6 and a product of 9. These are −3 and −3, so the equation factors to $(x - 3)(x - 3) = 0$. Notice that the two factors are the same, so this equation can be rewritten as $(x - 3)^2 = 0$. This looks similar to an equation that can be solved using the inspection method. Take the square root of both sides to get $x - 3 = 0$. (Remember that ±0 is the same as 0.) Add three to both sides to get $x = 3$. Now, consider instead this equation:

$$x^2 - 6x + 9 = 4$$

Again, you can factor the left side to get $(x - 3)^2 = 4$. Take the square root of both sides to get $x - 3 = \pm 2$. Consider both $x - 3 = 2$ and $x - 3 = -2$. In $x - 3 = 2$, add three to both sides to get $x = 5$. In $x - 3 = -2$, add three to both sides to get $x = 1$. Therefore the two solutions are $x = 1$ and $x = 5$.

This method can be used only when one side of the equation factors into a perfect square. A quadratic expression in the form $x^2 + bx + c$ is a perfect square if $c = \left(\dfrac{b}{2}\right)^2$. (In the case above, $b = -6$, so $\dfrac{b}{2} = \dfrac{-6}{2} = -3$ and $\left(\dfrac{b}{2}\right)^2 = \left(-3\right)^2 = 9 = c$.) But what if an equation doesn't have a perfect square? Let's look at an example.

---

3. If $x^2 + 4x - 8 = 13$, what are the possible values of x?

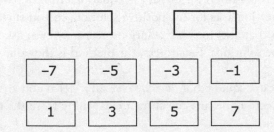

Here's How to Crack It

On the left side of the equation, the coefficient on the x term is 4. $\left(\frac{4}{2}\right)^2 = 4$, so this is not a perfect square. However, you can manipulate the equation to get a perfect square. Add 12 to both sides, you get $x^2 + 4x + 4 = 25$. Now, the left side is a perfect square. Factor the left side to get $(x + 2)^2 = 25$. Take the square root of both sides to get $x + 2 = \pm 5$. If $x + 2 = 5$, subtract two from both sides to get $x = 3$. If $x + 2 = -5$, subtract two from both sides to get $x = -7$. The correct answers are 3 and –7.

Quadratic Formula

On other equations, it will be more difficult to factor or complete the equation. For example,

$$3x^2 + 9x - 10 = 0$$

There is no simple way to solve this equation for x by find factors or by completing the square. However, there is a fall back plan for quadratics that will work no matter how easy or difficult the equation is. This fall back plan is called the *quadratic formula*. For an equation in the form $ax^2 + bx + c = 0$, $x = \dfrac{-b \pm \sqrt{b^2 - 4ac}}{2a}$. In the case above, $a = 3$, $b = 9$, and $c = -10$, so

$$x = \frac{-9 \pm \sqrt{9^2 - 4(3)(-10)}}{2(3)} = \frac{-9 \pm \sqrt{201}}{6}.$$

Let's look at another example.

---○---

4. Solve the equation for x.

$$2x^2 - 5x = 4$$

A. $x = 8$ and $x = -1$

B. $x = -8$ and $x = 1$

C. $x = \dfrac{5 \pm \sqrt{57}}{2}$

D. $x = \dfrac{5 \pm \sqrt{57}}{4}$

Here's How to Crack It

Use the answer choices as a hint that this may be difficult to factor. Use the quadratic equation:

$x = \dfrac{-b \pm \sqrt{b^2 - 4ac}}{2a}$. However, to use this, the equation must be in the form $ax^2 + bx + c = 0$.

Subtract four from both sides to get $2x^2 - 5x - 4 = 0$, so $a = 2$, $b = -5$ and $c = -4$. Thus,

$x = \dfrac{-(-5) \pm \sqrt{(-5)^2 - 4(2)(-4)}}{2(2)} = \dfrac{5 \pm \sqrt{57}}{4}$. The correct answer is (D).

---○---

Quadratic Equations Drill

You can check your answers in Part VIII: Answer Key to Drills.

1. Which of the following are the solutions to the equation $x^2 - 7x + 12 = 0$?

    A. $x = 3$ and $x = 4$
    B. $x = 6$ and $x = 2$
    C. $x = -6$ and $x = -2$
    D. $x = -3$ and $x = -4$

2. Which of the following equations has the same solutions as $x^2 - 10x + 16 = 0$?

    A. $(x - 5)^2 = 4$
    B. $(x - 5)^2 = 9$
    C. $(x + 5)^2 = 9$
    D. $(x + 5)^2 = 4$

3. Which of the following are the solutions to the equation $x^2 - 8x + 5 = 0$?

    A. $x = \dfrac{-8 \pm \sqrt{44}}{2}$

    B. $x = \dfrac{-8 \pm \sqrt{84}}{2}$

    C. $x = \dfrac{8 \pm \sqrt{84}}{2}$

    D. $x = \dfrac{8 \pm \sqrt{44}}{2}$

RATIONAL EXPRESSIONS

Rational expressions are fractions made up of polynomials. Because a rational expression is just a type of fraction, the same rules for adding, subtracting, multiplying, and diving fractions still apply.

Addition and Subtraction

Remember adding and subtraction fractions from Chapter 13? There were two methods: Bowtie and common denominator. When you're working with polynomials rather than numbers, the Bowtie may be too cumbersome of a method. However, common denominator works well. Let's look at an example:

---

1. Which of the following is equivalent to $\dfrac{x-2}{x} + \dfrac{2x+3}{2}$?

    A. $\dfrac{2x^2 + 5x - 4}{2x}$

    B. $\dfrac{2x^2 + x - 6}{2x}$

    C. $\dfrac{2x^2 - 6}{x + 2}$

    D. $\dfrac{3x - 5}{x + 2}$

Here's How to Crack It

Find the common denominator for the two fractions. The denominators are x and 2. Since these don't have any common factors, the common denominator is the product $2x$. Multiply the first fraction by $\dfrac{2}{2}$ and multiply the second by $\dfrac{x}{x}$. For the first fraction, $\dfrac{x-2}{x} \times \dfrac{2}{2} = \dfrac{2(x-2)}{2x} = \dfrac{2x-4}{2x}$.

For the second, $\dfrac{2x+3}{2} \times \dfrac{x}{x} = \dfrac{x(2x+3)}{2x} = \dfrac{2x^2 + 3x}{2x}$. Since the denominators are now the same, add the numerators to get $\dfrac{(2x-4) + (2x^2 + 3x)}{2x}$. Combine like terms in the numerator to get $\dfrac{2x^2 + 5x - 4}{2x}$. The correct answer is (A).

In the case above, the least common denominator is simply the product of the two denominators. That won't always be the case.

---

2. Which of the following is equivalent to

$$\frac{3x}{x^2-4} - \frac{5x^2+3x}{x^2-4x+4} ?$$

A. $\dfrac{-5x^2}{4x-8}$

B. $\dfrac{-2x^2-3x}{x^2-4x+4}$

C. $\dfrac{5x^3+11x^2}{x^3-2x^2-4x+8}$

D. $\dfrac{-5x^3-10x^2-12x}{x^3-2x^2-4x+8}$

Here's How to Crack It

The denominators are factorable polynomials, so it's possible that they have common factors. In the first fraction, $(x^2 - 4)$ factors to $(x - 2)(x + 2)$. In the second fraction, $(x^2 - 4x + 4)$ factors to $(x - 2)^2$. Since both denominators have a factor of $(x - 2)$, it is only necessary to multiply the first fraction by $\dfrac{x-2}{x-2}$ and the second by $\dfrac{x+2}{x+2}$.

In the first fraction $\dfrac{3x}{x^2-4} \times \dfrac{x-2}{x-2} = \dfrac{3x(x-2)}{(x^2-4)(x-2)} = \dfrac{3x^2-6x}{x^3-2x^2-4x+8}$. In the second,

$\dfrac{5x^2+3x}{x^2-4x+4} \times \dfrac{x+2}{x+2} = \dfrac{(5x^2+3x)(x+2)}{(x^2-4x+4)(x+2)} = \dfrac{5x^3+13x^2+6x}{x^3-2x^2-4x+8}$. Now that the denominators are

the same, subtract the numerators to get $\dfrac{(3x^2-6x)-(5x^3+13x^2+6x)}{x^3-2x^2-4x+8} = \dfrac{-5x^3-10x^2-12x}{x^3-2x^2-4x+8}$.

The correct answer is (D).

Multiplication and Division

Once again, the rules for multiplying and dividing rational expressions are the same as those for multiplying and dividing fractions. When multiplying rational expressions, there is no need to worry about a common denominator. Just line them up and multiply straight across.

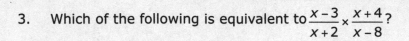

3. Which of the following is equivalent to $\dfrac{x-3}{x+2} \times \dfrac{x+4}{x-8}$?

A. $\dfrac{2x+1}{2x-6}$

B. $\dfrac{x^2-11x+24}{x^2+8x+8}$

C. $\dfrac{x^2+x-12}{x^2-6x-16}$

D. $\dfrac{x^2+7x+12}{x^2-6x-16}$

Here's How to Crack It

Multiply straight across: Multiply the numerator of the first fraction by the numerator of the second and multiply the denominator of the first fraction by the denominator of the second. For the numerators, $(x-3)(x+4) = x^2 + x - 12$. For the denominators, $(x+2)(x-8) = x^2 - 6x - 16$. Therefore the product of the fractions is $\dfrac{x^2+x-12}{x^2-6x-16}$. The correct answer is (C).

For dividing rational expressions, invert the second fraction and multiply.

4. Which of the following is equivalent to

$$\frac{x^2 - 6x + 9}{2x^2 + 10x - 48} \div \frac{x^2 - 7x + 12}{x^2 - 8x}?$$

A. $\dfrac{x}{2x - 4}$

B. $\dfrac{x}{2x - 8}$

C. $\dfrac{x - 4}{2x}$

D. $\dfrac{x^2 - 3x}{2x - 8}$

Here's How to Crack It

Since you're dividing fractions, flip the second and multiply to get $\dfrac{x^2 - 6x + 9}{2x^2 + 10x - 48} \times \dfrac{x^2 + 8x}{x^2 - 7x + 12}$.

This looks painful to multiply, but remember that you can reduce fractions by common factors when you multiply. You can do the same for rational expressions. Factor each polynomial.

For the numerator of the first fraction, $x^2 - 6x + 9$ factors to $(x - 3)^2$. For the denominator of the first fraction, first notice that 2 is a common factor of all three terms. Therefore, you can factor a 2 to get $2(x^2 + 5x - 24)$. Factor the polynomial inside the parentheses to get $2(x - 3)(x + 8)$. For the numerator of the second fraction, $x^2 + 8x$ factors to $x(x + 8)$. For the denominator of the second fraction, $x^2 - 7x + 12$ factors to $(x - 4)(x - 3)$. Therefore the product

becomes $\dfrac{(x-3)^2}{2(x-3)(x+8)} \times \dfrac{x(x+8)}{(x-4)(x-3)}$. Now reduce the fractions. The first fraction can be reduced by $(x - 3)$ to get $\dfrac{(x-3)}{2(x+8)} \times \dfrac{x(x+8)}{(x-4)(x-3)}$.

Remember that before you multiply, you can reduce fractions diagonally. Therefore, you can cancel a factor of $(x - 3)$ and a factor of $(x + 8)$ to get $\dfrac{1}{2} \times \dfrac{x}{(x-4)}$. Multiply straight across to get $\dfrac{x}{2(x-4)} = \dfrac{x}{2x-8}$. The correct answer is (B).

Rational Expressions Drill

You can check your answers in Part VIII: Answer Key to Drills.

1. Which of the following is equivalent to

$$\frac{3}{x^2 - 2x - 8} - \frac{2}{x - 4}?$$

   A. $\dfrac{1}{x^2 - 3x + 4}$

   B. $\dfrac{5}{x^2 - x - 12}$

   C. $\dfrac{-2x - 1}{x^2 - 2x - 8}$

   D. $\dfrac{2x + 7}{x^2 - 2x - 8}$

2. Which of the following is equivalent to

$$\frac{3x - 9}{x^2 - 6x + 9} \div \frac{x^2 + 8x + 15}{x^2 - 9}?$$

   A. $\dfrac{3}{x + 5}$

   B. $\dfrac{1}{x - 3}$

   C. $\dfrac{3x + 15}{x^2 - 6x + 9}$

   D. $\dfrac{3x^3 + 81}{x^4 - 48x^2 + 135}$

SIMULTANEOUS EQUATIONS

Solving a simple one-variable equation like $3x - 10 = 11$ can be done with the method described above. However, what if you were given the equation $3x - 10 = y$ and were asked to come up with a specific value for x? This would be impossible. Different values for y will result in different values for x. However, what if you were also given a second equation like $4x - 17 = y$? Although neither equation on its own can determine a value for x, the two of them together can, using a method called the substitution method. Since both equations are isolated for y, set

$$3x - 10 = 4x - 17$$

Subtract $3x$ from both sides to get

$$-10 = x - 17$$

Add 17 to both sides to get

$$7 = x$$

Need the value of y? Just substitute $x = 7$ into one of the above equations to get

$$y = 4(7) - 17 = 28 - 17 = 7$$

Look at an example.

———————◯———————

1. If $3x + 6y = 30$ and $2x + 5y = 26$, choose two numbers below that are possible values of x and y.

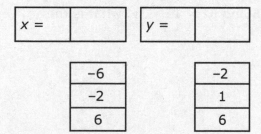

Here's How to Crack It

There are two equations and two variables. Isolate one of the variables in one of the equations. Take $3x + 6y = 30$ and isolate x. Subtract $6y$ from both sides to get $3x = 30 - 6y$. Divide both sides by 3 to get $x = 10 - 2y$. Now you have an expression for x. Substitute this expression for x into the other equation. $2x + 5y = 26$ becomes $2(10 - 2y) + 5y = 26$. Distribute 2 to get $20 - 4y + 5y = 26$. Combine like terms to get $20 + y = 26$. Subtract 20 from both sides to get $y = 6$. Now, to get x, substitute this value of y into one of the equations. Try the second one. $2x + 5y = 26$

becomes $2x + 5(6) = 26$ and $2x + 30 = 26$. Subtract 30 from both sides to get $2x = -4$. Divide both sides by 2 to get $x = -2$. Therefore, select -2 for x and 6 for y.

There is another method for solving this type of problem, called the linear combination method. Let's use the equations from the previous question. Stack the two equations as below.

$$3x + 6y = 30$$
$$2x + 5y = 26$$

To do this method, the first thing you want to do is make sure the coefficients on one of the variables are the same in both equations. In this case, you can multiply the first equation by 2 and the second equation by 3 to get

$$6x + 12y = 60$$
$$6x + 15y = 78$$

Now, the coefficients on the x variable are the same. Next, subtract the two equations by subtracting the lined up terms to get

$$6x + 12y = 60$$
$$\underline{-(6x + 15y = 78)}$$
$$-3y = -18$$

Divide both sides by -3 to get $y = 6$. To get the value of x, substitute this value into one the original equations to get $x = -2$, just as before.

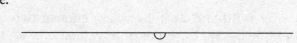

Try another example.

---

2. If $4x - 3y = 15$ and $5x = 12 - 3y$, what is the value of x?

    A. -3

    B. -1

    C. 1

    D. 3

Here's How to Crack It

To solve this using the linear combinations method, first get both equations in the same form. To do this, add $3y$ to both sides of the second equation to get $5x + 3y = 12$. Now line up the two equations to get

$$4x - 3y = 15$$
$$5x + 3y = 12$$

Notice that the coefficients on the y's are negation of each other. In this case, you can just add the two equations to get

$$
\begin{aligned}
4x - 3y &= 15 \\
+(5x + 3y &= 12) \\
\hline
9x &= 27
\end{aligned}
$$

Divide both sides by 9 to get $x = 3$. The correct answer is (D).

Simultaneous Equations Drill

You can check your answers in Part VIII: Answer Key to Drills.

1. If $x = 2y + 5$ and $x = 3y - 6$, what is the value of x?

    A.   11
    B.   22
    C.   27
    D.   33

2. If $3x + 4y = -5$ and $-2x - 5y = 8$, what is the value of y?

    A.   −2
    B.   1
    C.   3
    D.   7

3. At a certain fruit stand, apples cost 25 cents and bananas cost 30 cents. If Bill buys a total 8 apples and bananas for $2.15, how many bananas did Bill buy?

    A.   3
    B.   4
    C.   5
    D.   6

FUNCTIONS

Sometimes the GED® test will ask you about relations. A relation is a relationship between two variables: an input variable called the domain and an output variable called the range. The relations that the GED® test will be most interested in are called functions. Functions are relations in which each member of the domain corresponds to a unique member of the range. Look at the two relations below.

x	y
0	3
2	7
6	5
2	1

x	y
2	4
0	1
7	4
3	8

Are these relations functions? When a relation in is table notation, the domain is the variable on the left, in this case x, and the range is the variable on the right, in this case y. For the relation on the left, a member of the domain, 2, goes to two different members of the range, 7 and 1. Therefore, this is not a function. However, in the relation on the right, each member of the domain corresponds with only one member of the range, so this is a function. Does it matter that 2 and 7 from the domain correspond with 4 from the range? No. Each member of the domain has to correspond with a unique member of the range, but each member of the range need not correspond with a unique member of the domain.

Relations can also be put into graphical form.

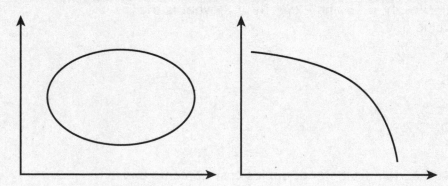

In the graphical form of a relation, the horizontal axis represents the domain and the vertical axis represents the range. (You'll see more about graphic functions in the next chapter.) Are these two relations functions? To determine this, use what is called the vertical line test. Since, in a function, every member of the domain corresponds with a unique member of the range, any vertical line drawn on the graph will hit the curve at only one point. If any vertical line touches the curve at more than one point, the relation is not a function. For the graph on the left, multiple vertical lines can be drawn that will touch the curve at more than one point. Therefore, this is not a function. However, for the graph on the right, any vertical line drawn will touch the curve at only one point. Therefore, this relation is a function. This can be seen in the following graphs.

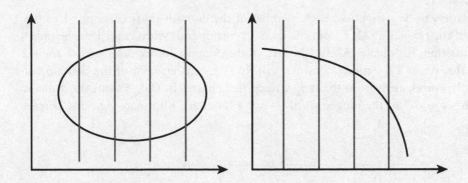

Sometimes the GED® test writers will test your ability to determine whether a relation is a function. Let's look at an example.

1.   Which of the relations below represents a function?

A.

x	y
1	2
5	6
3	2
1	1

B.

x	y
−1	6
4	1
2	4
4	−3

C.

x	y
−2	−4
3	−3
8	−3
5	−5

D.

x	y
3	−2
−5	3
2	−4
2	7

Here's How to Crack It

In order for a relation to be a function, each member of the domain must correspond with a unique member of the range. In (A), 1 from the domain corresponds with 2 and 1 in the range, so this is not a function. Eliminate (A). In (B), 4 from the domain corresponds with 1 and −3 in the range, so this is not a function. Eliminate (B). In (C), each element of the domain corresponds with only one element from the range. Keep this choice. In (D), 2 from the domain corresponds with −4 and 7 in the range, so this is not a function. Eliminate (D). The correct answer is (C).

Now let's look at a graphical example.

---

2. Which of the following graphs does NOT represent a function?

A.

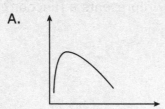

B.

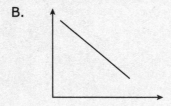

C.

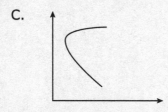

D.

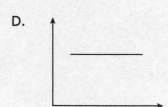

Here's How to Crack It

Since the question is asking whether graphs represent functions, use the vertical line test. In (A), no vertical line can be drawn that will touch the curve more than once. This represents a function. In (B), no vertical line can be drawn that will touch the curve more than once. This represents a function. In (C), several vertical lines can be drawn that will touch the curve more than once. This does not represent a function. In (D), no vertical line can be drawn that will touch the curve more than once. This represents a function. The only graph that does not represent a function is (C), so the correct answer is (C).

Another way to represent a function is using function notation. This is commonly $f(x)$, though a function could be represented with any letter other than f, as well. $f(x)$ can be stated as "f of x," "the function of x," or "f as a function of x." For example, look at the function $f(x) = x^2 + 5x$. If you were asked for the value of $f(3)$, plug the number inside the parentheses, 3 in this case, in for each appearance of x is the definition of the function. So $f(3) = 3^2 + 5 \times 3 = 9 + 15 = 24$. If you need $f(4)$, do the same thing. $f(4) = 4^2 + 5 \times 4 = 16 + 20 = 36$. Let's look at an example.

---

x	$g(x)$
1	2
2	6
3	10
4	14

3. Which of the following functions could represent the function described in the table above?

    A. $g(x) = 2x$

    B. $g(x) = 3x - 1$

    C. $g(x) = 4x - 2$

    D. $g(x) = 2x + 4$

Here's How to Crack It

For a question like this, use POE extensively. Start with the first row of the table, which says that $g(1) = 2$. Go through the answer choices and eliminate any choice for which $g(1)$ does not equal 2. In (A), $g(1) = 2 \times 1 = 2$, so keep this choice. In (B), $g(1) = 3 \times 1 - 1 = 2$, so keep this choice. In (C), $g(1) = 4 \times 1 - 2 = 2$, so keep this choice. In (D), $g(1) = 2 \times 1 + 4 = 8$, so eliminate this choice. Now look at the next row, which says that $g(2) = 6$, and go through the answer choices, eliminating any choice for which $g(2)$ does not equal 6. In (A), $g(2) = 2 \times 2 = 4$, so eliminate this choice. In (B), $g(2) = 3 \times 2 - 1 = 5$, so eliminate this choice. In (C), $g(2) = 4 \times 2 - 2 = 6$, so keep this choice, which is the only remaining choice. The correct answer is (C).

Some GED® questions will combine functions with translating. Let's look at an example.

---

4. A certain fruit stand sells only bananas. The fruit stand earns a profit of five dollars less than 3 dollars for each banana it sells. Which of the following is a function representing the stand's profits, p, as a function of the number of bananas sold, b?

    A. $p(b) = 5b - 3$
    B. $p(b) = -2b$
    C. $p(b) = 5 - 3b$
    D. $p(b) = 3b - 5$

Here's How to Crack It

Translate the information in the question into an equation. The profit is p as a function of b, which is written as $p(b)$. The profit is equal to "five dollars less than 3 dollars for each banana it sells." When you see "five dollars less than," leave some space and write _____ $- 5$. Then fill that space with whatever follows "than": in this case "3 dollars for each banana it sells." Since this translates to $3b$, the function becomes $p(b) = 3b - 5$. The correct answer is (D).

Functions Drill

You can check your answers in Part VIII: Answer Key to Drills.

x	$h(x)$
3	−1
5	4
3	y
−2	−6

1. For which of the following values of y does $h(x)$ represent a function?

   A. −6

   B. −1

   C. 3

   D. 4

2. If $g(x) = x^2 − 6x + 9$, which of the following is equal to $g(5)$?

   A. 2

   B. 4

   C. 5

   D. 9

3. Which of the following represents the statement, "The function of x is three times 4 more than the square of x"?

   A. $f(x) = 3(x^2 + 4)$

   B. $f(x) = 3x^2 + 4$

   C. $f(x) = 3(x + 4)^2$

   D. $f(x) = [3(x − 4)]^2$

PUTTING IT ALL TOGETHER

Now that you've seen all the elements of algebra separately, we'd like you to try a drill in which they are all mixed together. This will give you practice in recognizing the different types of problems so that you can zero in on exactly which technique you need to solve them quickly. Pay particular attention to spotting Backsolving questions, which our students find takes a bit of practice.

Algebra Drill

You can check your answers in Part VIII: Answer Key to Drills.

1. If $5x + 9 = 44$, then $x =$

    A. 12
    B. 10
    C. 7
    D. 6

2. Laura has $4 more than three times the amount of money Steven has. If x represents the amount of money Steven has, which expression shows how much money Laura has?

    A. $3x + 4$
    B. $3x - 4$
    C. $4x + 3$
    D. $x + 4(3)$

3. Evaluate $5x^2 - 4y$, if $x = 3$ and $y = 4$.

4. The Oakdale Preschool accepts 4-year-olds and 5-year-olds and has a total of 63 students. If the school has 7 more 4-year-olds than 5-year-olds, then how many of the children are 4 years old?

    A. 14
    B. 28
    C. 35
    D. 42

5. If $3m + 7 < 28$, then which of the following expressions gives all the possible values of m?

    A. $m < 9$
    B. $m < 7$
    C. $m > -5$
    D. $m > -7$

6. What is the sum of $2(x + y) + 3x + 2y$?

    A. $5x + 3y$
    B. $6x + 3y$
    C. $6x + 4y$
    D. $5x + 4y$

7. If $p = 4$, which of the following inequalities contains the number p?

    A. $x < 4$
    B. $x > 5$
    C. $2x < 3$
    D. $x < 5$

8. If 36 of the 120 workers in a factory work overtime, what percentage of the workers work overtime?

    A. 10%
    B. 20%
    C. 30%
    D. 40%

9. Multiply.

$$(4x - 8)(x + 2)$$

A. $4x^2 - 16$
B. $-4x + 2$
C. $4x^2 + 16x - 16$
D. $5x - 6$

10. Tony is 4 years older than Heather, and Heather is 5 years younger than Larry. If the sum of their ages is 69, how old is Tony?

A. 18
B. 20
C. 24
D. 25

11. If $3x + 2 = -2y$ and $-x + 3y = -14$, what is the value of y ?

A. -4
B. -2
C. 2
D. 4

x	$f(x)$
-2	
1	3
	19

12. If the table above represents the function $f(x) = 2x^2 + 1$, select possible values to complete the table.

| 5 | | 17 |

| -3 | | 19 |

| 9 | | -1 |

13. If $\dfrac{-2x+8}{x^2-3x-10} \times \dfrac{x^2-x-20}{x^2-16} = x+5$, which of following is a possible value of x ?

A. -4
B. -2
C. 3
D. 5

Chapter 16
Geometry

In this chapter, we'll cover all the geometry you need to know for the Mathematical Reasoning test—including lines and angles, triangles, rectangles, circles, volume, and graphing.

The good news is that the geometry on the GED® test covers only a fraction of what is covered in high school. Even if you never took geometry, you can learn everything you need to get the GED® geometry questions right just by reading this chapter and doing the exercises that follow.

Measuring Diagrams

One reason GED® geometry isn't too tough is that the diagrams are always roughly drawn to scale. As we showed you in our introduction to the Mathematical Reasoning test, this means that anytime there's a diagram, you always have a wonderful, concrete way to ballpark the problem. As we cover each of the geometry topics in this chapter, we'll show you how to measure the different types of diagrams.

What If There Is No Diagram?

If a geometry problem doesn't come with a diagram, then you should immediately draw your own. Believe us, it's a lot tougher to solve a geometric problem if you can't see it. Take a few seconds to sketch the information provided for you in the question, and if possible, try to draw your figure to scale so you'll have some idea of which answer choices are out of the ballpark.

Geometry Diagrams

If there's a diagram, use your eyes to estimate what the answer ought to be. If there's no diagram, draw one yourself.

The Formula List

On each GED® Mathematical Reasoning question, there is a clickable button to a list of many of the mathematical formulas you may need during the test. Here you will find the volume of a cube, the surface area of a pyramid, and the Pythagorean Theorem (don't worry if you don't know what that is yet).

You need to know the formulas for area and perimeter before taking the test—they will not be provided to you! You will be much more confident if you walk into the test room with these formulas already memorized and even more confident if you have practiced using the formulas on our two practice tests and the drills in this chapter.

Everything You Need to Know About GED® Geometry

Here are the topics that are tested on the Mathematical Reasoning test:

- Lines and angles
- Rectangles and squares
- Triangles and pyramids
- Circles and spheres
- Cones and cylinders
- Perimeter and area
- Surface area and volume
- Setup geometry
- Graphing points and functions
- Slope and the *y*-intercept

As in the previous chapters, we'll first cover a concept, then give you examples of how this concept is used on the GED® test, and then give you a short drill. At the end of the chapter, there will be a larger drill that covers all the geometry topics together.

LINES AND ANGLES

Here is a line:

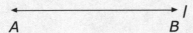

This particular line is labeled *l*, and like all lines, it extends forever to the left and to the right. *A* and *B* are points on the line, and the distance between them, *AB*, is called line segment *AB*.

How many degrees does a line contain? If the second hand on the face of a watch moves from 12 all the way around to 12 again, it has gone 360 degrees. A straight line drawn on the face of that watch from 12 straight down to 6 cuts the face of the watch in half: All straight lines create an angle of 180 degrees.

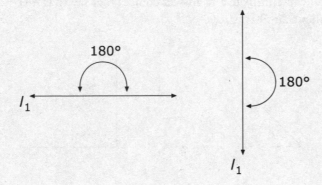

If that line is cut by another line, it divides that 180 degrees into two angles whose measures together add up to 180 degrees.

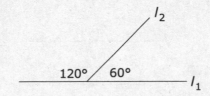

Perpendicular Lines

If the two lines cut across each other in such a way that they form two angles of 90 degrees each, then the two lines are called **perpendicular.** A 90-degree angle is also known as a **right angle.** On GED® diagrams, this is sometimes indicated by a little box drawn into the corner of the angles.

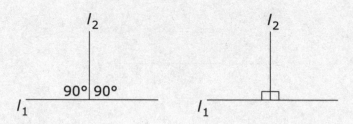

Using a Right Angle as a Measuring Tool

Whenever you see any angle on the Mathematical Reasoning test, it helps to compare it in your mind to a 90-degree angle. Take angle A below. Is it bigger or smaller than the 90-degree angle? If it's bigger, then you can eliminate any answer choices that say that A is less than 90. If it is smaller, then you can eliminate any answer choices that say that A is more than 90. In this case, angle A is smaller than 90 degrees.

Parallel Lines

If two lines are drawn so that they could extend into infinity without ever meeting, these lines are considered **parallel.** The two lines below are an example of parallel lines.

Lines and Angles Drill

You can check your answers in Part VIII: Answer Key to Drills.

Determine the value of angle *x* in each of the diagrams below.

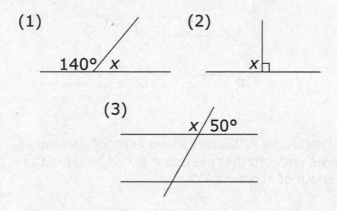

(1)   140° / x   (2)   x

(3)   x / 50°

RECTANGLES AND SQUARES

A rectangle is a four-sided object whose four interior angles are each equal to 90 degrees.

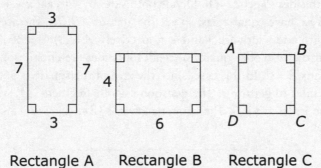

Rectangle A   Rectangle B   Rectangle C

The area of a rectangle is found by multiplying its length by its width. The area of rectangle A is 7 × 3, or 21. The area of rectangle B is 4 × 6, or 24.

The lengths of the opposite sides of a rectangle are always equal to each other. For example, in rectangle C, side *AB* is equal to side *DC*, and side *AD* is equal to side *BC*. To find the perimeter of a rectangle, you simply add the four sides together. The perimeter of rectangle A is 20. The perimeter of rectangle B is also 20.

A square is a rectangle whose four sides all happen to equal one another. The area of a square can still be found by multiplying length by width, but because the length and width in a square are the *same*, you can also say that the area of a square equals side squared.

Let's look at an example:

Square Rectangle Quiz

Q: Is a rectangle always a square, or is a square always a rectangle?

Turn the page for the answer.

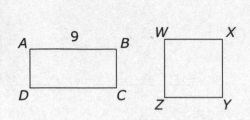

1. If rectangle *ABCD* has a perimeter of 26 and an area equal to that of square *WXYZ*, what is the length of segment $\overline{XY}$?

    A.   4
    B.   6
    C.   13
    D.   36

Here's How to Crack It

Since opposite sides in a rectangle are equal, side $\overline{DC}$ is also 9. Sides $\overline{AD}$ and $\overline{BC}$ are still unknown, but they must be equal, so call them *x*. Since the perimeter is the sum of the sides and the perimeter of *ABCD* is 26, then $9 + 9 + x + x = 26$. Simplify the left side to get $18 + 2x = 26$. Subtract 18 from both sides to get $2x = 8$. Divide both sides by 2 to get $x = 4$. The question says that *ABCD* and *WXYZ* have equal areas, so get the area of *ABCD*. The area of a rectangle is $A = lw$. Since the length and width are 9 and 4, respectively, $A = (9)(4) = 36$. Thus, *WXYZ* also has an area of 36. In the case of a square, since all four sides are equal, use the simplified version of $A = lw$, which is $A = s^2$. In this case, since the area of the square is 36, $36 = s^2$. Take the square root of both sides to get $6 = s$. The question asks for segment $\overline{XY}$, which is one of the sides of the square, so its length is 6. The correct answer is (B).

While area is always a two-dimensional measurement of flat objects on a page, volume is a three-dimensional measurement. Imagine a square metal lunch box. The volume of the box would represent how much space there is inside.

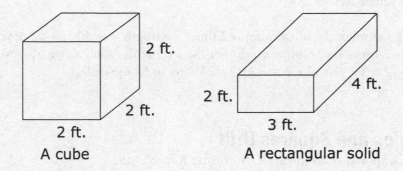

A cube

A rectangular solid

For rectangular solid objects, it is always easy to find the volume.

The formula for the volume of a cube is very simple. If you remember, the area of a square is side squared. The volume of a cube is side cubed. For the cube shown above, the volume would be 2^3, or 8 cubic feet.

The formula for the volume of a rectangular solid is also simple. It is length × width × depth. For the rectangular solid shown above, the volume would be $2 \times 3 \times 4$, or 24 cubic feet.

Here's how this might look on the Mathematical Reasoning test:

2. If Judy wants to fill a rectangular pool with water, approximately how many cubic feet of water will she need if the pool's dimensions are 10 feet wide by 12 feet long by 5 feet deep?

    A. 1,200
    B. 600
    C. 300
    D. 150

Here's How to Crack It
The key words in this problem are *volume* and *rectangular*. As soon as you see these words, you should know just what to do. The volume of a rectangular solid is length × width × depth. In this case, that means $12 \times 10 \times 5 = 600$. The correct answer is (B).

Rectangular solids and cubes also have surface area (SA), which is the combined areas of all of the two-dimensional sides combined. You could calculate the areas of each of the six sides, and then add all six together, or you could use the formulas for surface areas of each solid. For a cube, the formula is SA = 6 times the side squared. For the cube above, the surface area is 6×2^2, or 24 square feet.

For a rectangular solid, the surface area is 2 times the length × width, plus 2 times the length × depth, plus 2 times the width × depth. For the rectangular solid above, that would give us $(2 \times 2 \times 3) + (2 \times 3 \times 4) + (2 \times 2 \times 4) = 12 + 24 + 16$, or 52 square feet.

Rectangles and Squares Drill

You can check your answers in Part VIII: Answer Key to Drills.

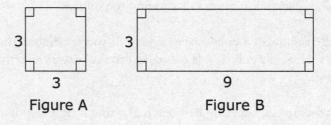

Figure A   Figure B

Answer the following questions based on the two figures above.

1. Identify Figure A.

2. Identify Figure B.

3. What is the area of Figure A?

4. What is the perimeter of Figure B?

5. How many Figure As would fit inside Figure B?

Square Rectangle Quiz

A: A square is always a rectangle. But a rectangle doesn't have to be a square.

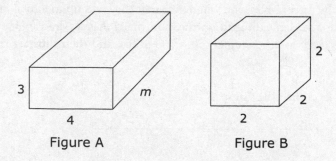

Figure A   Figure B

Answer the following questions based on the two figures above.

6. If the volume of figure A is 60 cubic feet, then what is the length of segment *m*?

7. Figure B is a tank in the shape of a cube. If this tank is to be filled halfway to capacity, how many cubic units will be in the tank?

8. Chen plans to wallpaper a rectangular room with the dimensions 10 feet by 12 feet by 9 feet high. If there are no windows, and only one door measuring 2 feet by 7 feet, and she does not wallpaper the ceiling or floor, approximately how much will it cost to wallpaper the room?

    A. $395
    B. $400
    C. $412
    D. Not enough information is given.

TRIANGLES AND PYRAMIDS

A **triangle** is a geometric figure with three sides. The three angles inside a triangle always add up to 180 degrees, no matter how the triangle is drawn.

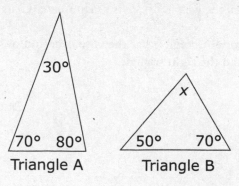

Triangle A   Triangle B

In triangle A, if you add up the three angles, you will notice that they add up to a total of 180 degrees. In triangle B, in order for the same thing to be true, how many degrees does angle *x* have to be? To find this out, add up the two other angles (50 + 70 = 120), and then subtract this from 180 (180 − 120 = 60).

Let's see how this would look on the GED® test.

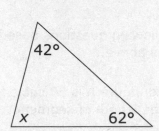

1. In the figure above, the triangle has three internal angles. One angle measures 42 degrees. Another angle measures 62 degrees. How many degrees does the third angle measure?

   A. 104 degrees
   B. 76 degrees
   C. 52 degrees
   D. Not enough information is given.

Here's How to Crack It

The three interior angles of *every* triangle have a total of 180 degrees. If the GED® test writers give you two out of the three angles, then you can find the third. Add up the two angles whose values you know (42 + 62 = 104). Now, just subtract the sum of the two angles from 180 (180 − 104 = 76). The correct answer to this question is (B).

Could you have *ballparked*? Of course. Look at the missing angle in the figure. Is it greater than or less than 90 degrees? Obviously it's a bit less, so we can eliminate (A). Now, compare it with the 62-degree angle directly across from it. Is it larger or smaller than 62 degrees? Come to think of it, it's still a little bit larger, isn't it. This lets us eliminate (C) as well.

The test writers have certain favorite triangles that they use over and over again on the tests. These are the **isosceles** triangle and the **right** triangle.

The Isosceles Triangle

There are two important things to know about an isosceles triangle: First, it has two equal sides; second, the angles opposite those sides turn out to be equal as well.

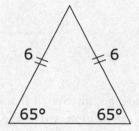

Generally, the test writers will tell you one of these two important things and then ask you to supply the other. Here's an example:

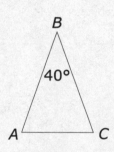

1. In the triangle above, if *AB* = *BC*, then what is the measure, in degrees, of angle *A*?

Here's How to Crack It

If side *AB* equals side *BC*, then the two angles opposite those sides (angles *A* and *C*) must be equal to each other as well. Although the problem doesn't mention it, this is in fact an isosceles triangle because of its two equal sides. First, find out the value of angle *A* plus angle *C*. The entire triangle has 180 degrees in it. If you subtract angle *B* (40 degrees) from the entire triangle, that leaves 140 degrees. Now, remember that angle *A* and angle *C* are equal to each other. How do you get the value of angle *A* alone? Divide by 2. The correct answer to this question is 70 degrees.

The Right Triangle

A right triangle contains one angle that equals 90 degrees.

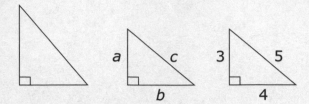

Pythagoras, a Greek mathematician, discovered that the sides of a right triangle always have a particular relationship, which can be expressed by the formula $a^2 + b^2 = c^2$, in which a and b are the two shorter sides of the triangle, and c is the longest side opposite the 90-degree angle. This longest side is called the **hypotenuse**.

The most common right triangle on the Mathematical Reasoning test is a triangle whose sides are in a ratio of 3-4-5 (shown above). Let's see if Pythagoras knew what he was talking about, by trying out his theorem with the 3-4-5 triangle. According to the formula, $3^2 + 4^2$ should equal 5^2. Does it? Yes! 9 + 16 does equal 25. The Pythagorean formula is provided on the Mathematical Reasoning test along with all the other formulas, and you may need it for other right triangles. But you won't need it for the writers' favorite, the 3-4-5 triangle, since that one you can just remember. Here's a sample problem:

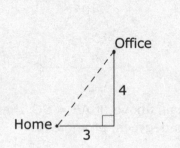

1.   To get to her office, Susan must drive due east for 3 miles and then due north for 4 miles, as shown in the figure above. If she could drive directly from her home to her office, how many miles would that route be if Susan traveled in a straight line?

     A.   2 miles
     B.   3 miles
     C.   5 miles
     D.   6 miles

Here's How to Crack It

The shortcut from her office to her home forms the hypotenuse of a right triangle, as the diagram shows. One side of the triangle is 3; the other side is 4. Do you need to plug these numbers into the Pythagorean Theorem? Not if you memorized the 3-4-5 triangle. The correct answer to this question is (C).

The Perimeter of a Triangle

The perimeter is the distance around the outside edge of any two-dimensional object. The perimeter of a triangle is the sum of the lengths of the three sides. What was the perimeter of the triangle in that last problem? 3 + 4 + 5 = 12.

The Area of a Triangle

The formula for the area of a triangle is

$$\frac{1}{2} (\text{base} \times \text{height}) \text{ or } \frac{(\text{base} \times \text{height})}{2}$$

where the base equals the length of the bottom side of the triangle, and the height equals the length of a perpendicular line from the base of the triangle to the triangle's highest point.

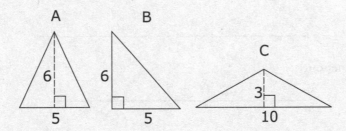

- In triangle A, the base equals 5, and the height equals 6, so the area is $\frac{1}{2}(5 \times 6)$, or 15.

- In triangle B, the base and height again equal 5 and 6, and the area of the triangle is again 15. However, note that because this is a right triangle, the height in this case is also the side of the triangle.

- In triangle C, the base equals 10, and the height equals 3, so the area is $\frac{1}{2}(10 \times 3)$, or 15.

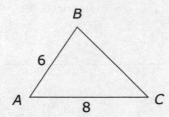

1. What is the area of the triangle above?

    A. 7
    B. 24
    C. 48
    D. Not enough information is given.

Here's How to Crack It

To find the area of a triangle, you need the base and the height. In this triangle, you know the base (8) but not the height. The number 6 is simply the length of one of the other sides of this triangle and would have been the height only if this were a right triangle with angle *A* equal to 90 degrees. Therefore, the correct answer to this question is (D), Not enough information is given.

Let's look at another one.

2. If a triangle has an area of 24 and a height of 8,
    what is the length of the base?

    A. 1.5
    B. 3
    C. 6
    D. 12

Here's How to Crack It

The question gives the area of a triangle. The formula for area of a triangle is $A = \frac{1}{2}bh$. The question states that the area is 24 and the height is 8, so plug these into the formula to get $24 = \frac{1}{2}b(8)$. Simplify the right side (by multiplying $\frac{1}{2} \times 8$) to get $24 = 4b$. Divide both sides by 4 to get $b = 6$. The correct answer is (C).

Pyramids

A **pyramid** is a three-dimensional shape made of triangular sides that sit atop a two-dimensional base. On the GED® test, this base will typically be a rectangle, so there will be four triangular sides.

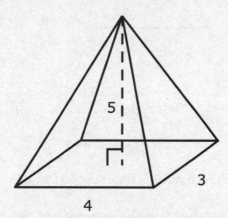

To find the volume of a pyramid, you must first find the area of the rectangular base, B, and the height, h, from the base to the top of the pyramid. The volume is the amount of space *inside* the shape.

$$V = \frac{1}{3}Bh$$

In the above example, the volume would be

$$V = \frac{1}{3}(3 \times 4)(5) = 20.$$

The area of the base, B, is $3 \times 4 = 12$. After that point, simply plug in values for the variables in the equation.

To find the surface area *(SA)*, you will need the perimeter, *p*, of the base, and the slant height, *s*, of a side of the pyramid. The surface area essentially adds up the areas of each side of the pyramid, including the base, *B*.

$$SA = \frac{1}{2}ps + B$$

Again, let's try this formula out with an example:

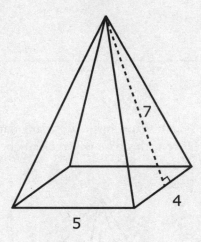

$$SA = \frac{1}{2}(18)(7) + (4 \times 5)$$

$$SA = 63 + 20 = 83$$

The perimeter, *p*, of the base in the above example can be found by adding $4 + 5 + 4 + 5 = 18$.

Don't worry about memorizing these formulas—they will be provided to you on the formulas page when you take the GED® test. Just familiarize yourself with them so that you know how to use them.

Triangles and Pyramids Drill

You can check your answers in Part VIII: Answer Key to Drills.

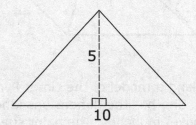

1. Michael is constructing a triangular garden as shown above. If the base of the garden is 10 feet long and the perpendicular distance from the base to the endpoint of the garden is 5 feet, then what is the area of the garden?

    A. 50
    B. 25
    C. 15
    D. Not enough information is given.

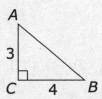

2. The distance from point *A* to point *B* is how much longer than the distance from point *A* to point *C*?

3. If a triangle has interior angles of 27 degrees and 53 degrees, then what is the measurement, in degrees, of the third angle?

    A. 26
    B. 80
    C. 100
    D. 154

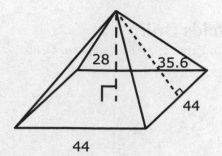

28   35.6

44

44

4. Sara is making a model of the Great Pyramid for math class. She has the dimensions labeled on the drawing above, in inches. The paint she plans to use on the outside of the model says that 1 can will cover 1,296 square inches. How many cans will Sara need to paint all the surfaces of her model pyramid?

    A.   1
    B.   2
    C.   3
    D.   4

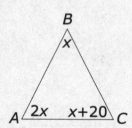

B

x

A $2x$ $x+20$ C

5. In triangle ABC above, the measures of the angles are shown in terms of x. What is the measure, in degrees, of angle A?

    A.   40 degrees
    B.   45 degrees
    C.   70 degrees
    D.   80 degrees

6. A pyramid with a square base has a volume of 320 and a height of 15. What is the perimeter of the base?

    A.   8
    B.   16
    C.   32
    D.   64

OTHER POLYGONS

A polygon is a closed figure made up of line segments. Squares, rectangles, and triangles are all examples of polygons. Although those are the most common types of polygons on the GED® test, other polygons will also appear on the test. Pentagons (five-sided polygons), hexagons (six-sided polygons), heptagons (seven-sided polygons), octagons (eight-sided polygons), and other polygons can appear of the GED® test. A **regular polygon** is one in which the measures of all sides are equal and the measures of all angles are equal. Squares and equilateral triangles are examples of regular polygons.

One concept tested on other polygons is perimeter. Luckily, determining perimeter on less common polygons is not very different from determining perimeter on the more common ones. Either way, the perimeter is just the sum of the sides. Let's look at an example.

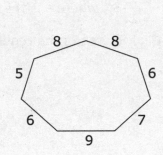

1. What is the perimeter of the polygon above?

Here's How to Crack It
To find the perimeter, add the length of each of the sides. In this case, the perimeter is 8 + 8 + 6 + 7 + 9 + 6 + 5 = 49. The correct answer is 49.

Other times they will ask you to find the area. Anytime this is done, they will provide you with the area formula.

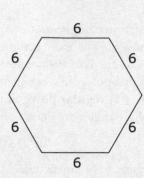

2. The area of a regular hexagon can be found with the formula $A = \dfrac{3\sqrt{3}}{2}s^2$, where s is the length of the side. What is the area of the regular hexagon shown above?

A. $18\sqrt{3}$

B. $27\sqrt{3}$

C. $54\sqrt{3}$

D. $108\sqrt{3}$

Here's How to Crack It

The question gives a formula for the volume in terms of the side of the hexagon. The figure gives you that the side is 6, so plug this in for s to get $A = \dfrac{3\sqrt{3}}{2}(6)^2 = \dfrac{3\sqrt{3}}{2}(36) = \dfrac{108\sqrt{3}}{2} = 54\sqrt{3}$.

The correct answer is (C).

Other Polygons Drill

You can check your answers in Part VIII: Answer Key to Drills.

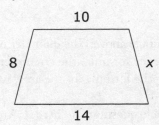

1. The figure above has a perimeter of 40. What is the value of *x* ?

   A. 4
   B. 8
   C. 16
   D. 72

2. A regular octagon has a perimeter of 56. If the area of a regular octagon can be found using the formula $A = 2\left(1 + \sqrt{2}\right)s^2$, where *s* is the side of the octagon, what is the area of the octagon?

   A. $49 + 49\sqrt{2}$
   B. $98 + 49\sqrt{2}$
   C. $49 + 98\sqrt{2}$
   D. $98 + 98\sqrt{2}$

CIRCLES, SPHERES, CYLINDERS, AND CONES

The distance from the center of a circle to any point on the circle is called the **radius.** The distance from one side of a circle through the center of the circle to the other side is called the **diameter.** The diameter of a circle is always equal to twice the radius. In the circle below, the radius is equal to 3, so the diameter is 2 × 3, or 6.

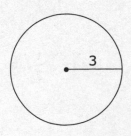

The **circumference** of a circle is the distance all the way around the outside edge of the circle. In other words, circumference is the name for a circle's perimeter. The formula for the circumference of a circle is πd, where d is the diameter of the circle, and π is a number with the approximate value of 3.14. A long time ago, mathematicians discovered that this number, when multiplied by the diameter, gave the value for a circle's circumference. The area of a circle is given by the formula πr^2.

What is the circumference of the circle above? The diameter of this circle is twice the radius, or 6. Therefore, using the circumference formula, the circumference of this circle is 6π. What is the area of the circle above? Using the formula for the area, we get $\pi 3^2$, or 9π.

One concept that is helpful on circle questions is CArd. CArd stands for Circumference, Area, radius, and diameter. If you know of one these, you can determine the other three. Look at the table below. In each row, there is one piece of the CArd puzzle. Fill in the other three.

Circumference	Area	radius	diameter
πd	πr^2	$\dfrac{d}{2}$	$2r$

C	A	r	d
		4	
	25π		
12π			
			18
		1	
π			

In the first row, $r = 4$. Therefore, $d = 2r = 8$, $C = \pi d = 8\pi$, and $A = \pi r^2 = 16\pi$.

In the second row, $A = 25\pi$. Since $A = \pi r^2$, $r = 5$, $d = 2r = 10$, and $C = \pi d = 10\pi$.

In the third row, $C = 12\pi$. Since $C = \pi d$, $d = 12$, $r = \dfrac{d}{2} = 6$, and $A = \pi r^2 = 36\pi$.

In the fourth row, $d = 18$. Therefore, $C = \pi d = 18\pi$, $r = \dfrac{d}{2} = 9$, and $A = \pi r^2 = 81\pi$.

In the fifth row, $r = 1$, so $d = 2r = 2$, $C = \pi d = 2\pi$, and $A = \pi r^2 = \pi$. (Remember that $1^2 = 1$ and

$1\pi = \pi$.)

In the last row, $C = \pi$. Since $C = \pi d$, $d = 1$, $r = \dfrac{d}{2} = \dfrac{1}{2}$, and $A = \pi r^2 = \pi\left(\dfrac{1}{2}\right)^2 = \dfrac{1}{4}\pi = \dfrac{\pi}{4}$.

With more practice, you'll be able to fill out CArd nearly instantaneously. Therefore, it can be a good habit to fill it out as routine anytime you're given one piece of CArd. You won't always need all four pieces. However, it will often take longer to figure which pieces you need than it will take you to figure out all four pieces. CArd can actually be a time-saver in the long run!

Spheres

Many objects, such as basketballs and baseballs, are spherical.

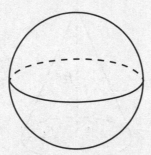

A **sphere** has a radius, r, and a diameter just like a circle. To find the volume of a sphere, use this formula (which is also provided on the formula page when you take the GED® test):

$$V = \frac{4}{3}\pi r^3$$

To find the surface area of a sphere, use

$$SA = 4\pi r^2$$

You need only the radius in order to find both the volume and the surface area.

Cylinders

A cylinder is essentially a circle with depth. Take a look at the following figure:

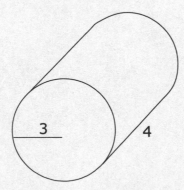

To find the volume of any cylinder, you must multiply the area of the circle at one end of the cylinder by its height. The formula for the area of a circle is πr^2. So the volume of a cylinder is $\pi r^2 h$. Thus, the volume of the cylinder in the figure above is $\pi 3^2(4)$, or 36π.

The surface area of a cylinder can be found by taking $2\pi rh + 2\pi r^2$. In the example above, the surface area would be 42π.

Again, all of these equations are provided to you on the formulas page when you take the test.

Cones

A **cone** has a circular base that has a radius, r. The height, h, is measured from the center of the circle to the tip of the cone.

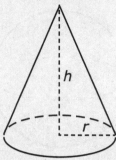

The volume of a cone can be found by taking

$$V = \frac{1}{3}\pi r^2 h$$

And the formula for surface area looks like

$$SA = \pi rs + \pi r^2$$

where s is the slant height, or the length from the outer edge of the base to the tip of the cone.

Circles, Spheres, Cylinders, and Cones Drill

You can check your answers in Part VIII: Answer Key to Drills.

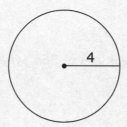

Using the figure above, answer the following questions.

1. What is the radius of this circle?

2. What is the diameter?

3. What is the circumference of this circle?

4. What is the area of this circle?

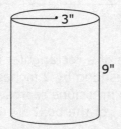

Figure C

5. The cylindrical box in Figure C is 9 inches tall. If the radius of the cylinder is 3 inches, what is the maximum volume that can fit in the box?

6. The diameter of a rubber ball is 4 inches. What is the total surface area of the ball?

    A. 16π
    B. 64π
    C. 128π
    D. 144π

7. If a cone has a volume of 100π and a circular base with an area of 25π, what is its height?

   A. 4
   B. 8
   C. 12
   D. 24

8. A sphere has a volume of 36π, what is the length of the diameter?

   A. 3
   B. 6
   C. 9
   D. 12

SETUP GEOMETRY

A few GED® problems will ask you to set up a geometry problem but then not solve it. Just like the setup problems we saw in the "Applied Arithmetic" chapter—which tested the same arithmetic concepts as all the other arithmetic problems—setup geometry tests the same concepts as regular geometry. Here's an example of a setup problem:

1. The dimensions of a rectangular box are 3 inches wide by 4 inches long by 2 inches deep. Which of the following expressions represents the volume (in cubic inches) of the box?

   A. 3(2)(4)
   B. 3 + 2 + 4
   C. 3(2) + 4
   D. 3(4) + 2

Here's How to Crack It

Essentially, this is almost exactly the same problem you just saw before. The key words again are *volume* and *rectangular*. The only real difference is that this time the question does not ask you to find the volume, but to set up the work involved in finding the volume.

As we said in the "Applied Arithmetic" chapter, take your time with these problems. It's easy to pick an answer choice that is almost (but not quite) right. You need to multiply length by width by depth. In this problem, that means $4 \times 3 \times 2$. The correct answer is (A).

GRAPHING

Graphing is a way of representing a point in two dimensions on what is known as a Cartesian grid or coordinate plane. This may sound intimidating, but it's actually pretty simple. Here's a Cartesian grid:

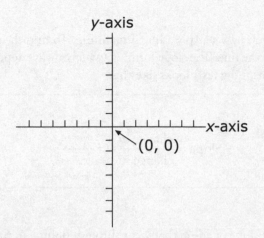

Graphing is a way of assigning points to this grid. Both the *x*-axis and the *y*-axis are number lines (as we discussed in Chapter 13) with positive and negative sides. These number lines cross at their zeros. Every point has two numbers assigned to it: an *x*-coordinate and a *y*-coordinate. Let's take the point *A* (3, 1). The first number is considered the *x*-coordinate. The second number is the *y*-coordinate. To plot this point on the graph, we start at (0, 0) and count over three to the right (the positive side) on the *x*-axis, and then count one up (the positive side of the *y*-axis). To find point *B* (5, 4), we count over five places to the right on the *x*-axis and then up four places.

Try plotting these two points on the graph above. Then, check your work by looking at the graph below.

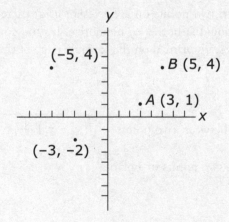

If the first number in an (*x*, *y*) point (in other words, the *x*-coordinate) is negative, then to graph this point, you count to the *left* along the *x*-axis. If the second number in an (*x*, *y*) point (in other words, the *y*-coordinate) is negative, then you count downward. Look at the graph above and see how points (–5, 4) and (–3, –2) were plotted.

GED® questions about graphing are fairly rare. There are three types of GED® graphing questions: questions in which you graph a point on the coordinate plane, questions about the slope of a line, and questions about the distance between two points.

Slope

The slope of a line tells you how sharply a line is inclining. To find the slope, you need to know two points anywhere on the line. The slope formula (which always appears on the formula page of the Mathematical Reasoning test) looks like this:

$$\textbf{Slope} = \frac{\text{change in } y}{\text{change in } x} = \frac{y_2 - y_1}{x_2 - x_1}$$

For example, to find the slope of a line that went through points (5, 6) and (3, 2), all you have to do is subtract one y-coordinate from the other (the result of this subtraction becomes your numerator—also sometimes known as the **rise**) and subtract one x-coordinate from the other (the result of this subtraction becomes your denominator—also known as the **run**):

$$\frac{6-2}{5-3} = \frac{4}{2} = 2$$

Therefore, the slope of the line that goes through points (5, 6) and (3, 2) is 2.

Distance

To find the distance between two points on a Cartesian grid, there is a long formula that we think is *one* equation you shouldn't bother to memorize. It's too complicated, it comes up too rarely on the test, and besides, it's printed on the formula page of the test.

Just for practice, here it is:

$$\text{Distance between two points} = \sqrt{\left(x_2 - x_1\right)^2 + \left(y_2 - y_1\right)^2}$$

where (x_1, y_1) and (x_2, y_2) are two points in a plane.

Let's find the distance between points (1, 2) and (5, 6). What we have to do is carefully plug these numbers into that long equation. Here's what it should look like:

$$= \sqrt{(5-1)^2 + (6-2)^2}$$
$$= \sqrt{4^2 + 4^2}$$
$$= \sqrt{32}$$

You can see why this doesn't come up often.

When You're Given a Graph

Most of the graphing problems on the Mathematical Reasoning test concerning slope or distance will actually give you a graph to look at. This can be very helpful in Ballparking your answers. Take a look at the following question:

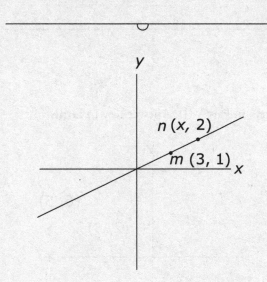

1. In the graph shown above, what is the

    x-coordinate of point n if the slope of the line

    mn is $\frac{1}{3}$?

    A.   9
    B.   6
    C.   3
    D.   2

Here's How to Crack It

First, let's get an idea of which answer choices are out of the ballpark. We are looking for the x-coordinate of point *n*. Well, before we start using complicated formulas, let's do a little measuring. The x-coordinate for point *m* is 3. This means that the horizontal distance from 0 to *m* is 3. Mark off this distance on your scratch paper. Now, try measuring the horizontal distance between 0 and point *n*. Did you get about 6? That's what we got. Because these figures are drawn only roughly to scale, we can't guarantee that the answer is going to be exactly 6, but it ought to be close to 6 anyway. So which answer choices can we get rid of? Choices (A), (C), and (D) are all out of the ballpark. The only possible answer this time is (B).

If you needed to get this one the traditional way, you would have to use the slope formula backward.

$$\text{Slope} = \frac{\text{change in } y}{\text{change in } x} \qquad \frac{1}{3} = \frac{2-1}{x-3}$$

The correct answer is (B).

Graphing Drill

You can check your answers in Part VIII: Answer Key to Drills.

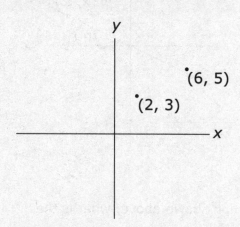

1. A line passes through the points (6, 5) and (2, 3). What is the slope of this line?

    A. $-\dfrac{1}{5}$

    B. $\dfrac{1}{4}$

    C. $\dfrac{1}{2}$

    D. 3

2. What is the distance between points (5, 0) and (12, 0) on the coordinate plane?

   A.   12
   B.   9
   C.   7
   D.   4

3. On the graph below, plot the following points: Point *A* (−3, −4), Point *B* (2, 3), and Point *C* (3, 5).

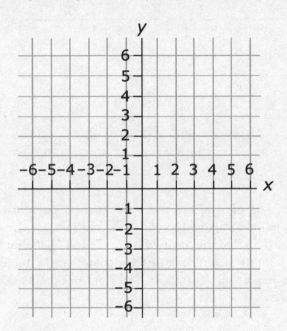

EQUATION OF A LINE

Sometimes the GED® test writers will give you an equation with two variables and ask you to graph a line representing the equation. The key is to get the equation into **slope-intercept** form

$$y = mx + b$$

in which *m* represents the slope and *b* represents the *y*-intercept. The *y*-intercept is the *y*-coordinate of the point on the line that crosses the *y*-axis and has an *x*-coordinate of 0.

If you need to sketch a graph of the equation $y = 2x + 3$, start out with the y-intercept, 3. Since the y-intercept is 3, the graph includes the point (0, 3). Plot this on the graph as below.

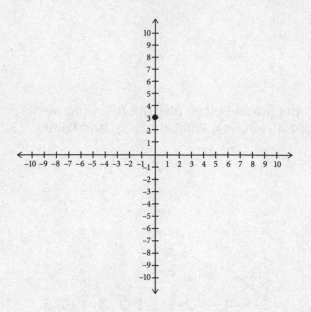

The slope is 2, so the y-coordinate increases by 2 as the x-coordinate increases by 1. Use this to plot additional points. Start with point (0, 3) and increase the x-coordinate by 1 and y-coordinate by 2 to get (1, 5). Do this again to get (2, 7) and (3, 9). Similarly, you can go backward. Go back to the point (0, 3) and decrease the x-coordinate by 1 and the y-coordinate by 2 to get (–1, 1) and again to get (–2, –1) and (–3, –3). Plot these points as well.

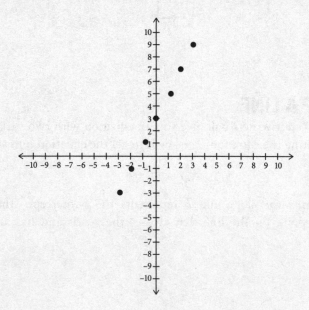

Finally, draw a line that goes through all these points as below.

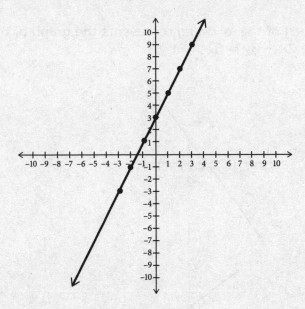

This line is a graphical representation of the equation. Try another one.

1. Which of the following represents the graph of the line $2x + 3y = 6$?

A.

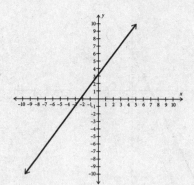

B.

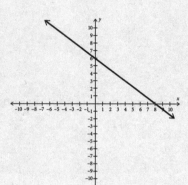

C.

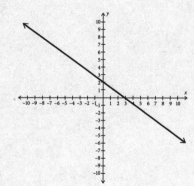

D.

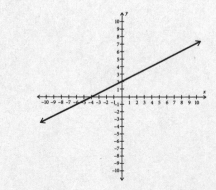

Here's How to Crack It

First, get the equation into $y = mx + b$ form. Take the given equation, $2x + 3y = 6$ and isolate y. First subtract $2x$ from both sides to get $3y = -2x + 6$. Now divide both sides by 3 to get $y = -\frac{2}{3}x + 2$. This equation has y-intercept 2, so eliminate (B). The equation also has a negative slope, meaning that the graph has to decrease as it goes from left to right. Eliminate (D). Now, since the slope is $-\frac{2}{3}$, the y-coordinate has to decrease by 3 as the x-coordinate increases by 2. Eliminate (A). The correct answer is (C).

Now try another one.

1. If $3x + 6y = 30$ and $2x + 5y = 26$, choose two numbers below that are possible values of x and y.

$x =$			$y =$	

x
−6
−2
6

y
−2
1
6

Here's How to Crack It

If this problem looks familiar, it's because you solved it in the previous chapter. Last chapter, you solved it using the linear combination method. This time, you'll solve it graphically. Graph one equation at a time. Start with $3x + 6y = 30$. Get this into slope-intercept form. Subtract $3x$ from both sides; then divide both sides by 6 to get $y = -\frac{1}{2}x + 5$. This graph has a y-intercept of 5 and a slope of $-\frac{1}{2}$. Graph this as follows.

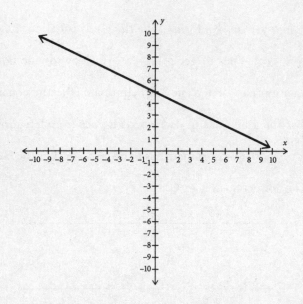

Now sketch the graph of the other line in the same axes. Take $2x + 5y = 26$, subtract $2x$ from both sides, and then divide both sides by 5 to get $y = -\dfrac{2}{5}x + \dfrac{26}{5}$. Therefore, this graph has a slope of $-\dfrac{2}{5}$ and a y-intercept of $\dfrac{26}{5} = 5.2$. Graph this to get the following:

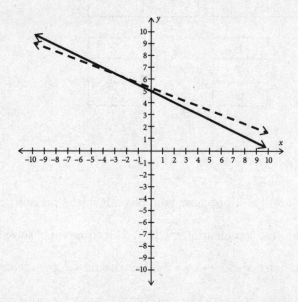

Look to see where the lines intersect. This appears to be at the point $(-2, 6)$. Therefore, $x = -2$ and $y = 6$.

Some GED® questions will ask you to determine the equation of a line. You know the slope-intercept form of a line equation, $y = mx + b$. Therefore, if given the slope and the y-intercept, you can plug the slope in form m and the y-intercept for b and get the equation of a line. For example, suppose you were told that a line had a slope of 3 and contained the point (0, –2). You're given slope, so you can plug this value in for m and get $y = 3x + b$. But what about the y-intercept? Since the y-intercept is the point on the line for which the x-coordinate is 0, the y-intercept of this line must be –2. Therefore, the equation of this line would have to be $y = 3x - 2$. What if they gave you the slope and a point other than the y-intercept? Let's look at an example below.

1. What is the equation of a line that goes through the point (1, 3) and has a slope of –2?

    A. $y = 5x - 2$
    B. $y = -2x + 3$
    C. $y = -2x + 5$
    D. $y = 3x + 2$

Here's How to Crack It

The equation of any line can be put into the form $y = mx + b$, with slope m and y-intercept b. Since the question tells you that the slope is –2, plug this in for m to get $y = -2x + b$. Therefore, you can eliminate (A) and (D), because they have the wrong slope. But what about the y-intercept? You don't have the y-intercept, but you do have a point on the line, (1, 3). This means that you have one pair of values for x and y. Plug these into the equation to get $3 = -2(1) + b$. Now, solve this equation for b. Multiply on the right side to get $3 = -2 + b$. Now, add 2 to both sides to get $5 = b$. Now, plug this into the original equation to get $y = -2x + 5$. The correct answer is (C).

Let's look at another one.

2. What is the equation of the line that goes through the points (−2, 5) and (8, 0)?

   A. $y = -\dfrac{1}{2}x + 4$

   B. $y = -\dfrac{1}{2}x + 8$

   C. $y = -2x + 4$

   D. $y = -2x + 8$

Here's How to Crack It

Once again, the equation of any line can be put into the form $y = mx + b$, with slope m and y-intercept b. You are not given the slope and, while it may appear that you're given the y-intercept, you're given a point in which the y-coordinate is 0, so this is actually the x-intercept. However, you can determine both the slope and the y-intercept. Remember the slope formula, $m = \dfrac{y_2 - y_1}{x_2 - x_1}$. Plug the points you're given into this formula to get $m = \dfrac{5 - 0}{-2 - 8} = \dfrac{5}{-10} = -\dfrac{1}{2}$. Plug this into the slope-intercept form of the line to get $y = -\dfrac{1}{2}x + b$. To get the value of b, plug in one of the points you're given. Try (8, 0). Plugging in this point gives you $0 = -\dfrac{1}{2}(8) + b$. Multiply on the right side to get $0 = -4 + b$. Add 4 to both sides to get $4 = b$. Plug this into the equation to get $y = -\dfrac{1}{2}x + 4$. The correct answer is (A).

Earlier in this chapter, we talked about parallel and perpendicular lines. In plane geometry, parallel means not intersecting, and perpendicular means intersecting at right angles. In coordinate geometry, this is also true, but parallel and perpendicular lines also have another interesting property relating to their equations. That's right; if you know the equations of the two lines, you can determine whether they're parallel and whether they're perpendicular without even needing to look at the graph. Simply use the facts that the slopes of parallel lines are equal and the slopes of perpendicular lines are negative reciprocals. (A reciprocal is a fraction flipped upside down, so a negative reciprocal is a fraction flipped upside down and with its sign reversed. The negative reciprocal of $\frac{5}{2}$ is $-\frac{2}{5}$. The negative reciprocal of 8 is $-\frac{1}{8}$.) Let's look at an example.

1. Which of the following represents the equation of a line that is parallel to the line represented by the equation $y = -3x + 1$?

    A. $y = 2x + 1$

    B. $y = -3x + 5$

    C. $y = 3x + 1$

    D. $y = \frac{1}{3}x + 5$

Here's How to Crack It

The question asks for which line is parallel to the given line. Your instinct might be to sketch the graph, but in this question there is no need. Parallel lines have equal slopes. Since the given line and the answer choices are in the form, $y = mx + b$, m represents the slope. The slope of the original equation is -3. Find the equation in the answer choices with the same slope, i.e. the same value of m. This is the equation $y = -3x + 5$. The correct answer is (B).

Let's look at another.

2. The line represented by the equation $3x + 6y = 4$ is perpendicular to the line represented by which of the following equations?

    A. $-4x - 8y = -5$

    B. $3x + 2y = 4$

    C. $2x - y = -1$

    D. $-3x + 6y = -4$

Here's How to Crack It

The slopes of perpendicular lines are negative reciprocals, which are any two numbers that have a product of –1 when multiplied together. However, neither the equation of the line given in the question nor those in the answer choices are in $y = mx + b$ form. Put them in this form. Start with the equation in the question: $3x + 6y = 4$. Subtract $3x$ from both sides to get $6y = -3x + 4$. Now, divide both sides by 6 to get $y = -\frac{1}{2}x + \frac{2}{3}$. Now that this is in $y = mx + b$ form, the slope is equal to m, which is $-\frac{1}{2}$. The slope of the perpendicular line is the negative reciprocal of $-\frac{1}{2}$, which is $\frac{2}{1}$, or 2. Now, do the same to the answer choices and stop when you find a line with a slope of 2. Choice (A) is $-4x - 8y = -5$. Add $4x$ to both sides to get $-8y = 4x + 5$. Divide both sides by –8 to get $y = -\frac{1}{2}x - \frac{5}{8}$. This is a possible trap answer since it is parallel to the line in the question. However, it is not perpendicular, so eliminate (A). Choice (B) is $3x + 2y = 4$. Subtract $3x$ from both sides to get $2y = -3x + 4$. Divide both sides by 2 to get $y = -\frac{3}{2}x + 2$. The slope is not 2, so eliminate (B). Choice (C) is $2x - y = -1$. Subtract $2x$ from both sides to get $-y = -2x - 1$. Divide both sides by –1 to get $y = 2x + 1$. Since the slope of this line is 2, the correct answer is (C).

Equation of a Line Drill
You can check your answers in Part VIII: Answer Key to Drills.

1. Which of the following is the equation of a line through the point (0, –2) with a slope of 4?

    A. $y = 4x - 2$

    B. $y = 4x + 4$

    C. $y = -2x - 2$

    D. $y = -2x + 4$

2. A line goes through the points (2, 2) and (−4, −1).
    Show below a possible equation for the line.

    $y = $ [   ] $x + $ [   ]

    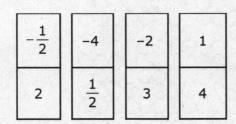

$-\dfrac{1}{2}$	−4	−2	1
2	$\dfrac{1}{2}$	3	4

3. Of the equations below, which best represents a
    line with a slope of −2 that goes through the
    point (−1, 3)?

    A. $y = -2x + 3$

    B. $y = 3x - 1$

    C. $y = -2x + 1$

    D. $y = 3x + 1$

4. What is true of the lines represented by the
    equations $2x + 8y = -5$ and $3x + 12y = 8$?

    A. They are parallel.

    B. They are perpendicular.

    C. They have the same x-intercept.

    D. They have the same y-intercept.

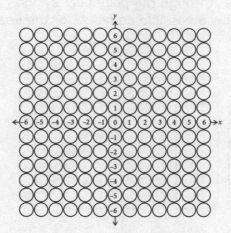

5. On the graph above, select the points on the line represented by the equation $y = -2x + 4$.

PROPORTIONS AND GRAPHS

In Chapter 14, we talked about ratios and proportions. Proportions can also be described as linear graphs through the origin. Remember that equations of lines can be expressed in the form $y = mx + b$. Since lines representing proportions go through the origin, the y-intercept, and therefore b is 0, so these lines can be expressed by the equation $y = mx$. In graphical terms, m represents the slope. In proportional terms, m represents the rate. Let's look at an example.

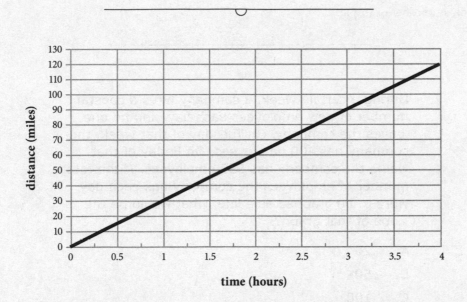

1. The graph above represents the distance traveled by a car driving at a constant speed. Which of the following is the constant speed?

   A.   10 mph
   B.   15 mph
   C.   30 mph
   D.   45 mph

Here's How to Crack It

Remember that the rate, in this case speed, is always equal to the slope of the line. To determine the slope, find two points on the line. To make this as easy as possible, make one of those points the origin (0, 0). Choose another point, say (1, 30). Then, the slope, i.e. the speed, is $\frac{30-0}{1-0} = 30$. The correct answer is (C).

Let's look at another example.

———————————————○———————————————

2. During a certain week, a company hires a constant number of new employees each day, and no one leaves the company. On Tuesday of that week, the company has 400 employees. On Friday of that week, the company has 550 employees. If the total number of employees the company has each day were to be graphed as a line, what would be the slope of that graph?

A. 25

B. 50

C. 100

D. 150

Here's How to Crack It

The slope of the graph is the rate of increase. Look at the data given. On Tuesday, there were 400 employees, and on Friday, there were 550. Therefore, over the course of 3 days, the number of employees increased by 150. The rate of increase, therefore, is $\dfrac{150}{3} = 50$. The correct answer is (B).

———————————————○———————————————

Proportions and Graphs Drill

You can check your answers in Part VIII: Answer Key to Drills.

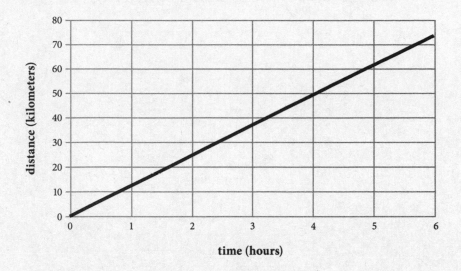

1. Elizabeth rides her bike over a period of 6 hours and records the distance she travelled in the graph above. If *d* represents her distance travelled in kilometers and *t* represents time, in hours, from the beginning of her trip, select the value that completes the equation below.

$$d = \boxed{} \; t$$

| 10 | 12 | 15 |

| 18 | 20 | 24 |

2. A certain toy store sells marbles only in boxes that contain 2 red marbles and 5 blue marbles. Which of the following plots the possible number of red marbles and blue marbles a customer can buy?

A.

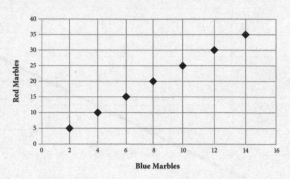

B.

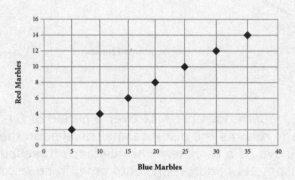

C.

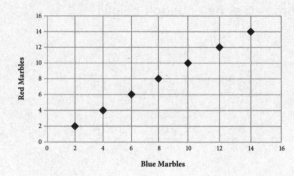

D.

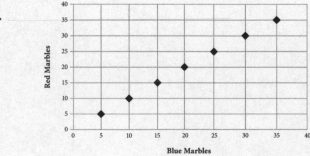

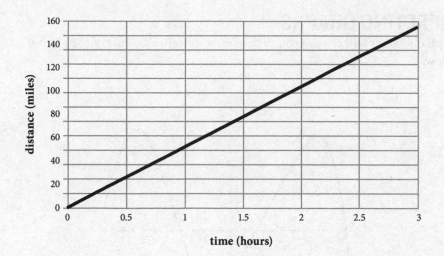

3. Lisa and Frank are both driving on a highway at different constant speeds. Lisa's driving is expressed by the graph above. Frank's driving is expressed by the equation $d = 40t$. Lisa's speed is

| Select... ▼ | Frank's speed.
| --- |
| greater than |
| the same as |
| less than |

INTERPRETING GRAPHS

Some graph questions will require you to determine certain elements of the graphs. Look at the graph below.

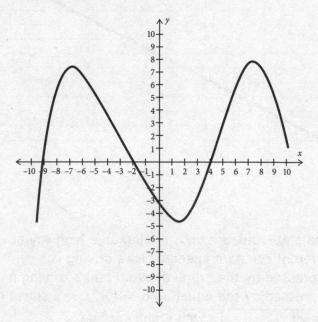

Let's identify some key elements. Start with the x- and y-intercepts, i.e., where the graph crosses the x-axis and y-axis, respectively. A graph, particularly a nonlinear graph, may have multiple x-intercepts. Where does the graph cross the x-axis? It crosses at three points: $(-9, 0)$, $(-2, 0)$, and $(4, 0)$. Therefore, these are the x-intercepts. If a graph is of a function, it can have only one y-intercept (otherwise it would fail the vertical line test). Where does this graph cross the y-axis? It crosses it about halfway between the hashmarks for -3 and -4, so the y-intercept is about $(0, -3.5)$.

Now determine where this graph is positive and negative. A graph is negative when it is below the x-axis and positive when it is above the x-axis. Use the x-intercepts to your advantage. The x-intercepts are -9, -2, and 4. To the left of the -9, the graph is below the x-axis, meaning that it is negative. Between -9 and -2, the graph is above the x-axis, meaning that it is positive. Between -2 and 4, the graph is below the x-axis, meaning that it is negative. To the right of 4, the graph is above the x-axis, meaning that it is positive. Therefore, the graph is negative at $-2 < x < 4$ and $4 < x < 10$ and positive at $-9 < x < -2$ and $4 < x < 10$.

Now determine relative maximums and minimums. These are points for which the y-coordinate is either greater or less than all the surrounding points. Look for peaks and valleys in the graph. The graph reaches peaks at about $(-6.5, 7.5)$ and at about $(7.5, 8)$. These are the relative maximums. The graph reaches a valley at $(1.5, -4.5)$. This is the relative minimum.

Now determine where the graph is increasing and decreasing. Use the relative maximums and minimums. The graph is increasing to the left of its relative minimum at $x = -6.5$. Then, it decreases to its relative minimum at $x = 1.5$. Then, it increases to its other relative maximum at $x = 7.5$. Then, it decreases to the right of this point. Therefore it increases from $-10 < x < -6.5$ and $1.5 < x < 7.5$ and decreases from $-6.5 < x < 1.5$ and $7.5 < x < 10$.

On the side of some graphs will be a mirror image of the other. Let's look at an example.

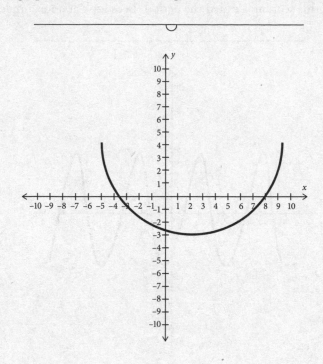

1. Which of the following represents the axis of symmetry in the graph above?

   A. $x = 2$
   B. $x = -3$
   C. $y = 2$
   D. $y = -3$

Here's How to Crack It

The axis of symmetry is the line that divides that graph into two mirror images. First, determine whether the axis of symmetry is horizontal or vertical. Since the left side of the graph is a reflection of the right side, the axis of symmetry is the vertical line separating the two sides. Since vertical lines have a constant x-value, they must be represented by "$x =$" and some constant. Eliminate (C) and (D). Imagine the lines represented by the two remaining choices. The line $x = 2$, the vertical line though 2 on the x-axis, does appear to divide the graph into mirror images. The line $x = -3$, the vertical line though -3 on the x-axis, clearly does not. The correct answer is (A).

Some graphs are periodic. Periodic means that the graph is made up of a repeating section. The horizontal length of this section is called the period. Let's look at an example.

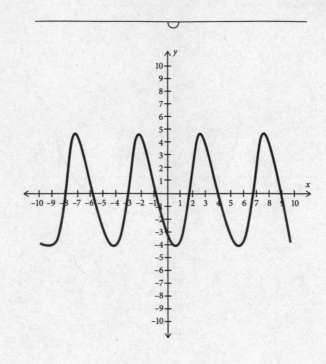

2. What is the period of the graph above?

A.   2

B.   5

C.   8

D.   10

Here's How to Crack It

This graph has a section that's repeating. To determine the length of this section, look at the relative maximums. The graph has a relative maximum at about $x = -7$, $x = -2$, $x = 3$, and $x = 8$. Since the difference between each of these relative maximums is 5, the period is 5. The correct answer is (B).

Interpreting Graphs Drill

You can check your answers in Part VIII: Answer Key to Drills.

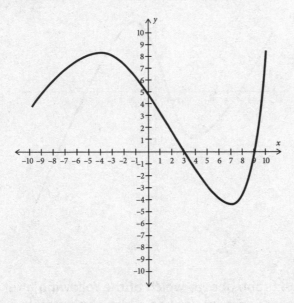

1. In the graph above, on which interval is the graph negative?

    A. $-10 < x < 0$

    B. $-4 < x < 7$

    C. $3 < x < 9$

    D. $5 < x < 7$

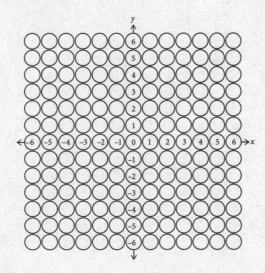

2. If a linear graph is represented by the equation $y = 2x + 4$, mark the point that represents the x-intercept and the point that represents the y-intercept on the graph above.

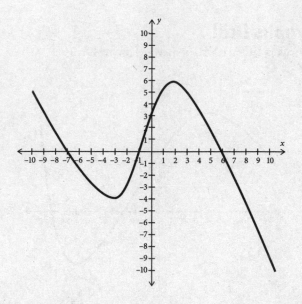

3. In the graph above, which of the following intervals represents the interval on which the graph is increasing?

A. $-7 < x < -1$ and $6 < x < 10$

B. $-3 < x < 2$

C. $-10 < x < -3$ and $2 < x < 10$

D. $-1 < x < 6$

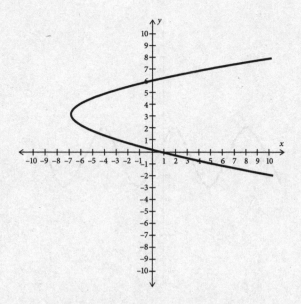

4. In the graph above, which of the following equations represents the axis of symmetry?

   A. $x = 3$

   B. $x = -7$

   C. $y = 3$

   D. $y = -7$

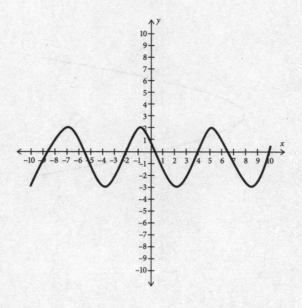

5. Which of the following is the period of the graph above?

   A. 3

   B. 6

   C. 12

   D. 24

PUTTING IT ALL TOGETHER

Now that you've seen the basics of geometry one topic at a time, we're going to give you a drill that mixes up all the different geometric concepts we've discussed in this chapter. This drill will help show you whether you're having trouble *recognizing* individual types of problems, as we've discussed in all the previous chapters. As you do this drill, make it a point to identify each question before you start calculating:

"This one is a triangle question."

"That is a setup volume problem."

"This one is a graphing question."

Examine every diagram to see if you can eliminate any answers that are out of the ballpark. Remember, if two answers are close together, you can't rely on the diagram to tell you which is exactly right. The figures are drawn only *roughly* to scale.

If there is no diagram provided, try to make your own. By taking something conceptual and making it concrete, you may be able to ballpark your *own* diagram.

Need More Math Practice?
Math Workout for the GED® Test contains nearly 500 practice questions.

Geometry Drill

You can check your answers in Part VIII: Answer Key to Drills.

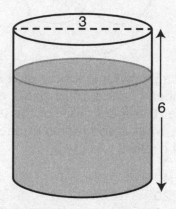

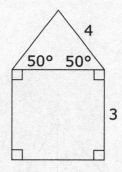

1. The cylindrical glass above is filled $\frac{3}{4}$ with water. What volume of water is in the glass, rounded to the nearest unit?

   A. 170
   B. 127
   C. 42
   D. 32

2. The radius of a circular traffic island is 7 feet. What is the approximate area of the traffic island?

   A. 154
   B. 148
   C. 21
   D. 15

3. The figure above shows a square attached to a triangle. If the triangle is isosceles, what is the perimeter of the <u>entire</u> figure?

   A. 12
   B. 17
   C. 20
   D. 34

4. A three-sided figure has sides in a ratio of 2 : 2 : 1. What type of figure is this?

   A. an equilateral triangle
   B. a square
   C. an isosceles triangle
   D. Not enough information is given.

5. If a cube has a volume of 27, which of the following is the length of one side of the cube?

   A. 3
   B. 9
   C. 81
   D. 144

6. An isosceles triangle has one internal angle of 45 degrees. What is the sum of the other two interior angles?

   A. 180 degrees
   B. 135 degrees
   C. 90 degrees
   D. 45 degrees

7. A rectangular flower garden has an area of 168 square feet. If the width of the garden is 12 feet, then what is the length of the garden?

   A. 23
   B. 20
   C. 15
   D. 14

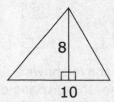

8. The triangle above has a base of 10 and a height of 8. Which of the following expressions gives the area of the triangle?

   A. $\frac{1}{2}(10)(8)$

   B. $2(10 + 8)$

   C. $\frac{1}{2}(10 + 8)$

   D. $\frac{1}{2}(10 - 8)$

9. Two circles with identical radii are inscribed inside a third circle, as shown above. If the diameter of the large circle is 20, what is the radius of one of the small circles?

   A. 40
   B. 20
   C. 10
   D. 5

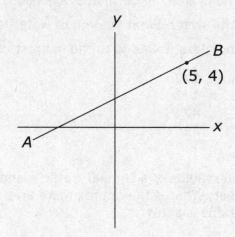

10. Point (5, 4) is on line AB as shown. Which of the following represents the slope of line AB?

   A. $\frac{4}{5}$

   B. $\frac{5}{4}$

   C. $\frac{4 \pm 5}{5 - 4}$

   D. Not enough information is given.

11. Which of the following represents the equation of a line that goes through the points (1, 2) and (−2, 8)?

   A. $y = -2x - 4$
   B. $y = -2x + 4$
   C. $y = 2x + 4$
   D. $y = 2x - 4$

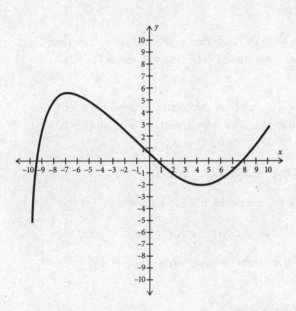

13. A regular hexagon has an area of $24\sqrt{3}$.

   If the area of a regular hexagon can be computed using the formula $A = \dfrac{3\sqrt{3}}{2}s^2$, where s is the side of the hexagon, what is the perimeter of the hexagon?

   A. 2
   B. 4
   C. 16
   D. 24

12. Which of the following intervals on the above graph is positive?

   A. $-9.5 < x < 1$ and $x > 8$
   B. $x < -9.5$ and $1 < x < 8$
   C. $x < -6.5$ and $x > 4$
   D. $-6.5 < x < 4$

Part V Summary

o The GED® Mathematical Reasoning test concentrates on only a few areas of math (and even these topics are not covered inclusively):

- Quantitative Problem Solving with Rational Numbers   25%
- Quantitative Problem Solving in Measurement   20%
- Algebraic Problem Solving with Expressions and Equations   30%
- Algebraic Problem Solving with Graphs and Functions   25%

o There are 46 questions on the Mathematical Reasoning test, to be done in 115 minutes. The first five questions will be in Part 1, in which calculators are not permitted. The rest will be in Part 2, in which calculators ARE permitted.

o At least 50 percent of the problems will be multiple choice. In these problems, a version of POE called Ballparking enables you to eliminate answer choices on the Mathematical Reasoning test that are out of the ballpark.

o Even if you know how to do the problem, Ballparking is useful as a reality check.

o Ballparking is even more useful if you don't know how to do the problem—as a guessing strategy.

o Look out for partial answers—answers that are on the way to the correct answer but stop too soon.

o Look out for red herrings—pieces of information in the problem that aren't necessary for its solution.

o Do each section of the Mathematical Reasoning test in two passes:

- The first pass for the problems you know immediately how to do
- The second pass for the problems you aren't sure of

o   Because you can't write on the computer screen, you'll have to get comfortable with using scratch paper. You will receive three erasable note boards on test day, but you can use scratch paper on our practice tests. Label each problem on your scratch paper so you can find your work again if you come back to it on the second pass.

o   Numbers to the left of zero on the number line are negative. Numbers to the right of zero on the number line are positive. Zero is neither positive nor negative.

o   Absolute value is the distance a number is from zero. It is always nonnegative.

o   When multiplying positive and negative numbers:
    • positive × positive = positive
    • positive × negative = negative
    • negative × negative = positive

o   When doing several operations, use PEMDAS to decide which operation to perform first.

o   A fraction is a $\frac{\text{part}}{\text{whole}}$. To compare fractions, use the Bowtie as outlined in Chapter 13.

o   You must know how to add, subtract, multiply, and divide fractions.

o   Always reduce fractions (when you can) before doing a complicated operation. This will reduce your chances of making a careless error.

o   A decimal is just another way of expressing a fraction.

o   A percentage is just a fraction whose denominator is always 100. You should memorize the percentage shortcuts we outline in Chapter 13.

o   In the setup problems on the GED® test, you don't have to find the answer—just the equation that will get the answer.

o   An average (or arithmetic mean) is the sum of all items, divided by the number of items. The median is the middle number of a group of ordered numbers. The mode is the number that appears the most often.

o   Any problem that uses the word "per" can be solved by the equation rate × time = distance.

o   An exponent is a shorter way of expressing the result of multiplying a number several times by itself.

o   When you multiply numbers with the same base, you simply add the exponents. When you divide numbers with the same base, you simply subtract the exponents.

o   The square root of a positive number x is the number that, when squared equals x. The square root of $9 = \sqrt{9} = 3$.

o   To find the probability that something is going to happen, you take the number of chances that the thing could happen and compare that to the total number of possible outcomes. Probabilities are usually expressed as fractions in which the number of chances that the thing could happen is the numerator and the total number of possible outcomes is the denominator.

o   Many algebra problems can be solved by Backsolving—working backward from the answer choices to see which one solves the problem.

o   Some problems can be "translated" from English to math:
   •   *is* means =
   •   *of* means ×
   •   *more than* means +
   •   *less than* means −

o   A line contains 180 degrees. A circle contains 360 degrees.

o   Triangles contain 180 degrees. A right triangle contains one 90-degree angle. An isosceles triangle has two equal sides, and two equal angles. An equilateral triangle contains three equal sides with three angles of 60 degrees each.

o   The area of a triangle is $\dfrac{\text{base} \times \text{height}}{2}$.

o   The circumference of a circle is $2\pi r$. The area of a circle is πr^2.

o   The volume of a rectangular solid is length $\times$ width $\times$ depth.

o   To graph an *x,y*-coordinate on a coordinate plane, count over to the right (for positive) or left (for negative) to plot the *x*-coordinate, then up (for positive) or down (for negative) to plot the *y*-coordinate.

o   The slope of a line is the change in *y* values (rise) divided by the change in *x* values (run). It is generally expressed as a fraction. Slope is just another word for the rate of change.

Part VI
Social Studies

Chapter 17
Social Studies
Overview

If you look in some of the other study guides for the GED® test, you may get the impression that you will have to memorize a huge number of facts for the GED® Social Studies test. In fact, the Social Studies test does not require *much* specific knowledge of history, economics, or geography (or any other social studies topics). Every question will be based on a document, chart, map, picture, or some type of graphic organizer, and the information you need to answer the question will almost always be contained in that accompanying piece of information.

The questions asked by the Social Studies test are twofold: They want to make sure you have a *background* in the ideas covered in a typical social studies curriculum, and they want to assess what we will call "social studies skills" (reading passages and charts for relevant information). Thus, a strong familiarity with the major topics of social studies along with a smart approach to locating key facts will be just what you need for success on this test. In the following chapters, we will cover both of these elements.

What Do the Questions and Passages Look Like?

You will have 70 minutes to answer 35 questions. While there may be a couple of stand-alone questions, almost all questions will require you to look for information contained in one of the following:

Document

Documents can include newspaper editorials, speeches, letters, pieces of legislation, Supreme Court opinions, essays, and Amendments to the Constitution.

This excerpt is from a speech given by Abraham Lincoln in 1863, following the Battle of Gettysburg.

> But, in a larger sense, we cannot dedicate—we cannot consecrate—we cannot hallow—this ground. The brave men, living and dead, who struggled here, have consecrated it, far above our poor power to add or detract. The world will little note, nor long remember what we say here, but it can never forget what they did here. It is for us the living, rather, to be dedicated here to the unfinished work which they who fought here have thus far so nobly advanced. It is rather for us to be here dedicated to the great task remaining before us—that from these honored dead we take increased devotion to that cause for which they gave the last full measure of devotion—that we here highly resolve that these dead shall not have died in vain—that this nation, under God, shall have a new birth of freedom—and that government of the people, by the people, for the people, shall not perish from the earth.

Map

Timeline

Events in the Civil Rights Movement

1954	*Brown v. Board of Education* Supreme Court decision
1955	Rosa Parks's arrest in Montgomery
1959	Little Rock Nine attend Central High School
1963	Martin Luther King Jr. delivers "I Have a Dream" speech
1964	Civil Rights Act is passed by Congress and signed by President Johnson

Chart, Graph, or Table

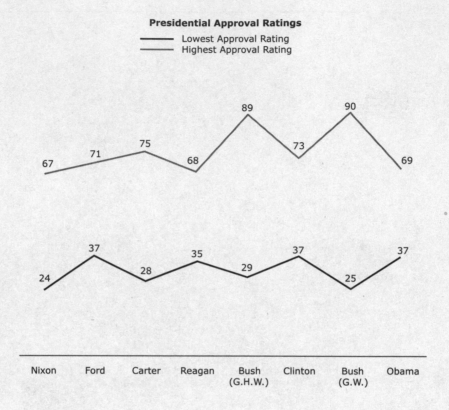

Presidential Approval Ratings

— Lowest Approval Rating
— Highest Approval Rating

67 71 75 68 89 73 90 69

24 37 28 35 29 37 25 37

Nixon   Ford   Carter   Reagan   Bush (G.H.W.)   Clinton   Bush (G.W.)   Obama

Graphic Organizer

Causes of the Great Depression			
Stock Market Crash of 1929	High tariffs against European countries	Bank failures	Widespread drought

Each of these sources will include one to three questions that can be answered with information found in the accompanying source.

Question Formats

Since the GED® test is to be taken on a computer, the test writers have included a few fancy kinds of question formats. You have seen these questions formats earlier in this book, but here are some examples of how they will look on the Social Studies test.

Multiple Choice

The following text is taken from the Articles of Confederation (1781).

> Each state retains its sovereignty, freedom, and independence, and every power, jurisdiction, and right, which is not by this Confederation expressly delegated to the United States, in Congress assembled.

1. According to the passage above, the Articles of Confederation gave priority to

   A. the development of a strong, central government.
   B. the rights of individuals.
   C. a powerful Congress.
   D. states maintaining self-determination.

Fill in the Blank

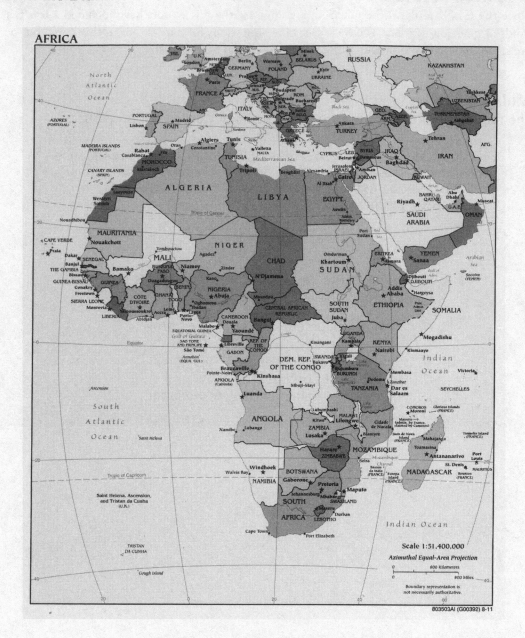

2. The country in Africa that can have trade ports on two oceans is [   ].

Drop Down

This excerpt is from Albert J. Beveridge's "The March of the Flag" (1898).

> The Opposition tells us that we ought not to govern a people without their consent. I answer, the rule of liberty that all just government derives its authority from the consent of the governed, applies only to those who are capable of self-government. We govern the Indians without their consent, we govern our territories without their consent, we govern our children without their consent. How do they know that our government would be without their consent? Would not the people of the Philippines prefer the just, human, civilizing government of this Republic to the savage, bloody rule of pillage and extortion from which we have rescued them?
>
> And, regardless of this formula of words made only for enlightened, self-governing people, do we owe no duty to the world? Shall we turn these peoples back to the reeking hands from which we have taken them? Shall we abandon them, with Germany, England, Japan, hungering for them? Shall we save them from those nations, to give them a self-rule of tragedy? … Then, like men and not like children, let us on to our tasks, our mission, and our destiny.

3. The perspective offered in this passage is most directly influenced by [Select... ▼].

   - Isolationism
   - Imperialism
   - Suffrage
   - Sectionalism

Drag and Drop

Natural gas reserves are plentiful throughout the planet. Most active sources for natural gas are located in central Asia and in the Americas. Iran and Russia each sit on approximately 33 trillion cubic meters of natural gas, which together combine for $\frac{1}{3}$ of the earth's natural gas supply. Qatar, which is a mere 150th the size of Iran contains $\frac{2}{3}$ of the oil reserves that Iran does. Rounding out the Asian natural gas powerhouses are Turkmenistan (18 trillion) and Saudi Arabia (8 trillion).

Despite the talk of the United States' dependence on foreign energy sources, it sits on between 9 and 10 trillion cubic meters of natural gas, making it the largest such resource holder in the Americas. Venezuela, the next most natural gas-rich country in the Americas has the equivalent of just over half of the United States' reserves.

4. Drag and place the appropriate country under the bar graph that best describes its natural gas reserves.

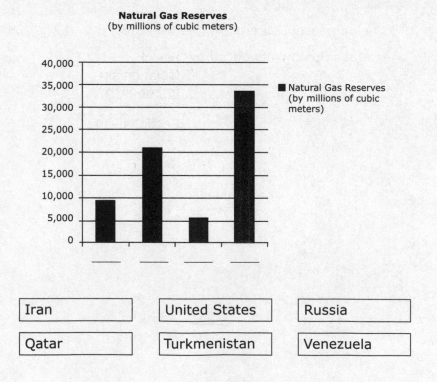

Natural Gas Reserves
(by millions of cubic meters)

| Iran | United States | Russia |
| Qatar | Turkmenistan | Venezuela |

Hot Spot

5. Click on a power that the executive branch has directly over the legislative branch.

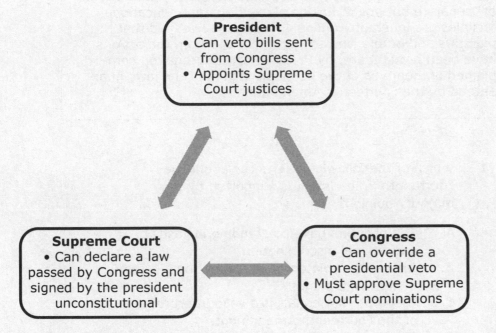

President
- Can veto bills sent from Congress
- Appoints Supreme Court justices

Supreme Court
- Can declare a law passed by Congress and signed by the president unconstitutional

Congress
- Can override a presidential veto
- Must approve Supreme Court nominations

Question Tasks

The following are the four types of question tasks that you'll be asked to perform on the Social Studies test.

Comprehension Questions

A comprehension question asks you to find a particular piece of information and then recognize it, slightly restated, among the answer choices. Occasionally, comprehension questions will ask you to go just a bit further to identify a logical implication of that information.

The following passage is taken from the Supreme Court's majority opinion in *Brown v. Board of Education* (1954).

> We conclude that, in the field of public education, the doctrine of "separate but equal" has no place. Separate educational facilities are inherently unequal. Therefore, we hold that the plaintiffs and others similarly situated for whom the actions have been brought are, by reason of the segregation complained of, deprived of the equal protection of the laws guaranteed by the Fourteenth Amendment.

1. Which of the following inferences about the Fourteenth Amendment is supported by the majority opinion?

   A. The plaintiffs have no standing in cases of educational discrimination.
   B. Institutions related to education may in some instances segregate.
   C. "Separate but equal" is a valid interpretation of the Fourteenth Amendment.
   D. The Fourteenth Amendment implies that schools may not segregate.

Comprehension Questions
These questions ask you to recognize information in a slightly altered form.

Here's How to Crack It

This is a comprehension question designed to see whether you understood what you read. The correct answer is (D) because the final sentence clearly states that segregated schools deprive students of a central guarantee of the Fourteenth Amendment. Since all segregation in schools violates the Fourteenth Amendment, (B) cannot work. Furthermore, the final sentence mentions that the court declared that the plaintiffs were wronged, so you can eliminate (A). Choice (C) is incorrect because the text declares that "separate but equal has no place."

Application Questions

To answer an application question, you must first understand the meaning of a concept conveyed in the document, chart, or map and then apply that concept to an entirely different situation.

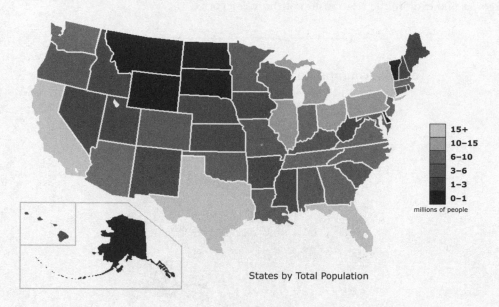

2007 United Status Population Distribution

	millions of people
	15+
	10–15
	6–10
	3–6
	1–3
	0–1

States by Total Population

2. Population density can be defined as the number of people living in an area, relative to the size of that area. Which area of the U.S. has the lowest population density?

A. The West Coast
B. The Southeast
C. The Northern Mountain region
D. New England

Application Questions
These questions ask you to apply a concept from one situation to another situation.

Here's How to Crack It
Here we have a population map, and we're asked about population density. Since we're looking for the lowest population density, we need to find big states with small populations. The West Coast contains large states, but they have higher populations, so we can eliminate (A). The Southeast has moderate-sized states, most of which also have medium-sized populations—plus Florida, which is very populous—so eliminate (B). That leaves us with the Northern Mountain region and New England. Both have low populations, but New England's area is also quite small, whereas the Northern Mountain region spreads its small population over a very large area. So, we can eliminate (D). Choice (C) is our answer.

Analysis Questions

An analysis question asks you to break down the accompanying information into more specific categories and explore the relationship of those categories.

The following poster was created during World War I.

Analysis Questions
These questions ask you to explore the relationship of implied categories within the passage.

3. This poster was most likely created with the intention to

    A. recruit soldiers to fight in the war.
    B. give factual information about the destruction caused by the German Empire.
    C. praise the military might of Germany.
    D. raise funds for the war effort.

Here's How to Crack It

The key to an analysis question is to understand the motives of the document's creator. The image shows a menacing figure of a person called a Hun and asks its audience to purchase war bonds. War bonds were sold to help fund the war effort, so (D) is correct. It is not asking for soldiers to fight in the war, so you can eliminate (A). The Huns were a Germanic people, so this poster does not seem to be praising Germans; rather, it depicts them as menacing and inhuman. Eliminate (C) and (B).

Evaluation Questions

To answer an evaluation question, you must make a judgment or prediction about the information provided in the passage—sometimes by applying outside knowledge.

———————————○———————————

4. Gadzooks Cola has been a favorite in the Pacific Northwest since its introduction five years ago. This year, it decided to finally raise the price it charges per bottle. This is most likely due to

    A. an increase in demand.
    B. a loss in profits.
    C. an increase in supply.
    D. deflation.

Evaluation Questions
These questions ask you to make a prediction based on the passage.

Here's How to Crack It

We are given an effect and have to imagine what cause is responsible for it. Work backward and see whether each answer choice would yield a price increase. The law of demand indicates that the more quantity demanded by consumers leads to price increases. Therefore (A) is correct. Choice (C) is incorrect because that would lead to a decrease in price. Deflation is also related to a decrease in price, so eliminate (D). Choice (B) is not necessarily true, as a loss in profits could mean low sales, which would necessitate a drop in prices.

———————————○———————————

Another type of evaluation question may ask you to distinguish fact from opinion or judgment in a primary or secondary source document.

Let's try a question.

The following text is adapted from President Richard Nixon's speech, "The Great Silent Majority" (November 3, 1969):

> Tonight I want to talk to you on a subject of deep concern to all Americans and to many people in all parts of the world, the war in Vietnam.
>
> I believe that one of the reasons for the deep division about Vietnam is that many Americans have lost confidence in what their Government has told them about our policy. The American people cannot and should not be asked to support a policy which involves the overriding issues of war and peace unless they know the truth about that policy.
>
> Now let me begin by describing the situation I found when I was inaugurated on January 20: The war had been going on for four years. Thirty-one thousand Americans had been killed in action. The training program for the South Vietnamese was beyond [behind] schedule. Five hundred and forty-thousand Americans were in Vietnam with no plans to reduce the number. No progress had been made at the negotiations in Paris and the United States had not put forth a comprehensive peace proposal.
>
> Tonight, I do not tell you that the war in Vietnam is the war to end wars, but I do say this: I have initiated a plan which will end this war in a way that will bring us closer to that great goal to which—to which Woodrow Wilson and every American President in our history has been dedicated—the goal of a just and lasting peace.

1. Click the selection of text in President Nixon's speech above that best represents an opinion, rather than a fact.

Here's How to Crack It

Facts are statements that can be proven true or false, whereas opinions are statements that can neither be proven nor disproven. In this question, the first highlighted quote (starting with "I believe") is the opinion, whereas the other two highlighted sentences are facts. There is no way to prove or disprove Nixon's statement that societal division about Vietnam was caused by Americans' lack of confidence in the government, but the other two statements are numerical and can thus be proven.

Yet another type of evaluation question, similar to the one above, may ask you to judge whether or not a particular author or source is credible and relevant to historical or modern political conversations.

Let's try a question.

⎯⎯⎯⎯⎯⎯⎯⎯⎯⎯○⎯⎯⎯⎯⎯⎯⎯⎯⎯⎯

The following text is adapted from President Barack Obama's speech on climate change delivered at Georgetown University (September 25, 2013):

> Now, we know that no single weather event is caused solely by climate change. Droughts and fires and floods, they go back to ancient times. But we also know that in a world that's warmer than it used to be, all weather events are affected by a warming planet. The fact that sea levels in New York, in New York Harbor, are now a foot higher than a century ago—that didn't cause Hurricane Sandy, but it certainly contributed to the destruction that left large parts of our mightiest city dark and underwater.

1. An analysis of which of the following sources would be most relevant to a thoughtful and unbiased discussion of the issue described above?

    A. an advertising campaign funded by a major coal mining company
    B. a political speech hosted by an environmentalist group
    C. a peer-reviewed academic paper published by a leading scientist
    D. a disaster film produced by one of Hollywood's most respected filmmakers

Here's How to Crack It

In order to determine whether a particular source or author is credible and relevant to a particular topic, one must consider the source's bias, credentials, level of expertise, etc. Since the issue above deals with climate change, any sort of advertising campaign would have inherent bias—especially an advertising campaign funded by a coal company; eliminate (A). Political speeches are rarely neutral, and those hosted by particular interest groups are less likely to be so; eliminate (B). A Hollywood film may provide the viewer with interesting things to think about, but a filmmaker is certainly not a credentialed expert on scientific matters; eliminate (D). The best answer is thus (C); among these four choices, a published and respected scientist is most likely to be unbiased and knowledgeable about the subject in question.

⎯⎯⎯⎯⎯⎯⎯⎯⎯⎯○⎯⎯⎯⎯⎯⎯⎯⎯⎯⎯

Graphic Material Questions

The Social Studies test will also include comprehension, application, analysis, and evaluation questions based on graphic materials. If you've already read the downloadable supplement, "Understanding Graphics," you're well on your way toward acing these questions. But there are three types of graphics that appear on the Social Studies test that the supplement didn't cover: cartoons, photos, and famous pieces of art.

The GED® Test Cartoon

The test writers want to see whether you can figure out the point behind these mostly political cartoons. Sometimes the cartoons will be fairly recent; other times they may be more than 200 years old. Here's an example from somewhere in between:

THE CROWNING ACHIEVEMENT   May 3 -16

THIS LATEST SUBMARINE VICTIM MAY BE THE LAST

1. This American World War I cartoon was published in 1916, before the United States entered the war. The U.S. ship has just been torpedoed by a German submarine. What is the sinking ship in the cartoon meant to imply?

A. The United States' patience with Germany was about to run out.

B. The ship was carrying illegal war supplies and was a legitimate war target.

C. The United States should be more patient.

D. In wartime, even innocent people can get hurt by mistakes.

Here's How to Crack It

Read this comprehension question carefully, and then study all information in the cartoon itself, including any words contained as a caption or inside the drawing itself. We know from the question that a U.S. ship has been torpedoed by a German submarine in the early days of World War I, before the United States entered the war. Even if you don't know much about World War I, you can imagine how the people of the United States probably felt about one of their ships being torpedoed: pretty mad.

The cartoonist has labeled the ship the *U.S. Patience*, and it's about to sink. What is the cartoonist implying by this? If you picked (A), you are doing just fine. The cartoonist was implying that the patience of the United States was about to run out in the face of Germany's sinking one of its ships—and, in fact, less than a year later, the United States did enter the war and helped to defeat Germany.

Choices (B) and (C) made new assumptions without any basis in information supplied in the cartoon or the question. Choice (D) certainly could have been true, but made no use of the important information contained in the drawing itself: the labeling of the ship as the *U.S. Patience*.

The GED® Test Photo

As with cartoon questions, the key to photo questions is to understand the point behind the photos and the relationship of the photo to any text that goes with it. Here's an example.

2. The men in this photograph are demonstrating against

    A. nationalism.
    B. segregation.
    C. fascism.
    D. suffrage.

Here's How to Crack It

Read this evaluation question carefully, and then study all information in the photo itself. Jim Crow is a symbol of the era of racial segregation, so (B) is correct. Nationalism, or pride in one's nation, is not depicted in this protest against segregation, so eliminate (A). Fascism was present in *Europe* during the 1930s and 1940s, not in the United States, the country indicated by the presence of the Jim Crow banner. Eliminate (C). Suffrage, the right to vote, was a cause for many Americans, but Jim Crow laws existed even after African Americans had the right to vote, so (D) is incorrect.

The GED® Test Famous Piece of Art

When the GED® test gives a famous piece of art as your information source, it will be of some historical significance. Fear not—there will be a historic document that will help you understand the context of the work of art. Here is an example of how they will present a famous piece of art.

The painting below depicts the signing of the Declaration of Independence:

The following text is taken from the Declaration of Independence:

> When in the Course of human events, it becomes necessary for one people to dissolve the political bands which have connected them with another, and to assume among the powers of the earth, the separate and equal station to which the Laws of Nature and of Nature's God entitle them, a decent respect to the opinions of mankind requires that they should declare the causes which impel them to the separation.

3. What event was ongoing when the meeting in the painting occurred?

    A. the Civil War
    B. the War of 1812
    C. the Revolutionary War
    D. World War I

Here's How to Crack It

Use the historic context surrounding the painting to determine its central issue. The Declaration of Independence was created to assert the United States' freedom from England. This is exactly why the Revolutionary War was fought, so (C) is correct. The United States had already gained its independence by the time the events in the other three answer choices occurred.

What Topics Are Covered on the Social Studies Test?

Here are the topics as they are described by the people who write the test:

Civics and Government	50%
United States History	20%
Economics	15%
Geography and the World	15%

This is a pretty vague list. Just trying to acquaint yourself with all the topics covered in high school economics classes alone would take a long time. Fortunately, we will be able to give you much more exact information in the two chapters that follow.

OUR APPROACH

While no particular knowledge of the facts of history, economics, or political science is necessary to do well on this test (you can virtually always find the correct answers contained in the passages), some *general* knowledge of these subjects and the specialized vocabulary that comes with them can be extremely helpful, if only because it will give you confidence. It's no fun answering questions about a topic you haven't heard about before.

We're going to discuss the topics that come up most often on the GED® Social Studies test. Don't try to memorize them. The idea is simply to become familiar with the subject matter and to practice answering social studies questions.

Chapter 18
Social Studies,
Part One

In this chapter, we'll go over some of the topics covered on the Social Studies test, including political systems, types of government, historical documents, civil rights, and United States history.

While it is impossible to predict *exactly* what is going to be on the GED® Social Studies test that you take, we can be pretty sure that it will include certain topics that come up on the test all the time. And while it isn't necessary to take any specific outside social studies knowledge to the test, some general understanding of the processes of social studies can be very useful.

In this chapter, we'll cover some of the GED® test writers' favorite social studies topics. After each review, we'll give you some helpful vocabulary words to think about, and we'll ask some GED®-type questions based on that particular area.

Learning how to think about the social studies questions is probably more important than learning facts, so at the end of each review, there will also be a short drill for you to try on your own.

Here are the topics we'll cover in this chapter:

- Political systems
- The U.S. government
- The documents on which the U.S. government is based
- Civil rights
- United States history

TYPES OF DEMOCRACIES

The American **constitutional democracy**—a system in which the people consent to the structure and limits of a government as outlined in a constitution—developed through its rejection of a **monarchy**, rule by a king or queen. Other kinds of democracies have both influenced and been influenced by the American system.

- **Parliamentary democracy**—system in which the elected legislators (lawmakers) appoint a person to be chief of government (e.g., United Kingdom)
- **Presidential democracy**—system in which the people elect a president to be the chief of government *and* head of state (e.g., United States)
- **Direct democracy**—a system in which the people decide on laws and decisions, as opposed to electing representatives to decide for them (e.g., ancient Athens)
- **Representative democracy**—a system in which people elect representatives to make decisions and create policies (e.g., United Kingdom and United States)

Let's try an example of a question dealing with types of democracies.

The following text comes from James Madison's *Federalist Paper #10.*

> ...a pure Democracy, by which I mean a Society consisting of a small number of citizens, who assemble and administer the Government in person, can admit of no cure for the mischiefs of faction. A common passion or interest will, in almost every case, be felt by a majority of the whole; a communication and concert result from the form of Government itself; and there is nothing to check the inducements to sacrifice the weaker party, or an obnoxious individual. Hence it is, that such Democracies have ever been spectacles of turbulence and contention.

1. In this text, James Madison most directly warns against

   A. presidential democracy.
   B. parliamentary democracy.
   C. representative democracy.
   D. direct democracy.

Here's How to Crack It

The text considers the "pure Democracy" to be "spectacles of turbulence and contention." This is a critical view of direct democracies, in which the people vote directly on decisions. Choice (D) is correct. No mention is made of a president, so (B) is incorrect. There is also no discussion of elected representatives, so eliminate (B) and (C).

THE U.S. GOVERNMENT

The formation of the United States government was highly influenced by the philosophers of the 1600s and 1700s. These philosophers emphasized the importance of **individual rights, popular sovereignty** (consent of the governed), and the rule of law over the arbitrary rule of monarchs.

In the U.S. Constitution, the country's founders created a government that embodied the idea of **checks and balances** (see explanation on the next page). The **legislative** branch of the government (called the U.S. **Congress**) is charged with making laws. It has two parts: the **Senate** (there are two senators from every state) and the **House of Representatives** (the number of representatives per state varies with the population of each state). The **executive** branch of the government consists of the president of the United States, his (or her) staff at the White House, and all the departments and agencies that enforce the laws enacted by the legislative branch.

The **judicial** branch of the government consists of the U.S. courts, which decide on the constitutionality of the laws proposed by the executive and legislative branches. The highest court in the land is the U.S. **Supreme Court**. Federal judges are appointed to the court for life.

Each branch of the government is designed to check the power of the others, ensuring that no one branch becomes too powerful. For example, if a president feels that a law proposed by Congress is wrong, the president can veto that law. If Congress still feels the law is correct, it can vote to override that veto. But if the Supreme Court feels that the law is contrary to the principles of the Constitution, it can declare the law unconstitutional. This process is called checks and balances.

Vocabulary

    veto—the power to prevent the carrying out of measures enacted by the legislature

    impeach—to challenge a public official in a public hearing

    separation of powers—the system of checks and balances that keeps any one of the parts of the U.S. government from controlling the others

    federalism—the system that permits the sharing of power between federal (national) and state governments

    constituent—a voter who is represented by a particular lawmaker

Let's try a question.

The following image is a political cartoon from 1833 featuring President Andrew Jackson.

1. The cartoonist most likely wishes to convey the idea that

    A. Andrew Jackson comes from royal lineage.
    B. the executive branch can disrupt the system of checks and balances by overusing the veto.
    C. President Jackson should be praised for his decisive leadership.
    D. the president opposes Congress's use of the veto.

Here's How to Crack It

Andrew Jackson is declared a king who is stomping on the Constitution, all the while holding a scroll that says "veto." This shows that the cartoonist sees Jackson as ignoring the Constitution and using the veto to overreach executive power. Therefore, (B) is correct. Choice (A) is wrong because it takes the symbolism of this political cartoon too literally. The cartoon is quite critical toward Jackson's approach, so (C) would not make sense. Choice (D) is incorrect because Congress does not have the power to use a veto.

POLITICS IN ACTION

As mentioned previously, the legislative branch is in charge of the lawmaking process. Congress is also empowered to propose **amendments**, or official changes, to the Constitution. If two-thirds of both houses approve an amendment, it may be ratified through one of two methods:

1. Passage by three-quarters of state legislatures
2. Passage by three-quarters of special state conventions

There are currently 27 amendments to the Constitution and only one has been ratified through the latter method.

Amendments, however, are rare. Instead, most of Congress's business deals with passing laws. Those laws are enforced by the executive branch through **federal agencies**. Federal agencies belong to **executive departments**, the primary units of the executive branch. The president appoints secretaries to head each department (the Department of State, the Department of Justice, and so on) and thereby oversees the execution of all federal laws and policies.

The GED® test may also ask questions that involve the political process from other angles. For instance, you should be familiar with the function of **political parties**, which are organizations composed of people with similar ideologies that seek to get like-minded candidates elected and pass laws consistent with their ideologies. Another influential political actor is an **interest group**. Interest groups represent a cause, a group of people, or even an industry. They attempt to get officials elected or laws passed that support their respective causes, groups, or industries.

Let's try a question.

The following chart describes the United States constitutional amendment process:

Amendment Proposal option 1: Congress approves of the Amendment by a 2/3 vote.		Amendment Proposal option 2: 2/3 of the states' legislatures request Congress to establish a national convention.	
Ratification option 1: The legislatures in 3/4 of the states ratify the amendment.	Ratification option 2: 3/4 of states ratify the amendment in state conventions.	Ratification option 1: The legislatures in 3/4 of the states ratify the amendment.	Ratification option 2: 3/4 of states ratify the amendment in state conventions.

1. It is NOT possible for an Amendment to be passed without the input of [Select... ▼].
    the president
    the state legislatures
    Congress
    state conventions

Here's How to Crack It

Since both methods of proposal involve Congress in some respect, it is not possible for an Amendment to be passed without its input. Therefore, **Congress** is the correct answer. The president is not officially involved at all in the process. State legislatures can be avoided with proposal option 1 and ratification option 2. "State conventions" is incorrect because they are involved only in ratification option 2.

THE DOCUMENTS THAT STARTED IT ALL

For nearly a millennium, societies have attempted to put forth the ideals later captured by the American system. Notably, in 1215, nobles from England wrote the **Magna Carta**, which sought to limit the power of the king and protect the rights of individuals. Centuries later, some of the first Europeans to arrive in the New World, the English Pilgrims, created the **Mayflower Compact** in 1620. All who signed this document consented to laws voted upon by the majority in exchange for protection and survival. Such constitutions became increasingly common in the New World and within a century and a half, the colonists were ready to cut ties with England.

Angered at Britain's refusal to grant them the rights of British citizens, the people of the 13 colonies decided to revolt. **The Declaration of Independence** was written by Thomas Jefferson in 1776. It said, in part,

We hold these truths to be self-evident, that all men are created equal, that they are endowed by their Creator with certain inalienable Rights, that among these are Life, Liberty, and the Pursuit of Happiness....

It went on to list the colonists' grievances against the king of England. The declaration was adopted on July 4, 1776.

During the war with England that followed (called the **Revolutionary War**), the colonists ruled themselves through an organization called the **Continental Congress**. However, after England was defeated, the former colonists wrote the **U.S. Constitution** in 1787, which created principles of government that are still in use today. The Constitution was designed to compromise between the need for autonomy of the individual states and the need for a strong central government. It began

We, the people of the United States...

The U.S. Constitution listed the powers of the states and the powers of the federal government and set up the system of government that we have described above. Worried that the rights of individuals were not sufficiently protected, the founding fathers wrote the first 10 amendments to the Constitution in 1791. These have come to be known as the **Bill of Rights**. These rights include freedom of speech, the right to bear arms, the right to a trial by jury, protection against illegal search and seizure, and protection against cruel and unusual punishment.

Let's try the following question.

The following text is taken from the Mayflower Compact:

> Having undertaken, for the Glory of God, and advancements of the Christian faith and honor of our King and Country, a voyage to plant the first colony in the Northern parts of Virginia, do by these presents, solemnly and mutually, in the presence of God, and one another, covenant and combine ourselves together into a civil body politic; for our better ordering, and preservation and furtherance of the ends aforesaid; and by virtue hereof to enact, constitute, and frame, such just and equal laws, ordinances, acts, constitutions, and offices, from time to time, as shall be thought most meet and convenient for the general good of the colony; unto which we promise all due submission and obedience.

1. Click the section of the text that best shows the authors' concern for all decisions being made with the common welfare of the Mayflower community in mind.

Here's How to Crack It

When reading the passage, look for clues related to "welfare" and "community." The "general good" is synonymous with welfare. Therefore "**the general good of the colony**" is most accurate.

THE CIVIL RIGHTS MOVEMENT

One group of immigrants came to this continent against their will. Beginning in the early 1600s, Africans were brought to America as slaves. In spite of the Civil War (fought largely over the North's resolve to free the slaves), the **Emancipation Proclamation** signed by Abraham Lincoln, amendments to the Constitution, and various other laws, the civil rights of African Americans were too often more theoretical than real in the 1950s. The phrase "**separate-but-equal**" came from the 1896 Supreme Court case *Plessy v. Ferguson* and was a way to excuse **segregated** facilities, including inferior schools. "Jim Crow" laws excluded many blacks from voting in elections.

The civil rights movement began to gather steam in the 1950s as black leaders began to rally support for nonviolent protest. In 1954, the *Brown v. Board of Education* Supreme Court decision made it illegal to segregate schools. In 1957, the first of a string of civil rights bills was passed by Congress—this one to protect the right of African American citizens to vote. There were sit-ins across the South and rallies in Washington, and from time to time, the anger spilled over and resulted in riots.

Civil rights legislation continued under the presidencies of Kennedy and Johnson, notably the Civil Rights Act of 1964, which banned discrimination based on "race, color, religion, or national origin"; the Voting Rights Act of 1965, which protected voting rights; and the Civil Rights Act of 1968, which banned discrimination in housing.

Let's look at this question.

The following passage comes from the majority opinion of *Plessy v. Ferguson* (1896):

> The argument...assumes that social prejudice may be overcome by legislation, and that equal rights cannot be secured except by an enforced commingling of the two races.... If the civil and political rights of both races be equal, one cannot be inferior to the other civilly or politically. If one race be inferior to the other socially, the Constitution of the United States cannot put them upon the same plane.

The following passage comes from the majority opinion of *Brown v. Board of Education* (1954):

A sense of inferiority affects the motivation of a child to learn. Segregation with the sanction of law, therefore, has a tendency to [retard] the educational and mental development of Negro children and to deprive them of some of the benefits they would receive in a racially integrated school system.... We conclude that, in the field of public education, the doctrine of 'separate but equal' has no place. Separate educational facilities are inherently unequal.

1. Drag the consequences of each Supreme Court decision into the proper box:

Legacy of *Plessy v. Ferguson*	Legacy of *Brown v. Board of Education*

desegregation of schools

increase of Jim Crow laws

further division between blacks and whites

some Southerners resisting forced integration

the rapid acceleration of the Civil Rights Movement

the creation of "separate but equal" facilities

Here's How to Crack It

Plessy v. Ferguson sets up the "separate but equal" doctrine. Therefore, any answer choice that deals with promoting segregation based on race will go in the box on the left. These are as follows: increase of Jim Crow laws, further division between blacks and whites, and the creation of "separate but equal" facilities. *Brown v. Board of Education* ended segregation in schools, effectively shooting down the "separate but equal" doctrine and jump starting the Civil Rights movement of the 1950s and 1960s. Any choice that shows the promotion of racial integration or the start of the Civil Rights movement should go on the right. These are as follows: desegregation of schools, some Southerners resisting forced integration, and the rapid acceleration of the Civil Rights Movement.

THE GED® TEST'S VERSION OF AMERICAN HISTORY

The following is the bulk of the American history you need to know for the GED® test.

- **1776–1789**—The American colonies proclaim their independence from England. The big movers and shakers are Benjamin Franklin, Thomas Jefferson, John Adams, and George Washington. After the Revolutionary War is won in 1781, the 13 colonies attempt to create a national government by drafting a constitution called the Articles of Confederation that fails due to its over-reliance on state sovereignty. The dissolution of the Articles of Confederation is followed up by discussions that will lead to the U.S. Constitution, which is ratified in 1789.

- **1789–1865**—The United States fights one more war with Great Britain (War of 1812) and goes on to expand its geography. Following Manifest Destiny, a belief that Americans are destined to settle the entire continent, the United States adds to its territories, buying some lands and gaining others through annexation and war. The Native Americans are gradually pushed off their land onto reservations. City populations explode as the Industrial Revolution gains force.

- **1860–1865**—The election of Abraham Lincoln on an antislavery ticket causes Southern states to secede from the Union. This begins the Civil War. During the war, Lincoln issues the Emancipation Proclamation, freeing the slaves in the seceding states.

- **1867–1877**—In the Reconstruction period, the Northern states ratify the Thirteenth, Fourteenth, and Fifteenth Amendments, extending Civil Rights and voting privileges to African Americans.

- **1877–1914**—The Industrial Revolution continues. Large industrial empires are born in the United States, including railroad and shipbuilding companies. These companies are major employers for the "new immigrants," groups of people from Southern and Eastern Europe who have arrived in major cities, such as New York, Philadelphia, and Chicago, to find new economic opportunities.

- **1914–1918**—World War I begins in Europe due to extreme nationalism and an alliance system among the countries. The United States enters the war in 1917 on the side of the Allies after it has civilian boats attacked by Germany. Russia, a strong member of the Allies, drops out due to its own communist revolution, but Germany still loses the war. The Allies develop the Treaty of Versailles (which the United States never actually ratifies) to punish Germany after the war. President Woodrow Wilson attempts to create a League of Nations with his Fourteen Point plan that will prevent such wars from happening in the future, but he is met with resistance from the Senate.

- **1918–1939**—War-weary Americans wish to practice isolationism following World War I. The Women's Suffrage movement culminates in the Nineteenth Amendment, which prohibits citizens from being denied the right to vote on the basis of sex. Franklin Delano Roosevelt is elected president and promises to try to bring the country back to prosperity. His New Deal policies bring more regulation to the business world, and his social programs employ hundreds of thousands.

- **1939–1945**—Germany, falling under control of the totalitarian Nazi party, is persuaded by a new leader, Adolf Hitler, to expand by invading other countries. Hitler begins to systematically persecute and kill Jews and political enemies as the Holocaust escalates. This begins World War II. The United States passes the Neutrality Acts to avoid entry but is forced to participate after Japan (an ally of Germany) bombs Pearl Harbor in 1941. The United States joins the Allies (Great Britain, Soviet Union, and others) to oppose the Axis Powers (Germany, Japan, Italy). During the war, the United States imprisons Japanese Americans out of fear that they may be spies. The war ends with an Allied victory and leads to a period of decolonization in which colonies in Africa and Asia gain independence. Soldiers return home to the United States greeted by the G.I. Bill, which allows veterans to get a college education and own a home.

- **1945–1953**—The United States enjoys a period of economic prosperity, although political tensions between the capitalist United States and communist Russia increase. The period begins what is known as the "Cold War," during which both sides start a nuclear arms race. The Truman Doctrine, articulated by President Truman, emphasizes the need to contain communism so that it will not follow the same path as the unchecked Nazism did. The United States forms NATO, which consists of allegiances with Western European countries that wish to stop the expansion of communism. The Soviets and Eastern European countries respond with the Warsaw Pact. Caught in the middle of this conflict is Germany, which is divided into East Germany and West Germany. Tensions grow early on as the Soviets block the United States from entering West Berlin, Germany, and the United States utilizes an airlift to take supplies to the region. From 1950 to 1953, the United States takes part in the Korean War in an attempt to prevent Korea from becoming a communist state.

- **1954–1963**—The Civil Rights movement begins. The Supreme Court rules school segregation unconstitutional. Martin Luther King Jr. becomes a national figure and delivers his "I Have a Dream" speech.

- **1963–1973**—The United States gradually gets entangled in the Vietnam War. The Civil Rights movement continues to gain ground, bolstered by a Supreme Court led by Earl Warren that is notable for its expansion of civil liberties and civil rights. President Johnson's Great Society plan champions equality and a war on poverty. The Watergate scandal forces President Nixon to resign and brings American confidence in its political system to a low point.
- **1973–1990s**—Nuclear armaments around the world begin to dismantle as the Cold War wanes. The USSR is disbanded, and many of the Eastern Bloc (formerly communist) countries begin to move toward capitalism. A new awareness of the environment leads to the ecology movement, and new technologies begin what would be called the Information Age.
- **2000–2010**—The September 11 attack on New York's World Trade Center in 2001 leads the United States to declare a "war on terrorism" resulting in the invasion of Afghanistan and Iraq. Several large natural disasters (including Hurricane Katrina) help propel global warming to the forefront of public debate. Both China and India come into their own as economic forces to be reckoned with, just as a credit and housing crisis in the United States leads to the bankruptcy of major banks and other financial institutions, resulting in a global recession.

Let's try a passage.

This excerpt is from a speech by President Harry Truman:

> Members of the Congress of the United States:
> The very existence of the Greek state is today threatened by the terrorist activities of several thousand armed men, led by Communists, who defy the government's authority at a number of points, particularly along the northern boundaries....
> Meanwhile, the Greek Government is unable to cope with the situation. The Greek army is small and poorly equipped. It needs supplies and equipment if it is to restore the authority of the government throughout Greek territory. Greece must have assistance if it is to become a self-supporting and self-respecting democracy...The United States must supply that assistance.

1. Based on the excerpt, what event was Truman addressing when he made this speech?

    A. the desegregation of the military
    B. the final stages of World War II
    C. his reelection campaign
    D. the early stages of the Cold War

Here's How to Crack It

There is a key phrase in this document that states rebellion in Europe is "led by Communists." Communism characterized the Soviet Union during the Cold War and the Soviets attempted to gain influence in Europe by infiltrating European governments. The U.S. response was containment policy, which aimed to disallow the spread of communism beyond Soviet borders. This is called the Truman Doctrine, which set the stage for the Cold War. Choice (D) is correct. While Truman is responsible for the desegregation of the military, there is no evidence in the text of this action, so (A) is incorrect. Truman oversaw the final stages of World War II as president, but did not declare the Truman Doctrine until after the war was over, so (B) is incorrect. There is no evidence of a political campaign, so eliminate (C).

Social Studies, Part One Drill

Try the following questions. You can check your answers in Part VIII: Answer Key to Drills.

<u>Question 1</u> refers to the following map.

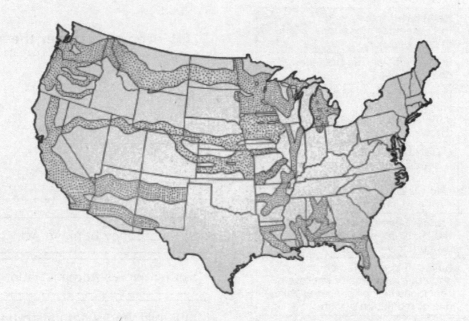

1. The shaded areas of this map from the late 1800s most likely indicate

    A. pathways of the Underground Railroad.
    B. land grants provided to railway companies.
    C. major rivers used for transporting manufactured goods.
    D. the Lewis and Clark trail.

2. The following chart lists many of the programs implemented under President Franklin D. Roosevelt's "New Deal":

1933	
Emergency Banking Act	Closed down all banks, examined their books, and reopened those that were solvent
Farm Credit Administration	Made low-interest, long-term loans to farmers for mortgages, equipment, and taxes
Economy Act	Proposed balancing the federal budget
Civilian Conservation Corps	Paid $30 a month to boys and young men to work in national parks and plant trees throughout the West
Federal Emergency Relief Administration	• Distributed $500 million to states for direct aid to families • Matched every $3 that cities and towns spent on relief projects with $1 in federal aid
Agricultural Adjustment Administration	Paid farmers to grow fewer crops, thus bringing prices up (later declared unconstitutional)
Tennessee Valley Authority	Built dams, provided electricity, and otherwise greatly improved conditions in the Tennessee Valley, one of the nation's poorest regions
Home Owners' Loan Corporation	• Made low-interest, long-term mortgage loans • Protected people from losing their houses
Banking Act of 1933	• Created the FDIC (see next row) • Authorized branch banking
Federal Deposit Insurance Corporation	Insured individual bank deposits of up to $5,000
National Recovery Administration	Regulated businesses by establishing minimum wages and other standards to protect workers
Public Works Administration	Contracted private firms to hire millions of people to build bridges, post offices, highways, and other structures
Civil Works Administration	Created millions of low-skill jobs such as cleaning city streets
1934	
Securities and Exchange Commission	Regulated companies that sold stocks and bonds
Federal Housing Administration	Insured all bank loans made for the construction and repair of houses

Which of the boxed New Deal programs to the left directly provided jobs to the unemployed?

Click on the programs you want to select and drag them into the box below. (For this drill, write the program letters in the box.)

Job Programs Under the New Deal

(a) Emergency Banking Act

(b) Civil Works Administration (CWA)

(c) Public Works Administration (PWA)

(d) Federal Housing Administration (FHA)

(e) Civilian Conservation Corps (CCC)

(f) Economy Act

3. "Laws permitting, and even requiring, their separation in places where they are liable to be brought into contact do not necessarily imply the inferiority of either race to the other, and have been generally, if not universally, recognized as within the competency of State Legislatures in the exercise of their police power. The most common instance of this is connected with the establishment of separate schools for white and colored children, which has been held to be a valid exercise of legislative power."

—*Plessy vs. Ferguson* (1896)

The above quote best exemplifies which of the following ideas?

A. civil rights and racial equality
B. separation of powers
C. racism
D. separate but equal

Chapter 19
Social Studies,
Part Two

In this chapter, we'll cover economics, statistics, geography, the environment, and human geography.

ECONOMICS

Economics is not just the study of money—it's the study of how a society meets its needs through the production and distribution of goods and services.

How successful a country is in meeting its needs is a function of many interconnected things such such as the following:

Natural resources: Every country has some natural resources. Some have oil or valuable metal deposits in their lands, others have rich farmland, and others have miles of coastline that can be used for fishing or shipbuilding.

The labor pool: Are the country's workers highly skilled or uneducated? Are there enough workers to meet the needs of production, or are there too many, leaving some unemployed?

The industrial base: Does a country have the technical know-how, the factories, and the ability to raise money to acquire new knowledge and new factories?

Types of Economies

Capitalism is a system in which the means of production and development are privately owned and traded. The concept of pure capitalism was first described in 1776 by a Scottish economist named Adam Smith, in a book called *The Wealth of Nations*. Smith advocated a **laissez-faire** (from the French "to let alone") economic system in which the government does not interfere with the free market at all, allowing the interplay of supply and demand to determine prices. In later years, other economists, such as John Maynard Keynes, argued that in the real world, governments must use a combination of tax and spending programs to stabilize a capitalist-based economy.

Some countries have installed economies based on **central planning**—in other words, government ownership of a country's resources and government control of its economic activities. **Communism**, as it was practiced in the former Soviet Union, is an example of such an economy. All the means of production in the Soviet Union were owned by the state, which decided what would be produced and when. **Socialism** is also an example of an economy based at least in part on central planning. In a socialist country, many of the largest industries (such as the transportation industry or the steel industry) are owned and operated by the government, as is a comprehensive system of public welfare.

The United States, like most countries today, practices a modified version of capitalism, sometimes called a **mixed economy**. The government regulates some aspects of business (for example, the Food and Drug Administration makes sure that products sold in our stores will not poison us) and offers some social welfare systems, but the majority of economic decisions are made by private individuals and companies. Such a system encourages **entrepreneurialism**, the practice of taking on the risk of starting a business with the hope of paying off in substantial profits.

Microeconomics

In a capitalist economy, prices are determined by supply and demand. **Supply** is the amount of goods and services available at a particular time. **Demand** is the consumers' need for those goods and services. For example, a sneaker company might produce 200,000 pairs of sneakers. This is its supply. The public might end up buying 150,000 pairs. This is the demand for this particular product. If supply and demand are equal, then the price will remain the same. However, if there is more supply than demand, then prices fall. For example, because there was a surplus of 50,000 pairs of sneakers that were not sold, the company is going to have to reduce its price to make the public want to buy them.

However, if there is more demand than supply, then prices rise. For example, if these sneakers become very popular, then there will be a shortage, and the sneaker company may charge more for the sneakers because they are scarce.

These forces work on a global scale, which is why the prices of oil, gold, and shares of stock in different companies go up and down every day in reaction to the supply and demand of the market.

> **Simple Economics**
> If supply is greater than demand, prices fall. If demand is greater than supply, prices rise.

If an economy is functioning properly, there is an ever-increasing demand for goods and services that is met by an ever-increasing supply. However, if there is too much demand and not enough supply, then **inflation** can result. Inflation is a general rise in prices. A little inflation is to be expected, but too much can start a spiraling effect in which prices rise so rapidly that a country's currency loses its value. During the 1930s in Germany, it was not uncommon to see people taking wheelbarrows full of money to the store to pay for their groceries.

When there is too little demand and too much supply, then **deflation** can result. Most of the countries of the world experienced deflation during the Great Depression.

Vocabulary

recession—a period during which employment and economic activity decline
depression—a longer period of drastic declines in the economy and employment
import—to buy goods from another country and bring them back to your own country for consumption
export—to sell goods to another country for consumption in that country

Let's try a problem.

1. A company produces and sells widgets. A demand curve for that product is shown below:

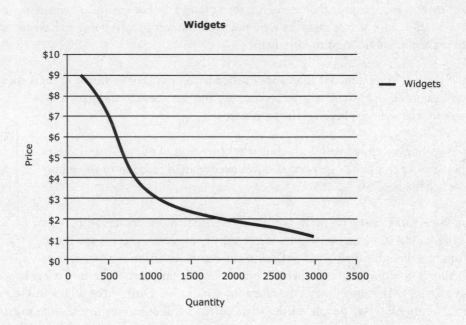

Widgets

If the price for a widget drops to $3, the company can expect to sell an amount of ⬚ widgets.

Here's How to Crack It

The demand curve shows us how much quantity a firm can expect to sell when it marks the product at a certain price. Look at the prices on the y-axis (vertical) and locate $3. Scan right until you find the line representing widgets. When you find the line, move straight down (to the x-axis) to see that the expected quantity sold is **1,000**.

Production

Capital is the primary catalyst for industrial production. Both material wealth and the ability to produce wealth are known as capital (hence the term *capitalism*). In many industries, the most important form of capital is human **labor**—the people who produce a given product.

Another factor in production is the concept of **incentives**. Incentives are anything that motivates or discourages economic behavior. For example, if a company receives tax breaks for hiring more employees, then it has an incentive to increase its labor force, thus increasing production. Other incentives occur at the consumer level. If a company wants to encourage people to purchase its product, it may create an incentive by lowering the price.

A further factor of production is **opportunity cost**. Opportunity cost is the option not chosen when a more advantageous option is chosen. For instance a person may choose to purchase Brand X or Brand Y. If she chooses Brand X, then Brand Y is the opportunity cost. In matters of production, opportunity costs can come in the form of materials used, the decision to hire more or fewer workers, the price set for a product, and other decisions related to economic behavior. The ability of a company in a particular country to produce its product at a lower opportunity cost than a company in another country is referred to as a **comparative advantage**.

Let's try a problem.

_____

Ben creates a company that sells and repairs musical instruments. When the economy experiences a recession and Ben's business slows down, he realizes that he cannot continue selling musical instruments. He decides to move into a smaller building with cheaper rent and continue his business by doing only musical instrument repairs.

1.   Click on the phrase that represents Ben's opportunity cost after the recession occurs.

Here's How to Crack It

Since opportunity cost refers to the option not taken, you want to look for something that Ben gave up. In this case, he stopped **selling musical instruments**, making that his opportunity cost. Since he is not forgoing a smaller building, cheaper rent, or instrument repairs (instead, he is choosing those options), these are not opportunity costs.

_____

Markets

A market is a system in which goods, services, and capital are exchanged. If one company controls an entire industry or becomes the only company to make a certain product, that company is said to have a **monopoly**. In the United States, this is illegal. If the government believes that one company is gaining control of an industry, it will institute an **antitrust** court action to force that company to let other companies into the field. An example of this was the antitrust action that forced AT&T to break up into smaller independent telephone companies. The case against Microsoft was another antitrust action.

Balance of Payments Quiz

Q: The United States buys more goods from Japan than it sells to Japan. Does it have a balance of payments deficit or a surplus?

Turn the page for the answer.

Because all countries lack some natural resources, each country trades certain goods and services in exchange for other goods and services that it needs. This is known as **international trade.** If a country buys more goods from foreign countries than it sells, it has a **balance of payments deficit.** If it sells more than it buys, it has a **balance of payments surplus.**

Vocabulary

    antitrust laws—laws designed to prevent the formation of monopolies
    GNP—the gross national product, the total value of the nation's production

Let's try a problem.

The graph below summarizes Country X's international trade:

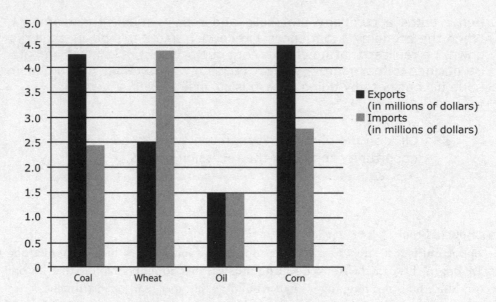

1.   For which product does Country X have a balance of payment deficit?

    A.   coal
    B.   wheat
    C.   oil
    D.   corn

Here's How to Crack It

The balance of payment deficit occurs when spending on imports exceeds revenue from exports. Therefore, you should look for the product with an import amount higher than its export amount. Wheat is the only product that has a higher bar for imports than exports. Both corn and coal have a balance of payment surplus, while oil is revenue neutral.

Macroeconomics

Instead of viewing individual markets, as the field of microeconomics does, **macroeconomics** looks at the entire economy. This is useful when it comes to government policies that attempt to strengthen the economy. There are two types of economic policies: **fiscal policy** and **monetary policy**.

Fiscal policy consists of the processes of taxation and government spending as they relate to the health of the overall economy. If there is widespread **unemployment**, the government may increase its spending to create programs that help people get back to work. In order to do this, the government must also increase its revenue by raising taxes. For obvious reasons, this may also have short-term drawbacks.

Monetary policy deals with the amount of money put into or taken out of the market. The intention of monetary policy is to adjust the value of currency in order to reverse inflation or deflation. For example, the rules of supply and demand tell us that the presence of too much money in a market lowers the value of an individual dollar. When the value of the dollar is low, people cannot easily afford the products they used to be able to purchase. This is called **inflation**. By removing some of the currency from the market, prices should drop back to normal levels.

Let's try a problem.

> **Balance of Payments Quiz**
> A: The United States has a balance of payments deficit with Japan.

The following text is from a radio address given by President Franklin Roosevelt in 1933:

Two months ago we were facing serious problems. The country was dying by inches. It was dying because trade and commerce had declined to dangerously low levels; prices for basic commodities were such as to destroy the value of the assets of national institutions such as banks, savings banks, insurance companies, and others... The legislation which has been passed or is in the process of enactment can properly be considered as part of a well-grounded plan.

First, we are giving opportunity of employment to one-quarter of a million of the unemployed, especially the young men who have dependents, to go into the forestry and flood prevention work. This is a big task because it means feeding, clothing, and caring for nearly twice as many men as we have in the regular army itself. In creating this civilian conservation corps we are killing two birds with one stone. We are clearly enhancing the value of our natural resources and second, we are relieving an appreciable amount of actual distress.

1. According to the speech, Franklin Roosevelt combated the economic crisis by

    A. cutting taxes to save federal money.
    B. saving banks to protect America's credit.
    C. selling natural resources to stabilize funds.
    D. allowing the government to spend money in order to invest in workers.

Here's How to Crack It
The text mentions that the government is "giving opportunity of employment to one-quarter of a million of the unemployed." This is closest to (D). Roosevelt's plan would actually raise taxes to pay for these programs. Therefore, (A) is incorrect. The phrase "savings banks" is located in the passage, but there is no evidence that Roosevelt sought to save banks. Choice (B) was meant to trick test takers who did not read for content. Natural resources are mentioned in the final sentence, but there is no evidence of selling them. Eliminate (C).

Economics Drill

Try the following questions. You can check your answers in Part VIII: Answer Key to Drills.

<u>Questions 1 and 2 refer to the graph below.</u>

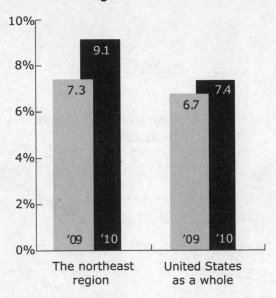

Percentage of the Labor Force Unemployed

1. According to the graph, the difference in the employment rate in the northeast region from 2009 to 2010 represented a change of what percent?

    A.   16.4%
    B.   10.9%
    C.   3.1%
    D.   1.8%

2. An evaluation of the graph above would show that the overall <u>economy</u> of the United States in 2010 probably performed

    A.   worse than it did in 2009.
    B.   worse than it did in the northeast region.
    C.   better than the economies of other nations.
    D.   better than it did in 2009.

STATISTICS

While you don't need to know much about statistics for the GED® test, one topic that occasionally shows up involves interpreting data in social studies contexts. You may, for example, be asked to distinguish between **correlation** (a mutual relationship or connection) and **causation** (the relationship between cause and effect). The main thing to remember in this context is that even if there is a close correlation between two variables, there is not necessarily a cause-and-effect relationship.

Let's try a question.

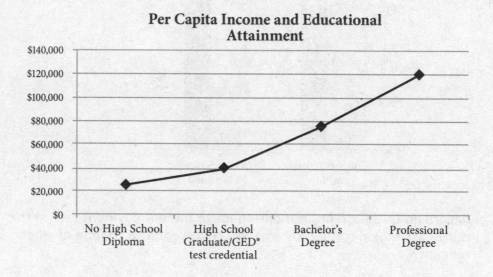

Per Capita Income and Educational Attainment

1. The graph above shows the relationship between average per capita income and educational attainment in the United States. Which of the following statements is best supported by the data?

    A. There is a causal relationship between educational attainment and per capita income.
    B. There is no causal relationship between educational attainment and per capita income.
    C. There is a correlation between educational attainment and per capita income.
    D. There is no correlation between educational attainment and per capita income.

Here's How to Crack It

According to the graph, average per capita income increases as educational attainment increases. Be careful, however—this is a correlation, and not necessarily a cause-and-effect relationship. Simply based on a correlation between two variables, it is impossible to state with certainty that one of those variables caused (or didn't cause) the other; eliminate (A) and (B). Since there is definitely a correlation between the two variables in question, eliminate (D) and choose (C).

A final area of statistics that is occasionally tested on the GED® test requires you to understand the difference between **average, median, mode,** and **range**. While this may seem like something that would fit better in the math chapter, the GED® test may ask you to apply these math concepts in a social studies context.

Vocabulary

   average (arithmetic mean)—the sum of a set of numbers divided by the number of numbers in that set
   median—the middle number in a set (when those numbers are arranged in increasing order); if there is an even number of numbers, the median is the average of the middle two numbers
   mode—the number that occurs most often in a set
   range—the difference between the highest and lowest numbers in a set

Let's try a question.

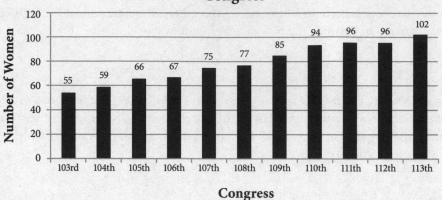

Women in the United States Congress

Number of Women (y-axis: 0, 20, 40, 60, 80, 100, 120)

Congress	Number of Women
103rd	55
104th	59
105th	66
106th	67
107th	75
108th	77
109th	85
110th	94
111th	96
112th	96
113th	102

Congress (x-axis)

1. The graph above shows the number of women serving in the United States Congress (both House and Senate) from the 103rd to the 113th Congress (1993–2015). Drag the average, median, mode, and range of the number of women serving in Congress during this period into the appropriate box below:

Average	Median	Mode	Range

> 47

> 77

> 79.$\overline{27}$

> 96

Here's How to Crack It

To find the average, you need to add up all the numbers in the chart and divide by the number of numbers: $(55 + 59 + 66 + 67 + 75 + 77 + 85 + 94 + 96 + 96 + 102) ÷ 11 = 79.\overline{27}$ To find the median, list the numbers in increasing order and find the one in the middle: 77. To find the mode, look for the number that occurs most often: 96. To find the range, subtract the smallest number from the largest number: $102 - 55 = 47$. Since finding the average is the most work-intensive of these four operations, you could also find the median, mode, and range first and then whatever answer choice is left over must be the average.

GEOGRAPHY

Geography is the study of the physical features of the earth and the ways in which these features affect the people who live on the earth. When most people think about geography, they think only of surface terrain, but the study of geography also includes the natural resources underneath the surface of the earth and the climates of, and atmosphere above, the various regions of the world.

Globes

A globe is a three-dimensional representation of the earth. On the GED® test, you may see two-dimensional drawings of a globe such as the one below:

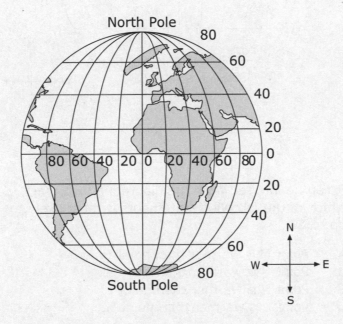

In this figure, you can see about half of the earth's surface. You are looking at Africa in the middle of the globe. Above Africa, you can see most of Europe. At the bottom left of the globe, you can see most of South America. The line running horizontally across the center of the globe is called the **equator**. This line, like all the lines on this map, is imaginary. If you go to the equator, you will not, of course, find a line drawn all the way around the globe. The part of the earth above the equator is called the **Northern Hemisphere.** The part below is called the **Southern Hemisphere.** The horizontal lines above and below the equator are called lines of **latitude.** Any point on the equator has a latitude of 0 degrees. A point 20 degrees above the equator would be called 20 degrees north. The vertical lines running along the globe are called lines of **longitude.** A longitude of 0 degrees describes an imaginary line that runs right through Greenwich, England, dividing the globe into the **Eastern and Western Hemispheres.** Using a combination of latitude and longitude, you can locate the position of any point on the earth.

Let's try a question.

Question 1 refers to the following diagram of the globe.

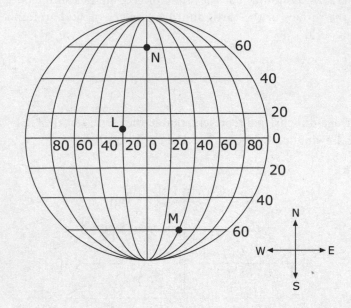

Map Lines
horizontal lines =
latitude
vertical lines =
longitude

1. It can be inferred from the diagram above that
    which of the following statements is most likely to
    be true?

    A. Point M is warmer than point L.
    B. Point N is warmer than point M.
    C. Point N is warmer than point L.
    D. Point L is warmer than point N.

Here's How to Crack It
The nearer the equator, the warmer the average temperature. Which point is nearest the equa-
tor? If you said point L, you are absolutely right. The correct answer to this analysis question is
(D).

Maps

A map is a drawing of a smaller part of the globe. Below, you can see one of the GED® test's favorites: a map of the United States.

■ population more than 10 million
(Source: U.S. Bureau of Census)

This map shows the different states of the United States. There's a similar one in the "Understanding Graphics" supplement. However, note that on this map, you are also given some additional information. States with a population more than 10 million are shaded. Almost certainly, this information will be necessary to answer the question that comes with this map. As we said in the "Understanding Graphics" supplement, the information you need to answer map questions is almost always located on the map itself. You will find that some maps include information on the population living in the area, others will show climate patterns, and others will give topographical information, such as how far the land is above sea level.

As with almost all maps, north is at the top of the page, which means that south is at the bottom, west is toward the left, and east is toward the right. Let's look at the question that went with this map:

1. According to the map above, the biggest concentration of states with large populations can be found in which region of the United States?

    A.   the central region
    B.   the southwestern region
    C.   the northwestern region
    D.   the northeastern region

Here's How to Crack It

Where are most of the high-population states? That's right, the top right-hand corner of the United States. Which region is that? If you're stuck, consult the paragraph right above the question. The correct answer to this comprehension question is (D).

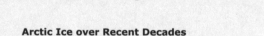

ENVIRONMENT

Humans have left an impact on the environment through their interaction with the world around them. Some of these can have harmful effects on the environment, such as pollution, while others can have positive effects, such as the protection of endangered species.

Policies that aim to maintain a healthy environment tend to aim for **sustainability**. Sustainable practices will theoretically allow an environment to remain stable, thus protecting its **natural resources** and **natural diversity** (the variety of living things in a region).

Let's try a problem.

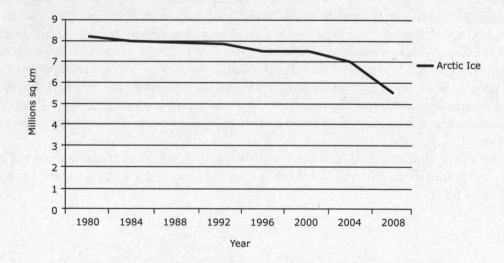

Arctic Ice over Recent Decades

1. In which set of years was the most significant change in arctic ice recorded?

    A.   1980–1984
    B.   1988–1992
    C.   1996–2000
    D.   2004–2008

Here's How to Crack It

The most significant change in arctic ice will be the part of the line with the steepest slope. The steepest part of this line is closest to 2004–2008, when arctic ice drops from around 7 to 5.5. Choice (D) is correct. From 1980 until 1992, the line is mostly flat, so eliminate (A) and (B). While the amount of arctic ice in 1996–2000 is less than that of previous years, it is relatively stable during this time period. Therefore, eliminate (C).

HUMAN GEOGRAPHY

Throughout history, humankind has migrated from one area to another in search of trade, food, adventure, and freedom. This dispersal of a population into new areas around the world is known as a **diaspora**.

The early settlers came to America to escape persecution in Europe. These were the first of a long line of immigrants who found a new beginning in our country. The United States is sometimes called a "melting pot" because of the rich brew of different cultures that has helped form the American culture. In melting pots such as the United States, **cultural diversity** can lead to the spread of practices beyond the original culture. This phenomenon is called **cultural diffusion**. For instance, Mexican food's popularity is not unique to Mexican Americans. Rather, it has diffused into mainstream American cultures, while undergoing some changes. Groups also practice **assimilation** as they sacrifice some of their cultural identity in order to fit into a new culture.

Vocabulary

refugee—someone fleeing from one country to another out of fear or necessity
immigrate—to enter a new country
emigrate—to leave your own country

Let's try a question.

The following is from an 1818 letter that an Irish immigrant to the United States wrote back to his family in Ireland six months after settling in America:

> One thing I think is certain that if the emigrants knew before hand what they have to suffer for about the first six months after leaving home in every respect they would never come here. However, an enterprising man, desirous of advancing himself in the world will despise everything for coming to this free country, where a man is allowed to...act and speak as he likes, abuse public men in their office to their faces, wear your hat in court and smoke a cigar while speaking to the judge as familiarly as if he was a common mechanic, hundreds go unpunished for crimes for which they would be surely hung in Ireland; in fact, they are so tender of life in this country that a person should have a very great interest to get himself hanged for anything!

1. What does the author of this letter indicate was a primary reason for his emigration?

    A. freedom of religion
    B. freedom of speech
    C. freedom of privacy
    D. freedom to work

Here's How to Crack It

The author says that one can "act and speak as he likes" and goes on to give examples of how this is possible in the United States. He most values his freedom of speech, which makes (B) the correct answer. There is no evidence that the author values religious freedom, privacy, or the right to work. Eliminate (A), (C), and (D).

Social Studies, Part Two Drill

Try the following questions. You can check your answers in Part VIII: Answer Key to Drills.

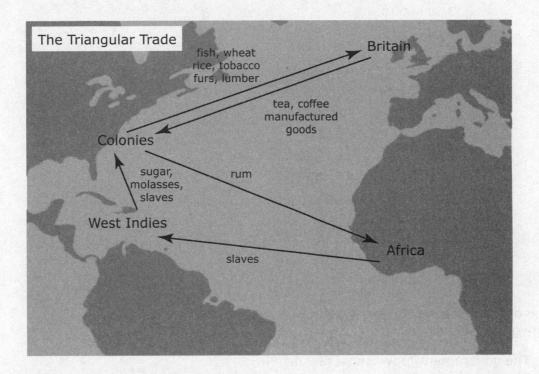

1. According to the map above, one of the colonies' major exports was

   A. tobacco.
   B. manufactured goods.
   C. slaves.
   D. sugar.

Paid Civilian Employment of the Federal Government, 1911–1970

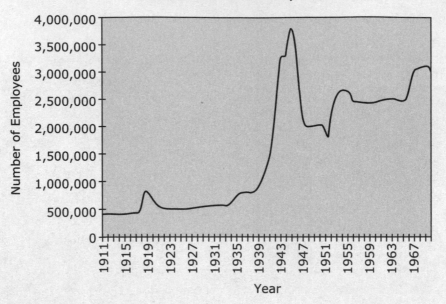

2. Which of the following is most supported by the graph above?

   A. The government grows most rapidly in wartime.
   B. The population of the country grew most rapidly during the 1940s.
   C. Civilian employment increased most rapidly during the Great Depression.
   D. Civilian employment was at its lowest levels in the years after World War I.

3. The following represents patterns of immigration to the United States from 1880 to 1930:

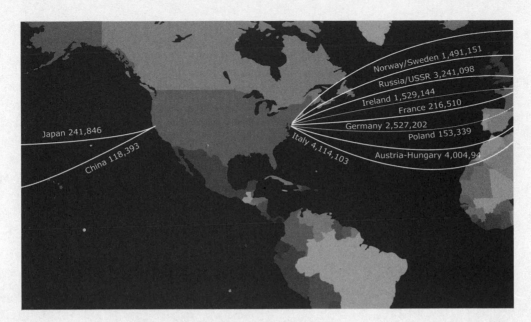

According to the map above, determine whether the following statements would be "True" or "False." Drag and drop the statements into the appropriate boxes. (For this drill, write the statement letters in the boxes.)

True	False

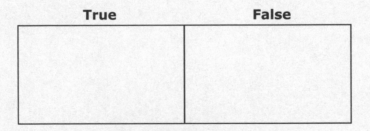

(a) European immigrants were more likely to arrive in the Eastern United States than in the West.

(b) Italian immigrants out-numbered Irish immigrants by at least 2 to 1.

(c) For a time, there were more Japanese than French immigrating to the United States.

(d) Chinese and Japanese immigrants did not settle in the East from 1880 to 1930.

Part VII
Science

Chapter 20
Science Overview

If you find that the idea of spending an hour and a half answering science questions sends you into a cold sweat, have no fear! While you will need to have some basic science knowledge in order to work the questions successfully, you won't need to memorize the periodic table or learn how to do quantum physics. In fact, you'll find that you can answer many of the questions in the Science test simply by reading the passages, charts, and graphs that the test provides, or by using scientific thinking. Some questions will require you to have outside knowledge, but in the chapters that follow we'll address the topics that the test covers, so that you'll be well prepared by the time that test day arrives.

What Does the Science Test Look Like?

To score well on the test, you first need to know what to expect on test day. On the GED® Science test you'll have 90 minutes to answer approximately 34 questions, although the number of questions can vary slightly from test to test. The questions will come in six different formats.

Question Formats

Multiple-choice questions give you a question with four possible answers, and your job will be to choose the best answer. For example, you may see a passage-based multiple-choice question, such as the one that follows.

> Biologists have long known that some types of electromagnetic radiation, such as X-rays and gamma rays, can be dangerous to human beings.
>
> However, until now, no one has ever suggested that microwave radiation might also be harmful. In preliminary test-tube laboratory results, a scientist has found elevated growth rates in cancer cells exposed to low doses of microwaves.
>
> These results are only preliminary because, first, there has been no controlled study of the effects of microwaves on human beings. Second, this study was of short duration, raising the possibility that the dangers of long-term exposure have not yet been assessed.
>
> Although federal guidelines for how much electromagnetic energy can be allowed to enter the work and home environment have been made more stringent since they were first implemented in 1982, the recent study poses troubling questions about the safety of microwaves.

1. According to the information presented, the cancer cells' increasing growth rates in the laboratory experiment was most likely due to

    A. the cancer cells' natural reproductive cycle.
    B. a short-term growth spurt that may not indicate a general trend.
    C. exposure to microwave radiation.
    D. accidental contamination of cell samples during laboratory procedures.

Fill-in-the-blank questions won't provide you with any answer choices; you'll just need to fill a word or number into a blank space in order to answer the question. Note that if the question requires you to do any calculations, you will generally receive access to an online calculator. After all, the Science test is about understanding science concepts and scientific thinking, not your ability to do math! Here's an example of a fill-in-the-blank question.

2. Each day for one week, doctors measured the flow rate—the amount of fluid passing through a given area of a pipe per second—of blood flowing through a patient's aorta. The day of the week, the velocity of the blood, and the flow rate are shown in the chart below.

Day	Blood Velocity	Flow Rate
Monday	40 cm/s	120 cm/s^3
Tuesday	38 cm/s	114 cm/s^3
Wednesday	39 cm/s	117 cm/s^3
Thursday	42 cm/s	126 cm/s^3
Friday	41 cm/s	123 cm/s^3
Saturday	39 cm/s	117 cm/s^3
Sunday	43 cm/s	129 cm/s^3

What is the mean of the flow rates shown in the chart above?

You may use the calculator.

Drop-down menu questions are similar to multiple-choice questions, but you'll need to choose your answers from a drop-down menu. Additionally, you may find that a single question will involve more than one drop-down menu. For example, you may see a question such as this one:

3. Scientists calculate the buoyant force, the upward force that a liquid exerts on an object submerged or floating in that liquid, by using the formula $F_B = \rho_f V g$, where F_B is the buoyant force, ρ_f is the density of the fluid, and g is a constant and is the acceleration due to gravity.

   Based on the information above, an object would

   experience a | Select... ▼ |
   | greater buoyant force |
   | lesser acceleration due to gravity |

   in a fluid that had | Select... ▼ |.
   | greater density |
   | lesser volume |

Hot-spot questions will typically provide you with a chart or a graph, and ask you to identify a point on the chart or graph that answers a particular question. You'll be able to select that point using your computer cursor. A typical hot-spot question might look like the following.

4. The term *solubility* refers to the amount of a substance (solute) that will dissolve in a given amount of a liquid substance (solvent). The solubility of solids in water varies with temperature. The graph below displays the water solubility curves for six crystalline solids.

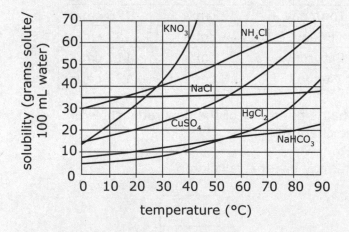

   Click the point on the graph at which the solubility of NaCl is equal to the solubility of CuSO$_4$.

Drag-and-drop questions will provide you with multiple options, and you'll be asked to select one or more of those options in order to complete the question. A typical drag-and-drop question may appear as follows.

5. The term *solubility* refers to the amount of a substance (solute) that will dissolve in a given amount of a liquid substance (solvent). The solubility of solids in water varies with temperature. The graph below displays the water solubility curves for six crystalline solids.

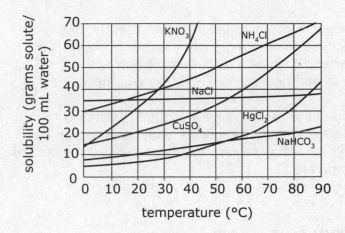

Identify the substances with the least change in solubility and the greatest change in solubility. Drag and drop your choices into the appropriate boxes.

Least change in solubility	Greatest change in solubility

NaCl

CuSO$_4$

NaHCO$_3$

HgCl$_2$

Short-answer questions are short essay questions in which you'll be asked to design an experiment, explain an issue, or answer a question. You should plan to spend about ten minutes answering each short-answer question, and you'll see two of these questions per test. A typical short-answer question might be similar to the one below.

6.   A marine biologist wishes to examine how the salt content in soil varies with distance from the ocean and with air temperature. She hypothesizes that, as the distance from the ocean increases, temperature increases and soil salt content decreases.

Design a controlled experiment that the biologist can use to determine whether her hypothesis is correct. Include a discussion of how she will collect data and how she will test her hypothesis.

Type your response on a computer, if one is available. Otherwise, write your response on paper. This task may require approximately 10 minutes to complete.

What Skills Will Be Tested?

In addition to knowing the format in which the questions will appear, you should also know which skills those questions will test. Fortunately, GED® Science questions really test only a few skills. Once you master those skills, then you'll find it much easier to ace the Science test!

Comprehension Questions

Comprehension questions ask you to find a particular piece of information from a passage, chart, or graph, and then recognize that information, slightly restated, in an answer choice. Comprehension questions may also ask you to go just a bit further and identify a logical implication of that information. The question that follows is a comprehension question related to a passage you've already seen.

Biologists have long known that some types of electromagnetic radiation, such as X-rays and gamma rays, can be dangerous to human beings.

However, until now, no one has ever suggested that microwave radiation might also be harmful. In preliminary test-tube laboratory results, a scientist has found elevated growth rates in cancer cells exposed to low doses of microwaves.

These results are only preliminary because, first, there has been no controlled study of the effects of microwaves on human beings. Second, this study was of short duration, raising the possibility that the dangers of long-term exposure have not yet been assessed.

Although federal guidelines for how much electromagnetic energy can be allowed to enter the work and home environment have been made more stringent since they were first implemented in 1982, the recent study poses troubling questions about the safety of microwaves.

1. According to the information presented, the cancer cells' increasing growth rates in the laboratory experiment was most likely due to

A. the cancer cells' natural reproductive cycle.
B. a short-term growth spurt that may not indicate a general trend.
C. exposure to microwave radiation.
D. accidental contamination of cell samples during laboratory procedures.

Here's How to Crack It

Before you begin the questions from any passage, you should always make sure that you understand the *structure* of the passage. For example, someone in a hurry might have read the first paragraph of *this* passage and gotten the impression that it was going to be about the danger of gamma rays and X-rays. However, if you looked past the first paragraph, you would realize that the introduction provides background historical context for the subject of the passage. It began by talking about the kind of rays scientists have "long known" to be dangerous and then segued in the second paragraph to another type of ray that may, it turns out *now*, be dangerous as well. The passage describes a laboratory study, gives two reasons that the results are only preliminary, and then summarizes. This question asks about a "laboratory experiment." Where does the passage discuss a laboratory experiment? Check out paragraph 2. Briefly reread the paragraph, and then use Process of Elimination to remove answers that don't agree with the information in the passage. The passage states that cancer cells exposed to microwave radiation experienced "elevated growth rates," so the increasing growth rates are due to microwave radiation, and are not natural. Eliminate (A). While the passage does state that the effects of microwave radiation are unknown, it doesn't provide any evidence that the growth spurt does not indicate a general trend, so (B) is incorrect. Choice (C) agrees with the passage, which states that "a scientist has found elevated growth rates in cancer cells exposed to low doses of microwaves." Thus, (C) is the correct answer. The passage doesn't mention accidental contamination, so (D) is not the correct answer.

Here's another example of a comprehension question. It's based on the same passage as the question on the previous page.

Scientists hypothesize that meteorologists who use remote sensing microwave radiometers to measure the temperature of objects and terrain may suffer adverse health effects due to frequent exposure to microwave radiation.

2. Which excerpt from the passage supports this hypothesis?

A. "These results are only preliminary, because, first, there has been no controlled study of the effects of microwaves on human beings."

B. "Biologists have long known that some types of electromagnetic radiation, such as X-rays and gamma rays, can be dangerous to human beings."

C. "A scientist has found elevated growth rates in cancer cells exposed to low doses of microwaves."

D. "Federal guidelines for how much electromagnetic energy can be allowed to enter the home and work environment have been made more stringent since they were first implemented in 1982."

Here's How to Crack It

In this question, you're asked about "adverse health effects due to frequent exposure to microwave radiation." Where can you find information about possible adverse health effects caused by microwave radiation? Check out paragraph 2, and then use Process of Elimination to remove answer choices that don't discuss adverse health effects and microwave radiation.

Choice (A) discusses the fact that there has been no controlled study of the effects of microwave radiation on humans. While this might suggest that the effects of microwave radiation on humans are unknown, it doesn't show that meteorologists have cause for concern regarding their health; it merely shows that they don't know whether they should be concerned. Thus, you can eliminate (A). Choice (B) does discuss the dangers of some types of electromagnetic radiation, but it discusses X-rays and gamma rays, rather than microwaves, so (B) is incorrect. Choice (C) mentions that microwaves may be associated with increased cancer cell growth rates, which is a potential health hazard associated with microwaves, and is the correct answer. Choice (D) discusses the fact that there are laws in place that regulate the amount of electromagnetic radiation allowed to enter homes and workplaces, but it does not deal specifically with microwave radiation, and does not state that the reason for such regulations is that such radiation poses a health hazard. Thus, (D) is also incorrect. The correct answer is (C).

Application Questions

To answer an application question, you must understand the meaning of a concept described in the passage and then apply that concept in a different context.

The following is an example of an application question.

––––––––––––––––––––○––––––––––––––––––––

1. Each day for one week, doctors measured the flow rate—the amount of fluid passing through a given area of a pipe per second—of blood flowing through a patient's aorta. The day of the week, the velocity of the blood, and the flow rate are shown in the chart below.

Day	Blood Velocity	Flow Rate
Monday	40 cm/s	120 cm/s^3
Tuesday	38 cm/s	114 cm/s^3
Wednesday	39 cm/s	117 cm/s^3
Thursday	42 cm/s	126 cm/s^3
Friday	41 cm/s	123 cm/s^3
Saturday	39 cm/s	117 cm/s^3
Sunday	43 cm/s	129 cm/s^3

What is the mean of the flow rates shown in the chart above?

You may use the calculator.

Here's How to Crack It

To find a mean, or average, you must add up all of the numbers given, and then divide your total by the number of numbers you added up. Be careful to make sure you're solving for the correct thing; in this case, you want to find the mean of the flow rates, not the blood velocity, so be sure to use the numbers given for flow rate. In this case, adding up all of the numbers given for flow rate gives you 120 + 114 + 117 + 126 + 123 + 117 + 129 = 846. Divide 846 by 7 to get 120.86.

––––––––––––––––––––○––––––––––––––––––––

Here's another application question.

---○---

2. A marine biologist wishes to examine how the salt content in soil varies with distance from the ocean and with air temperature. She hypothesizes that, as the distance from the ocean increases, temperature increases and soil salt content decreases.

    Design a controlled experiment that the biologist can use to determine whether her hypothesis is correct. Include a discussion of how she will collect data and how she will test her hypothesis.

Here's How to Crack It

> In a scientific experiment, the **independent variable** is the variable that is deliberately changed. The **dependent variable** changes as a result of changes in the dependent variable.
>
> Source: Encyclopaedia Britannica, Inc.

There are several possible ways that you might answer this question. However, start by considering what the biologist wants to test: "how the salt content in soil varies with distance from the ocean and with air temperature." Since she wants to see the effect that distance has on temperature and salt content, she'll want to get readings in which she varies distance. One way to do that might be as follows: She should collect soil samples at distances of 1 meter, 5 meters, 10 meters, 15 meters, 20 meters, and 25 meters from the ocean, and at each point she should also measure temperature. Keep in mind that experiments are concerned with both validity and reliability. Validity refers to whether or not a test measures what it is intended to measure and reliability refers to whether or not significant results are repeatable under identical conditions. Accordingly, the scientist must design the experiment with the goal of eliminating factors that could skew the results. In short, she needs to ensure she is accurately measuring the dependent variable by controlling for outside influences. To ensure that her results are accurate, she might repeat this process over several days; she would have multiple soil salt content and temperature results. She could then enter the data into a spreadsheet, and create two graphs: one that showed distance plotted against salt content, and another that showed distance plotted against temperature. If the biologist's hypothesis is correct, then the plot of distance versus salt content should show a line or curve with an increasing trend, and the plot of distance versus temperature should show a line or curve with a decreasing trend.

---○---

Try this final application question.

―――――――――――○―――――――――――

3. Scientists calculate the buoyant force, the upward force that a liquid exerts on an object submerged or floating in that liquid, by using the formula $F_B = \rho_f V g$, where F_B is the buoyant force, ρ_f is the density of the fluid, and g is a constant and is the acceleration due to gravity.

Based on the information above, an object would

experience a | Select... ▼ |
| greater buoyant force |
| lesser acceleration due to gravity |

in a fluid that had | Select... ▼ |.
| greater density |
| lesser volume |

Here's How to Crack It

The passage states that g, the acceleration due to gravity, is a constant. Thus, you can eliminate "lesser acceleration due to gravity" from the answer choices in the first drop-down menu, since acceleration due to gravity does not change. Thus, the correct answer in the first drop-down menu must be "greater buoyant force." Now check out the formula $F_B = \rho_f V g$. If density, or ρ_f, increases, then F_B, or the buoyant force, must also increase. On the other hand, if volume, or V, decreases, then F_B must actually decrease. Thus, the correct answer in the second drop-down menu is "greater density."

―――――――――――○―――――――――――

Analysis Questions

An analysis question asks you to break down information from a passage, chart, or graph into more specific categories, and then explore the relationships between those categories. An analysis question might be similar to this one.

1. The term *solubility* refers to the amount of a substance (solute) that will dissolve in a given amount of a liquid substance (solvent). The solubility of solids in water varies with temperature. The graph below displays the water solubility curves for six crystalline solids.

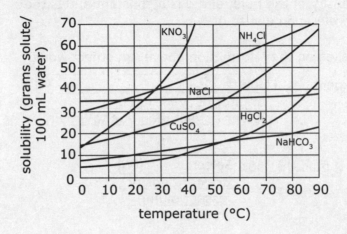

Identify the substances with the least change in solubility and the greatest change in solubility. Drag and drop your choices into the appropriate boxes.

Least change in solubility	Greatest change in solubility

NaCl

$CuSO_4$

$NaHCO_3$

$HgCl_2$

Here's How to Crack It

To find the substance with the least change in solubility, look at the slope of the graph of each of the substances. Note that NaCl has the flattest graph, which therefore means that it has the least change in solubility. The initial solubility of the substance is approximately 35 grams solute per 100 mL of water, and the final value is only approximately 38 grams solute per 100 mL of water. Thus, its change in solubility is very small. $CuSO_4$ has an initial solubility of approximately 15 grams solute per 100 mL of water, and a final solubility of approximately 68 grams solute per 100 mL of water, and does not have the flattest graph, so it does not have the least change in solubility. $NaHCO_3$ has an initial solubility of approximately 8 grams solute per 100 mL of water, and a final solubility of approximately 23 grams solute per 100 mL of water, and does not have the flattest graph, so it does not have the least change in solubility. Finally, $HgCl_2$ has an initial solubility of approximately 5 grams solute per 100 mL of water, and a final solubility of approximately 43 grams solute per 100 mL of water, and does not have the flattest graph, so it does not have the least change in solubility. Note that of the substances, $CuSO_4$ has the greatest difference between its initial solubility and its final solubility, and its graph has the steepest curve, so it is the substance with the greatest change in solubility.

Evaluation Questions

To answer an evaluation question, you must make a judgment or prediction about the information provided in a passage, chart, or graph—sometimes by applying outside knowledge or information that you bring with you to the test.

Biologists have long known that some types of electromagnetic radiation, such as X-rays and gamma rays, can be dangerous to human beings.

However, until now, no one has ever suggested that microwave radiation might also be harmful. In preliminary test-tube laboratory results, a scientist has found elevated growth rates in cancer cells exposed to low doses of microwaves.

These results are only preliminary because, first, there has been no controlled study of the effects of microwaves on human beings. Second, this study was of short duration, raising the possibility that the dangers of long-term exposure have not yet been assessed.

Although federal guidelines for how much electromagnetic energy can be allowed to enter the work and home environment have been made more stringent since they were first implemented in 1982, the recent study poses troubling questions about the safety of microwaves.

2. Which of the following, if true, would lend weight to the scientists' initial findings regarding microwaves?

I. Individuals who extensively use point-to-point telecommunications, which heavily utilize microwaves, have higher-than-average incidences of cancer.

II. A long-term study of cancer cells exposed to microwaves in the laboratory shows the same pattern of growth found in the short-term study.

III. A study of dental associates who regularly work with X-rays shows that such individuals have higher-than-normal incidences of cancer.

A. I only
B. II only
C. I and II
D. I and III

Here's How to Crack It

One of the most useful things you can know for the GED® Science test is the **scientific method.** We will cover it in the review that begins in the next chapter, but for now, you should know that evaluation questions often ask you to bring some knowledge of the scientific method to bear on the question—and that is certainly the case here.

Given what the passage said about the preliminary nature of the study and what needs to be done next, which of the answer choices would help to prove the initial findings? The passage gave two reasons that the findings were only preliminary. First, the study was only at the test-tube stage. No studies involving people have been done yet. Second, it was only a short-term study. To know for sure if microwaves cause increased growth in cancer cells, a long-term study is needed.

Now check out the possibilities. Statement I addresses the first reason presented in the passage—as yet there has been no study on human beings—and provides you with a study that supports the initial findings with new findings on human subjects. Statement II addresses the second reason presented in the passage—there has been no long-term study as of yet—by providing information from a long-term study of cancer cells exposed to microwaves. Statement III, however, focuses on people who have been exposed to X-rays, rather than microwaves. Since this study does not relate to microwaves, the results would not lend any weight to the initial results described in the passage. Thus, I and II, but not III, support the initial results, and the correct answer is (C).

What Topics Are Covered on the Science Test?

Here are the topics as they are described by the people who write the test:

Life Science	40%
Physics and Chemistry	40%
Earth and Space	20%

If this list seems slightly vague, have no fear. While trying to acquaint yourself with all of the topics covered in a high school biology class might take a long time, you don't need an in-depth knowledge of all of those topics in order to ace the Science test. In the chapters that follow, you'll discover just exactly what information you will need.

OUR APPROACH

While some questions won't require you to have any particular knowledge of biology, earth science, physics, or chemistry, others will require you to have some general knowledge of these topics, including a knowledge of their specialized vocabularies. As you read, you'll discover just exactly what basic knowledge of these subjects that you'll need. You may even find that science is more fascinating than you imagined, and may want to learn more about these topics!

Chapter 21
Life Science

In this chapter, we'll go over some of the topics covered on the Science test—including the scientific method, cell theory and the origins of life, genetics, evolution and natural selection, plants, ecosystems and food chains, the human body and human health, and fossils.

Sometimes science teachers can be long on knowledge and short on teaching skills. You may have had one of these teachers, in which case you are probably convinced that science is tough and deadly dull. In fact, science can be fun if you learn to look in the right places. The GED® test writers say that they frequently get their topics and ideas from *Discover, Science News, National Geographic, Popular Science,* and *American Health.* If you want some added confidence for the GED® Science test, you may consider reading one of these magazines from time to time as you prepare for the GED® test. It will help you get into a "science head," and besides, you may be astonished at how interesting you find these magazines. Not only that, but reading such articles may help you feel more comfortable with the topics tested on the science portion on the GED® test, and may therefore give you an important psychological advantage.

While it is impossible to predict *exactly* what you'll see on the Science test, the folks who write the test do indicate that there are certain topics that they test regularly. In this chapter, we'll review some of the test writers' favorite life science topics. After each review, we'll provide you with GED®-style practice questions based on those particular topics.

Here are the specific subjects we'll cover in this chapter:

- Scientific method
- Cell theory and the origins of life
- Genetics
- Evolution and natural selection
- Plants
- Ecosystems and food chains
- The human body and human health
- Fossils

THE SCIENTIFIC METHOD

How did scientists learn anything about biology, the solar system, or the movement of continents in the first place? In each case, a scientist first came up with a hypothesis to explain an event that was not yet understood. A **hypothesis** is simply a possible explanation of an event or a phenomenon. Once she has her hypothesis, the scientist performs experiments to see whether the hypothesis is correct. These experiments must be carefully designed to make sure that the information they provide is accurate and that each experiment tests only one phenomenon at a time. For example, if you were testing whether aspirin alleviates headaches, you would have to make sure that the test subjects took only aspirin—nothing else. A good scientist would properly wonder whether it might be the water the subjects took to swallow the aspirin that actually alleviated the headache. As you refine your hypothesis, you are attempting to remove any confounding external forces or internal sources of error. By controlling for both internal and external factors, you are establishing a controlled sample that reduces the potential of encountering issues with validity and reliability.

Often, an experiment will be repeated many times to make sure that the same results occur. Sometimes the scientist will use what is called a **control group.** A control group is a group of test subjects that are not subjected to the phenomenon being tested. For example, a scientist who is studying the effect of microwaves on cancer cells (like the man in the passage you just read in the last chapter) may also study a second group of cancer cells that are *not* exposed to microwaves. This is called the control group. The scientist will watch both groups closely. After all, how will he know if the cells exposed to microwaves behave abnormally if he doesn't know what normal is?

Only after other scientists have conducted the same experiments and obtained the same results is a hypothesis accepted as fact. And even then, scientists continue to re-examine their own thinking and the thinking of their predecessors. Sometimes accepted facts turn out to be wrong.

On the GED® Science test, you will occasionally be asked to evaluate the accuracy of information or the relevance of a method. These can be the most complicated questions on the test—and they almost always involve your thinking through the question based on the scientific method. Let's look at an example.

Scientists conducted a study to determine whether drinking a small amount of alcohol each day reduces one's chances of suffering from a heart attack. They tested 400 first-heart-attack survivors who maintained daily fitness routines and healthy diets by giving these individuals one alcoholic drink per day for 20 years. The results of the study are shown in the chart below, along with the incidence of second heart attacks among first-heart-attack survivors nationwide.

The Scientific Method Quiz

Q: If you were testing the effectiveness of a cream that's supposed to grow hair on bald men's heads, which of the following would be a good control group?

(1) a group of bald women

(2) a group of men with full heads of hair who are also given the cream

(3) a group of bald men who are given a harmless cream that has no effect

Turn the page for the answer.

Incidence of Second Heart Attacks Among Study Participants

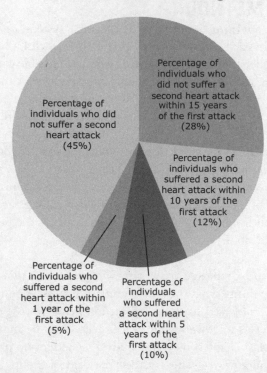

Percentage of individuals who did not suffer a second heart attack within 15 years of the first attack (28%)

Percentage of individuals who did not suffer a second heart attack (45%)

Percentage of individuals who suffered a second heart attack within 10 years of the first attack (12%)

Percentage of individuals who suffered a second heart attack within 1 year of the first attack (5%)

Percentage of individuals who suffered a second heart attack within 5 years of the first attack (10%)

Incidence of Second Heart Attacks Among Average First-Heart-Attack Survivors Nationwide

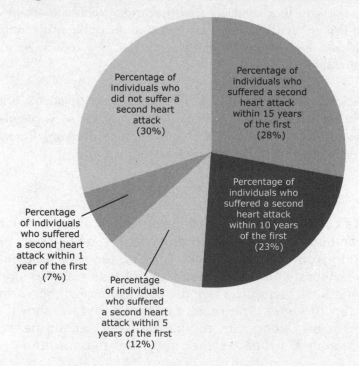

Percentage of individuals who did not suffer a second heart attack (30%)

Percentage of individuals who suffered a second heart attack within 15 years of the first (28%)

Percentage of individuals who suffered a second heart attack within 10 years of the first (23%)

Percentage of individuals who suffered a second heart attack within 1 year of the first (7%)

Percentage of individuals who suffered a second heart attack within 5 years of the first (12%)

1. Based on the results of the study, scientists concluded that drinking alcohol in small amounts lowers the risk of heart attack.

   Which of the following represents a flaw in the study above?

   A. The sample size of the study was too small to be effective.
   B. The study was not performed over a long enough period of time to provide reliable data.
   C. The exercise and diet routines of the subjects may have affected their incidence of heart attack.
   D. The scientists did not perform the study on animals before attempting to study humans.

Here's How to Crack It

As soon as you see the word "study," you can be pretty sure that this passage will concern the scientific method. Not every evaluation question is about a study or experiment, of course, but clearly this one is. You're asked to find a flaw in the study, so start by using Process of Elimination to get rid of some of the more clearly wrong answers first. Choice (A) would be a good answer if the number of study participants was small, but a sample size of 400 individuals seems large enough to be meaningful. Thus, (A) is incorrect. Similarly, the study was conducted over a period of 20 years, so the length of the study appears to be long enough to provide reliable data. Therefore, (B) is incorrect. Choice (D) seems unrealistic; even if testing animals before testing humans is preferable, you can't recommend a new form of treatment for mass human consumption without first testing it on at least a few human subjects. Choice (C), however, describes a serious flaw in the study. This choice points out that the study observed the effects not just of a single variable—alcohol consumption—but of other variables—exercise and diet routines. In this case, the lower incidence of second heart attacks among study subjects might be due, not to alcohol consumption, but to better-than-average exercise and diet routines. As noted above, it's much better to measure a single variable at a time than to attempt to measure multiple variables; otherwise, you don't know which of the variables is really responsible for the results.

If you found this question challenging, it might help to remember that when the GED® test writers select a passage about an experiment, they like to see how much you know about the scientific method. Typical flaws in experiments include relying on a sample size that is too small, failing to include a control group, and allowing a sample to be tainted by other possible causes of the phenomenon in question (as was the case in this question).

A: A control group should be a group that's representative of the group that you're testing but does not receive any medication or treatment. Since this study aims to test the effectiveness of the treatment on men, the control group should be men, rather than women. Thus, the first choice is incorrect. Additionally, since the study is testing the effects of the cream specifically on bald men, a control group of men with full heads of hair would not be appropriate. However, a control group of bald men who receive only a cream that has no effect would help scientists see bald men under normal conditions, so that they could see the difference between those who receive the cream and those who do not.

Vocabulary

control group—the group of people not being subjected to a phenomenon in a study

hypothesis—a possible explanation of an event or phenomenon

sample size—the number of subjects in a study

variable—an element that changes in a study

Scientific Method Drill

You can check your answers in Part VIII: Answer Key to Drills.

<u>Questions 1 through 3</u> refer to the following passage.

In the year 79 A.D., Mount Vesuvius erupted and covered the town of Pompeii in about 5m of ash, killing most of the inhabitants. However, much of the town was preserved under the volcanic debris which allowed researchers to learn a lot about the way of life in Pompeii when it was discovered 1,500 years later. Over the next two hundred years, it was determined that Pompeii must have had an intricate system for transporting water as well as an amphitheater that was used for entertainment and even a gymnasium for exercise.

Scientists found remains that also included many fossilized animals which have been used to better understand the wildlife that was present during that time period. Among the fossils was a bird that scientists believe to be part of a species that is now extinct. The bird had a slightly longer wing-to-body ratio than any known species that is alive today. It also has a stout and strangely pointed beak that may have given it a foraging advantage over competitors.

1. Based on the information in the passage, which of the following scientific conclusions is the most reasonable?

    A. The volcanic eruption at Pompeii was responsible for the extinction of this species.
    B. The bird did not live in Pompeii, but was on its way south for the winter.
    C. No one survived the volcanic eruption at Pompeii.
    D. The bird lived at the same time as the eruption.

2. How should scientists design a controlled experiment that can effectively determine whether or not an animal is a member of a known species today?

Type your response on a computer, if one is available. Otherwise, write your response on a separate sheet of paper.

3. Determine whether each of the following statements is a scientific observation or conclusion. For this drill, write the letters of the statements in the appropriate boxes.

Observations	Conclusions

(a) Mount Vesuvius erupted in 79 A.D.

(b) The bird would have been able to eat more than its competitors.

(c) The bird found at Pompeii is the only living version of that species that is alive today.

(d) The bird's wings are abnormally long.

CELL THEORY AND THE ORIGINS OF LIFE

All living organisms are made up of cells. Some organisms, such as amoebas, consist of single cells, while other organisms, such as humans, are composed of trillions of different cells. For instance, long tubular muscle cells, also known as myocytes, make up your muscle tissue, while your skin is comprised of skin cells. While the cells in your body may look different and have different functions, they are genetically identical.

Animal Cell

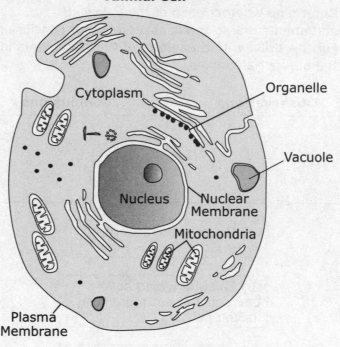

Cell Division Quiz

Q: If a cell divides into two cells, which process would ensure that each of the new cells had the same number of chromosomes as the original?
(1) mitosis
(2) meiosis

Turn the page for the answer.

There are two main types of cells: **prokaryotic cells**, which lack structure, and are generally found in single-cell organisms such as amoebas, and **eukaryotic cells**, which are very structured and which work together. Eukaryotic cells generally appear in more complex, multicellular living things.

All cells have a **nucleus** containing the essential genetic information of the organism of which they form a part. This information is made up of DNA and is contained in structures called **chromosomes.** Cells receive nourishment through **diffusion**, the process by which molecules spread from regions of high concentration to regions of low concentration. For example, the food that we eat is broken down and then transported in a watery solution throughout our bodies. The nutrients that individual cells need then diffuse through the permeable outer membrane of the cells, where the nutrients are converted to energy.

Most cells reproduce all by themselves in a process called **mitosis,** in which a cell splits into two new ones, each an exact copy of the original cell. Reproductive cells in animals divide by a different process called **meiosis,** in which the new cells contain only half the chromosomes of the original cell. Thus, when the sperm of a male unites with the egg of a female, together they make up the correct number of chromosomes, because the two "halves" (sperm cell and egg cell) make a "whole."

Single-cell organisms can be as complex in structure as the plantlike algae and the animal-like amoeba or as relatively simple in structure as **bacteria** and **viruses.** If a microbial organism can cause disease, it is called a **pathogen.** Many bacteria and viruses are considered pathogens, although some kinds of bacteria can be helpful to humans. For example, certain kinds of bacteria in the small intestine help us digest food.

In addition to being composed of cells, complex organisms such as humans require organ systems to assist them in completing activities necessary for life. These **essential functions of life** include the following:

- **Circulation.** This involves the movement of substances within an organism or its cells.
- **Excretion**. This process involves removal of waste, whether that waste be in the form of carbon dioxide, urine, or sweat.
- **Growth**. This is the process by which organisms increase the number of cells of which they are composed or increase in size.
- **Reproduction**. A single organism may not need to reproduce in order to maintain its own health, but each species as a whole cannot survive unless its organisms reproduce. There are two types of reproduction: asexual reproduction, which involves only one parent, and which produces offspring identical to that parent, and sexual reproduction, which requires two parents, and which produces offspring that possess features that are a combination of both parents.
- **Movement**. This simply involves a change in position of a living thing, and allows shifts in circulation, muscles, and other systems.
- **Nutrition.** This is the process in which living things take in substances that allow them to grow and repair themselves. There are two types of nutrition: autotrophic nutrition, in which living organisms make their own food, and heterotrophic nutrition, in which organisms acquire food from their environments.
- **Synthesis.** This is the process by which organisms take small, simple substances, and combine them to form larger, more complex substances.

Now that you know a few basics of cell theory, check out the question on the next page to discover how the GED® test writers might construct a question based on cell theory.

When a cell undergoes mitosis, it duplicates into two genetically exact replicas of itself, so that the new cells have exactly the same number of chromosomes as did the original cell. When a cell undergoes meiosis, it creates four cells, each with half the number of original chromosomes. Meiosis, unlike mitosis, takes place in two rounds.

Scientists conduct an experiment on a three different cells, and track the number of resulting cells and chromosomes after each cell undergoes either meiosis or mitosis, according to the cell type. The results are shown below.

Trial	Number of Initial Chromosomes	Number of Final Chromosomes in Each Resulting Cell	Number of Final Cells
1	6	6	2
2	4	2	4
3	46	x	4

1. In trial 3, the cell undergoes

    | Select... ▼ | and each resulting
    | meiosis |
    | mitosis |

    cell has | Select... ▼ | chromosomes.
    | 23 |
    | 46 |

Here's How to Crack It

Note that the final number of cells, after the cell in trial 3 divides, is 4. Thus, according to the information in the passage, the cell must have undergone meiosis, rather than mitosis. In meiosis, each resulting cell has half of the number of chromosomes of the original cell, so each resulting cell will have half of 46, or 23 chromosomes.

Vocabulary

organelle—specialized structures within a living cell

cytoplasm—area between the membrane and nucleus that contains organelles

mitochondria—the power houses of the cell that supply energy and break down food and sugar into water

vacuole—large water-filled sac that stores food, water, and waste

plasma membrane—boundary between the cell and environment that regulates the products that enter and exit the cell

nuclear membrane—boundary between the nucleus and the rest of the cell that is permeable to molecules like DNA, RNA, and ATP

permeable membrane—a barrier that lets certain molecules through it

prokaryotic cells—cells that lack structure

eukaryotic cells—cells that are structured and work together

nucleus—part of a cell containing its essential genetic information

chromosomes—structures of DNA

diffusion—the process by which molecules spread from regions of high concentration to regions of low concentration

mitosis—the process in which cells divide into new ones, each of which is an exact copy of the original

meiosis—the process by which cells split into new ones, each of which contains only half as many chromosomes as the original cell

pathogens—microbial organisms that can cause disease

essential functions of life—these include circulation, excretion, growth, reproduction, movement, nutrition, and synthesis

Cell Theory and the Origins of Life Drill

You can check your answers in Part VIII: Answer Key to Drills.

<u>Questions 1 through 3</u> refer to the following information.

Tuberculosis is caused by the mycobacterium, *Mycobacterium tuberculosis,* which kills approximately half of all infected patients. For many years, *M. tuberculosis* was susceptible to drug therapy; however, like many other disease-causing organisms, new drug-resistant strains of tuberculosis have emerged. Many theories have been postulated to explain the emergence of these resistant strains (also known as "superbugs") but most health-care professionals blame the over-prescription of antibiotics as well as their misuse by patients.

Today, before a tuberculosis patient can be treated, it is first necessary to find out which strain of bacterium is causing the disease and then to find a drug that will kill that particular strain. Fortunately, a new technique has been discovered that aids this process. Scientists can now insert *luciferase*, the enzyme that makes fireflies glow in the dark, into tuberculosis cells taken from the patient, which makes the tuberculosis cells glow in the dark (see Figure).

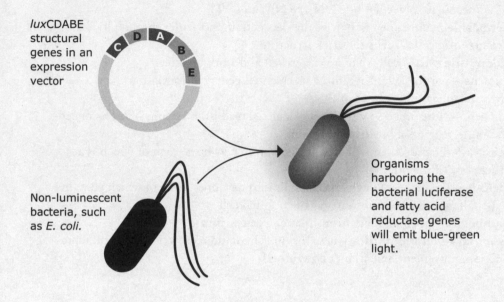

*lux*CDABE structural genes in an expression vector

Non-luminescent bacteria, such as *E. coli.*

Organisms harboring the bacterial luciferase and fatty acid reductase genes will emit blue-green light.

With their new glow-in-the-dark organisms, scientists can then test different drugs to see if they kill the bacteria (which stop glowing). This new test can be done in days, which is faster than previous tuberculosis tests which required up to five weeks.

1. If a tuberculosis cell with luciferase is treated with a drug but keeps on glowing, which of the following is most likely the case?

    A.   A higher dosage of the drug is needed.
    B.   The tuberculosis cell has been destroyed.
    C.   The cell is resistant to that particular drug.
    D.   Both A and C are correct.

2. What is likely to be the most important reason to save time on a tuberculosis test?

    A. The patient can begin effective drug therapy that much sooner.
    B. The scientists can perform twice as many tests and thus have more time for other experiments.
    C. The enzyme luciferase lasts almost indefinitely.
    D. Other types of bacteria have shown themselves less able to mutate.

3. The following chart depicts the dose response curve of *M. tuberculosis* to an antibiotic drug. If a scientist knows that an intensity score of 20 or less is considered acceptable (the remaining bacteria can be eradicated by the host's immune response), click on the dose of antibiotic that the scientist should recommend for patients. (For this drill, mark the dose with an X.)

Dose Response

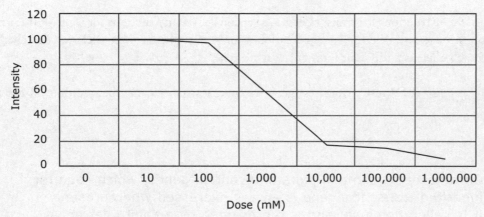

GENETICS

Genetics is the science of genes, and it involves the study of how parents pass on traits to their offspring. In order to begin learning the vocabulary of basic genetics, the first two genetics terms that you need to know are **genotype** and **phenotype.** A person's genotype is the genetic code that he or she carries, and it provides information about particular traits. Phenotypes are the expressions of those traits. For example, your hair color, which is an expression of instructions carried in your genetic code, is a phenotype. Phenotypes often depend upon genotype, but they can also result from environmental factors.

You have inherited many of your traits from your parents; perhaps people tell you that you have your mother's smile or your father's eyes. Your parents passed along these traits through chromosomes, which were introduced in the previous section, and which are made up of wound-up DNA. Each human chromosome pair consists of one chromosome from the father and another from the mother, which is why you resemble, at least to some extent, both your father and mother. You could think of the **genes**, or sections of DNA, as sets of instructions for proteins, or traits. Of course, children inherit multiple traits from their parents, so it's not surprising that human cells have not only more than one gene, but also more than one chromosome. In fact, human cells have 23 pairs of chromosomes, or 46 chromosomes each. Of those 23 pairs, one pair is made up of sex chromosomes. Male chromosomes are known as XY chromosomes, while female chromosomes are known as XX chromosomes. The remaining 22 pairs of chromosomes are called **autosomes**, and each autosome pair is a **homologous pair**, or a pair of chromosomes, one from the father and one from the mother, with the same structure.

If genes are instructions for traits, **alleles** are versions of the instructions for traits. For example, you might have an allele for attached earlobes, or you might have an allele for detached earlobes. Each allele is a different form of the same gene.

So how might GED® test writers test genetics concepts? Check out the question on the next page.

Chromosomes come in pairs and contain genes, which code for inherited traits. If a gene is always expressed when present, it is called dominant and is represented by a capital letter. A dominant gene will be expressed whether an individual is pure and has two copies of the dominant gene or is hybrid and contains one dominant copy and one copy of another gene. In the case of hybrids, the dominant gene hides the expression the recessive gene. A recessive gene is expressed only when it is pure, and it is represented by a lowercase letter.

In pea plants, the gene for round pea shape is dominant and the gene for wrinkled pea shape is recessive. A plant that produces wrinkled peas must be pure for the wrinkled gene, meaning it must contain two copies of the wrinkled gene. A plant that produces round peas can either be pure for the round gene or be hybrid and have one gene for round shape and one gene for wrinkled shape.

Punnett Squares are charts used to predict the odds of specific gene combinations in offspring. Below is a Punnett Square of a cross between a pea plant purebred for wrinkled peas and a pea plant that produces round peas.

Punnett Square—Shape in Pea Plants

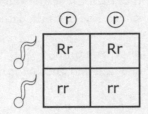

	(r)	(r)
	Rr	Rr
	rr	rr

○	egg cell of female parent
♪	sperm cell of male parent
R	dominant round shape gene
r	recessive wrinkled shape gene
?	unknown gene

1. Which of the following describes the offspring of this cross?

    A. Half produce round peas and half produce wrinkled peas.
    B. All produce wrinkled peas.
    C. All produce round peas.
    D. Half produce wrinkled peas and half produce both round and wrinkled peas.

Here's How to Crack It
Half of the offspring possess only the genes for wrinkled peas, and will therefore produce wrinkled peas. The offspring in the other half of the square possess one gene for wrinkled peas and one for round peas. Since the round gene is dominant over the wrinkled gene, these offspring will produce round peas. Thus, (A) is correct.

Vocabulary

genotype—genetic code that a person carries and that provides information about particular traits

phenotype—expressions of genetic traits and traits that result from interactions of the genotype with the environment

genes—sections of DNA

autosomes—pairs of chromosomes other than the sex chromosomes

homologous pair—a pair of chromosomes, one from the father and one from the mother, with the same structure

alleles—versions of the instructions for genetic traits

hybrid—having having one gene for one trait and another gene for a different trait

Genetics Drill

You can check your answers in Part VIII: Answer Key to Drills.

Questions 1 through 3 refer to the following information.

When an allele is represented by a capital letter, it is said to be dominant, and will always be expressed when coupled with another dominant allele. Recessive genes, which are represented by a lowercase letter, are only expressed when an individual is pure and has two copies of the allele.

In kittens, the gene for pointy ears is dominant and the gene for floppy ears is recessive. Kittens will express the pointy ear trait if the kitten is pure or has a hybrid of alleles. In order for floppy ears to be expressed on a kitten, the kitten must be pure for the recessive gene.

Punnett Squares are charts used to predict the odds of specific gene combinations in offspring. Below is a Punnett Square of a cross between two heterozygous parents.

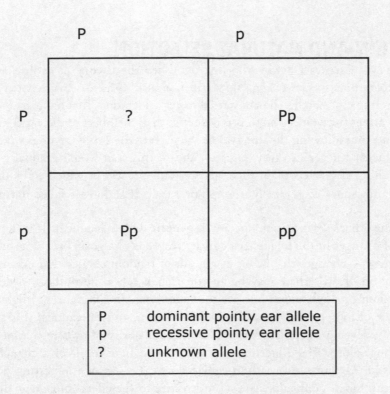

	P	p
P	?	Pp
p	Pp	pp

P	dominant pointy ear allele
p	recessive pointy ear allele
?	unknown allele

1. What is the probability that an offspring will have pointy ears?

2. According to the information presented, what genotype should replace the "?" in the Punnett Square?

   A. PP
   B. Pp
   C. pP
   D. pp

3. The genotypic ratio of this Punnett Square is best

   expressed as Select... ▼
   3:1
   1:3
   1:2:1
   2:1:2

EVOLUTION AND NATURAL SELECTION

It was Charles Darwin who first published the **theory of evolution.** This theory holds that species change slowly in response to factors in their environment. For example, if Earth's climate started to get colder, dogs that happened to have thicker, warmer fur would tend to survive better than members of their species with thinner fur, thus allowing the **survival of the fittest.** The surviving dogs would pass on the thicker fur gene to their puppies, and so this trait would gradually become a prevailing characteristic of their species. This process in which traits that help an organism survive gradually triumph over traits that don't is called **natural selection.**

The other way evolution operates is **genetic drift.** Genetic drift is the accumulation of changes in the frequency of alleles (versions of a gene) over time due to sampling errors—changes that occur as a result of random chance. For example, in a population of owls there may be an equal chance of a newly born owlet having long talons or short talons, but due to random breeding variances a slightly larger number of long-taloned owlets are born. Over many generations, this slight variance can develop into a larger trend, until the majority of owls in that population have long talons. These breeding variances could be a result of a chance event—such as an earthquake that drastically reduces the size of the nesting population one year. Small populations are more sensitive to the effects of genetic drift than large, diverse populations.

Just as new species are formed by natural selection and genetic drift, other species may become extinct. Extinction occurs when a species cannot adapt quickly enough to environmental change and all members of the species die.

Darwin theorized that all species on Earth descended from one or two very simple organisms that gradually evolved into different kinds of more complex organisms. Thus, according to Darwin, human beings are thought to have evolved from simple sea creatures that gradually changed over millions of years into a common ape-like ancestor that in turn gradually evolved into Homo sapiens.

Today, animals are divided into two categories: invertebrates and vertebrates. **Invertebrates** do not have a backbone—they include worms, jellyfish, and insects. **Vertebrates** *do* have a backbone and include most of the animals you know, including fish, birds, and mammals. **Mammals** are animals that nurse their young. The whale is the largest mammal. Homo sapiens (otherwise known as human beings) are also mammals.

Survival of the Fittest Quiz

Q: Which of the following is an example of natural selection?
(1) A frog survives by hiding under a rock.
(2) Over thousands of years, a frog species gradually changes color to mimic the color of the rocks it likes to sit on.

Turn the page for the answer.

Ready to try a question on evolution and natural selection? Work the problem below.

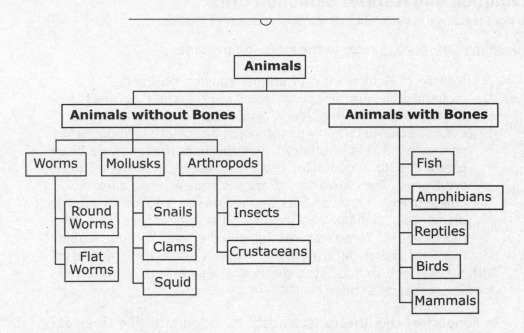

1. Based on the information in the chart above, which of the following animals are vertebrates?

    A. crustaceans
    B. amphibians
    C. insects
    D. round worms

Here's How to Crack It

Vertebrates are animals with bones, so look for an animal that appears on the right-hand side of the chart. Crustaceans, insects, and round worms are all animals that appear on the left-hand side of the chart, under "Animals without Bones," so (A), (C), and (D) are incorrect. Amphibians appear under the right-hand side of the chart, under "Animals with Bones," so (B) is the correct answer.

Vocabulary

survival of the fittest—another name for natural selection
adaptation—short-term changes in a species
evolution—long-term changes in a species
genetic drift—the accumulation of changes in the frequency of versions of a gene over time due to changes that occur as a result of random chance
invertebrates—animals without backbones
vertebrates—animals with backbones
mammals—animals that nurse their young

Evolution and Natural Selection Drill

You can check your answers in Part VIII: Answer Key to Drills.

<u>Questions 1 through 3</u> refer to the following passage.

Nearly 75% of plant and animal species on Earth, including all non-bird dinosaurs, went extinct during the Cretaceous-Paleogene (or Cretaceous-Tertiary) extinction event. Scientists have spent years speculating about what precipitated this extinction. Various hypotheses have been presented to account for the disappearance of these huge creatures. The prevailing theory is that a large asteroid collided with Earth and its impact raised a cloud of dust that prevented sunlight from reaching the planet's surface for many years. Temperatures fell rapidly, and without sunlight, much of the plant life on the planet's surface disappeared. Without warmth or food, the dinosaurs, as well as many other species, became extinct.

In support of this theory, scientists have found a thin layer of sediment in marine and terrestrial rocks that contains metals that are rare on Earth but abundant in asteroids. Additionally, a large crater was found in the Gulf of Mexico that must have hit Earth at roughly the same time as the extinctions took place.

Amid the destruction was opportunity for evolution. There were countless vacated ecological niches and the surviving organisms rapidly adapted and developed in order to occupy these niches. It is believed that several of the mammals, including primates, that are alive today developed during this time.

1. If the preceding information is true, which of the following is the most likely explanation for the fact that there is still life on Earth today?

    A. Some forms of life were able to survive in spite of the lack of sunlight.
    B. The dinosaurs went into hibernation.
    C. Sunlight is unnecessary for the survival of plant forms.
    D. There was no food at all on the planet's surface during these years.

2. If there had been time for the process of evolution to save the dinosaurs, which traits would have been most helpful for a dinosaur to survive during this time and why?

Type your response on a computer, if one is available. Otherwise, write your response on a separate sheet of paper.

3. If Charles Darwin read this passage, would he agree with the statements made in the last paragraph?

A. No. According to Darwin's theory of natural selection, organisms were destined to fulfill specific niches only when it was best for their evolutionary fitness.
B. No. Darwin would not have considered a tragedy to be an opportunity.
C. Yes. Darwin believed that slight differences between organisms can be selected for through natural selection and that this would be exacerbated in a time when there were many potential ecological niches.
D. Yes. Darwin believed that individual organisms were capable of evolution.

PLANTS

Most plants are made up of many cells. Plants make their own food through a fascinating process called **photosynthesis.** Plant cells contain a chemical called **chlorophyll,** which gives plants their green color. When a plant's leaves absorb sunlight, the chlorophyll in the leaves converts the sunlight into energy. Meanwhile, the roots of the plant have been drawing water from the ground all the way up into the leaves. The plant uses the energy it has just converted to split the water (H_2O) into its two components—hydrogen and oxygen. The hydrogen is used by the plant, along with carbon dioxide from the air, to create sugar and starches for its own nutrition. The oxygen is released into the atmosphere—incidentally making it possible for humans to go on breathing.

The growth process of plants is dependent on the seasons. Some plants last only one growing season and die during the winter. To carry on the species, these plants produce **seeds,** which lie fallow during the winter months and then **germinate** in the spring. Other plants, called **perennials,** live for many years. The upper shoots of a perennial wither and die during the winter, but the roots live through the winter and produce new shoots in the spring.

Trees are also a kind of plant whose stalks have become woody. Trees survive the winter because their trunks protect them from the cold. If you were to cut down a tree and look at a horizontal cross section inside, you would find many circular rings. This is because in the spring and summer, the tree grows more rapidly, producing wider pores. During the winter, the growth is slower, producing denser wood. By counting the rings of a tree, you can tell how old it is.

Check out the passage on plants below, and answer the question that follows.

When plants respond to an environmental stimulus by growing in a particular way, that response is called a tropism. There are five kinds of tropism:

phototropism—a response in which plants turn toward the light

geotropism—a response in which roots grow toward the earth and the shoots and flowers grow toward the sky

thigmotropism—a response in which plants curl around any object they touch

hydrotropism—a response in which plants' roots grow toward a source of water

chemotropism—a positive attraction of roots toward the presence of certain chemicals

A student decides to study the way in which a particular plant responds to sunlight over a six-month period. At the beginning of the study, the student moves the plant, which originally bent toward a nearby window, so that plant bends directly away from window and the angle between the direction in which the plant bends and the window is 180°. The graph below shows the changes in the way that the plant bends as the year progresses.

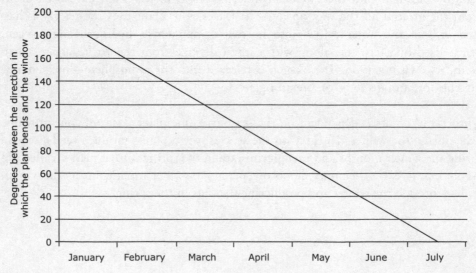

1. The plants movements toward the window are an expression of which of the following?

   A. phototropism
   B. geotropism
   C. thigmotropism
   D. chemotropism

Here's How to Crack It

This question is not about the roots but about the visible part of the plant above the soil. Based on that information, only two choices are possible: phototropism and thigmotropism. Because the question does not mention curling, and according to the graph, the plant bends toward the window at the end of the study, the correct answer to this question must be (A).

Vocabulary

stomates—the microscopic openings through which gases diffuse into and out of leaves during photosynthesis

pistil—female reproductive organs of a flower

stamen—male reproductive organs of a flower

photosynthesis—the process through which plants make their own food

chlorophyll—the chemical which provides plants with their green color

germinate—begin to grow or put out shoots

perennials—plants that live for many years

Plants Drill

You can check your answers in Part VIII: Answer Key to Drills.

<u>Questions 1 through 3</u> refer to the following passage.

If you cut a horizontal cross section through the trunk of a tree, you can see the tree's growth rings (also known as tree rings). Each ring inside the trunk of a tree represents the annual growth of the tree. There are two parts of a growth ring. The inner part is formed during the early growth season (spring and early summer in North America) and is relatively less dense. The outer part of each ring is denser and is formed during the late summer and autumn.

The growing conditions of a particular year will affect the size of a ring. In ideal growing conditions (such as adequate moisture and a relatively long growing season), a ring may be larger because the tree was able to grow more during that time. However, a cold summer or a drought can cause the ring size to be smaller than normal.

Researchers can use tree rings to learn about the growing conditions that were present during a particular time period. The tree depicted below was cut down at the end of the growing year in 2000.

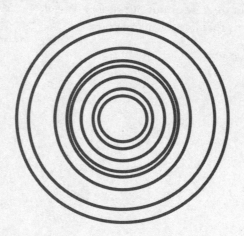

1. Based on the figure, which of the following years was the best growing season?

    A. 2000
    B. 1999
    C. 1998
    D. 1997

2. How old is the tree represented in the figure?

   A. 6 years
   B. 7 years
   C. 8 years
   D. 9 years

3. The following graph compares tree ring size to the average amount of monthly rainfall.

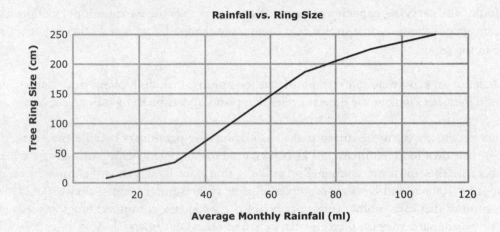

Rainfall vs. Ring Size

In the graph above, average monthly rainfall is the

Select... ▼
independent
dependent

variable, while tree ring size is the | Select... ▼ |
| --- |
| independent |
| dependent |

variable.

ECOSYSTEMS AND FOOD CHAINS

An **ecosystem** is a place where many organisms live and depend on other organisms for survival. For example, grass uses the energy of the sun to grow, a rabbit eats the grass, a hawk eats the rabbit. Every animal is eating something else to get energy, except for the grass, which gets its energy from sunlight through photosynthesis.

In any given ecosystem, the total number of resources is limited. A given region, for example, can support only so many rabbits before the rabbits begin to run out of grass to eat and their population begins to dwindle. When this happens, the hawk population will also begin to dwindle. The **carrying capacity** of a particular ecosystem is the maximum population size of a given species that can exist in that ecosystem given the food, water, and other resources available in the region.

To balance an ecosystem, all of the different organisms, including plants and animals, have certain jobs. Let's look at the different roles that plants and animals have in an ecosystem.

Plants get energy from the sun to make food. Plants are **producers** because they make (produce) their own food. Animals, unlike plants, need to eat to get energy. Animals are **consumers** because they must eat (consume) other living things for food. Primary consumers eat only producers. Rabbits and cows are examples of primary consumers because they eat only plants. A consumer that eats another consumer is called a secondary consumer. Frogs are secondary consumers because they eat flies, grasshoppers, and other consumers.

All primary consumers eat plants, and the scientific term for these consumers is **herbivores**. Secondary consumers that eat only animals and not any plants are called **carnivores**. Many consumers eat both plants and animals, depending on what is available. These consumers are called **omnivores**.

There are other organisms in an ecosystem besides producers and consumers. These organisms, like earthworms, bacteria, and fungi, eat dead organisms and return nutrients back to the soil for plants to use. These organisms are called **decomposers** because they break down other organisms to get energy.

The **food chain** is the process by which organisms pass energy from one to another. The first step in a food chain occurs when a green plant absorbs energy from the sun and converts it to chemical energy through photosynthesis. The second step occurs when an animal eats the plant, converting the energy contained in the plant into energy that the animal can store in its cells. Following this, a larger animal then eats the first animal, and stores the energy from that animal in its own cells. This process may continue through several steps. Eventually, at the top of the food chain, a fungus or bacterium breaks down decaying organic matter. The figure on the next page shows an example of a food chain.

Food Chains

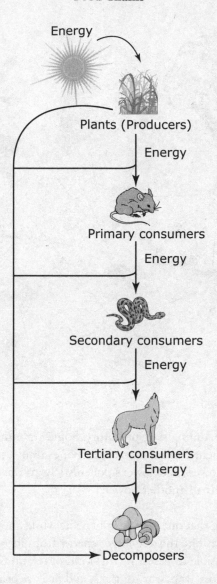

An alternative way to show how animals transfer energy to one another is by using a **food web**. This is a slightly more complicated chart that takes into account the fact that there is often more than one animal vying for a particular kind of food.

Food Web

Not all relationships between animals are predatory. Some are **mutualistic**, meaning that both organisms in a relationship benefit from each other. For example, insects that eat nectar from a flower are also helping the flower. The flower's pollen sticks to the insects as they eat, and then the pollen drops off as they fly to another flower.

Some are **parasitic**, meaning that one organism benefits while another organism suffers. Think about fleas on a dog. The fleas bite the dog to get energy from its blood and in return, the poor dog gets itchy welts and possible diseases. In this kind of relationship, the flea is called a parasite and the dog is called a host. Tapeworms, ticks, and lice are other examples of parasites.

Some exhibit **commensalism**, meaning that one organism is helped while the other organism is neither helped nor harmed. A great example of commensalism is the relationship between a remora and a whale. The remora has a sucker on the top of its head that attaches to the whale's top, mouth, or underside. Through this attachment, the remora can travel around more easily and eat any debris that falls from the whale. The whale is left unharmed.

1. A food web in an ecosystem is shown below:

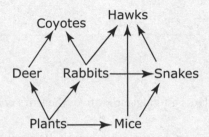

Select the producer from the list below, and drag it into the box.

Select the herbivores from the list below, and drag them into the box.

Select the carnivores from the list below, and drag them into the box.

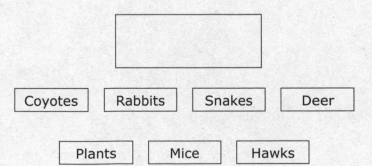

| Coyotes | Rabbits | Snakes | Deer |

| Plants | Mice | Hawks |

Here's How to Crack It

Plants make their own food, and are therefore producers. Thus, you'll want to select plants as the producers. Herbivores eat plants, and based on the food web, deer, rabbits, and mice eat plants, so you'll want to select these as the herbivores. Carnivores are animals that eat other animals. Coyotes eat deer and rabbits; hawks eat rabbits, mice, and snakes; and snakes eat mice. Therefore, coyotes, hawks, and snakes are carnivores.

Vocabulary

producers—green plants and algae that take the sun's energy and convert it into chemical energy

consumers—animals that eat the producers and/or sometimes each other

decomposers—saprophytic organisms like bacteria that break down organic matter into its basic ingredients and begin the life process all over again

ecosystem—a place where many organisms live and depend upon other organisms for survival

carrying capacity—the maximum population size of given species that a certain ecosystem can support

herbivores—primary consumers, or living things that eat plants

carnivores—secondary consumers, or animals that eat only animals

omnivores—animals that eat both plants and animals

food chain—the process by which organisms pass energy from one to another

food web—a chart that shows the way that organisms pass energy from one to another, and that takes into account the fact that there is often more than one animal vying for a particular kind of food

mutualistic relationships—relationships in which organisms benefit from helping each other

parasitic relationships—relationships in which one organism benefits while another suffers

commensalism—a class of relationships in which one organism benefits while another is neither helped nor harmed

Ecosystems and Food Chain Drill

You can check your answers in Part VIII: Answer Key to Drills.

<u>Questions 1 through 3</u> refer to the food web below.

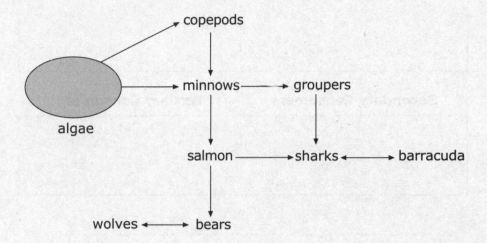

1. Which of the following organisms in the food web above are eaten by both land and sea creatures?

    A. minnows
    B. wolves
    C. salmon
    D. groupers

2. The absence of _____ on the food web above would most devastate the rest of the web?

    A. minnows
    B. wolves
    C. salmon
    D. algae

3. Drag and drop the organisms from the list below into the following categories. (For this drill, write the letter next to each organism into the appropriate category).

Primary Producers

Primary Consumers

Secondary Consumers

Tertiary Consumers

(a) Algae   (b) Copepods   (c) Minnows

(d) Groupers   (e) Salmon   (f) Sharks

(g) Bears   (h) Barracuda   (i) Wolves

THE HUMAN BODY AND HUMAN HEALTH

The human body is truly remarkable. Eleven different systems work together to keep your heart pumping, air in your lungs, and the rest of your body functioning. You'll need to know something about these systems in order to successfully tackle the GED® Science test, so you may find it helpful to familiarize yourself with them.

First, you have the **circulatory system**. This is the system that allows blood to circulate through your body and deliver oxygen, nutrients, and hormones to your cells, and carry away wastes such as carbon dioxide. It helps you to stay nourished, maintain a constant body temperature, and fight disease. Your **lymphatic system** is actually part of your circulatory system, and is composed of lymphatic vessels that carry lymph, a clear fluid, toward your heart. Each day, approximately 17 of your 20 liters of body's plasma are reabsorbed into your blood vessels, but 3 liters get left behind. The lymphatic system creates an alternative way for this plasma to return to your blood.

Next, there is the **integumentary system.** This system is composed of your skin, hair, and nails, and helps to protect your body from damage from its environment. The **urinary system**, otherwise known as the renal system, includes your bladder, kidneys, ureters, and urethra. This system is responsible for eliminating waste from your body, regulating blood pH, controlling your electrolyte and metabolite levels, and regulating your blood pressure and volume. Your lungs make up your **respiratory system,** moderate your intake of oxygen and expulsion of carbon dioxide. Your **muscular system** consists of your skeletal, cardiac, and smooth muscles, and allows you to move, remain upright, and circulate blood through your body. It works closely with your **nervous system**, which controls your muscular system and regulates both voluntary and involuntary motions by transmitting signals to various parts of your body. Your bones—all 270 of them at birth—make up your **skeletal system**, which supports your body and allows it to move, produces blood cells, regulates endocrine, and stores ions. Your **digestive system** includes your mouth, esophagus, stomach, intestines, anus, and rectum. It helps you break down food so that it can be absorbed into your body, and eliminate waste. The **reproductive system** is made up of the sex organs, as well as fluids, pheromones, and hormones, and allows humans to have offspring. Your **endocrine system** consists of glands that secrete hormones into your circulatory system, and is made up of glands that contribute to actions such as sweating and salivating.

Why do you need so many systems? One reason is that your body needs to maintain **homeostasis**, or stable internal conditions. For example, you need to maintain a constant internal temperature, a constant pH, and constant blood glucose levels. Your body's systems work together to maintain homeostasis.

Of course, nutrition and environment also strongly contribute to your health. Poor nutrition may cause diseases such as diabetes, scurvy (a disease that results from a lack of vitamin C), and cardiovascular disease, among others.

Try out the following human health and human body question.

The human body maintains itself through several systems. For example, the integumentary system, which is composed of skin, hair, and nails, helps to protect the body from harm. The endocrine system consists of glands that secrete hormones into your circulatory system, such as the mammary, pituitary, salivary, and sweat glands. Lungs make up the respiratory system, and moderate intake of oxygen and expulsion of carbon dioxide. The muscular system consists of skeletal, cardiac, and smooth muscles, and allows humans to move and remain upright, and circulates blood through the body. These, along with seven other systems, maintain homeostasis, or stable internal conditions. When the body is no longer in homeostasis, these systems act to bring the body back to equilibrium.

1. On a hot summer day, a runner quickly becomes overheated. In order to bring down his internal temperature, the runner's body releases sweat.

This is an example of the

Select... ▼
muscular
integumentary
endocrine

system glands being activated to

Select... ▼
return the body to homeostasis
circulate blood through the body
expel carbon dioxide

.

Here's How to Crack It

According to the passage, "the endocrine system consists of glands that secrete hormones into your circulatory system, such as the mammary, pituitary, salivary, and sweat glands." Thus, sweat glands are a part of the endocrine system, so the answer to the first question is "endocrine." The passage also states that the bodily systems listed, "along with seven other systems, maintain homeostasis, or stable internal conditions. When the body is no longer in homeostasis, these systems act to bring the body back to equilibrium." When a runner is overheated, he or she no longer has stable internal conditions, so the body's systems act to lower that temperature. Thus, the correct answer to the second question is "return the body to homeostasis."

Vocabulary

systems of the human body—the circulatory system, the lymphatic system, the integumentary system, the urinary system, the respiratory system, the muscular system, the nervous system, the skeletal system, the digestive system, the reproductive system, and the endocrine system

homeostasis—stable internal conditions

The Human Body and Human Health Drill

You can check your answers in Part VIII: Answer Key to Drills.

Questions 1 through 3 refer to the following information.

The human body maintains equilibrium through the use of multiple bodily systems. For example, the muscular system, which circulates blood through your body and allows you to move, is comprised of skeletal, cardiac, and smooth muscles. Working closely with the muscular system, the nervous system controls your muscular system and regulates both voluntary and involuntary motions by sending signals to parts of the body. Likewise, the skeletal system works in harmony with the muscular system, providing internal organs with protection and working with muscles to enable movement. Along with the other bodily systems, the muscular, nervous, and skeletal systems work together to keep the body in equilibrium.

1. Which of the following bodily systems from the list below play a role in movement? Choose all that apply. (For this drill, write the option letters in the box below.)

Bodily Systems that Play a Role in Movement

(a) Endocrine

(b) Muscular

(c) Skeletal

(d) Digestive

(e) Nervous

2. Susan suffered from a heart attack in February, which primarily impacted the [Select... ▼] / skeletal / cardiac / smooth

    muscles within the [Select... ▼] system. / muscular / skeletal / nervous

3. Franklin is walking through the desert when he comes upon a poisonous scorpion. Franklin's "flight or fight" response is initiated by his endocrine system and he then reacts by running in the opposite direction of the scorpion. Which system is responsible for triggering Franklin's movement?

    A. skeletal
    B. endocrine
    C. muscular
    D. nervous

BACTERIA AND VIRUSES

When we think of a disease, we often think of an illness (which can have a variety of symptoms and effects) that negatively impacts humans, animals, and plants. While you won't need to know the scientific names of every disease on the GED® test, you should have a general idea about the way in which disease spreads, the impact of disease on a population, and how to combat disease.

Bacteria are single-celled, living organisms. Despite their small size, bacteria have ribosomes and a single loop of DNA, which contains approximately 5,000 genes. Bacteria are also capable of reproduction through a process called **binary fission,** which occurs when the DNA replicates and the bacterial cell splits into identical daughter cells. So, how can you catch a bacterial infection? A bacterial infection can be transmitted through the air, tainted food or water, an insect bite, or direct contact with open sores on the body. Consider the bubonic plague, which was transmitted both through the air via fleabites, and dysentery, which is contracted when an individual consumes contaminated food or water. Thankfully, most harmful bacteria can be killed with chemicals or boiling water, and many bacterial infections can be treated with antibiotics, which are substances that can destroy or inhibit the growth of infectious bacteria by interfering with their cellular processes. It should be noted that not all bacteria are harmful. There are a number of "friendly" bacteria, such as L. acidophilus, that aid in the digestive process.

A **virus** is a piece of DNA or RNA encapsulated by a protein coat, or **capsid**. While a complex virus can have a hundred genes, all viruses are extremely small and no virus is alive. Viruses can't reproduce independently, don't perform any biological functions, and rely on living cells for replication through a process called **lysis**, or the lytic cycle. In the **lytic cycle**, a virus attaches to a host cell, injects its DNA or RNA into the host cell, and makes hundreds of copies of itself. Eventually, the host cell bursts, releasing the viral copies into the organism. Once replicated, viruses can be transmitted through either air or direct contact. For example, a child could contract the chicken pox through inhalation, but could contract AIDS only through direct contact with infected bodily fluids. Unlike bacterial infections, however, viral infections cannot be treated with antibiotics. Instead, the most effective preventative treatment against contracting a viral infection is **immunization** or **vaccination**, the process of stimulating the immune system to produce defenses against harmful viruses by introducing harmless, yet similar, viruses. Unfortunately, vaccines must be continually adapted, as many viruses (such as the common cold) are capable of rapid mutation.

Viral and bacterial **pathogens**, or disease-causing agents, can have devastating consequences on human, animal, and plant populations. During the Middle Ages, the bubonic plague spread throughout Europe, killing over one-third of the continent's population. Referred to as the Black Death, victims of the plague suffered from diarrhea, vomiting, chills, and blood-filled boils. Due to the lack of antibiotics and unsanitary living conditions during this time period, tens of millions had died by the time the plague ran its course. If a disease is particularly brutal, it can have a severe impact on the population demographics. In animal populations, for example, a virulent pathogen could cause the species to become extinct. While such fatal bacterial infections, such as the bubonic plague, sometimes occur today in pre-industrialized countries, modern medicine and sanitation practices have greatly reduced mortality rates due to bacterial infections. Conversely, modern sanitation and medicine have not been able to mitigate the consequences of many viral infections. Acquired immunodeficiency syndrome (**AIDS**), caused by the human immunodeficiency virus (**HIV**) and spread via bodily fluids, is perhaps the most notorious viral disease today. While cells in the immune system fight pathogens in a healthy individual, cells in the immune system are infected and attacked by HIV in an individual with AIDS. In turn, the individual's immune system is destroyed and the person becomes more susceptible to illness. Unfortunately, the sheer number of varieties and the rapidly mutating nature of HIV make the disease extremely hard to treat. AIDS can have a particularly devastating impact on populations of intravenous drug users or those that cannot afford, or do not emphasize, the use of birth control.

Vocabulary

AIDS—Acquired immune deficiency syndrome (AIDS) is a disease caused by HIV that is characterized by a greatly increased susceptibility to infection due to compromised cellular immunity. An individual with AIDS can develop a number of health conditions including pneumonia, tuberculosis, toxoplasmosis, and fungal infections. There is currently no cure for AIDS.

bacteria—Typically single-celled, prokaryotic organisms that exist in large groups. Bacteria can be either beneficial, such as bacteria that decompose organic matter, or harmful, such as bacteria that cause infections.

binary fission—A type of asexual reproduction most common in prokaryotes. Bacterial binary fission is the process utilized by bacteria to carry out cell division, reproduce, and increase the bacterial population.

capsid—A protein sheath that surrounds the genetic material of a virus.

disease—An atypical condition that compromises the normal bodily functions of an organism, typically associated with negative symptoms and feelings of pain and weakness

HIV—Human immunodeficiency virus (HIV) is a virus that attacks the immune system by destroying T-helper white blood cells, leaving an individual with a damaged immune system. HIV can be transmitted through the exchange of bodily fluids such as blood and semen. There is currently no cure for HIV and without antiretroviral treatment, HIV can progress to AIDS.

immunization—The process by which an organism is made immune or resistant to an infectious disease. Generally, immunization occurs via the administration of a vaccine.

infection—Occurs when a pathogen invades and multiplies within the tissues and organs of a living organism. An infection can cause the immune system to be activated, at which point symptoms and disease will present itself.

lytic cycle—A portion of the viral reproduction cycle during which the virus replicates itself, leading to the destruction of both the infected cell and its membrane.

pathogen—A bacterium, virus, fungus, or other microorganism that can cause disease.

vaccination—Allows an organism to achieve a state of immunity to a particular pathogen through artificial means. In active immunization, a weakened or inactive form of a pathogen is introduced to an organism that causes the immune system to respond and create immunological memory, or the ability to remember pathogens for future infections. Passive immunization involves the administration of specific antibodies that provide immediate, temporary protection against a pathogen.

virus—A small, nonliving, infectious agent that is composed of both nucleic acid and a protein coat. While a virus cannot reproduce on its own, a virus can invade an organism's cell, reproduce within the cell, and then destroy the cell.

You should now have a firm grasp of concepts related to disease transfer that will be tested on the GED® test. Let's try some sample questions.

Bacteria and Viruses Drill

You can check your answers in Part VIII: Answer Key to Drills.

Questions 1 through 3 refer to the following information.

Maria is a doctor at the World Health Organization who analyzes bacterial infections, which can be cured with antibiotics that disrupt the living cellular structures of the diseased cells, and viral infections, for which vaccines can be developed. Maria also analyzes the way in which the disease is transferred among individuals, determining whether an infection is spread through the air, contaminated water, animal bites, or direct contact.

Maria has been sent to Ezralia, a small, pre-industrialized state, where the majority of the population lives in squalor, with most homes lacking indoor plumbing and other innovations related to modern sanitation. Over the past six weeks, the people of Ezralia have been suffering from an unidentified disease, known as Mooshika, that is decimating the population. Maria interviews a number of individuals suffering from Mooshika and finds that the majority of the individuals who have suffered from Mooshika drink water from the well on the north side of town, and over 85% of the victims support themselves by raising goats and selling them at the local market.

1. After analyzing the disease, Maria determines that the infection is alive. Therefore, the disease is

| Select... ▼ | and can be addressed with
| viral |
| bacterial |

| Select... ▼ | .
| antibiotics |
| vaccinations |

2. Based on Maria's findings, how could Mooshika be transferred? Choose all that apply. (For this drill, write the option letters in the box below.)

Potential Methods of Transfer

```



```

(a) Contaminated Food or Water

(b) Air

(c) Blood

(d) Bite of Infected Animal

(e) Human Saliva

3. All of the following are potential ways to treat and prevent viral infections EXCEPT

    A. vaccination.
    B. quarantine infected animals.
    C. antibiotics.
    D. avoid contact with infected persons.

Chapter 22
Physical and Earth Sciences

In this chapter, we'll cover physical laws; solids, liquids, and gases; chemical reactions; the changing earth; glaciers, erosion, and the ice ages; and astronomy.

A study of any *one* of the physical sciences could take several hundred pages, but fortunately the GED® test writers don't delve very deeply into any of the subjects that make up the physical sciences—for the very good reason that they've already decided to ask nearly half of their questions about life sciences. This means that the remaining questions must be spread between three different topics: earth and space science, chemistry, and physics. In this chapter, we're going to show you the physical science topics that come up most on the GED® Science test. Here are the topics we'll cover in this chapter:

- Energy and Heat
- Physical Laws, Work, and Motion
- Waves and Radiation
- Solids, Liquids, and Gases
- Chemical Reactions
- The Changing Earth
- Glaciers, Erosion, and the Ice Ages
- Natural Resources and Sustainability
- Fossils
- Astronomy

ENERGY AND HEAT

No doubt you've been studying for the GED® test and at some point thought to yourself, "I just don't have the energy to study anymore right now." According to physics, you might be right. An object possesses **energy** if it has the ability to do work. So, if you don't have the energy to study, you don't have the ability to do work. Makes sense, right? All energy is either potential or kinetic. While **potential energy** cannot be observed, it is the amount of energy an object has due to its position or shape, which can be measured in terms of the amount of work an object *could* perform. Conversely, **kinetic energy** is directly related to motion, and can be thought of as the energy an object possesses because of its motion. Potential energy can be classified even further. **Gravitational potential energy** is energy that an object has due to its vertical or horizontal position in a gravitational field. The amount of gravitational potential energy an object has is dependent upon the mass of an object and its height in the environment. For example, if you were to hold a bowling ball a few inches from the ground, it would have less gravitational potential energy than would a bowling ball held a few feet from the ground. The second type of potential energy is **elastic potential energy**, which is the energy stored in elastic objects resulting from stretching and compressing. Elastic potential energy is based on both the mass and speed of an object. Consider the following. Imagine that you put a rock in a slingshot and pull back, increasing the tension of the slingshot. The further back you pull the slingshot, the more elastic potential energy the object acquires. When you release the slingshot, the elastic potential energy is converted into kinetic energy. An object's **mechanical energy** is the sum total of the object's gravitational potential energy, elastic potential energy, and kinetic energy. It is important to remember that energy can be transformed from one type to another. In fact, an important physics principle is the **law of conservation of energy**, which states that energy cannot be created or destroyed.

While an object can have mechanical energy, there are many other types of energy. Indeed, energy can come in many forms, such as light, sound, and electricity, but one important form of energy is heat. **Heat** is the energy transfer from the particles of one object to another because of the objects' different temperatures. It is important to note that energy will always move from a hotter object to a cooler object. An **exothermic reaction** occurs when heat is generated in a system and released to its surroundings, while an **endothermic reaction** is one that absorbs heat from its surroundings. Think about the last time you burned your tongue on a hot drink. You felt the burn as the energy transferred from the hotter liquid to your cooler mouth; this was an endothermic reaction, as your mouth absorbed the energy. The scale for measuring heat is **temperature**, or the kinetic energy of the molecules in an object, and is measured using either the **Celsius** or **Fahrenheit** scale. You should know that water freezes at 0° Celsius (32° Fahrenheit) and boils at 100° Celsius (212° Fahrenheit). Interestingly, the particles can stop moving altogether if the temperature is low enough—this point is referred to as **absolute zero** and is the basis of a third scale of measurement for temperature, the **Kelvin** scale. The amount of energy required to raise the temperature of 1 kg of a substance by 1°C is referred to as **specific heat**. Heat can also move through an object via either convection or conduction. **Convection** is a process that occurs in liquids and gasses when heated molecules carrying energy rise before eventually cooling and sinking, thus producing a continuous cycle of heat transfer; this cyclic process is known as a **convection current**. Heat can also be transferred through **conduction**. Conduction is a process of heat energy transfer that occurs when particles are in direct contact and have different temperatures.

The **kilogram (kg)** is the base unit of mass in the International System of Units (the Metric System).

Now, all this energy has to come from somewhere. Think about the activities you do on a daily basis: take a shower, cook food, waste time on Facebook, charge your phone, drive your car, and Google all sorts of amazing GED® vocabulary words. All the activities you do require energy and all the energy has to have a source. **Fossil fuels**, which consist of coal, oil, and natural gas, are the primary source of energy in the United States. While fossil fuels are nonrenewable and the cause of many environmental problems, such as pollution, acid rain, and ozone destruction, they remain the top energy choice for many countries. Another form of energy is **nuclear power**, a nonrenewable source of energy associated with nuclear fission. Despite the low cost associated with nuclear energy, there are many concerns with widespread use. Primarily, concerns regarding the radioactive waste produced by the fission process, coupled with the potential for tragic nuclear meltdowns as seen in Chernobyl, Ukraine and Fukushima, Japan, have halted the adoption of nuclear power. A number of renewable energy sources exist, including hydroelectric, solar, and wind power. **Hydroelectric power** produces energy via the systematic placement of river dams that spin turbines to produce electricity. Unlike the previous forms of energy, hydroelectric power does not generate any pollution and can be inexpensive. Unfortunately, the usefulness of hydroelectric power is limited by geography; after all, hydroelectric power would not be practical in a desert. Both **solar** and **wind power** are on the rise, as options become more readily available, cost effective, and reliable. Wind power can provide energy for a reasonable cost, but is not always practical in a given environment. For wind power to work, large windmills with turbines must be installed, which have been met with criticism due to their appearance and their deadliness to birds. Solar power, however, has seen a rapid adoption rate, as individuals and corporations alike install **photovoltaic cells**, which transform the sun's light into energy. Solar energy has limited impact upon the environment and many praise the economic benefits. Each form of energy, whether it is renewable or nonrenewable, has an environmental and economic impact. For the GED® test, just remember the basics about the different forms.

Vocabulary

absolute zero—Defined as 0° Kelvin, or –459.67° F, and is the lower limit of the thermodynamic temperature scale. At absolute zero, atoms would stop moving altogether and, therefore, is considered a physically impossible temperature to reach.

Celsius—In the Celsius scale of temperature, water will freeze at 0° and water will boil at 100° under normal conditions.

conduction—The flow of heat energy between substances that are in direct contact with one another. In conduction, heat energy flows from a higher temperature region to a lower temperature region.

convection—The flow of heat energy that occurs when warmer areas of liquid or gas rise to cooler areas within the liquid or gas. As the cooler substance takes the place of the warmer substances, a continuous circulation pattern, or convection current, results with thermal energy moving from hot areas to cooler areas.

convection current—Convection currents move gas or fluids when differences exist in density or temperatures within a substance.

elastic potential energy—Potential energy that is stored due to the application of force that deforms an elastic object. When the force is removed from the object, the energy is released, and the object returns to its original shape.

endothermic reaction—A chemical reaction during which heat is absorbed.

energy—The capacity to do work.

exothermic reaction—A chemical reaction during which heat is released.

Fahrenheit—In the Fahrenheit scale of temperature, water will freeze at 32° and water will boil at 212° under normal conditions.

fossil fuels—Nonrenewable, natural fuels comprised of hydrocarbon deposits that are formed from the remains of living organisms. Coal, oil, and natural gas are examples of fossil fuels.

gravitational potential energy—The energy held in an object due to the object's gravitational attraction to another object.

heat—Either the transfer of kinetic energy from an energy source to a medium or object or the transfer of kinetic energy from one medium or object to another. Heat transfer can occur as conduction, convection, or radiation.

hydroelectric power—A renewable energy source that harnesses the kinetic energy of water moving over a dam to produce electricity.

Kelvin—In the Kelvin scale of temperature, water will freeze at 273.15 kelvins and water will boil at 373.15 kelvins under normal conditions.

kinetic energy—The energy of an object due to the motion of the object.

law of conservation of energy—States that energy cannot be created or destroyed, but that energy can be changed from one form to another.

mechanical energy—The amount of work an object is capable of due to the object's potential and kinetic energies.

nuclear power—Energy produced by an atomic reaction. Nuclear fission, the current process used to create nuclear power, is a process during which a nucleus of an atom splits into two smaller nuclei, resulting in the release of energy. Nuclear power plants use uranium as fuel, which is a nonrenewable resource.

photovoltaic cells—Photovoltaic cells, which are generally composed of treated silicon, are used to convert solar energy to electrical energy.

potential energy—The energy of an object due to the position, shape, or condition of the object.

radiation—A form of heat transfer that does not rely upon any contact between the heat source and the heated object. Instead, heat is transmitted through empty space by thermal radiation.

specific heat—A quantity that dictates the amount of heat energy required to raise the temperature of a single unit of an object's mass 1° Celsius relative to the amount of heat energy required to raise the temperature of a single unit water's mass 1° Celsius, given constant volume and pressure.

solar power—A form of renewable energy power that involves converting the energy of the sun's rays into electricity. The most prevalent way of converting sunlight into electricity is through the use of photovoltaic cells.

temperature—A measure of the heat present in either a substance or an object that is defined according to a given scale. The three main temperature scales are Celsius, Fahrenheit, and Kelvin.

wind power—A form of renewable energy power that involves harnessing the kinetic energy of wind to generate electrical power. The most prevalent way of converting wind into electricity is by directing wind through turbines that generate power.

Great! You have now covered the material regarding energy transfer, heat, and sources of energy. Now, let's try some questions.

Energy and Heat Drill
You can check your answers in Part VIII: Answer Key to Drills.

Questions 1 through 3 refer to the following information.

The transfer of heat occurs when particles move from an object with a high temperature to an object with a low temperature. An exothermic reaction occurs when heat is released in an energy transfer, while an endothermic reaction occurs when heat is absorbed in the energy transfer. Heat transfer can occur via either conduction, which occurs when objects are in direct contact with one another, and convection currents, which involve the cyclic movement of fluid or gas, away from a heat source. Consider the following situation:

When setting up their campsite, Kristy and Eliz decide to build a campfire. After starting the fire, both girls felt much warmer than they did before the fire was made.

1. When Kristy and Eliz lit the campfire, an

    | Select...   ▼ | reaction took place
    | endothermic |
    | exothermic |

    because heat was | Select...   ▼ | .
    | absorbed |
    | released |

2. Based on the information provided, which of the following is true?

    A. Via conduction, the girls absorbed heat from the campfire.
    B. Via convection, the girls absorbed heat from the campfire.
    C. Via conduction, the campfire absorbed heat from the girls.
    D. Via convection, the campfire absorbed heat from the girls.

3. Suppose that Kristy takes a metal pole, places it in the fire, and burns her hand. Which of the following applies to the reaction that takes place when Kristy touched the pole? Choose all that apply. (For this drill, write the option letters in the box below.)

    The Chemical Reaction Is/Involves:

    | (a) Conduction |

    | (b) Convection |

    | (c) Endothermic |

    | (d) Exothermic |

    | (e) Heat Transfer |

PHYSICAL LAWS, WORK, AND MOTION

Physics studies the *behavior* of matter. Have you ever been in a car, and the car next to you began to go forward, but you felt as if you were moving *backward*? Interestingly, in relation to the car next to you, you were moving backward. This is because **motion** is a change in an object's position relative to time and a distinct reference point. Motion is a part of all matter in the universe and is affected by forces, which are push or pull factors that change an object's speed or direction.

Speed refers to how fast an object moves. When an object travels equal distances in equal amounts of time, the object is traveling at a **constant speed**. In order to calculate the speed of an object, you will use the equation $speed = \dfrac{distance}{time}$. Related to speed is the concept of **momentum**, which can be thought of as the amount of motion an object has or the power behind an object. Heavier objects (objects with greater mass) have more momentum than lighter objects. Consider a car and a truck that are traveling at the same speed and in the same direction. If the vehicles were asked to stop moving, it would be harder to stop the truck because it has greater momentum than the car. An object's momentum is dependent upon its mass and **velocity**, which refers to both the direction and speed of an object. Momentum can be calculated using the following equation: *momentum = mass × velocity*. If I say the word "accelerate," you may think of pushing the gas pedal down in a car to increase the speed. In physics, the meaning of **acceleration** is any change in velocity—i.e., either an increase or decrease in speed or a change in direction.

One of the basic physical laws that affects all matter is the law of **gravity**. Gravity is the force that attracts any two objects toward each other. The strength of the gravitational pull depends on the masses of the two objects and the distance between them. Earth's gravitational force keeps the moon orbiting around it, just as the sun's gravitational pull keeps Earth and the other planets orbiting around it. Earth's gravitational force also keeps your feet anchored firmly to the ground.

A scientist named Sir Isaac Newton, working in the early 1700s, came up with three laws of motion.

- **The First Law**—An object will remain at rest, or continue moving at the same speed and in the same direction, unless an unbalanced force acts on the object. This is called the law of **inertia**. Imagine an air hockey table: a puck moves at a constant speed in a straight line, until it hits the table bumper, or is struck by another player.
- **The Second Law**—If an object experiences an unbalanced force, it will accelerate. The acceleration depends on the size of the force (imagine kicking a soccer ball hard rather than softly) and the mass of the object (imagine kicking a bowling ball instead).

- **The Third Law**—If Object A exerts a force on Object B, then B will exert an equal force on A, but in the opposite direction. Gun recoil is a good example of this. While the forces are ALWAYS equal, different masses cause different accelerations (see above). A force propels the (small) bullet forward, and an equal force makes the (much larger) gun "kick" back.

When we think of work, we think of something we have to do and, usually, it requires us to expend some effort. If you have to mow the lawn, you use force to push the lawnmower forward across the grass—you are doing work. **Work**, when physicists use the term, occurs when a force moves an object in the direction of the force. Work is calculated using the following equation: *work = force × distance*. As you are probably aware, not all work is equal. After all, it would take a team of five people less time to mow a lawn than if you had to mow the same lawn by yourself. **Power** is the rate at which a certain amount of work is accomplished, and is calculated with the following equation: $power = \dfrac{work}{time}$. Power is measured in watts. One watt is the amount of power it takes to complete one joule of work in one second.

With all this work, wouldn't it be nice to catch a break? Thankfully, with the advent of machines, work is much easier than it was in the past. **Machines** are implements that make work easier by redirecting or multiplying forces. Just like work, not all machines are created equal. Machines that can complete work faster are said to have a **mechanical advantage**. The mechanical advantage of a simple machine is a ratio between the force put into the machine and the force put out by the machine.

There are *six* **simple machines** (machines that change the direction or magnitude of a force) that you should know for the GED® test. The **inclined plane** category of simple machines includes tools that both magnify and redirect force. An inclined plane can be thought of as a ramp, which requires less force to move an object than would be necessary with direct vertical movement. Historians often discuss the use of inclined planes in relation to the ancient pyramids in Egypt. Many researchers hypothesize that the Egyptians used a series of inclined planes to transport the giant stones that make up each pyramid. **Wedges** are inclined planes that redirect downward force into two forces pointing outward. **Screws** are spiral inclined planes that redirect a linear force into a rotational one, thus requiring less work. Levers and pulleys, which comprise the second category of simple machines, are tools in which the object and the force move in opposite directions. A **lever** consists of a long object, often a bar, and a **fulcrum**, or pivot point. When force is applied to one end of the bar, it pivots at the fulcrum, multiplying the force at the opposite end of the bar. There are three types of levers: first-class levers, such as a seesaw; second-class levers, such as a wheelbarrow; and third-class levers, exemplified by the act of hammering in a nail. Closely related to the lever is the **pulley**, which can be created by looping rope around two or more wheels to alter the direction of force, thus providing a mechanical advantage. The last simple machine is the **wheel and axle**, which consists of a wheel or lever connected to a shaft. When a small input of force is applied to the wheel, and the wheel is turned, the shaft turns as well, but with a larger, resulting output of force. Consider the steering wheel of a car; minor adjustments to the steering wheel result in much larger changes to the overall movement of the car.

Try the forces problem below.

Newton's Law of Gravity states that the gravitational force that two objects exert on each other is equal to the following:

$$F = \frac{G \times M \times m}{r^2}$$

In the equation,

F is the force of gravity;

G is a constant;

M is the mass of one of the objects;

m is the mass of the second object;

r is the distance between the centers of the objects.

1. If the distance between two objects doubles but the masses of the objects remain constant, then the force between the two objects will

Select... ▼
decrease by a factor of 4
decrease by a factor of 2
increase by a factor of 2
increase by a factor of 4

.

Here's How to Crack It

In the equation, the distance between the two objects is represented by the r^2 term in the denominator of the fraction. If the distance between the two objects doubles, then the denominator of the fraction becomes bigger. Making the denominator of a fraction larger makes the fraction as a whole smaller, so you can eliminate (C) and (D). Since the r in the equation is squared, then doubling the distance will give you a term of $(2r)^2$, or $4r^2$ in the denominator. Thus, the denominator increases by a factor of 4, making the fraction as a whole smaller by a factor of 4. Thus, the correct answer is that the force between the two objects will decrease by a factor of 4.

Vocabulary

motion—a change in an object's position relative to time and a distinct reference point

forces—push or pull factors that change an object's speed or direction

speed—how fast an object moves

constant speed—when an object travels equal distances in equal amounts of time

momentum—the amount of motion an object has or the power behind an object

acceleration—any change in velocity

work—occurs when a force moves an object in the direction of the force

power—the rate at which a certain amount of work is accomplished

machines—implements that make work easier by redirecting or multiplying forces

simple machines—inclined plane, wedge, screw, lever, pulley, axle and wheel

gravity—the force that causes all physical objects to attract each other

inertia—another term for Newton's First Law, which states that objects at rest tend to remain at rest unless acted upon by an outside force, and that objects in motion tend to remain in motion at constant velocity unless acted upon by an outside force

Physical Laws, Work, and Motion Drill

You can check your answers in Part VIII: Answer Key to Drills.

Questions 1 through 3 refer to the following information.

Bob pushes against a rock of mass 50 kg for 20 minutes exerting an average force of 100 N but the rock never budges. He really wants to move the rock so he asks his wife Barbara to come out and help. She pushes on the rock with another 100 N and eventually the rock starts to move. As the couple keeps pushing, it becomes easier and easier to move.

At the end of the driveway is a ledge and the couple push the rock off the ledge. The rock falls for 3 seconds and eventually crashes into the riverbed below.

1. Drag the correct force into the box that describes it. You might need to use a force more than once. (For this drill, write the force letters in the boxes.)

   Original scenario before Bob asks for help

   ```
   ┌─────────────────────────────┐
   │                             │
   │                             │
   └─────────────────────────────┘
   ```

   When Barbara is helping

   ```
   ┌─────────────────────────────┐
   │                             │
   │                             │
   └─────────────────────────────┘
   ```

   When the rock falls over the ledge

   ```
   ┌─────────────────────────────┐
   │                             │
   │                             │
   └─────────────────────────────┘
   ```

(a) Gravity
(b) Bob on the rock
(c) Barbara on the rock
(d) Friction
(e) Air resistance

2. According to a physicist, *work* is defined as the force applied to an object multiplied by the distance the object moves during the time the force is applied. Using this definition, how much work did Bob do before Barbara helped him?

   A.   none
   B.   more than was necessary
   C.   enough work to get the job done
   D.   20 minutes' worth

3. After Bob and Barbara push the rock over the cliff, it begins to free-fall. Initially during the free fall the rock accelerates but then it reaches a constant speed before it hits the riverbed. Why does the rock reach constant speed?

   Type your response on a computer, if one is available. Otherwise, write your response on a separate sheet of paper.

WAVES AND RADIATION

Generally, when we hear the word *wave*, we think either of the ocean's waves on the beach or of moving our hand. You don't have to go to the beach to be surrounded by waves—they surround us all the time. We use microwaves to cook our food, light waves help us see, and sound waves cause vibrations in our eardrums that allow us to hear. In physics, and for the science portion of the GED® test, you should know that a **wave** is a disturbance that carries energy from one point to another through a **medium** or space. A medium is the matter that carries a wave between locations. As noted in its definition, a wave is a disturbance. Usually, the disturbance is some sort of vibration that provides energy for the wave; for example, a plucked guitar string vibrates to cause sound waves, and friction between tectonic plates can cause shock waves. It is important to remember that waves transfer energy, *not* matter.

For the GED® test, you should know that all waves can be categorized as either **electromagnetic** or **mechanical**. Electromagnetic waves, such as light, radio, and microwaves, can travel through empty space and do not require a medium to transfer energy. Conversely, mechanical waves, such as sound and water waves, require a medium to transfer their energy.

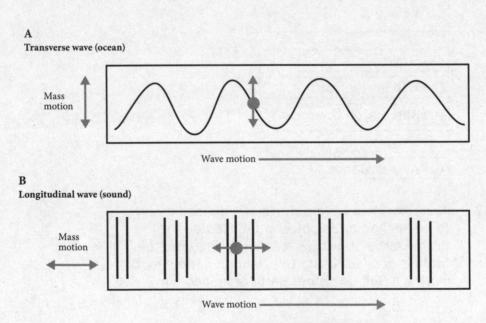

A
Transverse wave (ocean)

Mass motion

Wave motion

B
Longitudinal wave (sound)

Mass motion

Wave motion

Transverse and Longitudinal Waves

Mechanical waves can be further categorized based on the direction of the medium's particle motion in relation to the direction of the wave's motion. A **transverse wave** is one in which particle motion is perpendicular to the wave motion. As shown in the figure above, the direction of energy travel is at a right angle to the direction of the disturbance, or wave. Conversely, a **longitudinal wave** is a mechanical wave in which particle motion moves in the same direction as the wave motion. In a longitudinal wave, particles alternate between **compressions**, when particles are pushed together, and **rarefactions**, when particles are pulled apart.

In a wave, the highest point is known as the **crest** and the lowest point is called the **trough**. The height of a wave, which is referred to as **amplitude**, is found by dividing in half the vertical distance between the crest and the trough. As you notice in Figure A, a wave cycles, with each crest followed by a trough, when traveling from the origin to the final destination. A single **wavelength** is equal to the distance between two consecutive crests or troughs. The number of times a wave cycles in one second is referred to as **frequency**. Frequency is measured in **hertz**, or cycles per second. Related to frequency is the **period** of the wave, which is the time it takes for a single wave cycle, or the time between two consecutive crests of the wave. Waves that have a short period will have a high frequency, while waves that have a longer period will have a lower frequency.

Recall that, unlike mechanical waves, electromagnetic waves do not require a medium and travel through space. Electromagnetic waves are induced by disturbances, such as changes in magnetic and electric fields. Like transverse waves, charged particles move in a perpendicular direction to the direction of the wave's movement. The energy transferred through electromagnetic waves is referred to as **radiant energy**, or **radiation**.

The following electromagnetic waves are ordered from lowest to highest frequency: radio waves, microwaves, infrared waves, visible light, ultraviolet (UV) light, X-rays, and Gamma rays. Radio waves, microwaves, infrared rays, and visible light emit **non-ionizing radiation**, due to their ability to ionize atoms and break chemical bonds, and are considered relatively harmless. After all, you are exposed to radio waves when you watch television, microwaves when you make popcorn, infrared light when you change the channel using a remote control, and visible light when you walk outside.

Conversely, **UV light**, **X-rays**, and **Gamma rays** emit **ionizing radiation** and can be considered harmful. Thankfully, the earth's atmosphere filters out the majority of the harmful rays associated with electromagnetic waves such as ultraviolet light. However, we are not fully protected—you can thank the ionizing, electromagnetic radiation associated with UV light for that sunburn you got at the beach last year. X-rays are commonly used for medical exams, during which special precautions are taken to protect reproductive organs from harmful ionizing radiation. The true danger of ionizing radiation can be seen in cancer treatments like radiation therapy, which uses X-rays and Gamma rays to kill cancer cells. While effective at killing cancer cells, radiation treatment can also damage and kill normal, healthy cells. Thus, treatment sessions are generally short and spread out over time.

Vocabulary

amplitude—Refers to maximum displacement of points on a wave, or the height of a wave. The amplitude of a wave is equal vertical distance between the equilibrium point, or rest position, of the wave and the highest point, or crest, of the wave.

crest—The crest of a wave is the highest point on a transverse wave, where the displacement of the medium is at a maximum.

electromagnetic wave—A wave that does not require a medium to transfer energy and can travel through empty space. Examples of mechanical waves include light waves, radio waves, and microwaves.

frequency—The frequency of a wave, denoted by f, is the number of wavelengths per second. The frequency of a wave is inversely related to the period of a wave; i.e., a wave with a high frequency will have a small period and vice-versa.

Gamma rays—A type of high-frequency electromagnetic radiation that is used both in the medical and astronomical fields. Gamma rays are used to treat cancerous tumor cells.

hertz—Named after Heinrich Hertz, the unit hertz (Hz) is used to measure the frequency of a wavelength, or the number of wavelengths per second.

ionizing radiation—Any type of electromagnetic radiation that carries enough energy to remove electrons from an atom. While ionizing radiation, such as X-rays and Gamma rays, is used in many fields of research, prolonged exposure is harmful to humans and can cause illness, mutations, cancer, and death.

longitudinal wave—A mechanical wave in which the particle motion of the medium moves in the same direction as the motion of the wave.

mechanical wave—A wave that requires a medium to transfer energy. Examples of mechanical waves include both sound and water waves.

medium—Matter that carries mechanical waves between locations.

non-ionizing radiation—Any type of electromagnetic radiation that does not have enough energy to remove an electron from an atom. Accordingly, non-ionizing radiation, such as radio waves, microwaves, and UV light, is not harmful to humans.

period—The period of a wave, denoted by T, is the amount of time it takes a wave to complete a single cycle. The period of a wave is inversely related to the frequency of a wave; i.e., a wave with a large period will have a low frequency and vice-versa.

radiation—energy that travels by either waves or particles, such as heat or light.

transverse wave—A wave in which the particle motion of the medium is perpendicular to the motion of the wave.

trough—The lowest point on a transverse wave, where the displacement of the medium is at a minimum.

ultraviolet (UV) light—A type of high-frequency electromagnetic radiation produced by the sun, but invisible to the naked eye. In excess, UV light can be harmful to the human body.

wave—A disturbance that carries energy between locations through a medium or space.

wavelength—The distance between two consecutive crests or two consecutive troughs of a wave. A single wavelength is referred to as a cycle.

X-rays—A type of mid- to high-frequency electromagnetic radiation produced by accelerating electrons. X-rays are used in the medical field to create images, also known as X-rays, which penetrate soft tissues, but not bone. Prolonged exposure to X-rays can lead to negative health effects, as X-rays kill healthy cells.

Phew! You should now have a solid grasp of the wave and radiation concepts that will be asked on the GED® test. Now, let's try out some sample questions.

Waves and Radiation Drill

You can check your answers in Part VIII: Answer Key to Drills.

<u>Questions 1 through 3</u> refer to the following information.

Employees at GetWell research labs are analyzing mechanical waves, which require a medium to pass through, and electromagnetic waves, which travel through space. Jose Gonzalez IV is studying electromagnetic waves and their potential, real-world health and medical applications. He records the lengths of the various waves, noting that radio waves are the longest, while Gamma rays are the shortest. When calculating the frequency of the wave, or the number of wavelengths that occur in a distinct amount of time, Jose notes that there is an inverse relationship between the frequency of a wave and its period, which is the time it takes for a single wave to occur.

Wave Type	Wavelength Size	Application
Radio Waves	Greater than 30 cm	Aircraft Navigation, TV, AM/FM Radio
Microwaves	30 cm–1 mm	Microwave Ovens, Mobile Phones
Infrared Waves	1mm–700 nm	Remote Controls, Toasters, Night Vision
Visible Light	700 nm–400 nm	Physical Therapy, Light Bulbs, Photography
Ultraviolet Light	400 nm–60 nm	Sanitation, Air Purification, Forgery Detection
X-Rays	60 nm–1×10^4 nm	Medical Examination, Cancer Treatment
Gamma Rays	0.1 nm–1×10^5 nm	Cancer Treatment, Food Irradiation

1. Based on the information provided, as

   | Select... ▼ | waves pass through
   | electromagnetic |
   | mechanical |

   space, the | Select... ▼ | of a wave
   | period |
   | frequency |
   | amplitude |

   increases and the period of a wave

   | Select... ▼ |.
   | increases |
   | decreases |
   | stays the same |

2. Based on the information provided, which types of waves have potential medical applications? Choose all that apply. (For this drill, write the option letters in the box below.)

Waves with Potential Medical Applications

```



```

(a) Microwaves

(b) Radio Waves

(c) X-rays

(d) Ultraviolet Light

(e) Visible Light

(f) Gamma Rays

(g) Infrared waves

3. Jose identifies a new medical technology that utilizes a wave with a size of 1 nm. Which type of electromagnetic wave did Jose identify? (Write the name of the wave in the provided box— e.g., Microwaves, Infrared Waves, Gamma Rays, and so on.)

```


```

SOLIDS, LIQUIDS, AND GASES

Chemistry is the study of matter. All matter is made up of **molecules,** tiny invisible pieces of matter. However, even molecules are not the smallest particles in the world. Molecules are made up of **atoms,** which are in turn composed of **protons** and **neutrons** (at the atom's center, which is known as the **nucleus**) and **electrons** that circle the nucleus.

Certain types of atoms break down slowly over time. The nuclei of these atoms gradually decay over thousands of years and give off charged particles of energy. The particles that are discharged are called radioactive, and because they are coming from the nucleus of an atom, the process is called **nuclear radiation.** Some radioactive elements are highly dangerous—uranium comes to mind—but other elements are essentially harmless.

Matter exists in one of three states. When its temperature is low, matter exists in a **solid** state, with its molecules closely joined, barely moving. As the temperature increases, the molecules begin to move more freely, and the matter changes into a **liquid.** If the matter is heated even further, the molecules will break away from one another to form a **gas.** The point at which a solid turns into a liquid is called its **melting point.** The temperature at which a liquid turns into a solid is called its **freezing point.** Each element in nature changes from a solid into a liquid and from a liquid into a gas at different temperatures. Ice turns to a liquid (water) when the temperature is above 32 degrees Fahrenheit. Iron, however, does not turn into a liquid unless the temperature is much hotter.

Solids keep their own shape. Liquids will flow into any container but still have chemical bonds that hold the liquid together. Gases have no shape and will disperse unless they are contained. By increasing the temperature, in most cases you increase the volume of a substance. One exception is water, which actually increases slightly in volume *when frozen.*

An **element** is a substance that occurs in nature. For example, hydrogen and oxygen are elements. When two elements are mixed together, the result is called a **mixture.** However, if you mix the two elements and they bond together through a chemical interaction, then the new product formed is called a **compound.** For example, water (H_2O) is a compound. Many compounds can be classified either as an acid or a base. Acids, such as lemon juice, taste sour. Bases neutralize acids. An example of a base is baking soda.

When a substance such as salt is **dissolved** in water or another liquid, the result is called a **solution.** You can keep adding more of the substance until the solution reaches its **saturation point.** A higher temperature will often increase the saturation point.

Matter Quiz
Q: What happens if you freeze a pipe full of water?

Turn the page for the answer.

Try your skills at the solids, liquids, and gases problem below.

Ethylene glycol is the main ingredient in antifreeze and has the chemical structure shown below:

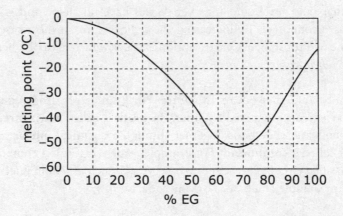

The figure below shows how the melting point (the temperature at which solid antifreeze would begin melting) of antifreeze varies with % EG.

1. A company that creates antifreeze wants to create an antifreeze solution that is effective at the coldest possible temperatures. Select the point on the graph that represents the ideal % EG that the company should use in its solution and the temperature that such an antifreeze solution could withstand before freezing. Mark the point with an X.

Here's How to Crack It
According to the graph, antifreeze is most effective when it is composed of approximately 65% EG. At that point, antifreeze melts at temperatures as low as approximately –52°C. Thus, the correct point on the graph is the point at (65%, –52°C).

Vocabulary

pH value—a scale to measure the baseness or acidity of a compound

evaporation—the process by which a liquid becomes a gas

half life—the amount of time it takes half of a radioactive element to decay

molecules—tiny particles of matter

atoms—tiny particles that make up molecules

nucleus—the center of an atom

protons—tiny, positively charged particles that make up an atom's nucleus

neutrons—tiny particles that make up an atom's nucleus, or center, and that do not have charge

electrons—tiny, negatively charged particles that circle the nucleus of an atom

nuclear radiation—the process in which the nuclei of certain atoms break down over time, releasing charged particles of energy

solid—a state of matter that occurs at low temperatures and in which the matter's molecules are closely joined and barely move

liquid—a state of matter that occurs at higher temperatures than does the solid state, and in which the matter's molecules move more freely than they do in the solid state

gas—a state of matter that occurs at higher temperatures than does the liquid state, and in which molecules break way from one another

melting point—the temperature at which a solid turns into a liquid

freezing point—the temperature at which a liquid turns into a solid

element—a substance that occurs in nature

compound—a substance that results when two elements bond together through chemical interaction

saturation point—the point at which a solution contains enough of a particular substance that it can no longer dissolve more of that substance

---

Matter Quiz

A: The pipe might break because when water freezes, it increases slightly in size.

Solids, Liquids, and Gases Drill

You can check your answers in Part VIII: Answer Key to Drills.

<u>Questions 1 through 3</u> refer to the following passage.

All matter exists in one of three phases: as a solid, liquid or gas. Solids are rigid in shape and usually the densest form of matter. Both liquids and gases are generally less dense and able to deform to take on the shape of a container, with gas molecules being the least constrained. The most notable exception to the density rule is water. Liquid water is actually denser than solid water (ice). You know that this is true because you have probably noticed that lakes and waterways freeze from the top down as opposed to the bottom up. For the same reason, ice cubes float in a glass of water.

Pressure and temperature affect the phase that matter is found in. For example, at high pressure and low temperature, matter is more likely to be solid. Conversely, at low pressure and high temperature, matter is often found in gaseous state. By changing pressure and temperature, researchers can change the phase of a substance. The following diagram depicts the phase that carbon dioxide will be found in based on the temperature and pressure.

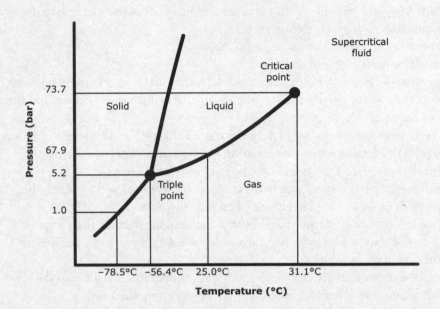

The dark black lines represent phase equilibriums where there is more than one phase present at a given temperature and pressure.

1. What can you do to increase the amount of gas that you can store in a fixed container?

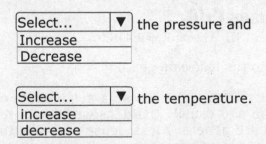

Select... ▼	the pressure and
Increase	
Decrease	

Select... ▼	the temperature.
increase	
decrease	

2. Adding salt to a pot of boiling water temporarily stops the water from boiling. Which of the following is the best explanation for this occurrence?

   A.   The salt raises the boiling point of the water.
   B.   Salt prevents water from ever boiling.
   C.   Salt neutralizes the water.
   D.   Salt water is easier to float in than freshwater.

3. Using the figure above, determine what phase change would occur if carbon dioxide at −70°C and 70 bar was heated to 25°C and held at the same pressure.

   A. melting
   B. freezing
   C. boiling
   D. condensing

CHEMICAL REACTIONS

While you won't need to memorize the periodic table or know how to do complex organic chemistry in order to succeed on the GED® test, you will find it helpful to be able to understand basic formulas for **chemical reactions.** A chemical reaction occurs when molecules interact to create a new substance. In order to show what happens in a chemical reaction, scientists use chemical equations. A typical example of a chemical reaction might be when hydrochloric acid combines with sodium hydroxide. In the equation that demonstrates this reaction, hydrochloric acid is denoted by HCl. This tells you that a molecule of hydrochloric acid is made up of one hydrogen atom (the H in HCl is for hydrogen) and one chlorine atom (the Cl in HCl is for chlorine). Sodium hydroxide is denoted by NaOH, which means that a molecule of sodium hydroxide is made up of one atom of sodium (Na), one atom of oxygen (O), and one atom of hydrogen (H). When these two substances interact, a chemical reaction occurs. The formula for the interaction is below.

$$NaOH + HCl \rightarrow NaCl + H_2O$$

This tells you that when sodium hydroxide and hydrochloric acid interact, they create one molecule of NaCl or sodium chloride, and one molecule of water, or H_2O. Note that NaCl is a molecule that contains one sodium atom (Na) and one chlorine atom (Cl). H_2O is a molecule that contains two hydrogen atoms (H_2) and one oxygen atom (O). The little 2 next to the H indicates that you have two, rather than one, hydrogen atom.

Sometimes you'll see equations that have a larger number out in front of one of the molecules in the equation. For instance, you might see $2H_2O$ in an equation. This would tell you that you had two water, or H_2O, molecules. Since each of those water molecules would have two hydrogen atoms, you would have four hydrogen atoms in total. However, each of those molecules would have only one oxygen atom, so you would have only two oxygen atoms in total.

Don't worry that you won't know the symbols for each of the elements. While the GED® test is tricky, it won't expect you to have an in-depth knowledge of chemistry! Generally, if you need to know what element a particular symbol refers to, the GED® test will give you that information. There are just three chemical symbols you may want to memorize: Hydrogen is denoted with an H, carbon is denoted with a C, and oxygen is denoted with an O. You should also know that water is H_2O.

How might you see chemical equations tested on the GED® test? Try out the following problem.

---

1. When propane interacts with oxygen, a chemical reaction occurs, creating carbon dioxide and water. The balanced chemical equation for this reaction is shown below.

    $$C_3H_8 + 5O_2 \rightarrow 3CO_2 + 4H_2O$$

    Based on the information above, which of the following is true?

    A. When one molecule of propane combines with five molecules of oxygen, one molecule of water results.
    B. When eleven molecules of propane combine with ten molecules of oxygen, three molecules of carbon dioxide result.
    C. When one molecule of propane combines with five molecules of oxygen, four molecules of water result.
    D. When one molecule of propane combines with five molecules of oxygen, one molecule of carbon results.

Here's How to Crack It

If you know that the $5O_2$ on the left-hand side of the equation represents oxygen, then you know that the C_3H_8 must represent the propane. Since there is no large number in front of the C_3H_8, you know that there is only one molecule of propane. Eliminate (B), since you do not have eleven units of propane. The right-hand side of the equation shows that the equation results in $4H_2O$, or four water molecules. Thus, you can eliminate (A), which says that one molecule of water results. Finally, the right-hand side of the equation also indicates that the reaction creates $3CO_2$. Since the $4H_2O$ represents the water molecules, the $3CO_2$ must represent the carbon dioxide molecules. Note that the number 3 appears in front, which means that you must have three carbon dioxide molecules. Eliminate (D), which states that the reaction creates one molecule of carbon dioxide. Only (C) remains, so it is the correct answer.

Vocabulary

chemical reaction—a process that occurs when molecules interact to create a new substance

Chemical Reactions Drill

You can check your answers in Part VIII: Answer Key to Drills.

<u>Questions 1 and 2</u> refer to the following information.

There are four basic types of chemical reactions, as shown in the table below.

Reaction Types	General Example
Combination	A + B → C
Decomposition	C → A + B
Single Displacement	A + BC → B + AC
Double Displacement	AB + CD → AC + BD

The balanced chemical equation describing the reaction between silver and hydrogen sulfide is shown below.

$$2Ag + H_2S \rightarrow Ag_2S + H_2$$

1. Which of the four basic types of chemical reactions is this?

   A. combination
   B. decomposition
   C. single displacement
   D. double displacement

2. Based on the information above, which of the following is true?

   A. When two atoms of silver combine with one molecule of hydrogen sulfide, the result is one molecule of silver sulfide and one molecule of hydrogen.
   B. When an atom of silver combines with one molecule of hydrogen, the result is one molecule of silver sulfide and two molecules of hydrogen.
   C. When two molecules of silver sulfide combine with two molecules of hydrogen, the result is two atoms of silver and one molecule of silver sulfide.
   D. When one molecule of hydrogen sulfide combines with one molecule of silver sulfide, the result is one molecule of hydrogen and one molecule of silver sulfide.

3. In a balanced chemical equation, the number of atoms associated with a given element is the same both before and after a chemical reaction. The balanced equation for photosynthesis is

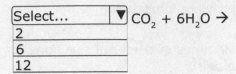 $CO_2 + 6H_2O \rightarrow$

Select... ▼
2
6
12

$C_6H_{12}O_6 + 6$ | Select... ▼ | $_2$.

Select... ▼
C
H
O

THE CHANGING EARTH

Although it generally feels pretty solid underfoot, the earth is undergoing constant change. We have discovered that the continents—that's right, entire *continents*—are actually moving slowly on the face of the earth. This is called **continental drift.** Looking at the map below, you will notice that if you pushed the continent of Africa up against the continent of South America, you would have an almost perfect fit.

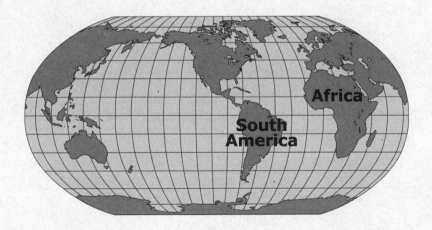

Scientists theorize that at one time, the two continents may have been joined together. Today, it is believed that the earth's crust is composed of several large pieces—called **tectonic plates**—that move slowly over the mantle of the earth. When these plates rub against one another, the friction between them causes **earthquakes.** The places where the plates rub together are called **fault lines.**

Earth's Plates

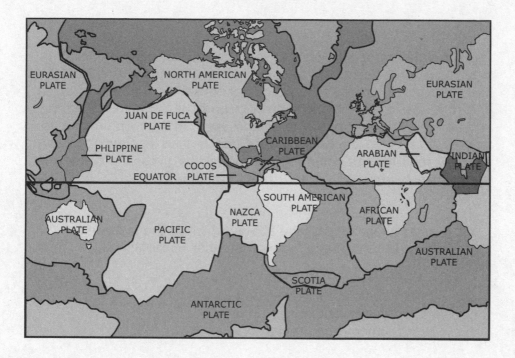

The inner portions of the earth are under enormous pressure and are very hot. Sometimes, when the pressure becomes too great, it forces hot molten rock to the surface of the earth. This is called a **volcanic eruption.**

So far, scientists have had little luck predicting earthquakes and volcanic eruptions, although one interesting avenue for exploration may be the fact that animals often seem to know when an earthquake is coming.

The earth is composed of several layers. The outer layer is called the **crust.** The next layer down is called the **mantle.** The center of the earth is called the **core.** The crust of the earth (the only part we generally ever get to see) is composed of several different kinds of rock. **Igneous** rock is formed from cooled **magma;** magma is rock from the mantle that is so hot it has turned to liquid. **Sedimentary** rock is made up of sediment from the earth—such as sand—that has been hardened by compression. **Metamorphic** rock is made up of either of the other two types of rock, but it has been subjected to either a great deal of pressure or heat way below the surface of the earth.

Let's look at how the GED® test writers might ask a question about the changing earth.

The rock cycle is a process by which old rocks are recycled into new rocks. In the rock cycle, time, pressure, and the earth's heat interact to create three types of rocks. Sedimentary rock is formed as sediment (eroded rocks and the remains of plants and animals) builds up and is compressed. Metamorphic rock is formed as a great deal of pressure and heat is applied to rock. Igneous rock results when rock is melted by pressure below the earth's crust into a liquid and then resolidifies.

1. Based on the passage above, which of the following would contain the greatest number of fossils?

    A. igneous rocks only
    B. sedimentary rocks only
    C. metamorphic rocks only
    D. igneous and metamorphic rocks

Here's How to Crack It

According to the passage, sedimentary rocks are formed from the eroded remains of plants and animals. Thus, sedimentary rocks would likely contain the greatest number of fossils, and the correct answer is (B).

Vocabulary

Richter scale—a scale used to measure the magnitude of earthquakes

epicenter—the place where an earthquake originates

dormant—a volcano that is inactive at the moment

strata—layers of rock

continental drift—the process in which continents move slowly across the face of the earth

tectonic plates—large pieces of earth that compose the earth's crust

earthquakes—events that occur when tectonic plates rub together and produce friction

fault lines—places where tectonic plates rub together

volcanic eruption—event that occurs when inner portions of the earth experience extreme heat and pressure, and pressure forces hot molten rock to the surface of the earth

crust—outer layer of the earth

mantle—layer of the earth below the crust

core—center of the earth

magma—rock from the earth's mantle that has become so hot that it has turned to liquid

igneous rock—rock composed of cooled magma

sedimentary rock—rock made up from sediment that has been hardened by compression

metamorphic rock—rock that is made up of either of the other two types of rock, but that has been subjected to extreme heat or pressure

The Changing Earth Drill

You can check your answers in Part VIII: Answer Key to Drills.

<u>Questions 1 through 3</u> refer to the passage below.

Scientists believe that earthquake activity is the result of friction between tectonic plates of the earth that causes the sudden release of energy creating seismic waves. These waves can be measured, using seismometers, to describe the magnitude of the earthquake. The Richter scale provides a local measurement of the strength of an earthquake. Anything measuring below 3 on the Richter scale is nearly imperceptible; however, a quake that exceeds 7 can cause major damage. The largest earthquakes recorded have measured over 9 on the Richter scale and caused enormous amounts of damage.

Earthquakes can occur at different depths and this has a significant effect on the amount of damage an earthquake causes. Shallow earthquakes, those that occur near to the earth's surface, cause the most damage. Earthquakes that occur on land have been known to cause volcanoes to erupt and landslides while earthquakes occurring offshore can initiate tsunamis.

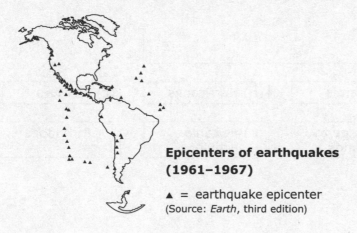

Epicenters of earthquakes (1961–1967)

▲ = earthquake epicenter
(Source: *Earth*, third edition)

Some locations on Earth are more prone to earthquakes than others. There has been a great deal of earthquake activity along the western coast of North and South America, as shown on the map above. Each point represents the epicenter of the earthquake, which is the point at ground level directly above where the initial rupture of the earthquake took place, referred to as the hypocenter or focus.

1. From the information presented above, which of the following statements can be concluded?

    A. The places marked on the map are the only places on Earth where earthquakes occur.

    B. Two tectonic plates are rubbing together along the west coast of the Americas.

    C. Two tectonic plates are rubbing together along the east coast of the Americas.

    D. Canada reports more earthquakes than the United States does.

2. Which of the following options from the list below can result due to an earthquake with magnitude 5 or greater? Choose all that apply. (For this drill, write the option letters in the box below.)

Outcomes of an Earthquake

(a) Tsunamis	(b) Hurricanes	(c) Tremors
(d) Damage to buildings	(e) Volcanic activity	(f) Tornadoes

3. You turn on the news to find out, for the first time, that an earthquake has taken place only a few miles from your home. You didn't feel anything, and there is no obvious sign of damage. The

earthquake probably measured [Select... ▼]
| 3 |
| 5 |
| 7 |

on the Richter scale and was probably

[Select... ▼] with respect to the
| deep |
| shallow |

earth's surface.

GLACIERS, EROSION, AND THE ICE AGES

Glaciers are giant pieces of ice that are many miles long. The glaciers in Greenland and Antarctica are nearly as big as continents. Glaciers begin as deposits of snow that gradually change to ice. They move very slowly by the process of gravity. At one time, these glaciers covered large parts of the earth. Over the course of time, the glaciers have advanced and retreated several times, for reasons that are still not yet entirely understood. These movements have caused large fluctuations in sea level, covering many shallow areas of land with water for long periods of time.

The advance of the glaciers led to periods called the ice ages. (During one of these, the Pleistocene age, ice covered much of North America.) As a glacier advances, it **erodes** the soil and bedrock in front of it, dragging large quantities of debris along with it. Other processes can also cause erosion. For example, a river gradually erodes the banks on either side of it. Even the wind can erode topsoil.

Let's try a question based on this material.

?

Glaciers Quiz
Q: If the glaciers suddenly melted, what would happen to the sea levels?

Turn the page for the answer.

The Cape Hatteras lighthouse is located on the Outer Banks, a chain of islands off the coast of North Carolina, and was built in 1870. After the lighthouse was built, citizens of the Outer Banks noted that the ocean was eroding the beach, bringing the shoreline progressively closer to the lighthouse. The chart below shows how the distance in meters between the shoreline and the lighthouse changed between 1870 and 1990.

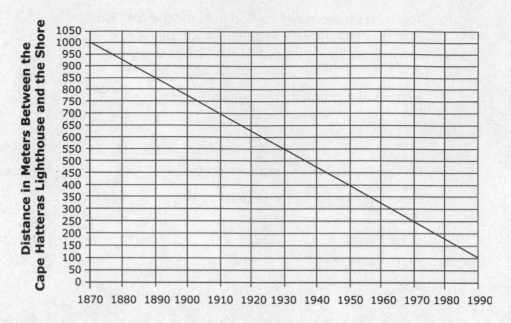

Distance in Meters Between the Cape Hatteras Lighthouse and the Shore

Year

1. In 1990, scientists studied the Cape Hatteras lighthouse to determine when local residents would need to move the lighthouse before it suffered damage. According to the information above, scientists could project that in the year 2000 the distance between the shore and the lighthouse would most likely be closest to

   A. 0 meters.
   B. 25 meters.
   C. 75 meters.
   D. 100 meters.

Here's How to Crack It

According to the chart, the distance between the shoreline and the lighthouse decreases by 75 meters every 10 years. In 1990, the distance between the shore and the lighthouse is 100 meters, so by 2000 the distance between the lighthouse and the shore should be 100 meters − 75 meters = 25 meters. Thus, the correct answer is (B).

Glaciers, Erosion, and the Ice Ages Drill

You can check your answers in Part VIII: Answer Key to Drills.

<u>Questions 1 through 3</u> refer to the passage below.

Scientists posit that ice ages, times when the temperature of the earth fell dramatically for reasons not well understood, took place as recently as 2.5 million years ago. There have been several ice ages during which glaciers covered much of the surface of the earth. In between ice ages and following the last one, the earth's temperature warmed up again for reasons not fully understood.

Evidence for the ice ages comes in three varieties: paleontological, chemical, and geological. Fossils have provided evidence of ice ages due to their distribution. Certain organisms that would have required warm conditions went extinct during these times while those that were better adapted to cooler climates survived and spread into warmer areas. Chemical variations in the isotopes found in fossils and sedimentary rock offer further evidence of ice ages. Finally, the valley cutting and scratching of rocks provides geological evidence of glacial movement.

1. Based on the information above, which of the following is most likely true?

   A. Glaciers begin melting when the temperature of the earth rises above freezing.
   B. Glaciers are found only near the equator.
   C. When glaciers melt, the level of water in the oceans goes down.
   D. Glaciers are affected by the gravitational pull of the moon.

   Glaciers Quiz
   A: Sea levels would rise.

2. Glaciers are formed over time as snow gradually turns to ice. Which of the following can be concluded about glaciers?

   A. When they move, glaciers move rapidly.
   B. Glaciers are composed of fresh water.
   C. Glaciers occur only in valleys.
   D. Glaciers will never again cover the earth.

3. Click on all of the points on the following graph that represent the ice ages. (For this drill, mark the points with an X.)

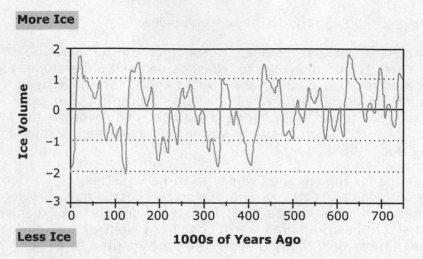

NATURAL RESOURCES

Remember when we discussed energy? Well, we are going to revisit the sources of our energy. On a daily basis, you perform a multitude of tasks that require power; e.g., you may brush your teeth, make toast, drive your car, use electricity, or a host of other power-sucking tasks. So, where does all that power come from? And, more importantly, what happens if the sources of power run dry? A large amount of energy is required to produce the power supplied throughout the world. In order to produce this energy, it is necessary to utilize a combination of human ingenuity and the earth's resources. There are two types of **natural resources:** renewable and nonrenewable.

Renewable resources are those that can be replenished or regenerated over the course of time by natural processes and can be replaced at a sustainable rate; i.e., the supply of the energy is able to meet the demand for energy. In the United States, eight percent of electricity is produced with five main renewable resources: biomass, hydroelectric power, geothermal energy, wind, and solar power. **Biomass**, or biofuels, is organic matter such as plants, animals, or waste products from organic sources that is burned in a biomass boiler to produce energy. Using biomass as an energy source is beneficial because it is low-cost, readily available and renewable, and better for the environment than fossil fuels. Biomass can also help reduce the amount of waste in landfills, as it relies on the burning of organic matter. The major downsides of biomass include the initial cost and large land mass required for installation of a biomass boiler. **Hydroelectric power** works via the systematic placement of river dams that spin turbines to produce electricity. Despite the fact that hydroelectric power does not generate any pollution and can be cost-effective, the usefulness of this resource is limited by geography. Hydroelectric power is practical only in areas that receive significant rainfall and are located near rivers. Environmentalists also note that hydroelectric dams require the diversion of waterways that leads to the disturbance, and often destruction, of habitats and ecosystems.

An increasingly researched renewable energy source is **geothermal energy**, which is produced by harnessing the earth's internal heat. (Fun fact: *Geo* means "from the earth," and *thermal* means "heat.") Geothermal energy is produced when heat, coming from steam or hot water reservoirs deep in the earth, is transferred through large pipes that drive an electrical generator. The benefits of geothermal energy are that it is reliable when installed, safe to use, and does not produce pollutants in the energy production process. Unfortunately, geothermal energy hasn't gained popularity, is expensive to install, and can potentially release toxic gas during the drilling process. Furthermore, the use of geothermal energy is limited by geography; if a location lacks a geothermal source, energy production cannot take place.

With recent advents in technology, both **solar** and **wind power** have become increasingly accessible, affordable, and reliable. Perhaps one of the greatest benefits of both resources is that they are indefinitely renewable. Wind power produces electricity through large windmills that harness wind that spins turbines. While wind power can provide energy for a reasonable cost, it has seen a slow adoption rate. Indeed, wind power is not always practical in a given environment, as large, unobstructed areas of land are needed for windmill placement. For wind power to work effectively, large windmills with turbines must be installed, which have been met with criticism for various reasons. One criticism is regarding the aesthetic nature of a windmill farm, which can stretch over vast swaths of land. Others note the deadliness of the wind turbines, which have been known to suck in and kill migrating birds. Solar power, however, has seen a rapid adoption rate, as individuals and corporations alike install **photovoltaic cells**, which transform the sun's light into energy. Two benefits of solar energy are that passive solar energy production produces no air pollutants and users can save significant amounts of money by receiving energy "off the grid." Unfortunately, the production of photovoltaic cells requires the use of fossil fuels, which have a detrimental impact on the environment, and the initial installation cost of a passive solar collection system is quite significant. Furthermore, areas that receive limited amounts of sunlight are not practical for solar energy systems.

In summation, it should be noted that there is a huge benefit associated with the use of renewable resources: Compared to nonrenewable energy, renewable energy is significantly less harmful to the environment and is considered **green technology**. Worldwide, renewable resources provide approximately 10 percent of the world's energy consumption. As technology continues to improve, and the world becomes increasingly aware of the environmental hazards associated with fossil fuels, researchers project that renewable resources will provide 15 percent of the world's energy by 2040.

Nonrenewable resources are those that exist in a limited supply and cannot be naturally replaced on a level to meet its consumption; i.e., the demand exceeds the supply. While **fossil fuels** are nonrenewable and the cause of many environmental problems, such as pollution, acid rain, and ozone destruction, they remain the top energy choice for many countries. Fossil fuels, such as coal, oil, and natural gas, are the world's primary sources of energy, comprising approximately 80 percent of the world's energy. Formed from fossilized remains of organic matter, fossil fuels are found deep within the earth. In order to locate fossil fuels, geologists dig **exploratory wells** to take samples from the earth and determine whether or not the area is a **proven reserve**, or a location known to house fossil fuel deposits. Once a proven reserve has been tapped, oil is pumped from the reserve up to the surface. This form of oil is **crude oil**, which can vary greatly in viscosity, sulfur output, and color. There are four main modes of oil extraction: primary extraction, during which oil is easily pumped to the surface; pressure extraction, during which water and CO_2 push oil out of the reserve; steam and gas extraction; and the newest mode, **fracking**, the process of injecting liquid at high pressure into the earth so existing fissures can be opened and oil can be extracted. Another major fossil fuel is **coal**, a combustible black rock composed of fossilized organic plant matter. Coal is extracted from the earth via **underground mining**, during which coal miners enter and manually retrieve coal from a series of underground tunnels. One major issue associated with coal mining is subsidence, which is the caving in of mine shafts. Many times throughout history, cave-ins have trapped men underground, in what would become their final resting place. Like other fossil fuels, coal releases harmful pollutants into the environment that destroy the ozone layer, pollute the air with smog and smoke, and produce **acid mine drainage**, or highly acidic water that can damage the areas surrounding the mine. Comprised mainly of methane and pentane, **natural gas** can be found deep in the earth where it is stored in the space between rocks. Like oil extraction, natural gas extraction occurs when gas is carried to the surface and harnessed to produce power. Unlike the other types of fossil fuels, natural gas does not produce harmful pollutants. However, natural gas is quite unstable and, if not properly controlled, intense explosions could occur. Another form of nonrenewable energy is **nuclear power**, which uses uranium in a process called **nuclear fission**, which occurs when an isotope of uranium-235 is split. Despite the low cost associated with nuclear energy, there are many concerns with widespread use. Primarily, concerns regarding the radioactive waste produced by the fission process, coupled with the potential for tragic nuclear meltdowns as seen in Chernobyl, Ukraine and Fukushima, Japan, has slowed the adoption of nuclear power. In the future, nuclear power will likely involve **nuclear fusion**, which is the process of fusing two nuclei to create power.

Keep in mind that nonrenewable resources will, eventually, run out. When they do, we better have perfected a form of renewable energy to sustain ourselves. Remember, for the GED® test, you need to know just the basics about renewable and nonrenewable resources and their respective costs and benefits.

Vocabulary

acid mine drainage—A direct negative environmental effect of the mining process that occurs when sulfides are exposed to air and water, forming sulfuric acid. Sulfuric acid that is released can then harm animals and plants.

biomass—A renewable resource that is comprised of organic materials found in plant and animal materials. Biomass is burned to create electricity or other types of power.

coal—A nonrenewable resource that is comprised of the carbonized remains of prehistoric plant matter.

crude oil—A nonrenewable resource that is composed of hydrocarbon deposits and prehistoric organic matter.

exploratory well—A deep hole that is drilled into the earth by an oil or gas company in order to determine if fossil fuels exist in a specific location.

fracking—The process of injecting liquid at high pressure into the earth in order to open existing fissures and extract oil from the earth. Fracking is a controversial process.

fossil fuels—Nonrenewable, natural fuels comprised of hydrocarbon deposits that are formed from the remains of living organisms. Coal, oil, and natural gas are examples of fossil fuels.

geothermal energy—A renewable resource that is produced by harnessing the earth's internal heat. Geothermal energy is produced when heat, coming from steam or hot water reservoirs deep in the earth, is transferred through large pipes that drive an electrical generator.

green technology—Technology that can be created through environmentally friendly means and produces energy that limits environmental harm.

hydroelectric power—A renewable energy source that harnesses the kinetic energy of water moving over a dam to produce electricity.

natural gas—A nonrenewable energy source that is composed mainly of methane gas. Considered the cleanest of the nonrenewable resources, natural gas is extracted from the earth and burned to produce electricity.

natural resources—Resources that exist naturally in the environment and prove beneficial to humans.

nonrenewable resources—Resources that exist in limited quantities and cannot be naturally replaced on a level to meet its consumption. Fossil fuels, such as coal, oil, and natural gas, are examples of nonrenewable resources.

nuclear fission—Nuclear fission, the current process used to create nuclear power, is a process during which a nucleus of an atom splits into two smaller nuclei, resulting in the release of energy.

nuclear fusion—Nuclear fusion is a process during which the nuclei of atoms fuse together to form a heavier nucleus, resulting in the release of energy. Nuclear fusion is the process that occurs in the sun, but has yet to be artificially perfected by scientists.

nuclear power—Energy produced by an atomic reaction. Generally, nuclear fission power plants use uranium, a nonrenewable resource, as fuel.

photovoltaic cells—Photovoltaic cells, which are generally composed of treated silicon, are used to convert solar energy to electrical energy.

proven reserve—A location that is known to house fossil fuel deposits.

renewable resources—Resources that can be naturally replaced or replenished on a level to meet its consumption and, therefore, is considered inexhaustible. Solar power, wind, and biomass are examples of renewable resources.

solar power—A form of renewable energy power that involves converting the energy of the sun's rays into electricity. The most prevalent way of converting sunlight into electricity is through the use of photovoltaic cells.

underground mining—A process of making tunnels that is used to gain access to minerals and ores in the ground. There are many detrimental issues associated with underground mining such as worker safety, ventilation, and environmental problems related to extraction.

wind power—A form of renewable energy power that involves harnessing the kinetic energy of wind to generate electrical power. The most prevalent way of converting wind into electricity is by directing wind through turbines that generate power.

Now that we've covered information regarding the extraction and use of natural resources, let's try some questions.

Natural Resources Drill

You can check your answers in Part VIII: Answer Key to Drills.

<u>Questions 1 through 3</u> refer to the following information.

Bashville is looking to reduce its carbon emissions by changing the type of power that's supplied to various parts of the city. Bashville also wants to reduce the amount of organic waste that has been accumulated in the town's landfills. Currently, the majority of the city's power comes from coal, oil, and other fossil fuels. When considering renewable energy sources, such as solar, wind, biomass, and hydroelectric power, Bashville must take into account the geographical limitations of the area. After all, Bashville is located in a large basin surrounded by mountains. Bashville also receives a large amount of rainfall each month and is situated near a system of rivers.

1. | Select... ▼ | energy sources
    | Renewable |
    | Nonrenewable |

    increase | Select... ▼ | emissions.
            | carbon |
            | oxygen |

2. Based on the information provided, which of the following would produce the greatest amount of carbon emission?

    A. solar power
    B. biomass
    C. coal
    D. hydroelectric power

3. Based on the information in the passage, which of the following renewable energy sources could Bashville potentially adopt? Choose all that apply. (For this drill, write the option letters in the box below.)

Bashville's Renewable Energy Choices

```
┌─────────────────────────────────────┐
│                                      │
│                                      │
│                                      │
└─────────────────────────────────────┘
```

(a) Solar

(b) Wind

(c) Biomass

(d) Hydroelectric

(e) Geothermal

FOSSILS

Much of what we know about both animal and plant life in ancient times comes from studying fossils—the preserved direct or indirect remains of ancient life. Millions of years ago, a tiny insect might have gotten caught in the mud of a riverbank. Eventually, if conditions were right, that riverbank became sedimentary rock, and although the organic matter of the insect decayed long ago, the rock preserved a perfect impression of that insect, waiting to be found and studied by man. Sometimes scientists can date the fossil by dating the material that surrounds it. For example, if it is known approximately when a volcanic eruption took place, any fossils found in the volcanic rock formed by the eruption can be assumed to come from the same period. Another method of discovering a fossil's age is to take a small sample of the organic material of the fossil (if any exists) and use a technique called **carbon-14 dating.** Carbon-14 is a mildly radioactive isotope of carbon that occurs naturally in all living things. It decays slowly over time. By measuring how much the isotope has decayed, scientists can date the fossil with a high degree of accuracy.

Let's try an example of a GED® test question on fossils.

Scientists study fossils to learn the conditions of Earth during certain periods of time. These fossils are found buried in rock layers. According to geological studies, rock layers develop chronologically, so older rocks are found deeper underground than newer rocks. Below is a cross section of rock layers currently being studied by geologists.

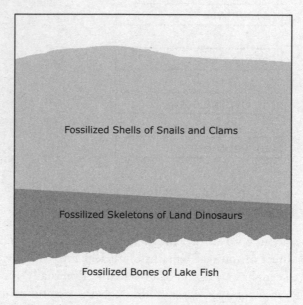

1. Based on the information above, scientists studying this region could infer which of the following?

A. The region has always been covered by water.

B. The region was first under an ocean, was later above sea level, and then was under a fresh water source.

C. This region was first under an ocean, was later above sea level, and then was under an ocean again.

D. This region was first under a fresh water source, was later above water level, and then was under an ocean.

Here's How to Crack It

According to the information in the passage, older rocks are buried deeper underground than are newer rocks. Therefore, the fossilized bones of lake fish must have appeared earlier than did the fossilized skeletons of land dinosaurs. Lakes are sources of fresh water, so the region must first have been under a fresh water source. Eliminate (B) and (C), since these choices indicate that the region was under an ocean first. Since the next layer of rocks contains fossils of land dinosaurs, the region must have later been above water. Thus, you can eliminate (A). Choice (D) matches the information in the figure, showing that the region was first under a fresh water source, which matches with the fact that the fossilized bones of lake fish were the first fossils to appear; then was above water, which matches with the idea that fossilized bones of land dinosaurs appeared next; and then was under an ocean, which matches up with the idea that fossilized shells of crabs and clams appeared next.

Vocabulary

carbon-14 dating—a technique that allows scientists to determine the age of a fossil with a high degree of accuracy and that involves the use of carbon-14, a mildly radioactive isotope that decays over time in living things

Fossils Drill

You can check your answers in Part VIII: Answer Key to Drills.

Questions 1 through 3 refer to the following passage.

When an organism is buried shortly after its death, it fills with groundwater that contains many minerals. Over time, these minerals precipitate forming detailed fossils that can reveal fascinating structural information about the organism. Oftentimes, the original remains of the organism dissolve over time so all that remains is the fossil.

Over many years, several layers of material can sediment over top of the fossilized organism burying it even further. Each of these layers is representative of a particular time period. Through carbon dating, scientists can determine when a particular layer of sedimentary rock was formed. If a particular organism was fossilized in that layer, the scientists can deduce that that organism most likely lived during that time period.

The half-life of carbon-14 (the radioactive isotope of carbon) is approximately 5,000 years. The following diagram depicts several rock layers.

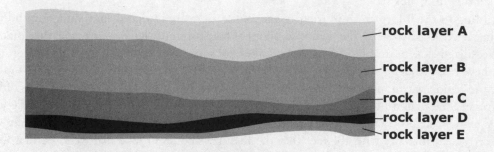

rock layer A
rock layer B
rock layer C
rock layer D
rock layer E

1. The organic material found in rock layer C is probably older than the material found in

    | Select... ▼ | and younger than the
    | layer A |
    | layer E |

    material found in | Select... ▼ |.
    | layer B |
    | layer D |

2. The passage states that the half-life of carbon-14 is about 5,000 years. This means that if you start with a sample of carbon-14 and wait for 5,000 years,

    A. you will have double the amount you started with.
    B. you will have half the amount you started with.
    C. the carbon-14 will have converted into carbon-7.
    D. you will have the same amount of carbon.

3. If rock layer D contains fossilized bones from a woolly mammoth, which lived about 200,000 years ago, which of the following statements must also be true?

    A. The rock formed over an area that was once a large ocean.
    B. Rock layer D formed 250,000 years ago.
    C. Rock layer A formed 10,000 years ago.
    D. Rock layer D contained minerals that were capable of fossilization

ASTRONOMY

Astronomy is the study of the universe beyond the earth. Astronomers study the moon, planets, solar system, galaxy, and everything farther away. It is one of the oldest branches of science, dating back to ancient times. In fact, some scientists theorize that the pyramids in Egypt were actually used for astronomical purposes. Thankfully, you won't be asked to know everything about the deepest reaches of space, but here are the basics of the universe.

Earth and the Solar System

We currently live on **Earth**, the third-closest planet to the **sun**. Earth is a part of the solar system, which in turn is part of the **Milky Way Galaxy**. All solar systems are made up of a sun and the objects revolving around it. For a long time, scientists believed that the earth was the center of the solar system. **Nicolaus Copernicus**, a Polish astronomer, was the first to introduce the idea of a heliocentric, or sun-centered, model of the solar system in the sixteenth century. It has since been proven that our solar system is indeed heliocentric. The following is a model of our solar system (not to scale):

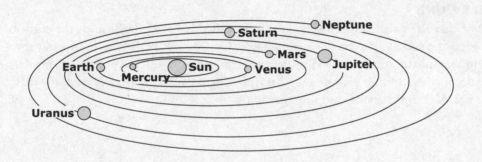

Astronomy Quiz

Q: Earth orbits the sun. What large body orbits Earth?

Turn the page for the answer.

Inner Planets

The four planets closest to the sun—Mercury, Venus, Earth, and Mars—are called the inner planets. They consist mainly of rock with metal cores. They notably do not have rings. Earth and Mars are the only inner planets that have moons; Earth has only one moon and Mars has two (called Phobos and Deimos).

Outer Planets

The four planets farthest from the sun—Jupiter, Saturn, Uranus, and Neptune—are called the outer planets. They are also sometimes called the Jovian planets because their structure is similar to that of Jupiter. These planets are the largest in the solar system (with Jupiter being the largest of them all) and are gas giants (meaning that they are not primarily made up of rock or solid matter). They all have numerous moons, ranging at the most recent count from 14 to 69. Also, all of these planets have rings, with Saturn's rings being the most notable and plentiful.

Pluto Demoted

Pluto, the outermost major body in the solar system, has been controversial since its discovery in 1930. Although it was once considered the smallest of the planets, in 2006 the International Astronomical Union (IAU) formally downgraded Pluto to a dwarf planet. It has five moons, with the largest, Charon, being roughly half its size, and its elliptical orbit sometimes brings it closer to the sun than Neptune.

Asteroids, Comets, and Meteoroids

The solar system also contains millions of smaller objects. **Asteroids** are large pieces of rock that orbit the sun, just as the planets do. Most asteroids are located between Mars and Jupiter in an area that is called the asteroid belt. **Meteoroids** are small pieces of rock and metal. Sometimes meteoroids enter the earth's atmosphere. When that happens, they are called meteors. Usually the meteor will burn up when passing through the atmosphere. However, on rare occasions, they hit the earth and are then called meteorites. **Comets** are made up of rock, dust, methane, and ice. Like asteroids, they also orbit the sun. The Kuiper Belt is a disk-shaped region past the orbit of Neptune that is thought to be the source of the short-period comets.

The Earth's Orbit

Did you know that the earth is moving, even as you read this book? Right now, the earth is traveling around the sun at an average speed of about 106,000 km per hour. The earth's revolution, or trip around the sun, takes 365 days (approximately one year). As the earth revolves around the sun, it is also spinning on its axis. This spinning is called rotation. It takes the earth 24 hours (or one day) to make one complete rotation.

The Sun

Ah the sun, the center of the solar system. There are two major facts you should know about the sun: The sun is very hot and very large. The outer layer (known as the corona) averages 2,000,000 degrees Celsius and the core (or center) is 15,000,000 degrees Celsius! The sun is about 109 times more massive than the earth, and it accounts for 99 percent of the total mass of the solar system.

Eclipses

An **eclipse** occurs when a planet or moon passes through the shadow of another. There are two types of eclipses that occur on Earth: solar eclipses and lunar eclipses. During a solar eclipse, the moon moves between the sun and the earth. The moon blocks the light of the sun and casts a shadow over a certain part of the earth. During a lunar eclipse, the earth moves between the sun and the moon. When this happens, the earth blocks the sunlight and casts a shadow on the moon.

Solar Eclipse

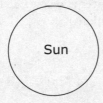

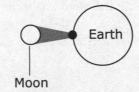
Earth

Moon

Astronomy Quiz
A: The moon orbits
Earth.

Lunar Eclipse

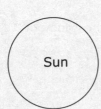

Earth's Shadow

Earth

Moon

Check out the astronomy question below.

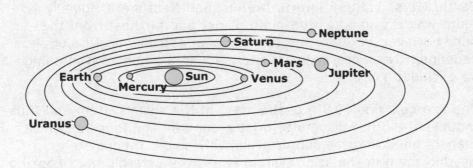

Neptune
Saturn
Mars
Earth   Sun   Jupiter
Mercury   Venus
Uranus

1. A year is the length of time it takes for a planet to complete one entire orbit around the sun. If each of the planets revolved around the sun at exactly the same speed, which of the planets would have the shortest year?

    A. Uranus
    B. Earth
    C. Mars
    D. Neptune

Here's How to Crack It

If all of the planets revolved around the sun at the same speed, then the planet with the smallest orbit would have the shortest year. Since, of the planets listed in the answer choices, Earth has the smallest orbit, Earth would have the shortest year under those conditions.

Vocabulary

solar system—a group of planets that orbit a star

galaxy—a group of stars; our galaxy is called the Milky Way

asteroid—a very small planet

meteoroids—small pieces of rock and metal

eclipse—event that occurs when a planet or moon passes through the shadow of another

Milky Way Galaxy—the galaxy containing Earth's solar system

Astronomy Drill

You can check your answers in Part VIII: Answer Key to Drills.

Questions 1 through 3 refer to the following passage.

Our solar system includes our sun, as well as the planets and other objects that orbit it. It was formed approximately 4.5 billion years ago and contains eight planets: Mercury, Venus, Earth, Mars, Jupiter, Saturn, Uranus, and Neptune. Originally, Pluto was classified as the ninth planet and farthest from the sun; however, in 2006, the International Astronomical Union redefined the necessary characteristics of a planet and in doing so excluded Pluto.

The sun contains 99.9% of the mass of the solar system and thus induces the other planets to orbit around it. The four innermost planets encircling the sun are relatively small. Immediately beyond them in the solar system is a rocky asteroid belt. Looking further out in the solar system one can find the largest planets, known as the gas giants. Many of the planets have secondary systems that include moons or planetary ring systems.

The following graph indicates the temperatures found on each planet based on its location relative to the sun. The maximum temperature in Kelvin is reported.

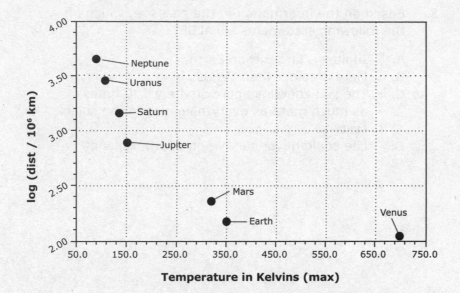

1. Click on the planet above that has the lowest surface temperature. (For this drill, mark the planet with an X.)

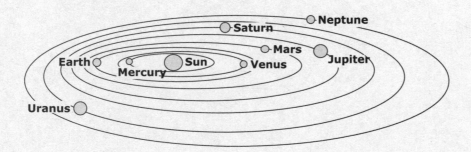

2. A year is the length of time it takes for a planet to complete one entire orbit around the sun. If each of the planets revolved around the sun at exactly the same speed, which of the planets would have the longest year?

    A. Mercury
    B. Venus
    C. Earth
    D. Mars

3. Based on the information in the passage, which of the following statements is FALSE?

   A. Jupiter is larger than Earth.
   B. Mars is colder than Venus.
   C. The sun contains approximately 100 times as much mass as everything else in the solar system.
   D. Life could never survive on another planet.

Part VII Summary

o   The Science test consists of approximately 34 questions based on short passages, graphs, and charts. You can find the answers to many of these questions within the informational sources provided by the test. There are six question formats: multiple choice, fill in the blank, drop down, hot spot, drag and drop, and short answer. The questions will test the following skills: comprehension, application, analysis, and evaluation.

o   The test covers **life sciences** (which include the scientific method, cell theory and the origins of life, genetics, evolution and natural selection, plants, ecosystems and food chains, the human body and human health, and viruses and bacteria), **physical sciences** (which include energy and heat; physical laws; waves and radiation; solids, liquids, and gases; and chemical reactions), and **Earth and space science** (which includes the changing earth; glaciers, erosion, the ice ages, natural resources and sustainability; fossils; and astronomy).

o   You should have a general understanding of the topics mentioned above. We recommend that you spend some time familiarizing yourself with these topics by reading Chapters 21 and 22, and answering the drill questions.

o   It can also be helpful to spend a little time reading articles from some of the science magazines that the GED® test writers say they use when they write questions: *Discover*, *Science News*, *National Geographic*, and *Popular Science*. Over time, these articles will help you get used to the kind of scientific writing that you will find on the test.

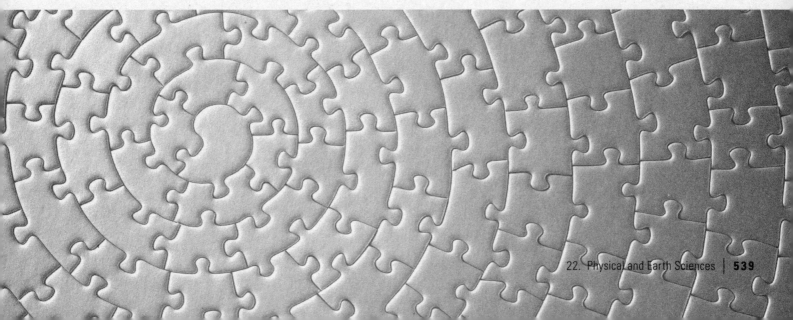

Part VIII
Answer Key to Drills

REASONING THROUGH LANGUAGE ARTS

Reading

Informational Passage Drill (Page 66)

1. **C** This is a structure question. Why are the senior executives and directors who crafted and approved this statement publicly dragging employees into the commitments they've made? Using Process of Elimination, (A) is gone quickly—the authors do take responsibility at the end, when they refer readers to the most senior leader, the Chairman and Chief Executive Officer. Eliminate (A) because the overall tone of the document is confidence and reassurance, not *worry*. Also eliminate (B), because the purpose of the passage is to show that *all* employees are a part of corporate responsibility, not just the ones the stakeholders are *dealing with*. Only (C) gives a reason that should result in a benefit to the company and to the authors: Now anyone who reads this document knows that meeting these responsibilities is part of everyone's job at Pine Trail Timber and will expect employees to behave accordingly.

2. **D** The context in which "obligations" is used will point the way to the best answer in this language use question. The word occurs in the sentence about suppliers—the companies that provide the products Pine Trail Timber uses in its own manufacturing—and is positioned as the second half of a two-part purchase transaction—specifying its requirements for the products it buys, and then meeting its obligations (i.e. to pay for those products). So while weak arguments could be made for (A), (B), and (C), choice (D) is the most accurate in this context.

3. **A** This question asks you to compare information about Pine Trail Timber given in two different formats—text and figures in a table. However, that information does not portray quite the same company image. The text statement presents a company committed to responsible resource management and concern for employees, including workers' safety. The table tells a rather different story. Even in Pine Trail Timber's largest operations (North America), only 20.8% of the workers have earned safety certification, and the largest percentage of remediation workers (still only 3.8%) is found in Central America, which is only the company's second largest area of activity.

   Now to find the *most significant* difference or similarity, use Process of Elimination. Choice (C) is eliminated because the text statement doesn't say anything about workers controlling their own safety, let alone being able to refuse dangerous work, as the table shows. Read the question carefully—you're comparing topics covered by *both* of the two sources. While (B) has some truth, it's hardly the most significant issue raised in a comparison. Choice (D) is also a weak similarity; having fewer than four percent of the workforce involved in remediation in even the area with the highest percentage isn't much of a commitment to restoring the land. Choice (A) is the correct answer, and you can see it more easily from the percentages than from the absolute numbers. Southeast Asia lags the other three areas on all measures of concern for workers' safety, for instance, while Africa has been more successful than the other areas in giving workers a voice in safety (through workers' committees and representatives, and through exercising the right to refuse dangerous work).

4. **B** The question is about the authors' motives for publishing the document, and there is no indication that they are required to do so, nor is there indication about what their competitors have done, so eliminate (A) and (C). Your answer choice should be based *only* on what's in the passage. Choice (D) is eliminated

because the CSR statement outlines the company's commitments in carrying out its mission, not the mission itself. That leaves only (B) as the correct answer: Overall, the document is intended to convey a positive public image of the company.

5.   This is an evaluation question that would be presented in an actual test in the drag-and-drop format. You're asked to decide how well the company supports its claims, or whether it supports them at all. The first and third claims—(a) and (c)—are supported by FSC certification and by the invitation to contact the company's Chairman and CEO. The references to a rising stock price and five years of dividend increases support the last claim (f). Since all six claims fit somewhere in the chart, the remaining three must go into the "not supported" column. Indeed, the second and fifth claims—(b) and (e)—are made without any support, and the fourth claim (d) isn't even directly made, let alone supported.

6. **A**   In this tricky main idea, or theme question, you need to find themes not only in the two paragraphs identified, but also in the CSR statement as a whole. Using your critical thinking skills, you'll recognize that the correct answer will identify something inconsistent in those themes. The only choice that does that is (A). If Pine Trail Timber is such a trustworthy custodian, why are there investigations and sufficiently large-scale events to create an impact beyond the company's operations? The need for remediation, mentioned in paragraph 15 of the "Respect for the Environment" section, reinforces the apparent disconnect between the image the company portrays and the actual results of its operations. Each of the other three choices may contain a grain of truth, but does not lead to the significant conclusion with relation to the overall theme of responsible corporate citizenship that (A) does.

7. **D**   This is a development question of the building block type. What is the most significant addition to the company's image as a responsible resource manager that is made by the concept of employees planting trees and teaching others how to care for them? Choice (C) can be eliminated quickly; it's doubtful a company in the business of felling trees would be attractive to environmentally conscious recruits. Choices (A) and (B) are true as far as they go, but this is a forestry company, so there's a more direct link than that. Choice (D) provides that direct link to the company's business by pointing out that employees help renew some of the resources the company uses.

Literary Passage Drill (Page 89)

1. **C**   To reach the correct answer for this structure question, you need to understand how the passage as a whole is built and then translate that understanding into a graphic shape. Think about the narrators: The passage begins with a first-person ("I") narrator who is talking to the Leopard Man; then the Leopard Man takes over the narration as he tells the story of Wallace and De Ville. It's (C)—a frame (the Leopard Man's story) within a frame (the first-person narrator's story about talking to the Leopard Man). None of the other shapes describes the structural characteristics of the passage. It doesn't begin with a large-scale picture and filter down to particular events or characters (A). It doesn't lead the reader through a confusing trail of dream sequences or shifts in time periods (B), and it doesn't keep circling back around the same circumstance (D).

2. **D**   Here we're looking at the author's purpose in giving such a detailed account of the Leopard Man's boredom. The Leopard Man doesn't think taming big cats is exciting or dangerous, he shrugs off his injuries and, for an hour, he can't even think of a thrilling circus story to tell the narrator. His attitude doesn't seem suited to his profession and neither does his small, weak physical build. The author considered that important enough to devote a lot of effort to conveying it. Why?

Let's start with Process of Elimination. Eliminate (A) because it's not the author's purpose to inform us about any profession; the passage focuses only on this one individual. Eliminate (B) because it's not the author's purpose to blame the Leopard Man's attitude on the result of aging, but rather to contrast that attitude with his profession. Choice (C) has some truth to it: Big, fearless Wallace the lion tamer is gone and the feeble, bored Leopard Man is still here. That's not the most important goal achieved by the detailed description of the Leopard Man, though.

The answer is (D). The narrator says, "He was the Leopard Man, but he did not look it" (paragraph 1). In the Leopard Man's story, De Ville hadn't taken his revenge for months, but that didn't mean he wasn't planning to. Things aren't always what they seem—that's one of the main points in the Leopard Man's story and in the narrator's description of the Leopard Man.

3. **C** Look at the context around the quote to find the answer to this language use question. The quote occurs right after the narrator mentions the Leopard Man's right arm, which "looked as though it had gone through a threshing machine" (paragraph 4). The quote doesn't apply to the whole man, as advancing age and boredom with a career would, so (B) and (D) are eliminated. That leaves (A) and (C), and you need to compare them carefully. The reference to "claws and fangs" suggests some type of damage, which both of those choices also suggest. Choice (A) specifies performing with leopards. In the passage, however, the Leopard Man also talks about fighting lions and a tigress. Choice (C), which refers to big cats, is therefore the correct answer.

4. **A** A couple of brief statements in the passage eliminate two choices in this comparison question. The Leopard Man admits, "I was beginning to think it all a scare over nothing" (paragraph 12) when nothing had happened for several months, so he ended up underestimating De Ville, too, eliminating (C). Wallace laughed off the Leopard Man's final warning, but "he did not look so much in Madame de Ville's direction after that" (paragraph 11), so he didn't completely ignore all warnings, eliminating (B). If you're not reading actively in a long passage such as this, it's easy to miss these little clues.

Now we're down to (A) and (D). Wallace "was afraid of nothing alive or dead" (paragraph 9), but there's no indication that he relied on physical strength for his courage, and the Leopard Man mentions only De Ville's quick temper, not his cleverness, so (D) is out. That leaves (A). The Leopard Man let his guard down after several months passed without any sign of revenge from De Ville, and Wallace let his guard down in the dressing tent; he was "too busy to notice" (paragraph 13) De Ville's look of hatred or De Ville passing close behind him.

5.   This plot development question is trickier than most because some of the events didn't happen in the passage. There are eight events and only five spots in the chart, so first try to eliminate the three that didn't occur. Those are the third one (c) (the Leopard Man, not Wallace, notices the hatred), the fifth event (f) (Wallace never tries to talk to De Ville), and the last one (h) (De Ville never reveals his intention to anyone).

Now you're ready to select the order of the five events that do take place in the passage. De Ville's wife looking at Wallace is what starts the whole chain of events, so that's the first one (d). Warnings from several people in the circus follow (g), and then Wallace stops looking at De Ville's wife after the Leopard Man gives his final warning (a)—those are the second and third events, respectively. The fourth event occurs when the Leopard Man watches De Ville walk behind Wallace, to plant the snuff (b). Augustus sneezing is what finishes Wallace off (e), so that's the last one.

6. **B**　In this evaluation question, you need to consider whether anything in the plot doesn't "add up."

There is some question of support in (A). There is no apparent relationship that would prompt the Leopard Man to care enough about Wallace's fate to warn him. On the other hand, there's no reason he wouldn't, either, especially when other people in the circus were giving warnings, too. So let's eliminate (A)—we're looking for the *weakest* support. Choice (C) is supported: Wallace isn't afraid of anything. Choice (D) is supported, too. Augustus didn't intend to bite Wallace's head off; he simply sneezed.

So we're left with (B). De Ville's months of hatred followed by his grisly revenge aren't explained in the passage. We're simply told that De Ville is quick to anger, not that he holds a grudge for months despite a correction in the behavior that caused it.

7. **A**　This is a version of the main idea or theme question as it applies to a literary passage. After reading all of the details, from your 10,000-foot perch, what moral is the author conveying in this passage?

Process of Elimination leads smoothly to the correct answer. There's no indication of a struggle with nature in the passage. The only "nature" is indicated by the big cats, who are represented as easy to manage (paragraph 3) or completely trusted (paragraph 8). That eliminates (B). Choice (C) is close: Wallace laughed off warnings about De Ville. However, he didn't see De Ville as an opponent, either, which eliminates this answer. Choice (D) is too general. In being attracted to another man's wife, Wallace may have been thinking the grass would be greener on the other side of the fence—a fatal error, in this case. However, that wouldn't necessarily apply in every situation, eliminating (D).

So we're left with (A). Wallace has the advantage in size and fearlessness (brawn), but De Ville has the advantage in brains, and that's what defeats Wallace. De Ville waits months before taking his revenge, lulling even the Leopard Man into a sense of false security; then he figures out how to get the trusted Augustus to do the job for him.

Language

Language Drill (Page 115)

The fourth choice is correct for the first drop-down question:

The harsh winter kept people at home more <u>this year, too, which meant fewer customers, even on weekends.</u>

The first answer presents a problem with word choice. "Less" is used for things that can't be counted or for units of measurement (e.g. He has less than 15 minutes to finish); "fewer" for people or things. This answer is also missing the signal word "too." While that's not necessarily a mistake, the signal word does improve clarity by helping the reader understand that the writer is building up points to support his explanation for the loss of business.

The second choice is too wordy. (A harsh winter most likely would have an effect since the beginning of the winter.) The third choice is wrong because there is no reason to capitalize "customers."

The second choice is correct for the second drop-down question.

I participated in a local trade fair, the recent "Home Grown Goodness" food exhibition, and sponsored a booth for a local charity at the fall fair.

The first choice (starting the sentence with "Participating" instead of "I participated," and then beginning a new sentence with "I sponsored") results in a sentence fragment. The third choice fails to set off the apposition with commas. (The trade fair and the "Home Grown Goodness" food exhibition refer to the same thing and perform the same function in the sentence.) This is the only choice that does not have those commas, which suggests that it's incorrect. The fourth choice has a couple of problems: The structure isn't parallel with the first part of the sentence, and the antecedent of "we" isn't clear.

The first choice is correct for the third drop-down question:

I would, of course, welcome any suggestions you can offer.

The second choice creates a sentence fragment. (A dependent clause starting with "although" cannot stand alone.) The third choice has a dangling modifier. (The modifier, "Welcoming any suggestions…," does not describe the subject of the sentence, "you." It describes the writer.) The third choice is also wordy. ("Suggestions" and "ideas" refer to the same thing.) The fourth choice is an ugly run-on sentence and is not consistent with the formal tone of the rest of the email.

In the final drop-down question, the third choice is correct:

However, I hope that my excellent credit record and my long business relationship with your bank would make me eligible for special consideration.

The first choice contains two pronoun errors: agreement ("their" is plural and bank is singular) and an unclear antecedent (it's not even clear whether the pronoun is supposed to refer to the bank). Switching from "I" to the third-person pronoun, "their," also creates a lack of parallel structure. The second choice is wordy (of course he was doing business with the bank during a long business relationship). It's also the only choice in which the transition word "however" is missing. That transition word improves clarity by marking a change in direction. The final choice lacks parallel structure again: It changes from a noun (the writer's credit record) to a verb ("I have").

Extended Response Drills

These two drills present different challenges that you might encounter in the Extended Response section. Below you'll find suggested approaches to these challenges, and chains of reasoning you might follow in creating your responses to the prompts.

Electric Vehicles Extended Response Drill (Page 148)

Building the Argument Use active reading to note each side's arguments and support in the charts. That evidence is quite clearly laid out in these passages although, as you'll read below, it's challenging because the authors' purposes are so different. Your chart might look like the one below.

Pro side (government document):

Argument	Support
increased energy security (Paragraph 3)	import 40% of petroleum (Paragraph 2) price spikes, supply disruptions (Paragraph 2)
better fuel economy (Paragraphs 4 and 5)	electricity cheaper than gas (Paragraph 5)
flexible fueling (Paragraph 6)	different charging locations, gas for PHEVs (Paragraph 6)
lower costs (Paragraph 8)	fuel cheaper, future price reductions, government incentives (Paragraph 8)
lower emissions (Paragraph 9)	none for EVs, lower for HEVs and PHEVs (Paragraph 9)

Con side (father's letter)

Argument	Support
limited range (Paragraph 14)	80 miles (Paragraph 14)
few charging stations (Paragraph 14)	5,000 in California (Paragraph 14)
long charging time (Paragraph 14)	8 hours (Paragraph 14)
high costs (Paragraph 15)	parts, batteries (5 years), initial price (2x) (Paragraph 15)
unsafe for highway (Paragraph 16)	70 mph maximum (Paragraph 16)
catch fire (Paragraph 17)	unspecified news reports (Paragraph 17)

Choosing Your Thesis Both sides give several arguments (although Dad has one more than the U.S. government). With one exception (the unspecified news reports of fires), the father also backs up his arguments with specific figures. The government document does in most cases, too, though. The U.S. government has more credibility as an author (one would hope the Department of Energy has professional experts who supplied the data), but the Office of Energy Efficiency and Renewable Energy also has a vested interest in promoting electric vehicles. Dad, on the other hand, has a parent's genuine passion for protecting his child.

One factor that might give the edge to the Department of Energy is the scope of its concern (the well-being of the nation) as opposed to the father's concern for one person. Other factors that weaken the father's case are his reasoning and his assumptions. His visions of Melissa hanging around an isolated charging station all night and sleeping unaware while her car burns outside seem alarmist; he doesn't provide any evidence to justify those leaps from electric vehicles to an endangered daughter. You could add to that the self-interest evident in his remark that, with the concern about safety on the highway, Melissa wouldn't be able to drive home to visit her parents.

If you think you could make a better case for the father's side being better supported, that would not be a wrong choice for a thesis. The Extended Response passages are designed to allow you to argue either side successfully. However, giving the edge to the government does seem an easier thesis to prove.

Organizing Your Argument Organizing specific pieces of evidence is a challenge in this example, since the authors' purposes (and therefore their arguments) don't overlap. Dad isn't the least bit concerned with the government's purpose (fostering energy security), and the government doesn't address the father's goal (safety).

The only minor overlap occurs in the discussion of cost; however, both sides approach that issue from different directions. For the government, the high initial cost of a vehicle is an acknowledged problem. (Any argument that acknowledges an opponent's position gains some credibility.) This cost disadvantage can be offset by lower fuel costs and government subsidies, it argues. The father doesn't mention those offsetting factors, and you have to wonder if he's concerned about having to subsidize repairs or a replacement battery down the road.

Given the general lack of overlap and the fact that cost isn't the main argument for either side, the best approach would be to discuss the evidence that proves your thesis first (the government's arguments) and then point out the alarmist reasoning and unsupported assumptions that weaken the father's case.

Writing the Essay You might take advantage of the two different purposes as an attention-getting opening question for your essay: "Energy security or driver safety: Which goal should decide the choice of a new car?" Your thesis statement and the high-level list of evidence come next: "In these two passages, the U.S. Department of Energy argues that electric vehicles would help protect the nation's energy supply, while a father raises rather alarmist concerns for his daughter's safety. The government's position is better supported in virtue of its credibility and the nationwide scope of its concerns about energy security and lower emissions."

That's the first paragraph. You'd likely end up with a four-paragraph essay here and that's fine, as long as your points are clearly organized in the middle two paragraphs. The second paragraph would discuss the evidence from the government's position, and the third paragraph would outline the evidence from the father's position, pointing out its weaknesses. As always, the final paragraph would restate the thesis in different words and remind readers about the evidence that proves the thesis.

Antibiotics in Farm Animal Feed Extended Response Drill (Page 152)

Building the Argument Here's a different version of the argument/support chart, with the arguments lined up beside each other. Arranging the chart in this way can help you decide which side you could do a better job of arguing.

For the ban (FDA media release)		Against the ban (online forum posting)	
Argument	Support	Argument	Support
contributes to anti-biotic resistance; raises the fatality rate for diseases that don't respond to antibiotics (Paragraph 3)	• all uses do (not just agriculture) (Paragraph 3) • world governments consider antibiotic-resistant diseases a major public health threat (Paragraph 3) • may not be prevent-able but need to slow it down (Paragraph 5) • using drugs that are also used in humans means they won't work in humans (Paragraph 4) • resistant bacteria entering food system can be transferred to people (Paragraph 7) • voluntary ban because it's faster (Paragraph 8) • working with the in-dustry (Paragraph 8) • authority of FDA name (Paragraph 8)	harmful effects not proven (Paragraph 11)	• studies inconclusive (Paragraph 11) • doctors overpre-scribing and unsafe food handling to blame (Paragraph 11) • hasn't reduced superbugs in Europe (Paragraph 12) • ban would be man-datory if FDA were sure (Paragraph 11)
		cost saving (Paragraph 10)	• cheaper to prevent disease (Paragraph 10)
		faster time to market at lower cost (Paragraph 10)	• faster weight gain using less feed (Paragraph 10)
		meet growing de-mand for food, lower costs for consumers, make exports com-petitive (Paragraphs 13 and 14)	• farmer feeds 155 people (6x increase) due to more efficient production (Paragraph 13)

Choosing Your Thesis Breaking these two passages down into an argument/support chart is quite revealing. The FDA has only one main reason for its pro-ban position, and it undercuts even that with statements such as "antimicrobial resistance may not be completely preventable" (paragraph 5) and "even appropriate therapeutic uses of antibiotics can promote the development of drug-resistant bacteria" (paragraph 7). Its strongest points are the weight of the FDA name and the fact that it has been working with stakeholders across the industry (drug companies, producers, veterinarians, and consumer groups).

On the other hand, the anti-ban side lays out four main reasons for its position. It counters the FDA's argument by pointing to studies that don't prove the link between antibiotic use and superbugs, as well as blaming other culprits (doctors who overprescribe antibiotics and consumers who don't handle food safely). The main argument of the anti-ban side, however, is economic: Adding antibiotics to feed allows farmers to feed more people at a lower cost, keeps food prices low for consumers, and makes agricultural exports competitive. The FDA doesn't even mention, let alone refute, those reasons. It also neglects an argument that would strengthen its own position: It makes only an indirect reference to the high cost (in human lives) of antibiotic-resistant diseases, and makes no mention of high costs to the health care system.

Regardless of your own opinion on the issue, it might be easier, looking at an argument/support analysis of the passage, to claim that the anti-ban side is better supported. Let's call that your "for" side. The writer refutes the FDA's reason for the ban and presents three economic reasons in favor of using antibiotics for growth and feed efficiency, including a specific number for the increase in farmers' productivity (155 people fed). The case would be even better supported if the author had cited specific studies and dollar figures.

Organizing Your Argument It would be ideal if each side's points lined up neatly, so you could discuss why your "for" side's Point A is better supported than your "against" side's Point A. Unfortunately, that doesn't usually happen.

In this example, you would have to include your "against" side's argument in favor of its position, since it makes only one and the prompt tells you to draw evidence from *both* passages. Luckily, your "for" side presents its case about the same point—the increase (proven or unproven) in antibiotic-resistant diseases as a result of antibiotics in farm animal feed. So that would be the first piece of evidence you'd discuss.

Your "for" side makes three more arguments, all of them tied to economic factors. It presents the strongest support for the argument about meeting the growing demand for food through more efficient production, since it gives a specific figure (the increase in the number of people fed per farmer) to support that argument. You'd discuss that point next, then.

The last two arguments can be combined neatly: Lower costs and faster time to market for the farmer mean lower food prices for consumers and more competitive exports. You might point out (if it occurred to you) that the FDA failed to present the economic argument it could have made: higher health care costs as a result of antibiotic-resistant illnesses. That would allow you to draw some more evidence for your thesis from the FDA passage.

Writing the Essay So now you have the thesis—the anti-ban case is better supported—and a plan for organizing your evidence.

It's time to start writing, using the template. The anti-ban author even provides a strong "startling fact" opening for your essay: "Each American farmer today feeds an average of 155 people, *six times* more than in 1960" (paragraph 13). Of course, you'd paraphrase this in your essay ("According to the online farmers' forum posting, each farmer feeds six times more people today than in 1960") or else put it in quotation marks with the paragraph reference.

Then you'd state your thesis (that the anti-ban position is the best supported) and briefly mention the evidence noted in your chart. You might say something like, "That increased productivity is the chief argument in favor of adding antibiotics to farm animal feed. It's the best supported argument, since it explains that the higher productivity leads to meeting ever-increasing demand for food and keeping costs low for both domestic and export customers. The side arguing for a ban on antibiotics doesn't support its one argument with credible evidence that the practice leads to the rise of antibiotic-resistant illnesses. In fact, it even undercuts its own argument by suggesting alternate causes for these illnesses."

The next three paragraphs—each one beginning with a topic sentence—will discuss the arguments you just mentioned (the antibiotic-resistant illnesses in paragraph 11, the higher productivity in paragraph 10, and the cost advantages in paragraph 12). In each paragraph, remember to explain *how* that evidence supports your thesis. The final paragraph restates your thesis in different words and wraps up your argument by summarizing the points you just made in the middle of the essay.

Reviewing Your Work Now, while you're practicing, you have time to ask yourself the questions listed in Chapter 10 (see page 127) to assess your own work. During the test, of course, you won't. Then you'll be reviewing your essay to revise it (Is something not clear? Is there a better way to say it?) and edit it (correcting grammar or spelling errors).

MATHEMATICAL REASONING

Number Line Drill (Page 176)

1. **less than**   Just use the values you were given to find the values of points A and B. A is −4 and B is −1, so A is less.

2. **C**   To find the distance, count the number of steps between A and B. The answer is 3.

3. **C**   Estimate. Roughly where will the midpoint of A and D fall? Point E will be between points 0 and 1.

Rounding Off Drill (Page 178)

1. **3,000**   3,400 is less than 3,500.

2. **3.5**   3.46 is greater than 3.45.

3. **600**   565 is greater than 550.

4. **$433**   432.70 is greater than 432.50.

5. **4.80**   This number already has a zero in the hundredths place.

Adding, Subtracting, Multiplying, and Dividing Positive and Negative Numbers Drill (Page 182)

1. **2**   Adding a negative is like subtracting.

2. **–11**

3. **18**

4. **–12**   Multiplying a negative by a positive always yields a negative.

5. **1**

6. **5**

7. **10**   Multiplying a negative by a negative always yields a positive.

8. **3**   Dividing a negative by a negative always yields a positive.

9. **–4**   Dividing a positive by a negative or a negative by a positive always yields a negative.

10. **–4**

Absolute Values Drill (Page 183)

1. **4**   The number 4 is four units from the number 0 on the number line, so $|4| = 4$.

2. **7**   The number –7 is seven units from the number 0 on the number line, so $|-7| = 7$.

3. **4**   The number 6 is four units to the right of 2 on the number line, so $|6 - 2| = 4$. Alternatively, $6 - 2 = 4$, so $|6 - 2| = |4|$. Since 4 is four units from 0 on the number line, $|4| = 4$. Either way, $|6 - 2| = 4$.

4. **2**   The number 3 is two units to the left of 5 on the number line, so $|3 - 5| = 2$. Alternatively, $3 - 5 = -2$, so $|3 - 5| = |-2|$. Since –2 is two units from 0 on the number line, $|-2| = 2$. Either way, $|3 - 5| = 2$.

5. **10 or –10** $|x| = 10$, so x is 10 units from 0 on the number line. It cannot be determined whether x is 10 units to the left or 10 units to the right of 0, so consider both possibilities. If x is 10 units to the left of 0, then subtract 10 from 0 to get $x = 0 - 10 = -10$. If x is 10 units to the right of 0, then add 10 to 0 to get $x = 0 + 10 = 10$. Therefore $x = 10$ or –10.

6. **4 or 14** $|y - 9| = 5$, so y is five units from 9 on the number line. It cannot be determined whether y is five units to the left or five units to the right of 9, so consider both possibilities. If y is five units to the left of 9, then subtract 5 from 9 to get $y = 9 - 5 = 4$. If y is five units to the right of 9, then add 5 to 9 to get $y = 9 + 5 = 14$. Therefore $y = 4$ or 14.

Order of Operations and Associative and Distributive Properties Drill (Page 187)

Use **PEMDAS** for these.

1. **–3**

2. **42**

3. **–12**

4. **–64**

5. **3**

Factors and Multiples Drill (Page 189)

1. **1, 2, 3, 4, 6, 9, 12, 18, 36**
   Start from the outside and work to the inside. Every number has 1 and itself as factors so 1 and 36 are factors. Now try 2. 36 ÷ 2 = 18, so 2 and 18 are factors. Now try 3. 36 ÷ 3 = 12, so 3 and 12 are factors. Now try 4. 36 ÷ 4 = 9, so 4 and 9 are factors. Now try 5. 36 ÷ 5 is a decimal, so 5 is not a factor. Try 6. 36 ÷ 6 = 6, so 6 is a factor. Since 6 has been repeated, stop here. The factors are 1, 2, 3, 4, 6, 9, 12, 18, and 36.

2. **1, 43**
   Start on the outside and work to the inside. Every number has 1 and itself as factors so 1 and 43 are factors. Now try 2. 43 ÷ 2 is a decimal, so 2 is not a factor. 43 ÷ 3 is also a decimal, so 3 is not a factor. 43 ÷ 4 is also a decimal, so 4 is not a factor. 43 ÷ 5 is also a decimal, so 5 is not a factor. 43 ÷ 6 is also a decimal, so 6 is not a factor. Continue through 42 to find that there are no other factors. Therefore, the only factors are 1 and 43.

3. **1, 2, 4, 5, 8, 10, 16, 20, 40, 80**
   Start on the outside and work to the inside: 1 and 80, 2 and 40, 4 and 20, 5 and 16, 8 and 10. Since 3, 6, 7, and 9 do not divide 80 even, these are not factors. Since the next number after 9 is 10, which is already on the list of factors, there are no other factors. The only factors are 1, 2, 4, 5, 8, 10, 16, 20, 40, and 80.

5. **7, 14, 21, 28, 35, 42, 49, 56, 63, 70**
   One way to find the first ten positive multiples of a number is to multiply the number by all the whole numbers from 1 through 10. 7 × 1 = 7. 7 × 2 = 14. 7 × 3 = 21. 7 × 4 = 28. 7 × 5 = 35. 7 × 6 = 42. 7 × 7 = 49. 7 × 8 = 56. 7 × 9 = 63. 7 × 10 = 70. Therefore, the first 10 positive multiplies of 10 are 7, 14, 21, 28, 35, 42, 49, 56, 63, and 70.

5. **9, 18, 27, 36, 45, 54, 63, 72, 81, 90**
   One way to find the first ten positive multiples of a number is to start with the number itself, then add the number 9 more times. In this case, start with 9, as 9 is a multiple of itself. Add 9 to get 18. Add 9 to get 27. Add 9 to get 36. Add 9 to get 45. Add 9 to get 54. Add 9 to get 63. Add 9 to get 72. Add 9 to get 81. Add 9 to get 90. Therefore, the first ten positive multiples of 9 are 9, 18, 27, 36, 45, 54, 63, 72, 81, and 90.

6. **16** Start by finding the factors of 32: 1 and 32, 2 and 16, and 4 and 8. Now, find the factors of 80: 1 and 80, 2 and 40, 4 and 20, 5 and 16, and 8 and 10. The common factors are 1, 2, 4, 8, and 16. The greatest of the common factors is 16. As a shortcut, first get the factors of 32, and then use the outside to inside method for finding factors of 80. The first common factor that is the greater number of a pair of factors must be the GCF. In this case, the first pair is 1 and 80. 80 is not a common factor. The second pair is 2 and 40. 40 is not a common factor. The third pair is 4 and 20. 20 is not a common factor. The fifth pair is 5 and 16. 16 is a common factor, so 16 is the GCF.

7. **63** List the multiples of 9 until one is also a multiple of 7. The first six positive multiples of 9 are 9, 18, 27, 36, 45, and 54. None of these are multiples of 7. The next multiple, however, is 63, which is a divisible of 7. Therefore, 63 is a common multiple of 7 and 9. Any other common multiple has to be greater, so 63 must be the least common multiple.

8. **24** Find the factors of 24: 1 and 24, 2 and 12, 3 and 8, and 4 and 6. Now begin to use the outside to inside method to find the common factors of 48. The first pair is 1 and 48. Since 48 is not a factor of 24, it is not the GCF. The next pair is 2 and 24. Since 24 is also a factor of 24, it is a common factor. The only greater factor of 48 is 48, which is not a common factor. Therefore, the greatest common factor of 24 and 48 must be 24.

9. **48** List the multiples of 48 until one is also a multiple of 24. 48 is a multiple of itself. $48 \div 24$ is a whole number, so 48 is a multiple of 24. Therefore, 48 is a common multiple and must be the least common multiple of 24 and 48.

Reducing Fractions Drill (Page 192)

1. $\dfrac{3}{4}$ Divide top and bottom by 3.

2. $\dfrac{1}{3}$ Divide top and bottom by 11.

3. $\dfrac{2}{5}$ Divide top and bottom by 7.

4. $\dfrac{4}{9}$ This fraction can't be reduced. If you said $\dfrac{2}{3}$, you found the square root of top and bottom by mistake.

5. $\dfrac{15}{8}$ This fraction can't be reduced.

Adding and Subtracting Fractions Drill (Page 196)

1. $\dfrac{4}{5}$ Use the Bowtie method.

2. $\dfrac{48}{35}$ 35 is the common denominator.

3. $\dfrac{5}{12}$ 12 is the common denominator.

4. $\dfrac{5}{9}$ If you use the Bowtie for the first two numbers, you will already have the same denominator as in the third number.

5. $-\dfrac{1}{21}$ 21 is the common denominator. You can have a negative fraction!

Multiplying, Dividing, and Converting Fractions Drill (Page 198)

1. $\dfrac{3}{10}$ First reduce the 4 on top and the 8 on bottom.

2. $\dfrac{3}{2}$ Invert and multiply. But before you multiply, divide top and bottom by 3 and then by 5.

3. $\dfrac{10}{54}$ or $\dfrac{5}{27}$ Invert and multiply, but before you multiply, divide top and bottom by 2.

4. $\dfrac{2}{5}$ Cancel the 3s and the 4s, and you won't have to multiply at all!

5. $\dfrac{1}{2}$ First, convert $1\dfrac{1}{3}$ to an improper fraction: $\dfrac{4}{3}$. Then cancel the 3s.

Fraction Word Problem Drill (Page 201)

1. **C**   Half of the 80 people tested originally had Lyme disease—that's 40 people. Of the other 40 people, one quarter later developed Lyme disease. One quarter of 40 is 10. So a total of 50 got Lyme disease out of 80 people. $\dfrac{50}{80} = \dfrac{5}{8}$.

2.   **August: 110**
   September: 121

   One tenth of 100 is 10, so in August they baked 110 pies. In September they increased production by another tenth. One tenth of 110 is 11. So in September, they baked 110 + 11 pies, or 121.

3. $\dfrac{4}{15}$ To work with these fractions, you need to find a common denominator: $\dfrac{1}{3} = \dfrac{5}{15}$ and $\dfrac{2}{5} = \dfrac{6}{15}$.

   So if $\dfrac{5}{15}$ go by public transportation, and $\dfrac{6}{15}$ go by car, that adds up to $\dfrac{11}{15}$—which means that $\dfrac{4}{15}$ walk to work.

Decimals Drill (Page 205)

1. **7.06**

2. **4.36**

3. **8.194** Forget the decimals and just multiply. Then add up the numbers to the right of the decimals in the original numbers. That is how many places to move the decimal to the left in your new number.

4. **3,200** Set this up like a normal division problem. Then move the decimal place of the divisor as many times as it takes to turn the divisor into an integer. Now move the decimal in the dividend the same number of places, and divide as usual.

5. **40** Use the same methods you used in Question 4.

Percents Drill (Page 210)

1. **16.6** Move the decimal over one place to the left, and then multiply by 2.

2. **4.5** Move the decimal over one place to the left, and then multiply by 3.

3. **288** Move the decimal over one place to the left, and then multiply by 4.

4. **2.1** Move the decimal over two places to the left, and then multiply by 3.

5. **9** Move the decimal over one place to the left, and then divide in half.

6. 100 + 15 = **115**

7. 9.8 + 4.9 = **14.7**

8. 3(14) + 7 = **49**

9. $\frac{1}{2}$ of 62 = **31**

10. $\frac{1}{4}$ of 144 = **36**

Percent Word Problems Drill (Page 214)

1. **greater than** Option X is 8% of $650, or $52. Option Y is 3% of $1,500, or $45.

2. **C** Think about what's left over: 40 percent of 1,200. Choice (A) was 60 percent of 1,200, which was a partial answer.

3. **903.61** Add the individual prices to get $120 + $635 + $74 = $829. $829 plus 9 percent of $829, or $74.61 for a total of **$903.61.**

4. **D** The $8,437.50 for the year before is a red herring: It doesn't have anything to do with this problem. The best way to do this problem is by working backward. Start with (B). What is 60 percent of $6,750? It's only $4,050, which is less than the $5,400 you're looking for. Go ahead and eliminate (A) and (B). Choice (D) is the next easiest answer to check. What is 80 percent of $6,750? That's right, it's $5,400. The answer to this problem is (D).

Basic Arithmetic Drill (Page 216)

1. **0.6 and $\dfrac{9}{15}$** To get the decimal, just divide 5 into 3, or think "one-fifth = 0.2, so three-fifths = 0.6."

   To get the fraction, multiply the numerator and the denominator by 3 to get the fraction $\dfrac{9}{15}$.

2. **greater than** The total bill is $14.65 + $1.47 = $16.12, so 20 percent is $3.22. This is much larger than the tax, $1.47.

3. **C** $\dfrac{2}{30} = \dfrac{x}{72}$. Ballparking will get rid of (A) and (B).

4. **B** Add $\dfrac{1}{4}$ and $\dfrac{1}{5}$, but look out for (A): It is a partial answer. We want what is left over, so subtract this from 1.

5.

6. **C** 11 percent of $275 is $30.25. Add the two amounts to find the total, $305.25, and then divide by 12.

7. **C** Divide both sides of the equation by 5. You should get $R - S = 7$.

8. **–1** Use PEMDAS, and be careful. The answer is –1.

9. **C** $\dfrac{30}{70} = \dfrac{3}{7} = \dfrac{x}{100}$, which you can round up to 43 percent. Ballparking shows it will be just under 50 percent.

10. **D** We can eliminate (A) and (B) because they are less than the amount paid. This is a good problem to do backward. Let's start with (D), $12,000. What is 80 percent of $12,000? You guessed it: $9,600.

11. $-\dfrac{4}{3}, -0.8, -\dfrac{1}{4}, 0.5, \dfrac{11}{8}, 2$

The question asks you to place fractions, decimals, and a whole number on a number line. Since decimals are easier to order than fractions, convert the fractions into decimals Turn $-\dfrac{4}{3}$ into a decimal by dividing 4 by 3 to get $3\overline{)4.00}$ with quotient $1.\overline{33}$.

$$\begin{array}{r} 1.\overline{33} \\ 3\overline{)4.00} \\ \underline{3\,0} \\ 10 \\ \underline{9} \\ 10 \end{array}$$

Bringing in the negative sign, $-\dfrac{4}{3} = -1.\overline{33}$. Turn $-\dfrac{1}{4}$ into a decimal by dividing 1 by 4 to get $4\overline{)1.00}$ with quotient 0.25.

$$\begin{array}{r} 0.25 \\ 4\overline{)1.00} \\ \underline{8} \\ 20 \end{array}$$

Bringing in the negative sign, $-\dfrac{1}{4} = -0.25$. Turn $\dfrac{11}{8}$ into a decimal by dividing 11 by 8 to get $8\overline{)11.00}$ with quotient 1.375,

$$\begin{array}{r} 1.375 \\ 8\overline{)11.00} \\ \underline{8} \\ 30 \\ 24 \\ \underline{60} \\ 56 \\ 40 \end{array}$$

so $\dfrac{11}{8} = 1.375$. Therefore, in decimal terms, the six numbers are 2, 0.5, $-1.\overline{33}$, -0.8, -0.25, and 1.375. Put these in order from least to greatest to get $-1.\overline{33}$, -0.8, -0.25, 0.5, 1.375, and 2. Place these in the boxes from left to right. The correct answer is $-\dfrac{4}{3}$, -0.8, $-\dfrac{1}{4}$, 0.5, $\dfrac{11}{8}$, and 2.

12.

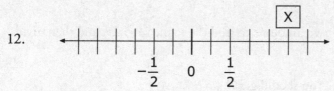

The question asks to place 1.25 on the number line. First determine the length of each interval. The tick mark for $\dfrac{1}{2}$ is 2 intervals to the right of 0. Therefore, each interval is $\dfrac{\frac{1}{2}}{2} = \dfrac{\frac{1}{2}}{\frac{2}{1}} = \dfrac{1}{2} \times \dfrac{1}{2} = \dfrac{1}{4}$. The number

1.25 is equal to $\dfrac{1.25}{1.00} = \dfrac{125}{100} = \dfrac{25}{20} = \dfrac{5}{4}$. Since 1.25 is $\dfrac{5}{4}$ and each interval is $\dfrac{1}{4}$, the number 1.25 must be

$\dfrac{\frac{5}{4}}{\frac{1}{4}} = \dfrac{5}{4} \times \dfrac{4}{1} = 5$ intervals to the right of 0.

12. **D** The question asks for the number of the factors of 14. Start on the outside and work inward. 1 and 14 are factors of 14. Since 14 ÷ 2 = 7, 2 and 7 are factors. Since 14 ÷ 3 is a decimal, 3 is not a factor. Since 14 ÷ 4 is a decimal, 4 is not a factor. Since 14 ÷ 5 is a decimal, 5 is not a factor. Since 14 ÷ 6 is a decimal, 6 is not a factor. Since 7 is already on the list, the list is complete. Therefore the factors are 1, 2, 7, and 14, and the sum of the factors is 1 + 2 + 7 + 14 = 24. The correct answer is (D).

13. **C** The question asks for which choice is NOT a multiple of 4. Divide each choice by 4. Any choice that can be divided evenly by 4 is a multiple. Choice (A) is 4. 4 ÷ 4 = 1, so 4 is a multiple of 4. Choice (B) is 12. 12 ÷ 4 = 3, so 12 is a multiple. Choice (C) is 34. 34 ÷ 4 = 8.5. Since this is a decimal, 34 is not a multiple. The correct answer is (C).

Setup Drill (Page 222)

1. **A**   8 times 6 times 4 times $5.50.

2. **B**   The new cost is the old cost ($12,000) plus 0.04 times the old cost.

Mean, Median, Mode, Range, and Weighted Mean Drill (Page 230)

1. **327.60**   An average is always equal to the sum of all the elements divided by the number of elements. So $23.40 = \dfrac{x}{14}$. x = $23.40 times 14, or $327.60.

Student Test Scores

2.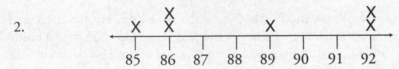

3. **C** Subtract the smallest amount, $35.77, from the largest amount, $73.23, to get $37.46.

4. **D** Add up the total number of cones and divide by the number of days: 595 divided by 5 = 119.

5. **B** Arrange the values in increasing order and then find the middle value.

6. **C** 50 percent is divided evenly between the midterm and final, each of which is weighted by 25 percent. The remaining 50 percent is divided evenly between the 5 tests, each of which is then weighted by 10 percent. Multiply the weight by each score and then add to get 88.2.

Ratios and Proportions Drill (Page 235)

1. **B** $\dfrac{5}{2} = \dfrac{x}{10}$

2. **B** $\dfrac{3}{2} = \dfrac{x}{2,500}$

3. **D** Not enough information is given. We have no method of comparison.

Rate Problems Drill (Page 238)

1. **4** If you set this up in the $R \times T = D$ format, it looks like this: $? \times 3 = 12$. The correct answer is **4** mph.

2. **C** Just divide 5,280 by 4.

3. **D** She drives 20 miles. If we deduct the hour she spent shopping, she drove the 20 miles in one hour.

Scale and Unit Conversion Drill (Page 241)

1. **D** First find 16 percent of 200 pounds, which is 32. Then multiply by 16 to find the number of ounces.

2. $5\frac{1}{2}$ **c. flour;** $2\frac{2}{3}$ **c. sugar;** $1\frac{1}{2}$ **c. butter; 2 eggs; 7 t. baking powder; 3 t. vanilla extract**

   If each of the 16 people eats 3 cookies, that is a total of 48 cookies. The original recipe makes 24, so double all the amounts to make 48.

Charts and Graphs Drill (Page 245)

1. **B** Let's say there were 100 telephones in all. If 45 of them were regular, then that number (45) is how many times greater than the number of cellular phones (15)? The answer is 3 times greater.

2. **C** To ballpark this problem, first compare bottles A and B (which have the same number of ounces), and bottles C and D (which also contain the same number of ounces). Bottle A is cheaper than B, and bottle C is cheaper than D, so eliminate B and D. To find the exact price per ounce of each bottle, divide the price by the number of ounces. Bottle A costs 5 cents per ounce. Bottle C costs 3.3 cents per ounce. Bottle E costs 5 cents per ounce. The answer is bottle C.

3. **B** Just ballpark, based on the chart.

Exponents and Square Roots Drill (Page 251)

1. **D** $2^3 = 8$. Just try out the answer choices until you find the one that equals 8.

2. **31** $27 + 4 = 31$

3. **D** $4 - 2 = 2$. Try out answers until you find the one that equals 2.

4. **A** Since the number has a fractional exponent, rewrite $\frac{5}{2}$ as $\frac{1}{2} \times 5$, and rewrite $(0.04)^{\frac{5}{2}}$ as

$$(0.04)^{\frac{1}{2} \times 5} = \left(0.04^{\frac{1}{2}}\right)^5 = \left(\sqrt{0.04}\right)^5.$$ Convert 0.04 into a fraction: $\frac{0.04}{1.00} = \frac{4}{100}$. Therefore,

$\sqrt{0.04} = \sqrt{\dfrac{4}{100}} = \dfrac{\sqrt{4}}{\sqrt{100}} = \dfrac{2}{10}$, so $\left(\sqrt{0.04}\right)^5 = \left(\dfrac{2}{10}\right)^5$. To raise a fraction to an exponent, apply the exponent to both the numerator and the denominator to get $\dfrac{2^5}{10^5} = \dfrac{32}{100{,}000}$. Convert this to a decimal by moving the decimal point in both the numerator and denominator 5 places to the left to get $\dfrac{0.00032}{1.0000} = 0.00032$. The correct answer is (A).

Scientific Notation and Probability Drill (Page 255)

1. **C** Multiply the 2,550 by 3 to get a total lumens of 7,650. Expand the answers until you find the one that matches this.

2. **B** Two out of six, or $\dfrac{1}{3}$.

3. **D** 3,400 + 41,000 = 44,400

Combinations and Permutations Drill (Page 259)

1. **D** Each choice is from a different source, so multiply by the number of possibilities from each source. This is $4 \times 5 \times 8 \times 3 = 480$. The correct answer is (D).

2. **C** Each cabinet member is appointed from the same pool of candidates. Since each position is different, the order matters. Look at the number of choices for each position one at a time. There are eight candidates for vice president. After one is selected, seven candidates remain for secretary. After one is selected, six candidates remain for treasurer. Multiply these numbers to get $8 \times 7 \times 6 = 336$. The correct answer is (C).

3. **B** The teacher is choosing three team members from nine candidates. Because no positions or rankings are specified and each candidate is simply selected or not selected, order doesn't matter. Look at the number of choices for each spot on the team, one at a time. There are nine choices for the first spot, leaving eight for the second, and seven for the third. Since order doesn't matter, divide by the number of possible ordering of three team members, $3 \times 2 \times 1$. This leaves $\dfrac{9}{3} \times \dfrac{8}{2} \times \dfrac{7}{1} = \dfrac{3}{1} \times \dfrac{4}{1} \times \dfrac{7}{1} = 84$. The correct answer is (B).

Applied Arithmetic Drill (Page 261)

1. **A** In this setup problem, you need to multiply 0.08 by $5,000 for one year, and then multiply that result by 2 for two years.

2. **B** If you set this up in the rate times time format, you have $5 \times ? = 17.5$. The correct answer is $3\frac{1}{2}$ hours. You could have eliminated (C) and (D) by Ballparking.

3. **D** 50 percent of 200 people is 100 and 40 percent of 200 people is 80. Subtract the two to find the difference.

4. **D** Try out answers to find the one that gives an average of 90.

5. **C** Don't bother multiplying further than you have to—it's clear (A) is way too big, for example. Five squared is 25 and the square root of 9 is 3. These values have a difference of 22, which is equivalent to (C).

6. **B** The square root of 9 is 3. This is the closest the answer choices come to the square root of 10.

7. $\frac{2}{7}$ There are a total of 7 possible cars. There are 2 sedans. The odds on this probablility problem are 2 out of 7.

8. **12** Rearrange the numbers in ascending order. The middle number is **12.**

9. **B** To answer this setup problem, just convert the words into math. She works 40 hours at $14.50 and 3 hours at one and a half TIMES the $14.50 rate. The correct answer is (B). Choices (C) and (D) are wrong because we are supposed to add the two numbers, not multiply.

10. **D** Expand out the scientific notation: 23,000 microns versus 32,000 microns. The difference is 9,000 microns.

11. **C** Marie is choosing three shows, so leave three spaces for the shows. There are 5 possible choices for the first show, 4 remaining possible choices for the second show, and 3 remaining choices for the third show. Since she has to choose an order, do not divide and simply multiply the three numbers. $5 \times 4 \times 3 = 60$.

12. **A** In the numerator, there are two factors with bases of 2. When multiplying numbers with the same base,

add the exponents: $(2^{12})(2^5) = 2^{17}$, so the fraction is equal to $\dfrac{(2^{17})(\sqrt{5})^4}{(2^{16})(5^3)}$. There is a factor with a base of

two in the denominator. When dividing numbers with the same base, subtract the exponents: $\dfrac{2^{17}}{2^{16}} = 2^1 = 2$,

so the fraction is equal to $\dfrac{(2)(\sqrt{5})^4}{(5^3)}$. In the numerator, there is a $\sqrt{5}$, which is equivalent to $5^{\frac{1}{2}}$, so the

fraction is equal to $\dfrac{(2)\left(5^{\frac{1}{2}}\right)^4 (5^3)}{(5^3)}$. When a number with an exponent is raised to another exponent, multiply

the exponents: $\left(5^{\frac{1}{2}}\right)^4 = 5^2$, so the fraction is equal to $\dfrac{(2)(5^2)}{(5^3)}$. Once again, numbers with the same base are divided. Subtract the exponents. Since the denominator is greater, keep the result in the denominator:

$\dfrac{5^2}{5^3} = \dfrac{1}{5^1} = \dfrac{1}{5}$, so the fraction is equal to $\dfrac{2}{5}$. The correct answer is (A).

Simple Equation Drill (Page 266)

1. **C** Add 5 to both sides of the equation, and then divide both sides by 2.

2. **15** Subtract 6 from both sides of the equation, and then divide both sides by 3.

3. **C** Just plug in 2 for x and 3 for y.

Inequalities Drill (Page 269)

1. **C** If the minimum age is five, then anyone five or older can ride the roller coaster.

2. **A** Just solve as if this were an equality.

3. **C** Plug in 4 into each inequality until one is a true statement.

Backsolving Drill (Page 274)

1. **A** First, ballpark. If Marcie sees more patients, then she must see more than half of them. The answer must be more than 8, which eliminates every answer choice but (A). If you didn't notice that, how could you have solved the problem? By Backsolving. Try (C) and say that Marcie saw 5 patients. If Marcie saw 2 more than Lewis, then Lewis saw 3 patients. When you add together Marcie and Lewis's patients, you are supposed to have 16. Could this be the right answer? No way. You need a bigger number. Try (B). If Marcie had 7 patients, Lewis has 5, and this is still too small. The correct answer must be (A).

2. **D** This is another good backsolve. Just try putting the values in the answer choices into the equation until you find one that works.

3. **B** Ballparking gets rid of (A) because the problem says there are some men workers as well. If you solve this algebraically, watch out for (D), which turns out to be the number of men. However, a good way to avoid any chance of making a mistake is not to use algebra—try Backsolving instead. Start with (B). If there are 60 women and 4 times as many women as men, then the number of men is $\dfrac{1}{4}$ of 60 or 15. If 60 + 15 = 75, then this is the answer. And it is.

4. **B** Again, it is much easier to backsolve. Start with (C), 10%. Ten percent of $45.00 is $4.50. This is too much, so go down one and find 9 percent of $45.00. This is the correct answer.

5. **D** You could use algebra, but Backsolving is just as easy. Start with (B), and see if it makes the equation work. No, we need a bigger number. Choice (C) doesn't work either, so the answer must be (D).

Translation Drill (Page 279)

1. **C** Choice (A) is just Sandra's weight alone. The combined weight of both of them is $x + (x + 5)$, which is equivalent to (C).

2. **B** The 2000 figure is just a red herring. It doesn't matter that the number of rabbits doubled in 2000 because by 2001 (the year we are interested in), the population is up five times.

3. **C** Choices (A) and (B) don't multiply Sam's age by 3. Choices (B) and (D) subtract years.

4. **C** There are a total of nine chips, so set up the equation $B + R = 21$. The blue chips are worth 5 points each, so they're worth $5B$ total. The red chips are worth 3 points each, so they're worth $3R$ total. Since the blue chips and red chips combined are worth 21 points, $5B + 3R = 21$.

Polynomial Drill (Page 286)

1. **A** Add up the total number of x's and y's.

2. **B** Start by factoring an x out of the first two terms and 3 out of the last two terms. Both leave you with a factor of $(x - 4)$.

3. **B** Even though the coefficients are fractions, follow the same method. The first two terms both have a factor

   of $\frac{1}{4}x$. Factor this to get $\frac{1}{4}x^2 + \frac{2}{4}x = \left(\frac{1}{4}x\right)(x+2)$. The other two terms both have a factor of $-\frac{2}{3}$, so

   factor this to get $-\frac{2}{3}x - \frac{4}{3} = -\frac{2}{3}(x+2)$. Thus the original expression factors to $\left(\frac{1}{4}x\right)(x+2) - \frac{2}{3}(x+2)$.

   Notice that the remaining terms both have factors of $(x + 2)$. Factor this to get $\left(\frac{1}{4}x - \frac{2}{3}\right)(x+2)$. The correct answer is (B).

4. **C** When multiplying polynomials, use the distributive property: $(x^2 + 2x + 8)(x - 4) = (x^2 + 2x + 8)(x) - (x^2 + 2x + 8)(4)$. Now use the distributive property on the remaining terms: $(x^2 + 2x + 8)(x) = x^3 + 2x^2 + 8x$ and $(x^2 + 2x + 8)(4) = 4x^2 + 8x + 32$. Therefore, the expression is $(x^3 + 2x^2 + 8x) - (4x^2 + 8x + 32)$. Distribute the negative to get $x^3 + 2x^2 + 8x - 4x^2 - 8x - 32$. Group like terms to get $x^3 + (2x^2 - 4x^2) + (8x - 8x) - 32$. Combine like terms to get $x^3 - 2x^2 + 0 + 32 = x^3 - 2x^2 - 32$. The correct answer is (C).

5. **B** Translate the pieces of the question. A player's score is the sum of the squares of the numbers on her cards. Let the two numbers be represented by x and y, respectively. The squares of the two numbers are x^2 and y^2, respectively, so their sum is $x^2 + y^2$. Jennifer's cards have a product of 24, so $xy = 24$. The pairs of factors of 24 are 1 and 24, 2 and 12, 3 and 8, and 4 and 6. Since the cards cannot have numbers greater than 10, eliminate 1 and 24 and 2 and 12 as possible pairs. The sum of Jennifer's cards is 11, so $x + y = 11$. Since that is the case, the two cards cannot be 4 and 6, since their sum is 10 rather than 11. Therefore, x and y must be 3 and 8. It cannot be determined whether $x = 3$ and $y = 8$ or $x = 8$ and $y = 3$. However, either possibility leads to the same result. Jennifer's score is $x^2 + y^2 = 3^2 + 8^2 = 9 + 64 = 73$. The correct answer is (B).

Quadratic Equations Drill (Page 293)

1. **A** Factor the equation. What two numbers have a sum of –7 and a product of 12. The factors of 12 are 1 and 12, 2 and 6, and 3 and 4. The factors 3 and 4 have a sum of 7. Since 7 is negative, the factors must both be negative, so the equation factors to $(x-3)(x-4)=0$. Set both factors equal to 0. If $x-3=0$, then add three to both sides to get $x=3$. If $x-4=0$, add four to both sides to get $x=4$. The correct answer is (A).

2. **B** The answer choices are in square form, so use the complete the square method. In this equation, $b=-10$, so, to have a perfect square, c has to equal $\left(\dfrac{-10}{2}\right)^2 = 25$. To get $c=25$, add 9 to both sides to get $x^2 - 10x + 25 = 9$. Factor the left side to get $(x-5)^2 = 9$. The correct answer is (B).

3. **D** The answer choices are in the form of the quadratic formula, so use $x=\dfrac{-b\pm\sqrt{b^2-4ac}}{2a}$. In the equation $x^2 - 8x + 5 = 0$, $a=1$, $b=-8$, and $c=5$. Plug these into the quadratic formula to get $x=\dfrac{-(-8)\pm\sqrt{(-8)^2-4(1)(5)}}{2(1)} = \dfrac{8\pm\sqrt{44}}{2}$. The correct answer is (D).

Rational Expressions Drill (Page 298)

1. **C** Find the common denominator for the two fractions. Start by factoring the first denominator. The denominator for the first fraction, $x^2 - 2x - 8$, factors to $(x-4)(x+2)$. To get the common denominator, multiply the second fraction by $\dfrac{x+2}{x+2}$ to get $\dfrac{2(x+2)}{(x-4)(x+2)} = \dfrac{2x+4}{x^2-2x-8}$. Since the denominators are the same, subtract the numerators to get $\dfrac{3-(2x+4)}{x^2-2x-8} = \dfrac{3-2x-4}{x^2-2x-8} = \dfrac{-2x-1}{x^2-2x-8}$. The correct answer is (C).

2. **A** To divide fractions (including rational expressions), invert the second and multiply: $\dfrac{3x-9}{x^2-6x+9} \times \dfrac{x^2-9}{x^2+8x+15}$. Look to simplify by finding common factors. Factor the numerators and denominators in each fraction to get $\dfrac{3(x-3)}{(x-3)(x-3)} \times \dfrac{(x-3)(x+3)}{(x+5)(x+3)}$. Cancel the $(x-3)$ in the first fraction and the $(x+3)$ in the second to get $\dfrac{3}{(x-3)} \times \dfrac{(x-3)}{(x+5)}$. Don't forget that you can cross cancel $(x-3)$ to get $\dfrac{3}{x+5}$.

The correct answer is (A).

Simultaneous Equations Drill (Page 301)

1. **C** Since both equations are isolated for x, set the two equal to each other, giving you $2y + 5 = 3y - 6$. Subtract $2y$ from both sides and add 6 to both sides to get $y = 11$. Plug the value back into one of the original equations to get $x = 27$.

2. **A** Line up the two equations. Since the question asks for the value of y, eliminate x. Multiply the first equation by 2 to get $6x + 8y = -10$ and second equation by 3 to get $-6x - 15y = 24$. Add the two equations to get $-7y = 14$. Divide by 7 to get $y = -2$.

3. **A** Translate the information into a system of equations. Let A represent the number of apples and B represent the number of bananas that Bill bought. Bill buys a total of 8 apples and bananas, so $A + B = 8$. Each apple costs 25 cents, so the cost of A apples is $0.25A$. Each banana cost 30 cents, so the cost of B bananas is $0.30B$. Since the total cost is $2.15, then $0.25A + 0.30B = 2.15$. Line up these two equations. Multiply the second equation by -4 to get $-A - 1.20B = -8.60$. Add the two equations to get $-0.20B = -0.60$. Divide both sides by -0.20 to get $B = 3$.

Functions Drill (Page 307)

1. **B** A relation is a function if every member of a domain corresponds with a unique member of the range. In the table, 3 corresponds with both -1 and y. In order for $h(x)$ to be a function, these values must be the same, so y must equal -1.

2. **B** Plug in 5 for each value of x, so $g(5) = 5^2 - 6 \times 5 + 9 = 25 - 30 + 9 = 4$.

3. **A** This is a translation problem. "The function of x" translates to $f(x)$. "Is" translates to =. "Three times" translates to 3( ), with whatever follows filling in the parenthesis. What follows translates to "four more than," so fill this is to get 3($+ 4$), with whatever follows filling in before the plus sign. Finally, what follows is "the square of x," which translates to x^2. Therefore, the entire function translates to $f(x) = 3(x^2 + 4)$.

Algebra Drill (Page 308)

1. **C** Subtract 9 from both sides, and then divide both sides by 5 or backsolve.

2. **A** Use translation: $3x + 4$.

3. **29** Just plug in 3 for x and 4 for y.

4. **C** This is a good Backsolving problem. If you start with (B), you'll see it's too small, so go up to the next biggest answer and try that.

5. **B** Treat this just like an equality: Solve for m.

6. **D** Just add up the total number of x's and y's.

7. **D** Plug 4 into each of the answer choices until you find the one that is true.

8. **C** You can ballpark this: 30 workers would be one-quarter, or 25 percent. 36 workers would be slightly more. Or work backward: What is 10 percent of the 120 workers? That's right: 12. Twenty percent? 24. Thirty percent? 36. Bingo!

9. **A** Use FOIL.

10. **C** This is a great Backsolving problem. Start with (B). You'll notice that you need a larger number. Choice (C) is correct.

11. **A** Put the two equations in the same form, so that you can use linear combinations. Take the first equation and subtract 2 from both sides and add $2y$ to both sides to get $3x + 2y = -2$. Now, to cancel x, multiply the second equation by 3 to get $-3x + 9y = -42$. Add the two equations to get $11y = -44$. Divide both sides by 11 to get $y = -4$.

12. To determine the blank space on the top right, plug -2 in for x to get $f(-2) = 2(-2)^2 + 1 = 9$. Select this for this blank space. To determine the blank space on the bottom left, plug in the answer choices to $f(x)$ and select the one for which $f(x) = 19$. Ballpark out 17 and 19, and try the remaining choices. $f(5) = 51$, so the answer has to be smaller. Ballpark out 9, as well. $f(-3) = 19$, so this is the correct answer. Select -3 for this blank.

13. **A** The question involves multiplication of rational expressions, so simplify the expressions by factoring. Factor -2 in the first numerator to get $-2(x - 4)$. Factor the denominator of the first fraction to get $(x - 5)(x + 2)$. The numerator of the second fraction factors to $(x - 5)(x + 4)$. The denominator of the second fraction factors to $(x + 4)(x - 4)$. Therefore, the factored form of the equation is

$\dfrac{-2(x-4)}{(x-5)(x+2)} \times \dfrac{(x+4)(x-5)}{(x-4)(x+4)} = (x+5)$. Now look to cancel. Cancel $(x + 4)$, $(x - 4)$, and $(x - 5)$ to get

$\dfrac{-2}{(x+2)} = (x+5)$. Get all the variables on one side of the equation by multiplying both sides by $(x + 2)$ to

get $-2 = (x + 5)(x + 2)$. Use FOIL on the right side to get $-2 = x^2 + 7x + 10$. Since the right side is now a

quadratic, get one side equal to 0 by adding 2 to both sides to get $0 = x^2 + 7x + 12$. Factor the right side

to get $0 = (x + 3)(x + 4)$. Set both factors equal to 0 to get $x + 3 = 0$ and $x + 4 = 0$. Subtract 3 from the

first equation to get $x = -3$ and 4 from the second to get $x = -4$. Since -4 is one of the choices, the correct

answer is (A).

Lines and Angles Drill (Page 315)

1. **40 degrees** $180 - 140 = 40$

2. **90 degrees** $180 - 90 = 90$

3. **130 degrees** $180 - 50 = 130$

Rectangles and Squares Drill (Page 318)

1. **square**   All sides are the same length.

2. **rectangle**   The sides are different lengths, but all angles are right angles.

3. **9**   Multiply length by width: $3 \times 3 = 9$

4. **24**   Add the four sides together: $3 + 3 + 9 + 9 = 24$. (The area of figure B would be 27.)

5. **3**   Divide the area of the rectangle by the area of the square: $27 \div 9 = 3$.

6. **5** $3 \times 4 \times ? = 60$

7. **4**   The entire volume of the cube equals 8, so halfway is 4.

8. **D**   Because you don't know how much the wallpaper costs, there is not enough information given for us to answer the question.

Triangles and Pyramids Drill (Page 327)

1. **B**   Area is base times height divided by two. If you picked (A), you forgot to divide by two.

2. **2**   This is a 3-4-5 triangle. The answer is $5 - 3 = 2$.

3. **C** $180 - (27 + 53) = 100$.

4. **D**   First, use the provided formula to find the surface area of the pyramid, 5,068.8. Since one can covers 1,296 square inches, two cans cover 2,592 square inches, 3 cans cover 3,888, and 4 cans cover 5,184. Only (D) is large enough to cover the surface area.

5. **D**   Adding up the three angles of the triangle, you get $4x + 20 = 180$. Solving for x, you get 40 degrees—but the question is asking for angle A, which is $2x$ or 80 degrees.

6. **C** The question gives the volume of a pyramid. The formula for volume of a pyramid is $V = \frac{1}{3}Bh$, where B represents the volume of the base and h represents the height of the pyramid. The question gives the volume and height, so plug these into the formula to get $320 = \frac{1}{3}B(15)$. Simplify the right side to get $320 = 5B$. Divide both sides by 5 to get $B = 64$. Therefore, the area of the base is 64. Since the question says that it is a square base, use the area formula $A = s^2$. Plug in $A = 64$ to get $64 = s^2$. Take the square root of both sides to get $8 = s$. The question asks for the perimeter of the base. Perimeter is the sum of the lengths of all sides. Since the base is a square, all sides have a length of 8. Therefore, the perimeter is $8 + 8 + 8 + 8 = 4(8) = 32$. The correct answer is (C).

Other Polygons Drill (Page 331)

1. **B** The perimeter is the sum of the sides, so $8 + 10 + x + 14 = 40$. Simplify the left side to get $32 + x = 40$. Subtract 32 from both sides to get $x = 8$. The correct answer is (B).

2. **D** The question asks for the area of the octagon and gives a formula in terms of the side. Although the side is not given, the perimeter is given as well as the fact that it is a regular octagon. A regular octagon has eight equal sides, so the perimeter $P = 8s$. Since $P = 56$, $56 = 8s$, and $s = 7$. Plug this into the formula to get $A = 2\left(1+\sqrt{2}\right)(7)^2 = 2\left(1+\sqrt{2}\right)(49) = 98\left(1+\sqrt{2}\right)$. None of the answer choices are in factored form, so distribute the 98 to get $A = 98 + 98\sqrt{2}$. The correct answer is (D).

Circles, Spheres, Cylinders, and Cones Drill (Page 335)

1. **4**

2. **8**   Multiply the radius by 2: $4 \times 2 = 8$.

3. **8π**   The diameter is 8, so multiply that by π to get the circumference.

4. **16π**   Use the formula for area: $\pi 4^2 = 16\pi$.

5. **81(π)**   The area of the circle is $9(\pi)$. $9(\pi) \times 9 = 81(\pi)$.

6. **A**   If the diameter is 4, then the radius is 2.

7. **D** The formula for volume of a cone is $V = \frac{1}{3}\pi r^2 h$. The question says that the volume is 100π, so plug this in to get $100\pi = \frac{1}{3}\pi r^2 h$. The questions asks for h, so you'll need to determine the value of r. The question also says that the area of the circular base is 25π. The formula for the area of a circle is $A = \pi r^2$. Plug in $A = 25\pi$ to get $25\pi = \pi r^2$. Divide both sides by π to get $25 = r^2$. Take the square root of both sides to get $5 = r$. Plug $r = 5$ into the volume formula to get $100\pi = \frac{1}{3}\pi(5)^2 h$. Simplify the right side to get $100\pi = \frac{25\pi}{3}h$. (Alternatively, note that $A = \pi r^2$ and plug 25π into the formula directly bypassing the need to find the radius.) Multiply both sides by $\frac{3}{25\pi}$ to get $h = 100\pi \times \frac{3}{25\pi} = \frac{100\pi}{1} \times \frac{3}{25\pi} = \frac{4}{1} \times \frac{3}{1} = 12$. The correct answer is (D).

8. **B** The formula for volume of a sphere is $V = \frac{4}{3}\pi r^3$. Plug in $V = 36\pi$ to get $36\pi = \frac{4}{3}\pi r^3$. Divide both sides by π to cancel the π's and get $36 = \frac{4}{3}r^3$. Multiply both sides by $\frac{3}{4}$ to get $r^3 = 36 \times \frac{3}{4} = \frac{36}{1} \times \frac{3}{4} = \frac{9}{1} \times \frac{3}{1} = 27$. Take the cube root of both sides to get $r = 3$, which is (A), but this is not the answer. The question asks for the diameter. Since $d = 2r = 2(3) = 6$, the correct answer is (B).

Graphing Drill (Page 340)

1. **C** To find the slope, take the difference in y-values, and put that over the difference in x-values. In this case, that is $\frac{2}{4}$ or $\frac{1}{2}$.

2. **C** Did you need the distance formula this time? No way! The y-values were the same for both numbers. All we had to do was subtract 5 from 12. If you didn't notice this, you could have sketched it out. Seeing what the problem really looks like almost always makes it easier to solve.

3. To graph point A, count 3 left and 4 down. To graph point B, go right 2 and up 3. For point C, count 3 right and 5 up.

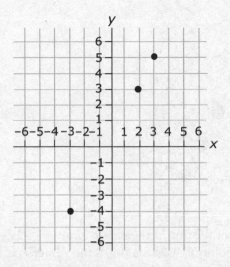

Equation of a Line Drill (Page 350)

1. **A** You want $y = mx + b$ form, in which m is the slope and b is the y-intercept. The question says that the slope is 4, so plug this in for m. Since at the y-intercept, the x-coordinate is 0, the (0, –2) represents the y-intercept, so plug in –2 for b.

2. $y = \dfrac{1}{2}x + 1$

    You want $y = mx + b$ form, in which m is the slope and b is the y-intercept. First get the slope. Plug the

    points you have into the slope formula to get $m = \dfrac{2-(-1)}{2-(-4)} = \dfrac{3}{6} = \dfrac{1}{2}$. Select this for the first box. To get

    the y-intercept, plug in the slope and one of the points into the slope intercept form to get $2 = \dfrac{1}{2}(2) + b$.

    Solve to get $b = 1$. Select this for the second box.

3. **C** You want $y = mx + b$ form, in which m is the slope and b is the y-intercept. Since the slope is –2, the equation is in the form $y = -2x + b$. Plug in the point (–1, 3). $3 = -2(-1) + b$. Solve to get $b = 1$, so the equation of the line is $y = -2x + 1$.

4. **A** Get the two equations into $y = mx + b$ form. The first equation, $2x + 8y = -5$, can be put into the

    form $y = -\dfrac{1}{4}x - \dfrac{5}{8}$. The second equation, $3x + 12y = 8$, can be put into the form $y = -\dfrac{1}{4}x + \dfrac{2}{3}$.

    Since the slopes are the same, the lines are parallel.

5.

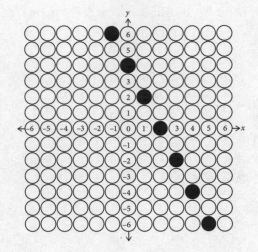

You are given the equation of the line in $y = mx + b$ form: $y = -2x + 4$. Therefore, the slope is –2 and the y-intercept is 4. Mark the point (0, 4), since this is the y-intercept. Since the slope is –2, mark the point that is up 2 and left 1, (–1, 6). Now, go in the other direction and mark the points that are down 2 and right 1: (1, 2), (2, 0), (3, –2), (4, –4) and (5, –6).

Proportions and Graphs Drill (Page 355)

1. **12** The speed traveled is equal to the slope of the line. To get the slope, you need two points, so use the points (0, 0) and (5, 60). The speed is $\dfrac{60-0}{5-0} = 12$.

2. **B** Each box contains 2 red marbles and 5 black marbles, so the number of red marbles must always be a multiple of 2, and the number of black marbles must always be a multiple of 5. Start with one box. If a customer buys one box, he or she will have 2 red marbles and 5 black marbles. The only graph that has this point is (B).

3. **greater than**

   To get Lisa's speed, find the slope of the line. Use the points (0, 0) and (2, 100) to get a speed of $\dfrac{100-0}{2-0} = 50$.

   To get Frank's speed, take the coefficient on t, which is 40. Therefore, Lisa's speed is greater.

Interpreting Graphs Drill (Page 361)

1. **C** A graph is negative when it is below the x-axis. Look to see where the graph crosses the x-axis. This happens at $x = 3$ and at $x = 7$. Between these points is where the graph is below the x-axis and, therefore, negative.

2.

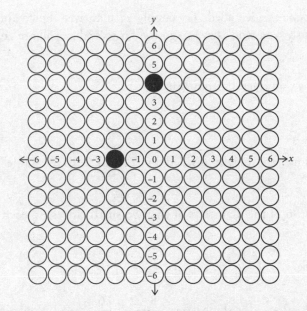

Since the equation of the line is in $y = mx + b$ form, the y-intercept is represented by the b term, in this case 4. Therefore, the y-intercept is the point (0, 4). To get the x-intercept, set $y = 0$ to get $0 = 2x + 4$. Solve for x to get $x = -2$, so the x-intercept is the point (−2, 0).

3. **B** Find the peaks and valleys. In this case, there is only one of each. The graph hits a valley, i.e. a relative minimum at the point (−3, −4) and a peak, i.e. a relative maximum, at the point (2, 6). The graph is increasing between these two points, so over the interval −3 < x < 2.

4. **C** The axis of symmetry is the line that divides the curve into two mirror images. Sketch the graph on scratch paper and draw each line from the answer choices. The only one that divides it into mirror images is $y = 3$.

5. **B** To determine the period, find the peaks in the graph. The graph reaches peaks at (−7, 2), (−1, 2), and (5, 2). Since the distance between each of these peaks is 6, the period is 6.

Geometry Drill (Page 365)

1. **D** 3 is the diameter, so the radius is 1.5. Use the area formula and then multiply by $\frac{3}{4}$.

2. **A** The area is $7^2 \times \frac{22}{7}$, or 154.

3. **B** Each side of the square has the same length, 3. The two sides of an isosceles triangle that are opposite equal angles also have the same length, 4. The correct answer is 17.

4. **C** Any three-sided figure is a triangle. If two of the sides have the same length, as the ratio tells you, then it is an isosceles triangle.

5. **A** You could backsolve this. The volume of a cube is side cubed. Try cubing each answer choice until you find one that gives you the value 27. Obviously, you won't have to go too far to realize you are going to need a pretty small number.

6. **B** The sum of all three angles must equal 180, so subtract 45 from 180.

7. **D** Divide 168 by 12. The correct answer is 14.

8. **A** The area of a triangle equals the base times the height divided by 2, which is the same as $\frac{1}{2}$ times the base times the height.

9. **D** The diameter of the large circle equals the sum of the diameters of the two small circles, so each small circle has a diameter of 10 and a radius of 5.

10. **D** You need *two* points on a line to find its slope.

11. **B** Get the line in $y = mx + b$. Start by getting the slope. The slope is $m = \frac{8-2}{-2-1} = \frac{6}{-3} = -2$. Now plug this in for m and the point $(1, 2)$ in for x and y into the equation to get $2 = -2(1) + b$. Solve for b to get $b = 4$, so the equation is $y = -2x + 4$.

12. **A** To determine where a graph is positive, start with where the value is 0, i.e. the x-intercepts. The x-intercepts are -9.5, 1, and 8. The graph is above the x-axis, and therefore positive, between -9.5 and 1 and to the right of 8. Therefore, it is positive when $-9.5 < x < 1$ and when $x > 8$.

13. **D** Both the area of the hexagon and the formula for area are given, so set $24\sqrt{3} = \frac{3\sqrt{3}}{2}s^2$. Multiply both sides by 2 to get $48\sqrt{3} = 3\sqrt{3}s^2$. Divide both sides by $\sqrt{3}$ to get $48 = 3s^2$. Divide both sides by 3 to get $16 = s^2$. Take the square root of both sides to get $4 = s$. This is (B), but the question asks not for the length of the side but for the perimeter. There are six sides in a regular hexagon and all sides are equal; the perimeter is $6s = 6(4) = 24$. The correct answer is (D).

SOCIAL STUDIES

Social Studies, Part One Drill (Page 409)

1. **B** The shaded areas generally run in stripes from east to west. You may remember that the Underground Railroad was an escape route for slaves going from the South to Canada, so rule out (A). Lewis and Clark were explorers who traveled the West using only one main trail, not the complex network of trails on this map, so rule out (D). Choice (C) looks tempting, but remember that manufactured goods were primarily made in the East and these shaded regions don't extend into any of the major cities of the East. So, that leaves (B). The shaded regions represent the major railroad trails running east to west: the Transcontinental, Northern Pacific, and Southern Pacific.

2. The three New Deal programs that provided jobs to the unemployed were the following:

   - **Event (b): Civil Works Administration**

   - **Event (c): Public Works Administration**

   - **Event (e): Civilian Conservation Corps**

   Reading the descriptions in the chart, all three of these programs were specifically designed to put people to work. Federal Housing Administration is tempting, but nowhere does it say that people were hired to *build* houses, only that the government would assist people to get loans.

3. **D** The quote states that "separate schools for white and colored children, has been held to be a valid exercise of legislative power." The words "separation" and "power" make (B) tempting, but this a trap. It cannot be (C), since the quote states that limits to contact "do not necessarily imply the inferiority of either race to the other." On the other hand, the civil rights movement had not gained any influence until the 1960s, so rule out (A). That leaves (D). The quote states that separate schools are "valid," but that this does not imply "inferiority."

Economics Drill (Page 421)

1. **D** For this question, we are interested only in the northeastern region, represented by the figure on the left. Just subtract the '09 figure from the '10 figure. Calculate as follows: $9.1 - 7.3 = 1.8$, or (D).

2. **A** This is a tough evaluation problem that requires you to make generalizations about the economy based on unemployment figures. If a country's unemployment figures are up, we can make a general assumption that the country's economy is not healthy. Of course, from this chart, we have no idea about the economies of other nations. According to the data in the chart, the unemployment rate in 2010 was higher than it was in 2009. From this data, we can infer that the overall economic situation was worse in 2010 than it was in 2009.

Social Studies, Part Two Drill (Page 431)

1. **A** Notice that the arrows are pointing in different directions. An export is a good that a country sends TO another country, not something that it receives. The arrow going from the Colonies to Britain lists "tobacco" as one of the exports, so (A) is the best answer. Manufactured goods (B) are an import from Britain, not an export from the Colonies. Slaves (C) are imported from Africa, and sugar (D) is imported from the West Indies.

2. **A** Recalling that World War II took place during the 1940s will help you to select (A). Otherwise, use POE. Choice (B) is a trap, since the graph measures employment, not population. The Great Depression was in the 1930s, not the 1940s, so rule out (C). Choice (D) is not true, since civilian employment was low throughout the early part of the graph. Also, we cannot say what is true of employment in the years not measured by the graph.

3. TRUE: Statements (a), (b), and (c). All of the countries listed on the right side of the map (the East) are European countries, so statement (a) is true. Italy had over 4,000,000 immigrants, while Ireland had less than 2,000,000, so this ratio is at least "2 to 1" (two times bigger). Looking at the numbers for Japan and France, Japan is slightly higher at 241,000, so statement (c) is true. Statement (d) is deceptive. It certainly looks like Japanese and Chinese immigrants largely landed in the West, but we do not know where they ultimately "settled." Many of them may have migrated East after they landed. Statement (d) is FALSE.

SCIENCE

Scientific Method Drill (Page 458)

1. **D** In order for the bird to be found in the lava from the Pompeii eruption, the bird must have lived during that period or it would not end up preserved in that rock—(D) is correct. This was an evaluation question. The passage mentions that the bird's species is believed to be extinct, but there is no mention of how this happened and we cannot assume that the extinction was due to the volcano, so eliminate (A). While it is possible that the bird did not live in Pompeii and was just caught in the wrong place at the wrong time, this is unlikely and cannot be determined from the information in the prompt, so eliminate (B). Choice (C) does not define whom it is referring to (no one who lived in Pompeii or no one in general). Obviously the eruption did not kill all humans or we would not be here today. Also, the passage doesn't mention the extent of the casualties at Pompeii, so eliminate (C).

2. The passage alludes to the fact that scientists typically compare physical traits of the newly found animal to other physical traits of similar species that are alive today. Physical traits can include, but are not limited to, body shape, ratios of key features, specifics such as beak or wing size/shape, and so on. This should be done systematically; as soon as a direct physical trait comparison is not the same, the scientists should move on to the next organism. Only when all known similar species are determined to have fundamental physical differences should the scientists conclude that they must be dealing with a new species.

3. The only two observations are that the bird's wings are abnormally long and that Mount Vesuvius erupted in 79 A.D. The belief that the bird would have been able to eat more than its competitors is a conclusion that the scientists could have made based on its unique beak. Finally, (c) is not supported by the passage and does not fit into either category.

Cell Theory and the Origins of Life Drill (Page 463)

1. **D** According to the passage, bacteria that keep glowing are still alive so the drug must not be able to kill them. There are two possible explanations for this; first, the drug may not be the correct type (as the passage explains, it is imperative that the correct drug be chosen based on the particular strain) or, secondly, the drug might not have been administered at a high enough dose [(D) is correct while (A) and (C), while correct, do not include the other option and are eliminated]. If the cell continues to fluoresce, it must not have been destroyed—eliminate (B).

2. **A** Timing is critical to the test so that the patient can be placed on the correct course of treatment as soon as possible to prevent the spread of infection [(A) is correct]. Choice (B) is a nice feature of the new test but certainly not the most important reason, so eliminate (B). There is not enough information in the passage to know how long the enzyme lasts but, even if this were true, it would not support the need for expediency with respect to the test, so eliminate (C). Choice (D) is vague and can be eliminated since the passage does not specifically describe other types of bacteria.

3. The 10,000 mM point on the *x*-axis should be clicked on as this represents the dose at which the intensity falls below 20, which the question stem indicates is acceptable.

Genetics Drill (Page 468)

1. **25%**

   This question wants you to look at the Punnett Square and figure out how often an offspring will have pointy ears. The information in the passage states that the trait will be expressed if the gene is pure or composed of mixed alleles. Accordingly, the probability a cat will have pointy ears is $\frac{1}{4}$ or 25% or 0.25.

2. **A** You need to understand how a Punnett Square works in order to answer this question. You must cross each column with each row in order to find the possibilities; e.g., the first column, which has the allele P, is crossed with the first row, which also has the allele P, to give us the gene PP. Thus, the answer is (A).

3. The genotypic ratio is the pattern of offspring distribution based on genotype. In this example, we have one instance of PP, two instances of Pp, and one instance of pp. Thus, the genotypic ratio is **1:2:1**.

Evolution and Natural Selection Drill (Page 472)

1. **A** In order for some life forms to survive, they would have needed to have the ability to survive despite the conditions described in the passage. One such ability would be to be able to survive without sunlight— (A) is correct. The dinosaurs went extinct; they did not hibernate. If this was true, we would expect to still see dinosaurs, so eliminate (B). As we know, sunlight is critical to the survival of plants, which use it for photosynthesis—eliminate (C). There must have been some food on the planet or else no organisms would have survived, so eliminate (D).

2.   Dinosaurs would have had to be able to withstand all of the hardships in the passage, so they would have needed traits that apply to those. They would have needed a way of staying warm, generating heat, or surviving in very cold temperatures. They would have also needed to be able to hunt for prey in the dark and consume organisms that did not depend on the sun for survival. They would also have to be able to attract a mate and care for young despite the lack of heat and light.

3. **C** This is a good example of a fifty-fifty question because you can probably eliminate two answer choices immediately by thinking about the question. Darwin would very likely agree with this passage because of his belief in natural selection and the conditions under which it occurs. Moreover, he did not believe in destiny—so eliminate (A)—or consider tragedy in his theory, so eliminate (B). Choice (C) closely describes Darwin's views—(C) is correct—while (D) implies that evolution took place at the level of individual organisms, a common misconception about Darwin's theory, which described species and populations but not individuals. Eliminate (D).

Plants Drill (Page 476)

1. **B** The passage states that the tree was cut down at the end of the growing season in 2000, meaning that the outermost ring must correspond to the growth that took place in 2000. You can see that the second-most outer ring has a larger size than this and the next two closest to it, which represent 1998 and 1997, respectively. Therefore, (B) (1999) is the correct answer.

2. **C** Counting the rings reveals that there are 8 complete rings; hence the tree is 8 years old. Choice (C) is correct, so eliminate the other answer choices.

3.   The correct answers are, in order, **independent** and **dependent**.

Ecosystems and Food Chain Drill (Page 483)

1. **C** Use the arrows to determine which organism is consuming the other. The arrow originates at the organism that is getting eaten and terminates at the organism that is preying on it. The only organism that is eaten by both land and sea creatures is the salmon, which is eaten by both bears and sharks, so (C) is correct. Minnows are eaten only by sea creatures, so eliminate (A). Wolves are eaten only by bears—eliminate (B)—and groupers are eaten only by minnows, so eliminate (D). Note that (B) and (D) could be eliminated immediately because they are eaten only by one animal.

2. **D** The absence of algae, (D), would have the greatest impact on the rest of the food chain since it is a primary producer.

3.   Primary producers: algae. Primary consumers: copepods, minnows. Secondary consumers: salmon, groupers. Tertiary consumers: sharks, bears, barracuda, wolves.

The Human Body and Human Health Drill (Page 487)

1.   Based on the passage provided, the muscular system allows the body to move, the skeletal system works in conjunction with the muscular system to enable movement, and the nervous system regulates both voluntary and involuntary motion. Thus, the correct answers are (b), (c), and (e). Neither the endocrine nor digestive system is mentioned in the passage and, therefore, neither is incorrect.

2. We are told that Susan suffered from a heart attack, which would primarily impact the **cardiac**, or heart, muscles within the **muscular** system.

3. **D** According to the passage, the nervous system controls your muscular system and regulates both voluntary and involuntary motions by sending signals to parts of the body. Therefore, prior to the act of running, the nervous system must send signals to the muscular and skeletal systems. Thus, (D) is the correct answer. Don't fall for (B), as this is a trap! The question states that the endocrine system initiates the flight-or-fight response, not the movement itself.

Bacteria and Viruses Drill (Page 490)

1. Based on the passage provided, bacterial infections, unlike viral infections, are living. Therefore, if the disease is alive, it is bacterial. The passage also states that bacterial infections can be treated with antibiotics. Thus, the disease is alive and can be addressed with antibiotics; i.e., **bacterial** and **antibiotics** are correct.

2. According to the passage, the majority of individuals infected drink water from the same well and work with goats. Thus, the likely mode of disease transfer involves drinking contaminated water and exposure to infected animals. Choice (a) aligns with the contaminated water theory and, therefore, is correct. There is no indication that the disease is airborne, blood-borne, or transferred via human saliva, so eliminate (b), (c), and (e). The only other option is (d), the bite of an infected animal. Since we are told that the infected are exposed to goats, which could transfer disease via the bites of infected fleas, (d) is also a potential method of transfer.

3. **C** According to the passage, a viral infection can be prevented via the use of vaccination. Thus, eliminate (A). Quarantining animals and avoiding contact with infected persons can prevent the spread of disease by eliminating contact, so (B) and (D) can be eliminated. The passage also states that *bacterial*, not viral, infections can be treated with antibiotics. Therefore, (C) is correct.

Energy and Heat Drill (Page 497)

1. According to the passage, an exothermic reaction occurs when heat is released in an energy transfer, while an endothermic reaction occurs when heat is absorbed in the energy transfer. When Eliz and Kristy started the fire, heat was released into the atmosphere. Thus, an **exothermic** reaction took place because heat was **released**.

2. **B** Based on the passage, conduction occurs when objects are in direct contact with one another. Since Kristy and Eliz were not in direct contact with the fire, conduction did not take place. Therefore, you can eliminate (A) and (C). Choice (B) states that the girls absorbed heat, while (D) states that the campfire absorbs heat. Since Kristy and Eliz were the ones who became warmer and absorbed the heat, the correct answer is (B).

3. **D** Here, you need to determine what happens when Kristy burns her hand. Since she uses a metal pole that is in direct contact with the fire, heat is transferred by means of conduction. Thus, select (a) and (e). Since an exothermic reaction occurs when heat is released to surrounding objects, which become warmer when they absorb the heat, the reaction is exothermic; heat from the fire was released and transferred to her hand. Thus, select (d).

Physical Laws, Work, and Motion Drill (Page 502)

1. To answer this question, break it up into the three parts. First, Bob is the only one pushing on the rock. He is providing a force and so is friction. Note that gravity is supplying a force in all the scenarios. In the second scenario, the first three forces are the same but now there is also the force from Barbara. Finally, when the rock is over the ledge, neither Bob nor Barbara is pushing. Gravity is still a force and so is air resistance.

2. **A** Work is defined as the force (F) multiplied by the distance moved (d). Since the rock didn't move, the work done is zero [(A) is correct].

3. Objects in free fall reach constant speed because the vertical forces that are acting on them cancel out. The forces are the force of gravity, which is constant and acts in a downward direction, and the force of air resistance, which increases as velocity increases and acts in the upward direction. When the object gets going fast enough, these forces cancel out. Since there is no net force on the object, there is no acceleration and the object falls at constant speed.

Waves and Radiation Drill (Page 507)

1. According to the passage, electromagnetic waves pass through space, while mechanical waves require a medium. The passage also states that there is an inverse relationship between the frequency of a wave and its period. Therefore, as **electromagnetic** waves pass through space, the **frequency** of a wave increases as the period of a wave **decreases**.

2. In order to answer this question, you need to look at the "Applications" section of the provided table and select waves that relate to medical research. According to the chart, Visible Light is used in physical therapy, Ultraviolet Light is used in sanitation and air purification, and both X-Rays and Gamma Rays are used to treat cancer. Thus, you should select (c), (d), (e), and (f).

3. Here, you need to use the table to find the wave type that corresponds to a wavelength size of 1 nm. Make sure you don't fall into the trap of reading the wavelength size as 1 *mm*, as the question asks about nanometers, not millimeters. According to the table, a wavelength size of 60 nm $- 1 \times 10^4$ nm is associated with X-Rays. Thus, the correct answer is *X-Ray*.

Solids, Liquids and Gases Drill (Page 511)

1. The correct sentence reads as follows: **Increase** the pressure and **decrease** the temperature.

2. **A** Saltwater boils at a higher temperature than freshwater. This is due to a colligative property. The salt dissolves into its constituent ions in the water and the charged ions anchor water molecules down in the liquid. This means that it takes more energy for the water molecules to escape into the gas phase than normal. As a result, the boiling point is increased—(A) is correct. The water can still boil; it just takes longer, so eliminate (B). Also be wary of extreme wording in answer choices such as this one. Water is already neutral—eliminate (C)—and the fact that salt water is easier to float in has nothing to do with its boiling point, so eliminate (D).

3. **A** This is a difficult question because you have to use the graph and then interpret your findings. Start by finding the first point (–70°C and 70 bar). This corresponds to solid carbon dioxide. If this solid CO_2 is heated and kept at the same pressure, it will become a liquid. A solid-to-liquid phase transition is melting, so (A) is correct. Freezing is the opposite process, so eliminate (B). Boiling and condensing are processes that describe the phase transition that takes place between liquids and gases, so eliminate (C) and (D).

Chemical Reactions Drill (Page 515)

1. **C** In this chemical reaction, $2Ag + H_2S \rightarrow Ag_2S + H_2$, the sulfur atom is originally bonded to the hydrogen atoms. However, after the reaction takes place, the sulfur atom bonds to the silver atoms. Therefore, a single displacement occurs in this reaction; i.e., (C) is the correct answer.

2. **A** In this chemical equation, $2Ag + H_2S \rightarrow Ag_2S + H_2$, two atoms of silver combine with one molecule of hydrogen sulfide to produce one molecule of silver sulfide and one molecule of hydrogen. Therefore, (A) is the correct answer.

3. **6, O**

    In order to have a balanced chemical equation, the number of atoms associated with a particular element must be equal in both the reactants and the products. The balanced equation for photosynthesis is $6CO_2 + 6H_2O \rightarrow C_6H_{12}O_6 + 6O_2$. Notice that after the reaction occurs, 1 molecule of glucose is produced, which contains 6 carbon atoms. Since there are 6 carbon atoms after the reaction occurs, there must be 6 carbon atoms prior to the reaction occurring; thus, the first blank is 6. Furthermore, prior to the reaction, there are 12 oxygen atoms associated with carbon dioxide, 6 oxygen atoms associated with the water, and 18 total oxygen atoms. After the reaction, 6 oxygen atoms are associated with the glucose, leaving 12 unaccounted oxygen atoms; thus, the missing element for the first blank is O.

The Changing Earth Drill (Page 519)

1. **B** The figure shows that several earthquakes have taken place along the Western coast of the United States— eliminate (C)—and appear to follow a line down below that. Collectively, this suggests that there must be tectonic plates that rub together along this fault line, so (B) is correct. The map shows only the Americas, and there is no reason to suspect that this is the only location on Earth that earthquakes occur—eliminate (A). As the map indicates, more earthquakes occur in the United States than in Canada, so eliminate (D).

2.   The correct answer would be to include tsunamis, tremors, damage to buildings, and volcanic activity in the drop box. These four outcomes are all mentioned in the passage as being caused by earthquakes, while the others—hurricanes and tornadoes—are not.

3.   The correct answer is that the earthquake was probably low on the Richter scale (**3**) and **deep** because it was imperceptible and there was no sign of damage.

Glaciers, Erosion, and the Ice Ages Drill (Page 523)

1. **A** Glaciers are made of ice, which begins to melt once it warms up to slightly above zero degrees Celsius, so (A) is correct. Glaciers were found all over the earth but predominantly near the poles, not the equator, so eliminate (B). The opposite of (C) is true as well. As glaciers melt, the water that they were comprised of must go somewhere so it ends up in the oceans and other waterways, which causes their levels to rise— eliminate (C). Finally, while glaciers will certainly feel the gravitational pull of the moon, they are too large and heavy to be truly affected by it, so eliminate (D).

2. **B** Glaciers move extremely slowly—eliminate (A)—and they are made up of fresh water, just like snow. Choice (B) is correct. Glaciers occur in many geographical locations—eliminate (C)—and there is no evidence to suggest that they will never again cover the earth, so eliminate (D).

3.   You should select the peaks of the trend line, as these correspond to the times when the ice was thickest and were likely ice ages.

Natural Resources Drill (Page 528)

1.   According to the passage, Bashville uses fossil fuels, which are nonrenewable energy sources, to power the town. Furthermore, the town is looking to decrease carbon emissions, by switching to renewable energy sources. Thus, select **nonrenewable** energy sources, as they increase **carbon** emissions.

2. **C** Based on the passage, Bashville wants to reduce carbon emissions by switching from fossil fuels to renewable energy sources. Therefore, fossil fuels, such as coal, would produce the greatest amount of carbon emission. Choice (C) is the correct answer.

3.   Here, you need to determine which renewable energy sources that Bashville could potentially adopt. The passage states that Bashville receives significant rainfall and is located in a basin surrounded by mountains. Thus, solar power and wind power are not viable options. Furthermore, the passage does not mention geothermal energy. Therefore, choices (a), (b), and (e) are incorrect. According to the passage, Bashville is located near a number of rivers and receives a significant amount of rainfall each month. Accordingly, (d), hydroelectric power, is a viable renewable energy option for the people of Bashville. The passage also states that Bashville is located in a large basin and the town wants to reduce the amount of organic waste. Therefore, choice (c), biomass, is also a potential renewable energy choice for Bashville.

Fossils Drill (Page 531)

1.   The sentence should read as follows: The organic material found in rock layer C is probably older than the material found in **layer A** and younger than the material found in **layer D**. As the passage describes, the layers sediment over time so the oldest material will be on the bottom, while the youngest material will be on the top.

2. **B** After one half-life has transpired, there will be half of the original amount left [(B) is correct and (A) and (D) are incorrect]. Half-lives do not change the element to something new and carbon-7 does not exist—(C) is incorrect.

3. **D** It is unlikely that this area was once an ocean; (A) is false and eliminated. The rock layer could not have formed before the woolly mammoth roamed the earth, so eliminate (B). There is not enough information to determine when layer A formed, so eliminate (C). There must have been the appropriate conditions for fossilization, so (D) is correct.

Astronomy Drill (Page 536)

1.   According to the graph in the passage, the coldest *planet* is Neptune so the correct answer is to click on Neptune.

2. **D** Being farthest from the sun, Mars has the longest orbital distance. Therefore, if all planets were to travel at the exact same speed, Mars would complete its orbit in the greatest amount of time—(D) is correct. Note that this question asks for an extreme answer. Even if you don't know the right answer, you can eliminate the two answers that are not the extremes (Earth, Venus) right away.

3. **C** The correct answer to this question will be one that is not supported by the evidence in the passage. Process of Elimination is a good strategy to use for questions like this one. According to the passage, the outermost planets are the larger ones, so eliminate (A). The graph indicates that the maximum temperature of Mars is less than Venus, so eliminate (B). The passage does not speculate on the likelihood of life on other planets—(D) is neither supported nor contradicted so it is eliminated. The passage states that the sun contains 99.9% of all mass in the solar system, indicating that it is about 1,000 times as massive as everything else in the solar system, not 100 times—(C) is false and therefore the correct answer.

Part IX
Practice Tests

DIRECTIONS FOR THE PRACTICE TESTS

The questions in these two full-length practice tests are modeled closely on actual GED® test questions in terms of what content they cover, their levels of difficulty, and the various formats you should expect to encounter. We have adapted the following formats to allow you to answer most of the questions by **writing directly in this book.** If you prefer NOT to write on the tests themselves, we have provided **two custom answer sheets** at the end of the book, one for each practice test, which you may also download and print out when you register your book online.

Here are some guidelines on how to answer questions for each of the seven GED® question formats:

- **Multiple choice:** If you are writing directly in the book, circle the letter of the answer choice you select. If you're using an answer sheet, bubble in your choice.
- **Drag and drop:** Write in the correct answer or answers in the space provided.
- **Drop down:** Circle or check your selection from the drop-down menu.
- **Fill in the blank:** Write the correct answer in the box or blank provided.
- **Hot spot:** Mark an X or dot on the graphic as indicated.
- **Short answer and Extended Response:** If you have access to a computer, we recommend typing your response; doing so will give you the closest possible experience of taking the GED® test. Otherwise, you may write your response on a separate sheet of paper.

Before you begin, make sure to have the following items on hand:

- Pencils
- A notepad for scratch paper—and for writing your responses to short-answer and Extended Response questions, if you will not be using a computer
- A Texas Instruments T1-30XS calculator. You may also use the online calculator at web2.0calc.com.
- A clock or watch to help you keep track of time

Good luck!

Chapter 23
Practice Test 1

Reasoning Through Language Arts

Welcome!

Here is some information that you need to know before you start this test:

- You should not spend too much time on a question if you are not certain of the answer; answer it the best you can, and go on to the next question.
- If you are not certain of the answer to a question, you can mark your answer for review and come back to it later.
- This test has three sections.
- You have **35 minutes** to complete Section 1.
- When you finish Section 1, you may review those questions.
- You may not go back to Section 1 once you have finished your review.
- You have **45 minutes** to complete the Extended Response question in Section 2.
- After completing Section 2, you may take a 10-minute break.
- You have **60 minutes** to complete Section 3.
- When you finish Section 3, you may review those questions.

Turn the page to begin.

GO ON TO THE NEXT PAGE

Questions 1 through 8 refer to the following passage.

Excerpt from *A Popular Schoolgirl*
by Angela Brazil

1   The Saxons were spending their summer holidays at a farm near the seaside, and for the first time in four long years the whole family was reunited. Mr. Saxon, Egbert, and Athelstane had only just been demobilized, and had hardly yet settled down to civilian life. They had joined the rest of the party at Lynstones before returning to their native town of Grovebury. The six weeks by the sea seemed a kind of oasis between the anxious period of the war that was past and gone, and the new epoch that stretched ahead in the future. To Ingred they were halcyon days. To have her father and brothers safely back, and for the family to be together in the midst of such beautiful scenery, was sufficient for utter enjoyment. She did not wish her mind to venture outside the charmed circle of the holidays. Beyond, when she thought about it all, lay a nebulous prospect, in the center of which school loomed large.

2   On this particular hot August afternoon, Ingred welcomed an excursion in the sidecar. She had not felt inclined to walk down the white path under the blazing sun to the glaring beach, but it was another matter to spin along the high road till, as the fairy tales put it, her hair whistled in the wind. Egbert was anxious to set off, so Hereward took his place on the luggage-carrier, and, after some back-firing, the three started forth. It was a glorious run over moorland country, with glimpses of the sea on the one hand, and craggy tors on the other, and round them billowy masses of heather, broken here and there by runnels of peat-stained water. If Egbert exceeded the speed-limit, he certainly had the excuse of a clear road before him; there were no hedges to hide advancing cars, neither was there any possibility of whisking round a corner to find a hay-cart blocking the way. In the course of an hour they had covered a considerable number of miles, and found themselves whirling down the tremendous hill that led to the seaside town of Chatcombe.

3   Arrived in the main street they left the motorcycle at a garage, and strolled on to the promenade, joining the crowd of holiday-makers who were sauntering along in the heat, or sitting on the benches watching the children digging in the sand below. Much to Ingred's astonishment she was suddenly hailed by her name, and, turning, found herself greeted with enthusiasm by a schoolfellow.

4   "Ingred! What a surprise!"

5   "Avis! Who'd have thought of seeing you?"

6   "Are you staying here?"

GO ON TO THE NEXT PAGE

7   "No, only over for the afternoon."

8   "We've rooms at Beach View over there. Come along and have some tea with us, and your brothers too. Yes, indeed you must! Mother will be delighted to see you all. I shan't let you say no!"

9   Borne away by her hospitable friend, Ingred presently found herself sitting on a seat in the front garden of a tall boarding-house facing the sea, and while Egbert and Hereward discussed motor-cycling with Avis's father, the two girls enjoyed a confidential chat together.

10   "Only a few days now," sighed Avis, "then we've got to leave all this and go home. How long are you staying at Lynstones, Ingred?"

11   "A fortnight more, but don't talk of going home. I want the holidays to last forever!"

12   "So do I, but they won't. School begins on the twenty-first of September. It will be rather sport to go to the new buildings at last, won't it? By the by, now the war's over, and we've all got our own again, I suppose you're going back to Rotherwood, aren't you?"

13   "I suppose so, when it's ready."

14   "But surely the Red Cross cleared out ages ago, and the whole place has been done up? I saw the paperhangers there in June."

15   "Oh, yes!" Ingred's voice was a little strained.

16   "You'll be so glad to be living there again," continued Avis. "I always envied you that lovely house. You must have hated lending it as a hospital. I expect when you're back you'll be giving all sorts of delightful parties, won't you? At least that's what the girls at school were saying."

17   "It's rather early to make plans," temporized Ingred.

18   "Oh, of course! But Jess and Francie said you'd a gorgeous floor for dancing. I do think a fancy-dress dance is about the best fun on earth. The next time I get an invitation, I'm going as a Quaker maiden, in a gray dress and the duckiest little white cap. Don't you think it would suit me? With your dark hair you ought to be something Eastern. I can just imagine you acting hostess in a shimmery sort of white-and-gold costume. *Do* promise to wear white-and-gold!"

GO ON TO THE NEXT PAGE

19   "All right," laughed Ingred.

20   "It's so delightful that the war's over, and we can begin to have parties again, like we used to do. Beatrice Jackson told me she should never forget that Carnival dance she went to at Rotherwood five years ago, and all the lanterns and fairy lamps. Some of the other girls talk about it yet. Hullo, that's the gong! Come indoors, and we'll have tea."

1.   Which quotation from the story supports the idea that Ingred's relatives have had military experience?

    A.   "Mr. Saxon, Egbert, and Athelstane had only just been demobilized, and had hardly yet settled down to civilian life."

    B.   "The six weeks by the sea seemed a kind of oasis between the anxious period of the war that was past and gone, and the new epoch that stretched ahead in the future."

    C.   "By the by, now the war's over, and we've all got our own again, I suppose you're going back to Rotherwood, aren't you?"

    D.   "To have her father and brothers safely back, and for the family to be together in the midst of such beautiful scenery, was sufficient for utter enjoyment."

2.   Which definition best matches the use of the word "native" in paragraph 1?

    A.   natural
    B.   wild
    C.   original
    D.   inherited

3.   Read the following sentence from paragraph 2.

> It was a glorious run over moorland country, with glimpses of the sea on the one hand, and craggy tors on the other, and round them billowy masses of heather, broken here and there by runnels of peat-stained water.

The detailed description of the landscape enhances the story by

    A.   revealing the dangerous nature of the motorcycle trip.

    B.   further emphasizing Ingred's feelings about her summer home.

    C.   showing the contrast between the sea and the cliffs.

    D.   introducing Egbert as a secondary character.

GO ON TO THE NEXT PAGE

4. Read the sentences from paragraph 14.

> "But surely the Red Cross cleared out ages ago, and the whole place has been done up? I saw the paperhangers there in June."

What is the significance to Ingred of the "place" mentioned in the passage?

A. It is Ingred's family home which had been occupied by wartime personnel.
B. It is the town where Ingred lives, which has a Red Cross military hospital.
C. It is a popular ballroom that has been undergoing renovations in preparation for a dance.
D. It is one of the new buildings at Ingred's school, where she dreads returning.

5. In paragraph 15, which characteristic does the passage reveal about Ingred as she responds to Avis?

A. reluctance
B. agreement
C. exhaustion
D. enthusiasm

6. Drag and drop the events into the chart to show the order in which they occur in the excerpt. (For this practice test, write the event letters in the chart.)

Order of Events

```
┌─────────────────┐
│                 │
└─────────────────┘
        ↓
┌─────────────────┐
│                 │
└─────────────────┘
        ↓
┌─────────────────┐
│                 │
└─────────────────┘
        ↓
┌─────────────────┐
│                 │
└─────────────────┘
```

(a) Egbert drives Ingred to the beach.

(b) Ingred is invited to tea.

(c) Avis talks about a fancy-dress dance.

(d) The Saxons unite at Lynstones.

GO ON TO THE NEXT PAGE

7. Drag and drop each word that describes Ingred into the character web. (For this practice test, write each word in the web.)

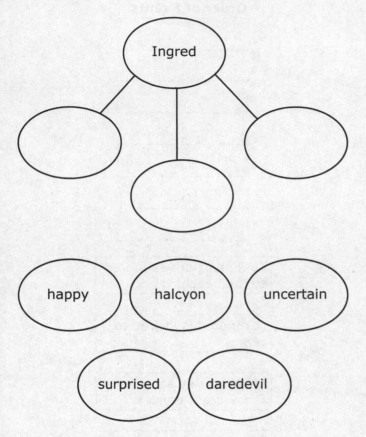

8. Based on the details in the story, what can readers predict about Avis?

    A.   She will be going to school with Ingred for the first time in September.

    B.   She will plan and host a dance after school starts.

    C.   She will travel to Lynstones when the afternoon is over.

    D.   She will return to her hometown before Ingred does.

GO ON TO THE NEXT PAGE

Questions 9 through 16 refer to the following article.

Devices and Additives to Improve Fuel Economy and Reduce Pollution—Do They Really Work?

By the U.S. Environmental Protection Agency

Watch Out!

1   Have you seen advertisements for products that "Double Your Fuel Economy," or "Clean-up Your Car's Tailpipe Exhaust"? Be careful about these products; don't be fooled by erroneous claims.

Fuel Additives

2   Some advertisements claim that certain fuel additives have been approved by the EPA. While the EPA requires fuel additives to be "registered," the EPA does not test additives for engine efficiency, emissions benefits, or safety as part of the registration. To register an additive, manufacturers report the chemical composition and technical, marketing, and health effects information. The EPA does NOT endorse or certify fuel additives; registration with the EPA does not imply anything about the claims made by the manufacturer.

Aftermarket Devices to Improve Fuel Economy or Reduce Emissions

3   If a device has significant benefits, the manufacturer may apply for EPA testing through the Voluntary Aftermarket Retrofit Device Evaluation Program. Very few manufacturers have applied for this program in the past 10 years. Most devices tested in earlier years had a neutral or negative effect on fuel economy and/or exhaust emissions. Without this report, the EPA has no information about the safety of the device or its impact on fuel efficiency or the environment.

   Popular Devices and Their Effects

   • Devices that turn water into fuel: The EPA has received no credible and complete data showing fuel economy benefits from devices that split water molecules into hydrogen and oxygen gas, which is then burned with your fuel. Some devices' installation instructions include adjustments that the EPA would consider tampering. Tampering with your car's emissions control system is punishable by significant fines.

   • Fuel line devices: Some devices heat, magnetize, ionize, irradiate, or add metals to the fuel lines. EPA testing of

GO ON TO THE NEXT PAGE

such devices has shown no substantive effect on fuel economy or exhaust emissions. Installation of devices that retard timing or adjust the air-fuel ratio of the vehicle may be considered tampering.

- Mixture enhancers: The EPA has received no credible and complete data showing fuel economy benefits from devices that claim to increase fuel efficiency by creating aerodynamic properties or turbulence that improves the air-fuel mix prior to combustion.

Aftermarket Alternative Fuel Conversions

4   Aftermarket alternative fuel conversions are sometimes alleged to improve fuel economy and reduce pollution. However, it is difficult to re-engineer a vehicle to operate properly on a different fuel, and especially difficult to ensure that the vehicle will meet emission standards. So, before choosing a vehicle conversion, consider these factors:

- It is not the fuel alone but the integration of engine, fueling, exhaust and evaporative emission control system designs that determines how clean a vehicle will be. Vehicle conversion systems must retain a similarly integrated design and functionality to retain low emissions.

- Gaseous and alcohol fuels are less energy dense than conventional fuels, so your fuel efficiency per gallon of fuel will decrease compared to gasoline or diesel.

- Be sure to check whether your vehicle's manufacturer will honor the warranty after conversion.

If the conversion manufacturer has not followed EPA guidelines, you may be violating the tampering prohibition and/or increasing the release of harmful exhaust and evaporative emissions.

5   Therefore, thoroughly research any aftermarket part or additive before purchasing, and remember the old adage, "If it sounds too good to be true, it probably is."

Improve Your Fuel Economy

By the U.S. Department of Energy

Fuel-Saving Habits

6   There are several things you can do obtain the best possible fuel economy and produce the lowest possible emissions.

- Avoid idling. Idling gets 0 miles per gallon and costs as much as $0.04 per minute.

GO ON TO THE NEXT PAGE

- Keep tires inflated to the recommended pressure, and use the recommended grade of motor oil, which can improve fuel economy by up to 5%.

- Drive more efficiently. Each 5 MPH you drive over 60 MPH can reduce your fuel economy by 7%.

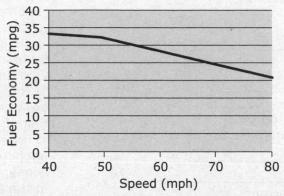

- Keep your car in shape. Fixing a car that is out of tune can improve your gas mileage by about 4%.

- Combine your trips. Many short trips taken from a cold start can use twice as much fuel as one multipurpose trip.

- Avoid carrying unneeded items. An extra 100 pounds can decrease fuel economy by 1%–2%.

Fuel-Saving Technology Highlight: Start-Stop Systems

7   An energy-saving feature is now available that can help you save fuel in stop-and-go traffic, at red lights, and in other situations where your car would normally waste fuel idling. Start-stop systems turn off the engine when a vehicle comes to a stop and automatically start it back up when the brake is released or when the accelerator or clutch is pressed. It usually takes half a second or less to restart. Until recently, these systems were mostly found on hybrid vehicles, but as of the 2014 model year, they are available on about one hundred conventional vehicle models. By turning off the engine when it's not needed, start-stop systems can improve fuel economy by around 4 to 5 percent on average. Unlike a hybrid system, which can add thousands of dollars to a vehicle's cost, a start-stop system typically adds only a few hundred dollars. A start-stop system doesn't require you to drive differently, but it may take some time for you to get used to the way the vehicle operates or feels. Most systems are robust and easy to use. If you spend significant drive time idling, a vehicle equipped with a start-stop system might just be right for you!

Sources: Adapted and abridged from *Devices and Additives to Improve Fuel Economy and Reduce Pollution—Do They Really Work?*, U.S. Environmental Protection Agency, 2012, and *Model Year 2014 Fuel Economy Guide*, U.S. Department of Energy, 2016.

GO ON TO THE NEXT PAGE

9. Drag and drop two statements that express the EPA's purposes for writing its article into the empty boxes. (For this practice test, write the statement letters in the boxes below.)

EPA's Purposes

| |
| |
| |

(a) To promote start-stop systems as a method to increase fuel economy

(b) To list the many harmful effects that emissions can have on the environment

(c) To caution consumers about deceptive advertising

(d) To give information about the role of the EPA in evaluating fuel additives and devices

(e) To list ways to increase fuel economy

10. Which conclusion is best supported by the Department of Energy article?

   A. Because of the advent of start-stop systems, other methods to improve fuel economy and reduce pollution are no longer necessary.
   B. Start-stop systems offer better fuel economy benefits than aftermarket alternative fuel conversions.
   C. Consumers seeking to save on fuel costs should adopt better driving habits.
   D. Consumers should research any devices marketed to improve fuel economy, to make sure they have been tested and endorsed by the EPA.

11. What was the author's purpose for including the sentence "Very few manufacturers have applied for this program in the past 10 years" (paragraph 3) in the Environmental Protection Agency article?

   A. to emphasize that the EPA program is competitive and takes a long time to complete
   B. to suggest that the claims made by many manufacturers cannot be verified
   C. to show that only a few devices are effective enough to pass EPA testing
   D. to urge more manufacturers to apply for the program, so that consumers will have better choices in the future

12. How does the chart extend the information in the article by the Department of Energy?

   A. by showing that fuel economy improves 5% with every 5 MPH a driver slows down
   B. by showing that reducing driving speed is more effective than vehicle maintenance
   C. by illustrating the effects of safer driving
   D. by highlighting the optimum speed for every driving condition

13. How are the two articles similar?

   A. Both articles list methods to help reduce emissions.
   B. Both articles mention devices that are reported to increase fuel economy.
   C. Both articles use statistics to support their assertions about fuel economy.
   D. Both articles describe a way to verify the claims made about a marketed device.

GO ON TO THE NEXT PAGE

14. Which idea about the effect of aftermarket fuel economy devices is included in the article by the EPA?

    A. Installation of the devices might be more costly than expected.
    B. The devices can improve economy 4 to 5 percent.
    C. The devices can be tested and registered by the EPA.
    D. There is no information about the safety of these devices.

15. How does the "Fuel-Saving Habits" section (paragraph 6) of the Department of Energy article relate to the "Fuel-Saving Technology Highlight" section (paragraph 7)?

    A. The "Fuel-Saving Habits" section lists changes drivers can make to save fuel, while the "Fuel-Saving Technology Highlight" contradicts this list by claiming there is no need to drive differently.
    B. The "Fuel-Saving Habits" list begins by cautioning against a bad driving habit; the "Fuel-Saving Technology Highlight" builds on this advice by recommending a device that automatically reduces this habit.
    C. The "Fuel-Saving Habits" section implies that there are several ways to reduce fuel consumption, while the "Fuel-Saving Technology Highlight" implies that one of these ways is more effective than the others.
    D. The "Fuel-Saving Habits" section focuses only on ways to operate a vehicle while the "Fuel-Saving Technology Highlight" focuses on devices that can be installed in vehicles.

16. In the Department of Energy article, what is the effect of the use of the word "robust" in paragraph 7?

    A. It reassures the reader that the start-stop system is sturdy and well-made.
    B. It informs the reader that the start-stop system will not be hard to drive.
    C. It cautions the reader that the start-stop system is fairly bulky and may increase the weight of the car.
    D. It advises the reader that the start-stop system is not expensive.

GO ON TO THE NEXT PAGE

17. The passage below is incomplete. For each "Select" option, choose the option that correctly completes the sentence. (For this practice test, circle your selection.)

Macy Redizas
5366 Ardenhall Lane
Laughing Pines, NJ

Dear Ms Redizas:

As a fellow member of the Laughing Pines community, I am sending this to you with great concern for our quality of life. Surely you enjoy living in such a quiet and peaceful

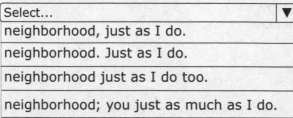

Select... ▼
neighborhood, just as I do.
neighborhood. Just as I do.
neighborhood just as I do too.
neighborhood; you just as much as I do.

As it happens, in order to ensure a "quiet and peaceful" community, one sometimes must take precautions.

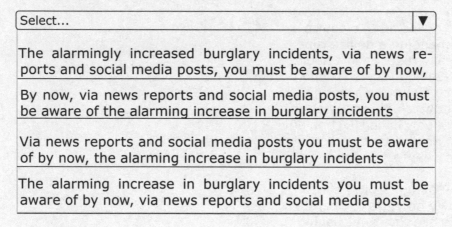

Select... ▼
The alarmingly increased burglary incidents, via news reports and social media posts, you must be aware of by now,
By now, via news reports and social media posts, you must be aware of the alarming increase in burglary incidents
Via news reports and social media posts you must be aware of by now, the alarming increase in burglary incidents
The alarming increase in burglary incidents you must be aware of by now, via news reports and social media posts

in our neighborhood during the past few years. While police may assert that this is an expected result of the continuing economic slump, that is no consolation to those whose homes have been targeted.

GO ON TO THE NEXT PAGE

We have determined not to meet this danger unprepared. The additional cost to double nighttime security patrols by Protect Pro will be approximately $25,000 to $30,000 annually. There are no additional funds in our budget available to cover such an unexpected, but necessary, expense. Therefore,

Select... ▼
concerning our community, as we all do
as we all were concerned about our community,
as we are all concerned about our community,
having concern about our community, as were we all,

I propose that every resident consider personally contributing to the security control budget. I am willing to spearhead this initiative with my own business. For every $2 raised in the community to cover the additional security costs, IntelliTech will donate $1 more.

Please make a donation today to support this much-needed cause for the common good. You can visit either one of our two stores and deposit your donation in the boxes provided near the front cash registers. Alternatively, if you can't make it to the store, please send a check or money order, payable to "ProtectPro Security Patrol" and mail

Select... ▼
them
it
that
one

to the address listed below.

With neighborly goodwill,

Gracie Wishton
IntelliTech Design
823 Askward St.
Laughing Pines, NJ

GO ON TO THE NEXT PAGE

Reasoning Through Language Arts, Section 2

Extended Response Answer Guidelines

Please use the guidelines below as you answer the Extended Response question on the Reasoning Through Language Arts test. Following these guidelines as closely as possible will ensure that you provide the best response.

1. **You will have up to (but no more than) 45 minutes to complete this task.** However, don't rush through your response. Be sure to read through the passage(s) and the prompt. Then think about the message you want to convey in your response. **Be sure to plan your response before you begin writing.** Draft your response and revise it as needed.

2. As you read, think carefully about the **argumentation** presented in the passage(s). "Argumentation" refers to the assumptions, claims, support, reasoning, and credibility on which a position is based. Pay close attention to **how the author(s) use these strategies to convey his or her (their) positions.**

3. When you write your essay, be sure to
   - **determine which position presented** in the passage(s) is **better supported** by evidence from the passage(s)
   - **explain why the position you chose is the better-supported one**
     - **remember, the better-supported position is not necessarily the position you agree with**
   - **defend your assertions with multiple pieces of evidence** from the passage(s)
   - **build your main points thoroughly**
   - **put your main points in logical order** and tie your details to your main points
   - **organize your response carefully** and consider your **audience, message, and purpose**
   - **use transitional words and phrases** to connect sentences, paragraphs, and ideas
   - **choose words carefully** to express your ideas clearly
   - **vary your sentence structure** to enhance the flow and clarity of your response
   - **reread and revise your response** to correct any errors in grammar, usage, or punctuation

GO ON TO THE NEXT PAGE

Reasoning Through Language Arts, Section 2

The following article presents both the successes and criticisms of emissions trading. Proponents and critics disagree about the practice's overall impact on emissions.

In your response, analyze both positions presented in the article to determine which one is best supported. Use relevant and specific evidence from the article to support your response.

Type your response, if a computer is available. Otherwise, write your response on paper. This task may require approximately 45 minutes to complete.

Emissions Trading

1   "Cap-and-trade" is a market-based policy tool for controlling large amounts of harmful emissions, such as sulfur dioxide (SO_2) and nitrogen oxides (NO_x), from a group of sources. A cap-and-trade program from the Environmental Protection Agency (EPA) first sets an aggressive "cap," or maximum limit, on emissions. Businesses and industries covered by the program then receive authorizations to produce emissions in the form of emissions permits, with the total amount of permits limited by the cap. Each business or industry can develop its own strategy to comply with the overall reduction requirement, including the sale or purchase (the "trade") of permits, installation of pollution controls, and implementation of efficiency measures, among other options. Businesses and industries must also completely and accurately measure and report all emissions in a timely manner to guarantee that the overall cap is met.

Indications that Cap-and-Trade Works

2   Under the right circumstances, cap-and-trade programs have proven extremely effective, providing certainty in allocations, rules, and penalties; substantial emission reductions; cost-effective, flexible compliance choices for regulated sources; complete accountability, unprecedented data quality, and public access to program data and decisions; and minimized administrative costs for industry and government. EPA's cap-and-trade programs have the force of federal and state standards behind them, including national health-based air quality standards. This ensures that local public health needs are met in conjunction with achievement of regional or national emission reductions.

3   Examples of successful cap-and-trade programs include the nationwide Acid Rain Program (ARP) and the regional NO_x Budget Trading Program in the Northeast. Additionally, EPA issued the Clean Air Interstate Rule (CAIR) on March 10, 2005, to build on the success of these programs and achieve significant additional emission reductions.

GO ON TO THE NEXT PAGE

4   The programs have had measurable results:

- Since the 1990s, SO_2 emissions have dropped 40%, and according to the Pacific Research Institute, acid rain levels have dropped 65% since 1976.

- NO_x reductions due to the NO_x Budget Trading Program have led to improvements in ozone and particulate matter, saving an estimated 580 to 1,800 lives in 2008.

- Ozone season NO_x emissions decreased by 43 percent between 2003 and 2008, even while energy demand remained essentially the same during the same period.

- The EPA estimates that by 2010, the overall costs of complying with the program for businesses and consumers will be $1 billion to $2 billion a year, only one fourth of what was originally predicted.

5   Therefore, cap-and-trade has been proven to be effective in protecting human health and the environment. Successful cap-and-trade programs reward innovation, efficiency, and early action and provide strict environmental accountability without inhibiting economic growth.

Criticisms of Cap-and-Trade

6   Critics have several objections to cap-and-trade. Skeptical environmentalists have argued that reductions in emissions occurred due to broad trends unconnected to the program. For example, there were many other regulations that impacted emissions at the time the ARP was implemented. Therefore, the effectiveness of the emissions trading element of the ARP in reducing emissions has been questioned, since the EPA also used other regulations in conjunction with the ARP during the time period the emissions reduction took place.

7   "Carbon leakage" occurs when there is an increase in carbon dioxide emissions in one country as a result of an emissions reduction by a second country with a strict climate policy. If one country has a strict emissions policy that raises production costs, then production may move offshore to the cheaper country with lower standards, and global emissions will not be reduced. Furthermore, cheap "offset" carbon credits are frequently available from the less developed countries, where they may be generated by local polluters at the expense of local communities.

8   Regulatory agencies run the risk of issuing too many emission credits, which can result in a very low price on emission permits. This reduces the incentive for companies to cut back their emissions, since permits are cheap. On the other hand, issuing too few permits can result in an excessively high permit

GO ON TO THE NEXT PAGE

price. Another issue with cap-and-trade programs has been overallocation, whereby the cap is high enough that sources of emissions do not need to reduce their emissions.

9   The price and supply of permits can result in perverse incentives. If, for example, polluting firms are given free emission permits, this may create a reason for them not to cut their emissions. A firm making large cuts in emissions could then be granted fewer emission permits in the future. This perverse incentive can be alleviated if permits are sold, rather than given, to polluters.

10   Some environmentalists argue that offsets for emission reductions are not a substitute for actual cuts in emissions, and that offsets are an excuse for business as usual, since expensive long-term changes will not be made if there is a cheaper source of carbon credits. Environmental protection will require more radical change than the modest changes driven by pollution trading schemes. These critics advocate solutions that leave most remaining fossil fuels underground.

> You may take a 10-minute break before proceeding to Section 3.

GO ON TO THE NEXT PAGE

Questions 18 through 25 refer to the following passage.

Excerpt from *Across America by Motorcycle* by C. K. Shepherd

1   I found a hotel that, from the outside, just suited my fancy. Plain, large and unpretentious, it described itself in an illuminated sign as the "National." I booked a room at three dollars and sallied forth to see the sights.

2   I was impressed with Washington. It is truly a city of beautiful streets and magnificent buildings. Undoubtedly it is the city de luxe of America. Being the capital, wealth is lavished upon it. No factories or barren wastes disfigure its graceful countenance. Every street or avenue glistens at night with a bewildering multitude of illuminated signs. This method of advertising is typically American. The first impression of a stranger visiting a large American city at night is that he is in a children's luminous palace. There are illuminations and decorations of every conceivable nature. Sometimes a single sign advertising perhaps some particular brand of chewing-gum or cigarette or motor-car has thousands and tens of thousands of lights wonderfully displayed in different colors and arranged in different series, one series flashing into view as another disappears, then a few seconds later giving place to another still more wonderful, and finally there comes a grand climax in which all the colors and all the series and all the figures blaze forth in an indescribable orgy of light.

3   When I found myself finally back in my hotel, I was to be the victim of still another disillusionment. No country anywhere could rival America for hotels, I had thought. But I had not then experienced the "National" at Washington. The room allotted to me was literally an outrage. It was of the very poorest that one would expect to find in an East End boarding-house in the Old Kent Road. It had one window, which faced on to an unimaginably dreary "area." The carpet was threadbare and colorless. The furniture, consisting of one bed, one dressing-table, one wardrobe and one chair was obviously suffering from advanced senile decay. There was a washbasin in one corner that boasted of two taps and a piece of wood to stop the hole up with. The door showed signs of having been minus a lock for many a long day. I was too tired, however, to bother about trivialities of detail, so putting my revolver under the blanket near me in case of possible eventualities, I laid me down in peace to sleep.

4   Nothing occurred, however, to disturb my peace of mind or body throughout the night. When I came to square up that morning I paid my respects and three dollars to the management.

GO ON TO THE NEXT PAGE

5   "See here, Mister Manager," I said in such a tone that everyone within hearing distance had the benefit of it as well, "I've done a bit of travelling here and there, but never in ANY city at ANY time have I struck ANY hotel that for sheer rottenness compares with THIS one!"

6   I have an idea at the back of my mind that that manager-man doesn't love Englishmen!

18.   Which definition best matches the use of the word "unpretentious" in paragraph 1?

    A.   lacking excessive ambition
    B.   free-spirited, easygoing
    C.   without excessive ornament
    D.   straightforward, direct

19.   How does the nighttime view of the city of Washington affect the narrator?

    A.   The narrator is overwhelmed by the city's confusing illumination.
    B.   The narrator wonders at the number of lights used in the signs.
    C.   The narrator rejoices in the splendor of the nighttime cityscape.
    D.   The narrator is disillusioned to find it typical of American cities.

20.   Why does the narrator describe an American city at night as a "children's luminous palace"?

    A.   to show that there is a magical innocence about cities at night
    B.   to illustrate the size and number of illuminated advertisements
    C.   to make a poetic statement about the regal nature of America
    D.   to downplay the importance of American cities

21.   What does the phrase "still another disillusionment" reveal about the narrator's journey?

    A.   Not all the narrator's assumptions about America have been correct.
    B.   The narrator was disappointed with the nighttime landscape of Washington.
    C.   The narrator had not had time to see the "National" at Washington.
    D.   The narrator was reluctant to return to the hotel.

22.   Why does the author use "senile" in paragraph 3?

    A.   to give the reader a sense of the advanced age of the hotel
    B.   to show that the chair in the room was old while the other furniture was new
    C.   to empathize with the elderly manager of the hotel
    D.   to emphasize that the condition of the furniture matches the rest of the room

GO ON TO THE NEXT PAGE

23. In this excerpt the narrator puts a revolver under the blanket before going to sleep. What characteristic does this action reveal about the narrator?

    A. fear about being in a rough neighborhood
    B. exhaustion so extreme that the narrator is too tired to put the revolver away properly
    C. a naturally violent temper that leads to being armed at all times
    D. preparation for questionable situations a traveler might encounter

24. Read this sentence.

    > "I have an idea at the back of my mind that that manager-man doesn't love Englishmen!"

    Why does the author conclude the excerpt with this sentence?

    A. to give a humorous slant to the scene by using an understatement
    B. to offer a guess about the manager's personal preferences
    C. to show the narrator's suspicions about the manager that will be addressed in the next segment
    D. to express regret over having complained to the manager

25. What can the reader infer about the narrator?

    A. The narrator's overall impression of Washington is negative.
    B. The narrator is not native to the United States.
    C. Washington is the first stop on the narrator's trip.
    D. The narrator is loud-mouthed and argumentative.

GO ON TO THE NEXT PAGE

Questions 26 through 33 refer to the following article.

Excerpt from "State Lotteries"
By A. A. Milne

1   The popular argument against the State Lottery is an assertion that it will encourage the gambling spirit. The popular argument in favor of the State Lottery is an assertion that it is hypocritical to say that it will encourage the gambling spirit, because the gambling spirit is already amongst us. Having listened to a good deal of this sort of argument on both sides, I thought it would be well to look up the word "gamble" in my dictionary, and I can now tell you all about it.

2   To gamble, says my dictionary, is "to play for money in games of skill or chance." Now, to me this definition is particularly interesting, because it justifies all that I have been thinking about the gambling spirit in connection with Premium Bonds. I am against Premium Bonds, but not for the popular reason. I am against them because there is so very little of the gamble about them. And now that I have looked up "gamble" in the dictionary, I see that I was right. The "chance" element in a state lottery is obvious enough, but the "game" element is entirely absent.

3   We play for money in games of skill or chance. But it isn't only of the money we are thinking. We get pleasure out of the game. If you are only throwing dice, you are engaged in a personal struggle with another man, and you are directing the struggle to this extent, that you can call the value of the stakes, and decide whether to go on or to stop. And is there any man who, having made a fortune at Monte Carlo, will admit that he owes it entirely to chance? Will he not rather attribute it to his wonderful system, or if not to that, at any rate to his wonderful nerve, his perseverance, or his recklessness?

4   This, then, is the gambling spirit. It has its dangers, certainly, but it is not entirely an evil spirit. It is possible that the State should not encourage it, but it is not called upon to exorcise it. I am not sure that I should favor a State gamble, but my arguments against it would be much the same as my arguments against State cricket or the solemn official endowment of any other jolly game. However, I need not trouble you with those arguments now, for nothing so harmless as a State gamble has ever been suggested. Instead, we have from time to time a State lottery offered to us, and that is a very different proposition.

GO ON TO THE NEXT PAGE

5   For in a State lottery—with daily prizes of £50,000—the game (or gambling) element does not exist. Buy your £100 bond, as a thousand placards will urge you to do, and you simply take part in a cold-blooded attempt to acquire money without working for it. You can take no personal interest whatever in the manner of acquiring it. Somebody turns a handle, and perhaps your number comes out. More probably it doesn't. If it doesn't, you can call yourself a fool for having thrown away your savings; if it does—well, you have got the money.

6   Moreover, the State would be giving its official approval to the unearned fortune. In these days, when the worker is asking for a week of so many less hours and so many more shillings, the State would answer: "I can show you a better way than that. What do you say to no work at all, and £20 a week for it?" At a time when the one cry is "Production!" the State adds (behind its hand), "Buy a Premium Bond, and let the other man produce for you." After all these years in which we have been slowly progressing towards the idea of a more equitable distribution of wealth, the Government would show us the really equitable way; it would collect the savings of the many, and re-distribute them among the few. Instead of a million ten-pound citizens, we should have a thousand ten-thousand-pounders and 999,000 with nothing. That would be the official way of making the country happy and contented. But, in fact, our social and political controversies are not kept alive by such arguments as these, nor by the answers which can legitimately be made to such arguments. The case of the average man in favor of State lotteries is, quite simply, that he does not like Dr. Clifford. The case of the average man against State lotteries is equally simple; he cannot bear to be on the same side as Mr. Bottomley.

Source: Abridged and adapted from "State Lotteries," *If I May,* A. A. Milne, London: Methuen & Co Ltd, 1920

GO ON TO THE NEXT PAGE

26. Drag and drop two statements that express Milne's purposes for writing the essay into the empty boxes. (For this practice test, write the statement letters in the boxes below.)

Milne's Purpose

(a) To propose a way to achieve a more equitable distribution of wealth

(b) To persuade the reader that playing a State Lottery isn't really gambling

(c) To analyze the dual character-istics of the definition of the word "gamble"

(d) To argue that a State Lottery should be adopted

(e) To emphasize the dangers of gambling

27. Why does the author use the phrase "behind its hand" (paragraph 6)?

    A. to show that the idea of "no work at all" is shameful and should be kept discreet
    B. to illustrate that the messages from the State are contradictory
    C. to imply that the State functions like a human body, with hands to do its work
    D. to show that gambling is illegal and conducted in secret

28. In paragraph 3, what role does the image of the gambler in Monte Carlo play in the passage?

    A. It establishes Monte Carlo as a place where fortunes are made.
    B. It is an example of the personal struggle with chance discussed in the previous sentence.
    C. It underscores the recklessness of gambling.
    D. It illustrates the aspects of gambling discussed in the previous paragraph.

29. Read this sentence from paragraph 6.

    > "The case of the average man in favor of State lotteries is, quite simply, that he does not like Dr. Clifford."

    What can the reader infer from this sentence?

    A. Dr. Clifford is opposed to State lotteries.
    B. Dr. Clifford is a supporter of State lotteries.
    C. The average man is simple and unintelligent compared to Dr. Clifford.
    D. The average man would not favor anything represented by Dr. Clifford.

GO ON TO THE NEXT PAGE

30. Which detail in Milne's essay supports the claim that people get pleasure out of games of skill and chance?

    A. "Somebody turns a handle, and perhaps your number comes out." (paragraph 5)
    B. "That would be the official way of making the country happy and contented." (paragraph 6)
    C. "...it justifies all that I have been thinking about the gambling spirit..." (paragraph 2)
    D. "Will he not rather attribute it to his wonderful system, or if not to that, at any rate to his wonderful nerve..." (paragraph 3)

31. What is the impact of the use of the term "cold-blooded" in paragraph 5?

    A. It prejudices the reader to view those who play the lottery as ruthless.
    B. It offers a contrast to the warm, engaged description of gambling in paragraph 3.
    C. It underscores the evil nature of gambling discussed in paragraph 4.
    D. It sets a tone for the scenario that leaves "999,000 with nothing" in paragraph 6.

32. In paragraph 3, the author addresses the reader with direct questions. How do the questions contribute to the development of the author's essay?

    A. They raise issues that will be answered in the following paragraphs.
    B. They illustrate that the nature of gambling is always in question and can never be conclusively defined.
    C. They inspire the reader to consider the personal characteristics of a gambler.
    D. They influence the reader to agree with the author's point that "game" is essential to gambling.

33. What can the reader infer about the author's opinions regarding Premium Bonds?

    A. The author would not vote in favor of them.
    B. The author views them as an appropriate method for redistributing public funds.
    C. The author feels that they are a prime example of gambling as defined in his dictionary.
    D. The author thinks they encourage hypocrisy.

GO ON TO THE NEXT PAGE

Questions 34 through 41 refer to the following article.

Career Myths That Stop People Cold
by Olivia Crosby

1   Some career myths are less about occupations than about the working world in general. Myths like these can derail a career search and sap motivation. Here are five common myths, and realities, about careers.

2   **Myth**: There is one perfect job for me.

3   **Reality**: There are many occupations—and many jobs—that you would enjoy. Focusing on finding a single, perfect career is not only intimidating, it's limiting. If you're like most people, you will have several jobs and careers in your life, and each will have positive and negative aspects to it. Furthermore, your job preferences are apt to change over time as you gain experience, skill, and self-knowledge. Keeping your options open is a position of strength, not weakness.

4   **Myth**: I will use all of my talents and abilities in this job.

5   **Reality**: No one job uses all of your talents. And trying to find one that does will derail your job search. Learning a variety of tasks helps you to sharpen abilities that might not be needed in one job but could be invaluable in another. Especially at the start of your career, you should expect to spend time acquiring experience and skills. This is one reality about careers that, career counselors say, many new graduates fail to grasp. Counselors remind jobseekers to be patient. New workers should expect to start in entry-level positions and be willing to do routine tasks as they gain experience.

6   **Myth**: My job has to match my college major or vocational training.

7   **Reality**: You need not restrict your job search to careers related to your degree or training. Most jobs do not specify which college major is needed, even if they require that workers have a college degree. Many computer specialist positions, for example, are filled by workers whose degree is in a subject unrelated to computers. Vocational training is often more closely related to specific occupations. But even this kind of training can open the door to a wider array of jobs than people think. Consider that electrical technicians are now repairing fuel cells, for example, or that veterinary technicians become pharmaceutical sales workers. Often, technical skills are applicable to many settings—and most workers learn the specifics of an occupation on the job.

GO ON TO THE NEXT PAGE

8   **Myth**: No one will hire me because I lack experience, have low grades, have gaps in my work history, etc.

9   **Reality**: People overcome all kinds of challenges to find satisfying work. Experts say that how you handle adversity is a good indicator of your ability to persevere. Need experience? Get it! Volunteer, work in a related occupation, or focus on school projects that are relevant to your desired career. Low grades are the problem? Highlight other parts of your resume, and remember that grades usually matter only for that first job after graduation. Gaps in your work history? Overcome them with a well-designed resume that focuses on skills rather than chronology, and then get a little interviewing practice. For most entry-level jobs, employers are looking for general attributes such as communication skills, interpersonal abilities, and enthusiasm.

10   **Myth**: It's too late to change my career.

11   **Reality:** It's never too late to change careers. Workers who change careers come from many backgrounds, age groups, and situations. There's the doctor who decided she'd rather be a chef, the retiree who enrolled in college to become an accountant, the construction worker who wanted a steadier income without moving to a warmer climate. For each of these workers, the desire for job satisfaction outweighed the desire for status quo. To make the change easier, look at your past work and education to see what skills relate to the job you want. Most jobs' entry requirements are more flexible than people think. Gain needed skills with volunteer work, internships, or a class, and don't be afraid to start at the bottom to get the career you want. If you are out of school and want expert advice, consider a local One-Stop Career Center or the counseling center at a nearby school.

Source: U.S. Department of Labor, Bureau of Labor Statistics

GO ON TO THE NEXT PAGE

34. The author's tone toward the reader is one of

    A. condescension.
    B. reassurance.
    C. intimidation.
    D. satisfaction.

35. What is the author's primary purpose in writing this article?

    A. to encourage readers to develop new abilities and seek new experiences
    B. to caution workers against changing jobs by exposing the myths about career change
    C. to showcase the types of jobs that will accept workers with low grades and work history gaps.
    D. to encourage job seekers to use all of their prior experience and training

36. Read this sentence from paragraph 7:

    > Consider that electrical technicians are now repairing fuel cells, for example, or that veterinary technicians become pharmaceutical sales workers.

    The sentence enhances the article by

    A. giving examples of the types of careers readers should pursue.
    B. presenting a scenario to illustrate the fact that readers should apply for jobs that match their college majors.
    C. emphasizing the value and versatility of technical skills in the job market.
    D. offering an example to show that skills acquired in one kind of training can be transferred to another field.

37. In paragraph 9, the author asks and answers a series of questions. How does the question-and-answer structure help the author's point?

    A. It shows that gaps in work history are no worse than low grades.
    B. It supports the point in the next paragraph that it's never too late to change careers.
    C. It shows that the concerns raised in the previous paragraph can be addressed.
    D. It raises concerns that readers may not have considered.

38. Which definition best matches the use of the word "overcome" in paragraph 9?

    A. overpower
    B. shock
    C. outlive
    D. surmount

39. Read this sentence from paragraph 11:

    > For each of these workers, the desire for job satisfaction outweighed the desire for status quo.

    What can be inferred about the "workers" in this sentence?

    A. They had all undergone a significant change in work.
    B. They were concerned with staying in a familiar field.
    C. They liked the status that came from professional jobs.
    D. They returned to school in order to widen their career options.

GO ON TO THE NEXT PAGE

40. The author claims that prospective employees can take steps to better their odds of employment. Drag two actions that the author uses to support this claim into the boxes below. (For this practice test, write the action letters in the boxes.)

(a) Work for good grades in college to make up for lack of experience

(b) Donate your time to charitable organizations

(c) Apply for jobs within your college major to increase your odds of landing a job

(d) Carefully explain gaps in work history

(e) Anticipate questions that might arise when applying for a job

41. What can the reader infer about the article's intended audience?

A. The article is written specifically for first-time job seekers.
B. The article is written to students currently in college.
C. The article is written to help those who are uncertain about finding a job.
D. The article is written to help job seekers address gaps in their work history.

GO ON TO THE NEXT PAGE

Questions 42 through 49 refer to the following article.

Susan B. Anthony: Rebel, Crusader, Humanitarian
by Alma Lutz

1   "If Sally Ann knows more about weaving than Elijah," reasoned eleven-year-old Susan with her father, "then why don't you make her overseer?"

2   "It would never do," replied Daniel Anthony as a matter of course. "It would never do to have a woman overseer in the mill."

3   This answer did not satisfy Susan and she often thought about it. To enter the mill, to stand quietly and look about, was the best kind of entertainment, for she was fascinated by the whir of the looms, by the nimble fingers of the weavers, and by the general air of efficiency. Admiringly she watched Sally Ann Hyatt, the tall capable weaver from Vermont. When the yarn on the beam was tangled or there was something wrong with the machinery, Elijah, the overseer, always called out to Sally Ann, "I'll tend your loom, if you'll look after this." Sally Ann never failed to locate the trouble or to untangle the yarn. Yet she was never made overseer, and this continued to puzzle Susan.

4   The manufacture of cotton was a new industry, developing with great promise in the United States, when Susan B. Anthony was born on February 15, 1820, in the wide valley at the foot of Mt. Greylock, near Adams, Massachusetts. Enterprising young men like her father, Daniel Anthony, saw a potential cotton mill by the side of every rushing brook, and young women, eager to earn the first money they could call their own, were leaving the farms, for a few months at least, to work in the mills. Cotton cloth was the new sensation and the demand for it was steadily growing. Brides were proud to display a few cotton sheets instead of commonplace homespun linen.

5   When Susan was two years old, her father built a cotton factory of twenty-six looms beside the brook which ran through Grandfather Read's meadow, hauling the cotton forty miles by wagon from Troy, New York. The millworkers, most of them young girls from Vermont, boarded, as was the custom, in the home of the millowner; Susan's mother, Lucy Read Anthony, although she had three small daughters to care for, Guelma, Susan, and Hannah, boarded eleven of the millworkers with only the help of a thirteen-year-old girl who worked for her after school hours. Lucy Anthony cooked their meals on the hearth of

GO ON TO THE NEXT PAGE

the big kitchen fireplace, and in the large brick oven beside it baked crisp brown loaves of bread. In addition, washing, ironing, mending, and spinning filled her days. But she was capable and strong and was doing only what all women in this new country were expected to do. She taught her young daughters to help her, and Susan, even before she was six, was very useful; by the time she was ten she could cook a good meal and pack a dinner pail.

42. How does being told "it would never do to have a woman overseer in the mill" affect young Susan?

    A.   She sees the truth of the words after she watches the workers in the mill.

    B.   She questions her father's judgment.

    C.   She learns that what she is told does not always match her observations.

    D.   She decides to go to work in the mill to rebel against her father.

43. How do the details about Susan's home life in paragraph 5 enhance the narrative?

    A.   They give a portrait of the kinds of work customary for women at the time.

    B.   They reveal how overworked Susan's mother was because her father was away building the cotton factory.

    C.   They show that working at home was much harder than working in the mill.

    D.   They demonstrate how difficult it was to board the millworkers.

44. Which quotation from the passage supports the idea that Susan is learning skills that enhance independence?

    A.   "young women, eager to earn the first money they could call their own, were leaving the farms"

    B.   "Sally Ann never failed to locate the trouble or to untangle the yarn."

    C.   "she was fascinated by the whir of the looms, by the nimble fingers of the weavers, and by the general air of efficiency."

    D.   "by the time she was ten she could cook a good meal and pack a dinner pail."

45. In this excerpt the overseer speaks to Sally Ann when there is trouble with the machinery. What does this action reveal about Sally Ann?

    A.   She is a more efficient weaver than the other women who work at the factory, which suggests that she is the best person to be overseer.

    B.   Her mechanical aptitude is recognized by the other workers, which suggests that she would be a competent overseer.

    C.   She has a habit of getting in trouble for tangling the yarn in her machinery, which confirms Susan's father's statement that she should not be overseer.

    D.   She enjoys being asked for help, which shows she hopes to be made overseer someday.

GO ON TO THE NEXT PAGE

46. Based on the story, what was Susan's father's attitude about the cotton mills?

   A. The mills were an acceptable place for women to work.
   B. The new cotton industry only had places for enterprising young men.
   C. Cotton cloth made in the mills would be sure to replace homespun entirely, creating new jobs for both women and men.
   D. He thought of the mills as places that proved that men were generally more efficient than women.

47. Drag and drop into the character web each word that describes Susan as she watches the mill workers. (For this practice test, write the words in the web.)

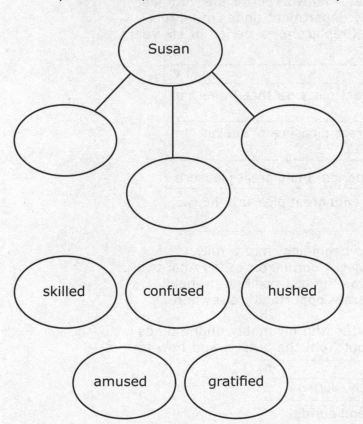

48. What can readers infer about the mill that Susan's father built?

   A. It was located in Troy, New York, to take advantage of industrial development.
   B. It was staffed by workers who boarded at the mill.
   C. Construction on the mill was begun in 1820 in a valley.
   D. It had to be located near a source of running water.

49. Based on the details in the story, what can readers tell about the women workers in Susan's father's mill?

   A. Most of the weavers were qualified to become overseers.
   B. For some of them, the job at the mill was their first paying job.
   C. They lived on farms and traveled to their jobs in the mill.
   D. They helped Susan's mother with the housework.

GO ON TO THE NEXT PAGE

50. The passage below is incomplete. For each "Select" option, choose the option that correctly completes the sentence. (For this practice test, circle your selection.)

August 25, 2010

Ms. Roberta Alvarez
Manager, Marketing Services
Zetacorp, Inc.
554 Alacor Drive
Stamford, CT 06907

Dear Ms. Alvarez:

In response to your request, I am writing to provide a letter of recommendation for Jorge Garcez who worked for me until last year. Jorge Garcez worked in my department under my direct supervision at Readywise ImageGraphics for a period of six years ending in June 2009.

Select... ▼
During that period, it is with great pleasure that I see him developing
During that period, I had the great pleasure of seeing him develop
Seeing him develop during that period, I had great pleasure
As I saw him during that period, with great pleasure, he was developing

from a paste-up assistant at the beginning, into a fully functioning Graphics Design Project Coordinator in his final two years with the company. That was the last position he held before moving on to a better career opportunity elsewhere.

Jorge is a hard-working self-starter who invariably understands exactly what a project is all about from the outset, and how to get it done

Select... ▼
quickly and effectively, during
quickly, effectively, and during.
quickly and effectively. During
quick and effectively. During

his two years as Graphics Design Project Coordinator, he met every deadline, often ahead of schedule. His projects were

GO ON TO THE NEXT PAGE

rendered with the utmost quality, requiring very little revision after the first presentation. He was very budget-minded, finding creative ways to fund his team's needs within the allocated funds. Resourceful, creative, and solution-oriented, Mr. Garcez often found innovative and refreshing approaches to the challenges involved in his everyday tasks. He is flexible as a team

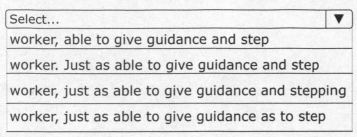

Select... ▼
worker, able to give guidance and step
worker. Just as able to give guidance and step
worker, just as able to give guidance and stepping
worker, just as able to give guidance as to step

back and take direction when another is leading the group.

Jorge's written and communication skills are excellent, and he was well liked by everyone on our staff. He served as a mediator on our interdepartmental committee to ensure smooth cooperation from all project levels, helping department heads communicate their needs to one another. On the interpersonal side, Mr. Garcez gets along well with all colleagues, customers, and even competitors!

When he told us, regretfully, that he was leaving to fill a new position with a larger company, we were saddened to see him leave. Still, we wished him success and happiness in his new position and endeavors.

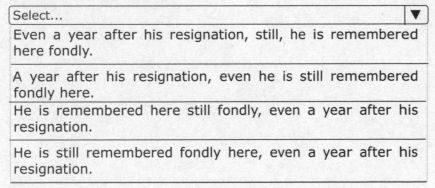

Select... ▼
Even a year after his resignation, still, he is remembered here fondly.
A year after his resignation, even he is still remembered fondly here.
He is remembered here still fondly, even a year after his resignation.
He is still remembered fondly here, even a year after his resignation.

Therefore, I can recommend Jorge Garcez most heartily to fill any senior graphic design position you might have. I hope these details have illuminated Mr. Garcez's capabilities. If I can provide any further information, please feel free to call me at (417) 555-4495.

Sincerely,

Rita Cassat
Senior Vice President
Readywise ImageGraphics

END OF TEST

THIS PAGE INTENTIONALLY LEFT BLANK.

Mathematical Reasoning

Welcome!

Here is some information that you need to know before you start this test:

- You should not spend too much time on a question if you are not certain of the answer; answer it the best you can, and go on to the next question.
- If you are not certain of the answer to a question, you can mark your answer for review and come back to it later.
- You have **115 minutes** to complete this test.
- This test has two parts.
- When you finish Part 1, you may review those questions.
- You may not go back to Part 1 once you have finished your review.
- You may not use a calculator in Part 1. You may use a calculator in Part 2.

Turn the page to begin.

GO ON TO THE NEXT PAGE

Mathematics Formula Sheet

Area of a:

square	$A = s^2$
rectangle	$A = lw$
parallelogram	$A = bh$
triangle	$A = \dfrac{1}{2}bh$
trapezoid	$A = \dfrac{1}{2}h(b_1 + b_2)$
circle	$A = \pi r^2$

Perimeter of a:

square	$P = 4s$
rectangle	$P = 2l + 2w$
triangle	$P = s_1 + s_2 + s_3$
Circumference of a circle	$C = 2\pi r$ OR $C = \pi d$; $\pi \approx 3.14$

Surface Area and Volume of a:

rectangular prism	$SA = 2lw + 2lh + 2wh$	$V = lwh$
right prism	$SA = ph + 2B$	$V = Bh$
cylinder	$SA = 2\pi rh + 2\pi r^2$	$V = \pi r^2 h$
pyramid	$SA = \dfrac{1}{2}ps + B$	$V = \dfrac{1}{3}Bh$
cone	$SA = \pi rs + \pi r^2$	$V = \dfrac{1}{3}\pi r^2 h$
sphere	$SA = 4\pi r^2$	$V = \dfrac{4}{3}\pi r^3$

$(p = \text{perimeter of base } B; \pi \approx 3.14)$

Data

mean	mean is equal to the total of the values of a data set, divided by the number of elements in the data set
median	median is the middle value in an odd number of ordered values of a data set, or the mean of the two middle values in an even number of ordered values in a data set

Algebra

slope of a line	$m = \dfrac{y_2 - y_1}{x_2 - x_1}$
slope-intercept form of the equation of a line	$y = mx + b$
point-slope form of the equation of a line	$y - y_1 = m(x - x_1)$
standard form of a quadratic equation	$y = ax^2 + bx + c$
quadratic formula	$x = \dfrac{-b \pm \sqrt{b^2 - 4ac}}{2a}$
Pythagorean Theorem	$a^2 + b^2 = c^2$
simple interest	$I = prt$ $(I = \text{interest}, p = \text{principal}, r = \text{rate}, t = \text{time})$
distance formula	$d = rt$
total cost	total cost = (number of units) × (price per unit)

GO ON TO THE NEXT PAGE

Mathematical Reasoning, Part 1
You may NOT use a calculator in Part 1.

1. If $z = -3$, what is $\dfrac{z^3 + 2z + 3}{z^2 + 1}$?

   A. 3
   B. −1.8
   C. −3.6
   D. −3

2. Each of 4 CDs can contain up to 3.6 hours of recorded music. If each of the CDs is at least half full, which of the following expressions represents the total amount of music, x, contained on all 4 CDs?

   A. $0 < x < 7.2$
   B. $0 < x < 14.4$
   C. $7.2 < x < 14.4$
   D. $1.8 < x < 3.6$

3. Traveling at an average speed of 58 miles per hour, Terence drives 145 miles. Three hours later, Terence makes the return trip at the same speed. How much total time elapses between Terence's original departure and final return?

   A. 2.5
   B. 5
   C. 5.5
   D. 8

4. The average temperature, in degrees Fahrenheit, in the month of July in Clark City is 4 times the average temperature in the month of February. If the average temperature in July was 82 degrees, which of the following equations could be used to determine the average temperature in February (t)?

   A. $t + 4 = \dfrac{82}{4}$

   B. $4t = 82$

   C. $\dfrac{t}{4} = 21$

   D. $4t = 21$

5. If 20% of a shipment of 50,000 tomatoes is crushed during transport and then 5% of the remaining tomatoes are lost to insects, then how many tomatoes remain?

   ☐

GO ON TO THE NEXT PAGE

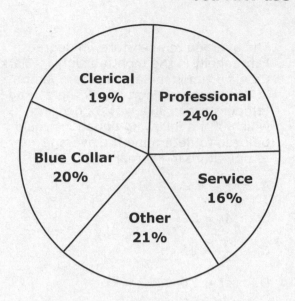

6. The figure above shows the worker distribution in a given country. If the total population of workers is 2.3 million, how many workers are employed neither in clerical nor in professional occupations?

A.   1,311,000
B.   1,048,800
C.   990,000
D.   552,000

7. Miriam and Betty buy a total of 42 stamps. Miriam bought 6 more stamps than Betty did. How many stamps did Miriam buy?

A.   18
B.   24
C.   30
D.   36

Questions 8 and 9 refer to the following number line.

$$-1\ 0\ 1$$

P Q   R S T

8. Select the point on the number line that corresponds to the value P + S. (For this practice test, mark the point with an X.)

9. Select the point on the number line that corresponds to |Q − R| − T. (For this practice test, mark the point with an X.)

10. Since its formation 10,000 years ago, Niagara Falls has eroded upstream a distance of 9.8 miles. Which of the following equations indicates the distance D that Niagara Falls, continuing at this rate will erode in the next 22,000 years?

A. $\dfrac{9.8}{10,000} = \dfrac{D}{22,000}$

B. $\dfrac{9.8}{10,000} = \dfrac{D}{12,000}$

C. $D = 9.8 + \dfrac{22,000}{10,000}$

D. $D = 9.8 \times \dfrac{10,000}{22,000}$

GO ON TO THE NEXT PAGE

11. A science class compares the relative strength of two telescopic lenses. Lens X produces a magnification of 3×10^5, and Lens Y produces a magnification of 6×10^2.

Which of the following statements accurately describes the relationship between the two lenses?

A. Lens X produces a magnification 200% that of lens Y.
B. Lens X is 200 times as strong as Lens Y.
C. Lens X produces a magnification 500% that of lens Y.
D. Lens X is 500 times as strong as Lens Y.

12. If Mark can mow $\frac{2}{3}$ of a lawn in 1 hour, how many hours does it take him to mow the entire lawn?

A. $\frac{2}{3}$
B. $1\frac{1}{3}$
C. $1\frac{1}{2}$
D. 2

Question 13 refers to the diagram below.

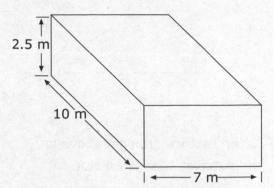

13. The dimensions of a box are shown in the diagram above. A designer wishes to paint the four larger sides of the box, leaving the smallest two sides unpainted. What will be the total surface area in square meters of the four sides the designer paints?

A. 175
B. 190
C. 225
D. 280

14. Evaluate $3x(x - 2a)^{-x}$, if $x = -2$ and $a = 0.5$.

GO ON TO THE NEXT PAGE

Question 15 is based on the following figure.

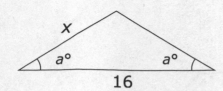

15. Given that the triangle above is an isosceles triangle, if side

    $x =$ | Select... ▼ |, then the perimeter
    | 9 |
    | 10 |
    | 13 |
    | 16 |

    of the triangle will be | Select... ▼ |.
    | 27 |
    | 31 |
    | 34 |
    | 41 |

16. Mrs. Carter decides to buy a computer system for her son. She spends $1,500 for a computer and LCD monitor, $650 for a color laser printer, and $250 for an external hard drive. What would be the total cost of the system if the cost of the computer and monitor cost 10% more?

    | |

17. Universal Products has 78 employees. If twice as many women work for Universal as men, how many women work for Universal?

    A. 52
    B. 42
    C. 26
    D. 16

18. In a study of bird migration, a researcher recorded, on a certain day a total of 262 birds, consisting of 65 geese, 84 ducks, and 113 robins in the skies. Show below a possible equation for calculating the probability that a random bird chosen from among these is not a duck. (For this practice test, write the numbers in the boxes below.)

    $$\frac{\boxed{} + \boxed{}}{\boxed{}}$$

    | 65 |

    | 84 |

    | 113 |

    | 262 |

19. Which of the following expressions is equivalent to $2a(a - 3b^2) + a^2$?

    A. $2a^2 - 6ab^2$
    B. $3a^2 - 3b^2$
    C. $2a(a - 3b^2)$
    D. $3a(a - 2b^2)$

GO ON TO THE NEXT PAGE

Questions 20 and 21 are based on the following graph.

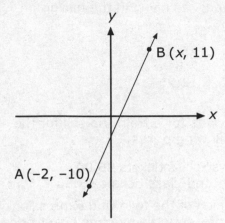

20. If the slope of the line shown is 3, then what is the x-coordinate of point B?

    A.   −5
    B.   −3
    C.   3
    D.   5

21. Given that the slope of the line is 3, what is the equation of the line?

    A. $y = 3x - 3$
    B. $y = 3x - 4$
    C. $y = 3x - 5$
    D. $y = 3x - 10$

22. Working for 4 hours a day, a typist earns $65.40 a day after taxes. At the same rate of pay, what would he earn per day if he worked for 7 hours a day? (Let N represent after-tax earnings.)

    A. $N = \frac{4}{7}(65.40)$

    B. $N = \frac{7}{4}(65.40)$

    C. $N = 4(65.40)$

    D. $N = 7(65.40)$

GO ON TO THE NEXT PAGE

Questions 23 and 24 refer to the following graph.

Movie Survey, by %

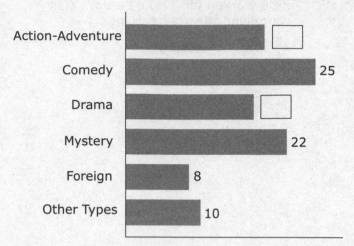

- Action-Adventure: [ ]
- Comedy: 25
- Drama: [ ]
- Mystery: 22
- Foreign: 8
- Other Types: 10

23. The graph above shows the results of a survey that asked moviegoers to choose their favorite type of movie. If the chart represents all the people surveyed and if each person chose only one type of movie, then choose two numbers below that could properly complete the graph, showing values for Action-Adventure and for Drama. (For this practice test, write the numbers in the boxes.)

Action-Adventure	Drama

10	15	17
18	19	25

24. Which of the following correctly represents the ratio of Comedy to Other Types, as given in the bar graph?

- A. 5:2
- B. 25:12
- C. 2:5
- D. 12:25

25. Tickets for a train trip sell for the following prices:

First-class tickets $6.00
Second-class tickets $3.50

Which of the following expressions represents the average ticket price for all tickets sold if the station sells 110 first-class and 172 second-class tickets?

A. $\dfrac{110 + 172}{2}$

B. $\dfrac{110(6.00) + 172(3.50)}{2}$

C. $\dfrac{(110 + 172) \times 4.75}{110 + 172}$

D. $\dfrac{110(6.00) + 172(3.50)}{110 + 172}$

26. If $\dfrac{(4x + 3)^2}{2} = 72$ and $x > 0$, then $x =$

[ ]

GO ON TO THE NEXT PAGE

Mathematical Reasoning, Part 2

<u>Question 27</u> refers to the following diagram.

7 miles	8 miles	2 miles	6 miles	12 miles

A   B   C   D   E   F

27. The towns in Maple County are located along a 35-mile section of an interstate at the points A, B, C, D, E, and F as shown in the diagram above. The Maple County Post Office is located midway between points A and E. The location of the post office is between which of the following two points?

   A.   D and E
   B.   C and D
   C.   B and C
   D.   A and B

28. The total bill for four friends eating at a restaurant (including tax) is $36.00. The friends wish to add a 20% tip and then to divide the bill evenly among the four of them. How much will each person pay?

   A. $7.20
   B. $9.00
   C. $10.80
   D. $16.20

<u>Question 29</u> refers to the following coordinate plane grid.

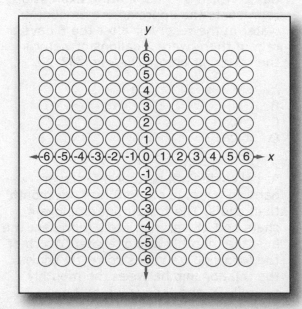

29. If the equation of a line is $y = \frac{1}{2}x + 3$, then mark on the graph the point where the line crosses the y-axis and the point where the line crosses the x-axis.

30. Karen puts 60% of her paycheck into her savings account. If Karen put $120 into her savings account, what was the amount of her entire paycheck?

GO ON TO THE NEXT PAGE

Mathematical Reasoning, Part 2

31. A rainfall doubled the original amount of water in a reservoir in 1 day and quadrupled the original amount in 5 days. Which of the following expressions represents the approximate amount of water in the reservoir after the 5 days of rain, if there were x gallons of water in the reservoir before the rainfall?

    A. $x + 4$
    B. $x + 6$
    C. $4x$
    D. $5x$

32. At Lakeside Park restaurant, servers earn an average of $840 less per month than chefs. The restaurant employs 4 chefs and 18 servers. Let c represent the average monthly pay of a chef. Which of the following functions correctly shows the relationship between the monthly payroll (P) and the wages of these employees?

    A. $4c + 18c - 840$
    B. $4(c - 840) + 18c$
    C. $22c - 840$
    D. $4c + 18(c - 840)$

33. The town of Woodgreen offers billboard space along the highway. A 5 foot by 8 foot rectangular advertising space costs $140. The price ($p$) of a sign is proportional to its area. A new sign erected in the billboard space costs $336. If the new sign is 8 feet tall, then what is its length?

    A. 11 feet
    B. 12 feet
    C. 16 feet
    D. 42 feet

34. Team A has won 28 of 35 games so far this season. There are a total of 44 games in the entire season. How many of the remaining games must team A win in order to have an overall win percentage of 75%?

    A. 3
    B. 5
    C. 9
    D. 33

Question 35 refers to the following diagram.

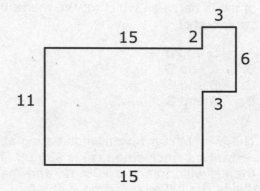

35. What is the area of the figure above?

    A. 55
    B. 132
    C. 165
    D. 183

36. A certain chest (a rectangular solid) has the following dimensions: 1.5 feet wide, 2.5 feet long, and 2 feet deep. If the chest currently holds 3 blankets that individually occupy 1 cubic foot each, then how much additional space is available in the chest?

     ft^3

GO ON TO THE NEXT PAGE

37. Michelle had a medical bill of $850. After she paid the deductible of $500, her insurance company paid 80% of the remainder. How much more of the bill did Michelle have to pay?

    A. 70
    B. 100
    C. 170
    D. 280

Questions 38 and 39 refer to the following diagram.

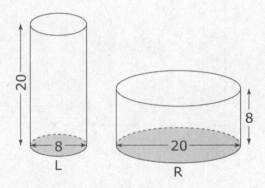

38. The volume of cylinder L is

Select...   ▼
less than half
slightly smaller than
equal to
slightly larger than
more than twice

    the volume of cylinder R.

39. If cylinder L is filled with water and then emptied into cylinder R (which was previously empty), then what will the height of the water in cylinder R be?

    A. 3.2
    B. 4
    C. 4.6
    D. 8

40. An airplane can hold 325 passengers, 30 in first class and the rest in coach. If a first-class ticket costs $700 and a coach ticket costs $250, then what is the minimum revenue that the airplane will gross on a flight in which exactly 3 seats remain empty?

    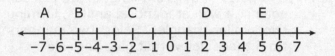

Questions 41 and 42 refer to the following number line.

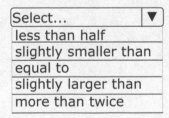

41. Let x be the distance between points A and E as shown on the number line above. Indicate where the point $\frac{x}{3}$ would appear on the number line. (For this practice test, write an X on the number line.)

42. Indicate where on the number line the point (B − C) − D would appear. (For this practice test, write an X on the number line.)

GO ON TO THE NEXT PAGE

Mathematical Reasoning, Part 2

<u>Question 43</u> refers to the following diagram.

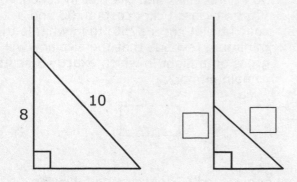

43. Two poles of different lengths are placed against a wall at identical angles, forming two similar triangles. Select two numbers from those below that give possible values for the length of the shorter pole and the height up the wall that it reaches. (For this practice test, write the numbers in the boxes above.)

4	5	6

8	11

44. AJ was prescribed an antibiotic that must be taken as one tablet every 8 hours. Following the instructions, he took the first tablet at 2 pm on Monday and took the last tablet three days later, on Thursday at 2 pm. How many tablets of antibiotic did AJ take?

45. Over an 8-year period, Katrina's $14,000 investment in the stock market increased by 180%. What was the value of her investment at the end of that period?

A. $16,520
B. $25,200
C. $39,200
D. $252,000

<u>Question 46</u> refers to the following diagram.

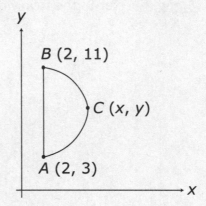

46. For the semicircle above, point C represents the midpoint of arc AB. Which of the following represent the coordinates of point C?

A.   (6, 7)
B.   (7, 7)
C.   (4, 6)
D.   (7, 6)

END OF TEST

Social Studies

Welcome!

Here is some information that you need to know before you start this test:

- You should not spend too much time on a question if you are not certain of the answer; answer it the best you can, and go on to the next question.
- If you are not certain of the answer to a question, you can mark your answer for review and come back to it later.
- You have **70 minutes** to complete this test.

Turn the page to begin.

GO ON TO THE NEXT PAGE

<u>Questions 1 through 3</u> are based on the following information.

The Department of Labor operates under the mandate that the most important capital is human capital. Particular attention is paid to the future workforce of America—the children. To this end, legislation was enacted to safeguard youngsters' opportunities to receive schooling without the burden of a full-time or health-threatening occupation. The Fair Labor Standards Act (FLSA) has provisions designed to protect children. Employment for minors now must conform to the following restrictions, which apply to all labor except farm labor. First, 16- or 17-year-olds may legally obtain employment as long as the job is not determined to be dangerous or ruinous to their health or well-being. Second, 14- or 15-year-olds may also work during specific hours at certain jobs as long as their employment does not negatively affect their health, schooling, or well-being. Employment of children under 14 years of age is usually prohibited. The Department of Labor has already classified 17 nonagricultural occupations as being unsuitable for minors.

1. According to the regulations described, all of the following could legally be used to deny a minor employment EXCEPT

   A. age.
   B. gender.
   C. hazard level.
   D. type of job.

2. Which of the following beliefs is the basis for the regulations?

   A. Minors should judge the appropriateness of their own employment.
   B. Employment of minors must be controlled to protect them from harm.
   C. Minors should not be employed under any circumstances.
   D. School children should focus on their studies and not be burdened with jobs.

3. It can be inferred that support for the passage of the FLSA most likely came from

   A. factory owners.
   B. child protection agencies.
   C. workers' unions.
   D. small companies.

GO ON TO THE NEXT PAGE

Questions 4 through 6 refer to the following sources.

TAB 1: **Timeline of events following the end of World War II**

1945: Yalta Conference: The Allies of World War II (the USA, the USSR, Great Britain, and France) divide Germany into four occupation zones.

1947: Marshall Plan: A comprehensive program of economic assistance for the war-ravaged countries of Western Europe.

1948: Berlin Airlift: In response to Soviet Premier Joseph Stalin's attempt to block supplies to Berliners, France, Britain, and the United States launch the Berlin Airlift to supply the citizens of Berlin by air.

1949: North Atlantic Treaty Organization (NATO): Western nations unite in order to resist Communist expansion.

1955: Warsaw Pact: Soviet Union and Eastern European Communist nations unite to oppose NATO.

TAB 2:

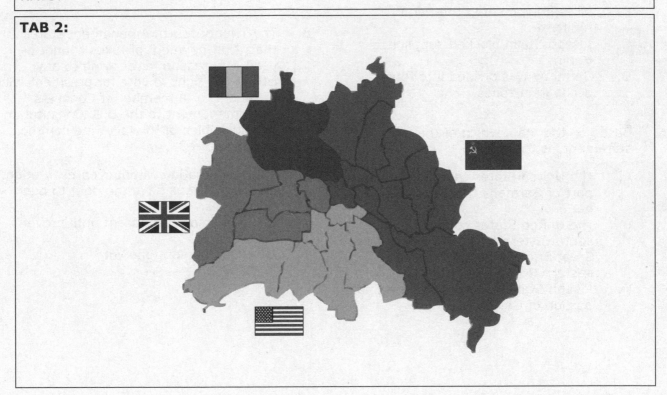

GO ON TO THE NEXT PAGE

4. Why was the Berlin Airlift necessary?

   A. The Yalta Conference had impoverished the citizens of Berlin.
   B. The Marshall Plan had successfully assisted the citizens of Berlin to recover economically.
   C. The creation of the Warsaw Pact had prevented Berliners from accessing food supplies.
   D. The Soviets had closed supply routes to Berlin.

5. What event was a response to the formation of the North Atlantic Treaty Organization (NATO)?

   A. Communist countries united under the Warsaw Pact.
   B. Allies implemented the Berlin Airlift.
   C. Joseph Stalin blocked supplies to Berlin.
   D. Germany was divided into four occupation zones.

6. Based on the map, which of the following statements is true?

   A. The United States controlled a larger part of Germany than any other nation.
   B. The United States controlled the southwestern portion of Germany.
   C. Great Britain controlled much of eastern Germany.
   D. Joseph Stalin controlled only a small portion of Germany.

"Ulysses S. Grant concluded by 1863 that the very nature of a war to preserve the Union states would have the effect of changing those states and thus altering the Union."

7. Which of the following historical developments best supports Grant's conclusion?

   A. Grant had predicted a Northern triumph.
   B. In 1917, the United States entered the First World War.
   C. Women received the right to vote in 1919.
   D. The emancipation of the slaves affected the society of the entire nation.

8. The Twenty-fourth Amendment states that "Non-payment of taxes cannot be used as a reason for denying to any citizen the right to vote for president, vice president, or a member of Congress." This amendment to the U.S. Constitution upholds which of the following common law principles?

   A. No taxation without representation.
   B. All citizens have the right to bear arms.
   C. A person is innocent until proven guilty.
   D. One person, one vote.

GO ON TO THE NEXT PAGE

Social Studies

Questions 9 and 10 are based on the following information.

> Most of them were disappointed in their search for gold. Many of those who failed as prospectors settled in towns such as San Francisco and Monterey. There they found jobs working for the canneries that sprang up as a result of the booming fishing industry or digging in the gold mines that others had found.

9. Which of the following best explains why the men described in the passage traveled west?

   A. to live near the ocean
   B. to start families
   C. for economic and other opportunities
   D. to escape religious persecution

10. According to the information, which of the following is a conclusion that best explains why many of those who headed west settled in coastal towns?

    A. They were able to find jobs there.
    B. There was no available land.
    C. Monterey rivers were rich in gold.
    D. The mountains were not open to settlement.

Questions 11 and 12 refer to the following excerpt from the First Amendment to the U.S. Constitution.

> "Congress shall make no law respecting an establishment of religion, or prohibiting the free exercise thereof; or abridging the freedom of speech, or of the press; or the right of the people peaceably to assemble, and to petition the Government..."

11. Which statement describes the primary purpose of the First Amendment?

    A. The First Amendment protects the right to bear arms.
    B. The First Amendment increases the government's restriction of individual freedoms, such as the freedom of religion, of speech, and of the press.
    C. The First Amendment protects essential individual freedoms, such as the freedom of religion, of speech, and of the press.
    D. The First Amendment prohibits Congress from making laws.

12. All of the following are guaranteed by the First Amendment EXCEPT

    A. the freedom to vote.
    B. the freedom of petition.
    C. the freedom of speech.
    D. the freedom of the press.

GO ON TO THE NEXT PAGE

Question 13 is based on the following graph.

How Children Are Being Educated

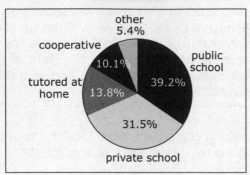

13. Which statement is supported by information in the graph?

A. Private schools provide a better education than do other types of schooling.
B. Children prefer the educational arrangements their parents have made for them.
C. Tutoring at home is the most popular method of educating children.
D. Most children attend either public or private schools.

Questions 14 and 15 refer to the following information.

Economic systems can be classified according to the degree of government intervention and the type of control that the government exerts.

A command economy is one in which the government takes a very active role. If the government chooses to use its control of the economy to redistribute all of the money equally among all of the members of society, this is a command socialist system. If the government controls the economy but allows the money to be unevenly distributed, this is known as a command capitalistic system.

An economy in which the government takes no active role is known as a pure market economy. The only things that control the distribution of money in a pure market economy are market forces that no one person or organization can control.

14. It can be inferred from the passage that which of the following would NOT be found in a pure market economy?

A. monopolies
B. small businesses
C. unemployed workers
D. taxes and welfare

15. Of the following groups, which would probably benefit the least from a transition from a market economy to a socialist economy?

A. government employees
B. the unemployed
C. small shop owners with small profits
D. highly skilled labor

GO ON TO THE NEXT PAGE

Social Studies

Question 16 refers to the following photo.

Source: Shutterstock

16. While today's car owners sometimes have difficulties, car owners in the early 20th century had to cope with quite a number of different problems.

Which of the following would have been the biggest concern for the people shown in the photo above?

A. a lack of unleaded gas, which resulted in pollution

B. a lack of seatbelts and other safety features

C. a shortage of lightweight building materials, which led to much heavier cars than we have today

D. a scarcity of gas stations

Question 17 refers to the following source.

"In the spring of 1879, thousands of colored people, unable longer to endure the intolerable hardships, injustice, and suffering inflicted upon them by a class of Democrats in the South, had, in utter despair, fled panic-stricken from their homes and sought protection among strangers in a strange land. Homeless, penniless, and in rags, these poor people were thronging the wharves of Saint Louis, crowding the steamers on the Mississippi River, and in pitiable destitution throwing themselves upon the charity of Kansas. Thousands more were congregating along the banks of the Mississippi River, hailing the passing steamers, and imploring them for a passage to the land of freedom, where the rights of citizens are respected and honest toil rewarded by honest compensation. The newspapers were filled with accounts of their destitution, and the very air was burdened with the cry of distress from a class of American citizens flying from persecutions which they could no longer endure."

Report and Testimony of the Select Committee of the United States Senate to Investigate the Cause of the Removal of the Negroes from the Southern States to the Northern States, 46th Congress, 1880.

17. According to the passage, why did many African Americans migrate to the North in 1879?

A. to seek religious freedom

B. to find employment in factories

C. to escape poverty and racial discrimination

D. to escape lynchings

GO ON TO THE NEXT PAGE

Question 18 refers to the following graph.

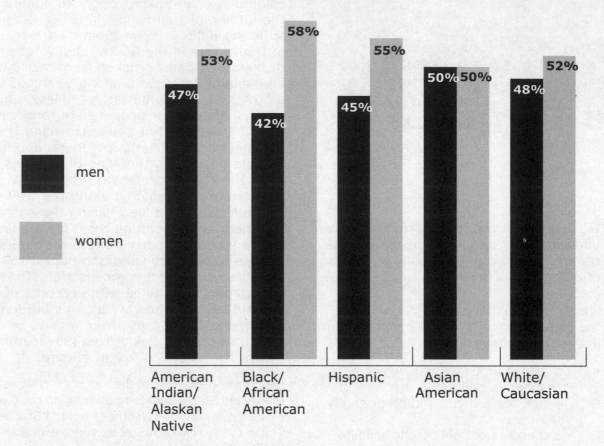

Profile of SAT Takers by Ethnic Group

men

women

	American Indian/ Alaskan Native	Black/ African American	Hispanic	Asian American	White/ Caucasian
men	47%	42%	45%	50%	48%
women	53%	58%	55%	50%	52%

18.   Which statement is clearly supported by evidence in the graph?

   A.   American women perform better on the SAT than American men do.
   B.   There has been a decline in the number of Asian American men taking the SAT.
   C.   The number of women in general taking the SAT has increased.
   D.   More women than men take the SAT.

GO ON TO THE NEXT PAGE

Social Studies

19. A plutocracy may be defined by the political principle of rule by the wealthy, that is, those who have accumulated wealth either through inherited property or financial success.

According to this statement, which of the following is <u>inconsistent</u> with a plutocratic form of government?

A. Citizens must abide by the decision of the select group in power.
B. Monetary interests are valued above human interests.
C. Leaders are determined by popular vote.
D. A farmer is excluded from holding office.

<u>Question 20</u> refers to the following quotation.

"The [oil monopoly] molds public opinion in a manner creating a complete misunderstanding of the petroleum situation and influences the judgment and acts of unknowing and unwise public officials to a point where they fall to these interests of monopoly as against the welfare of the people whom they are supposed to serve."

—Andrew Mellon

20. Which of the following is an opinion most likely held by the speaker above?

A. Those who profit from monopolies should not try to serve the public by running for office.
B. The interests of the people are secondary to those of public officials.
C. All should profit from the rewards gained by a monopoly.
D. Public officials should value the interests of the people they serve over the interests of any one business.

<u>Question 21</u> refers to the following paragraph.

The U.S. government is structured with separate powers at the state and federal levels. Some political scientists have referred to this organization as a "wagon wheel," with the hub, or center, representing the federal government and the spokes representing the various state governments. This means that each state is separate, but the federal government maintains some level of centralized power.

21. Which of the following best illustrates how the "wagon wheel" analogy applies to the U.S. system of government?

A. A wagon wheel is one of four wheels needed to stabilize a wagon.
B. The hub of a wagon wheel holds in place the spokes, which strengthen the structure of the wheel.
C. A wagon wheel's hub and spokes are made of different materials.
D. A wagon wheel is created in several pieces and then assembled.

Questions 22 through 24 relate to the following map.

Non-English-Speaking Children*

*Children aged 5 to 17 who speak a foreign language at home and who don't speak English well or who don't speak it at all

New York

California

Arizona

Texas   Florida

Number of counties with 500 or more non-English-speaking children

■ 10 or more
▨ 5–9
▨ 1–4
☐ none

22. Which of the following best explains the distribution of non-English-speaking children shown on the map?

    A. Income taxes are lower on the coasts than in the middle of the country.

    B. Fewer children are born in states with cold climates.

    C. There are fewer English courses offered in the northern part of the United States.

    D. Recent immigrants to the United States have tended to settle in border and coastal states.

23. Which factor would have the least effect upon the distribution of non-English-speaking children in the United States?

    A. migration patterns
    B. climate
    C. ESL programs
    D. immigration laws

24. Which generalization is supported by the evidence in the map?

    A. Non-English-speaking children are distributed evenly across the United States.

    B. There are more non-English-speaking children in Arizona than in California.

    C. In Texas and California, more children are unable to speak English than are able to speak English.

    D. There are fewer non-English-speaking children in the northern middle portion of the United States than in other parts of the country.

GO ON TO THE NEXT PAGE

Questions <u>25 through 27</u> refer to the following paragraph.

> The Constitution, the laws made in accordance with that Constitution, and any treaties that the United States has signed constitute the supreme law of the land, to which the judges in any state must adhere. Any state laws incompatible with this supreme law of the land are unconstitutional, and therefore null and void.

25. Which of the following is an example of the concept of supreme law?

   A. The president of the United States makes political appointments to the Supreme Court.
   B. The freedoms outlined in the Bill of Rights can't be denied by the government.
   C. The House of Representatives contains two representatives from each state.
   D. The president is elected to four-year terms.

26. Which of the following is an example of a state law that would be incompatible with the Constitution?

   A. a law that prohibits protests by a steelworkers' union
   B. a law that lowers the speed limit on a highway to 50 miles per hour
   C. a law that limits state senators to two six-year terms each
   D. legislation that requires reductions in emissions from factories

27. Which of the following is an example of a law compatible with the Constitution?

   A. legislation that prohibits the practice of certain religions
   B. a law that protects the rights of convicted criminals
   C. a law that suspends the right to trial by jury
   D. a law that prevents non-English-speakers from voting

GO ON TO THE NEXT PAGE

Questions 28 and 29 are based on the following paragraphs.

> According to several prominent professors of economics, it is impossible to be completely accurate when predicting the long-term performance of any given stock. The professors' arguments are that the various political, social, and economic pressures that affect the success of any company are constantly changing and that their combined effects are extremely unpredictable.
>
> This would explain why an amateur investor can very often do as well as a professional stock trader in long-term investments. The professors likened predicting stock performance to predicting weather patterns. Weather predictions are usually accurate up to a few days into the future, but the farther ahead the prediction, the greater the likelihood that unforeseen events render the prediction inaccurate. The same may be true of long-term stock predictions.

28. After analyzing the success of long-term stock predictions, some business professors reported that

   A. professional predictions of stock performance are usually accurate.
   B. stocks that are currently performing well will continue to do so.
   C. amateur stock investors do very poorly in long-term investments.
   D. even careful analysis of current stock performance is no guarantee of accurate long-term predictions.

29. If it is true that a company's performance is affected by many factors, one can conclude that

   A. two companies producing the same goods will perform equally well.
   B. a company's success is dependent on amateur investors.
   C. it is possible to lose money by investing in a company that has been very successful.
   D. an amateur stock investor will automatically make more money than a professional.

30. **Laissez-faire** is an economic environment in which transactions between private parties are largely free from government restrictions.

   Choose THREE characteristics that best exemplify laissez-faire economics:

   ```
   ┌─────────────────────┐
   │                     │
   └─────────────────────┘

   ┌─────────────────────┐
   │                     │
   └─────────────────────┘

   ┌─────────────────────┐
   │                     │
   └─────────────────────┘
   ```

(a) Deregulation	(b) Labor Laws
(c) Building Codes	(d) Free Trade
(e) Antitrust Laws	(f) Non-Interference

   Drag and drop your choices into the three slots above. (For this practice test, write the letters of three characteristics in the slots.)

GO ON TO THE NEXT PAGE

Social Studies

Question 31 refers to the photo below.

Source: Photofest Archives

Question 32 refers to the following cartoon.

A MAN KNOWS A MAN

"Give me your hand, Comrade! We have each lost a LEG for the good cause; but, thank GOD, we never lost HEART."

31. The golden age of transatlantic passenger ships was quickly coming to an end in this photo taken of six ocean liners at dock in New York City circa 1953. Which of the following events was probably the most important reason for the end of the era of crossing the Atlantic by ship?

    A.   A series of highly publicized liner accidents made the public too nervous to take ships.
    B.   A major war made overseas travel impossible.
    C.   The advent of passenger airlines cut down the time it took to get to Europe, leaving ships outmoded.
    D.   The cost of travel by boat became prohibitively expensive.

32. This cartoon from the Civil War era depicts two veterans of the Civil War (which was fought over the emancipation of African American slaves) greeting each other. What did the cartoonist mean to imply by the caption?

    A.   These two men were equals in each other's eyes.
    B.   These two soldiers who had lost their legs were not to be pitied because they were still men.
    C.   These soldiers had previously met.
    D.   Although they may have met before, these veterans had nothing in common.

GO ON TO THE NEXT PAGE

Social Studies

Questions 33 through 35 refer to the following sources.

TAB 1:

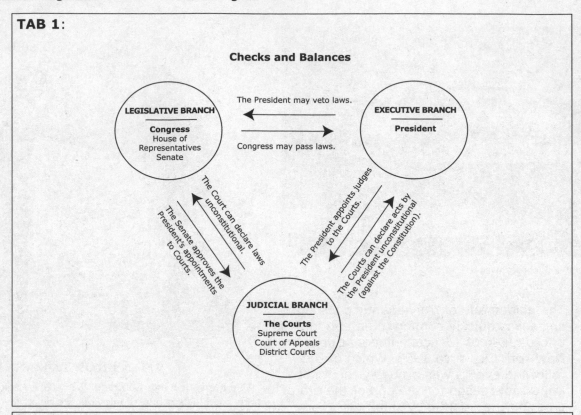

Checks and Balances

LEGISLATIVE BRANCH

Congress
House of
Representatives
Senate

The President may veto laws.

Congress may pass laws.

EXECUTIVE BRANCH

President

The Court can declare laws unconstitutional.

The Senate approves the President's appointments to Courts.

The President appoints judges to the Courts.

The Courts can declare acts by the President unconstitutional (against the Constitution).

JUDICIAL BRANCH

The Courts
Supreme Court
Court of Appeals
District Courts

TAB 2:

"It is emphatically the province and duty of the Judicial Department [the judicial branch] to say what the law is. Those who apply the rule to particular cases must, of necessity, expound and interpret that rule. If two laws conflict with each other, the Courts must decide on the operation of each."

–Justice John Marshall, *Marbury vs. Madison*, 1803

TAB 3:

"You seem to consider the judges as the ultimate arbiters of all constitutional questions; a very dangerous doctrine indeed, and one which would place us under the despotism of an oligarchy. Our judges are as honest as other men, and not more so. They have, with others, the same passions for party, for power, and the privilege of their corps.... Their power [is] the more dangerous as they are in office for life, and not responsible, as the other functionaries are, to the elective control."

–Thomas Jefferson, in response to *Marbury vs. Madison*

GO ON TO THE NEXT PAGE

33. What is a primary duty of the Legislative Branch?

   A. to veto laws
   B. to pass laws
   C. to implement *Marbury vs. Madison*
   D. to nominate and appoint judges to the Supreme Court

34. What was Thomas Jefferson's opinion of *Marbury vs. Madison*?

   A. It balanced federal power by giving federal judges the right to override unjust laws.
   B. It conferred too much power to the Executive Branch.
   C. It made judges as honest as other men.
   D. It gave too much power to the Judicial Branch.

35. In context, what is the best substitute for the word "oligarchy"? (TAB 3)

   A. tyranny
   B. democracy
   C. passion
   D. honesty

END OF TEST

THIS PAGE INTENTIONALLY LEFT BLANK.

GO ON TO THE NEXT PAGE

Science

Welcome!

Here is some information that you need to know before you start this test:

- You should not spend too much time on a question if you are not certain of the answer; answer it the best you can, and go on to the next question.
- If you are not certain of the answer to a question, you can mark your answer for review and come back to it later.
- You have **90 minutes** to complete this test.
- There are two Short Answer questions on this test.
- You should plan to spend about 10 minutes on each Short Answer question.

Turn the page to begin.

GO ON TO THE NEXT PAGE

Question 1 refers to the following photograph and chart.

Source: Shutterstock

Average Temperature of Various Large Bodies of Water	
Atlantic Ocean	46 degrees Fahrenheit
Arctic Ocean	36 degrees Fahrenheit
Baltic Sea	45 degrees Fahrenheit
Great Lakes of North America	44 degrees Fahrenheit
Gulf of Mexico	60 degrees Fahrenheit

1. Hurricanes such as the one pictured above gather strength as they pass over warm water. According to the chart above, over which of the following bodies of water would a hurricane gather the most strength?

    A. Baltic Sea
    B. Atlantic Ocean
    C. Arctic Ocean
    D. Gulf of Mexico

2. Blood is made up of two main elements: (1) plasma, which is largely water and proteins, and (2) the solid components of blood—red blood cells, white cells, and platelets (important for forming clots). If a patient has lost a lot of blood, he or she may receive a transfusion of "whole blood," which includes red blood cells and plasma. However, sometimes the patient needs only an increase in the *volume* of liquid in the bloodstream, in which case plasma alone may be substituted.

    A person must be tested for blood type before receiving certain kinds of transfusions because of differences in the ways that red blood cells react to one another. Under what conditions would such testing be necessary?

    A. for whole blood transfusions only
    B. for plasma transfusions only
    C. for both whole blood transfusions and plasma transfusions
    D. if the patient has not lost any blood

GO ON TO THE NEXT PAGE

Science

Questions 3 through 5 are based on the following information.

Coal is formed from the material of plants and other organisms that lived on land and whose remains were covered by mud, which later became rock. Coal is classified by carbon content.

Types of Coal

Peat	=	The remains of plants and organisms that, because they were covered in bogs, were prevented by a lack of oxygen from completely decaying. Still a porous, soft brown mass, peat has a carbon content of 52%–60%.
Lignite	=	In time, peat turns into lignite, a soft coal-like substance that is 60%–65% carbon.
Subbituminous coal	=	With more time, heat, and pressure, lignite changes into subbituminous coal, which is about 65%–75% carbon.
Bituminous coal	=	After even more heat and pressure, subbituminous coal turns into bituminous coal with a carbon level of 75%–85%.
Anthracite	=	This is bituminous coal subjected to another million years of heat and pressure. Anthracite has a carbon level of 85%–95% and will burn only at extremely high temperatures.

3. A researcher analyzes a piece of coal and finds that it is unusually dense and burns only when subjected to very intense heat. What is the lowest percentage of carbon that this coal is likely to contain?

4. Steel is made in a process in which iron is combined with carbon at extremely high temperatures. Which of the following types of coal might be most useful in this process?

   A. peat
   B. lignite
   C. subbituminous coal
   D. anthracite

5. Drag and drop the appropriate type of coal into each box. (For this practice test, write the appropriate letter in each box.)

The type of coal most likely found closest to the surface of the earth:	The type of coal that contains the greatest amount of carbon per kilogram:

(a) Peat	(c) Bituminous coal
(b) Lignite	(d) Anthracite

GO ON TO THE NEXT PAGE

Science

Questions 6 and 7 are based on the following information.

Most seeds will germinate when they have moisture, oxygen, and the right temperature, but different seeds need differing proportions of each of these ingredients. Most seeds require a temperature of between 15 degrees and 27 degrees centigrade to germinate, although some seeds, such as the maple, can germinate in far colder climates, and some other seeds, such as corn, require warmer temperatures. Before germination, seeds must absorb water, but too much absorption of water will encourage the growth of fungus, which can halt the germination process.

6. Which of the following environments would be most suitable for the germination of corn seeds?

    A. a moist, sealed container at 26 degrees centigrade
    B. an arid desert plain
    C. a moist, plowed field at 30 degrees centigrade
    D. an environment suitable for maple seed growth

7. Based on the information in the passage, which of the following is most likely true?

    A. Maple seeds can germinate in any temperature.
    B. Corn is difficult to grow.
    C. Water, in limited amounts, is vital to the germination process.
    D. Maple seeds and corn seeds require different amounts of oxygen for germination.

8. During periods of intense activity, the cells of the body need more oxygen than the body is supplying, a situation known as oxygen debt. During these periods, the body's cells briefly switch to "anaerobic respiration," which produces lactic acid. The buildup of lactic acid in the tissues signals the brain to increase breathing and heart rates, thus supplying the body with more oxygen.

    After which of the following activities would lactic acid most likely be found in the body?

    A. walking to work
    B. playing an intense game of chess
    C. taking an aerobics class
    D. watching a scary movie

9. During periods that are unfavorable for growth, some plants become dormant. Woody plants are protected during such periods by their bark. Perennial plants die above ground, but their roots remain alive. Annual plants die, but their seeds survive to continue the life of the species.

    Which of the following would most likely be a time of year during which plants might lie dormant?

    A. winter
    B. spring
    C. summer
    D. fall

GO ON TO THE NEXT PAGE

Question 10 refers to the following diagram.

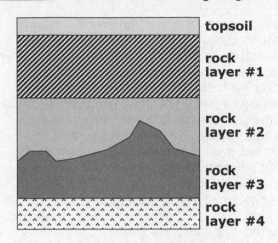

10. The diagram above shows various layers of rock that have been deposited over time. Drag and drop the rock layers into the appropriate boxes. (For this practice test, write the letters in the boxes.)

The oldest rock layer:	The newest rock layer:

(a) rock layer #1	(c) rock layer #3
(b) rock layer #2	(d) rock layer #4

Question 11 refers to the following diagram.

Food Chain

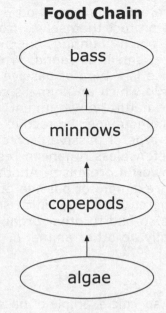

11. Which of the following conclusions is most likely to be true regarding the food chain above?

A. Bass are the only fish that eat minnows.
B. Minnows are bigger than bass.
C. Bass benefit in some ways from the existence of copepods.
D. Bass could simply eliminate the middlemen by eating algae.

GO ON TO THE NEXT PAGE

Question 12 is based on the following passage.

Passive protection is a method by which organisms protect themselves from predators, not by fighting, but by their appearance, smell, or sound. Protective resemblance is a type of passive protection in which an animal's coloring mimics the natural environment, acting as a kind of camouflage. Protective mimicry is another type of passive protection in which a defenseless organism resembles a more powerful organism. Another interesting example of passive protection is the Monarch butterfly, which smells and tastes so bad to other organisms that virtually no other animal or insect will eat it.

12. Give a specific example of passive protection and explain how that type of passive protection might protect an animal. Be sure to discuss an example not mentioned in the passage. Include pieces of information from the text to support the fact that your example is a type of passive protection.

Type your response on a computer, if one is available. Otherwise, write your response on paper. This task may require approximately 10 minutes to complete.

13. The density of seawater is 1,029 kilograms/meter^3. 1 kilogram/liter = 1,000 kilograms/meter^3. What is the density of seawater in kilograms/liter?

You may use a calculator.

A. 0.0001029
B. 0.1029
C. 1.029
D. 1,029,000

Question 14 refers to the following scenario.

Researchers in a particular city theorize that decreasing the greenhouse gas emissions in that city will result in better respiratory health for its citizens. In order to test this theory, they institute two programs. The first program provides commuters with financial incentives to take public transportation, and the second program initiates a respiratory care education campaign and provides free clinics for citizens suffering from respiratory health issues.

During the five years after the researchers institute the two programs, greenhouse gas emissions in the city decrease by 50%, and a city-wide survey reveals that cases of illness due to respiratory problems have decreased by 65%. Researchers therefore conclude that their theory was correct: Decreasing greenhouse gas emissions resulted in better respiratory health for local citizens.

14. Briefly explain the problem with the researchers' results. Why can they not accurately conclude that a decrease in greenhouse gas emissions resulted in better respiratory health for local citizens?

Type your response on a computer, if one is available. Otherwise, write your response on paper. This task may require approximately 10 minutes to complete.

GO ON TO THE NEXT PAGE

15. Lobsters are crustaceans commonly found in the waters of the Atlantic Ocean off the North American coast between Maine and North Carolina. Researchers studied the weights of these creatures over a period of a few years. Some of the results are displayed in the table below.

Year	Average Weight (kg)
2005	0.43
2006	0.41
2007	0.37
2008	0.43
2009	0.38

The researchers hope to find the most commonly occurring lobster weight for the lobsters studied during the five-year period shown above. The researchers must calculate the [Select...] ▼
- average
- mode
- median
- range

of the weights, which is [Select...] ▼.
- 0.04 kg
- 0.40 kg
- 0.41 kg
- 0.43 kg

You may use a calculator.

16. Amy tracks the monthly snowfall in two areas over a period of several months. One area is a region of high elevation, and the other is an area of low elevation. The table below displays her results.

Month	Area	Meters
November	low elevation	0.2
November	high elevation	0.4
December	low elevation	0.2
December	high elevation	0.8
January	low elevation	0.9
January	high elevation	1.7
February	low elevation	1.3
February	high elevation	1.8
March	low elevation	0.9
March	high elevation	1.1

What is the mean of the data shown in the table?

You may use a calculator.

[   ] meters

GO ON TO THE NEXT PAGE

17. Scientists calculate the pressure within a gas by using the following equation:

$$P = \frac{N \times k \times T}{V}$$

In the equation:

P is the pressure of the gas;
N is the number of particles in the gas;
k is a constant;
T is the temperature of the gas;
V is the volume of the gas.

If the number of particles in the gas decreases, which of the following changes will increase in the pressure of the gas?

A. decreasing both the volume and the temperature of the gas
B. increasing both the volume and the temperature of the gas
C. increasing the volume and decreasing the temperature of the gas
D. decreasing the volume and increasing the temperature of the gas

18. There are four basic types of chemical reactions, as shown in the table below.

Reaction Type	General Example
Combination	$A + B \rightarrow C$
Decomposition	$C \rightarrow A + B$
Single displacement	$A + BC \rightarrow B + AC$
Double displacement	$AB + CD \rightarrow AC + BD$

The balanced chemical equation describing the reaction between hydrogen and fluorine is shown below.

$$H_2 + F_2 \rightarrow 2HF$$

Which of the four basic types of chemical reactions is this?

A. combination
B. decomposition
C. single displacement
D. double displacement

GO ON TO THE NEXT PAGE

Question 19 refers to the following graph.

Projected AIDS Deaths 2011–2020

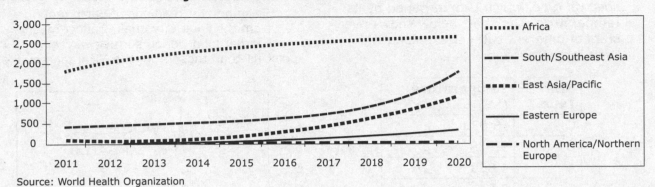

Source: World Health Organization

19. According to the chart above, which of the following regions will have the largest projected increase in the number AIDS deaths between 2011 and 2020?

A. Africa
B. South/Southeast Asia
C. North America/Northern Europe
D. East Asia/Pacific

GO ON TO THE NEXT PAGE

20. Scientists classify stars according to the following categories: O, B, A, F, G, K, M. A star's category depends upon its *spectral type*, which is determined by its temperature. The chart below shows five stars of different categories, along with their temperatures.

Star Type	Temperature (°F)
O	18,033
B	9,978
A	4,839
F	3,644
G	3,422

However, rather than measuring star temperature in degrees Fahrenheit, scientists typically measure star temperature in units of Kelvin. The conversion from Kelvin to Fahrenheit is given by the following formula:

$$K = \frac{5}{9}(°F - 32) + 273.$$

What is the approximate temperature of the A-type star in Kelvin?

You may use a calculator.

A. 2,569
B. 2,822
C. 2,929
D. 2,944

Questions 21 and 22 refer to the following graph.

Waves That Foretell Tidal Waves
Seismometer readings of Earth motion from the Fault City quake reflect much larger long-period surface waves at point R1 than those from the Nicaragua quake.

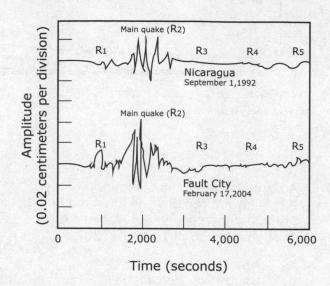

21. According to the information above, which of the following statements is true?

A. The Nicaragua main quake had a larger amplitude than did the Fault City quake.
B. The Fault City main quake had a larger amplitude than did the Nicaragua quake.
C. A seismometer was used to measure the Nicaragua quake but was not used to measure the Fault City quake.
D. The long-period surface waves at the point R1 were larger during the Nicaragua quake than during the Fault City quake.

22. Select the point on the graph that would be of the most importance in foretelling an earthquake in Nicaragua. (For this practice test, write an X on the graph.)

GO ON TO THE NEXT PAGE

Questions 23 and 24 refer to the following article.

23. For years, paleontologists have debated whether the archaeopteryx, a creature that lived 150 million years ago, was an early species of bird or a dinosaur that spent most of its time on the ground. Its feathers and wings were of only limited use, they say, and could not sustain flight.

Ornithologists, on the other hand, believe that archaeopteryx was first and foremost a bird. As evidence, they point to fossil remains of the creature that show its claws were curved so that it could perch on tree limbs. Curved claws would have prevented the animal from walking or running quickly on the ground.

According to paleontologists, the archaeopteryx was incapable of

A. perching.
B. running.
C. flying.
D. walking.

24. According to the theory advanced by ornithologists, which of the following is most likely to have been a modern-day descendant of the archaeopteryx?

A. the lizard
B. the alligator
C. the crow
D. the mosquito

25. In science, work is defined as the component of force parallel to motion multiplied by displacement. One reason that individuals use ramps, rather than lifting heavy items straight up, is that using a ramp increases total displacement, but reduces the amount of force required to move an object by exactly the same amount as the increase in displacement, provided that the ramp's surface is frictionless.

According to the information in the paragraph, using a ramp with a frictionless surface will have which of the following effects?

A. The total amount of work required to move an object will decrease.
B. The total amount of work required to move an object will increase.
C. The total amount of work required to move an object will remain the same.
D. The amount of work required to move an object will initially increase, but will later decrease.

26. Below is a table listing the concentrations of chemicals found in human blood and urine.

	Albumin mg/dL	Chloride mg/dL	Glucose mg/dL	Phosphate mg/dL	Urea mg/dL
Blood	4.1	92	95	2.5	4.5
Urine	—	53	—	0.15	1.6

Based on the table above, which of the following chemicals is not normally found in urine?

A. albumin only
B. chloride only
C. glucose only
D. albumin and glucose

GO ON TO THE NEXT PAGE

27. In a certain forest, foxes prey on rabbits. A virus that infects only rabbits spreads through the forest, killing many rabbits.

Which of the following is most likely to occur to the fox population?

A. It will decrease, because the foxes will not have enough food.
B. It will decrease, because the foxes will suffer from the virus.
C. It will increase, because the foxes will no longer need to compete with the rabbits for food.
D. It will increase, because the foxes will evolve to become more resistant to disease.

28. A solar eclipse is a celestial event during which the sun appears partially or totally obstructed when viewed from a certain location on Earth. The diagram below shows a solar eclipse.

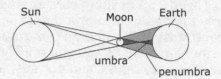

Based on the information above, which of the following is mostly likely to be true during a solar eclipse?

A. The entire moon is in the penumbra, or shadow, of the earth, so that the moon is no longer visible from the earth.
B. The moon is directly between the sun and the earth, thus placing certain regions of the earth within the moon's umbra, or deepest part of the shadow, so that the sun's rays are not visible from those regions.
C. Light rays from the earth intercept those from the sun, thus creating an umbra, or dark shadow, around the moon so that the sun is no longer visible from the earth.
D. The sun is in the umbra, or deepest part of the shadow, cast by the earth, and is therefore invisible from the earth.

GO ON TO THE NEXT PAGE

Science

Questions 29 and 30 refer to the following passage.

Pathogenic microbes, microorganisms that cause disease, include viruses, bacteria, fungi, and protozoa. Such microbes can invade hosts through several pathways, including through the air, through direct or indirect physical contact, through blood, and through other bodily fluids.

Medical researchers are currently attempting to find better treatments for microbial diseases by developing new pharmaceuticals. Currently, many doctors prescribe penicillin, which is derived from the spores of a fungus and which prevents the growth of new bacteria, to treat bacteria-induced microbial diseases, and antiviral compounds to combat viruses. However, such treatments do not always eradicate the relevant diseases, and while some microbe-induced illnesses, such as chicken pox, may not be life-threatening, others, such as those that cause ebola, can be deadly.

29.   Below is a chart of some common microbe-induced illnesses and their causes.

Illness	Cause
Common Cold	Rhinovirus
Strep Throat	Streptococcal bacterium
Athlete's Foot	Candida yeast
Malaria	Malaria protist

Which of the following is most likely treatable with penicillin?

A.   common cold
B.   strep throat
C.   athlete's foot
D.   malaria

30.   Medical researchers fear that preventing those suffering from microbial diseases from having physical contact with others may not be sufficient to stop the spread of such diseases. Which of the following quotes from the passage supports this idea?

A.   "Many doctors prescribe penicillin, which is derived from the spores of a fungus and which prevents the growth of new bacteria, to treat bacteria-induced microbial diseases."
B.   "Such treatments do not always eradicate the relevant diseases, and while some microbe-induced illnesses, such as chicken pox, may not be life-threatening, others, such as those that cause ebola, can be deadly."
C.   "Pathogenic microbes, microorganisms that cause disease, include viruses, bacteria, fungi, and protozoa."
D.   "Such microbes can invade hosts through several pathways, including through the air, through direct or indirect physical contact, through blood, and through other bodily fluids."

GO ON TO THE NEXT PAGE

Questions 31 and 32 refer to the following passage.

Hereditary traits are encoded by genes that are located on chromosomes. Chromosomes come in pairs, and the pair of genes for a particular feature determines the characteristics of that trait. In many cases, genes exhibit a pattern called classical dominance. In such cases, the gene for a dominant trait is always expressed when present. An individual may have only a dominant gene and have two copies of that gene, or an individual may be hybrid and have one dominant gene and one recessive gene. In hybrids, the dominant gene hides the expression of the recessive gene. A recessive gene is expressed only when both copies of the gene are recessive. In literature, dominant genes are represented by capital letters, while recessive genes are represented by lowercase letters.

In pea plants, pea color is a hereditary trait. Green comes from a dominant gene, and yellow comes from a recessive gene, so that if a plant has one gene for green and one gene for yellow, that plant will produce green peas.

The following Punnett Square shows the results when two hybrid pea plants produce new plants. Punnett Squares predict the likelihood of a specific gene combination occuring. Approximately 75% of the offspring in this case are green, and the rest are yellow.

Punnett Square—Color in Pea Plants

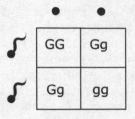

> sperm cell of male parent
> • egg cell of female parent
> G dominant green color gene
> g recessive yellow color gene

31. Which of the following is the best explanation for the results displayed in this Punnett Square?

A. One parent plant had only the yellow gene.
B. One parent plant had only the dominant gene.
C. Neither parent plant had the hidden gene for yellow.
D. Both parent plants were hybrids and carried the hidden gene for yellow.

32. Dimples result from a dominant gene, and a lack of dimples results from a recessive gene. Based on the information in the passage, which of the following will be true for an individual who is a hybrid?

A. That individual will have dimples.
B. That individual has an equal chance of either having or not having dimples.
C. That individual will have a dimple on one side of his or her face, but not on the other.
D. That individual will have no dimples.

GO ON TO THE NEXT PAGE

Science

Questions 33 and 34 refer to the following graph.

The graph below shows a science experiment in which a sample of ice at −20 degrees C is heated to 120 degrees C. During the experiment, the ice melted into water and then the water boiled and turned into steam.

Heat and Temperature of Water

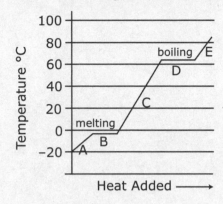

33. Based on the information presented above, which of the following statements is most accurate?

   A. The temperature of the sample increased at the same rate throughout the experiment.
   B. The sample remained as ice throughout most of the experiment.
   C. The sample increased in temperature, then melted, then increased in temperature again, then boiled, and then increased in temperature.
   D. The sample melted and increased in temperature at the same time.

34. Select the area on the graph during which the entire sample consists of liquid water. (For this practice test, write an X on the graph.)

35. Bees are insects that play an important role in any ecosystem that has flowering plants. Bees serve as primary pollinators, and enable flowering plants to reproduce. Scientists estimate that nearly one-third of the human food supply consists of plants that depend on bees for pollination.

   Based on the information above, which characteristic of bees is most important to an ecosystem?

   A. Bees create honey for human consumption.
   B. Bees serve as pollinators.
   C. Bees sting harmful insects that would otherwise eat and destroy plants.
   D. Bees transfer their genes to plants.

END OF TEST

Chapter 24
Practice Test 1:
Answers and
Explanations

REASONING THROUGH LANGUAGE ARTS

Section 1

1. **A** This development question asks which sentence from the passage supports the idea that Ingred's relatives have had military experience. Since several quotations are related to the major theme of the recent war, consider what is implied as well as what is directly stated. Choice (A) is correct: It talks about "Mr. Saxon, Egbert, and Athelstane" which follows the first sentence in paragraph 1 which states that the family has been reunited; therefore, these are members of the Saxon family. Additionally, the word "demobilized" and the phrase "had hardly yet settled down to civilian life" support the idea that these members of Ingred's family had served in the war. Choices (B) and (C) are incorrect because, while they do mention that there has been a war, neither choice mentions Ingred's family. Although (D) indicates that Ingred's relatives have returned from somewhere, there is no mention of the war. The correct answer is (A).

2. **C** This language use item requires test takers to determine which definition of the word "native" matches its use in paragraph 1. Each of the answer options reflects an actual definition of the word "native," so look closely at the way the word is used in context. The word is used as a part of the sentence "They had joined the rest of the party at Lynstones before returning to their native town of Grovebury." Here, there is a contrast drawn between where the family is at the time of the narrative—the summer home at Lynstones—and their final destination, which is their family home at Grovebury. Here, "native" means "place of origin." Choices (A) and (B) are incorrect, because while there are many descriptions of the "natural" and perhaps "wild" beauty of Lynstones, "native" here refers to Grovebury, which is not described as a place in nature. Choice (C) is correct: "original" means "first" or "earliest" which is consistent with the idea that the Saxons are returning to their "place of origin." Finally, (D) is incorrect, because while the Saxon family home might indeed be "inherited," there is no evidence to support this in the text. The correct answer is (C).

3. **B** This structure question asks about how the sentence describing the landscape enhances the story. The passage uses the phrase "glorious run" to emphasize Ingred's positive feelings during the trip, and paints a detailed picture of the landscape with phrases like "glimpses of the sea," "craggy," and "billowy masses." Altogether, the sense is of an appreciation of the natural scenery. Choice (A) is incorrect: While the next sentence does mention that "Egbert exceeded the speed-limit," it goes on to say, "he had the excuse of a clear road before him," so the passage emphasizes that the trip is picturesque, not dangerous. Choice (B) is correct: Since the contrast between Ingred's feelings about her summer holidays versus returning to school is a main theme of this excerpt (first described in paragraph 1), the description of nature and use of "glorious" reinforces Ingred's feelings about her summer vacation home. Choice (C) is incorrect because although the quotation does describe the sea and the cliffs as having different characteristics, the difference between the sea and the cliffs is not a major theme of the story. Even though Egbert appears in this part of the narrative, the quoted description of the landscape does not reveal anything about his character or function in the story, so (D) is incorrect. The correct answer is (B).

4. **A** This structure question asks about the significance of the "place" mentioned in the quotation. The sentence included in the question says, "But surely the Red Cross cleared out ages ago," meaning that the "place" had been used by the Red Cross during the war. To find out exactly what the "place" is, look further in paragraph 12. Avis asks Ingred, "I suppose you're going back to Rotherwood, aren't you?" Since one of the major themes of the passages is Ingred's feelings about having to return to her family home as soon

as the summer is over, the "going back to Rotherwood" Avis mentions must be that return to the Saxon family home. Therefore, (A) is correct. Choice (B) is incorrect because, while the passage does mention the Red Cross, Avis is specifically referring to a house, not a town, in paragraph 16: "I always envied you that lovely house." Choice (C) is incorrect: even though the quotation mentions that the "whole place has been done up," there is no evidence that this was done to a ballroom for the purpose of a dance. Choice (D) is incorrect, because the "place" is Ingred's home, not her school. The correct answer is (A).

5. **A** This character development question asks about Ingred's character based on her response to Avis. Use the dialogue that ends with Ingred's response in paragraph 15 to get a sense of the entire exchange between the characters. When Avis asks, in paragraph 12, whether Ingred is going back to Rotherwood, Ingred gives a vague response. When Avis persists, "But surely the Red Cross cleared out ages ago," then Ingred responds, "Oh, yes!" (paragraph 15) in a voice "a little strained." Since Ingred's voice is "strained" when she discusses her return, this is consistent with previous information that Ingred enjoys her holidays and does not want to think about the time beyond summer (paragraph 1) when she will return to her family home. Therefore, (A) is correct: Ingred is reluctant to talk about going back to Rotherwood. Choice (B) is incorrect, because while Ingred is technically "agreeing" with Avis, the strain in her voice shows reluctance. Choice (C) is incorrect, because while "strained" does sometimes mean "exhausted," in paragraph 15 "strained" means "forced," showing that Ingred does not really want to think about her eventual return. Choice (D) is incorrect because even though Ingred says "Oh, yes!" emphatically, her inner emotion is not one of enthusiasm. The correct answer is (A).

6. This plot development item asks the reader to arrange the sequence of events in the excerpt in order in a chart. The correct order from first to last:

1. Event (d): The Saxons unite at Lynestones. This occurs early in the narrative in paragraph 1: The first sentence says "the whole family was reunited" and the third sentence says "They had joined the rest of the party at Lynstones."

2. Event (a): Egbert drives Ingred to the beach. Following the general description of Ingred's feelings in paragraph 1, a specific day is described in paragraph 2, during which Egbert takes Ingred for a motorcycle ride: "Egbert was anxious to set off, so Hereward took his place on the luggage-carrier, and, after some back-firing, the three started forth."

3. Event (b): Ingred is invited to tea. After arriving at the seaside, Ingred meets Avis, who invites her to tea: "Come along and have some tea with us," (paragraph 8).

4. Event (c): Avis talks about a fancy-dress dance. As Avis and Ingred talk, Avis becomes enthusiastic about the idea of dancing: "I do think a fancy-dress dance is about the best fun on earth," (paragraph 18).

7. This character development item asks the reader to identify three adjectives that accurately describe Ingred. The three correct adjectives:

- **Happy.** Ingred's feelings of happiness are referenced in paragraph 1: "To have her father and brothers safely back, and for the family to be together in the midst of such beautiful scenery, was sufficient for utter enjoyment."

- **Uncertain.** Ingred's inner thought process is highlighted with words like "nebulous" (paragraph 1) and is further suggested by the fact that her voice is "a little strained" (paragraph 15) and the fact that she says "It's rather early to make plans," when talking about her eventual return. Therefore, Ingred is uncertain about her future after she returns to her family home and to school.

- **Surprised.** Ingred is surprised to meet Avis at the seaside: "Much to Ingred's astonishment she was suddenly hailed by her name" (paragraph 3).

8. **D** This development item requires making a prediction about Avis based on an overall understanding of the details that relate to her. Avis appears in the narrative in paragraphs 3–20, so use the details in these paragraphs to eliminate answers that don't conform to the passage. Choice (A) is incorrect: Avis is described as "a schoolfellow" (paragraph 3), so she has been to school with Ingred before. Choice (B) is incorrect because Avis doesn't mention hosting, but talks of Ingred possibly giving parties: "you'll be giving all sorts of delightful parties, won't you?" (paragraph 16). Eliminate (C), because it is Ingred who is visiting for the afternoon, not Avis (paragraph 7). Choice (D) is correct, because Avis sighs "only a few days now," and Ingred tells Avis she is staying "a fortnight more (paragraphs 10–11). Even without knowing the definition of fortnight, Ingred indicates that she is staying "more" than Avis, so the correct answer is (D).

9. This item asks the reader to identify statements that express the EPA's purposes for writing its article. The two correct statements:

- **Statement (c): To caution consumers about deceptive advertising.** The EPA begins the article with a warning "Be careful about these products" (paragraph 1) and ends the article with the old adage: "If it sounds too good to be true, it probably is" (paragraph 5).

- **Statement (d): To give information about the role of the EPA in evaluating fuel additives and devices.** Paragraph 2 informs the reader about the registration process for additives and paragraph 3 explains the option for testing aftermarket devices to improve fuel economy. The EPA purposefully explains the process and the limitations of registration and testing to help the consumer properly evaluate any claims by manufacturers.

10. **C** This question asks which answer is supported by the Department of Energy article, which covers methods of fuel economy. Choice (A) is incorrect, because the article never states that other methods are replaced or "no longer necessary" due to the start-stop system. Choice (B) is incorrect because aftermarket alternative fuel conversions are mentioned only in the other article, not the Department of Energy article. Choice (C) is correct: This article is about methods of fuel economy, including better driving habits (paragraph 6). Choice (D) is incorrect, because this is the main idea of the EPA article, not the Department of Energy article. The correct answer is (C).

11. **B** This structure question asks about the EPA's purpose for including a particular detail, in this case, the sentence, "Very few manufacturers have applied for this program in the past 10 years." The main idea of this passage is to warn the reader about fuel additives and devices to improve fuel economy, so consider how this detail relates to the main idea. Choice (A) is incorrect: There is no information about how long the program takes. Choice (B) is correct: Paragraph 3 goes on to say, "Without this report, the EPA has no information about the safety of the device or its impact on fuel efficiency." So the EPA cannot verify the claims of manufacturers who do not apply for the program, and consumers should be wary. Choice (C) is incorrect: This sentence in the question refers to applying for the program, not the testing that occurs later. Choice (D) is also incorrect: The tone and purpose of the EPA article is directed not at the manufacturer but at the consumer. The correct answer is (B).

12. **C**   This structure question asks about how a figure relates to the overall purpose of the article by the Department of Energy, which covers methods of fuel economy. The chart illustrates the guideline about driving speed in paragraph 6: "Each 5 MPH you drive over 60 MPH can reduce your fuel economy by 7%." Choice (A) is incorrect, however, because reducing fuel economy 7% by speeding does not equate to improving fuel economy 5% by slowing down. Choice (B) is incorrect because this is a question about the role of the figure in the article, and the chart does not reflect data about vehicle maintenance. Choice (C) is correct: The chart visually illustrates the loss of fuel economy with increased speed. Finally, (D) is incorrect because the chart has no information about driving conditions. The correct answer is (C).

13. **B**   This is a comparison question about the similarities in the two articles. Both articles address fuel economy, but the first article warns about devices and the second article recommends a device. Choice (A) only reflects the second passage by the Department of Energy, so this answer is incorrect. Choice (B) is correct: The EPA warns about aftermarket devices while the Department of Energy recommends the start-stop system. Again, (C) only reflects the second passage by the Department of Energy, so this answer is incorrect. Choice (D) is wrong because neither passage offers a way to verify advertisers' claims. The correct answer is (B).

14. **A**   This structure question asks which specific detail is included in the EPA's article. Choice (A) is correct: Paragraph 3 warns, "Tampering with your car's emissions control system is punishable by significant fines," so there are potential hidden costs when taking these measures. Choice (B) contradicts the passage: The EPA says, "Most devices tested in earlier years had a neutral or negative effect on fuel economy" (paragraph 3). Eliminate (C), which also contradicts the passage: While the EPA registers additives (paragraph 2), it makes no similar claims about devices. Finally, (D) is too strong: Although paragraph 3 states, "Without this report, the EPA has no information about the safety of the device," it's possible that the EPA does have reports on some devices so some information is available. The correct answer is (A).

15. **B**   This question asks the reader to examine the structural relationships in paragraphs 6 and 7 of the Department of Energy's article. Choice (A) is incorrect: The phrase "doesn't require you to drive differently" (paragraph 7) refers to driving with a start-stop system, not driving in general, so the parts of the article do not contradict one another. Choice (B) is correct: The first item in the list of recommended habits is to avoid idling (paragraph 6), and paragraph 7 offers a system that virtually eliminates idling. Choice (C) is incorrect because paragraph 7 does not directly compare the start-stop system to other methods that reduce fuel consumption. Finally, (D) is incorrect because the start-stop system is not installed aftermarket, but comes with new vehicles ("as of the 2014 model year, they are available on about one hundred conventional vehicle models"). The correct answer is (B).

16. **A**   This language use question asks the reader to examine the effect of the use of the word "robust" in the Department of Energy's article. Paragraph 7 recommends start-stop systems. This section acknowledges "it may take some time for you to get used to" but then immediately follows with "Most systems are robust and easy to use," to reassure and persuade the reader, since "robust" means "sturdy." Therefore, (A) is correct. Choice (B) is incorrect, because even though the sentence claims the system is "easy to use," this is not the meaning of the word "robust." Choice (C) is incorrect because although another meaning of "robust" is "hefty," that does not fit the context of the paragraph. Choice (D) is incorrect, because even though paragraph 7 claims the system is "only a few hundred dollars," this is not the meaning of the word "robust." The correct answer is (A).

17.   The option that correctly completes the sentence for each "Select" option:

Drop-Down Item 1: Sentence fragments and run-ons

Option 1 is correct: Appropriate punctuation (a comma) separates the dependent clause "just as I do" from the independent clause "Surely you enjoy living in such a quiet and peaceful neighborhood."

Option 2 is incorrect because it incorrectly uses a period, creating a sentence fragment. Option 3 provides punctuation between the independent and dependent clause, creating a run-on sentence. Option 4 treats a somewhat lengthy phrase as though it is an independent clause, separated by a semicolon. However, this phrase is actually a sentence fragment and therefore cannot be separated by a semicolon.

Drop-Down Item 2: Misplaced modifiers or illogical word order

Option 2 is correct: In this sentence, the phrase "you must be aware of" appropriately refers to "the alarming increase in burglary incidents," while "via news reports and social media reports," modifies "you must be aware." The phrases appear in an appropriate order with no dangling modifiers or unclear antecedents.

Option 1 is incorrect: In this order, the phrases appear to indicate that the "burglary incidents" are "via news reports." Option 3 is incorrect: In this option, the phrase "you must be aware of by now" seems to refer to "social media posts" and creates a sentence fragment. Option 4 is incorrect, because this option presents the construction "social media posts in our neighborhood" so that it appears the social media posts (instead of the burglaries) happen in the neighborhood.

Drop-Down Item 3: Verb tense, parallelism

Option 3 is correct: This option correctly uses the present tense "are concerned" to parallel "propose" and "consider" later in the sentence.

Option 1 is incorrect: The use of "concerning" and "we all do" results in the meaning "we all do concern our community" rather than "we are all concerned about our community." Option 2 is incorrect, because the past tense "were" does not match the present tense "propose" and "consider" later in the sentence. Option 4 is incorrect because the past tense "were" does not match the present tense "propose" and "consider".

Drop-Down Item 4: Pronoun usage

Option 2 is correct: The option correctly uses the singular objective pronoun case "it" to match to "check or money order."

Option 1 is incorrect: The sentence is asking the reader to "send a check or a money order," only one, not both, so a singular pronoun is required. Option 3 is incorrect: Although "that" can function as a pronoun, the word "that" refers to something specific that is clearly understood, as in "that cat (of several cats)." For "that" to work in the context, a more complete phrase like "that payment" would be required. Option 4 is incorrect for similar reasons: For "one" to work in context, the entire phrase "one of them" would be required.

Section 2: Extended Response

As noted in Chapter 10, the Extended Response essay is evaluated based on three traits. You can earn up to 2 points for each trait for a possible maximum of 6. Here, we've provided two sample responses to give you an idea of what a score of 1 and 2 looks like for each trait.

Sample Response A

The argument of whether or not cap-and-trade is beneficial is best supported by the benefits of cap-and-trade. The environment and air quality is very important and so emissions control is needed. Cap-and-trade is something that has been implemented with success and that saves lives. It is a way for the EPA to control emissions by giving businesses and industries permits.

Since nitrous oxide and sulfur dioxide are harmful it makes sense to try to control them to try to keep the air clean. The benefits argument uses studies that have shown that SO_2 emissions have dropped 40% since the 1990s, and acid rain levels have dropped 65% since 1976. Also the benefits argument mentions cap-and-trade has reduced emissions because businesses are willing to be part of a low-cost program. These are all good points for the benefits of cap-and-trade. If cap-and-trade was an idea that didn't work, it wouldn't have been in use for so long, starting from 1976.

The argument against cap-and-trade states that the results are brought into question because there were other regulations happening at the same time as the Acid Rain Program. They also claim that the permit process causes bad incentives because free permits mean companies might not try very hard to reduce emissions. They claim that if a company reduces emissions, then their cap might be lower next year, so a company might try not to reduce emissions. But there are no statistics to show that this would happen.

If those are the argments that are made then people just need to rely on the actual results. Read the statistics and see how the Acid Rain Program and other programs are actually working. The EPA does a good job of making sure businesses can't pollute too much.

Trait 1—Creation of Arguments and Use of Evidence

Score: 1

The writer of this response makes an argument in favor of cap-and-trade ("The argument of whether or not cap-and-trade is beneficial is best supported by the benefits of cap-and-trade") through a somewhat unsophisticated analysis. The response contains some evidence from the source text to support the central position, but this evidence is presented as references that only summarize the source text ("The benefits argument uses studies that have shown SO_2 emissions have dropped 40% since the 1990s, and acid rain levels have dropped 65% since 1976"). There is some analysis of the issue and evaluation of the evidence for the arguments, but it is minimal ("If those are the argments that are made then people just need to rely on the actual results" and "These are all good points for the benefits of cap-and-trade"). Overall, the writer makes an argument supported by some analysis and some evidence from the source text. Therefore, this Response A earns a score of 1 for Trait 1.

Trait 2—Development of Ideas and Organizational Structure

Score: 1

The writer establishes an organizational structure in this response by providing a comparison of the two arguments presented. In the introduction, the writer takes a position ("The argument of whether or not cap-and-trade is beneficial is best supported by the benefits of cap-and-trade"). The second paragraph addresses the benefits of cap-and-trade and shows a clear progression of ideas. In the paragraphs, main points are developed in a general sense, but the details are not as well developed. In the second paragraph, a new thought is presented about the benefits of cap-and-trade ("If cap-and-trade was an idea that didn't work, it wouldn't have been in use for so long, starting from 1976."). The third paragraph focuses on the unwelcome possibilities of cap-and-trade, summarizing the source text and offering an assessment ("They claim that if a company reduces emissions, then their cap might be lower next year, so a company might try not to reduce emissions. But there are no statistics to show that this would happen."). The conclusion is a general explanation of why the second position is better supported. The writer's word choice is sufficiently competent and the response's tone is acceptable. Overall, the response is somewhat organized and focused, but the ideas are underdeveloped. Therefore, Response A earns a score of 1 for Trait 2.

Trait 3—Clarity and Command of Standard English Conventions

Score: 1

This brief response shows generally correct sentence structure, but without sentence variety. There is unreliable control of standard English conventions with regard to subject verb agreement ("The environment and air quality is very important") and punctuation usage. These errors do not interfere with comprehension, however, and this response is an acceptable example of draft writing. Therefore, Response A earns a score of 1 for Trait 3.

Sample Response B

There is much debate about whether cap-and-trade as a strategy for controlling emissions is effective. It is an important debate because air quality is a pressing issue today and addressing harmful emissions can possibly save lives. In this discussion of cap-and-trade, the proponents have made the better argument. They bring up several benefits to cap-and trade, including advantages to business. The pro cap-and-trade article then uses statistics to support its position. The second article from the critics' standpoint uses mostly hypothetical assertions and warnings of what might happen, with no statistical data to support the position.

In the first article, an outline of the benefits of cap-and-trade are supplied to show what makes the practice was effective—cost, accountability, and the support of federal and state standards. The first argument then provides examples of some specific successful programs: the nationwide Acid Rain Program (ARP) and the regional NO_x Budget Trading Program. The first article then cites several statistics pointing to improvements in both SO_2 and NO_x. According to the article, improvements in emissions mean saved lives, and saving lives is very strong evidence for using cap-and-trade.

The second article then calls the statistical evidence into question by pointing out that, in addition to cap-and-trade, there were other regulations in effect that impacted emissions. While the article began with a good observation here, it did not follow through. If the article had provided the exact regulations in effect, and the statistical impact on emissions, this would have been a more direct counter the statistics presented in the previous article, and the second article may well have won the argument.

Another topic mentioned by both arguments is the cost of cap-and-trade. The first article claims that cap-and-trade provides cost-effective, flexible compliance choices for regulated sources and minimized administrative costs. This argument is supported by the statistical citation that the overall costs of complying with the program will be only one fourth of what was originally predicted. Including the information about low costs for industry and government is very important evidence for the pro-cap-and-trade side. The low costs indicate that businesses will be more likely to want to comply with this program. The second argument brings up the same point about low cost, but claims that the low cost can actually result in perverse incentives, because a low price on emission permits reduces the incentive for companies to cut back their emissions. However, the critics' argument fails for two reasons. First, the second article did not offer statistics to support this assertion. Second, the critic's argument did not consider that the program's low cost might have a positive incentive as well—encouraging companies to participate in the program at all. The point the second article was trying to make is that the negative incentives outweigh the positive ones, but the evidence is not strong enough to prove this point.

The final objection used by critics of cap-and-trade claims that expensive long-term changes will not be made if there is a cheaper source of carbon credits and that environmental protection needs better solutions. However, the statistics provided by the pro-cap-and-trade article indicate that these programs have been in place since 1976, so the changes reported by the statistics are definitely seen in the long term. As for "better solutions," the critics' article continues to make the same faults: it does not supply any data to support the objection. It does not even offer any specific programs that would be the kind of solutions that the critics advocate. The second article does raise an interesting point about how one solution can prevent a better solution. If the critics of cap-and-trade had managed to supply some facts to prove this point, the second article would have made the better argument.

Because of the lack of supportive facts or concrete details for the arguments in the second article, it is clear that the first article contains the better researched and supported argument. The first argument supplies specific, concrete data in support of the claim that cap-and-trade is effective. If the second article were to go beyond its vague warnings and use specific data in its objections, then the second article would have a more significant impact simply because the first argument does not seem to consider the possible drawbacks of the cap-and-trade structure. In that case, article two would win the argument.

Trait 1—Creation of Arguments and Use of Evidence

Score: 2

The introduction of this essay contains a position ("In this discussion of cap-and-trade, the proponents have made the better argument") and then provides a developed explanation ("The pro cap-and-trade article then uses statistics to support its position. The second article uses mostly hypothetical assertions and warnings of what might happen, with no statistical data to support the position."). The writer reinforces this claim with an analysis of the evidence for the arguments in the source text, first focusing on the strength of the proponents' argument ("The first article then cites several statistics pointing to improvements in both SO_2 and NO_x. According to the article, improvements in emissions mean saved lives, and saving lives is very strong evidence for using cap-and-trade."). The writer then moves on to the inadequacy of the opposing argument ("The article began with a good observation here, but it did not follow through.").

As further support, the writer introduces alternative interpretations of the evidence ("the second article did not consider that the program's low cost might have a positive incentive as well"). Finally, the writer pinpoints the critics' unsupported assertions about better solutions ("It does not even offer any specific programs that would be the kind of solutions that the critics advocate"). Overall, the response offers a well-developed, logical, and organized argument focused on the validity of the arguments in the source text. Therefore, Response B earns a score of 2 for Trait 1.

Trait 2—Development of Ideas and Organizational Structure

Score: 2

The response shows a clear structure, beginning with the importance of emissions control to frame the issue, then discussing points made by both sides of the argument, and finally concluding with an analysis. This structure permits a development of generally logical ideas that are sufficiently explored. The response establishes a clear connection between the main idea and supporting details within paragraph 2. The writer points to hypotheses about possible negative outcomes of cap-and-trade in paragraph 3 and then discusses why the claims are not supported. The writer goes on to explore the idea that the "concrete data in support of the claim that cap-and-trade is effective" outweighs the use of "vague warnings" by the opposition. The writer uses appropriate vocabulary and formal tone to express ideas, resulting in a response that is structured, focused, and developed. Therefore, Response B earns a score of 2 for Trait 2.

Trait 3—Clarity and Command of Standard English Conventions

Score: 2

This writer shows competency with several standard English rules, including subject-verb agreement, word usage, and the rules of capitalization and punctuation. The response offers a largely correct sentence structure, and the writer blends simple and complex sentences while maintaining clarity ("The second argument brings up the same point about low cost, but claims that the low cost can actually result in perverse incentives, because a low price on emission permits reduces the incentive for companies to cut back their emissions. However, this argument fails for two reasons. First, the second article did not offer statistics to support this assertion."). Transitional words and phrases are used throughout ("in that case," "however," "while"). Overall, the response indicates a strong command of the English language and the level is appropriate for on-demand draft writing. Therefore, Response B earns a score of 2 for Trait 3.

Section 3

18. **C** This language use question requires test takers to determine which definition of the word "unpretentious" matches its use in paragraph 1. Each of the answer options reflects an actual definition of the word "unpretentious," so look closely at the way the word is used in context. The word is used as a part of the sentence "Plain, large and unpretentious, it described itself in an illuminated sign." Here, the word "unpretentious" is part of a list of adjectives, beginning with the word "plain," that describe the hotel mentioned in the previous sentence. So here the word "unpretentious" is used to mean "not fancy." Choice (A) is incorrect, because the passage is not claiming that the hotel lacks ambition. Nor would a hotel be "easygoing," so eliminate (B). Choice (C) is correct: "without excessive ornament" means "not fancy." Finally, (D) is incorrect, because "straightforward, direct" is a characteristic that describes a person's manner or an idea, not a building. The correct answer is (C).

19. **C** This development question asks specifically how the nighttime view of the city (paragraph 2) affects the narrator. Consider all of the details in paragraph 2 to get a sense of the narrator's attitude. The narrator uses phrases like "a city of beautiful streets and magnificent buildings," "Every street or avenue glistens at night," "another still more wonderful," and "indescribable orgy of light." Therefore, the author is impressed by the beauty of the city, especially the illumination. Choice (A) is incorrect. While the narrator does mention "a bewildering multitude of illuminated signs," there is nothing to indicate that the narrator is overwhelmed. Eliminate (B) because, while the author does mention the number of lights in the phrase "tens of thousands of lights wonderfully displayed," the phrase "wonderfully displayed" does not mean that the narrator is "wondering at" the number of lights. Rather, the narrator uses this phrase to express admiration for the signs. Choice (C) is correct: "rejoices" reflects all the positive language the narrator uses to describe the city at night. Choice (D) is incorrect, because the narrator is not "disillusioned" or disappointed by the city, but rather admires it. The correct answer is (C).

20. **B** This structure question asks why the author chose to use a certain phrase, so locate the detail and consider the context of the surrounding text. The phrase occurs in paragraph 2: "The first impression of a stranger visiting a large American city at night is that he is in a children's luminous palace." The passage goes on to say "There are illuminations and decorations of every conceivable nature." All of these descriptions refer to the "advertising" mentioned in the sentence, so the quotation in the question is referring to advertising signs, and "every conceivable nature" shows that the narrator is impressed by the number of signs. Choice (A) is incorrect: Although the use of the word "children" might seem to imply "innocence," the author never observes "innocence" about the city. Choice (B) is correct, indicating that the author is impressed with how many advertisements there are in the city. Eliminate (C), because while the phrase "children's luminous palace" is certainly a poetic representation of the narrator's feelings, there is nothing about the "regal nature of America" anywhere in the excerpt. Choice (D) is incorrect because it is contrary to the author's purpose: The author is admiring the nighttime city. The correct answer is (B).

21. **A** This is actually a plot development question, because the phrase suggests something about the author's broader experiences. Paragraph 3 states, "When I found myself finally back in my hotel I was to be the victim of still another disillusionment." The passage continues "No country anywhere could rival America for hotels, I had thought." So the "disillusionment" refers to the mistaken thought the author had about American hotels. "Still another" implies that the narrator has had mistaken thoughts about America before. Choice (A) is correct: This phrase indicates that the author has been mistaken before. Choice (B) contradicts the passage: All the details in paragraph 2 indicate that the narrator admires the city at night. Choice (C) is incorrect because the "National" is the hotel where the narrator is staying (paragraph 3), which reveals the mistaken assumption the author had about hotels. Choice (D) is incorrect because in

paragraph 1 the author feels satisfied with the hotel ("I found a hotel that, from the outside, just suited my fancy,") and so would not have been reluctant to return. The correct answer is (A).

22. **D** This is a structure question about the use of "senile" in paragraph 3, so locate the detail and consider the context: "The furniture, consisting of one bed, one dressing-table, one wardrobe and one chair was obviously suffering from advanced senile decay." This sentence occurs within a larger description of the shabby appearance of the room overall. Therefore, "senile" repeats the emphasis that all parts of the room are worn out, by emphasizing the age of the furniture. Choice (A) is incorrect: Although the use of the word is intended to mean "advanced age," it applies to the furniture, not the hotel. Choice (B) is incorrect, because the author applies the word "senile" to all the furniture in the list—nothing in the room is new. Eliminate (C) because this paragraph discusses the room, not the manager. Choice (D) is correct: All the items of furniture are old, which builds on the author's description of the room overall. The correct answer is (D).

23. **D** This question asks about the character development of the narrator as shown through certain actions. Paragraph 3 directly states, "putting my revolver under the blanket near me in case of possible eventualities, I laid me down in peace to sleep." The use of the phrase "possible eventualities" suggests that the narrator is preparing for anything that may happen, specifically because the door was "minus a lock for many a long day." So, the narrator places the revolver in preparation for what may happen because of the unlocked door. Choice (A) is contradictory because "laid me down in peace" indicates that the author is not fearful, and the neighborhood is never described as rough. Choice (B) is incorrect: Even though the narrator states, "I was too tired, however, to bother," the action of placing the revolver under the blanket is not due to tiredness, but a purposeful response to the unlocked door. Eliminate (C) because nothing in the excerpt indicates that the author has a naturally violent temper. Choice (D) correctly indicates that the narrator's action is done in deliberate preparation for a possibly dangerous situation (the unlocked door). The correct answer is (D).

24. **A** This question asks about the author's purpose in choosing that sentence for the conclusion. So, consider the role the last sentence plays in the excerpt as a whole. Paragraph 5 relates the speech the narrator gives to the manager regarding the shabby hotel room: "never in ANY city at ANY time have I struck ANY hotel that for sheer rottenness compares with THIS one!" The manager would likely be outraged at hearing such a criticism, so for the excerpt to conclude, "I have an idea at the back of my mind that that manager-man doesn't love Englishmen!" is an ironic understatement about the manager's true feelings. Thus, (A) is correct. Choice (B) is incorrect because the purpose of the sentence is to close the scene with humor or irony, not guess about the manager's preferences. Eliminate (C), because the narrator is angry about the condition of the room, not suspicious of the manager. Choice (D) is contradictory to the passage: The narrator does not show regret for complaining, but instead makes an ironic comment. The correct answer is (A).

25. **B** This question asks about the narrator, so at first it may seem like a character development question. However, the entire passage is about the narrator, so use the main idea. A major theme is that the narrator is a foreigner visiting America, as is suggested by the title and the words "a stranger visiting a large American city" (paragraph 2). Choice (A) contradicts the passage: All the details in paragraph 2 indicate that the narrator admires the city. Choice (B) is correct since paragraph 6 indicates the narrator is from England. Eliminate (C) because the sentence "No country anywhere could rival America for hotels, I had thought" (paragraph 3) strongly indicates that the narrator has been to other places in America before. Even though the narrator shouts once in paragraph 5, there is no evidence to indicate that the narrator is loud-mouthed in general, so eliminate (D). The correct answer is (B).

26.   This item asks the reader to identify statements that express the author's purposes for writing this article. The two correct statements:

- **Statement (b): To persuade the reader that playing a State Lottery isn't really gambling.** The author begins the essay with a definition of gambling and then analyzes that definition and argues that the State Lottery doesn't fit this definition (paragraph 2).

- **Statement (c): To analyze the dual characteristics of the definition of the word "gamble".** The author analyzes the aspects of "chance" and "game" using a detailed scenario (paragraph 3).

27. **B**   This structure question asks why the author uses the phrase "behind its hand" (paragraph 6). This phrase comes in the context of this sentence: "At a time when the one cry is 'Production!' the State adds (behind its hand), 'Buy a Premium Bond, and let the other man produce for you.'" This sentence shows a contrast between the two actions of the state, almost a hypocrisy. Choice (A) is incorrect; this phrase doesn't refer to the "no work at all" proposition in the previous sentence. Choice (B) is correct: This phrase is part of a contrast between the two actions of the state. Choice (C) is incorrect, because the analogy of the state to a human body is never made in this essay. Choice (D) is contradictory to the passage, because the author has a somewhat positive, rather than negative, view of gambling (paragraph 3). The correct answer is (B).

28. **D**   This structure question asks about the role that a detail—the image of the Monte Carlo gambler (paragraph 3)—plays in the passage as a whole. The author draws out this scenario to illustrate the aspects of "chance" and "game" that comprise "gambling" according to the dictionary definition (paragraph 2). Therefore, (A) is wrong; the author is not trying to make a statement about Monte Carlo as a place. Choice (B) is also incorrect; while "struggle" is mentioned, it is mentioned as a part of "game," the aspect that the author is exploring. Choice (C) is contradictory to the author's tone: The author has a generally neutral to positive view of gambling, so "reckless" is too strong. Choice (D) is correct: The image of the gambler is there to complete the picture begun with the definition of gambling. The correct answer is (D).

29. **A**   This structure question asks about what inference can be made from the sentence. The author asserts, "The case of the average man in favor of State lotteries is, quite simply, that he does not like Dr. Clifford." The author implies that favoring lotteries is not based on logic but instead on personal dislike for Dr. Clifford. If the average man in favor of lotteries does not like the doctor (or his views), then it follows that the man is in favor of lotteries, simply because the doctor is not. Therefore, (A) is correct and (B) is wrong. Choice (C) is incorrect because intelligence is not addressed in the essay. Choice (D) is far too broad an assertion to make based on that one sentence—there's no evidence that the average man would not favor anything represented by the doctor. The correct answer is (A).

30. **D**   This evaluation question asks about which detail supports the claim that people get pleasure out of games of skill and chance (paragraph 3). Immediately following this claim, the author draws out the scenario of the gambler in Monte Carlo. Choice (A) is incorrect because it is the bland description of the State Lottery. Choice (B) is incorrect; although it refers to making the country "contented" (paragraph 6), it doesn't refer back to getting pleasure out of a game of chance. Choice (C) is incorrect; this quote (paragraph 2) just refers to the author's consideration of the definition of "gambling." Therefore, (D) is correct—the repeated use of "wonderful" indicates the gambler's elation. The correct answer is (D).

31. **B**   This language use question asks the reader to examine the effect of the term "cold-blooded" in paragraph 5. The sentence reads, "and you simply take part in a cold-blooded attempt to acquire money without working for it." Here the use of the term "cold-blooded" indicates a pragmatic pursuit of the lottery as opposed to the exciting language used to describe the Monte Carlo gambler's experience. Therefore, (A)

is incorrect—the author is depicting the players as passionless, not ruthless—and (B) is correct. Choice (C) contradicts the passage, since the author says gambling is not entirely evil (paragraph 4). Choice (D) is incorrect because this choice describes the consequences to society, rather than the experience of the individual in playing the lottery. The correct answer is (B).

32. **D** This development question asks about how the author's use of direct questions in paragraph 3 contributes to the author's essay. Paragraph 3 states, "And is there any man who, having made a fortune at Monte Carlo, will admit that he owes it entirely to chance? Will he not rather attribute it to his wonderful system, or if not to that, at any rate to his wonderful nerve...?" These questions to the reader are rhetorical, designed to encourage thinking about the topic and convince the reader of the author's perspective on gambling. Choice (A) is incorrect because there are no answers to these rhetorical questions. Choice (B) is contradictory to the passage, since the essay begins with a definition. Choice (C) is incorrect because the personality of the gambler is not under discussion. Choice (D) is correct—the questions cause the reader to consider the "game" or pleasure of gambling. The correct answer is (D).

33. **A** This question asks about the author's opinions regarding Premium Bonds. The author declares, "I am against Premium Bonds, but not for the popular reason. I am against them because there is so very little of the gamble about them" (paragraph 2). Thus, (A) is correct. Choice (B) is wrong because the author's tone when discussing the redistribution of funds (paragraph 6) is definitely satirical: "Instead of a million ten-pound citizens, we should have a thousand ten-thousand-pounders and 999,000 with nothing. That would be the official way of making the country happy." Choice (C) is contradictory because the author feels that Premium Bonds "have so very little of the gamble about them." Choice (D) is incorrect because the author mentions "hypocritical" in paragraph 1 as the views of others, not his own view. The correct answer is (A).

34. **B** This point of view question asks about the author's tone toward the reader, so examine the passage for tone indicators. In several places the author gives opinions and addresses the reader directly: "There are many occupations—and many jobs— that you would enjoy" (paragraph 3), "You need not restrict your job search to careers related to your degree" paragraph (7), and "It's never too late to change careers" (paragraph 1). Overall, the author offers encouragement to the reader or job seeker. Choice (A) is incorrect, because "condescension" means talking down to someone, which is not what the author is doing. Choice (B) is correct: The author is offering information to reassure and help job seekers. Choice (C) is incorrect, because the author is not trying to intimidate the reader. Choice (D) is incorrect because "satisfaction" expresses a concern with the self. However, this author is concerned primarily with the reader. The correct answer is (B).

35. **A** This question asks about the author's primary purpose in writing the article. The author's identification as part of the Department of Labor suggests that the author is familiar with the realities of the working world, and paragraph 3 asserts "There are many occupations—and many jobs—that you would enjoy." The final paragraph, paragraph 11, states, "It's never too late to change careers." Therefore, the author is trying to help people persist in a job search despite temporary setbacks. Choice (A) is correct, because the author emphasizes "keeping your options open" (paragraph 3) and "learning a variety of tasks helps you to sharpen abilities" (paragraph 5). Eliminate (B) because the author's tone is encouraging, not cautionary. Choice (C) is incorrect, because while the article mentions low grades and work history gaps, it does not mention the specific types of jobs that accept people with these limitations. Choice (D) contradicts the passage: Paragraph 5 states, "no one job uses all your talents."

36. **D** This structure question asks how this sentence relates to the article as a whole. The sentence "Consider that electrical technicians are now repairing fuel cells, for example, or that veterinary technicians become pharmaceutical sales workers." This sentence appears in the context of a paragraph that begins with "You need not restrict your job search to careers related to your degree," (paragraph 7). Therefore, the sentence in question offers support for that topic sentence. Choice (A) is incorrect: While the sentence does present examples of specific careers, the author is not advocating that readers pursue these careers. Eliminate (B) because it contradicts the topic sentence of the paragraph. Choice (C) may seem attractive, because the last sentence of paragraph 7 reads "Often, technical skills are applicable to many settings." However, the purpose of paragraph 7 is to address the flexibility of skills in general, not just technical skills, so (D) is correct.

37. **C** This purpose question asks you to analyze the author's rhetorical technique of question-and-answer in paragraph 9. The topic sentence of this paragraph states, "People overcome all kinds of challenges to find satisfying work." The paragraph then goes on to raise the same challenges that were brought up in paragraph 8 and offer solutions to those challenges one by one. Choice (A) is incorrect because the paragraph does not address which challenges are "worse" or not. Choice (B) is incorrect because paragraph 9 is a response to paragraph 8 (the previous paragraph), not support for the next paragraph. Choice (C) is correct: Paragraph 9 uses the question-and-answer format to address the concerns raised in paragraph 8. Choice (D) is incorrect because the question-and-answer format does not help the author's point by *raising* the concerns; it helps the author's point by offering solutions for those concerns. The correct answer is (C).

38. **D** This language use item requires test takers to determine which definition of the word "overcome" matches its use in paragraph 9. Each of the answer options reflects an actual definition of the word "overcome," so look closely at the way the word is used in context. The word is used as a part of this sentence: "People overcome all kinds of challenges to find satisfying work," which is connected to the later phrase "how you handle adversity." So here, the word "overcome" is used to mean "rise above" the challenges or the adversity. Choice (A) is incorrect, because "overpower" means to "defeat in physical contest" or "overwhelm the senses"; neither makes sense with "challenges." Choice (B) is also incorrect, because "shock the challenges" would not make sense either. Choice (C) might seem attractive because of the phrase "a good indicator of your ability to persevere"; however, "People outlive all kinds of challenges" would not make sense in a paragraph advising job seekers to assertively handle adversity. Choice (D) is correct: "surmount" means "rise above." The correct answer is (D).

39. **A** This question asks you to make an inference about the "workers" mentioned in the quotation. To answer this question, refer to the paragraph mentioned and read beyond the sentence to find out more about the "workers." The topic sentence of paragraph 11 is "It's never too late to change careers" followed by examples of workers who move into very different fields. Therefore, (A) is correct. Choice (B) contradicts the passage, which states, "For each of these workers, the desire for job satisfaction outweighed the desire for status quo." Eliminate (C) because "status quo" means "current state" not "prestige." Choice (D) is incorrect because the workers in the example did not all return to school—only one did. The correct answer is (A).

40. This item asks the reader to choose two examples the author uses to support the claim that prospective employees can take steps to better their odds of employment. Answer (a) is wrong because the author advocates working to gain skills as a remedy for lack of experience. Answer (c) is wrong because it contradicts paragraph 6. Answer (d) is wrong because author advocates a focus on skills rather than chronology to address gaps in work history (paragraph 9). The two correct answers are as follows:

- **Action (b): Donate your time to charitable organizations.** In paragraph 11, the author recommends "Gain needed skills with volunteer work."

- **Action (e): Anticipate questions that might arise when applying for a job.** The author also advises to "get a little interviewing practice." (paragraph 9).

41. **C** This is a purpose question about the author's intended audience, so use the main idea from the passage as a starting point. This author is concerned with correcting "career myths" so that these myths won't "derail a career search and sap motivation" (paragraph 1). Therefore, the author is addressing job seekers who might be affected or "derailed" by these myths. Choices (A) and (B) are incorrect: There is nothing in the article to indicate that the information is targeted specifically at first-time job seekers or college students. Choice (C) is correct: The article addresses myths that cause people to doubt their ability to get a job (paragraphs 8 and 10). Choice (D) is incorrect because addressing work history gaps is just one detail in the passage, not the purpose of the whole article. The correct answer is (C).

42. **C** This character development question asks specifically how her father's words affect young Susan. After the sentence "It would never do to have a woman overseer in the mill," (paragraph 2), the very next sentence conveys Susan's reaction: "This answer did not satisfy Susan and she often thought about it" (paragraph 3). Choice (A) is incorrect: As she watched the mill workers, the fact that women weren't overseers "continued to puzzle Susan" (paragraph 3). Eliminate (B) because, while Susan questions her father *before* being told "it would never do to have a woman overseer," there is no indication that Susan questions her father's judgment *after* being told this. Choice (C) is correct: Susan sees that her father's words do not match what she observes happening in the mill. Choice (D) is incorrect because nothing in this excerpt indicates that Susan goes to work in the mill or rebels against her father. The correct answer is (C).

43. **A** This structure question asks about how the details about Susan's home life enhance the narrative, so connect these details to the main idea. The main idea of the passage is about the kinds of work considered appropriate for women. The description starts with the second sentence of paragraph 5, indicated by "in the home of the millowner." At home, Susan's mother cared for three daughters and eleven boarders, and that her days were filled with cooking, washing, ironing, mending, and spinning. Then the passage states, "But she was capable and strong and was doing only what all women in this new country were expected to do." So, the description of Susan's home life shows both her mother's capabilities and the enormous workload women were expected to handle. Therefore, Choice (A) is correct. Choice (B) is incorrect because the passage does not indicate that Susan's father is absent; rather, her mother's workload is depicted as a typical amount of daily duties. Choice (C) is incorrect because the housework and the millwork are not compared in the passage. Even though boarding the millworkers is part of Susan's mother's work, it is only one part of it, not the primary reason to give all the details of home life. Therefore, eliminate (D). The correct answer is (A).

44. **D** This evaluation question asks which sentence from the passage supports the idea that Susan is learning skills that enhance independence. Since several answers contain quotations related to the major themes of women's work or independence, consider what is implied as well as what is directly stated. Choices (A) and (B) are incorrect, since these sentences refer to the women who work in the mills, not Susan. Choice (C) is incorrect; even though this quotation describes Susan, she is only observing other workers, not learning skills. Choice (D) is correct: It is part of the sentence that states, "Susan, even before she was six, was very useful" (paragraph 5), so this quotation highlights Susan's ability to care for herself and do grown-up work. The correct answer is (D).

45. **B** This development question asks about the character of Sally Ann as shown through the overseer's actions. The reference is located in paragraph 3: "When the yarn on the beam was tangled or there was something wrong with the machinery, Elijah, the overseer, always called out to Sally Ann." The passage goes on to say "Sally Ann never failed to locate the trouble or to untangle the yarn." This shows that Sally Ann's mechanical ability was known and relied upon. Choice (A) is incorrect, because the overseer is not relying

upon Sally Ann's weaving abilities in these sentences, nor does the passage indicate that she is a more efficient weaver than the other women. Choice (B) is correct: The overseer (another worker) recognizes her mechanical ability. Choice (C) is somewhat contradictory since Sally Ann is the person who untangles the yarn. Choice (D) can be eliminated because there is no information about Sally Ann's hopes or whether she enjoys being asked for help. The correct answer is (B).

46. **A** This question asks about Susan's father's attitude about the cotton mills. Susan's father's point of view is a major theme of the passage: He has definite ideas about the women who work in his mills. Since the cotton mills are discussed throughout most of the excerpt, use the passage to either confirm or eliminate answers based on details in the choices. That the mills were an acceptable place for women to work is not directly stated in the passage but is strongly implied by the fact that Susan's father employs women weavers, so keep (A) and eliminate (B), since that answer directly contradicts the fact that Susan's father employed women. Choice (C) can be eliminated because even though the passage states, "Brides were proud to display a few cotton sheets instead of commonplace homespun linen" (paragraph 4), there is no indication in the passage that Susan's father felt cotton would replace homespun entirely. Eliminate (D), because even though paragraph 3 states the mill had a "general air of efficiency," there is no indication that Susan's father considered men generally more efficient than women. The correct answer is (A).

47. This character development item asks the reader to identify three adjectives that accurately describe Susan as she watches the mill workers. This scene is found in paragraph 3. Here are the three correct adjectives:

- **Hushed.** The second sentence in paragraph 3 states, "to stand quietly and look about," when describing Susan's experience of the mill, so she is quiet as she watches.

- **Confused.** The last sentence of paragraph 3 reveals that as Susan observes Sally Ann doing a task the overseer can't, the fact that Sally Ann isn't an overseer herself "continued to puzzle Susan."

- **Amused.** The mill is described as "the best kind of entertainment" from Susan's point of view, and paragraph 3 states that Susan was "fascinated."

48. **D** This question asks about the mill that Susan's father built. Since different details about cotton mills are discussed in paragraphs 3, 4, and 5, use the passage to either confirm or eliminate answers based on details in the choices. Choice (A) is incorrect: The first sentence of paragraph 5 directly states that cotton had to be brought *from* Troy to the mill, a distance of 40 miles. Choice (B) is incorrect, because paragraph 5 states that the workers boarded at the home of the millowner, not the mill. Eliminate (C) because the passage states that Susan was born in 1820 (paragraph 4) and Susan's father built the mill when she was two years old (paragraph 5). Choice (D) is correct: Paragraph 5 states that Susan's father's mill was built beside a brook, and paragraph 4 states that "men like her father, Daniel Anthony, saw a potential cotton mill by the side of every rushing brook," implying that a source of running water is necessary for a mill. The correct answer is (D).

49. **B** This development question asks about the women workers in Susan's father's mill. The women mill workers are shown at work in paragraph 3, their backgrounds are discussed in paragraph 4, and their living conditions are mentioned in paragraph 5. Choice (A) is incorrect, because only Sally Ann is presented as a worker possibly qualified to be overseer—there is no information about the others. Choice (B) is correct: It accurately summarizes the sentence in paragraph 4: "young women, eager to earn the first money they could call their own, were leaving the farms, for a few months at least, to work in the mills." Choice (C) directly contradicts the passage, which states in paragraph 5 that the workers lived at the home of the millowner. Eliminate (D) because Susan's mother wasn't helped by the mill workers but by "a thirteen-year-old girl who worked for her after school hours," (paragraph 5). The correct answer is (B).

50.   The option that correctly completes the sentence for each "Select" option is as follows:

Drop-Down Item 1: Verb tense and Misplaced modifier/illogical word order

Option 2 is correct: In this sentence, the verb "had" (the simple past tense of "have") is used appropriately in a sentence that refers to a period in the past.

Option 1 is incorrect, because the present tense "I see him developing" does not fit in this sentence about a "a period of six years ending in June 2009." Past tense is needed here. Option 3 is incorrect: This option results in illogical construction: "I had great pleasure from a paste-up assistant at the beginning, into a fully functioning Graphics Design Project Coordinator." Option 4 is incorrect, because this option results in ambiguous construction that could be read "with great pleasure, he was developing" instead of "As I saw him, with great pleasure."

Drop-Down Item 2: Parallelism and run-ons

Option 3 is correct: This option correctly divides two independent clauses with a period and keeps the items in the list in parallel adverbial form: "quickly and effectively."

Option 1 is incorrect: A comma is too weak to divide the two independent clauses and so this option results in a comma splice. Option 2 incorrectly merges "quickly, effectively, and during" into a list form, resulting in a comma splice as the two independent clauses are connected with a comma. Option 4 is incorrect because the items in the list (connected by "and") are not parallel: "quick" is an adjective and doesn't match the adverb "effectively."

Drop-Down Item 3: Parallelism

Option 4 is correct: This option keeps the structure parallel by pairing an infinitive with an infinitive in a comparison structure: "just as able to give guidance as to step."

Option 1 is incorrect because it results in the construction "able to give guidance and step back and take direction" which is a run-on structure. A list of three items should be written "give guidance, step back, and take direction." Option 2 is incorrect, because the dependent clause is separated from the rest of the sentence with a period, forming the sentence fragment "Just as able to give guidance and step back and take direction when another is leading the group." Option 3 is incorrect because the construction "to give guidance and stepping" is not parallel, as it pairs an infinitive with a gerund.

Drop-Down Item 4: Misplaced modifiers or illogical word order

Option 4 is correct: In this sentence, the words "still" and "fondly" are correctly placed next to "remembered," which they both modify. The word "even" is placed next to "a year" to emphasize the time period, so that the sense of "still remembered" matches "even a year."

Option 1 is incorrect: In this order, the placement of the word "fondly" makes it appear to modify the word "here" when it should modify "remembered." Option 2 is incorrect: In this option, the placement of the word "even" makes it appear to modify "he," resulting in the phrase "even he" which distinguishes a person from other people. However, since no other people are the subject of discussion, "even he" is unnecessary and confusing. The word "even" should modify "year," to distinguish a time period. Option 3 is incorrect: The placement of the word "still" seems to modify "fondly" when it should modify "remembered" so that the emphasis on time in "still remembered" would match "even a year."

MATHEMATICAL REASONING

Part 1

1. **D** Replace every z with -3 and solve the equation. Remember that when you square a negative number, it becomes positive, but when you cube a negative number, it stays negative. So,

$$\frac{z^3 + 2z + 3}{z^2 + 1} = \frac{(-3)^3 + 2(-3) + 3}{(-3)^2 + 1} = \frac{(-27) + (-6) + 3}{9 + 1} = \frac{-30}{10} = -3$$

2. **C** To calculate the minimum amount of music (7.2 hours), divide 3.6 by 2 and then multiply the result by 4. To calculate the maximum amount (14.4 hours), multiply 3.6 by 4. The total must be between these numbers. If you chose (D), you gave the range for a single CD instead of for all 4.

3. **D** The total time must include the trip there, the 3 hours in between, and the trip back. To calculate the time for the trip there (2.5 hours), divide 145 by 58. The trip back is also 2.5 hours, so for total time add 2.5 + 2.5 + 3.

4. **B** The July temperature should equal four times the February temperature, so $4t$ (remember that t represents the February temperature) is equal to 82. If you chose (C) or (D), you solved for the February temperature and got 21 and incorrectly made that a part of the equation. Note that the question asks for the formula not the solution.

5. **38,000**

First calculate the number of tomatoes that were crushed (20% of 50,000 = 10,000 tomatoes) and subtract this number from the original 50,000. Now calculate 5% of the remaining tomatoes, keeping in mind that there are 40,000 tomatoes now not 50,000. So 5% of 40,000 = 2,000 tomatoes. Subtracting from 40,000 leaves 38,000 tomatoes.

Part 2

6. **A** The total number of workers employed in neither clerical nor professional jobs is equal to the total number of workers (2,300,000) minus the number of clerical workers (19% of 2,300,000 = 437,000) minus the number of professional workers (24% of 2,300,000 = 552,000). If you answered (C), you found the total workers in those two professions but forgot to subtract it from the total workforce

7. **B** This question can be solved algebraically or by plugging in answer choices for Miriam and seeing which number works. To solve algebraically, set Betty's stamps equal to $m - 6$. Now, $m + m - 6 = 2m - 6 = 42$. Solving, $m = 24$.

8.

Since point P is at –5 and point S is at 3, $P + S = -2$.

9.

Since point Q is at –3, point R is at 1, and point T is at 4, $|Q - R| - T = |(-3) - 1| - 4 = |-4| - 4 = 4 - 4 = 0$. Don't forget to do the operation inside the absolute value sign before applying the absolute value.

10. **A** To solve this equation, set up the rate of erosion as a ratio of distance divided by time. Since the rate of erosion remains constant, this ratio will remain constant. Therefore the original distance divided by the original time $\left(\dfrac{9.8}{10,000} \right)$ is equal to the new distance divided by the new time $\left(\dfrac{D}{22,000} \right)$.

11. **D** The question asks how many times stronger lens X is than lens Y, so divide the strength of lens X by the strength of lens Y. $3 \times 10^5 \div 6 \times 10^2 = 300,000 \div 600 = 500$. If you chose (C), remember that 500% of a number is equivalent to multiplying by 5 not by 500. If you chose (A) or (B), you probably divided 6 by 3 instead of 3 by 6.

12. **C** One good way to solve this equation is with ratios. Mark's rate of mowing, which is equal to the amount mowed divided by time, remains constant. So $\dfrac{\frac{2}{3}\, lawn}{1\, hour} = \dfrac{1\, lawn}{x\, hours}$. Solve this equation using cross multiplication to determine that $x = \dfrac{3}{2}$.

13. **B** First you must recognize that the front and the back of the box are the smallest two sides, since they have the smallest dimensions (2.5×7). So now, using the surface area formula, add up the other 4 sides and leave off the front and the back. The perimeter of the base is $2.5 + 2.5 + 7 + 7 = 19$, so surface area $19 \times h = 19 \times 10 = 190$.

14. **–54**

First substitute the values of x and a into the equation and then solve, being careful about order of operations. $3x(x - 2a)^{-x} = 3(-2)(-2 - 2 \times (.5))^2 = (-6)(-2 - 1)^2 = (-6)(-3)^2 = (-6) \times -54$, if $x = -2$ and $a = 0.5$.

15. **9, 34**

The task here is to find a value in the first pull-down menu that will give a perimeter found in the second pull-down menu. Just start plugging in values from the first menu until you get a perimeter that is in the second menu. If $x = 9$, then perimeter $= 9 + 9 + 16 = 34$.

16.   **2,550**

The laser printer and hard drive do not change price so they will still cost $650 and $250 respectively. The price of the computer, however, goes up 10%, so calculate 10% of $1,500 and add that to the previous price. So now the computer costs $1,500 + $150 = $1,650. The total bill therefore would be $1,650 + 650 + 250 = $2,550.

17.   **A**   This is a hard algebra problem but an easy Backsolving problem. Always start with a middle answer choice, such as (C). Say there are 26 women at Universal. If there were twice as many women as men, that means there would be 13 men. Altogether, there are *supposed* to be 78 employees, but your numbers add up to only 39. Could (C) be the right answer? Nope, too small. You need a bigger number. Move up to (B) and say there are 42 women, which means there would be 21 men. You're supposed to get 78 employees, but 42 + 21 equals only 53 employees. Still too small. That must mean the correct answer is (A).

18. $\dfrac{65 + 113}{262}$ or $\dfrac{113 + 65}{262}$

Probability questions always ask for a part divided by a whole. To calculate the probability that a random bird is not a duck, you need to divide the total number of non-ducks by the total number of birds. The total number of non-ducks is equal to the number of geese plus the number of robins.

19.   **D**   This question tests distribution. Be sure to distribute the term outside the parentheses to both of the terms inside the parentheses, and then combine like terms and simplify. $2a(a - 3b^2) + a^2 = 2a^2 - 6ab^2 + a^2 = 3a^2 - 6ab^2$. But this is not an answer choice. If you chose (A), you forgot to add the a^2. If you chose (B), you did not distribute the $2a$. Notice that both terms now are divisible by $3a$, so you can get (D) by pulling $3a$ out front. You may also try plugging in for values of a and b in the original equation and checking the answer choices to see which is equivalent.

20.   **D**   Use the slope equation to find the missing point. $\dfrac{y_2 - y_1}{x_2 - x_1} = m$ (*slope*). Since the slope of the line is given as 3, therefore, you find that $3 = \dfrac{11 - (-10)}{x - (-2)} = \dfrac{11 + 10}{x + 2} = \dfrac{21}{x + 2}$. Multiply both sides by the denominator, so $3(x + 2) = 21$, and $x = 5$.

21.   **B**   To write the equation of a line in the form $y = mx + b$, you need to know the slope m (here given as 3) and the y-intercept b, which is not given. To calculate b, plug in the point on the line that you know $(-2, -10)$ and solve. So $-10 = 3(-2) + b$. Solving, $b = -4$.

22.   **B**   The answer choices should clue you in that this is a setup problem: There is no need to complete the algebra. To find out how much the typist is earning per hour, divide $65.40 (his daily pay) by 4 (the number of hours he is currently working). This is the typist's hourly rate. Now, multiply that by 7 hours to find out what he would be paid if he worked 7 hours a day: $7 \times \$65.04 \div 4$. The correct answer is (B).

23.   **Action-Adventure 18, Drama 17.** The total of the values on the chart must add up to 100%, since the chart represents all the people surveyed. The current values add up to 65. Subtract this from 100 to get 35, which should be the sum of the missing numbers. Looking at the length of the bars on the chart, you

can see that 10 is much too small and that 25 is too large. Try numbers until you find two that add up to 35. The only options are 17 and 18. Since Action-Adventure is a longer bar than Drama, place the 18 by Action-Adventure and the 17 by Drama.

24. **A** The ratio of Comedy to Other Types is 25:10, but this is not one of the answer choices. You must reduce the ratio just like you reduce a fraction. Divide both 25 and 10 by 5 and you get 5: 2.

25. **D** The question asks for an average price, so you need to divide the total price of the tickets by the total number of tickets. The total price of the first-class tickets is 110(6.00), the total price of the second-class tickets is 172(3.50), and the total number of tickets is 110 + 172.

26. $\dfrac{9}{4}$ or **2.25**

   Be careful about order of operations. First multiply both sides by 2 to eliminate the fraction. So $(4x + 3)^2 = 144$. Take the square root of both sides. $4x + 3 = 12$ and $4x = 9$.

27. **C** The post office is located halfway between points A and E. Using the diagram, we can calculate that the distance between A and E is 23 miles. Therefore, the post office is located 11.5 miles from A and 11.5 miles from E, right in the middle. Start at point A and go 11.5 miles to the right. You will be between B and C.

28. **C** First add the tip to the given bill, so multiply $36 by 20% and then add $36. So the total bill is $43.20. Now divide this by 4.

29.

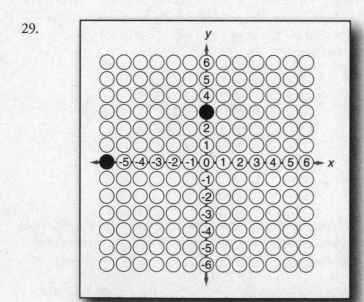

Remember that when a point lies on the y-axis, that means the x-coordinate is 0, and when a point lies on the x-axis, the y-coordinate is 0. Given the equation, $y = \dfrac{1}{2}x + 3$, when x is 0 then y is 3. So mark the point (0, 3) on the y-axis. Then set $y = 0$ in the equation and solve for x. $\dfrac{1}{2}x + 3 = 0$, so $\dfrac{1}{2}x = -3$. amd $x = -6$. So mark point (−6, 0) on the x-axis.

30. **200**

The classic mistake here is to find 60 percent of $120, or $72. However, the $120 is 60 percent of Karen's entire paycheck. In other words, you need to find 60 percent of a number we don't know yet, and set that equal to $120. Since $120 is 60 percent of the paycheck, this means that $120 = \frac{60}{100} x$. Solving for x, the answer is 200.

31. **C** In this problem, there was more information given than you really needed. After one day, the amount of water in the reservoir had doubled from its original amount. After five days, the amount of water had quadrupled from its original amount. If all we need to know is how much water there was after *five* days, the fact that it doubled after the *first* day is irrelevant. If x represents the original amount, the correct answer is $4x$.

32. **D** There are 4 chefs, and each one averages c per month. There are 18 servers, and each one averages $840 less than the chefs' wages (c). Subtract $840 from c and multiply that by 18 servers. Add the totals of the two groups to get the monthly payroll.

33. **B** First calculate the area of the new sign using a ratio of area to price. $\frac{40 \text{ ft}}{\$140} = \frac{x}{\$336}$. Cross multiply and solve for $x = 96$. So the area of the large sign is 96. Now divide area by height to get the length = 12.

34. **B** Since the total number of games team A will play is 44, take 75% of 44 to calculate the total number of games that team A must win. 75% of 44 is 33 games, so that is their target. So far team A has won 28 games, so they need to win an additional 5 games.

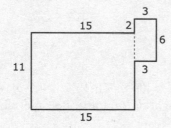

35. **D**

In order to find the area of a more complicated figure, divide the figure into more manageable shapes. Here if you draw in the dotted line shown, you will have two rectangles. The area of the larger rectangle is 15 × 11 = 165. The area of the smaller rectangle is 3 × 6 = 18. So the area of the whole figure is 165 + 18 = 183.

36. **4.5**

To find the empty space, find the volume of the entire chest by multiplying the three dimensions (length, width, depth): 2.5 × 1.5 × 2 = 7.5 cubic feet. Then subtract the size of the blankets (3 total cubic feet, since 3 blankets) to get 4.5 cubic feet of empty space.

37. **A** After Michelle paid the deductible of $500, there was $350 remaining. The insurance company paid 80% of that, so $350 × 0.8 = $280. Michelle had to pay the remaining $70 ($350 − $280 = $70).

38.   The volume of cylinder L is **[less than half]** the volume of cylinder R.

Use the formula for the volume of a cylinder to calculate the volume for each cylinder. Although the numbers in both cylinders (8 and 20) are the same, the volumes are not equal. The reason is that the formula for volume requires that the radius of a cylinder be squared. Therefore, the radius has a greater effect on volume than height does. As a result, the volume of the cylinder with the larger radius (20) has a greater volume. Volume of cylinder L $= \pi r^2 h = \pi 4^2 \times 20 = 320\pi$. Volume of cylinder R $= \pi 10^2 \times 8 = 800\pi$. So the second cylinder is much larger in volume.

39. **A** First calculate the volume for each cylinder L $= \pi r^2 h = \pi 4^2 \times 20 = 320\pi$. So this is the volume of the water poured into cylinder R. The water in cylinder R now forms a cylinder that comes part of the way up the side of cylinder R. To determine the height, use the volume equation again: $320\pi = \pi r^2 h = \pi 10^2 h$. So $320 = 10^2 \times h$ and h (the height of the water) $= 3.2$.

40.   **92,650**

To calculate the minimum revenue, consider which empty seats will cost the airline the most money. 3 empty first-class seats will reduce the total revenue much more than 3 empty coach seats. So calculate the total income from (30 – 3) = 27 first-class passengers and (325 – 30) = 295 coach passengers. So Total minimum revenue $= 27 \times \$700 + 295 \times \$250 = \$18,900 + \$73,750 = \$92,650$.

41.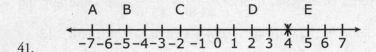

The distance between two points on a number line is found simply by subtracting (and distance is always positive). So $5 - (-7) = 12$. $\frac{1}{3} \times 12 = 4$ so you should mark 4 on the number line.

42.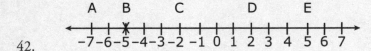

Insert the values from the number line into the equation and solve. $((-5) - (-2)) - 2 = (-3) - 2 = -5$. Remember that subtracting a negative number will move to the right on a number line and subtracting a positive number will move to the left.

43.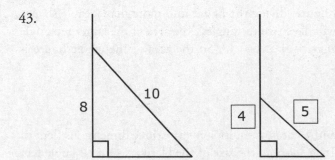

When two triangles are similar, respective sides must have the same proportion. So in this case, the ratio of the height to the length must be 8:10. Look for two numbers among those available that give the same ratio. 4 and 5 are the only possibilities. Note that $\frac{8}{10}$ reduces to $\frac{4}{5}$.

44. **10** Count 'em up! On Monday, he takes 2 tablets: one at 2 p.m. and then one 8 hours later at 10 p.m. On Tuesday and Wednesday, he takes 3 tablets a day, at 6 a.m., 2 p.m., and 10 p.m. On Thursday, he takes 2 tablets: one at 6 a.m. and the last one at 2 p.m. 2 + 3 + 3 + 2 = 10 tablets.

45. **C** Notice that the question says her investment *increased* by 180%. That means that the difference between the new value and the old is equal to 180% of $14,000. 180% of $14,000 is $25,200. Add this to the original ($14,000) to get $39,200—the current value of her investment.

46. **A** Diameter *AB* has length 8, so the radius of the circle is 4. Since *AB* is a semicircle, the center of the circle must be directly between points *A* and *B* at point (2,7). Point *C*, then, must be directly to the right of the center, since it is the midpoint of the arc. Therefore, its *x*-coordinate will also be 6 (since the radius is 4) and its *y*-coordinate will be 7.

SOCIAL STUDIES

1. **B** This EXCEPT question is asking you to decide which answer choice CANNOT be used to deny a child employment. Each of the choices is mentioned in the passage as a possible reason to keep children from working—except for one: (B), gender. Age is mentioned in the second half of the passage as a restrictor to employment, so eliminate (A). As for (C), the actual phrase "hazard levels" is not in the passage, but the third sentence from the end says, "as long as the job is not determined to be dangerous or ruinous to their health or well-being," which basically means the same thing. This sentence also rules out (D). Only gender is NOT discussed as a reason to deny a child employment.

2. **B** Choice (A) says that it should be up to kids to decide when and whether they want to take a job—but the passage says this is decided by the Department of Labor, so you can eliminate this one. Choice (C) says kids can't work under any circumstances, which directly contradicts the entire passage, so you can eliminate this one, too. Choice (D) is saying the same thing as (C) using different words. The correct answer, which sums up the reason for the need for regulations, is (B).

3. **B** Who would be likely to support regulations to protect children? Factory owners *may* be kindhearted, but then again, there have been a lot of factory owners who have exploited child labor—so eliminate (A). Child protection agencies would seem very likely to protect children; let's hold onto (B) while we look at the other choices. Worker's unions might well also support regulations to protect children, so let's hold onto (C) as well. Small companies and agricultural workers *might* be kindhearted too, but we don't know that they will be, so eliminate (D). We have two choices left: (B) and (C). Which is better? The correct answer is (B).

4. **D** The passage states that the Berlin Airlift was "in response to Soviet Premier Joseph Stalin's attempt to block supplies to Berliners." This is closest to (D). Choice (C) is tempting, but the creation of the Warsaw Pact happened *after* the Berlin Airlift. Choice (A) is unsupported by the timeline and (B) does not work, since if the Marshall Plan had been completely successful, Berliners would not have needed assistance.

5. **A** According to the timeline, the Warsaw Pact was created after the formation of NATO. All remaining answers include events that happened before NATO.

6. **B** The American flag is located next to the lower-left, southwestern region of the map. Choice (A) is not true, since this region is smaller than the eastern region. Great Britain controlled the west, not the east, so (C) is wrong. Choice (D) is incorrect, since Stalin is Soviet and thus controlled much of eastern Germany.

7. **D** In the passage, Grant says that the Civil War would change the nation as a whole. Which historical development best supports that? The triumph by one side in a civil war isn't an example of how the country was changed by the war. Eliminate (A). The entry of the United States into World War I does not seem to be directly related to the Civil War either. Eliminate (B). Women's winning the right to vote also doesn't seem like a direct result of the Civil War. Eliminate (C). The correct answer is (D). The Civil War was waged to free the African American slaves—which profoundly changed the entire nation.

8. **D** You may have been tempted to pick (A) because it concerned taxation, but the principle of "taxation without representation" means that a government doesn't have the right to tax its citizens unless those citizens have the right to elect the government and thus have a say in how much they will be taxed. This was one of the principles that drove the 13 colonies to declare independence from England in 1776. Choices (B) and (C) have nothing to do with the Twenty-fourth Amendment as outlined in the question. Only (D) does: Just because a person doesn't pay his taxes does not mean his right to vote can be taken away.

9. **C** The passage says that the young men went west in search of opportunities such as finding gold and striking it rich. Which of the answer choices says that? The correct answer is (C). Choices (A), (B), and (D) didn't appear in the passage itself—and while these all *might* have been reasons for someone to head west, the correct answer to a GED® Reading passage is almost always going to come from within the passage.

10. **A** The only reference to towns in the passage comes in the second sentence, and it refers to San Francisco and Monterey. The next sentence reads, "There they found jobs…." So why did people settle in those towns? The correct answer is (A). You might have been tempted by (C) because it refers to Monterey and the gold to be found there—but by the time they got to these towns, the passage says that the settlers had given up on being prospectors and just needed jobs. Choices (B) and (D) contain information not found in the passage itself.

11. **C** The First Amendment protects five essential freedoms, three of which are listed in (C), the correct answer. The Second Amendment protects the right to bear arms (A). (D) is obviously wrong: The primary role of Congress is to make laws.

12. **A** The First Amendment does not guarantee the right to vote. Rather it makes five guarantees: those listed in (B) through (D) and also the freedom of assembly.

13. **D** Before you turn to the question, make sure that you understand the pie chart. The title says that it is about how children are being educated. It says that 39.2 percent are being educated in public school, 31.5 percent are being educated in private school, and the rest of the children are being educated in other ways. Which statement is supported by the information in the pie chart? Choices (A) and (B) imply value judgments that are not supported by the chart. Who knows which is better, or which ones the children prefer? Choice (C) contradicts what we can see from the chart. If tutoring at home were the most popular method, it would have the largest percentage of kids doing it. The correct answer is (D).

14. **D** This was a tough question, because it asked you to do some analysis. A pure market economy, according to the passage, is one in which the forces of the market control what happens; in other words, there is no government control whatsoever. So which of the answer choices would NOT be found in a pure market economy? Monopolies could occur in a pure market economy because there would be no government rules to prevent them. Small businesses would probably flourish—at least until monopolies put them out of business. There would certainly be unemployment because the markets would hire people only when they needed them. And presumably, stocks and bonds (which provide capital for new businesses) would be found in large numbers. The only things you would NOT find in a pure market economy, as unlikely as it seems, would be taxes and welfare (both of which are controlled by the government). The answer to this difficult question is (D).

15. **D** The passage says that in a socialist economy, all the money is distributed equally among the members of a society. So which of the groups in the answer choices would benefit the *least* from the switch to a socialist economy? Choices (B) and (C) would benefit quite a bit, because these are relatively poor people who would get a bigger slice of the pie than they have now. Eliminate (B) and (C). Between the two choices we have left, who benefits the *least*? The correct answer is (D), highly skilled labor, because presumably they were being well paid for their unique skills, and would lose money in the redistribution of wealth. Government employees in socialist systems usually tend to gain power because they get to decide who receives the wealth.

16. **D** As you study the photograph, you will probably notice two things: (1) The car in the photo is quite old, and (2) it isn't working. The people in this old photograph are pushing the car instead of riding in it. The question itself says that while today we sometimes have difficulties with cars, the people back then had to deal with another kind of problem. What was it? Does it seem as if the people in that photo are concerned about pollution? We didn't think so. Are they concerned about seatbelts? Not when most of them are pushing the car. Are they concerned about heavy cars? Now, we're getting warmer. If you were pushing a car, you would probably want it to be as light as possible. But let's read the last answer choice before we pick: Could the people in the photo be concerned with a shortage of gas stations? Aha! This answer gets to the heart of *why* they are pushing the car in the first place: It is out of gas. The correct answer to this question is (D).

17. **C** Religion, factories, and lynchings are simply not mentioned anywhere in the passage, so eliminate all but (C).

18. **D** Read the graph carefully before looking at the questions. We see bars representing men and women who take the SAT, broken down by ethnic group. From this graph, we can see that in all but one group, more women than men take the SAT. The one group where this does not appear to be true is that of Asian Americans. Looking at the answers, (A) makes a claim not supported by the graph. We are not given any information about how men and women perform on the test—just the fact that they took it. Choices (B) and (C) make statements of fact not supported by the graph. We have no idea whether numbers are declining or increasing from year to year. This graph is of a single snapshot in time. The correct answer is (D): According to the chart, clearly more women than men take the SAT.

19. **C** The question is basically asking, "Which of the following is NOT an example of a plutocratic government?" The best answer is (C), in which the leaders are elected by popular vote. In a plutocracy, the leaders are chosen because they are the wealthiest citizens. This means that there is no vote. All the other choices reflect situations that could occur in a plutocracy.

20. **D** You don't have to know anything about Andrew Mellon to realize that, in this statement at least, he is on the side of the people. He writes that "unwise" public officials "fall to these interests of monopoly as against the welfare of the people of whom they are supposed to serve." So we are looking for an answer choice that is sympathetic to the people and critical of officials who lose sight of the people's welfare. Choice (A) seems possible at first, but goes too far: Mellon doesn't suggest that public officials who profit from a monopoly shouldn't run for office. Choice (B) is wrong because it sides with the public officials over the interests of the people. Choice (C) goes too far, because Mellon never says the profits of monopolies should be shared by all. This leaves us with (D), which is a simple restatement of what Mellon says in the passage.

21. **B** The passage compares the relationship between the federal and state governments to, respectively, the hub and spokes of a wagon wheel. This is called an analogy (which means a comparison between two things to help you understand one of them better). You have to find an answer choice that illustrates the analogy. Choice (A) is no good because, in the analogy, the entire government is represented by one wheel. What purpose would three other wheels serve? This might have been a good analogy if we were talking about four separate countries, each with its own wagon wheel helping to support the world-wagon—but that's a different analogy. Choice (B) basically restates the analogy—and is the correct answer. Choices (C) and (D) extend the analogy in some meaningless way.

22. **D** The map of the United States shows which areas have a high number of non-English-speaking children. You'll notice that the highest concentrations tend to be on the outside edges of the country, not the interior. Question 22 asks you to pick the best geographic explanation for the areas that have the highest numbers of non-English-speaking children. Choice (B) is irrelevant because we aren't concerned with the total number of children in the country—only the children who can't speak English. Choice (C) is irrelevant because, according to the map, some of the heaviest areas of non-English-speaking kids are in the north, such as New York and Washington. Choice (A) seems possible at first, because lower income taxes might attract new immigrants, but then again, wouldn't they attract just about everyone? Let's hold onto this as we look at (D): If recent immigrants settled in border and coastal states, wouldn't that be a pretty logical explanation for why these areas contain the most non-English-speaking kids? Choice (D) is a much better answer than (A).

23. **B** All of the answer choices would have an effect on the distribution of these kids EXCEPT (B), climate. In general, new immigrants would seem to make decisions based more on the availability of ESL programs, immigration laws, social services, and even migration patterns (where immigrants have gone before) than on climate. One of the states with the largest number of non-English speakers (according to the chart) is New York (which has a colder climate) while others include California and Florida, with warmer climates.

24. **D** To answer this question, you have to consider each answer choice in turn. Are non-English-speaking children evenly distributed across the entire country? The map says no. Eliminate (A). Are there more of these kids in Arizona than in California? No, according to the map, California has the highest level of counties with at least 500 non-English-speaking kids. Arizona has between five and nine counties with 500 or more non-English-speaking children, but not as many as California, so we can eliminate (B). And while Texas and California *do* have the highest levels of kids who don't speak English, could that really mean that they have more kids who can't speak English than kids who *can*? The map does not show information that compares these two groups of children, so eliminate (C). The correct answer is (D) because it best reflects what the map tells us: In the middle states in the north of the United States, there are fewer non-English-speaking children.

25. **B** The passage tells us that the Constitution and other laws "made in accordance" with the Constitution can't be set aside by judges or any other laws. So, which is an example of this? The correct answer is (B),

which says that the Bill of Rights (the first ten amendments of the Constitution) can't be denied by any arm of the government. Choices (A), (C), and (D) are all irrelevant to this concept.

26. **A** Lowering the speed limit, limiting senators to two terms, reducing pollution, or creating town zoning—none of these deprives people of their constitutional rights. However, prohibiting protests by a union takes away a fundamental right guaranteed by the Constitution: the right to free speech. Thus, the correct answer is (A).

27. **B** Freedom of religion is a fundamental right guaranteed by the Constitution—so we can eliminate (A). A right to a trial by jury is also guaranteed by the Constitution—so we can eliminate (C). The right to vote is also guaranteed to citizens by the Constitution—so we can probably eliminate (D), because even if they don't speak English, people can be citizens. The correct answer is (B).

28. **D** The passage states that the economics professors say there are too many factors to be able to make long-term stock-market predictions. Choice (D) accurately restates that idea. Choices (A), (B), and (C) all make statements that contradict the passage.

29. **C** Because so many different factors can affect stock prices, there can be no guarantee that two companies producing the same goods will do equally well—so we can eliminate (A). While amateur investors are mentioned in the passage, their behavior is not the most important factor on a stock's success—so eliminate (B). The passage says that amateurs may do as well as a professional stock trader, but it does not say that they will do better—so we can eliminate (D). The correct answer must be (C), because past success does not ensure future performance—a concept always mentioned in stock prospectuses, but often forgotten in practice.

30. Since laissez-faire economics is free from government restrictions, labor laws, building codes, and antitrust laws would all be incorrect choices. Deregulation (a), free trade (d), and non-interference (f) all imply a lack of government oversight in business.

31. **C** What caused the end of the era of transatlantic ship-crossings? Do you think it was a series of accidents, a major war that disrupted routes, the cost of travel by boat, or the fact that sea travel fell out of fashion? Nope, it was something much more basic—the airplane. The correct answer is (C).

32. **A** In this cartoon, the two Civil War veterans, one African American, one white—each missing a leg—are shaking hands. Always read the caption carefully in a cartoon or photograph. The two soldiers are calling each other comrade and saying they each lost a leg for a good cause. The best answer is (A), which reflects what the Civil War was fought over: the right of all men to be free and equal to each other. Both (C) and (D) suggest information that is impossible to know about these two individuals, while not reflecting the point of the cartoon. Choice (B), while true, again did not reflect the larger point behind the conflict.

33. **B** The flowchart indicates that Congress is responsible for passing laws. They do not veto; that is the president's role. TAB 2 indicates that the Judicial Branch gained power in *Marbury vs. Madison*, so eliminate (C). Choice (D) is tempting, but there is no indication that the Congress nominates judges. The president does this.

34. **D** In TAB 3, Jefferson states that "judges as the ultimate arbiters of all constitutional questions" is "a very dangerous doctrine." He made this statement in response to *Marbury vs. Madison*. The quote also indicates that "their power is…dangerous." This matches best with (D). Choices (A) and (C) are too positive in tone to match with the Jefferson quote. Choice (B) is close, but *Marbury vs. Madison* pertains to the Judicial Branch, not the Executive Branch.

35. **A** Jefferson is using negative language, such as "dangerous." The only negative word in these answers is "tyranny." It is not a literal definition of "oligarchy," but is the only word that captures the spirit of Jefferson's opinion regarding *Marbury vs. Madison*.

SCIENCE

1. **D** The question states that hurricanes gather strength over warm water, so a hurricane should gather the most strength over the warmest body of water. Since the Gulf of Mexico has the highest average temperature of the bodies of water listed, the correct answer is (D).

2. **A** According to the passage, patients must receive tests for blood type before certain kinds of transfusions because of the ways in which different red blood cells interact with each other. Therefore, blood type tests must be necessary only when there is going to be an exchange of red blood cells. Since the passage states that whole blood transfusions involve both red blood cells and plasma, blood type tests must be necessary before whole blood transfusions. Since plasma transfusions do not involve red blood cells, you can eliminate (B) and (C). The passage states that patients may receive transfusions when they have lost a lot of blood, not when they have not lost any blood. Therefore, (D) is not supported by the passage and is incorrect. Thus, (A) is the best answer.

3. **85%**

    According to the information given, coal turns into anthracite only after the coal has been subjected to heat and pressure for more than a million years. Thus, this type of coal is likely very dense, or hard. Additionally, the passage indicates that anthracite burns only when subjected to very high temperatures. Thus, the question most likely describes anthracite, which is 85–95% carbon, so the lowest level of carbon the coal is likely to contain is 85%.

4. **D** According to the question, steel is formed when iron combines with carbon at very high temperatures. Since you need carbon to form steel, you likely do not want all of the carbon to burn up before it combines with the iron. Additionally, the form of coal that contains the highest percentage of carbon is likely to be the most effective for this process. Since anthracite burns only at very high temperatures, and contains the highest percentage of carbon of the coals listed, the correct answer is (D).

5. **Peat (a); Anthracite (d).** Peat turns into lignite, which in turn becomes subbituminous coal, which in turn becomes anthracite. Notice that these changes require both heat and pressure, which would result from the coal being farther and farther underground. Additionally, anthracite is millions of years old, and therefore is likely to become covered by dirt over the centuries. Therefore, peat is likely to be closest to the surface. According to the chart, the carbon with the highest level of carbon is anthracite.

6. **C** According to the passage, seeds need moisture and oxygen. Additionally, while most seeds require temperatures between 15 and 27 degrees centigrade, corn seeds require even higher temperatures. Therefore, the correct answer must involve temperatures higher than 27 degrees centigrade. Eliminate (A). Since "arid" means "without moisture," corn seeds likely will not germinate in an arid environment, so (B) is not the credited answer. Choice (C) mentions an environment that is moist, has plenty of oxygen, and is warmer than 27 degrees centigrade, so (C) is the correct answer. Since the passage states that maple trees can germinate in temperatures lower than 15 to 27 degrees centigrade, an environment that is suitable for maple trees will not necessarily be suitable for corn seeds. Thus, (D) is incorrect.

7. **C** According to the passage, maple seeds can germinate in low temperatures. However, that does not necessarily mean that they can germinate in any temperature; there may still be temperatures that are either too high or too low for them to germinate. Thus, (A) is incorrect. The passage does state that corn seeds require temperatures higher than 27 degrees centigrade in order to grow, but that does not necessarily mean that corn is difficult to grow. Therefore, (B) is incorrect. The passage states that "most seeds will germinate when they have moisture." So, some water is necessary for the germination process. Choice (C) is supported by the passage and is the credited answer. The passage states that maple seeds and corn seeds germinate in different temperatures, but does not mention the respective amounts of oxygen that they require. Choice (D) is not supported by the passage and is therefore incorrect.

8. **C** The passage states that the body produces lactic acid during periods of intense activity. Therefore, you'll want to examine the answer choices to find one that describes intense activity. Walking to work is not likely to involve intense activity, so you can eliminate (A). While (B) does describe the chess game as "intense," this intensity is of a mental, rather than a physical nature. Since the passage is discussing physical activity, you can eliminate (B). An aerobics class is likely to involve intense physical activity, so (C) is the correct answer. A scary movie may be intense, but watching a movie does not involve physical activity, so (D) is not the credited answer.

9. **A** The passage states that plants lie dormant during periods that are unfavorable for growth. Winter is generally the season least favorable for growth, so the correct answer is (A).

10. Unless volcanic activity has occurred, the oldest rock layers are the ones located deepest within the ground. Therefore, rock layer #4 is the oldest rock layer, and rock layer #1 is the newest rock layer.

11. **C** According to the information in the food chain, bass do eat minnows. However, the food chain does not provide any information as to whether any other fish also eat minnows. Since minnows may have more than one predator, (A) is not supported by the information in the food chain. The food chain begins with microscopic algae and ends with the much larger bass. In general, the living things on the food chain seem to be ordered from smallest to largest. Since bass are higher on the food chain than are minnows, bass are likely larger than minnows, rather than the other way around. Therefore, you can eliminate (B). Bass eat minnows, which in turn eat copepods. Therefore, if there were no copepods, minnows would have fewer food options and would likely suffer. In turn, bass would suffer since they would have fewer minnows to consume. Choice (C) is supported by the information in the food chain and is the credited answer. Since bass may derive benefits from minnows that they could not derive from algae, there is no evidence that (D) is true.

12. Answers may vary but should include a discussion of a specific animal that uses passive protection. For example, the chameleon changes color to blend in with its surroundings. The passage states that one type of passive protection involves changing color to mimic the surrounding environment. Thus, this example agrees with the passage's definition of passive protection. When a chameleon changes color in this manner, it is no longer easily visible to predators, and thus may escape predation.

13. **C** According to the information in the question, 1 kilogram/liter = 1,000 kilograms/meter^3. Divide both sides by 1,000 to find that 0.001 kilograms/liter = 1 kilogram/meter^3. Now multiply both sides by 1,029 to find that 1.029 kilograms/liter = 1,029 kilograms/meter^3. Therefore, the correct answer is (C).

14. Answers may vary, but a thorough explanation should discuss the fact that the researchers did not properly use the scientific method. Because they not only decreased greenhouse gas emissions, but they also took steps to ensure that citizens received better respiratory care, the resulting improvement in the citizens' health could have been due to the respiratory care education campaign and the free clinics. In order to improve their study, the researchers would have had to change only one variable at a time, rather than both.

15. **Mode, 0.43.** The mode is defined as the most commonly occurring number, so in this case the researchers would need to find the mode of the weights. Since the weight 0.43 kg occurs most frequently in the list, the correct answer to the second question is 0.43.

16. **0.93**

    To find the mean of a list of numbers, add up all of the numbers and then divide by the number of numbers that you have. $0.2 + 0.4 + 0.2 + 0.8 + 0.9 + 1.7 + 1.3 + 1.8 + 0.9 + 1.1 = 9.3$. You have ten numbers, so divide this result by ten: $9.3/10 = 0.93$.

17. **D** Decreasing the volume of the gas will make the denominator of the fraction smaller, and will contribute toward making the fraction as a whole larger. However, decreasing the temperature of the gas will make the numerator smaller, and will contribute toward making the fraction as a whole larger. Therefore, decreasing both the volume and the temperature of the gas will not necessarily increase the pressure within the gas, and you can eliminate (A). Increasing the volume of the gas will make the denominator of the fraction larger, and will therefore make the fraction as a whole smaller, so you can eliminate both (B) and (C). Decreasing the volume of the gas will make the denominator smaller, and will thus make the fraction as a whole larger. Increasing the temperature of the gas will make the numerator of the fraction larger, and will thus make the fraction as a whole larger. Thus, only (D) will cause an increase in the pressure within the gas.

18. **A** According to the table, a combination occurs when A + B —> C. Note that this matches the reaction described in the equation. In this case, H_2 = A, F_2 = B, and 2HF = C. All of the other types of reactions have additions on the right sides of the equations, so (B), (C), and (D) are incorrect. The credited answer is (A).

19. **B** Use the chart and estimate. According to the chart, the number of AIDS deaths in 2011 was approximately 1,800, and will be approximately 2,500 in 2020. Therefore, the increase in AIDS deaths in Africa between the two years will be about $2,500 - 1,800 = 700$. The number of AIDS deaths in 2011 in South/Southeast Asia was approximately 500, and will be approximately 1,500 in 2020. Therefore, the increase in AIDS deaths in South/Southeast Asia between the two years will be about $1,500 - 500 = 1,000$. Eliminate (A), since (B) gives you a larger answer. The number of AIDS deaths in 2011 in Eastern Europe was approximately 0, and will be approximately 250 in 2020. Therefore, the increase in AIDS deaths in Easter Europe between the two years will be about 250. Eliminate (C). Finally, the number of AIDS deaths in North America/Northern Europe was approximately 0 in 2011, and will be just slightly more than 0 in 2020, so you can eliminate (D). The correct answer is (B).

20. **D** The type-A star has a temperature of 4,839 degrees Fahrenheit, so plug 4,839 into the formula in place of F. You then have $K = \frac{5}{9}(4,839 - 32) + 273$. Simplify inside the parentheses first to get $K = \frac{5}{9}(4,807) + 273$. Multiply the $\frac{5}{9}$ and the 4,807 so that you have $K = 2670.55 + 273$. Finally, add to get $K = 2943.55$. The correct answer is (D).

21. **B** Amplitude is a measure of the difference between the middle height of a wave to the top (or bottom) of a wave. If you look at the two waves, you will see that the distance from the middle height to the top of the Fault City wave is much greater than the distance from the middle height to the top of the Nicaragua wave. Therefore, the Fault City wave had a much greater amplitude. You can eliminate (A), and the correct answer is (B). The information in the caption indicates that a seismometer was used to measure the Fault City quake, so (C) is incorrect. Finally, the long-period surface waves at point R1 were larger during the Fault City quake than during the Nicaragua quake, so (D) is incorrect.

22. **R1**. Since you're looking for a point that would allow you to identify signs of an earthquake before the earthquake actually occurred, you need a point before the earthquake. Points R2, R3, R4, and R5 are all located on the timeline at points after the earthquake. Only point R1 is before the earthquake, and is a point at which signs of seismic activity actually occur.

23. **C** The passage mentions that ornithologists have observed that the archaeopteryx could perch on tree limbs, but does not state whether paleontologists agree with this observation. Eliminate (A). According to the passage, ornithologists believe that the archaeopteryx could not run quickly, but again the passage does not state whether paleontologists agree with this view, so (B) is not the credited answer. Paragraph 1 indicates that paleontologists believe that the archaeopteryx "could not sustain flight." Thus (C) is supported by the passage and is the correct answer. Paragraph 2 states that ornithologists believe that the archaeopteryx may not have been able to walk quickly, but the passage does not state whether paleontologists agree with this view, so (D) is incorrect.

24. **C** According to ornithologists, the "archaeopteryx was first and foremost a bird." Of the animals listed in the answer choices, only the crow is a bird. Therefore, the correct answer is (C).

25. **C** According to the information in the paragraph, work is equal to force multiplied by displacement. The paragraph also states that if you use a ramp to move an object rather than lifting the object straight up, then the amount of force required decreases, while displacement increases by exactly the same amount that the force decreased. Thus, the net product of force times displacement should not change. The correct answer is therefore (C).

26. **D** Look at the chart, and read horizontally across the row for urine. Note that the columns for both albumin and glucose have dashes for entries, signaling that neither is generally present in urine. Therefore, the correct answer is (D), albumin and glucose.

27. **A** The passage states that the foxes prey on rabbits, so if there are fewer rabbits in the forest, the fox population will suffer because one of its food sources will be depleted. Choice (A) is therefore supported by the passage and is the correct answer. The passage indicates that the virus infects only rabbits, so you can eliminate (B). Since the foxes rely on the rabbits for food, the foxes are not in competition with the rabbits for food, so you can eliminate (C). Finally, because the virus infects only rabbits, the foxes are unlikely to evolve to become more resistant to disease under these circumstances, so (D) is not the credited answer.

28. **B** According to the introductory sentence, a solar eclipse occurs when the sun cannot be seen from the earth. Choice (A) claims that a solar eclipse occurs when the moon is no longer visible from the earth, so you can eliminate (A). Based on the information in the figure, a solar eclipse occurs when the moon is situated directly between the earth and the sun. Note that in the figure, parts of the earth are in the umbra, or deepest part of the shadow, of the moon. Since this is the situation that (B) describes, (B) is the correct answer. If light rays intercepted one another, the resulting light would likely be brighter, rather than darker, so (C) is not the credited answer. The figure shows that the earth, not the sun, is in the moon's umbra, so you can eliminate (D).

29. **B** According to the passage, penicillin prevents the growth of new bacteria. Therefore, the correct answer should involve an illness caused by bacteria. The chart indicates that streptococcal bacteria cause strep throat. Therefore, penicillin is likely to be an effective treatment for strep throat.

30. **D** The question asks you to find the quote that supports the idea that simply preventing those with microbial diseases from having physical contact with others will not stop the spread of such microbial diseases. Choice (A) discusses treating the diseases with penicillin, rather than preventing direct physical contact, so (A) is not the credited answer. Choice (B) also discusses the effectiveness of penicillin, rather than the effectiveness of preventing physical contact, so (B) is incorrect. Choice (C) mentions only the different types of microbes, and does not discuss the effectiveness of preventing physical contact, so you can eliminate (C). Choice (D) mentions several ways that microbes can invade hosts: through the air, through direct or indirect physical contact, through blood, and through other bodily fluids.

31. **D** According to the passage, both plants were green and were hybrids, so you can eliminate answers (A), (B), and (C), leaving only (D). If both parents carry a hidden yellow gene, then some of the offspring may be yellow, so the passage supports (D).

32. **A** The passage states that in hybrids the dominant gene hides the expression of the recessive gene. Therefore, an individual who has both the dominant gene for dimples and the recessive gene for a lack of dimples will have dimples. The correct answer is (A).

33. **C** According to the graph, the temperature increases, then remains constant while the sample melts, then increases, then stays constant while the sample boils, and then increases. Since this is the scenario that (C) describes, the correct answer is (C). Note that a horizontal line means that the variable on the y-axis, in this case, temperature, is not changing.

34. Point C represents the sample at the point when it is between melting and boiling. Such a sample would be liquid, so if you selected a point near point C, then you selected the correct region of the graph. Before the sample melted, it would be entirely solid, so the region of the graph near point A would not represent a time during which the sample would be liquid. During melting, some of the sample would be solid and some of the sample would be liquid, so the region of the graph near point B would not represent a time during which the sample would be liquid. During boiling, some of the sample would be liquid and some of the sample would be gas, so the region of the graph near point D would not represent a time during which the sample would be liquid. After boiling, the sample would be entirely gas, so the region of the graph near point E would also not represent a time during which the sample would be liquid.

35. **B** The passage states that bees are important because they pollinate flowering plants, so (B) is supported by the passage. While (A) describes another role of bees, that role is not mentioned in the passage. Choices (C) and (D) do not describe actions that bees take, and are therefore both incorrect.

Chapter 25
Practice Test 2

Reasoning Through Language Arts

Welcome!

Here is some information that you need to know before you start this test:

- You should not spend too much time on a question if you are not certain of the answer; answer it the best you can, and go on to the next question.
- If you are not certain of the answer to a question, you can mark your answer for review and come back to it later.
- This test has three sections.
- You have **35 minutes** to complete Section 1.
- When you finish Section 1, you may review those questions.
- You may not go back to Section 1 once you have finished your review.
- You have **45 minutes** to complete the Extended Response question in Section 2.
- After completing Section 2, you may take a 10-minute break.
- You have **60 minutes** to complete Section 3.
- When you finish Section 3, you may review those questions.

Turn the page to begin.

GO ON TO THE NEXT PAGE

Questions 1 through 8 refer to the following passage.

Niagara
by Mark Twain

1   Niagara Falls is a most enjoyable place of resort. The hotels are excellent, and the prices not at all exorbitant. The opportunities for fishing are not surpassed in the country; in fact, they are not even equaled elsewhere. Because, in other localities, certain places in the streams are much better than others; but at Niagara one place is just as good as another, for the reason that the fish do not bite anywhere, and so there is no use in your walking five miles to fish, when you can depend on being just as unsuccessful nearer home. The advantages of this state of things have never heretofore been properly placed before the public.

2   The weather is cool in summer, and the walks and drives are all pleasant and none of them fatiguing. When you start out to "do" the Falls you first drive down about a mile, and pay a small sum for the privilege of looking down from a precipice into the narrowest part of the Niagara River. A railway "cut" through a hill would be as comely if it had the angry river tumbling and foaming through its bottom. You can descend a staircase here a hundred and fifty feet down, and stand at the edge of the water. After you have done it, you will wonder why you did it; but you will then be too late.

3   Then you drive over to Suspension Bridge, and divide your misery between the chances of smashing down two hundred feet into the river below, and the chances of having the railway-train overhead smashing down onto you. Either possibility is discomforting taken by itself, but, mixed together, they amount in the aggregate to positive unhappiness.

4   When you have examined the stupendous Horseshoe Fall till you are satisfied you cannot improve on it, you return to America by the new Suspension Bridge, and follow up the bank to where they exhibit the Cave of the Winds.

5   Here I followed instructions, and divested myself of all my clothing, and put on a waterproof jacket and overalls. This costume is picturesque, but not beautiful. A guide, similarly dressed, led the way down a flight of winding stairs, which wound and wound, and still kept on winding long after the thing ceased to be a novelty, and then terminated long before it had begun to be a pleasure. We were then well down under the precipice, but still considerably above the level of the river.

6   We now began to creep along flimsy bridges of a single plank, our persons shielded from destruction by a crazy wooden railing, to which I clung with both hands—not because I was afraid, but because I wanted to. Presently the descent became steeper and the bridge flimsier, and sprays from the American Fall began

GO ON TO THE NEXT PAGE

to rain down on us in fast increasing sheets that soon became blinding, and after that our progress was mostly in the nature of groping. Now a furious wind began to rush out from behind the waterfall, which seemed determined to sweep us from the bridge, and scatter us on the rocks and among the torrents below. I remarked that I wanted to go home; but it was too late. We were almost under the monstrous wall of water thundering down from above, and speech was in vain in the midst of such a pitiless crash of sound.

7   In another moment the guide disappeared behind the deluge, and, bewildered by the thunder, driven helplessly by the wind, and smitten by the arrowy tempest of rain, I followed. All was darkness. Such a mad storming, roaring, and bellowing of warring wind and water never crazed my ears before. I bent my head, and seemed to receive the Atlantic on my back. The world seemed going to destruction. I could not see anything, the flood poured down savagely. I raised my head, with open mouth, and the most of the American cataract went down my throat. If I had sprung a leak now I had been lost. And at this moment I discovered that the bridge had ceased, and we must trust for a foothold to the slippery and precipitous rocks. I never was so scared before and survived it. But we got through at last, and emerged into the open day, where we could stand in front of the laced and frothy and seething world of descending water, and look at it. When I saw how much of it there was, and how fearfully in earnest it was, I was sorry I had gone behind it.

1. The author's overall tone in paragraph 1 is one of

  A. fearful prediction.
  B. ironic contrast.
  C. appreciative description.
  D. satisfied recollection.

2. Read this sentence from paragraph 2.

> After you have done it, you will wonder why you did it; but you will then be too late.

Why does the author choose to conclude the paragraph with this sentence?

  A. to show how important it is to arrive at the falls on time
  B. to offer advice to any readers who might consider visiting Niagara Falls
  C. to show the narrator's acquaintance with the motives of the reader
  D. to predict a tourist's feelings about the effort needed to view the site

3. Which quotation from the passage stands out in direct contrast to the main theme of the passage?

  A. "The weather is cool in summer, and the walks and drives are all pleasant and none of them fatiguing."
  B. "You can descend a staircase here a hundred and fifty feet down, and stand at the edge of the water."
  C. "Either possibility is discomforting taken by itself, but, mixed together, they amount in the aggregate to positive unhappiness."
  D. "Here I followed instructions, and divested myself of all my clothing, and put on a waterproof jacket and overalls."

GO ON TO THE NEXT PAGE

4. In paragraph 6, the narrator says, "I remarked that I wanted to go home." Which characteristic does this remark reveal about the narrator?

   A. homesickness
   B. melancholy
   C. apprehension
   D. nostalgia

5. Read the following sentences from paragraph 7.

   > Such a mad storming, roaring, and bellowing of warring wind and water never crazed my ears before. I bent my head, and seemed to receive the Atlantic on my back.

   This detailed description of the author's surroundings enhances the story by

   A. revealing the author's predicament after falling into the Atlantic.
   B. further emphasizing the flimsy nature of the bridges the author must cross.
   C. showing the fury of the storm that catches the author off guard.
   D. using exaggeration to illustrate the volume of water the author experiences.

6. Which definition best matches the use of the phrase "in earnest" in paragraph 7?

   A. serious
   B. vigorous
   C. sincere
   D. ardent

7. Drag and drop the events into the chart to show the order in which they occur in the excerpt. (For this practice test, write the event letters in the chart.)

   Order of Events

   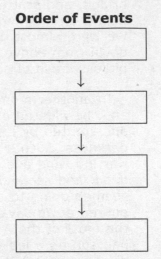

   (a) Horseshoe Fall is included as a stop in the visit.

   (b) The Suspension Bridge is described.

   (c) The narrator mentions a view of the river.

   (d) The narrator goes behind the falls.

8. Which fact can the reader infer about Niagara Falls?

   A. Part of it is located outside the United States.
   B. It is a good spot for fishing.
   C. It is a short drive from the exhibit of the Cave of the Winds.
   D. Hotels there are expensive.

GO ON TO THE NEXT PAGE

Questions 9 through 16 refer to the following passage.

Should American Cities Adopt a Commission Form of Government?

by Leverett S. Lyon

The Affirmative:

1   During the last quarter-century, municipal organization has trended toward concentration of powers. Some cities have recognized the wisdom of such action, but have unwisely attempted to concentrate only the executive power whereas the real solution lies in concentrating all governmental authority in one responsible body.

2   So evident is the need for this solution that there is now a charter revision committee meeting in New York to consider eliminating the separate council entirely, and creating in its place a small commission possessing both legislative and administrative authority.

3   What is true of New York is true of scores of other cities. Within the past two years more than a dozen states have provided for a commission form of government, while within the past year more than a dozen cities have thrown away their old forms and assumed the commission system.

4   The success of a separate legislative body in state and national government is the only excuse for its retention in our cities, yet such a government is unsuited to modern municipalities. Unlike the state, the work of a city is largely administrative and of a business character, and does not require a separate council to legislate. We do not find, as in the state, the necessity of a large and separate body to represent the various localities. The city has a large population living in a restricted territory; in the state it is scattered.

5   The present principle of separation makes possible concentration of power, without a corresponding concentration of responsibility. When one branch of the government dominates, checks and balances between the departments are lost. The system of checks and balances failed in New York, where the mayor is supreme, and where the city has been plundered of sums estimated at 7 percent of the total valuation of real estate. It failed in St. Louis, where the council dominated, and where "Boss Butler" paid that body $250,000 to pass a street railway franchise. Neither did it work in Philadelphia, which has been plundered of an amount equal to 10 percent of her real estate valuation.

GO ON TO THE NEXT PAGE

6   Therefore, we must concentrate municipal authority; we must co-ordinate departments, eliminate useless boards and committees and fix individual responsibility. This, we propose to do by establishing a commission form of government, where all governmental authority is vested in one small body of men, who individually act as the heads of administrative departments, but who collectively pass the needed legislation. Thus, instead of a council with restricted powers and divided authority, we have a few men assuming positions of genuine responsibility, as regards both the originating and enforcing of laws.

The Negative:

7   We do not defend the evils of present city organization. We believe that far-reaching reforms must be instituted. The issue then is, does the commission form offer a satisfactory solution of our municipal problems?

8   In many forms today, as the gentlemen have depicted, the relations between the legislative and executive departments are such that responsibility cannot be fixed. But every conspicuous example of municipal success is based upon the proper correlation between these departments. Municipal success in Europe is an established fact. There we find the cabinet form, in which governing power is vested in the legislative body, which then delegates administrative functions to the cabinet. Charleston, S. C., Elmira, New York, Los Angeles, Cal., are a few of the typical American cities which have successfully adopted the mayor and council form by utilizing the model charter of the National Municipal League.

9   Therefore, in whatever form, the principle of a proper division of functions must be embodied. The Affirmative must admit that, after fifteen years of misrule under the commission form in Sacramento, the freeholders by unanimous choice again adopted distinct legislative and administrative bodies; and that the commission form has lately operated but a few years in a few small cities.

10   Evils in our cities are due to bad social and economic conditions, and to state interference in purely local affairs. In the United States the city may not act except where authorized by the state. In Europe the city may do anything it is not forbidden to do, and municipal success there is based on this freedom. The European city makes its own local laws, not in conflict with, but in addition to, state law. But in the United States the state legislature failed to distinguish between matters of interest to the state government and those of exclusive interest to the cities.

11   The remedy lies in restoring to the city its proper field of legislation. Already thirty states have passed constitutional amendments granting greater legislative powers to the cities. Five states now allow cities to amend their own charters. But in

GO ON TO THE NEXT PAGE

direct opposition to this movement for municipal home rule, the commission form takes the last step in the destruction of the city's legislative body and fosters continued state interference. President Eliot says that the functions of the commissioners will be defined by the state.

12   We have shown the real causes of municipal evils, and they are to be remedied without tampering with the fundamental principles proved by time and experience. The Affirmative say: change the fundamental principle. The Negative say: retain the principle of distinct legislative and administrative bodies, but observe a proper correlation between them. We would remedy bad social and economic conditions, and, most important of all, give the city greater freedom in powers of local self-government.

Source: Adapted and abridged from *Elements of Debating*, by Leverett S. Lyon, 1919.

9.   What evidence does the Affirmative use to support their claims? Drag and drop four pieces of evidence into the chart. (For this practice test, write the statement letters in the chart.)

Claim	Evidence	Evidence
The need for concentrating all power into a commission is evident.		
When one branch of the government dominates, checks and balances between the departments are lost.		

(a) There is a charter revision committee meeting in New York.

(b) More than a dozen cities have thrown away their old forms.

(c) Some cities have lost funds due to a corrupt administration.

(d) The city has a large population living in a restricted territory; in the state it is scattered.

(e) The council in St. Louis took a bribe to pass a street railway franchise.

(f) During the last quarter-century, municipal organization has trended toward concentration of powers.

GO ON TO THE NEXT PAGE

10. Which idea about city government is included in the Affirmative?

    A. City governments require a separate council to legislate business and administrative concerns.
    B. The deplorable conditions of the cities are caused by economic and social factors.
    C. Checks and balances between departments are the only way to guarantee successful government.
    D. Many cities have completely revised the structure of their municipal governments.

11. Which conclusion is supported by the argument of the Negative?

    A. The cabinet form of city government is currently found only in Europe.
    B. The cabinet form of city government is preferable to the mayor and council form.
    C. Separation of departments is partly responsible for corruption in city government.
    D. There are guidelines to help cities set up a successful form of government.

12. Read the following sentence from paragraph 11:

    > Already thirty states have passed constitutional amendments granting greater legislative powers to the cities.

    What idea mentioned by the Negative does this sentence support?

    A. The remedy is to give the city greater freedom in powers of local self-government.
    B. In Europe the city may do anything it is not forbidden to do.
    C. Retain the principle of distinct legislative and administrative bodies.
    D. Far-reaching reforms must be instituted.

13. Which detail in the Negative's argument supports the idea that there are disadvantages associated with the commission form of government?

    A. "...a few of the typical American cities which have successfully adopted the mayor and council form by utilizing the model charter of the National Municipal League..." (paragraph 8)
    B. "...the freeholders by unanimous choice again adopted distinct legislative and administrative bodies..." (paragraph 9)
    C. "...Evils in our cities are due to bad social and economic conditions..." (paragraph 10)
    D. "...the commission form has lately operated but a few years in a few small cities..." (paragraph 9)

GO ON TO THE NEXT PAGE

14. How does the Negative build the argument that the Affirmative's position is incorrect?

    A. The Negative brings up alternative city models that the Affirmative fails to acknowledge.
    B. The Negative denies the Affirmative's assertion that general city government is in need of reform.
    C. The Negative calls into question the use of the sample cities presented by the Affirmative.
    D. The Negative demonstrates that the Affirmative is uninformed about the true workings of city government.

15. How are the conclusions of the Affirmative and the Negative similar?

    A. Both base their conclusions on the premise that current city conditions are problematic and need to be addressed.
    B. Both convey a dedication to the fundamental principles on which the broader U.S. government is based.
    C. Both advocate for the concentration of municipal power into one unified body with full responsibility.
    D. Both conclude that the balancing of powers is essential to the proper workings of city government.

16. Based on the information in the two articles, the Affirmative and the Negative share which perspective?

    A. There is one form of government that is best suited to cities.
    B. The states interfere too much into matters best left to local policymakers.
    C. The current conditions in the cities are in serious need of reform via the commission model.
    D. The city has concerns distinct from those of the state.

GO ON TO THE NEXT PAGE

17. The passage below is incomplete. For each "Select" option, choose the option that correctly completes the sentence. (For this practice test, circle your selection.)

September 20, 2011

Ms. Celine Margot
Chair, AIM Foundation
1235 Deer Park Road
Rochester, NY

Dear Ms. Margot,

I was so honored to meet you last week at the AIM Foundation Benefit. When I walked in the door, I had no idea I was about to be introduced to a Phi Kappa sister: Although, I should not really have been surprised; the members of our sorority

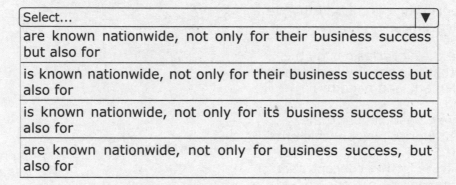

Select... ▼
are known nationwide, not only for their business success but also for
is known nationwide, not only for their business success but also for
is known nationwide, not only for its business success but also for
are known nationwide, not only for business success, but also for

their works of charity. I was touched to hear the outreach that AIM is doing, helping poor villages in several countries have access to clean water. Clearly, your foundation has a commitment to bettering the lives of those communities who live closest to subsistence level.

As we discussed that night, my company, Clear Image has great experience helping organizations

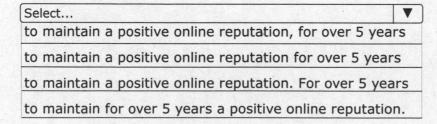

Select... ▼
to maintain a positive online reputation, for over 5 years
to maintain a positive online reputation for over 5 years
to maintain a positive online reputation. For over 5 years
to maintain for over 5 years a positive online reputation.

GO ON TO THE NEXT PAGE

we have been at the forefront of social media and viral image marketing and during that time the clients we have had range from Fortune 500 companies to philanthropic fraternities. We produce content highlighting your activities via blogs and user

Select... ▼
profiles, maintain a watch on major search engines for traffic to your site,
profiles, maintain a watch on major search engines for traffic to your site, and
profiles, maintaining a watch on major search engines for traffic to your site,
profiles, major search engines are maintained on watch for traffic to your site, and

collect news reports with a bearing on your organization's goals.

After we connected at the fundraiser, it occurred to me that with AIM approaching 10 whole years of community service, the time would be right for a major media push touting AIM's accomplishments to date. We have, in fact, initiated special media events for several companies. As AIM's 10th anniversary nears, your board of directors has probably been considering ways to make that anniversary special. To that end, I suggest we meet so that I could present some of the promotional work we have done and give you a sense of the nuances of what

Select... ▼
it
they
to
we

offer. Clear Image might be the perfect partner to

handle the celebration of "10 Years of AIM."

Feel free to call me at 748-555-2398 if you'd like to explore how Clear Image can make AIM more prominent in the world of philanthropy.

Yours truly,

Misha Ayakusi
Coordinator, Philanthropy & Social Service Image Enhancement

GO ON TO THE NEXT PAGE

Extended Response Answer Guidelines

Please use the guidelines below as you answer the Extended Response question on the Reasoning Through Language Arts test. Following these guidelines as closely as possible will ensure that you provide the best response.

1. **You will have up to (but no more than) 45 minutes to complete this task.** However, don't rush through your response. Be sure to read through the passage(s) and the prompt. Then think about the message you want to convey in your response. **Be sure to plan your response before you begin writing.** Draft your response and revise it as needed.

2. As you read, think carefully about the **argumentation** presented in the passage(s). "Argumentation" refers to the assumptions, claims, support, reasoning, and credibility on which a position is based. Pay close attention to **how the author(s) use these strategies to convey his or her (their) positions.**

3. When you write your essay, be sure to
   - **determine which position presented** in the passage(s) is **better supported** by evidence from the passage(s)
   - **explain why the position you chose is the better-supported one**
     - **remember, the better-supported position is not necessarily the position you agree with**
   - **defend your assertions with multiple pieces of evidence** from the passage(s)
   - **build your main points thoroughly**
   - **put your main points in logical order** and tie your details to your main points
   - **organize your response carefully** and consider your **audience, message, and purpose**
   - **use transitional words and phrases** to connect sentences, paragraphs, and ideas
   - **choose words carefully** to express your ideas clearly
   - **vary your sentence structure** to enhance the flow and clarity of your response
   - **reread and revise your response** to correct any errors in grammar, usage, or punctuation

GO ON TO THE NEXT PAGE

The following article presents both the benefits and drawbacks of a possible minimum wage increase. Proponents and critics disagree about the results of a minimum wage increase.

In your response, analyze both positions presented in the article to determine which one is best supported. Use relevant and specific evidence from the article to support your response.

Type your response, if a computer is available. Otherwise, write your response on paper. This task may require approximately 45 minutes to complete.

Assessing the Proposed $10.10 Minimum Wage

1   The minimum wage (first introduced as law in 1938) is the lowest hourly wage that employers may legally pay to workers. During the historic 1963 civil rights march on Washington, Bayard Rustin, a march organizer, called to increase the minimum wage from $1.15 an hour to $2 "so that men may live in dignity." Adjusted for inflation, $2 an hour in 1963 would be equivalent to $13.39 an hour in 2014.

2   Recently there has been debate about whether the minimum wage of workers should be raised. Present-day minimum-wage workers seek a raise from $7.25 an hour (established in 2009) to $10.10 an hour.

How raising the minimum wage might harm workers

3   While there has been much talk about increasing the minimum wage to $10.10, it is important to examine who exactly is earning minimum wage. The majority of minimum wage earners work in the service industry or fast food industry, for large nationwide food chains or big-box store corporations. So far, the demand for a higher wage seems reasonable: couldn't these multibillion-dollar corporations afford to pay their employees more? However, the truth is that many of these corporations are made up of innumerable small franchises, and the franchises are the true employers of the minimum-wage workers.

4   Each franchise operates as a very small independent company with little overhead to meet unexpected expenses. If these franchises were forced to pay a $10.10 wage, layoffs would likely occur, if there were not sufficient funds to retain all the employees. The remaining employees would then have to do extra work to compensate for their fired coworkers.

5   Even if the franchise finds it can "make do" with fewer workers, those laid off due to the wage increase are unlikely to

GO ON TO THE NEXT PAGE

be rehired. If a franchise does try to retain all its workers with a $10.10 wage, then it must struggle to remain in business, risking the jobs of all its employees in the process. Businesses in this situation also have no financial room to create new jobs, causing stagnation in the economy. And any jobs that remain are now priced out of the reach of unskilled workers, pushing them further into poverty.

6   Additionally, many economists feel that $10.10 represents too much compared to other wages in the economy. The current median wage in the U.S. is a bit less than $17 per hour, so this proposed increase would make the minimum wage nearly 60% of the median. Canadian studies show that workers lose jobs and have increased workloads when the minimum wage is more than half the median wage. In these studies, the lost jobs might have meant a franchise that migrated to the U.S., or the hiring of undocumented workers at a substandard wage.

7   But the same studies showed that a minimum wage of less than 45% of the median would have almost none of those undesired results. The current federal minimum wage of $7.25 is 43% of the median. So, opponents claim, according to the Canadian studies, maintaining the current minimum wage would be the best measure to guarantee jobs. Opponents of the $10.10 an hour minimum wage claim that guaranteeing jobs in the long term should outweigh any short-term gains from a severe hike in pay, and any rise in the minimum wage should follow an upward trend in national wages overall.

How an increase in the minimum wage benefits the economy

8   Supporters of the $10.10 minimum wage point out that the wages earned by minimum workers are much more likely to return to the economy than wages earned by those in higher-income brackets. From 2002 to 2012, wages have stagnated or declined for those at the bottom of the wage ladder, which translates to stifled spending. As time goes on, a greater percentage of available jobs become low-wage jobs, as jobs for the middle class are gradually lost. Some economists estimate that by 2020, 48% of U.S. jobs will be retail, food services, domestic services, and health-care support, the core fields that employ minimum-wage workers. Often, these are jobs that can be neither outsourced nor automated, contradicting the objection that a wage increase would force employers to shed workers or relocate.

9   Those in higher economic brackets don't spend the same proportion of their income as minimum wage workers do, and they don't spend it on the same types of goods. Rich people can afford not to spend: when they do spend, they buy luxury items from luxury sellers. By contrast, poor people dedicate most or

GO ON TO THE NEXT PAGE

all of their income to subsistence-level items and in the process contribute to the salaries of other low-wage earners: grocery clerks and gas station attendants. In this model of "parallel economies," wealth does not "trickle down" to minimum-wage earners; instead, funds cycle rapidly in the "poor economy" with some funds moving upwards to the "rich economy." So, supporters argue, increasing the minimum wage increases the health of the economy overall, enabling more people to buy cars, clothing, and food from our nation's businesses.

10   Another argument in support of raising the minimum wage is the large number of minimum-wage workers who are also receiving benefits from social services to fill in the gaps left by their small incomes. The Congressional Budget Office report in 2012 indicates that the lowest-income households receive about $8,800 in annual assistance from the federal government, for a total of $316 billion spent on social service programs annually. This assistance translates to basic food and medical care for employees of those mega-corporations that choose to pay their employees as little as possible. In essence, these corporations shift their labor costs to the taxpayers. With a higher minimum wage, supporters say, the government would experience significant relief from these payouts, and put the duty of providing a living wage on the shoulders of the employers.

> You may take a 10-minute break before proceeding to Section 3.

GO ON TO THE NEXT PAGE

Questions 18 through 25 are based on the following passage.

"The Wives of General Houston"
From *Famous Affinities Of History: The Romance Of Devotion Volume III of IV*
by Lyndon Orr

1   In 1828 Governor Houston was obliged to visit different portions of the state, stopping, as was the custom, to visit at the homes of "the quality," and to be introduced to wives and daughters as well as to their sportsman sons. On one of his official journeys he met Miss Eliza Allen, a daughter of one of the "influential families" of Sumner County, on the northern border of Tennessee. He found her responsive, charming, and greatly to be admired. She was a slender type of Southern beauty, well calculated to gain the affection of a lover, and especially of one whose associations had been chiefly with the women of frontier communities.

2   To meet a girl who had refined tastes and wide reading, and who was at the same time graceful and full of humor, must have come as a pleasant experience to Houston. He and Miss Allen saw much of each other, and few of their friends were surprised when the word went forth that they were engaged to be married.

3   The marriage occurred in January, 1829. They were surrounded with friends of all classes and ranks, for Houston was the associate of Jackson and was immensely popular in his own state. He seemed to have before him a brilliant career. He had won a lovely bride to make a home for him, so that no man seemed to have more attractive prospects. What was there which at this time interposed in some malignant way to blight his future?

4   It was a little more than a month after his marriage when he met a friend, and, taking him out into a strip of quiet woodland, said to him:

5   "I have something to tell you, but you must not ask me anything about it. My wife and I will separate before long. She will return to her father's, while I must make my way alone."

6   Houston's friend seized him by the arm and gazed at him with horror.

7   "Governor," said he, "you're going to ruin your whole life! What reason have you for treating this young lady in such a way? What has she done that you should leave her? Or what have you done that she should leave you? Every one will fall away from you."

GO ON TO THE NEXT PAGE

8   Houston grimly replied:

9   "I have no explanation to give you. My wife has none to give you. She will not complain of me, nor shall I complain of her. It is no one's business in the world except our own. Any interference will be impertinent, and I shall punish it with my own hand."

10   "But," said his friend, "think of it. The people at large will not allow such action. They will believe that you, who have been their idol, have descended to insult a woman. Your political career is ended. It will not be safe for you to walk the streets!"

11   "What difference does it make to me?" said Houston, gloomily. "What must be, must be. I tell you, as a friend, in advance, so that you may be prepared; but the parting will take place very soon."

12   Little was heard for another month or two, and then came the announcement that the Governor's wife had left him and had returned to her parents' home. The news flew like wildfire, and was the theme of every tongue. Friends of Mrs. Houston begged her to tell them the meaning of the whole affair. Adherents of Houston, on the other hand, set afloat stories of his wife's coldness and of her peevishness. The state was divided into factions; and what really concerned a very few was, as usual, made everybody's business.

13   There were times when, if Houston had appeared near the dwelling of his former wife, he would have been lynched or riddled with bullets. Again, there were enemies and slanderers of his who, had they shown themselves in Nashville, would have been torn to pieces by men who hailed Houston as a hero and who believed that he could not possibly have done wrong.

14   However his friends might rage, and however her people might wonder and seek to pry into the secret, no satisfaction was given on either side. The abandoned wife never uttered a word of explanation. Houston was equally reticent and self-controlled. In later years he sometimes drank deeply and was loose-tongued; but never, even in his cups, could he be persuaded to say a single word about his wife.

GO ON TO THE NEXT PAGE

18. Which definition best matches the use of the word "refined" in paragraph 2?

    A. processed, distilled
    B. purified, cleansed
    C. delicate, intricate
    D. cultivated, civilized

19. Drag and drop each word that describes Houston into the character web. (For this practice test, write each word into the web.)

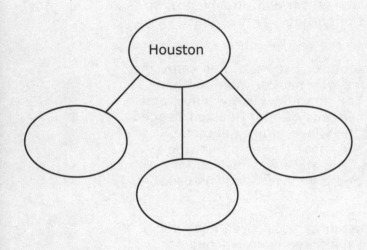

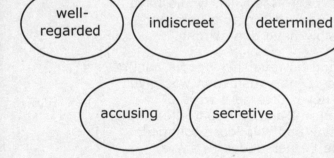

20. Read the following sentences from paragraph 3.

> He seemed to have before him a brilliant career. He had won a lovely bride to make a home for him, so that no man seemed to have more attractive prospects. What was there which at this time interposed in some malignant way to blight his future?

The detailed description of Houston's situation enhances the story by

    A. elaborating on Houston's character with details from his life.
    B. providing a contrast to the story development in the following paragraphs.
    C. comparing Houston to other politicians of his time.
    D. adding to the narrative by revealing the fact of Houston's marriage.

21. What can readers infer about Houston?

    A. His frequent drinking contributed to the break-up of his marriage.
    B. Unlike his wife, he was not widely read.
    C. He was loose-tongued about the details of his separation.
    D. He held public office in Tennessee.

GO ON TO THE NEXT PAGE

22. Which quotation from the story supports the inference that Houston was not accustomed to "refined" society?

    A. "In 1828 Governor Houston was obliged to visit different portions of the state, stopping, as was the custom, to visit at the homes of "the quality," and to be introduced to wives and daughters as well as to their sportsman sons."

    B. "There were times when, if Houston had appeared near the dwelling of his former wife, he would have been lynched or riddled with bullets."

    C. "He had won a lovely bride to make a home for him, so that no man seemed to have more attractive prospects."

    D. "She was a slender type of Southern beauty, well calculated to gain the affection of a lover, and especially of one whose associations had been chiefly with the women of frontier communities."

23. In paragraph 11, Houston says, "What difference does it make to me?" What characteristic does this reveal about Houston?

    A. indifference about the consequences of the separation from his wife

    B. sadness so extreme that the loss of his career appears of little importance

    C. curiosity about the effect that the separation will have on him

    D. irritation at his friend's repeated protests

24. Why does the author use the phrase "gazed at him with horror" in paragraph 6?

    A. to illustrate how unexpected and unbelievable the news was to Houston's friend

    B. to emphasize how afraid of him Houston's friend was

    C. to inform the reader that Houston's appearance had become grotesque

    D. to show that the friend has become speechless

25. Based on the details in the story, what can readers conclude about the marriage between Houston and Eliza Allen?

    A. Only the "influential families" were present at the wedding.

    B. Because of their different backgrounds, their friends were surprised to hear of the marriage.

    C. The marriage helped Houston's public image.

    D. Eliza Allen did not want the marriage as much as Houston did.

GO ON TO THE NEXT PAGE

Questions 26 through 33 are based on the following article.

Excerpt from "How To Tell a Story"

by Mark Twain

1   I do not claim that I can tell a story as it ought to be told. I only claim to know how a story ought to be told, for I have been almost daily in the company of the most expert story-tellers for many years.

2   There are several kinds of stories, but only one difficult kind— the humorous. I will talk mainly about that one. The humorous story is American, the comic story is English, the witty story is French. The humorous story depends for its effect upon the manner of the telling; the comic story and the witty story upon the matter.

3   The humorous story may be spun out to great length, and may wander around as much as it pleases, and arrive nowhere in particular; but the comic and witty stories must be brief and end with a point. The humorous story bubbles gently along, the others burst.

4   The humorous story is strictly a work of art—high and delicate art—and only an artist can tell it; but no art is necessary in telling the comic and the witty story; anybody can do it. The art of telling a humorous story—understand, I mean by word of mouth, not print—was created in America, and has remained at home.

5   The humorous story is told gravely; the teller does his best to conceal the fact that he even dimly suspects that there is anything funny about it; but the teller of the comic story tells you beforehand that it is one of the funniest things he has ever heard, then tells it with eager delight, and is the first person to laugh when he gets through. And sometimes, if he has had good success, he is so glad and happy that he will repeat the "nub" of it and glance around from face to face, collecting applause, and then repeat it again. It is a pathetic thing to see.

6   Very often, of course, the rambling and disjointed humorous story finishes with a nub, point, snapper, or whatever you like to call it. Then the listener must be alert, for in many cases the teller will divert attention from that nub by dropping it in a carefully casual and indifferent way, with the pretense that he does not know it is a nub.

7   Artemus Ward used that trick a good deal; then when the belated audience presently caught the joke he would look up with innocent surprise, as if wondering what they had found to laugh at. Dan Setchell used it before him, Nye and Riley and others use it to-day.

GO ON TO THE NEXT PAGE

8   But the teller of the comic story does not slur the nub; he shouts it at you—every time. And when he prints it, in England, France, Germany, and Italy, he italicizes it, puts some whooping exclamation-points after it, and sometimes explains it in a parenthesis. All of which is very depressing, and makes one want to renounce joking and lead a better life.

Source: *How To Tell A Story And Other Essays*, Mark Twain, 1897, Harper & Brothers.

26. Drag and drop two statements that express Twain's purposes for writing the essay into the empty boxes. (For this practice test, write the statement letters in the boxes.)

Twain's Purpose

```
┌─────────────────────────────┐
│                             │
└─────────────────────────────┘
```

```
┌─────────────────────────────┐
│                             │
└─────────────────────────────┘
```

(a) To compare the techniques of storytelling from different cultures

(b) To criticize the rambling and disjointed humorous story

(c) To relate the practices of the world's most expert storytellers

(d) To satirize the habits of comic storytellers, whether writing or speaking

(e) To defend humorous and comic storytelling as a work of art

27. Read this sentence from paragraph 8.

All of which is very depressing, and makes one want to renounce joking and lead a better life.

Why does the author conclude the essay with this sentence?

A. to show that the methods of comic storytelling are counterproductive
B. to give insight into the mental state of the author and instill empathy in the reader
C. to subtly criticize humorous storytelling as immoral
D. to give an alternative to the career of a professional storyteller

GO ON TO THE NEXT PAGE

28. Why does the author describe the humorous story as "difficult"?

  A. Because attempting to tell a humorous story is so strenuous it can result in depression
  B. Because, if done incorrectly, the audience will view the teller as pathetic
  C. Because it is a form that requires patience and self-control
  D. Because it takes many years of study to fully master the form

29. Which statement expresses the central theme of this essay?

  A. Humor is more a matter of style than of substance.
  B. No story is truly humorous that is not based on truth.
  C. Anybody can be humorous, as long as you tell the story with delight.
  D. Humor is a universal human characteristic, found throughout the world.

30. Drag and drop the sentences into the correct location in the chart. (For this practice test, write the sentence letters in the boxes.)

The humorous story	The comic story

(a) It compares the techniques of storytelling from different cultures.

(b) It never has a point.

(c) It is told seriously.

(d) Anybody can tell it.

(e) The listener must be alert at the end.

(f) It is pathetic to hear.

GO ON TO THE NEXT PAGE

31. What technique does the author use to make his point about the different types of stories?

    A. The author draws an analogy between the stories of America and those of England and France.
    B. The author uses exaggerated imagery to highlight a contrast between the methods of storytelling.
    C. The author cites storytelling experts from each type of story tradition.
    D. The author draws from his own history and experience with storytelling.

32. What can the reader infer about the author's feelings regarding writers and tellers of comedic stories in England, France, and Germany?

    A. The author appreciates that they go out of their way to make the story seem exciting with punctuation.
    B. The author feels they overemphasize the ending of a joke too much, so that the humor in the story is not allowed to stand on its own.
    C. The author applauds them for originating the modern comedic story form, which has taken root in America.
    D. The author is critical of them for telling a story too gravely, rambling, and never getting to the point.

33. Drag and drop each word that applies to the author into the character web. (For this practice test, write the statement letters in the boxes.)

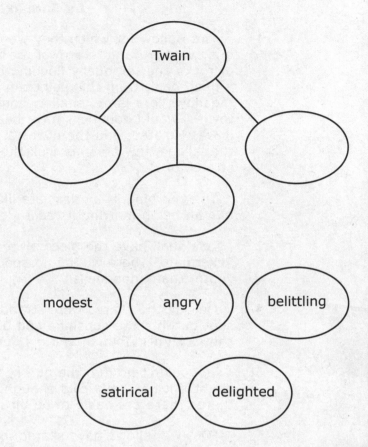

GO ON TO THE NEXT PAGE

Questions 34 through 41 are based on the following passage.

Excerpt from *Steve and the Steam Engine*
by Sara Ware Bassett

1   The Hollow for which they were bound lay in a deserted stone quarry where a little arm of the river had penetrated the barrier of rocks and, gradually flooding the place, made at one end a deep pool; from this point the water spread itself over the meadows in a large, shallow pond. Had the spot been nearer the town it would doubtless have been overrun with skaters; but as it was isolated, and there was a larger lake near the center of the village, few persons took the trouble to seek out this remote stretch of ice.

2   This morning it lay desolate like a gleaming mirror, not a human being marring its solitude.

3   "We shall have the place all to ourselves!" exclaimed Mr. Ackerman. "There will be no spectators to watch me renew my youth, thank goodness!"

4   Quickly the skates were strapped on and the young people shot out into the sunshine and began to circle about. More cautiously Mr. Tolman and his guest followed.

5   "I wouldn't go into the quarry," shouted Mr. Tolman, "for I doubt if it has been cold enough yet to freeze the ice very solidly there. There are liable to be air holes where the river makes in."

6   "Oh, we fellows have skated in the quarry millions of times, Dad," Stephen protested. "It is perfectly safe."

7   "There is no way of telling whether it is or not," was the response, "so suppose for to-day we keep away from it."

8   "But—"

9   "Oh, don't argue, Stevie," called Doris. "If Dad doesn't want us to go there that's enough, isn't it?"

10   "But half the fun is making that turn around the rocks," grumbled Stephen, in a lower tone. "I don't see why Dad is such a fraid-cat. I know this pond better than he does and—"

11   "If your father says not to skate there that ought to go with you," cut in Dick. "He doesn't want you to—see? Whether it is safe or not has nothing to do with it."

12   "But it's so silly!" went on Stephen. "Why—"

GO ON TO THE NEXT PAGE

13   "Oh, cut it out! Can it!" exclaimed the East Side lad. "Your dad says *No* and he's the boss."

14   The ungracious retort Steve offered was lost amid the babble of laughter that followed, and the skaters darted away up the pond. Indeed, one could not long have cherished ill humor amid such radiant surroundings. There was too much sunshine, too much sparkle in the clear air, too much jollity and happiness. Almost before he realized it Stephen's irritation had vanished and he was speeding across the glassy surface of the ice as gay as the gayest of the company.

15   He never could explain afterward just how it happened that he found himself around the bend of the quarry and sweeping with the wind toward its farther end. He had not actually formulated the intention of slipping away from the others and invading this forbidden spot. Nevertheless, there he was alone in the tiny cove with no one in sight. What followed was all over in a moment,— the breaking ice and the plunge into the frigid water. The next he knew he was fighting with all his strength to prevent himself from being drawn beneath the jagged, crumbling edge of the hole. To clamber out was impossible, for every time he tried the thin ice would break afresh under his hands and submerge him again in the bitter cold of the moving stream. Over and over he tried to pull himself to safety but without success. Then suddenly he felt himself becoming numb and helpless. His teeth chattered and he could no longer retain his hold on the frail support that was keeping his head above water. He was slipping back into the river. *He was not going to be able to get out!*

16   With a piercing scream he made one last desperate lunge forward, and again the ice that held him broke and the water dashed over his ears and mouth.

17   When he next opened his eyes it was to find himself in his own bed with a confusion of faces bending over him.

18   "There!" he heard some one say in a very small, far-away voice. "He is coming to himself now, thank God! It was chiefly cold and fright. He is safe now, Tolman. Don't you worry! You'd better go and get off some of your wet clothing, or you will catch your death."

GO ON TO THE NEXT PAGE

34. Drag and drop the events into the chart to show the order in which they occur in the excerpt. (For this practice test, write the event letters in the chart.)

Order of Events

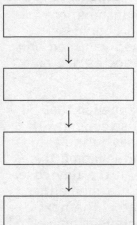

(a) The lake ice breaks.

(b) Stephen objects to his father.

(c) Stephen is at home.

(d) The quarry is deserted.

35. What can readers infer about the skating trip?

A. Stephen deliberately planned to disobey his father by skating around the quarry.

B. Stephen's father was the one who pulled him from the water.

C. The quarry was deserted because it had a reputation for being unsafe.

D. The trip was planned for the purpose of restoring Mr. Ackerman's health.

36. Which quotation from the story best supports the idea that Dick's father is not the only adult in the skating party?

A. "There will be no spectators to watch me renew my youth, thank goodness!"

B. "Quickly the skates were strapped on and the young people shot out into the sunshine and began to circle about."

C. "If your father says not to skate there that ought to go with you," cut in Dick.

D. "He is safe now, Tolman. Don't you worry!"

37. Which definition best matches the use of the word "cherished" in paragraph 14?

A. preserved
B. embraced
C. harbored
D. honored

38. Based on the details in the story, what can readers tell about Dick?

A. He is Stephen's brother, and warns Stephen to obey their father.

B. He is the son of Mr. Ackerman, who is friends with Stephen's father.

C. He disagrees with Stephen about whether the quarry is safe to skate around.

D. He and Stephen have different views of parental authority.

GO ON TO THE NEXT PAGE

39. Read the following sentences from paragraph 1.

> The Hollow for which they were bound lay in a deserted stone quarry where a little arm of the river had penetrated the barrier of rocks and, gradually flooding the place, made at one end a deep pool; from this point the water spread itself over the meadows in a large, shallow pond.

The detailed description of the landscape enhances the story by

A.   giving some evidence for the claim that some parts of the ice may be safer than others.

B.   establishing the geological history of The Hollow.

C.   introducing the skating area that lies near the village.

D.   showing that the group had to cross a river before arriving at the skating area.

40. Drag and drop each word that describes Stephen into the character web. (For this practice test, write each word into the web.)

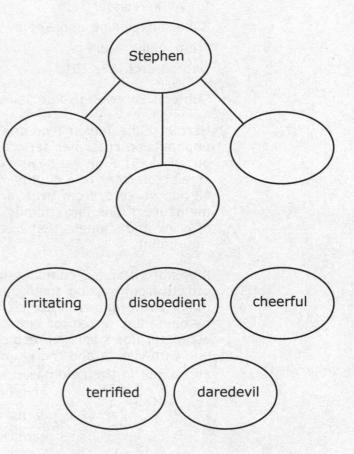

irritating   disobedient   cheerful   terrified   daredevil

41. Why does the narrator use the phrase "a confusion of faces"?

A.   to show that Tolman is disoriented by the lake experience

B.   to emphasize that the people caring for Stephen are confused by his condition

C.   to represent Stephen's mental state after the skating trip

D.   to indicate that the people Stephen sees are strangers to him

GO ON TO THE NEXT PAGE

42. The passage below is incomplete. For each "Select" option, choose the option that correctly completes the sentence. (For this practice test, circle your selection.)

To: All Personnel
Billie Tanker Pipe and Supply
From: Billie Tanker
Date: March 18, 2013

Subject: Farewell to Ron Jensen

Here at Billie Tanker Pipe and Supply, we take pride in our unparalleled customer service and the unquestionable quality of our work. Though we have expanded our operations from one small storefront to a county-wide franchise, we continue to see all our workers, from truck drivers to senior management, as members of one large family. Therefore, it is with a mixed sense of pride and sadness that I congratulate Ron Jensen on his retirement.

Ron started at our company fifteen years ago and was a part of growth from making small business "housecalls" to servicing major corporations in our city. Many customers got to know Ron by name and asked for him personally when they needed an estimate. Ron's service record is outstanding. His work one-on-one with clients and the knowledge he's gained from a decade and a half in the field [Select... ▼] many referrals from

| earn him |
| earns him |
| earn them |
| earns them |

valued customers. While many of his peers went on to positions in management, Ron remained at the "front lines," where he could "get his hands dirty" with the renovations and retrofits that he preferred to desk work.

At his retirement [Select... ▼]

| party, ceremoniously, Ron will present the password for his workstation |
| party Ron's presentation of the password for his workstation will be ceremonious |
| party, Ron will ceremoniously present the password for his workstation |
| party, Ron's workstation will have its password ceremoniously presented |

to his colleague of many years, Belle Sanchez. His coworkers will then stage a humorous "This Was Your Life" retrospective,

GO ON TO THE NEXT PAGE

highlighting Ron's career successes, and relating humorous anecdotes about his adventures in engineering.

Ron plans to retain a consultant relationship with our company to best serve his [Select... ▼]

| colleagues and project managers and his |
| colleagues and project managers. His |
| colleagues, his project managers, and, his |
| colleagues, his project managers, and his |

long-time clients, providing guidance necessary to make his transition to retirement as smooth as possible for all parties. Ron will work with new technicians as they take over existing projects, to ensure our [Select... ▼] best performance.

| Company, |
| company's |
| companies' |
| companies |

Please join me in thanking Ron for his outstanding tenure of service and commending him on a successful career. All employees are invited to Ron's retirement party on Friday, at 7pm, in the main conference room of our downtown office location: 2121 Main Street. Come wish him a happy retirement.

GO ON TO THE NEXT PAGE

Questions 43 through 50 refer to the following articles.

Addresses and Proceedings of the Second National Conservation Congress

Held At Saint Paul, Minnesota   September 5–8, 1910

Article 1: Address by the President of the United States by President William Howard Taft

1   We have, then, excluding Alaskan forests, a total of about 144,000,000 acres of forests belonging to the Government, which are being treated in accord with the principles of scientific forestry. The law now prohibits the reservation of any more forest lands in Oregon, Washington, Idaho, Montana, Colorado and Wyoming, except by act of Congress. I am informed by the Department of Agriculture that the Government owns other tracts of timber lands in these States which should be included in the forest reserves. I expect to recommend to Congress that the limitation herein imposed shall be repealed. In the present forest reserves there are lands which are not properly forest land, and which ought to be subject to homestead entry. We are carefully eliminating such lands from forest reserves or, where their elimination is not practicable, listing them for entry under the forest homestead act.

2   The Government timber in this country amounts to only one-fourth of all the timber, the rest being in private ownership. Only three percent of that which is in private ownership is looked after properly and treated according to modern rules of forestry. The usual destructive waste and neglect continue in the remainder of the forests owned by private persons and corporations. It is estimated that fire alone destroys $50,000,000 worth of timber a year. The management of forests not on public land is beyond the jurisdiction of the Federal Government. If anything can be done by law, it must be done by the State legislatures. I believe that it is within their constitutional power to require the enforcement of regulations, in the general public interest, as to fire and other causes of waste in the management of forests owned by private individuals and corporations.

3   Exactly how far these regulations can go and remain consistent with the rights of private ownership, it is not necessary to discuss; but I call attention to the fact that a very important part of Conservation must always fall upon the State legislatures, and that they would better be up and doing if they would save the waste and denudation and destruction through private greed or accidental fires that have made barren many square miles of the older States.

GO ON TO THE NEXT PAGE

4   I have shown sufficiently the conditions as to Federal forestry to indicate that no further legislation is needed at the moment except an increase in the fire protection to National forests and an act vesting the Executive with full power to make forest reservations in every State where Government land is timber-covered, or where the land is needed for forestry purposes.

Article 2: Report of the Western Forestry and Conservation Association by E. T. Allen, Forester

5   Let us not, during excursions into Constitutional problems, State rights, and other bewildering issues, forget that first of all comes protection from destruction and waste! The great danger now is that our resources will disappear while we are deciding to whom they shall belong.

6   In our five States from Montana to California stands half the merchantable timber in the United States, the majority in private hands. To preserve it for the fullest use, to replace it when used, if possible—this is the timber-owner's duty. Nowhere else has he realized this so promptly and acted so adequately as in the Pacific Northwest.

7   You have all read of the recent fires in our northwestern country. They have been greatly exaggerated, the area injured really being very limited. Nevertheless, while we talk here of generalities, bands of weary, half-blind men are still battling to prevent fresh outbreaks; the smoke still curls over the blackened forms of those who met a fearful death to save the lives of others; scores who fought till they could fight no more still lie bandaged and sightless in the extremity of mortal agony. We of the West owe a sacred debt to them, one and all, and not least to the men of the Forest Service whose training made them as efficient as they were brave. But side by side with the bravest, equally efficient, equally trained and disciplined, worked the patrolmen of our fire associations. Conservationists are employed by private effort. In the Coeur d' Alene fires alone, a single one of our Associations put 850 men in the field.

8   The way to prevent fire is to prevent it, not fight it when almost or quite beyond control. The only solution of the fire question is better enforcement of better laws, better public sentiment, and better patrol. It is in this that our Associations now lead all other agencies. They handle the fire situation in a much better and more comprehensive manner than even the Government

GO ON TO THE NEXT PAGE

has ever done, because they spend three times as much money per acre for patrol. Thoroughly excellent as are the methods in the National Forests—they are identical with those of the most progressive practical timberman—Congress does not sustain them adequately.

9   Our own system is by no means perfect yet. We need more men and more money from our own brethren, and heartier cooperation from public, State, and Government. And when, as already in Washington last year, one Association protects 8,000,000 acres with a loss of but 1,000 acres; when this small loss was caused by less than 6 fires out of 1,200 extinguished; when in this historic year of 1910 we have controlled our countless fires so that actual disasters can be counted on the fingers, and our loss as a whole is insignificant—we feel that no one has done more to prove his willingness and competence to practice Conservation that counts than the northwestern forest owner.

43. President Taft mentioned the fraction of timber owned by public organizations in order to

   A.   show that waste and neglect of forests is mostly due to private owners.
   B.   emphasize that not enough forested land was designated for public use.
   C.   support the idea that some lands are not properly forest lands, and should be re-categorized.
   D.   prove that federal laws about management of forests not on public land should not be enacted because the fraction is so small.

44. What approach did the author of the report by the Western Forestry and Conservation Association take to support the idea that northwestern forest owners have effective conservation practices?

   A.   The author explored several different definitions of "conservation" and evaluated them.
   B.   The author offered statistics to illustrate the effectiveness of the private associations in protecting private forest lands.
   C.   The author compared the number of Forest Service members to the number of members in fire patrols of the private associations.
   D.   The author offered a critique of the government's conservation methods.

GO ON TO THE NEXT PAGE

45. Read this quotation from the report:

> "...we feel that no one has done more to prove his willingness and competence to practice Conservation that counts than the northwestern forest owner."

Why does E. T. Allen, in responding to President Taft, conclude the report with this sentence?

- A. to counter the idea that private owners of forested lands are guilty of waste and neglect
- B. to clearly define the kind of Conservation "that counts"
- C. to prove that Congress does not adequately maintain the forested lands
- D. to show that the private owners can protect their forested lands without further laws

46. Drag and drop the phrases into the correct location on the chart. (For this practice test, write the phrase letters in the chart.)

President Taft's Address	E. T. Allen's Report

(a) There are lands which should be removed from the forest reserves.

(b) States should make laws for fire safety.

(c) Private fire patrols are more costly per acre than National Forest patrols.

(d) The private Northwest forest owners have an imperfect fire safety system.

47. How does Article 1 (the president's address) relate to Article 2 (the excerpt of the report by E. T. Allen)?

- A. The president's address mentions the limitations on national reserved forests, and the report by E. T. Allen defends these limitations.
- B. The president's address calls for more laws regarding fire safety, and the report by E. T. Allen denies the necessity of such laws.
- C. The report by E. T. Allen calls for laws to enforce fire safety, while the president's address discusses how those laws impact property rights.
- D. The president's speech spends equal time on the classification of forests and problems of regulation, while the report by E. T. Allen gives priority to the details of forest protection.

48. Based on Article 1, what was President Taft's attitude about laws regarding the regulation of forested lands?

- A. No further legislation is currently needed.
- B. The states do not have constitutional power to require the enforcement of such regulations.
- C. The laws regarding limitations on forested reserves should remain.
- D. The federal government should not make laws about forests that are not public.

GO ON TO THE NEXT PAGE

49. Which quotation expresses the primary purpose of President Taft's address?

    A. "I call attention to the fact that a very important part of Conservation must always fall upon the State legislatures."

    B. "We have, then, excluding Alaskan forests, a total of about 144,000,000 acres of forests belonging to the Government, which are being treated in accord with the principles of scientific forestry."

    C. "The usual destructive waste and neglect continue in the remainder of the forests owned by private persons and corporations."

    D. "No further legislation is needed at the moment except an increase in the fire protection to National forests and an act vesting the Executive with full power to make forest reservations."

50. What can readers infer about the forest homestead act?

    A. The act was passed to make sure pioneers could have homesteads in the forests.

    B. The act was passed to reallocate the forest lands that had been restricted in the northwest states.

    C. The act provided another way of categorizing government forest lands that had been assigned to the forest reserve.

    D. The act applied to one-fourth of the timber in the country.

END OF TEST

Mathematical Reasoning

Welcome!

Here is some information that you need to know before you start this test:

- You should not spend too much time on a question if you are not certain of the answer; answer it the best you can, and go on to the next question.
- If you are not certain of the answer to a question, you can mark your answer for review and come back to it later.
- You have **115 minutes** to complete this test.
- This test has two parts.
- When you finish Part 1, you may review those questions.
- You may not go back to Part 1 once you have finished your review.
- You may not use a calculator in Part 1. You may use a calculator in Part 2.

Turn the page to begin.

GO ON TO THE NEXT PAGE

Mathematics Formula Sheet

Area of a:

square	$A = s^2$
rectangle	$A = lw$
parallelogram	$A = bh$
triangle	$A = \frac{1}{2}bh$
trapezoid	$A = \frac{1}{2}h(b_1 + b_2)$
circle	$A = \pi r^2$

Perimeter of a:

square	$P = 4s$
rectangle	$P = 2l + 2w$
triangle	$P = s_1 + s_2 + s_3$
Circumference of a circle	$C = 2\pi r$ OR $C = \pi d$; $\pi \approx 3.14$

Surface Area and Volume of a:

rectangular prism	$SA = 2lw + 2lh + 2wh$	$V = lwh$
right prism	$SA = ph + 2B$	$V = Bh$
cylinder	$SA = 2\pi rh + 2\pi r^2$	$V = \pi r^2 h$
pyramid	$SA = \frac{1}{2}ps + B$	$V = \frac{1}{3}Bh$
cone	$SA = \pi rs + \pi r^2$	$V = \frac{1}{3}\pi r^2 h$
sphere	$SA = 4\pi r^2$	$V = \frac{4}{3}\pi r^3$

(p = perimeter of base B; $\pi \approx 3.14$)

Data

mean	mean is equal to the total of the values of a data set, divided by the number of elements in the data set
median	median is the middle value in an odd number of ordered values of a data set, or the mean of the two middle values in an even number of ordered values in a data set

Algebra

slope of a line	$m = \dfrac{y_2 - y_1}{x_2 - x_1}$
slope-intercept form of the equation of a line	$y = mx + b$
point-slope form of the equation of a line	$y - y_1 = m(x - x_1)$
standard form of a quadratic equation	$y = ax^2 + bx + c$
quadratic formula	$x = \dfrac{-b \pm \sqrt{b^2 - 4ac}}{2a}$
Pythagorean Theorem	$a^2 + b^2 = c^2$
simple interest	$I = prt$ (I = interest, p = principal, r = rate, t = time)
distance formula	$d = rt$
total cost	total cost = (number of units) × (price per unit)

GO ON TO THE NEXT PAGE

Mathematical Reasoning, Part 1

You may NOT use a calculator in Part 1.

1. The Great Pyramid in Egypt has a height of approximately 150 meters and a base of 50,000 square meters. In cubic meters, what is its approximate internal volume?

   A. 7,500,000
   B. 5,000,000
   C. 2,500,000
   D. 750,000

2. If a woman sleeps only 6 hours per night and spends $\frac{4}{9}$ of her waking hours at work, then what fraction of the total 24-hour day (on a work day) is the woman at work?

   A. $\frac{1}{9}$

   B. $\frac{1}{3}$

   C. $\frac{4}{9}$

   D. $\frac{3}{4}$

3. A class with 87 students has an average test score of 76 points. The number of students who scored above the average score is less than the number of students who scored below the average test score. Only 1 student scored exactly 76 points. It follows that the median student score

Select... ▼	76.
$\leq$	
$<$	
$=$	
$>$	
$\geq$	

4. A moving company charges $50 per hour for each person working, plus an additional $.50 per mile driven. If Fritz hires 3 movers for 2 hours of work apiece and the total distance driven is 40 miles, which of the following represents the equation for his total cost?

   A. $\$50 \times 3 + 40 \times (\$.5) \times 2$

   B. $\dfrac{\$50 \times 3}{2} + 40 \times (\$.5)$

   C. $\$50 \times 3 \times 2 + 40 \times (\$.5)$

   D. $\$50 \times 3 \times 2 + \dfrac{40}{(\$.5)}$

5. Mindy invested $500 in a savings account. After one year, her account balance was $515. What percent yearly interest did her bank pay?

GO ON TO THE NEXT PAGE

Mathematical Reasoning, Part 2

You MAY use a calculator in Part 2.

6. By law, a bus driver may drive a maximum of 9 hours per day. If the speed limit is 65 miles per hour and if a driver needs to cover 4,287 miles, then what is the minimum number of days in which the driver can make the trip?

   A. 7
   B. 8
   C. 25
   D. 66

7. Zarbini's gourmet grocery buys pickles in barrels that are 4 feet tall and measure 24 inches in diameter. What is the approximate volume (in cubic feet) of pickles that will fill a barrel with these dimensions?

   A. 4
   B. 12.6
   C. 25.2
   D. 150.7

Questions 8 and 9 refer to the following diagram.

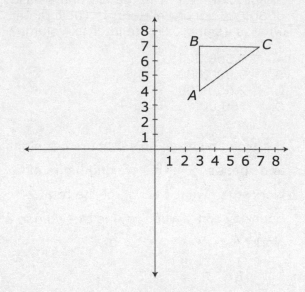

8. The sum of the lengths of line segments *AB* and *BC* is [Select... ▼]
   greater than
   less than
   equal to
   equal to the square of

   the length of line segment *AC*.

9. What is the difference between the area of the triangle and the length of the hypotenuse of the triangle?

   A. 1
   B. 5
   C. 6
   D. 7

GO ON TO THE NEXT PAGE

Mathematical Reasoning, Part 2

<u>Questions 10 and 11</u> refer to the following graph.

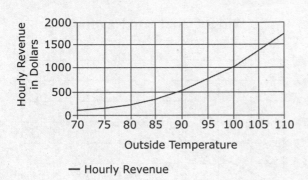

— Hourly Revenue

<u>Question 12</u> refers to the following diagram.

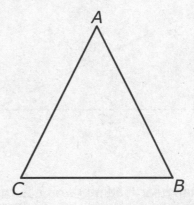

10. A shaved ice stand located near a beach records its hourly revenue as well as the temperature outside, as shown on the graph above. Approximately how much more revenue would be expected during a 3-hour shift with a temperature of 100° than at a shift of the same duration with a temperature of 90°?

   A. $150
   B. $500
   C. $750
   D. $1,500

11. The owner of the shaved ice stand institutes a policy to close the stand on any day on which the average revenue is likely to fall below $250 per hour as predicted by the graph. On a given day, the temperature at the beginning of the shift is 70° and the temperature is expected to rise at a constant rate to 95°. Should the owner close the ice stand?

   A.   No, because the average temperature during the day will be greater than 80° so the stand is likely to make more than $250 per hour.
   B.   No, because the sum of the revenue at the beginning of the day and the revenue at the end of the day will be more than $250 per hour.
   C.   Yes, because the midpoint between the revenue at the beginning of the day and the revenue at the end of the day is less than $250 per hour.
   D.   Yes, because for at least half the day, the stand will be bringing in less than $250 per hour.

12. For the triangle shown in the diagram above, both angle *A* and angle *C* measure 60°. If side *AB* has a length of 4 inches, what is the sum (in inches) of sides *AC* and *BC*?

   A.   12
   B.   10
   C.   8
   D.   6

GO ON TO THE NEXT PAGE

Mathematical Reasoning, Part 2

<u>Question 13</u> refers to the following diagram.

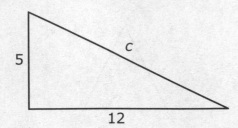

13. A triangular loading ramp has the dimensions shown in the figure above. Side c is the length. If a new ramp is made for a dock that is twice as high off the ground as the one with length c but with the same incline, what will the new ramp's length be (in feet)?

   A.   6.5
   B.   13
   C.   17
   D.   26

<u>Questions 14 and 15</u> refer to the following graph.

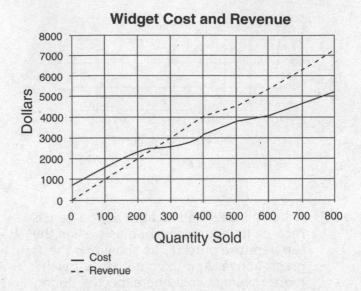

14. Indicate on the revenue line the minimum number of widgets that must be sold in order to avoid losing money. (For this practice test, write an X on the revenue line.)

15. Indicate on the revenue line the quantity sold for which the profit will be $2,000. (For this practice test, write an X on the revenue line.)

GO ON TO THE NEXT PAGE

<u>Questions 16 and 17</u> refer to the following graph.

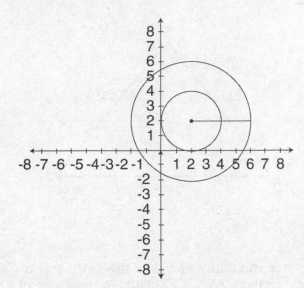

16. The larger circle has [Select... ▼]
 - twice
 - three times
 - four times

the diameter and [Select... ▼]
 - twice
 - four times
 - eight times

the area of the smaller circle.

17. If *a* represents the point on the larger circle with the largest *y*-value, and if *b* represents the point on the smaller circle with the smallest *y*-value, then what is the distance from point *a* to point *b*?

A.   2
B.   4
C.   6
D.   8

18. If a plane travels at 280 miles per hour, how many miles will it travel in 12 minutes?

A.   56
B.   45
C.   36
D.   28

19. A can of fruit weighs *w* ounces. The fruit itself, without the can, weighs *f* ounces. Which equation can be used to find *C*, the weight of the empty can?

A. $C = w + f$
B. $C = w - f$
C. $C = f - w$
D. $C = f$

20. A square has sides that measure 5 inches. The square is then divided in half vertically and horizontally, creating 4 smaller squares. What would the total perimeter of the 4 smaller squares be (in inches)?

A.   5
B.   6.25
C.   25
D.   40

21. If $\frac{1}{5}$ of *x* = 15, what is $\frac{4}{3}$ of *x*?

A.   4
B.   25
C.   75
D.   100

GO ON TO THE NEXT PAGE

22. A jar of marbles contains two sizes of marbles: normal and jumbo. There are 84 normal size marbles. If $\frac{2}{9}$ of the marbles are jumbo size, then how many marbles total are in the jar?

   A.   19
   B.   103
   C.   108
   D.   378

23. For her first 3 years with a company, Marissa earned $45,200 each year. For the next 5 years she earned $55,400 per year. What was the average amount that Marissa earned per year over the 8-year period?

   A. $49,075
   B. $50,300
   C. $51,575
   D. $52,100

24. To rent a convention hall costs a $400 base fee, plus an additional $5 per attendee. If x legionnaires are attending an event, which of the following equations indicates (in dollars) the average cost per legionnaire C of renting the hall?

   A. $C = 400 + 5x$

   B. $C = \dfrac{400 + 5x}{x}$

   C. $C = \dfrac{400 + 5x}{5}$

   D. $C = \dfrac{400 + 5x}{400}$

Questions 25 and 26 refer to the following diagram.

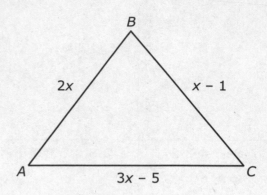

25. In the figure above, if the perimeter of triangle ABC is 27, what is the value of x?

26. Given that the perimeter of the triangle is 27, indicate below the correct relationship among the 3 angles of the triangle. (For this practice test, circle your selections.)

Select... ▼		Select... ▼	
A		A	
B	<	B	<
C		C	

Select... ▼
A
B
C

GO ON TO THE NEXT PAGE

Mathematical Reasoning, Part 2

27. A farmer purchases 200 lbs. of feed each month to support 35 cows. How much total feed (in lbs.) will he need per month, at this rate, if he acquires an additional 245 cows?

  A. 43
  B. 243
  C. 1,400
  D. 1,600

28. To rent a community center for a school prom costs a base fee of $550 and an additional fee of $6 per person in attendance. The organizers expected 350 attendees, but in fact a total of 377 people attended. How much greater was the actual fee than the fee the organizers had expected to pay?

  A. $162
  B. $712
  C. $2,262
  D. $2,812

Questions 29 and 30 refer to the following coordinate axis.

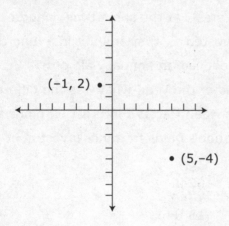

29. What are the coordinates of the midpoint of the two points shown on the coordinate axis above?

  A. (2, −1)
  B. (3, −3)
  C. (3, −1)
  D. (2, −2)

30. Which of the following equations represents the line that passes through the two given points?

  A. $y = 2x - 14$
  B. $y = 2x + 3$
  C. $y = -x - 1$
  D. $y = -x + 1$

31. At a law firm, new associates earn an average of $2,800 more per month than new paralegals do. The firm employs 15 new associates and z more new associates than new paralegals. If the the average pay for a new paralegal is represented by p, then use numbers and variables from the figure bank to indicate the correct equation for the total monthly payroll of these new employees. (For this practice test, write the figures in the boxes.)

$$Total = \left(\boxed{} \times \left(\boxed{} + p \right) \right) + \left(\left(15 + \boxed{} \right) \times \boxed{} \right)$$

$$\boxed{p}$$

$$\boxed{12}$$

$$\boxed{z}$$

$$\boxed{2,800}$$

$$\boxed{15}$$

32. The scale on a map of the moon's surface indicates that 0.4 inches = 100 miles. Sen wants to know the distance between two large craters. If on the map, the distance between the two craters is 7.4 inches, then what is the actual distance, in miles, between the two craters?

  A. 74 miles
  B. 296 miles
  C. 1,850 miles
  D. 2,960 miles

GO ON TO THE NEXT PAGE

Mathematical Reasoning, Part 2

Questions 33 through 35 refer to the following table.

Migration Sightings			
Bird Type	**2008**	**2009**	**2010**
Cardinal	24	31	
Finch	40	37	
Grosbeak	19	23	
Harrier	31	38	
Sparrow	28	24	

33. Choose from the figure box below to indicate the correct relationship among the three types of birds that showed an increase in the number of sightings from 2008 to 2009. The bird types are to be ordered from least percent increase in sightings to greatest percent increase in sightings. (For this practice test, circle your selections.)

% increase of [Select...   ▼]
| Cardinal |
| Finch |
| Grosbeak |
| Harrier |
| Sparrow |

< % increase of [Select...   ▼]
| Cardinal |
| Finch |
| Grosbeak |
| Harrier |
| Sparrow |

< % increase of [Select...   ▼]
| Cardinal |
| Finch |
| Grosbeak |
| Harrier |
| Sparrow |

34. Considering only these 5 bird types, what was the total percentage increase in sightings from 2008 to 2009? (Round your answer to the nearest integer.)

   A. 7%
   B. 8%
   C. 14%
   D. 18%

35. Assume that in 2010, the new sightings levels for each bird type increased or decreased by identical amounts as they had from 2008 to 2009. Select the appropriate sightings numbers from the figure box below, and write them in the 2010 column to complete the chart. (Not all of the numbers will be used, but all of the empty boxes should be filled).

20	26	27	30

33	34	38	45

36. One year ago Harold invested $24,000 in a bank bond that offers 3% annual interest. At the same time, Maude invested $\frac{1}{3}$ that amount in a fund that produced an annual yield of 8%. At the end of the year, what was the difference between Harold's interest earnings and Maude's gains from her investment yield?

   A. $80
   B. $240
   C. $640
   D. $5,040

GO ON TO THE NEXT PAGE

37. Each number below is a possible solution for $2x^2 - 3 \leq 15 - x$ EXCEPT

    A. −3
    B. 0
    C. 1
    D. 3

38. A pizza store sells two sizes of pizzas, one with a circumference of 22π inches and a larger with a circumference of 27π inches. Each pizza is cut from edge to center into 8 identical slices and the length of the smaller slice (measured along the edge from the tip to the end of the crust) is compared to the length of the larger slice. How much longer, in inches, is the edge of the larger pizza slice?

    A. 2.5
    B. 3
    C. 5
    D. 5π

39. 384 conference attendees need to take tour shuttles into the city. If each bus can carry a maximum of 26 passengers, then what is the minimum number of shuttle trips required to transport all the passengers?

    ☐

40. A small copy shop spent 24% of its monthly revenue on supplies, 17% on renting the building, and 33% on payroll and taxes. If after paying these expenses, $7,384 dollars in profit is left, then how much did the copy shop spend on rent?

    A. $3,976
    B. $4,828
    C. $19,198
    D. $28,400

41. If $x^2 - x = 12$, then which of the following could be the value of x^2?

    A. 1
    B. 9
    C. 36
    D. 144

GO ON TO THE NEXT PAGE

<u>Questions 42 and 43</u> refer to the following pie chart.

2012 Allocation of Endowment Funds for University X

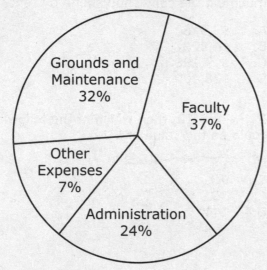

42. If the total income from the endowment in 2012 was $1.2 million, then how much more money went to Faculty salaries than to Administration?

    A. $130,000
    B. $156,000
    C. $180,000
    D. $684,000

43. If in 2013, the income from the endowment increases from $1.2 million to $1.6 million, and the percentage distribution remains constant, then by how much will the funds available for "other expenses" increase? (Enter your result in dollars.)

44. Currently a sports league has 33 teams with 24 players each. If the membership of each team is going to be reduced to 18 players, then how many additional teams will need to be formed to include all the remaining players?

45. If the equation of two lines is given by $y = -28x - 4$ and $y = 2x + 11$, then at which of the following points do the two lines intersect?

    A. $\left(-\frac{9}{2}, 2\right)$

    B. $(2, 15)$

    C. $\left(-\frac{1}{2}, 10\right)$

    D. $(-26, 7)$

46. A bell rings every 2 hours. A second bell rings every 3 hours. A third bell rings every 4 hours. If all three bells ring at 9:00 am, when will all three bells ring again?

    A.   12:00 pm
    B.   2:00 pm
    C.   6:00 pm
    D.   9:00 pm

END OF TEST

Social Studies

Welcome!

Here is some information that you need to know before you start this test:

- You should not spend too much time on a question if you are not certain of the answer; answer it the best you can, and go on to the next question.
- If you are not certain of the answer to a question, you can mark your answer for review and come back to it later.
- You have **70 minutes** to complete this test.

Turn the page to begin.

GO ON TO THE NEXT PAGE

Social Studies

Questions 1 and 2 refer to the following interpretation of the U.S. Constitution.

> The first ten amendments to the U.S. Constitution are called the Bill of Rights. They were originally added to grant both individual citizens and states certain rights that could not be violated by the federal government. The 14th Amendment, which was adopted in 1868 as part of the settlement of the Civil War, widened the applications of the Bill of Rights. One sentence of this amendment states: "No state shall make or enforce any law which shall abridge the privileges or immunities of citizens of the United States; nor shall any state deprive any person of life, liberty or property, without due process of law, nor deny to any person...equal protection under the law."
>
> This amendment has since been interpreted as protecting the individual citizen's rights from encroachment by the states.

1. Which of the following descriptions of the authors of the amendments to the Constitution is supported by the passage?

    A. They were legal scholars.
    B. They believed that the government and the church should be united.
    C. They believed that the best type of government would have ultimate authority.
    D. They were wary of giving the government too much power over individual rights.

2. All of the following actions by a particular state would violate the 14th Amendment EXCEPT

    A. a zoning law prohibiting naturalized citizens from operating ethnic restaurants.
    B. legislation requiring citizens to pay taxes regardless of their beliefs.
    C. a bill requiring children of citizens of a particular ethnic origin to attend separate public schools.
    D. sentencing a person accused of murder without a trial.

Question 3 refers to the following statement about Amelia Earhart.

> When Amelia Earhart made her first successful trip across the Atlantic with her colleague, Captain Manning, she was greeted on arrival by the mayor of Southampton in England. Despite most of the favorable reactions of the press to her accomplishment, one of the London papers stated that she was "a pleasant young woman who should be capable of spending her time to better advantage in domestic pursuits." Many members of the American press characterized her as a "foolhardy girl" and as a publicity seeker. Perhaps as a result, Earhart resolved to tackle her next mission alone.

3. In the author's opinion, what factor contributed to Amelia Earhart's decision to fly alone?

    A. a love of her country
    B. the public's ignorance of aviation
    C. the patriotism of the British
    D. a lack of respect by some members of the press for women's abilities

GO ON TO THE NEXT PAGE

Social Studies

Question 4 refers to the following chart.

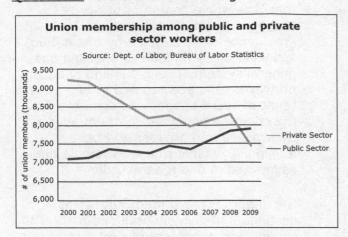

Question 5 refers to the following chart.

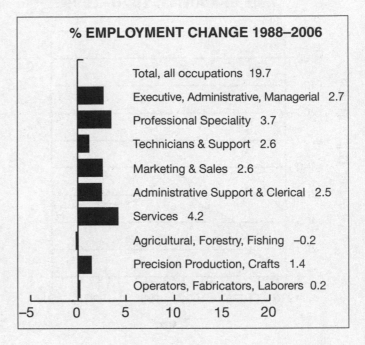

4. Determine whether or not each statement below is supported by the information in the graph. Drag the statements into the "Yes" box if so and the "No" box if not. (For this practice test, write the statement letter in the correct box.)

Yes	No

(a) "There were about 7,500,000 public sector union members in 2007."

(b) "There were about 9,000,000 private sector employees in 2002."

(c) "There was an increase in both private and public sector union membership from 2006 to 2008."

(d) "For the years shown, the number of public sector employees peaked in 2009."

(e) "Combined union membership in both public and private sectors generally decreased from 2000 to 2009."

5. The information in the chart supports the conclusion that from 1988 to 2006 there has been

A. an increase in agricultural jobs.
B. more growth in administrative support jobs than in any other occupation.
C. more growth in administrative support jobs than in services and technicians and support jobs combined.
D. less growth in precision production than in professional specialties.

GO ON TO THE NEXT PAGE

GDP per capita in Southeast Asia and Africa, 1970–1995

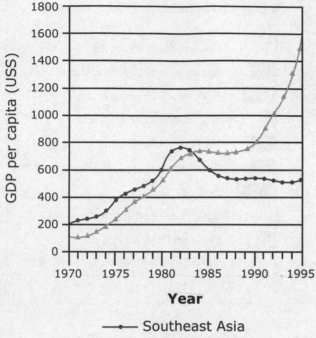

Legend:
— Southeast Asia
— Sub-Saharan Africa

GDP, or Gross Domestic Product, per capita is the average value of the goods and services produced by the citizens of a country in a year. Economists use GDP to compare wealth between individuals and nations.

6. Based on this information, which statement is an OPINION, rather than a fact, about the GDP per capita of these nations?

    A. The GDP per capita for Southeast Asia has increased substantially in recent years.
    B. The GDP per capita of Southeast Asia is now higher than that of Sub-Saharan Africa.
    C. Sub-Saharan Africa is in desperate need of foreign aid in order to sustain its economy.
    D. For many years, Southeast Asia and Sub-Saharan Africa had similar patterns of economic growth.

7. President John Quincy Adams wrote that "the whole continent of North America appears to be destined by Divine Providence to be peopled by one nation, speaking one language, professing one general system of religious and political principles, and accustomed to one general tenor of social usages and customs. For the common happiness of them all, for their peace and prosperity, I believe it is indispensable that they should be associated in one federal Union."

    The idea that the United States was destined and divinely ordained by God to expand across the entire North American continent is called

    A. Manifest Destiny.
    B. capitalism.
    C. imperialism.
    D. eminent domain.

GO ON TO THE NEXT PAGE

Questions 8 and 9 refer to the following graph.

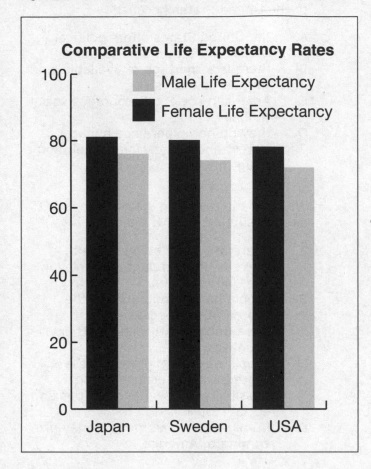

Comparative Life Expectancy Rates

Male Life Expectancy
Female Life Expectancy

Japan   Sweden   USA

8. According to the above graph, a member of which of the following groups is likely to have the shortest life span?

A. Japanese women
B. Swedish women
C. American men
D. Japanese men

9. Which statement is the most likely explanation for the differences in life expectancy shown in the graph?

A. Asian men tend to work more hours per week than do men from other countries.
B. Life expectancy is higher in North American countries.
C. Japan provides free or low-cost health care for all Japanese citizens.
D. There are fewer natural disasters in Japan than there are in other parts of the world.

GO ON TO THE NEXT PAGE

Social Studies

Questions 10 through 12 refer to the following interpretation of the role of immigrants in American society.

The society of the United States, perhaps more than that of any other country, is a "melting pot" society. America is a nation of immigrants and is reputed to be a haven for the oppressed and a land of equal opportunity for all. Symbols such as the Statue of Liberty and rags-to-riches success literature reinforce this reputation. Immigrants to the United States come in search of new opportunities, increased social mobility, and an environment free from political unrest and oppression.

On the other hand, America is not free from bigotry. In the past, each new immigrant group has been greeted with prejudice and discrimination by the groups that settled before them.

There have been many steps taken in recent history to make American society as free and equal as our founders had intended. There has been much legislation passed over the last three decades to help to ensure the equal treatment of all individuals and groups. With this legislation and improved public awareness, perhaps American society can live up to its "melting pot" image.

10. Which of the following observations about immigration to the United States is supported by the article?

A. Americans are always friendly to every group of people making a new home here.
B. Immigrants come to the United States expecting not to find jobs.
C. The United States wants to shed its reputation as a "melting pot" society.
D. Efforts have been made to ensure that America is receptive to immigrants.

11. According to the article, people immigrate to the United States because

A. the United States offers political stability and economic opportunity.
B. there is a shortage of available land in their countries.
C. American society discourages social mobility.
D. they do not experience political unrest and oppression in their home countries.

12. Which of the following statements is NOT directly supported by the article?

A. There are steps being taken to decrease the amount of bigotry in the United States.
B. People have immigrated to the United States because they were unhappy with life in other countries.
C. People have immigrated to the United States because of the possibility of new opportunities and social mobility.
D. Immigrants make more money after coming to America.

GO ON TO THE NEXT PAGE

Question 13 refers to the following photo.

13. This 1852 advertisement expresses opposition to "foreign pauper labor" and "foreigners holding office." With which of the following policies would the writer of this advertisement be likely to disagree?

A. a trade embargo to keep cheap foreign goods out of the United States

B. a new law that prevents immigration unless the immigrant is rich

C. a voter registration drive that targets only American-born persons

D. a constitutional amendment giving new immigrants voting rights

GO ON TO THE NEXT PAGE

Social Studies

Question 14 refers to the following sources.

TAB 1:

The right of citizens of the United States to vote shall not be denied or abridged by the United States or by any State on account of sex. Congress shall have power to enforce this article by appropriate legislation.

–Nineteenth Amendment to the United States Constitution (ratified in 1920)

TAB 2:

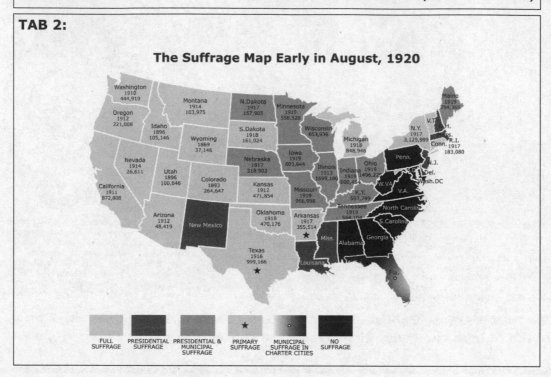

The Suffrage Map Early in August, 1920

---

14. Which conclusion is best supported by the information in the passage and the map?

   A. American women had no legal right to vote in presidential elections before 1920.

   B. The Nineteenth Amendment guaranteed full economic and political equality for women.

   C. Most Western states had guaranteed full suffrage to women before 1920.

   D. Women in Alaska and Hawaii had no voting privileges before 1920.

GO ON TO THE NEXT PAGE

<u>Question 15</u> refers to the following sources.

TAB 1:

The following excerpt is taken from the Preamble to the Constitution of the Unites States of America:

"We the People of the United States, in Order to form a more perfect Union, establish Justice, insure domestic Tranquility, provide for the common defence, promote the general Welfare, and secure the Blessings of Liberty to ourselves and our Posterity, do ordain and establish this Constitution for the United States of America."

TAB 2:

The following excerpt is taken from the Declaration of Independence:

"We hold these truths to be self-evident, that all men are created equal, that they are endowed by their Creator with certain unalienable Rights, that among these are Life, Liberty and the pursuit of Happiness."

---

15. According to the excerpts provided, which of these principles is mentioned in the Preamble to the Constitution but NOT in the Declaration of Independence?

    A. the desire for freedom
    B. a united defense
    C. the desire for happiness
    D. the equality of all citizens

GO ON TO THE NEXT PAGE

Question 16 refers to the following graph.

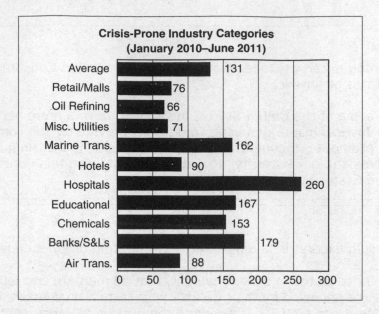

16. According to the graph, which of the following types of industries was least likely to experience a crisis?

A. education
B. chemical
C. hotel
D. oil refining

GO ON TO THE NEXT PAGE

Social Studies

Questions 17 and 18 are based on the following graph:

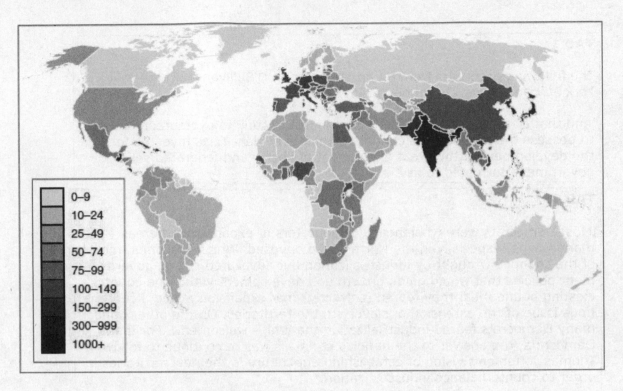

Number of People Per Square Mile

17. According to the graph, what are the most densely populated continents?

   A.   South America and Europe
   B.   Asia and North America
   C.   Europe and Asia
   D.   South America and North America

18. What factors are the most influential in determining population density?

   A.   climate and geography
   B.   race and language
   C.   religion
   D.   public sanitation and health

GO ON TO THE NEXT PAGE

<u>Question 19</u> refers to the following sources:

TAB 1:

The following excerpt is from an article by Brian O'Sullivan from the *New York Morning News*, December 1845:

"And that claim is by the right of our manifest destiny to overspread and to possess the whole of the continent which Providence has given us for the development of the great experiment of liberty and federated self-government entrusted to us."

TAB 2:

"Most Democrats were wholehearted supporters of expansion, whereas many Whigs (especially in the North) were opposed. Whigs welcomed most of the changes wrought by industrialization but advocated strong government policies that would guide growth and development within the country's existing boundaries; they feared (correctly) that expansion raised a contentious issue of the extension of slavery to the territories. On the other hand, many Democrats feared industrialization the Whigs welcomed....For many Democrats, the answer to the nation's social ills was to continue to follow Thomas Jefferson's vision of establishing agriculture in the new territories in order to counterbalance industrialization."

–John Mack Faragher et al. *Out of Many: A History of the American People*

TAB 3:

Westward Expansion of the United States

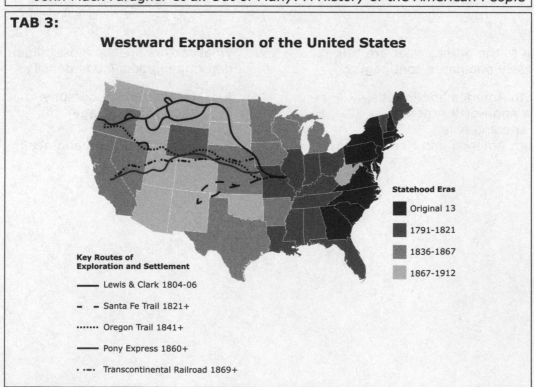

Key Routes of Exploration and Settlement

—— Lewis & Clark 1804-06

– – Santa Fe Trail 1821+

······· Oregon Trail 1841+

—— Pony Express 1860+

·–·–· Transcontinental Railroad 1869+

Statehood Eras
- Original 13
- 1791-1821
- 1836-1867
- 1867-1912

GO ON TO THE NEXT PAGE

19. Which of the following conclusions is most consistent with the excerpts and map?

   A. Elected in 1828, President Andrew Jackson was a Democrat who opposed Westward Expansion.
   B. Inspired by the principle of Manifest Destiny, President James K. Polk, a Democrat elected in 1845, sought to secure American control of the Southwest after the Mexican-American War.
   C. Whig presidents such as William Henry Harrison, elected in 1841, failed to gather support from the American people because of their insistence on Westward Expansion.
   D. Many Democrats, including Franklin Pierce, elected in 1853, opposed the Transcontinental Railroad, since it threatened to expand slavery to Western territories.

20. The following is a quote by President Abraham Lincoln:

   > "A majority held in restraint by constitutional checks and limitations, and always changing easily with deliberate changes of popular opinions and sentiments, is the only true sovereign of a free people."

   The above quote most closely describes which of the following forms of government?

   A. a constitutional republic
   B. a monarchy
   C. a pure democracy
   D. anarchy

21. With improvements in technology, production becomes more efficient, increasing the output per worker of a given industry. Product quality rises, profits and wages increase, and the economy improves overall. In short, both workers and employers benefit.

   Which of the following opinions contradicts the above conclusion about improvements in technology?

   A. New technology will cause companies to decrease the size of their workforce in order to cut costs.
   B. Product quality increases consumer satisfaction, which leads to greater company profits.
   C. When businesses succeed, more money is reinvested into the economy.
   D. Efficiency is a key factor in ensuring a business's success.

GO ON TO THE NEXT PAGE

Question 22 refers to the following maps:

TAB 1:

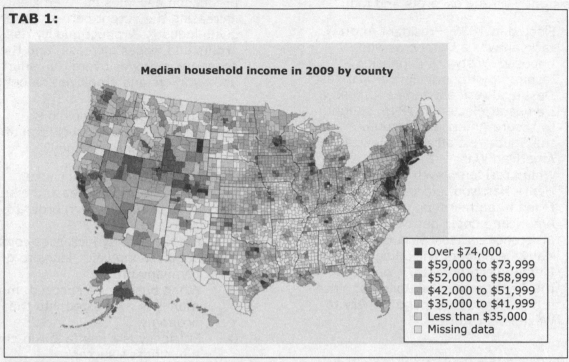

Median household income in 2009 by county

- ■ Over $74,000
- ■ $59,000 to $73,999
- ■ $52,000 to $58,999
- ▨ $42,000 to $51,999
- ▨ $35,000 to $41,999
- ☐ Less than $35,000
- ☐ Missing data

TAB 2:

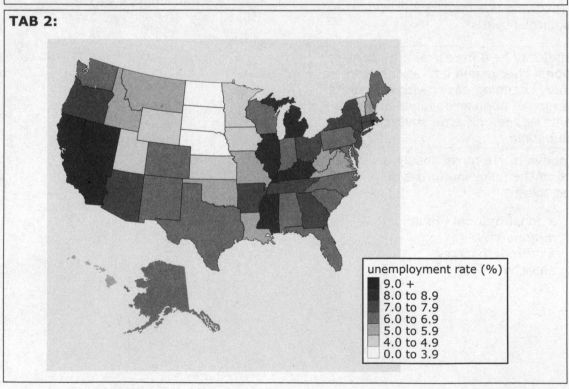

unemployment rate (%)
- ■ 9.0 +
- ■ 8.0 to 8.9
- ■ 7.0 to 7.9
- ▨ 6.0 to 6.9
- ▨ 5.0 to 5.9
- ☐ 4.0 to 4.9
- ☐ 0.0 to 3.9

GO ON TO THE NEXT PAGE

22.   Based on this data, which conclusion
      about the U.S. economy is true?

      A.   All counties with household incomes
           of $74,000 or more in 2009 had the
           lowest unemployment rates.
      B.   Southeastern states generally
           have a lower median income than
           Northeastern states.
      C.   Only Plains states have
           unemployment rates below 5.0%.
      D.   Hawaii has a lower rate of
           employment than Alaska.

GO ON TO THE NEXT PAGE

Question 23 refers to the following sources:

TAB 1:

The following excerpt is taken from the Fourteenth Amendment to the United States Constitution:

"**Section 1.** All persons born or naturalized in the United States, and subject to the jurisdiction thereof, are citizens of the United States and of the State wherein they reside. No State shall make or enforce any law which shall abridge the privileges or immunities of citizens of the United States; nor shall any State deprive any person of life, liberty, or property, without due process of law; nor deny to any person within its jurisdiction the equal protection of the laws."

TAB 2:

"We consider the underlying fallacy of the plaintiff's argument to consist in the assumption that the enforced separation of the two races stamps the colored race with a badge of inferiority. If this be so, it is not by reason of anything found in the act, but solely because the colored race chooses to put that construction upon it."

–Justice Henry B. Brown, U.S. Supreme Court, *Plessy vs. Ferguson,* 1896

TAB 3:

"We conclude that, in the field of public education, the doctrine of "separate but equal" has no place. Separate educational facilities are inherently unequal. Therefore, we hold that the plaintiffs and others similarly situated for whom the actions have been brought are, by reason of the segregation complained of, deprived of the equal protection of the law."

–from U.S. Supreme Court, *Brown vs. Board of Education,* 1954

GO ON TO THE NEXT PAGE

23. Which of the following conclusions is best supported by the passages?

   A. In *Brown vs. Board of Education*, the Supreme Court relied on past legal decisions to help shape its ruling.
   B. *Plessy vs. Ferguson* upheld the Fourteenth Amendment's guarantee of "equal protection" under the law.
   C. *Brown vs. Board of Education* upheld the doctrine of "separate but equal."
   D. *Brown vs. Board of Education* found that "separate but equal" facilities were a violation of the Fourteenth Amendment.

24. The modern cotton gin was patented in 1794 by Eli Whitney. It allowed for the easier separation of cotton fibers from their seeds. Why was the cotton gin so revolutionary?

   The cotton gin

   A. caused the massive growth of the wool industry in America.
   B. caused the economic destruction of rural farmland.
   C. ended the need for slavery.
   D. caused the expansion of the cotton industry in the American South.

GO ON TO THE NEXT PAGE

Question 25 refers to the following passage.

> Interpreting the U.S. Constitution is so complex a task that it has become its own legal specialty, constitutional law. One example of the complexity of the Constitution is an interpretation of the 13th Amendment, which states that there shall be no "involuntary servitude" except as a punishment for a crime. Due to this interpretation, Congress was reluctant for a long time to pass any draft resolutions in times of peace. Finally, in 1940, only one year before our entrance into World War II, Congress approved the first peacetime draft in our history.

25. What conclusion is supported by this statement about the interpretation of the Constitution?

   A. A document that needs amendments is not a reliable guide for government policy.
   B. A document that can be reinterpreted is not an adequate method for resolving legal questions.
   C. A text that causes controversy does more harm than good.
   D. Interpretations of the Constitution can change, which in turn affect decisions made by lawmakers.

Question 26 refers to the following graph.

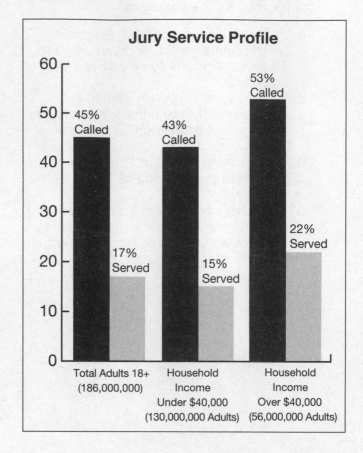

26. Which of the following statements is supported by the survey on jury service represented in the table?

   A. People with incomes under $40,000 are twice as likely to be called as are those with higher incomes.
   B. A greater percentage of adults from households with incomes of more than $40,000 have served on juries than the percentage of those from households with lower incomes.
   C. People with lower incomes are more likely to want to serve on juries.
   D. Most jurors have incomes between $30,000 and $35,000.

GO ON TO THE NEXT PAGE

Social Studies

Questions 27 through 29 refer to the following information about energy production.

Three of the most common sources of energy are fossil fuels, nuclear power, and hydroelectric power. Each of these three methods of energy production has its advantages and disadvantages.

Fossil fuels are the most widely used energy source in the United States. The burning of oil and coal derivatives releases energy that is used to boil water. The released steam turns turbines and produces energy. Today, fossil fuels are relatively abundant, which makes this form of energy production inexpensive. However, one of the problems with fossil fuels is that burning oil and coal derivatives releases chemicals that are harmful to the environment.

Nuclear power harnesses the energy contained in atoms. The energy released is used to convert water to steam, which in turn drives turbines. This form of energy production has proven to be even less expensive than fossil fuels, but there is no foolproof method for storing all of the dangerous by-products from nuclear power plants.

Hydroelectric power is produced by using the force of a river to turn turbines. This is the cleanest of the three methods of energy production, but not all communities have access to rivers, and rivers with hydroelectric plants are much more vulnerable to the effects of erosion.

27. Which of the following would most likely result in an increase in the use of nuclear power?

   A. the invention of a safe radioactive-waste disposal method
   B. the discovery of a cleaner method of burning coal
   C. a decrease in taxes on fossil fuels
   D. increased oil exploration in Alaska

28. What do all three forms of energy production have in common?

   A. smoke
   B. smog
   C. erosion
   D. turbines

29. Which of the following communities would most likely use hydroelectric power?

   A. a desert community with little or no fossil fuel resources
   B. a town adjacent to a large river
   C. a community with large oil reserves
   D. a community in coal-rich West Virginia

GO ON TO THE NEXT PAGE

Question 30 refers to the following cartoon:

"The Big Stick in the Caribbean Sea"

Question 31 refers to the following excerpt from U.S. history.

Development in California during the gold rush of 1849 was characterized by exploitation of the wilderness for economic gains. Entire forests were razed for lumber, and beautiful valleys were dammed up and lost forever to provide water pressure for strip mining. Such atrocities continued unhindered until one man stepped forward to argue on the behalf of the wilderness. John Muir almost single-handedly convinced President Roosevelt to create one of the nation's first national parks in Yosemite Valley, thereby protecting that portion of land from the dangers of development.

30. The above cartoon depicts which famous American in which major war?

    A. Theodore Roosevelt in the Spanish-American War
    B. Douglas MacArthur in World War II
    C. Count Frontenac in King William's War
    D. Norman Schwarzkopf in the Persian Gulf War

31. Which of the following might describe John Muir's opinions regarding the California wilderness?

    A. Economic interests should outweigh sentimental interests.
    B. It is acceptable to destroy natural beauty in some cases.
    C. Things that humans value should be used for human benefit.
    D. Some things have value that cannot be measured in monetary terms.

GO ON TO THE NEXT PAGE

Social Studies

Question 32 refers to the following globe.

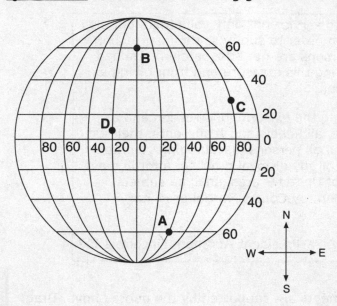

32. Which of the following lists the points on the globe from west to east?

   A. D, A, C, B
   B. C, B, D, A
   C. A, C, B, D
   D. D, B, A, C

33. Hurricanes are most seriously a threat to cities along the coast of the Atlantic Ocean and the Gulf of Mexico. Which city is NOT seriously threatened by hurricanes?

   A. Orlando, Florida
   B. New Orleans, Louisiana
   C. Chicago, Illinois
   D. Virginia Beach, Virginia

GO ON TO THE NEXT PAGE

Question 34 refers to the following excerpt from a proclamation.

> "Whereas, it has become necessary to call into service not only volunteers but also portions of the militia of the States by draft in order to suppress the insurrection existing in the United States, and disloyal persons are not adequately restrained by the ordinary processes of law from hindering this measure and from giving aid and comfort in various ways to the insurrection;
>
> Now, therefore, be it ordered, first, that during the existing insurrection and as a necessary measure for suppressing the same, all Rebels and Insurgents, their aiders and abettors within the United States, and all persons discouraging volunteer enlistments, resisting militia drafts, or guilty of any disloyal practice, affording aid and comfort to Rebels against the authority of United States, shall be subject to martial law and liable to trial and punishment by Courts Martial or Military Commission."
>
> –President Abraham Lincoln, 1862

34. Determine whether or not the following statements are supported by the quote above. Drag and drop the statements into the "Yes" box if so and the "No" box if not. (For this practice test, write the statement letters in the appropriate boxes.)

Yes	No

(a) "Felons previously convicted in civilian courts would be subject to court-marshal and punishment."

(b) "Those attempting to suppress rebels and insurgents would be subject to court-marshal and punishment."

(c) "Those resisting the military draft would be subject to court-marshal and punishment."

(d) "Volunteers for the militia would be subject to court-marshal and punishment."

GO ON TO THE NEXT PAGE

Social Studies

Question 35 refers to the following excerpt from a speech.

"I have never been a quitter. To leave office before my term is completed is abhorrent to every instinct in my body. But as President, I must put the interest of America first. America needs a full-time President and a full-time Congress, particularly at this time with problems we face at home and abroad. To continue to fight through the months ahead for my personal vindication would almost totally absorb the time and attention of both the President and the Congress in a period when our entire focus should be on the great issues of peace abroad and prosperity without inflation at home. Therefore, I shall resign the Presidency effective at noon tomorrow. Vice President Ford will be sworn in as President at that hour in this office."

–President Richard Nixon, August 1974

35.   The above quote supports the conclusion that, after the Watergate scandal, President Nixon

A.   was forced to leave office after being impeached by the Congress.
B.   resigned before completing his term of office.
C.   appointed Vice President Ford as interim president.
D.   continued on as full-time president, despite pressure from Congress.

END OF TEST

THIS PAGE INTENTIONALLY LEFT BLANK.

GO ON TO THE NEXT PAGE

Science

Welcome!

Here is some information that you need to know before you start this test:

- You should not spend too much time on a question if you are not certain of the answer; answer it the best you can, and go on to the next question.
- If you are not certain of the answer to a question, you can mark your answer for review and come back to it later.
- You have **90 minutes** to complete this test.
- There are two Short Answer questions on this test.
- You should plan to spend about 10 minutes on each Short Answer question.

Turn the page to begin.

GO ON TO THE NEXT PAGE

1. The table below lists the normal ranges of various chemicals found in human blood.

Substance	Normal Range
total cholesterol	125–200 mg/dL
HDL cholesterol	under 40 mg/dL
LDL cholesterol	under 130 mg/dL
triglycerides	under 150 mg/dL

Which of the following statements is accurate based on the table above?

A.   A total cholesterol level of 150 is considered normal.
B.   A triglyceride level of 180 is considered normal.
C.   An LDL cholesterol level of 110 is considered above normal.
D.   A triglyceride level of 100 is considered abnormal.

2. Cardiac output is the amount of blood a human heart pumps out per minute. Increases in heart rate, blood pressure, and cardiac muscle strength all lead to higher cardiac output. Below is a graph that shows the effects of blood pressure on cardiac output.

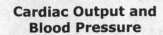

Cardiac Output and Blood Pressure

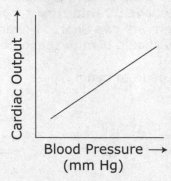

Which of the following conclusions is best supported by the graph?

A.   As blood pressure increases, cardiac output decreases.
B.   As blood pressure increases, cardiac output increases.
C.   Cardiac output is measured in mm HG.
D.   Cardiac output increases and decreases irregularly as blood pressure changes.

GO ON TO THE NEXT PAGE

Science

Questions 3 and 4 are based on the passage and food web shown below.

A food web is a diagram that shows which organisms feed on which other organisms in a community. The arrows point from the food sources to the consumers. Some animals are herbivores, meaning that they eat only plants, while some are carnivores, meaning that they eat only animals. Still others are omnivores, meaning that they eat both plants and animals. Below is a food web for a grassland ecosystem.

FOOD WEB

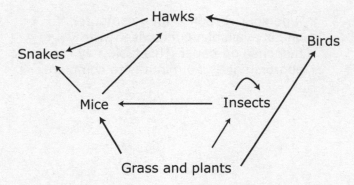

3. Which organisms in this food web are carnivores only?

   A. hawks only
   B. snakes only
   C. both snakes and hawks
   D. hawks, snakes, and insects

4. Hawks consume rabbits as well as the other animals listed in the food web. If rabbits are herbivores, which of the following food webs accurately includes rabbits in the grassland ecosystem?

A.

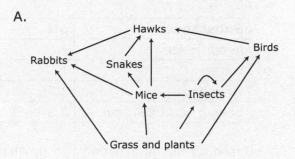

B.

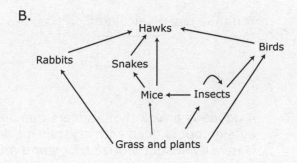

C.

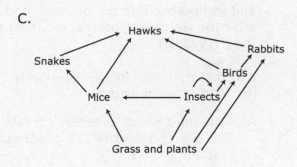

D.

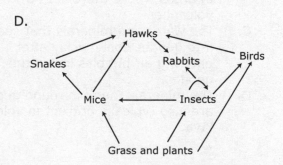

GO ON TO THE NEXT PAGE

5. Whether a substance is classified as acidic, basic, or neutral is determined by its pH. A pH below 7 is acidic, a pH of 7 is neutral, and a pH above 7 is basic. Below is a table of common substances and their pH values.

Substance	pH
lemon juice	2
water	7
vinegar	2.2
baking soda solution	8.3

Based on the information above, what percent of the substances in the table are basic?

You may use a calculator.

%

6. A geode is a rock that appears dull on the outside but is filled with crystals inside. Many scientists theorize that some round geodes are formed when lava bubbles as it cools after a volcanic eruption. Minerals and water seep into the bubbles, and after the water evaporates, the minerals form crystals.

Which of the following best supports the theory discussed above?

A. Round geodes generally contain fewer crystals than do geodes of other shapes.
B. Some geodes have been discovered in areas where there are no volcanoes.
C. The water and minerals that seep into geodes cool quickly after entering air bubbles inside the geodes.
D. The minerals found in round geodes are also typically present in volcano lava.

7. A scientist wishes to determine whether using compost and nitrogen-rich fertilizer together will be more effective than using either alone. She hypothesizes that if she uses a combination of compost and nitrogen-rich fertilizer, then the plants that she grows will be taller and will grow more abundantly than they would if she used either independently.

Design an experiment that the scientist can use to test this theory. Include descriptions of the materials that the scientist will need, and the most appropriate methods of data collection. Discuss how the scientist will be able to determine whether her theory is accurate.

Type your response on a computer, if one is available. Otherwise, write your response on paper. This task may require approximately 10 minutes to complete.

GO ON TO THE NEXT PAGE

Science

Question 8 is based on the passage below.

Hereditary traits are encoded in genes, which in turn are located on chromosomes. Chromosomes come in pairs, and the pair of genes associated with a particular feature determines the characteristics of that trait. Often, there are several varieties of genes associated with a given trait. A gene is expressed when it is pure, meaning that it is expressed when both genes in a pair are alike. A hybrid pattern occurs when two genes in a pair are different, and in cases of incomplete dominance the two traits will blend together to make a new trait.

Flower color in carnations follows an incomplete dominance pattern. When both genes in a pair are associated with the color red, then the plant produces red flowers. When both genes in a pair are associated with the color yellow, the plant produces yellow flowers. When a plant is hybrid, and has one gene associated with the color red and another associated with the color yellow, then the two traits blend to produce orange flowers.

Below is a Punnett Square showing the results when a carnation with yellow flowers and a carnation with red flowers are crossed to produce offspring. Punnett Squares predict the likelihood of specific gene combinations occuring.

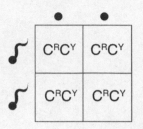

	egg cell of female parent
♪	sperm cell of male parent
C^R	gene for red color
C^Y	gene for yellow color

8. What color are the flowers of the offspring shown in the Punnett Square?

   A.   All are red.
   B.   All are yellow.
   C.   All are orange.
   D.   Half are red, and half are yellow.

GO ON TO THE NEXT PAGE

Science

Water is constantly being naturally recycled on Earth. Below is a picture of the water cycle, which depicts the natural processes that affect the flow of water.

Water Cycle

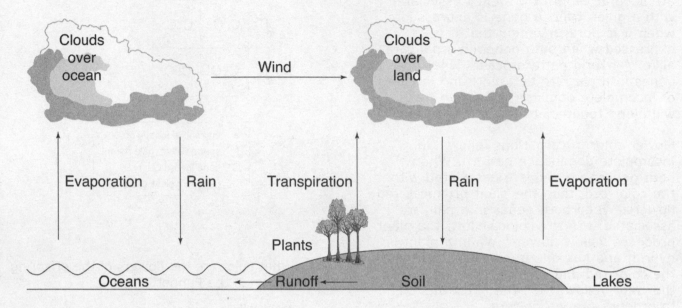

9. Based on the figure, which of the following processes deliver(s) water to clouds?

   A. evaporation only
   B. evaporation and transpiration
   C. transpiration only
   D. evaporation and precipitation

10. The balanced equation below represents the oxidation process for propane.

    $$C_3H_8 + 5O_2 \rightarrow 3CO_2 + 4H_2O$$

    Which of the following describes the reaction shown above?

    A. Oxygen reacts with propane to create carbon dioxide and water.
    B. Oxygen and propane react to create water.
    C. Oxygen is converted into carbon dioxide.
    D. Propane is converted into water.

GO ON TO THE NEXT PAGE

11. Below is a table showing the percentage of total blood volume for several components of human blood.

Percent Composition of Human Blood	
Dissolved Gases	1%
Nutrients	3%
Red Blood Cells	43%
Water	51%
White Blood Cells	2%

What percentage of human blood is not made up of cells?

You may use a calculator.

%

12. An enzyme speeds up a chemical reaction by interacting with an initial substance and making it easier for that substance to form a product. In most cases, an enzyme can interact with only one molecule of the initial substance at a time.

The graph below shows the results of an experiment that measured the rate of product formation as the concentration of an initial substance was increased. A limited amount of the enzyme was present during the experiment.

Enzymes and Product Formation

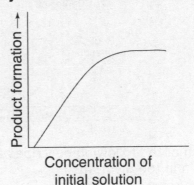

Which of the following best describes the results shown in the graph? As the concentration of the initial substance increased, the rate of product formation

A. increased continually.
B. initially increased and then became constant.
C. increased and then decreased.
D. remained constant.

GO ON TO THE NEXT PAGE

<u>Question 13</u> is based on the following information.

Plants use carbon dioxide to make food, and then that food is consumed by animals and eventually returns to the soil or atmosphere. The diagram below shows the carbon cycle.

The Carbon Cycle

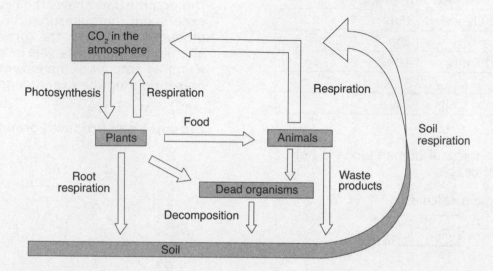

13. Which of the following describes a process shown in the diagram?

A. Plants absorb CO_2 from the atmosphere, and transfer some of that CO_2 to animals in the form of food, after which animals release waste products and transfer some of that CO_2 to the soil.

B. Animals absorb CO_2 from the atmosphere and from dead organisms, and then transfer some of that CO_2 into the soil through waste products.

C. Plants absorb CO_2 from the soil through respiration, and then transfer some of that CO_2 to the soil through root respiration, after which the soil transfers that CO_2 to the atmosphere through soil respiration.

D. Plants absorb CO_2 from the soil through root respiration, and then transfer some of that CO_2 to animals in the form of food, after which the animals become dead organisms and transfer some of that CO_2 into the soil.

GO ON TO THE NEXT PAGE

14. In most environments, there are a limited number of nutrients. As a result, living organisms must compete for food and resources. The graph below shows the results of two experiments, one in which an amoeba was cultured alone and one in which it was cultured with a mixture of other single-celled organisms. The same nutrients were provided to each culture.

Amoeba Population Growth

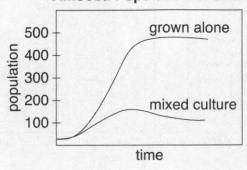

Which of the following conclusions can be drawn from the graph above?

A. This species of amoebas is more likely to thrive if cultured in a mixed culture than if cultured alone.
B. This species of amoebas is more likely to reproduce rapidly if cultured alone than if cultured in a mixed culture.
C. The population of this species of amoebas will continue to increase indefinitely if the amoebas are cultured alone.
D. If cultured in a mixed culture, this species of amoebas will initially increase in population, but will eventually die out.

15. Scientists use the following formula to calculate the force of gravity that two objects exert on each other:

In the equation

$$F = \frac{G \times M \times m}{r^2}$$

F is the force of gravity;
G is a constant;
M is the mass of one of the objects;
m is the mass of the second object;
r is the distance between the centers of the objects.

If an object with a given mass m is replaced by an object of half its mass, which of the following will increase the force of gravity?

A. increasing mass M and doubling the distance between the objects
B. reducing mass M and doubling the distance between the objects
C. reducing mass M and halving the distance between the objects
D. increasing mass M and halving the distance between the objects

GO ON TO THE NEXT PAGE

16. The table below shows an analysis of the composition of soil taken from a canyon in the desert.

Material	Percent Composition
Silt	25
Clay	15
Calcium Carbonate	14
Sedimentary Rock	13
Metamorphic Rock	11
Gypsum	8
Caliche	6
Salt	4
Zinc	2
Boron	2

What is the median of the numbers listed in the table above?

You may use a calculator.

Questions 17 and 18 both refer to the graph below.

17. The graph below shows the amount of rainfall during the spring and summer months in the city of Mayfair.

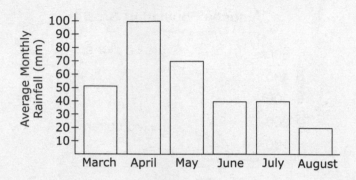

Between which two months was the increase in average monthly rainfall the greatest?

A. March and April
B. April and May
C. May and June
D. June and July

18. What was the mode of rainfall for the months shown above?

You may use a calculator.

A. 40
B. 45
C. 50
D. 55

GO ON TO THE NEXT PAGE

Questions 19 and 20 are based on the information below.

An atom contains neutrons, protons, and electrons. The atomic number of an element is the number of protons in one atom of that element, and the atomic weight is equal to the sum of the number of protons and the number of neutrons. The chart below lists the numbers of protons, neutrons, and electrons in three common elements.

Element	Protons	Neutrons	Electrons
Carbon	6	6	6
Nitrogen	7	7	7
Oxygen	8	8	8

19. Drag and drop the appropriate element into each box. (For this practice test, write the element letters in the boxes.)

The element with an atomic weight of 16:	The element with an atomic number of 7:	The element with an atomic weight of 12:

(a) Carbon

(b) Nitrogen

(c) Oxygen

20. Based on the information and the table, which of the following is true?

A. A nitrogen cation, which has one fewer electron than does an ordinary nitrogen atom, has an atomic number of 7.

B. Fluorine, which has an atomic number of 9, has more protons than does oxygen.

C. Boron, which has an atomic weight of 10 and an atomic number of 5, has more neutrons than does carbon.

D. An oxygen anion, which has more electrons than does an ordinary oxygen atom, has an atomic weight of 15.

GO ON TO THE NEXT PAGE

Science

Questions 21 and 22 are based on the information and chart below.

The Richter scale measures seismic activity, or energy released in the form of heat and vibration during earthquakes. The scale is a logarithmic, base-10 scale, which means that an earthquake measuring 3.0 on the Richter scale has a shaking amplitude 100 times more powerful than does an earthquake measuring 2.0.

The chart below shows the classifications and effects of various earthquakes and their measurements on the Richter scale.

Richter Magnitude	Classification	Effects
less than 2.0	micro	not felt
2.0–3.9	minor	may be felt
4.0–4.9	light	noticeable shaking but damages are unlikely
5.0–5.9	moderate	may cause damage to unstable structures
6.0–6.9	strong	can cause damages in areas up to 100 miles
7.0–7.9	major	can cause damages in areas several hundred miles large
8.0–8.9	great	can cause damages in areas several thousand miles large

21. An earthquake causes severe structural damage to a house located within 150 miles of the epicenter of the quake. Which of the following is the best likely description of the earthquake?

   A. The earthquake was less than moderate, measuring below 5.0 on the Richter scale.
   B. The earthquake was moderate, measuring between 5.0 and 5.9 on the Richter scale.
   C. The earthquake was strong, measuring between 6.0 and 6.9 on the Richter scale.
   D. The earthquake was major or great, measuring more than 7.0 on the Richter scale.

22. An earthquake in California measures 4.0 on the Richter scale, and an earthquake in Taiwan measures 6.0 on the Richter scale. According to the information in the passage, what is the ratio of the shaking amplitude of the earthquake in California to the shaking amplitude of the earthquake in Taiwan?

   You may use a calculator.

   A. 1:100
   B. 1:200
   C. 1:1,000
   D. 1:10,000

GO ON TO THE NEXT PAGE

Questions 23 and 24 refer to the following information.

In an ecosystem, each living thing plays a specific role in the food chain. For example, in the forest, mice eat leaves, and snakes eat mice. The path that energy takes can be shown through the following food chain:

leaves → mice → snakes

A food web is another way to demonstrate how energy is transferred from one species to another within an ecosystem. The figure shows a food web for an ocean ecosystem. In a food web, living creatures fall into the following categories:

Autotrophs create their own food, and do not gain their nutrition from other creatures.

Primary consumers, or herbivores, eat plants, algae, and other producers.

Secondary consumers eat primary consumers.

Tertiary consumers eat secondary consumers.

Apex predators are at the top of the food chain, and have no predators other than humans.

Consumers can be carnivores (creatures that eat meat) or omnivores (creatures that eat both plants and animals).

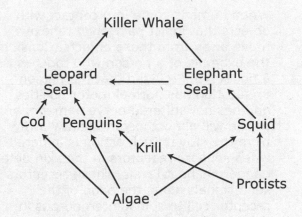

23. Which term accurately describes the role that the elephant seal plays in this ecosystem?

   A.   autotroph
   B.   primary consumer
   C.   secondary consumer
   D.   apex predator

24. In the ecosystem above, if the population of krill were depleted, which of the following consumers would be most affected?

   A.   cod
   B.   squid
   C.   leopard seals
   D.   elephant seals

GO ON TO THE NEXT PAGE

25. When humans come into contact with objects that inflict pain, they reflexively move away from those objects. Consider the example of a person who touches a hot stove. Provided that the person in question has normal motor abilities and has not suffered nerve damage, he or she will almost instantly draw away from the stove. Such action is initiated when sensory receptors in the skin detect dangerous heat levels. These receptors send signals along the axon of the receptor cell to spinal interneurons in the spinal cord. The spinal interneurons excite the motor neurons that control the arm muscles, which in turn send signals to the muscle cells. The muscle cells then contract, causing the arm to move away.

Using the information above, drag and drop the steps that show the process that occurs when an individual touches a dangerously hot object into the diagram below. (For this practice test, write the letters in the boxes.)

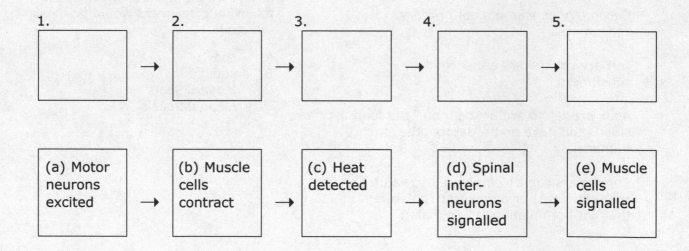

1. [   ] → 2. [   ] → 3. [   ] → 4. [   ] → 5. [   ]

(a) Motor neurons excited → (b) Muscle cells contract → (c) Heat detected → (d) Spinal inter-neurons signalled → (e) Muscle cells signalled

GO ON TO THE NEXT PAGE

26. A research team plans to conduct an experiment to test whether a certain chemical compound causes outbreaks of hives in average adults. In total, 1,000 adults volunteer for the study.

    Design an experiment that the team could conduct, and explain how the team can determine whether the results show that the chemical compound does or does not cause hives.

    Type your response on a computer, if one is available. Otherwise, write your response on paper. This task may require approximately 10 minutes to complete.

27. A particular aircraft has a mass of 1,800 kilograms, and has engines that provide 90,000 Newtons of thrust force. A second aircraft has a mass of only 1,500 kilograms, but has engines that provide exactly the same acceleration. What amount of thrust force do that aircraft's engines provide?

    You may use a calculator.

    Force [Newtons] =
    mass [kilograms] × accelation [meters/second²]

    A. 50 Newtons
    B. 60 Newtons
    C. 75,000 Newtons
    D. 108,000 Newtons

28. Scientists use index fossils to identify the times at which unidentified fossils and certain sediments were deposited. They hypothesize that if a particular fossil is found near an index fossil, in the same layer of rock, then the two fossils were likely from the same time period. The shorter the lifespan of the index fossil species, the more precisely scientists are able to correlate that species with a particular era. Therefore, it is not surprising that ideal index fossils are therefore from short-lived, common, and easy-to-identify species.

Which of the following is an example of the effective use of index fossils?

A. Scientists fix the time that *Mesolenellus hyperborea* existed in the late *Nevadella* era, because they find *Mesolenellus hyperborea* near and in the same level of rock as *Limniphacos perspiculum*, a recognized index fossil that existed in that period.
B. Scientists determine that *Mesolenellus hyperborea* were probably mud bottom-dwellers, because hyolitha, which existed during the same time period as *Mesolenellus hyperborean*, were also bottom dwellers.
C. Scientists hypothesize that *Mesolenellus hyperborea* were wiped out by a sudden climate change that occurred at the end of the Devonian period, when many other trilobites were wiped out.
D. Scientists determine that *Mesolenellus hyperborea* did not exist in Iceland, because *Petrianna fulmenta,* a similar trilobite, did not exist in Iceland.

GO ON TO THE NEXT PAGE

29. Boyle's law explains some aspects of the behavior of gases, such as those in our atmosphere. The law states that if temperature remains constant, volume decreases as pressure increases. The graph below illustrates Boyle's law for one gas.

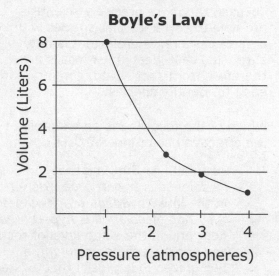

Boyle's Law

Which of the following is supported by the information in the graph above?

A. Pressure and volume are directly proportional.

B. As the pressure rises from 1 atmosphere to 3 atmospheres, the volume increases from 2 liters to 8 liters.

C. As the pressure rises from 1 atmosphere to 2 atmospheres, the volume decreases from 8 liters to 2 liters.

D. If the trend in the graph continues, then when the pressure reaches 5 atmospheres, the volume will near $\frac{1}{2}$ liter.

30. Mass is an indicator of the amount of matter that an object possesses. Scientists determine the weight of an object by multiplying its mass by the acceleration that the object experiences due to gravity. The acceleration due to gravity on the moon is approximately $\frac{1}{6}$ the acceleration due to gravity on the earth.

Based on the information above, a person would have

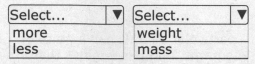

Select... ▼	Select... ▼
more	weight
less	mass

on the moon.

31. Scientific theory holds that convergent evolution occurs when different species independently evolve analogous structures, or features that may appear different, but perform the same function. Creatures evolve such structures in order to adapt to their environments.

A scientist argues that bats and birds have analogous structures. Which of the following supports his argument?

A. Bats use echolocation to track their prey, while birds rely primarily on sight.

B. Unlike bird wings, bat wings are composed primarily of membrane, but both types of wings provide flight capabilities.

C. Baby bats gain nourishment from their mother's milk, while baby birds eat worms and bugs brought by their mothers.

D. Both bats and birds frequently make their homes in trees, bridges, and attics.

GO ON TO THE NEXT PAGE

Questions 32 and 33 are based on the information below.

A scientist conducts a study to determine the effects that certain substances have on those who suffer from polyuria, or excessive urine production. During a two-week period, the 500 volunteers participating in the study drink two liters of water per day, and do not consume any other liquids. During the next two-week period, the same 500 volunteers drink two liters of caffeinated diet soda per day, and do not consume any other liquids. During a final two-week period, the same 500 volunteers drink two liters of water containing a mild amount of salt per day. The scientist tracks each volunteer's urine output each day. The volunteers all followed exactly the same diet in the first week as they did in the second week and in the third week. The average daily urine output per volunteer for each of the two-week periods is shown below.

Urine Production after Consuming Different Substances

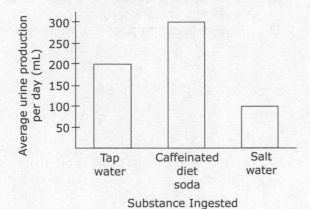

32. The data support which of the following conclusions?

A. Individuals suffering from polyuria may benefit from drinking caffeinated diet sodas.

B. Individuals who drink water with a high salt content are more likely than others to suffer from polyuria.

C. Individuals who suffer from polyuria should avoid consuming large amounts of caffeinated diet soda.

D. Individuals who suffer from polyuria should vary their liquid consumption by drinking some water, some caffeinated diet sodas, and some slightly salty water.

33. The passage indicates that the volunteers followed the same diet during each week of the study. Why was this important?

A. Had the volunteers varied their diets throughout the study, the differences in urine production may have been attributable to differences in solid food consumption, rather than in liquid consumption.

B. Had the volunteers varied their diets throughout the study, they may have craved different amounts of liquid each week.

C. By eating the same foods each week, the volunteers ensured that they did not suffer from any nutritional imbalances throughout the study.

D. By feeding the volunteers the same foods each week, the scientist ensured that the volunteers produced that same amount of urine as each other per day.

GO ON TO THE NEXT PAGE

34. Chemicals can be classified as acidic, neutral, or basic, depending on their pH measurements. A pH below 7 indicates that a substance is acidic, a pH of 7 means that a substance is neutral, and a pH above 7 means that a substance is basic. An indicator is a chemical compound that, when added to a substance, changes color based on the pH of the solution. For example, cabbage juice is an indicator that turns blue when added to a basic substance.

Liquid	pH
apple juice	3
water	7
acid rain	5
ammonia	11

Based on the information and the table above, which of the following substances, if combined with cabbage juice, would cause the cabbage juice to turn blue?

A.   apple juice and acid rain
B.   water
C.   acid rain
D.   ammonia

35. Geologists classify rocks in three main categories: igneous, sedimentary, and metamorphic. Igneous rock forms when melted rock cools and hardens. Below ground, igneous rock forms when melted rock known as magma cools in small pockets. Above ground, igneous rock forms when volcanoes erupt and spew lava that cools and hardens into igneous rock. Sedimentary rock forms when minerals or organic particles accumulate and settle in a specific place on the earth's surface or within a body of water. Metamorphic rock forms when existing rocks are transformed by heat and pressure, and as a result experience profound chemical and physical changes.

A student discovers a rock that he hypothesizes may be igneous. Which of the following supports the student's hypothesis?

A.   The rock has undergone profound chemical changes at some point in its history.
B.   The rock was found within an underground lake.
C.   The rock was found near the site of a recent volcano eruption.
D.   The rock is composed of minerals.

END OF TEST

Chapter 26
Practice Test 2:
Answers and
Explanations

REASONING THROUGH LANGUAGE ARTS

Section 1

1. **B** This point of view question asks about the author's overall tone in paragraph 1. This paragraph begins by introducing Niagara Falls and moves on to a discussion about its "opportunities for fishing." The author states, "at Niagara one place is just as good as another, for the reason that the fish do not bite anywhere," and then goes on to say "The advantages of this state of things have never heretofore been properly placed before the public" (paragraph 1). In a discussion about opportunities for fishing, to call the fact that "the fish do not bite anywhere" an "advantage" is a strong contrast, used to convey humor through the use of paradox. Choice (A) is incorrect, because the author does not express fear until later in the passage, beginning in paragraph 3. Choice (B) is correct: The author is offering a contrast to indicate irony, which is the use of language that normally signifies the opposite. Eliminate (C), because even though the paragraph begins by calling Niagara an "enjoyable place of resort," the majority of the paragraph involves the ironic contrast. Choice (D) is incorrect; while the author may be recollecting in this narrative, there is not a particular sense of satisfaction in the discussion of Niagara's opportunities for fishing. In fact, because of the use of irony, the author's true feelings are more negative than positive. The correct answer is (B).

2. **D** This structure question asks why the author chooses to conclude paragraph 2 with that sentence. So, consider the role the sentence plays in the paragraph as a whole. Paragraph 2 relates how someone approaches the Falls: "you first drive down about a mile" and then details how to get a close look: "You can descend a staircase here a hundred and fifty feet down, and stand at the edge of the water." Therefore, the concluding sentence shows what the author thinks the tourists' feelings will be about climbing down all that way: "you will wonder why you did it; but you will then be too late" (that is, it will be too late for the tourist to take back all that effort). Choice (A) is incorrect; even though the author says "you will be too late," this refers to the effort, not the arrival at the falls. Choice (B) is incorrect because the sentence aims to estimate a tourist's reaction, not to advise future visitors. Eliminate (C), because even though the sentence uses the second person "you," this doesn't mean that the author is personally acquainted with the reader. Choice (D) is correct: The author is expressing a prediction about a tourist's attitude after climbing a lengthy stairway. The correct answer is (D).

3. **A** This question asks which sentence from the passage stands out in direct contrast to the main theme of the passage, so focus on the main idea, and consider what is implied as well as what is directly stated. Even though this passage begins with a positive statement about Niagara Falls: "Niagara Falls is a most enjoyable place of resort," (paragraph 1), most of the passage highlights the dangers of the Falls and the author's discomfort while being there. This negative opinion is shown throughout the passage by the use of words like "precipice" (paragraph 2), "misery" (paragraph 3), and "flimsy" (paragraph 6) and the description of the dangerous trip under the falls in paragraph 7. Therefore, (A) is correct, because this sentence offers only positive qualities about the Falls, in contrast to the more negative theme. Choice (B) is incorrect, since this sentence offers only facts about the falls, with no words indicating opinion. Choice (C) is contradictory; the negative tone (shown by "discomforting" and "unhappiness") is consistent with the main idea, not contrasting with it. Choice (D) is incorrect; once again this sentence contains only factual details about the author's actions, without indications of tone. The correct answer is (A).

4. **C** This character development question asks about the author's character based on the statement "I remarked that I wanted to go home." Use the sentences that precede this statement to get a sense of the context. Immediately before the remark about wanting to go home, the author states, "Now a furious wind began to rush out from behind the waterfall, which seemed determined to sweep us from the bridge, and scatter us on the rocks and among the torrents below." So in this context, the remark about wanting to go home is a reaction to a dangerous situation. Choices (A) and (B) are incorrect because nothing in the passage overall indicates that the author is constantly longing for home or has a depressed (melancholic) attitude. Choice (C) is correct: With the statement about wanting to go home, the author is emphasizing the feelings of apprehension—wanting to leave a dangerous situation. Choice (D) is incorrect because nothing in the passage indicates that the author is pining for an earlier era. The correct answer is (C).

5. **D** This structure question asks about how the sentence describing the author's surroundings enhances the story. The passage uses the phrase "storming, roaring, and bellowing of warring wind and water" to emphasize the intense pressure and strength of the waterfall. The phrase "seemed to receive the Atlantic on my back" builds on this image by calling the waterfall the Atlantic, an exaggerated comparison to the Atlantic Ocean. Altogether, the sense is of an enormous, threatening amount of water. Choice (A) takes the use of the word Atlantic literally, as if the author were in the Atlantic. However, the passage is not about the Atlantic, so eliminate this answer. Choice (B) is incorrect: Even though the author mentions the bridges in the previous paragraph, these particular sentences describe the waterfall itself. Choice (C) is incorrect because the use of the word "storming" describes the pressure and the sound of the water, not an actual weather storm. Choice D is correct: The narrator exaggerates the experience of the waterfall by using words like "storming" and "Atlantic," to convey a sense of the intensity and amount of water pouring down from the waterfall. The correct answer is (D).

6. **B** This language use item requires test takers to determine which definition of the phrase "in earnest" matches its use in paragraph 7. Each of the answer options reflects an actual definition of the phrase "in earnest," so look closely at the way the word is used in context. The word is used as a part of the phrase "how fearfully in earnest it was." The "it" refers to the "seething world of descending water" in the previous sentence. So here, "in earnest" describes the "descending water," so look for a word would indicate "seething," which means "storming" or "furious." Choice (A) is incorrect, because "serious" would not match with the violent descriptions of the waterfall found in this paragraph. Choice (B) is correct: The movement of the water is vigorous, or fast-moving. Choice (C) is incorrect, because water cannot be sincere, which means true or heartfelt. Finally, (D) is incorrect, because "ardent" means emotionally enthusiastic, which doesn't fit with the waterfall. The correct answer is (B).

7. This plot development item asks the reader to arrange the sequence of events in the excerpt in order in a chart. Here is the correct order from first to last:

   1. **Event (c): The narrator mentions a view of the river.** This occurs in paragraph 2: "When you start out to "do" the Falls you first drive down about a mile, and pay a small sum for the privilege of looking down from a precipice into the narrowest part of the Niagara River."

   2. **Event (b): The Suspension Bridge is described.** Following the initial description of the view of the river in paragraph 2, the narrator continues the description of a trip to Niagara. The first sentence of paragraph 3 reads as follows: "Then you drive over to Suspension Bridge, and divide your misery between the chances of smashing down two hundred feet into the river below, and the chances of having the railway-train overhead smashing down onto you."

3. **Event (a): Horseshoe Fall is included as a stop in the visit.** After the description of the bridge, the author mentions Horseshoe Fall: "When you have examined the stupendous Horseshoe Fall till you are satisfied you cannot improve on it, you return to America by the new Suspension Bridge," (paragraph 4).

4. **Event (d): The narrator goes behind the falls.** The final two paragraphs describe the harrowing trip underneath the waterfall: "When I saw how much of it there was, and how fearfully in earnest it was, I was sorry I had gone behind it," (paragraph 7).

8. **A** This question asks which detail the reader can infer about Niagara Falls, so check the details in the answer choices against the information in the passage. Choice (A) is correct: Paragraph 4 states, "When you have examined the stupendous Horseshoe Fall till you are satisfied you cannot improve on it, you return to America by the new Suspension Bridge." This means that part of the Falls (the Horseshoe Fall) is outside of the United States. Choice (B) is incorrect; this is not a good fishing resort because paragraph 1 states, "the fish do not bite anywhere." While (C) might be attractive, it is incorrect, since the Cave of the Winds is listed as a part of Niagara, and this choice would indicate that the two are separate. Choice (D) directly contradicts the passage, because paragraph 1 states, "The hotels are excellent, and the prices not at all exorbitant." The correct answer is (A).

9. This Evaluation item asks the reader to identify evidence for claims made by the Affirmative side. The claims and their corresponding evidence:

Claim: The need for concentrating all power into a commission is evident.

- **Evidence (a):** There is a charter revision committee meeting in New York.

- **Evidence (b):** More than a dozen cities have thrown away their old forms.

Paragraph 2 begins "So evident is the need for this solution that there is now a charter revision committee meeting in New York." Paragraph 3 follows this with "What is true of New York is true of scores of other cities…within the past year more than a dozen cities have thrown away their old forms."

Claim: When one branch of the government dominates, checks and balances between the departments are lost.

- **Evidence (c):** Some cities have lost funds due to a corrupt administration.

- **Evidence (d):** The council in St. Louis took a bribe to pass a street railway franchise.

The Affirmative lists examples of instances in which the checks and balances "failed" in paragraph 5, including New York City, Philadelphia, and St. Louis.

10. **D** This structure question asks which idea about city government is included in the Affirmative. Choice (A) contradicts the passage, because the Affirmative advocate "concentrating all governmental authority in one responsible body," (paragraph 1) not retaining separate bodies. Choice (B) is incorrect because this is an assertion made by the Negative in paragraph 10. Choice (C) also contradicts the passage, as the Affirmative advocates for one, not several, governing bodies. Choice (D) is correct: Paragraph 3 states "within the past year more than a dozen cities have thrown away their old forms." The correct answer is (D).

11. **D** This structure question asks which detail is supported by the argument of the Negative. Choice (A) is incorrect because it is too narrow: The passage did not claim that the cabinet form of city government is found only in Europe. Neither did the Negative claim that the cabinet form is preferable to the mayor and council form, so (B) is also incorrect. Choice (C) is incorrect because the Affirmative is the side that blames separation of departments for corruption (paragraph 5). Choice (D) is correct: Paragraph 8 mentions "cities which have successfully adopted the mayor and council form by utilizing the model charter of the National Municipal League." The correct answer is (D).

12. **A** This evaluation question asks about which claim by the Negative a detail supports. The sentence from paragraph 11 immediately follows this one: "The remedy lies in restoring to the city its proper field of legislation." Therefore, (A) is correct. Choice (B) is incorrect because it is another piece of evidence for the same idea found in (A). Choices (C) and (D) are incorrect because while they are assertions made by the Negative, the selected sentence from paragraph 11 is not evidence for these assertions. The correct answer is (A).

13. **B** This structure question asks which specific detail by the Negative supports the idea that there are disadvantages to the commission form of government. Choice (A) is incorrect because this quote refers to the mayor and council form. Choice (B) is correct: The full sentence asserts that the city again adopted distinct legislative and administrative bodies after years of "misrule" by the commission form. Choice (C) is incorrect, because this refers to the current municipal system that needs reform, not the solution proposed by the Affirmative of the commission form. While (D) indicates that the commission form may be too recent to evaluate, there is no indication in this quote of a disadvantage. The correct answer is (B).

14. **A** This evaluation question asks how the Negative side builds the argument that the Affirmative's position is incorrect. The Negative begins in paragraph 7 by acknowledging that there is a problem with current city government, but questioning the solution proposed by the Affirmative. Therefore, (A) is correct: The Negative offers different solutions to the problem—the cabinet form or mayor and council form (paragraph 8). Choice (B) contradicts the passage because the Negative does acknowledge the need for reform. Choice (C) is incorrect because the Negative never addresses the specific examples used by the Affirmative; instead, the Negative uses alternate, additional examples. Choice (D) is incorrect because the Negative never implies that the Affirmative is uninformed. The correct answer is (A).

15. **A** This is a comparison question about the similarities in the two arguments. Both the Negative and the Affirmative state that the cities are in need of reform or reorganization (paragraph 5 and paragraph 7). Therefore, (A) is correct. Choice (B) is incorrect because only the Negative is concerned with preserving fundamental principles (paragraph 12). Choice (C) is incorrect because only the Affirmative wishes to concentrate power into one governing body (paragraph 1). Choice (D) is incorrect because the balancing of powers is the concern of the Negative only. The correct answer is (A).

16. **D** This is a comparison question about a perspective the two arguments share. Choice (A) is incorrect because while the Affirmative may think there is one best form of government (commission), the Negative advocates both the cabinet form and mayor and council form (paragraph 8). Choice (B) is incorrect because only the Negative is concerned with preserving fundamental principles (paragraph 12). Choice (C) is incorrect because only the Affirmative wishes to use the commission model. Choice (D) is correct: The Affirmative describes the distinct duties of the cities in paragraph 4, while the Negative claims that the cities have distinct concerns in paragraph 10. The correct answer is (D).

17.   The option that correctly completes the sentence for each "Select" option:

Drop-Down Item 1: Subject-verb agreement, pronoun usage, parallelism

Option 1 is correct: The plural verb "are" appropriately agrees with the subject "the members," which is then appropriately referenced by the plural pronoun "their." The pronoun is necessary for parallelism in this list structure, since the second item in the list includes a pronoun: "their works of charity."

Options 2 and 3 are incorrect because they incorrectly use the singular verb "is," which does not agree with the plural subject "the members." Option 4 omits the plural pronoun "their," so this option presents a list that is not parallel.

Drop-Down Item 2: Sentence fragments and run-ons

Option 3 is correct: Appropriate punctuation (a period) separates the independent clause beginning "Clear Image has great experience helping organizations" from the independent clause beginning "For over 5 years we have been at the forefront."

Option 1 is incorrect: A comma is too weak to divide the two independent clauses and so this option results in a comma splice. Option 2 provides no punctuation between the two independent clauses, creating a run-on sentence. Option 4 does end an independent clause with a period. However, the word "we" after the period is not capitalized, so this option is incorrect.

Drop-Down Item 3 Parallelism

Option 2 is correct: This option keeps the structure parallel with a consistent verb structure throughout the list, and properly uses a comma series and the conjunction "and" to connect the last list item: "We produce content...maintain a watch...and collect news reports."

Option 1 is incorrect because it omits the conjunction "and" for the last item, resulting in a run-on sentence. Option 3 is incorrect because the construction "produce content...maintaining a watch...collect news reports" is not parallel, as it inserts a gerund into the list; it also omits the conjunction "and" for the last item, resulting in a run-on sentence. Option 4 is incorrect, because the construction "produce content... major search engines are maintained...and collect news reports" is not parallel, as the list switches from active to passive voice with "engines are maintained."

Drop-Down Item 4: Pronoun usage

Option 4 is correct: This sentence is a meeting proposal from the writer to the recipient, so the use of the first-person plural subjective "we" in "I suggest we meet" is appropriate. The option correctly uses the plural pronoun "we" to form the phrase "what we offer," to continue the proposal begun with "I suggest we meet."

Option 1 is incorrect: The pronoun "it" is singular, which does not agree with the verb "offer," resulting in the erroneous construction "it offer." Option 2 is incorrect: Although "they" is plural and agrees with "offer," there is no antecedent for this plural pronoun—the nouns "end" and "work" both require the singular pronoun "it," and while the word "nuances" is plural, if this were the antecedent, then the literal translation would then be "give you a sense of the nuances of what the nuances offer," which is redundant and confusing. Option 3 results in the construction "give you a sense of the nuances of what to offer." In this option, it is unclear which party is offering the nuances—the writer or the recipient. Because of this lack of clarity, this option is incorrect.

Section 2: Extended Response

As noted in Chapter 10, the Extended Response essay is evaluated based on three traits. You can earn up to 2 points for each trait for a possible maximum of 6. Here, we've provided two sample responses to give you an idea of what a score of 1 and 2 looks like for each trait.

Sample Response A

When the marchers on Washington listed their demands, people considered $2 an hour a "living wage." Because that would translate to $13 today, perhaps it is not surprising that workers making a $7.25 minimum wage today feel they need more money. But, raising the minimum wage has more problems than solutions. It is more sound that the current minimum wage keeps people employed. This is obvious through the statistics and through sound basic economics.

Economists continually debate which is better: to regulate business, and give laws and standards for hiring, and limit the freedom of employers? Or, on the contrary, to allow a completely free and unrestricted market, trusting that the business will work out to what's fair for all. While there have been constant agitations throughout history to raise the minimum wage, it is more evident that these agitations do not always merit action. The current minimum wage is the right one for our present economy, as is evident by basic economics and common wisdom. Even the civil rights marchers in 1963 would have agreed. If they could have foreseen the long-term consequences.

At first glance into the issue before us, the answer is apparent through basic economics. As noted by "How raising the minimum wage might harm workers" much of the argument for the minimum wage increase is aimed at the so-called megacorporations" but these megacorporations are actually many small businesses that are just trying to get by with a few employees each. If anyone argues for increasing the minimum wage, they are arguing for bankrupting these small businesses, and the small business owner who may have started as a minimum wage worker in the same business, with dreams of owning a franchise.

Even if the franchises fight to stay alive, they must do this through laying off some workers and making the others work more. With fewer workers the business still suffers; perhaps the quality of the product goes down and so does the reputation. This is not just a guess, but is based on studies from Canada proving that people lose jobs when the minimum wage goes up too high.

The statistics given by the opponents are sound and convincing. If the studies show that there is a definite correlation between the median wage and the minimum wage, in terms of good effects, then by all means the economists and lawmakers should listen to that wisdom and not risk the jobs of low-wage workers.

Those who want a higher minimum wage point to how many people hold low income jobs and the fact that poor people have to buy poor things. But that is just a basic fact of life. Someone has to be at the bottom, and if the minimum wage is raised, then everyone's wages have to go up to compensate.

It is true that minimum wage workers have to work hard for little, and maybe even have to get on welfare. But some possible short-term gains that might be made through a higher wage cannot counterbalance the drawbacks shown by the studies that indicate that a higher minimum wage harms workers. In the final say, definite speeches about class differences and ideals about a perfect economy cannot overcome the fact that hard studies by economists show that minimum wage increases cause a loss of jobs.

Trait 1—Creation of Arguments and Use of Evidence

Score: 1

The writer of this response shows a clear connection to the prompt in the introduction and takes a position opposing an increase in the minimum wage using a rather simplistic analysis: "But, raising the minimum wage has more problems than solutions. It is more sound that the current minimum wage keeps people employed." The response cites some evidence from the source text to support the central position (as noted by "How raising the minimum wage might harm workers," much of the argument for the minimum wage increase is aimed at the so-called megacorporations") and also references specific studies mentioned in the source text. There is some analysis of the issue and evaluation of the evidence for the arguments, but it is minimal ("This is obvious through the statistics and through sound basic economics" and "Someone has to be at the bottom, and if the minimum wage is raised, then everyone's wages have to go up to compensate"). Overall, the writer makes an argument supported by some evidence from the source text with a partial analysis. Therefore, this Response A earns a score of 1 for Trait 1.

Trait 2—Development of Ideas and Organizational Structure

Score: 1

The writer establishes an organizational structure in this response by giving the background of the issue in the introduction, and then taking a position ("But, raising the minimum wage has more problems than solutions. It is more sound that the current minimum wage keeps people employed"). However, the second paragraph just repeats the same information. In paragraphs three, four, and five, the writer cites evidence from the opposing position ("the argument for the minimum wage increase is aimed at the so-called megacorporations" but these megacorporations are actually many small businesses that are just trying to get by with a few employees"), but the organization is not clear; for example, the fifth paragraph is just a continuation of the summary of the source-text statistics made at the end of the fourth paragraph. In the second paragraph, a new thought is presented about the ramifications of layoffs ("With fewer workers the business still suffers; perhaps the quality of the product goes down and so does the reputation"). The sixth and seventh paragraphs summarize the "pro"-wage increase position and dismiss these arguments rather simplistically. The conclusion is a general explanation of why the opponent's position is better supported. The writer's word choice is sufficiently competent and the response's tone is acceptable. Overall, the response is minimally organized and focused, but suffers from repetition in the early portion of the essay, and from choppy transitions in the later portion. Therefore, Response A earns a score of 1 for Trait 2.

Trait 3—Clarity and Command of Standard English Conventions

Score: 1

This brief response shows generally correct sentence structure, but with a very few errors of sentence fragments ("If they could have foreseen the long-term consequences.") and run-ons ("In the final say, definite speeches about class differences and ideals about a perfect economy cannot overcome the fact that hard studies by economists show that minimum wage increases cause a loss of jobs"), but these errors do not interfere with comprehension. There is generally reliable control of standard English conventions with regard to subject-verb agreement and punctuation usage, so this response is an acceptable example of draft writing. Therefore, Response A earns a score of 1 for Trait 3.

Sample Response B

The federal minimum wage is implemented throughout the United States as the lowest wage that employers can pay their workers. This article presents both the views of the opponents and the supporters of an increased minimum wage. Both sides claim that their position represents better economic sense. Taking into consideration the two positions presented, the one for increasing the minimum wage from $7.25 to $10.10 per hour makes the better argument.

The minimum wage has been around for a long time (1938) and for a long time folks have been asking for it to be raised; in the 1963 Civil Rights march, for example. What is clear, then, is that the minimum wage does not stay stagnant over time; it responds to the needs of the economy.

The first point that the supporters of an increased minimum wage make is that there are more and more minimum-wage jobs all the time, and nearly half of all jobs will be service or food industry work (often minimum wage) by 2020. The supporters rightly point out that many of these jobs cannot be automated or outsourced. If the predictions are right, and the minimum wage is not increased, then the nation is well on the way to sentencing half the nation to live in poverty, which would have disastrous consequences for the economy as a whole. The "pro" minimum wage increase position points out that giving more money to the people on the low end of the ladder is exactly the way to safeguard the economy as a whole, since the money that poor people make goes directly back in to the economy as they use their wages to address their immediate needs, and in the process employ other people on the low end of the spectrum. In this sense, giving money to poor people helps poor people. Giving money to rich people does not help nearly as much, as the wealthy do not participate in the economy in the same fashion, or even in the same economy, as the supporters' article points out.

By far, however, the most compelling reason the supporters give in favor of the minimum wage increase is the fact that low-wage earners fill their wage gaps via social service programs. The government is giving billions of dollars of assistance to big-box stores and fast food chains that refuse to pay their workers a livable wage. At this point, the issue of minimum wage is no longer a private matter between employer and employee: we are ALL funding that wage gap with taxes.

Those opposed to a minimum wage increase try to counter the notion that megacorporations are just stingy by insisting that they are really small franchises. But this argument is deliberately vague and misleading. Who set up the franchise system? Whom does it serve? The franchise system is a feudal system that allows the parent corporation to reap all of the profits while evading the responsibilities. There is no law preventing a parent corporation from investing in the employees of the franchise.

Perhaps the only argument from the opponents worth looking at is the sentence "Canadian studies show that workers lose jobs and have increased workloads when the minimum wage is more than half the median wage." Once again, though, the sentence is vague. How much more than half is meant? Since $10.10 would be 60% of the current median wage, that is not very much more than half. Some more precise numbers would help the opponents' point; as it stands, the argument is weak. Also, the studies are from Canada which has a different economy and different laws from the United States. The application of these studies to this situation is therefore questionable.

Therefore, overall, the arguments against an increase in the minimum wage hold little weight. It may be that there is some validity to the studies quoted, but without further explanation of the nature of the studies, and their application to the United States, this cannot be determined. For that reason, the arguments for an increased minimum wage, with their focus on the distinct proportions of the U.S. economic make-up and the real numbers of dollar cost to the government, are more convincing.

Trait 1—Creation of Arguments and Use of Evidence

Score: 2

The introduction of this essay gives a background of the issue and contains a clear statement of position ("Taking into consideration the two positions presented, the one for increasing the minimum wage from $7.25 to $10.10 per hour makes the better argument"). The writer reinforces this claim with an analysis of the evidence, first focusing on the strength of the proponents' argument: "The supporters rightly point out that many of these jobs cannot be automated or outsourced" and "By far, however, the most compelling reason the supporters give in favor of the minimum wage increase is the fact that low-wage earners fill their wage gaps via social service programs." The writer then moves on to the inadequacy of the opposing argument: "Those opposed to a minimum wage increase try to counter the notion that megacorporations are just stingy by insisting that they are really small franchises." As further support, the writer introduces alternative interpretations of the evidence ("Who set up the franchise system? Whom does it serve? The franchise system is a feudal system that allows the parent corporation to reap all of the profits"). Finally, the writer critiques the opponents' use of statistics ("It may be that there is some validity to the studies quoted, but without further explanation of the nature of the studies, and their application to the United States, this cannot be determined."). Overall, the response offers a well-developed, logical, and organized argument focused on the validity of the arguments in the source text. Therefore, Response B earns a score of 2 for Trait 1.

Trait 2—Development of Ideas and Organizational Structure

Score: 2

The response shows a clear structure, beginning with some historical facts about minimum wage to introduce the issue, then analyzing what that history indicates ("What is clear, then, is that the minimum wage does not stay stagnant over time; it responds to the needs of the economy"), then highlighting the strong points of the proponents argument, and finally dismissing the points of the opponents' argument. This structure permits a development of generally logical ideas that are sufficiently explored. The response establishes a clear connection between the main idea and supporting details within paragraphs 3, 4, and 5. The writer points to hypotheses about the structure of the franchise system and then discusses why that structure invalidates the opponents' claim. The writer uses appropriate vocabulary and formal tone to express ideas, resulting in a response that is structured, focused, and developed. Therefore, Response B earns a score of 2 for Trait 2.

Trait 3—Clarity and Command of Standard English Conventions

Score: 2

This writer demonstrates largely correct sentence structure and competency with several standard English rules. The response makes good use of subject-verb agreement, word usage, and the rules of capitalization and punctuation, and the writer blends simple and complex sentences while maintaining clarity ("But this argument is deliberately vague and misleading. Who set up the franchise system? Whom does it serve? The franchise system is a feudal system that allows the parent corporation to reap all of the profits while evading the responsibilities."). Transitional words and phrases are used throughout ("since," "however," "by far"). Overall, the response indicates a strong command of the English language and the level is appropriate for on-demand draft writing. Therefore, Response B earns a score of 2 for Trait 3.

Section 3

18. **D** This language use item requires test takers to determine which definition of the word "refined" matches its use in paragraph 2. Each of the answer options reflects an actual definition of the word "refined," so look closely at the way the word is used in context. The word is used to describe Eliza Allen as "a girl who had refined tastes and wide reading, and who was at the same time graceful and full of humor." Here, the word "refined" is used in conjunction with the words "wide reading," so "refined" is used to mean something like "widely read, educated." Choices (A) and (B) are incorrect, because the passage is not claiming that Eliza Allen is "distilled" (A) or "purified" (B). Choice (C) is incorrect: While Eliza Allen *might* be delicate, that is not how the word "refined" is used in this sentence. Finally, (D) is correct, because "cultivated" is a characteristic that describes someone who is "widely read." The correct answer is (D).

19. This character development item asks the reader to identify three adjectives that accurately describe Houston. The three correct adjectives are as follows:

    - **Well-regarded.** The fact that Houston was well-regarded is mentioned in paragraph 3: "Houston was the associate of Jackson and was immensely popular."

    - **Determined.** Houston's determination is mentioned in several places. In paragraph 11, he says, "What must be, must be." Furthermore, Houston persists in his course of action despite public outcry (paragraphs 12–13) and paragraph 14 subsequently describes Houston as "self-controlled." Therefore, the passage clearly indicates that Houston is very determined in the matter of his separation.

    - **Secretive.** The passage states that "never, even in his cups, could he be persuaded to say a single word" (paragraph 14).

20. **A** This structure question asks about how the sentences describing Houston's situation enhance the story. The excerpt uses the phrase "brilliant career" and "attractive prospects" to emphasize that Houston's situation in life is promising. However, the next sentence poses a question about these "prospects," indicating that something might "blight his future." Immediately afterward, the passage begins to relate the tale of Houston's separation. Altogether, the sense is of a positive description combined with a negative prediction about the future, a prediction that is fulfilled later in the passage. Therefore, (A) is correct: The positive description stands in contrast to the negative developments later in the passage. Choice (B) is incorrect: Although the passage contains details from Houston's life, these details are about his prospects, not his

character. Choice (C) is incorrect: Even though paragraph 3 mentions that Houston was "an associate of Jackson," this passage does not compare Houston to another politician. Finally, (D) is incorrect, because Houston's marriage is revealed before this paragraph. The correct answer is (A).

21. **D** This is a development question about Houston, whose character is discussed throughout the passage. Use the passage to either confirm or eliminate answers based on details in the answer choices. Choice (A) is incorrect: The last sentence of paragraph 14 states that "sometimes in later years he drank deeply," but doesn't say this happened frequently. Choice (B) is incorrect, because even though the passage states that Eliza Allen had "refined tastes and wide reading" (paragraph 2), there is no information about whether Houston did or did not have the same qualities. Eliminate (C) because paragraph 14 states, "However his friends might rage, and however her people might wonder and seek to pry into the secret, no satisfaction was given on either side," meaning that the cause of the separation remained unknown. Choice (D) is correct: Paragraph 1 states that Houston was Governor, and had to "visit different portions of the state," on the "northern border of Tennessee." The correct answer is (D).

22. **D** This structure question asks which sentence from the passage supports the idea that Houston was not accustomed to "refined" society. Since this question asks you to make an inference, consider what is implied as well as what is directly stated. The word "refined" is used in paragraph 2 to describe Eliza Allen, who is also described as a member of the "influential families." Look for an answer choice that indicates Houston was not used to this kind of society. Choice (A) is incorrect: While this answer indicates that Houston was introduced to the Tennessee "influential families," it does not indicate that he was unaccustomed to this kind of society, since there is not evidence of whether he had met similar people before. Choice (B) is incorrect: It indicates that his wife's family was hostile, but this is attributed to the separation, not Houston's unfamiliarity with refined society. Choice (C) is incorrect because this answer choice mentions that he has "attractive prospects" after his marriage. In (D), the phrase "one whose associations had been chiefly with the women of frontier communities" refers to Houston, indicating that he was not accustomed to women like Eliza Allen, who was "refined." The correct answer is (D).

23. **B** This question asks about the character of Houston as shown through the declaration "What difference does it make to me?" so locate this phrase and read for context, to link this phrase back to Houston's character. When his friend expresses distress at his separation, Houston utters this phrase "gloomily," and goes on to say "what must be, must be." This reinforces his attitude in paragraph 8 when he replies "grimly." So, the phrase is said with an overall attitude of gloominess or grimness, which highlight's Houston's emotion while speaking of his separation. Choice (A) is incorrect: "gloomily" shows that Houston is definitely speaking with emotion, not indifference. Choice (B) is correct, because Houston feels grim, or sad, when speaking of his separation, so much that future events do not seem to matter: "what must be, must be." Eliminate (C) because even though Houston is asking a question, it is not out of curiosity, but to make a point about his emotional state. Choice (D) is incorrect because Houston is responding to his friend's predictions, not requests. The correct answer is (B).

24. **A** This is a structure question about the use of the phrase "gazed at him with horror" in paragraph 6, so locate the detail and consider the context. The phrase occurs immediately after Houston breaks the news of the separation from his wife in the previous paragraph, so the "horror" is his friend's response to this news. Therefore, Choice (A) is correct: The separation comes as a complete shock to his friend, so his expression is one of "horror." Choice (B) is incorrect, because the same paragraph states, "Houston's friend seized him by the arm," which he would not do if he were afraid of Houston. Eliminate (C) because this scene does not contain any description of Houston's appearance or indication that Houston had become grotesque. Choice (D) is incorrect because immediately following the phrase "gazed at him with horror," the friend begins speaking (paragraph 7), so he is not speechless. The correct answer is (A).

25. **C** This development question asks about the marriage between Houston and Eliza Allen. Since the marriage is the primary subject of the whole passage, use the passage to either confirm or eliminate answers based on details in the answer choices. Choice (A) is incorrect: Paragraph 3 states, "They were surrounded with friends of all classes and ranks." Choice (B) is incorrect, because paragraph 2 states that "few of their friends were surprised when the word went forth that they were engaged to be married," meaning that the marriage was expected. Choice (C) is correct: Because paragraph 3 notes that Houston seemed to have a "brilliant career" ahead, and immediately follows this with "He had won a lovely bride to make a home for him; so that no man seemed to have more attractive prospects." Furthermore, his friend notes that Houston's separation will cause "everyone to fall away" from him (paragraph 7). Therefore, Houston's marriage had an impact on his public image. Eliminate (D): There is no information about how much Eliza Allen wanted the marriage. The correct answer is (C).

26. This item asks the reader to identify statements that express the author's purposes for writing this article. The two correct statements:

   - **Statement (a): To compare the techniques of storytelling from different cultures**. The author begins the essay with a description of comic, witty, and humorous stories, from England, France, and America, (paragraph 2) and then analyzes the methods of storytelling in the later paragraphs.

   - **Statement (d): To satirize the habits of comic storytellers, whether writing or speaking**. The author emphasizes the over-the-top delivery of the comic story (paragraphs 5 and 8) and uses words like "pathetic" and "depressing" ironically juxtaposed with the images of "laughter" and "delight."

27. **A** This development question asks why the author uses this sentence to conclude the essay. This sentence immediately follows the over-the-top storytelling technique of the comedic storyteller (paragraph 8) that the author is satirizing. Therefore, (A) is correct—the designation "very depressing" shows weariness from the heavy-handed delivery of the comedic storyteller. Choice (B) is incorrect—the author seeks to make a point about the futility of the comedic storytelling method, not his own mental state. Choice (C) is too extreme—"immoral" is too strong a word for the author's satirical view of the comedic storyteller. Choice (D) is also incorrect—storytelling as a profession is not under discussion. The correct answer is (A).

28. **C** This language use question asks the reader to examine the use of the term "difficult" to describe the humorous story in paragraph 2. The author expands this idea in paragraphs 4 and 5: "The humorous story is strictly a work of art—high and delicate art—and only an artist can tell it...The humorous story is told gravely; the teller does his best to conceal the fact that he even dimly suspects that there is anything funny about it." Therefore, (A) is incorrect—the difficulty is not in the effect on the teller, but the execution. Choice (B) is also wrong, because if done correctly the audience will laugh, as illustrated by the examples in paragraph 7. Choice (C) is correct; the humorous story takes pretense and self-control to deliver. Choice (D) is incorrect—there is no mention of formal study to learn the form. The correct answer is (C).

29. **A** This main idea question asks about the central theme of the essay. Early in the essay, the author asserts: "The humorous story depends for its effect upon the manner of the telling; the comic story and the witty story upon the matter" (paragraph 2). So (A) is correct—it correctly juxtaposes the "manner" and "matter" in the same fashion as the author does. Choice (B) is wrong because the author never asserts that stories must be based on truth. Choice (C) contradicts the author, who contrasts the truly "humorous" story, which only an "artist" can accomplish, with the "comedic" story, which "anyone" can do. Choice (D) also contradicts the author, who asserts that the humorous story is found only in America. The correct answer is (A).

30. This development item asks the reader to make specific comparisons between similar topics and place the correct details into the correct categories. The correct assignment of details to categories:

The humorous story
- **It is told seriously. (Paragraph 5)**
- **The listener must be alert at the end. (Paragraph 6)**

The comic story
- **It must be brief and end with a point. (Paragraph 3)**
- **Anybody can tell it. (Paragraph 4)**

31. **B** This development question asks about how the author makes his point about the different types of stories. Choice (A) is incorrect because an analogy highlights how items are alike, and the author instead makes a contrast between the stories of America and those of England and France. Choice (B) is correct—the author uses imagery like "burst," "shouts," "whooping," and "exclamation" to describe the comedic storyteller, and imagery like "delicate" and "bubbling" to describe the humorous story. Choice (C) is incorrect—the author mentions experts of only the humorous story form, not the other types. Choice (D) contradicts the author, who states, "I do not claim that I can tell a story as it ought to be told" (paragraph 1). The correct answer is (B).

32. **B** This structure question asks about the author's feelings regarding writers and tellers of comedic stories in England, France, and Germany. The author satirizes these tellers in the last paragraph by emphasizing how these tellers spoil a joke with too much emphasis on the punchline. Therefore, (A) is incorrect and (B) is correct. Choice (C) contradicts the author, who states, "The art of telling a humorous story—understand, I mean by word of mouth, not print—was created in America" (paragraph 4). Choice (D) reverses the methods of these European storytellers and the methods of the humorous story, so this choice is incorrect. The correct answer is (B).

33. This development item asks the reader to identify three adjectives that accurately describe the author. The three correct adjectives:

- **Modest.** In the first paragraph, the author states, "I do not claim that I can tell a story as it ought to be told," indicating modesty about his own abilities.

- **Satirical.** The author uses grandiose exaggeration to convey a dislike of the comic story.

- **Belittling.** When describing the teller of the comic story, the author writes, "It is a pathetic thing to see" (paragraph 5), and the author looks down on the method of comic story.

34. This plot development question item asks the reader to arrange the sequence of events in the excerpt in order in a chart. Here's the correct order from first to last:

1. **Event (d): The quarry is deserted.** This occurs early in the narrative in paragraph 1: The first sentence says "The Hollow for which they were bound lay in a deserted stone quarry."

2. **Event (b): Stephen objects to his father.** Following the general description of the quarry, the party prepares to skate. When Stephen's father warns the others away from the quarry, Stephen responds, "'Oh, we fellows have skated in the quarry millions of times, Dad,' Stephen protested" (paragraph 6).

3. **Event (a): The lake ice breaks.** After skating into the quarry, Stephen falls through the ice: "What followed was all over in a moment—the breaking ice and the plunge into the frigid water." (paragraph 15).

4. **Event (c): Stephen is at home.** After Stephen falls through the ice, the next scene begins "When he next opened his eyes it was to find himself in his own bed with a confusion of faces bending over him." (paragraph 17).

35. **B** This development question asks about the skating trip. Since the skating trip is the primary topic of the narrative, use the passage to either confirm or eliminate answers based on details in the answer choices. Choice (A) is incorrect because Stephen skates to the quarry without planning it: "He never could explain afterward just how it happened that he found himself around the bend of the quarry" (paragraph 15). Choice (B) is correct: In paragraph 18, someone says "He is safe now, Tolman. Don't you worry! You'd better go and get off some of your wet clothing." The "Tolman" referred to is Stephen's father; his wet clothes and the assurance that Stephen is safe both imply that Mr. Tolman pulled Stephen from the water. Choice (C) might be tempting, because the quarry is indeed both deserted and unsafe; however, this choice is incorrect: The quarry is deserted because it is far from town (paragraph 1). Choice (D) is incorrect: Although Mr. Ackerman jokes that he might "renew his youth," (paragraph 3) there is nothing to indicate the trip was made for this purpose. The correct answer is (B).

36. **A** This structure question asks which quotation from the passage supports the idea that Dick's father is not the only adult in the skating party. Since several quotations are related to the major theme of the skating party, consider what is implied as well as what is directly stated. Choice (A) is correct: This quotation is found in paragraph 3 and is stated by Mr. Ackerman, suggesting that Mr. Ackerman is no longer young. Choices (B) may be tempting because it distinguishes "young people," but this quotation by itself does not indicate that there are adults in the party as well. Choice (C) is incorrect because, while this indicates that there are more people in the party besides Stephen's family, Dick is not presented as an adult. Although (D) indicates that someone is addressing Mr. Tolman in an informal fashion ("He is safe now, Tolman!"), suggesting an adult, this occurs away from the quarry "in his own bed" and so the speaker may not have been in the skating party. The correct answer is (A).

37. **C** This language use item requires test takers to determine which definition of the word "cherished" matches its use in paragraph 14. Each of the answer options reflects an actual definition of the word "cherished," so look closely at the way the word is used in context. The word is used as a part of the sentence "Indeed, one could not long have cherished ill humor amid such radiant surroundings," and is followed by "There was…too much jollity and happiness." So, ill humor is not possible because of too much happiness; so one could not long have "held on to" ill humor. Look for a word that means "held" or "kept" in the answers. Choice (A) is incorrect, because "preserved" means "kept from damage." It would not make sense to say "could not long have kept from damage ill humor." Choice (B) is not quite right, because embraced means "hugged" or "happily accepted," and "could not long have happily accepted ill humor" doesn't make sense with the following "too much jollity and happiness." Choice (C) is correct because harbored means "kept" or "made a place for," so "could not long have made a place for ill humor" is consistent with "too much jollity and happiness. Finally, (D) is incorrect, because this would result in "could not long have honored ill humor." The correct answer is (C).

38. **D** This character development item requires making an inference about Dick based on an overall understanding of the details that relate to her. Dick appears in the narrative in paragraph 11, so use the details in this paragraph to eliminate answers that don't conform to the passage. Choice (A) is incorrect: Since Dick says "your father," to Stephen, this suggests that Stephen and Dick do not share the same father. Choice (B) is incorrect because there is no evidence that Mr. Ackerman is Dick's father. Choice

(C) may be tempting, because Dick does disagree with Stephen. However, Dick says, "Whether it is safe or not has nothing to do with it," so eliminate this answer. Choice (D) is correct, because Stephen claims "I know this pond better than he does," (paragraph 10), meaning that his father should listen to Stephen. In contrast, Dick says, "If your father says not to skate there that ought to go with you," advising Stephen to obey Mr. Tolman because his father's desires should be enough—the issue of safety is irrelevant. The correct answer is (D).

39. **A** This structure question asks about how the sentence describing the landscape enhances the story. The passage offers a very specific description of the quarry to set the scene for the skating narrative that follows: "at one end a deep pool; from this point the water spread itself over the meadows in a large, shallow pond." This description gives the necessary context for the reader to understand the physical layout of the scene. Therefore, Choice (A) is correct, because this description is the reason Mr. Tolman later claims in paragraph 5 that parts of the skating area may be unsafe while others are safe: the depth of the water varies. Choice (B) is incorrect: While paragraph 1 does state that an arm of the river had penetrated the quarry, this is not a geological history of the area. Choice (C) contradicts the passage because paragraph 1 states, "Had the spot been nearer the town it would doubtless have been overrun with skaters," so eliminate this answer. Even though the skating area is formed by a river, nothing indicates the group had to cross this river, so (D) is incorrect. The correct answer is (A).

40. This character development item asks the reader to identify three adjectives that accurately describe Stephen. The three correct adjectives are as follows:

- **Cheerful.** Even though Stephen begins by being irritated by his father, this feeling changes to enjoyment: "Stephen's irritation had vanished and he was speeding across the glassy surface of the ice as gay as the gayest of the company" (paragraph 14).

- **Disobedient.** Stephen does disobey his father, though he does not plan to: "He had not actually formulated the intention of slipping away from the others and invading this forbidden spot. Nevertheless, there he was," (paragraph 15).

- **Terrified.** Stephen is terrified that he will die after falling through the ice: The description of his thoughts at the end of paragraph 15 and the phrase "With a piercing scream he made one last desperate lunge" (paragraph 16) all indicate his extreme fear.

41. **C** This structure question asks why the author chose to use a certain phrase, so locate the detail and consider the context of the surrounding text. The phrase occurs in paragraph 17: "When he next opened his eyes it was to find himself in his own bed with a confusion of faces bending over him." This sentence occurs right after the description of Stephen's fall through the ice, so the "he" in paragraph 17 is Stephen, who is just waking up after the traumatic experience, and the "confusion of faces" represents what he sees upon waking. Choice (A) is incorrect: The use of "Tolman" in the following paragraph refers to someone besides Stephen—his father, who was named Mr. Tolman in paragraph 5. Eliminate (B) because the "confusion" represents what Stephen sees, not how he looks to others. Choice (C) is correct: Stephen is disoriented after the traumatic experience, so what he sees as he just awakens is confusing to him. Choice (D) is incorrect because those around Stephen may not be strangers: The use of the phrase "confusion of faces" indicates that Stephen cannot immediately tell who is around him; whether or not they are familiar faces, they are unrecognizable at first. The correct answer is (C).

42.   The option that correctly completes the sentence for each "Select" option:

Drop-Down Item 1: Pronoun usage, subject-verb agreement

Option 1 is correct: The compound subject "His work…and the knowledge" is plural (two items: work and knowledge), the plural form "earn" is appropriate. Also, the singular objective pronoun "him" is appropriately used to refer to "Ron."

Option 2 is incorrect: The verb "earns" would agree only with a singular subject (one person *earns*, two people *earn*). Option 3 is incorrect: The pronoun "they" is plural, and does not agree with the antecedent "Ron"; instead, this option makes it appear as if the "work and knowledge" are the subjects which are receiving "many referrals," which is confusing. Option 4 is incorrect: In this option, the verb "earns" does not agree with the plural subject, and the pronoun "they" does not properly refer to "Ron."

Drop-Down Item 2: Misplaced modifiers or illogical word order

Option 3 is correct: In this sentence, the adverb "ceremoniously" is correctly placed next to the verb "will present," which it modifies. The subject of the verb "will present" is "Ron," which correctly agrees with the following pronoun construction "his colleague."

Option 1 is incorrect: in this option, the placement of the word "ceremoniously" is confusing: it appears to modify the phrase "at the party" when it should modify the verb "will present." Option 2 is incorrect: in this option, the subject of the sentence is now "Ron's presentation" (making it seem as if the "colleague" later is the colleague of the presentation), which is a passive construction that divides the idea of "ceremonious" from what it modifies: the presentation. Option 4 is incorrect: in this option, the subject of the sentence is now "Ron's presentation" resulting in a passive construction with a confusing mix of pronouns ("will have its password ceremoniously presented to his colleague").

Drop-Down Item 3: Parallelism, run-on sentences, and sentence fragments

Option 4 is correct: This option keeps the structure parallel with a consistent verb structure throughout the list, and properly uses a comma series and the conjunction "and" to connect the last list item: "his colleagues, his project managers, and his long-time clients."

Option 1 is incorrect because it results in the construction "his colleagues and project managers and his long-time clients" which is a run-on structure. A list of more than two items should be set off with commas and use "and" to connect the last items. Option 2 is incorrect, because this option breaks up the list, separating a dependent clause from the rest of the sentence with a period, forming the sentence fragment "His long-time clients, providing guidance necessary to make his transition to retirement as smooth as possible for all parties. "Option 3 is incorrect because this option provides an extra comma after the word "and."

Drop-Down Item 4: Possessives and the placement of apostrophes

Option 2 is correct: In this sentence, the word "company's" is appropriately singular and possessive, indicating that the "best performance" belongs to the company.

Option 1 is incorrect because it is singular but omits the possessive. Option 3 is incorrect because it is possessive but improperly uses the plural form. Option 4 is incorrect because it is plural and omits the possessive.

43. **A** This evaluation question asks about the reason President Taft mentioned the fraction of timber owned by public organizations in his address. In paragraph 2, Taft mentions that the government owns only one-fourth of all the country's timber, and states, "Only three percent of that which is in private ownership is looked after properly and treated according to modern rules of forestry. The usual destructive waste and neglect continue in the remainder." Therefore, the mention of the small fraction of public timbered lands highlights the larger proportion of private lands, which are maintained with "waste and neglect," so (A) is correct. Choices (B) and (C) may be tempting, because the limitations on forests reserved for public use and "lands which are not properly forest land" are discussed in paragraph 1. However, the fraction of timber that is Government timber is specifically presented in paragraph 2, which is about the neglect and poor management of forests not on public land, so eliminate these choices. Choice (D) is incorrect because President Taft declares such federal laws are " beyond the jurisdiction of the Federal Government," not that the fraction of timber is too small to enact the laws. The correct answer is (A).

44. **B** This evaluation question asks about the approach the author of the report by the Western Forestry and Conservation Association takes to support the idea that northwestern forest owners have effective conservation practices. Therefore, find the quoted material in the paragraph and locate the information given in support of this idea. In paragraph 9, the author states, "we have controlled our countless fires so that actual disasters can be counted on the fingers, and our loss as a whole is insignificant—we feel that no one has done more to prove his willingness and competence to practice Conservation that counts." This assertion immediately follows statistics that show the number of fires that have been controlled compared to the relatively small amounts of loss. Choice (A) is incorrect: There are no multiple definitions of "conservation" in this article. Choice (B) is correct: The author uses statistical evidence to prove that the private owners are effective at protecting forest lands. Choice (C) may be tempting, because author did compare the Forest Service to the private fire patrols in paragraph 7; however, the author just says these groups are "equally trained" and does not mention their numbers. Choice (D) is contradictory because paragraph 8 claims the methods in the National Forests are "excellent," so eliminate this answer. The correct answer is (B).

45. **A** This structure question asks why the author chooses that sentence to conclude the report, in responding to President Taft. So, consider the role the last sentence plays in Article 2 as a whole, and how that relates to Article 1. The "northwestern forest owners" are the private landholders. In Article 1, President Taft claims that the management of the privately owned forests is neglectful (paragraph 2). By contrast, the last sentence of Article 2 asserts that "no one has done more to prove his willingness and competence to practice Conservation that counts than the northwestern forest owner," so this concluding sentence is a refutation of Taft's suggestion that the private owners are neglectful. Thus, (A) is correct. Choice (B) is incorrect because the purpose of the sentence is not to define "conservation" but to defend the owners. Eliminate (C), because this particular sentence is a defense of the private owners, not a criticism of the government. Choice (D) is contradictory: The report advocates *for* more legislation. The correct answer is (A).

46. This item asks the reader to make specific comparisons between similar themes or topics and place the correct details into the correct categories. The correct assignment of details to categories:

President Taft's Address

- **Phrase (a): There are lands which should be removed from the forest reserves.** Paragraph 1 states, "In the present forest reserves there are lands which are not properly forest land, and which ought to be subject to homestead entry...We are carefully eliminating such lands from forest reserves."

- **Phrase (b): States should make laws for fire safety.** In paragraph 2, Taft states, "If anything can be done by law it must be done by the State legislatures. I believe that it is within their constitutional power to require the enforcement of regulations."

E.T. Allen's Report

- **Phrase (d): The private Northwest forest owners have an imperfect fire safety system.** Paragraph 9 of Article 2 states, "Our own system is by no means perfect yet."

- **Phrase (c): Private fire patrols are more costly per acre than National Forest patrols.** Paragraph 8 states, "They handle the fire situation in a much better and more comprehensive manner than even the Government has ever done, because they spend three times as much money per acre for patrol."

47. **D** This comparison question asks the reader to examine the structural relationships between the two articles, so look at the organization of each article. Article 1, the president's address, gives some background information about forested lands, public and private, and then brings up the problem of waste and mismanagement. Article 2, the report, starts with the warning "The great danger now is that our resources will disappear while we are deciding to whom they shall belong," and then goes on to discuss forest fire measures in great detail. Choice (A) is incorrect, because E. T. Allen's article does not defend the limitations on national reserved forests. Eliminate (B), because Article 2 claims the solution to the problem of fire is "better laws" (paragraph 8), so this answer is contradictory. Choice (C) is incorrect, because President Taft says "Exactly how far these regulations can go and remain consistent with the rights of private ownership, it is not necessary to discuss" (paragraph 3). Choice (D) is correct because it accurately reflects the structures of both articles: The president's address spends as much time on the classification of forest lands as on the problems of mismanagement, whereas E. T. Allen's report focuses almost exclusively on fire prevention and management in forests. The correct answer is (D).

48. **D** This point of view question asks about President Taft's attitude concerning the laws regarding the regulation of forested lands, so locate the specific information in the passage. In Article 1, President Taft asserts that the federal government should not make laws to regulate the management of privately owned forested lands (paragraph 2), and if any laws are made, the States should make them. Choice (A) is incorrect, because the President states, "No further legislation is needed at the moment except an increase in the fire protection to National forests" (paragraph 4). Eliminate (B), because it contradicts President Taft's assertion that the States must make the laws. Choice (C) can be eliminated because it contradicts paragraph 1: "I expect to recommend to Congress that the limitation herein imposed shall be repealed." Choice (D) is correct: President Taft states, "The management of forests not on public land is beyond the jurisdiction of the Federal Government" (paragraph 2). The correct answer is (D).

49. **D** This question asks which sentence from the passage best expresses the primary purpose of the president's address, so look at the overall structure and theme of Article 1. The address gives some background information about forested lands, public and private, and then brings up the problem of waste and mismanagement. Look for an answer choice that expresses these two major themes. Choice (A) is incorrect, because while lawmaking is an important part of the president's address, this sentence does not express the ideas of allocations of lands. Eliminate (B) because this sentence merely introduces the topic by giving the total acres of public forests. Choice (C) is incorrect: This sentence emphasizes the idea of mismanagement, but doesn't encompass the entire theme. Choice (D) is correct: This sentence occurs in the conclusion of the president's address and expresses the president's evaluation of legislation, forest management problems (fire protection), and classification of forest lands (forest reservations). The correct answer is (D).

50. **C** This question asks about the purpose of the forest homestead act. Since this is a detail question, locate the specific information and verify each answer choice against the passage. The phrase appears in paragraph 1: "We are carefully eliminating such lands from forest reserves or, where their elimination is not practicable, listing them for entry under the forest homestead act." The "such lands" refers to the "lands which are not properly forest land" in the previous sentence. Choice (A) is incorrect, because the passage does not mention pioneers or the intentions of the act. Choice (B) is incorrect, because again there is no information about why the act was passed. Choice (C) is correct: The act apparently allows the government to classify forest lands in another way, under the "forest homestead act. Choice (D) is incorrect: Even though the government controls one-fourth of the timbered lands, the forest homestead act would be used only for those "lands which are not properly forest land." The correct answer is (C).

MATHEMATICAL REASONING

Part 1

1. **C** Check your formula sheet. Volume Pyramid = $\frac{1}{3} Bh$. B refers to the area of the square base of the pyramid and is given as 50,000 and h = 150, so simply apply the formula. So $\frac{1}{3} \times 50{,}000 \times 150 = 2{,}500{,}000$. Since you don't have a calculator for this question, it will be much easier if you calculate $\frac{1}{3} \times 150 = 50$ (to get rid of fractions) and then multiply 50 by 50,000.

2. **B** If the woman sleeps 6 hours, then she is awake for 24 − 6 = 18 hours per day. She works $\frac{4}{9}$ of this, so she works $\frac{4}{9} \times 18 = 8$ hours per day. The question asks for what fraction of the total day she works, so divide the hours she works by the total hours in a day. $\frac{8}{24} = \frac{1}{3}$.

3. **<** Since more than half the students scored below a 76, the median score (the score of the middle student) must be below 76. The median cannot possibly be equal to or greater than 76, so the correct expression is *median* < 76.

4. **C** The total cost of the workers should be the rate per worker multiplied by the number of workers and the number of hours. $50 \times 3 \times 2$. Eliminate (A) and (B). The cost for mileage should be the mileage rate multiplied by the number of miles. So the correct answer is $50 \times 3 \times 2 + 40 \times (\$0.5)$.

5. **3** She earned $15 in interest, so you must determine what % of $500 this is. Percentage means "amount per 100" so the easiest solution is to use a proportion to find out how much interest she earned for each $100 in her account. $\frac{\$15}{\$500} = \frac{x}{\$100}$. Reduce the fraction on the left by cancelling 5 from both the top and bottom to determine that $\frac{\$3}{\$100} = \frac{x}{\$100}$. Therefore $x = 3$.

Part 2

6. **B** Multiply the number of miles per hour, 65, by the maximum number of hours per day, 9, to determine the maximum distance the driver can travel each day: $9 \times 65 = 585$. Since the total distance is 4,287, divide this by the distance per day to get the number of days: $4{,}287 \div 585 = 7.3$ (approximately). So the trip cannot be completed in 7 days, but will require at least 8.

7. **B** A barrel is a cylinder, so write down the formula from the formula sheet: $V = \pi r^2 h$. Notice also that the diameter is currently given in inches, so you will need to convert 24 inches to 2 feet. Since the diameter is 2, then the radius is 1. Now use the formula. $V = \pi \times 1^2 \times 4 = 4 \times \pi = {\sim}12.6$.

8. **Greater Than**

   The sum of two sides of a triangle is always greater than the length of the third side. If you chose **Equal to the Square of**, you were thinking of the Pythagorean theorem, but that formula would require the sum of the squares of the other two sides, not just the sum of the other two sides.

9. **A** According to the graph, the length of AB is 3 and the length of BC is 4. Therefore, by the Pythagorean Theorem, the length of the hypotenuse is 5. The area of the triangle is $\frac{1}{2}bh = \frac{1}{2} \times 3 \times 4 = 6$. The question asks for the difference between the two, which means subtraction, so the answer is 1.

10. **D** At 90°, the stand brings in approximately 500 per hour. At 100°, it brings in 1,000 per hour. The difference is 500. Multiplied by 3 hours, the total difference in revenue is 1,500.

11. **A** If the temperature rises at a constant rate, then the average temperature will be the midpoint between 70 and 95, which is 82.5. At that temperature, the stand is bringing in more than 250 per hour. Since revenue also rises more quickly during the warmer part of the day (the slope of the curve is steeper on the graph), it follows that the stand will average more than 250 per hour. Choices (B), (C), and (D) are all factually incorrect.

12. **C** The three angles of a triangle total 180°. If two of the angles are 60° each (60° + 60° = 120°), the third angle must also be 60° (180° − 120° = 60°). If all three angles are equal, then all three sides must be equal. Since side AB is 4 inches, the other two sides, AC and BC, are also 4 inches each. $AC + BC = 8$.

13. **D** Use the Pythagorean Theorem to find side c: $a^2 + b^2 = c^2$. So $(5)^2 + (12)^2 = c^2$. $25 + 144 = c^2$. $169 = c^2$. $13 = c$. Since the new ramp is going to be twice as high off the ground, but the angles will be the same, each side of the triangle will be twice as long. The new ramp will be $13 \times 2 = 26$.

14.

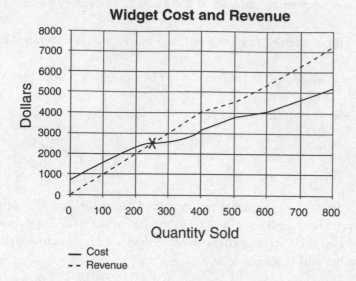

Widget Cost and Revenue

— Cost
-- Revenue

The widget factory will lose money wherever cost is greater than revenue. The minimum number of sales, therefore, that will not lose money is where the revenue line crosses the cost line at Quantity Sold = approximately 250.

15.

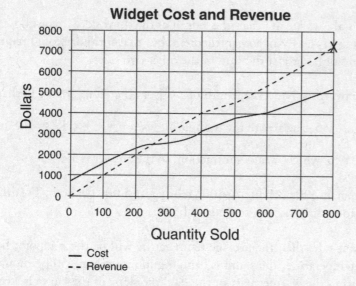

Widget Cost and Revenue

— Cost
-- Revenue

In order to make a profit of $2,000, the widget factory must sell enough widgets that Revenue dollars exceed cost by 2,000. On the chart, $2,000 represents two grid intervals' difference, so look at the chart for a place where the revenue line is two full intervals above the cost line. The profit reaches this level only at Quantity = 800.

16. **Menu 1: twice. Menu 2: four times**

The radius of the smaller circle is 2 and the radius of the larger circle is 4. Therefore, the diameter of the small circle is 4 and the diameter of the large circle is 8. The area of the smaller circle is $\pi r^2 = \pi \times 4 = 4\pi$. The area of the larger circle is $\pi r^2 = \pi \times 16 = 16\pi$, which is four times the area of the smaller circle.

17. **C** The point on the larger circle with the largest *y-value* is (2, 6). The point on the smaller circle with the lowest *y-value* is (2, 0). The distance between these points is 6.

18. **A** For a rate question, use the formula *Distance = rate multiplied by time*. The question has one extra step, however, because the rate and time are given in different units: hours vs. minutes. At the beginning of the problem, choose the unit that will be simpler to use. In this situation, divide 12 minutes by 60 minutes per hour to get 0.2 hours. Now *distance = rate $\times$ time* = $280 \times 0.2 = 56$.

19. **B** The weight of the empty can, *C*, is equal to the weight of the full can (*w*) minus the contents of the can (*f*). If we express the sentence as an equation, we get $C = w - f$.

20. **D** The smaller squares have sides that are exactly $\frac{1}{2}$ the side length of the larger square, so each side of the smaller square will be 2.5 inches. There are a total of 16 sides to the 4 small squares, so the total perimeter is $16 \times 2.5 = 40$ inches.

21. **D** $\frac{1}{5}x = 15$ so multiply both sides by 5 to get $x = 75$. Now calculate $\frac{4}{3} \times 75 = \frac{300}{3} = 100$.

22. **C** Be sure that you apply the fraction to the correct number. The question says $\frac{2}{9}$ of the total, not $\frac{2}{9}$ of the normal marbles. The easiest method is to plug in the answers, particularly if you notice that you need an answer choice divisible by 9 (the number of marbles must be an integer). Try out one of the middle answers: 108. $\frac{2}{9} \times 108 = 24$, the number of jumbo marbles. Since $84 + 24 = 108$, this is indeed the correct answer. If you solved with algebra, your equation should be $(\frac{2}{9} \times total) + 84 = total$.

23. **C** To calculate average, take the total salary over the 8 years divided by the number of years. Total salary will be ($45,200 \times 3$) + ($55,400 \times 5$) = $135,600 + $277,000 = $412,600. Now divide the total by 8 to get $51,575.

24. **B** First calculate the total cost, which is equal to the base cost plus the cost of the legionnaires. Since there are *x* legionnaires and each adds $5 to the price, the total cost = $400 + 5x$. However the question asks for the total cost per legionnaire. "Per" always means division, so you must divide by *x*, the number of legionnaires. $C = \dfrac{\$400 + 5x}{x}$.

25. **5.5** The perimeter is the sum of the three sides, so add up the three sides algebraically to get a formula for perimeter. $27 = 2x + (3x - 5) + (x - 1) = 6x - 6$. Now solve and $x = 5.5$.

26. **$A < C < B$**

   In any triangle, the smallest angle will also be opposite the smallest side and the largest angle will be opposite the largest side. Since $x = 5.5$ (calculated in the previous question), the three sides are 4.5, 11, and 11.5. Angle A is opposite 4.5, so angle A is the smallest. Angle B is opposite 11.5, so angle B is the largest.

27. **D** First calculate the total number of cows: $245 + 35 = 280$. Now set up a proportion for the ratio of feed to cows: 200lbs/35 cows. Write an equation with the proportion you are given on one side and the quantity you are looking for on the other, making sure to keep the pounds of feed in the numerator and the number of cows in the denominator: $\dfrac{200}{35} = \dfrac{x}{280}$. Cross multiply the fractions and solve for x. $200 \times 280 = 45x$ and $x = 1{,}600$.

28. **A** The actual fee will be greater than expected because of the extra 27 (i.e., $377 - 350$) people. Since the cost per person is $6, just multiply 27 by $6 to get $162.

29. **A** The formula for the midpoint is $\dfrac{x_1 + x_2}{2}, \dfrac{y_1 + y_2}{2}$. Plugging into the formula, we get

   $\left(\dfrac{5 + (-1)}{2}, \dfrac{(-4) + 2}{2} \right)$ which simplifies to $(2, -1)$.

30. **D** The equation of a line is written in form $y = mx + b$ where m is the slope and b is the y-intercept. First calculate the slope, using the formula $m = \dfrac{y_2 - y_1}{x_2 - x_1}$. So $m = \dfrac{2 - (-4)}{(-1) - 5} = -1$. The answer must be either (C) or (D). Plug in one of the given points into the equation $y = (-1)x + b$ in order to solve for b. So $-4 = (-1 \times 5) + b$ and $b = 1$. Note that you could also just plug both of the given points into each formula in order to find the only answer choices for which both points would work.

31. **Total = 15 × (2,800 + p) + (15 + z) × p**

   The total payroll will be the sum of the payroll for associates and the payroll for paralegals. Solve for each independently to figure out where to enter appropriate terms in the equation. Payroll for associates is equal to the number of associates multiplied by the average payroll for associates. The average pay for associates is $2,800 more than p, or $(2,800 + p)$. This must go within the parentheses in the first term of the equation. Therefore the first blank in the first term must be the number of associates = 15. The second term of the equation now must be the payroll for paralegals. The number of paralegals is $(15 + z)$ and the average pay per paralegal is p.

32. **C** Set up a proportion relating distance on the map to actual distance. We know that 0.4 miles on the map corresponds to 100 miles in actual distance, so $\dfrac{0.4 \text{ inches}}{100 \text{ miles}} = \dfrac{7.4 \text{ inches}}{y}$, where y is the real distance between the craters. Solve for y by cross multiplying: $(0.4)y = 100 \times 7.4$ and $y = 1{,}850$.

33. **% Increase of Grosbeaks < % Increase of Harriers < % Increase of Cardinals**

The three bird types that increased are Cardinals, Grosbeaks, and Harriers. To calculate percentage increase, take the difference between the two years divided by the original 2008 sightings figure. Cardinals % increase = $\frac{7}{24} \times 100 = 29.2\%$. Grosbeaks % increase = $\frac{4}{19} \times 100 = 21.1\%$. Harriers % increase = $\frac{7}{31} \times 100 = 22.6\%$.

34. B To calculate percentage increase, take the total increase in sightings divided by the original 2008 total sightings. 2008 sightings (adding the five types) is 142. The 2009 sightings figure is 153. So the increase in sightings is 11. % Increase = $\frac{11}{142} = 7.7\%$. The question asks you to round to the nearest integer, so the answer is 8%.

35.

Migration Sightings			
Bird Type	2008	2009	2010
Cardinal	24	31	**38**
Finch	40	37	**34**
Grosbeak	19	23	**27**
Harrier	31	38	**45**
Sparrow	28	24	**20**

This question asks you to find the change in sightings between 2008 and 2009, and to continue the pattern (an arithmetic sequence) for 2010. So, for example, Cardinals increased by 7 from 2008 to 2009. In 2010, therefore, Cardinals should increase 7 more to 38.

36. A Since Harold invests $24,000 at 3% interest, his interest earnings are $24,000 × .03 = $720. Maude invests $8,000 ($\frac{1}{3}$ of $24,000) at 8% interest, so her earnings are $8,000 × .08 = $640. The difference is $80.

37. D Plug in the answer choices to find the choice that does not fit the inequality. $2 \times 3^2 - 3 = 15$, and $15 - 3 = 12$. So $x = 3$ does not fit the inequality.

38. A Circumference = $2\pi r$. The length of each pizza slice, extending from edge to center is equivalent to the radius. So for the larger pizza, $27\pi = 2\pi r$ and $r = 13.5$ For the smaller wheel, $22\pi = 2\pi r$ and $r = 11$. The difference is 2.5.

39. 15 Divide the total number of attendees by the number of buses. 384 divided by 26 is 14.8, so the minimum number of buses required will be 15.

40. **B** The various expenses add up to 74% of revenue, which means that the profit must equal 26% (100 − 74) of revenue. So to calculate total revenue, the equation should be $7,384 = 26% of revenue = (0.26) × r. Solving, r = $28,400. Be careful, though, because the question does not ask for revenue, but instead asks for rent. So take 17% of revenue. $28,400 × (0.17) = $4,828.

41. **B** This is a quadratic equation, so first write it in the correct form: $x^2 - x - 12 = 0$. Factor this expression to get $(x − 4)(x + 3) = 0$ so $x = − 3$ or $x = 4$. The question asks for x^2 so the correct answer is 9. (16 would also have been a possible answer.)

42. **B** Since Faculty accounts for 37% of the endowment and Administration accounts for 24%, the difference between them is 13% of the endowment. Take 13% of the endowment: (0.13) × 1,200,000 = 156,000.

43. **28,000**

    The 2012 Other Expenses = (0.07) × 1,200,000 = $84,000. The 2013 Other Expenses will be (0.07) × 1,600,000 = $112,000. The difference is $28,000.

44. **11** First calculate the total number of players: $33 × 24 = 792$. When these players are divided into teams of 18 players each, that will mean that there are $\frac{792}{18} = 44$ teams. So 11 = (44 − 33) new teams will need to be formed.

45. **C** The correct answer must give an x-coordinate and y-coordinate that satisfy both equations. Either test each pair of coordinates in each equation, or solve algebraically by combining the two equations (substituting for y in the second equation) to get $-28x − 4 = 2x + 11$. Combine like terms: $-30x = 15$, so $x = -\frac{1}{2}$. Plugging this x value into either equation will give you $y = 10$.

46. **D** Write it out: Bell 1 rings every 2 hours. Beginning at 9 a.m. it will ring again at 11 a.m., 1 p.m., 3 p.m., 5 p.m., 7 p.m., and 9 p.m. Bell 2 will ring every 3 hours: 9 a.m., 12 p.m., 3 p.m., 6 p.m., and 9 p.m. Bell 3 rings every 4 hours: 9 a.m., 1 p.m., 5 p.m., and 9 p.m. So all 3 bells will ring again at 9 p.m.

SOCIAL STUDIES

1. **D** Read *all* the choices before you make up your mind. Although it is possible that the authors of the amendments were legal scholars, this isn't stated in the passage, so (A) doesn't seem likely. Nor is there any mention of the relationship between church and state, so you can safely eliminate (B). (Of course, in the United States, we have always kept church and state separated, but you didn't need to know that to start thinking this isn't the answer—it is enough to know it wasn't mentioned in the passage.) Choice (C) says that the writers of the amendments believed in government with ultimate authority—but that seems to go against the idea of granting citizens rights that can't be taken away by the government. Choice (D) basically restates what was in the passage: The writers didn't want to give the government too much power. The correct answer is (D).

2. **B** At first glance, *all* of these answer choices seem to be things people wouldn't like—but only one of them doesn't violate the Fourteenth Amendment: Choice (B) requires all citizens to pay taxes, regardless of their beliefs. Choices (A) and (C) deny equal protection under the law. Choice (D) denies due process of the law.

3. **D** Amelia Earhart made her historic flights in an earlier era when women were often expected to take a backseat to men. Choices (A), (B), and (C) raise issues that were not mentioned in the passage and seem irrelevant. The correct answer is (D).

4. This is a tricky question. You must read the statements carefully. Notice the graph measures only *union* employees, *not* total numbers of employees. Thus statements (b) and (d) are unsupported by the data. Statements (a), (c), and (e) are consistent with the data given.

5. **D** Always read the chart first; in this case, it shows changes in employment in a number of fields. Now, go through the answer choices. Was there an increase in agricultural jobs? Actually, no, there was a decline, so eliminate (A). Was there more growth in administrative support than in any other occupation? No, services had more growth, so eliminate (B). Was there more growth in administrative support than there was in services and technicians and support jobs combined? No, services *alone* had a bigger increase, so eliminate (C). Was there less growth in precision production than in professional specialties? Well, yes, as a matter of fact, there was! The correct answer is (D).

6. **C** Do not let the academic language of the prompt throw you off. While it may sound intimidating, GDP is just a measure of wealth. For this question, the definition does not even matter because it asks you to select the *opinion* from among the facts. Choices (A), (B), and (D) can be verified from the data in the graph. They do not express personal opinions. So long as the data from the graph is accurate, they cannot be disputed. Choice (C), however, expresses a political opinion, not a fact.

7. **A** President Adams believes "the whole continent of North America" is "destined by Divine Providence" to be part of one "Union." The belief that God ordained the expansion of the United States from the Atlantic Ocean to the Pacific Ocean is known as "Manifest Destiny," (A). Choice (C) is not quite right, since imperialism implies interfering in the politics of other nations. Choices (B) and (D) are irrelevant to the quote.

8. **C** The chart shows the life expectancy rates for men and women in different countries. This question wants to know which group will have the shortest life span. As you look at the chart, you'll notice that women live longer than men in all three countries—which eliminates (A) and (B). Whose life span is shorter: American men or Japanese men? The chart shows the correct answer is (C).

9. **C** Japan's life expectancy is just a bit higher than those of the other countries. Which of the answer choices accounts for that? Choices (A) and (B) don't supply a reason why Japanese people live longer. Choice (A) discusses Asian men—which could include men from many other Asian countries and doesn't address Japanese women. Choice (B) seems to be a reason that Americans should live longer. Choice (D) is in the right direction at least, but for the most part, natural disasters don't come along that often, and statistically don't change life expectancy much. Actually, there are more earthquakes in Japan than there are in the United States. The correct answer is (C) because it supplies a possible reason why people live longer in Japan: free health care.

10. **D** America is a great place, but (A) is unfortunately a little too optimistic. Choice (B) incorrectly says that immigrants do not expect to find jobs in the United States. The passage states that they come "in search of new opportunities." The passage makes clear that the United States fosters its reputation as a melting pot by putting up symbols of its openness such as the Statue of Liberty, so we can eliminate (C). The correct answer is (D), which restates what is said in the passage.

11. **A** The answer to this question can be found in the last sentence of the first paragraph: "new opportunities… and an environment free from political unrest and oppression." The correct answer is (A), which simply restates that sentence.

12. **D** Choice (A) can be found in paragraph 3. Choices (B) and (C) can be found in the last sentence of paragraph 1. Only (D) is not directly supported by the article.

13. **D** This advertisement shows an example of the bigotry shown to new immigrants back in the 1850s. The writer of the advertisement clearly doesn't want any new immigrants coming to the United States or holding office here. So which of the answer choices would this writer disagree with? The correct answer is (D), which proposes a law giving immigrants the right to vote—something the writer clearly would have hated. All the other answer choices were suggestions of ways to keep immigrants or their goods out of the country.

14. **C** "Suffrage" is the right to vote. According to the map, many women had full suffrage prior to 1920, so (A) is wrong. The Nineteenth Amendment gave all American women the universal right to vote, but "full economic and political equality" is too strong. Eliminate (B). According to the map, most Western States had given women full suffrage before 1920, so (C) is the most supported by the data. Alaska and Hawaii (neither of which became states until 1959) are not represented by the map, so (D) is unsupported.

15. **B** Both passages mention "liberty," so (A) is wrong. The preamble mentions "tranquility," while the Declaration mentions "happiness," so eliminate (C). Choice (D) is definitely mentioned in the Declaration. "Defense" is mentioned only in the Preamble and not in the Declaration, so (B) is the best answer.

16. **D** The graph shows that the least crisis-prone industry is oil refining, which is (D). You may have felt that in this day and age, oil refining is actually pretty crisis-prone. But on the GED® test, all we have to do is read the graph and write down what it says.

17. **C** This question requires you to pay attention to the information in the graph. The most densely populated continents are, in fact, Europe and Asia, (C). Two of the world's most populous nations, China and India, are found in Asia. They contain nearly 2.5 billion of the earth's 6.5 billion inhabitants between them.

18. **A** Population density is determined most importantly by climate and geography. Deserts, extreme arctic environments, and highly mountainous regions have few human inhabitants. Therefore (A) is correct.

19. **B** TAB 1 defines "manifest destiny" as the desire to "possess the whole of the continent" (i.e., Westward Expansion). TAB 2 tells us that Democrats supported Westward Expansion, while Whigs did not. Don't worry; you don't need to know anything about the presidents mentioned in the answers. Just stick to the facts. Since Democrats supported Westward Expansion, eliminate (A). Since Whigs opposed Westward Expansion, eliminate (C). Choice (D) is impossible, since, according to the map key, the Transcontinental Railroad was built around 1869, well after Pierce's presidency. That leaves (B). Polk was a Democrat, and thus supported the notion of manifest destiny.

20. **A** "Pure democracy" is a system in which the majority is not "held in restraint," so eliminate (C). In a monarchy, (B), a king or queen makes law; we do not have mention of that. Anarchy, (D), is the complete absence of government, so the best answer is (A).

21. **A** Choices (B), (C), and (D) all give opinions that paint a rosy picture of improvements in technology. Only (A) predicts a negative consequence: that new technology will enable companies to cut their workforce, throwing people into unemployment.

22. **B** "All counties" makes (A) too extreme to be true. Choice (C) is untrue, since Vermont has a low unemployment rate. Choice (D) is the opposite; lighter-shaded states have a lower rate of unemployment, thus a HIGHER rate of employment. Choice (B) is supported by TAB 1, since there are more dark portions in the Northeast than in the Southeast.

23. **D** TAB 2 shows that *Plessy vs. Ferguson* considered the notion of "enforced separation of the two races" as "a badge of inferiority" as a fallacy (a false idea). TAB 3 shows that *Brown vs. Board of Education* ruled that "separate but equal has no place," thus directly going against the *Plessy vs. Ferguson* ruling. *Plessy vs. Ferguson* was NOT upholding civil rights, so eliminate (B). *Brown vs. Board of Education* did NOT uphold "separate but equal," (C); it struck it down, (D). Choice (A) is wrong because it goes beyond what is directly supported by the sources. Choice (D) is the correct answer.

24. **D** The cotton gin "caused the expansion of the cotton industry in the American South," (D), by making the production of cotton much more efficient. None of the other answers address this impact.

25. **D** Each of the first three answer choices says bad things about the U.S. Constitution, which does not make any of them likely contenders to be correct. So the correct answer must be (D), which says that our interpretations of the Constitution have changed over time. This is illustrated by the example of Congress finally changing its mind about a peacetime draft.

26. **B** This graph shows some statistics about people called to jury duty, broken down by household income. Choice (A) is contradicted by the graph because a greater percentage of higher-income people are called than lower-income people. Choice (C) is contradicted by the graph because only 15 percent of the lower-income people called actually served on juries, a lower percentage than the higher-income people called. Choice (D) is not in any way supported by the passage.

27. **A** According to the passage, the problem with nuclear power is where to store dangerous by-products. If there was a better way to store these by-products, there might be an increased use of nuclear power. That is exactly what (A) proposes. The other answer choices all propose options that would increase use in non-nuclear sources of energy.

28. **D** All three forms of energy production involve turbines. Erosion is a problem only with hydroelectric power. Waste, smoke, and smog are produced only with fossil fuels and nuclear power.

29. **B** Choices (C) and (D) would make no sense, because a community with large coal or oil reserves would presumably be less likely to use hydroelectric power. A desert community might want to use hydroelectric power, but would have little chance to use one without a source of water. Choice (B) is the best answer.

30. **A** Studying the cartoon, we notice that the man carrying the "big stick" is walking through the area near the Caribbean Sea. The Spanish controlled these territories, so (A) is the most logical choice. Kudos to you if you recognized the face of Theodore Roosevelt and his famous quote: "Speak softly and carry a big stick."

31. **D** Muir was clearly a conservationist. He would have hated (A) and (B) because they are all rationalizations for destroying the environment. Choice (C) is vague and thus not a great answer: "Human benefit" could mean almost anything. The correct answer is (D).

32. **D** The global map shows four points. From west to east, the four points are D, B, A, and C. The correct answer is (D).

33. **C** The only city not located near the Atlantic Ocean or the Gulf of Mexico is Chicago, (C).

34. Studying Lincoln's quote, we notice that he proclaimed "all persons discouraging volunteer enlistments, resisting militia drafts, or guilty of any disloyal practice, affording aid and comfort to Rebels against the authority of United States, shall be subject to martial law and liable to trial and punishment by Courts Martial." This is consistent only with statement (c). All other statements are unsupported by the information provided.

35. **B** Nixon stated, "Therefore, I shall resign the Presidency effective at noon tomorrow." This matches (B), not (D). The passage says nothing about impeachment (A). Choice (C) is tempting, but we don't know if Nixon actually appointed Ford.

SCIENCE

1. **A** According to the table, the normal total cholesterol level range is between 125 and 200 mg/dl. Choice (A) is correct because a total cholesterol level of 150 fits into this normal range.

2. **B** The graph shows a straight line moving up and to the right. Such a line shows a constant increase in both cardiac output and blood pressure. Therefore, as cardiac output increases, blood pressure also increases. Choice (B) is thus the credited answer.

3. **C** The passage defines a carnivore as an animal that eats other animals. Hawks are carnivores because they eat both snakes and mice, and snakes are carnivores because they eat mice. Since insects eat both plants and other insects, they are omnivores, rather than carnivores, so (D) is incorrect.

4. **B** The question states that hawks consume rabbits, so an accurate food web should have an arrow pointing from rabbits to hawks. Choices (A) and (D) reverse the direction of this arrow, making it appear as though rabbits eat hawks, so you can eliminate both of these choices. The question also indicates that rabbits are herbivores, meaning that they eat only plants. However, (C) includes an arrow from birds to rabbits, making it appear as though rabbits eat birds. Therefore, (C) is incorrect. Choice (B) correctly includes an arrow from grass and plants to rabbits, showing that rabbits eat grasses and plants, and also includes an arrow from rabbits to hawks, showing that hawks eat rabbits. Thus, (B) is the correct answer.

5. Based on the information provided, a substance is basic when its pH is above 7. Of the four substances listed, 1 has a pH above 7, so $\frac{1}{4}$, or 25%, of the substances are basic.

6. **D** The theory does not discuss the differences between the number of crystals that round geodes contain and the number of crystals that geodes of other shapes contain, so (A) is incorrect. The theory states that round geodes form when lava bubbles as it cools after a volcanic eruption. Therefore, (B) actually weakens the theory and is not the credited answer. The theory does not discuss the speed with which water and minerals cool inside geodes, so (C) is incorrect. Choice (D) strengthens the theory by providing a link between geodes and the lava that accompanies a volcanic eruption, so (D) is correct.

7.   Answers may vary but should discuss the fact that the scientist should test her idea using four groups of plants: one that receives only compost, another that receives only nitrogen-rich fertilizer, another that receives both, and a control group that receives neither. She should regularly measure and record the growth rates over a period of several days or weeks, and track the progress of each group. If, at the end of the study period, the group that receives both the compost and the nitrogen-rich fertilizer has the tallest and most abundant plants, then the scientist's hypothesis is correct.

8. **C** The passage states that a flower with one yellow gene and one red gene will have orange flowers. In the Punnett Square, all of the offspring have one red gene and one yellow gene, so all of the offspring will have orange flowers. The correct answer is therefore (C).

9. **B** Upward arrows show the water being delivered to clouds, and the upward arrows are labeled evaporation and transpiration, so (B) is correct. Precipitation is represented by a downward arrow and shows water leaving the clouds, so (D) is not the credited answer.

10. **A** On the left, the $5O_2$ term represents oxygen, so the C_3H_8 must represent propane. On the right, the $3CO_2$ represents carbon dioxide, and the $4H_2O$ term represents water. Since the resulting substance is composed of both carbon dioxide and water, only (A) describes the reaction. Choice (B) mentions only water, so (B) is incorrect. The oxygen alone is not responsible for the water, so (C) is incorrect. Finally, the oxygen alone does not become carbon dioxide, so (D) is not the credited answer.

11. **55** Dissolved gases, nutrients, and water are components that are not blood. Add up the percentages of each of these to find the percent of blood that is not composed of cells: 1% + 3% + 51% = 55%.

12. **B** Initially the graph shows a curve going up and to the right, which means that the rate of product formation initially increased. Later, however, the graph shows the curve leveling off, which means that the rate of product formation became constant. Therefore, (B) is the correct answer. Choice (A) is incorrect because, while the rate of product formation initially increased, it eventually leveled off. Choice (C) is incorrect because the rate of product formation never decreased. Finally, (D) is incorrect because the rate of product formation was constant only at the very end.

13. **A** The diagram shows an arrow labeled *photosynthesis* that points from CO_2 in the atmosphere to plants, showing that plants absorb CO_2 from the atmosphere through photosynthesis. Another arrow labeled *food* points from plants to animals, showing that plants transfer CO_2 to animals through food. Next, an arrow labeled *waste products* points from animals to soil, showing that animals transfer CO_2 to the soil through waste products. This is the process that (A) outlines, so (A) is the correct answer. The arrow labeled *respiration* points from animals to CO_2 in the atmosphere, showing that animals release CO_2 into the atmosphere. Choice (B) reverses this relationship, suggesting that animals instead absorb CO_2 from the atmosphere. Therefore, (B) is incorrect. The arrow labeled *respiration* points from plants to CO_2 in the atmosphere, showing that plants release CO_2 into the atmosphere through respiration. Since (C) reverses this relationship by suggesting that animals absorb CO_2 through respiration, you can eliminate (C). The arrow labeled *root respiration* points from plants to the soil, showing that plants release CO_2 into the soil through root respiration. Choice (D) reverses this relationship by suggesting that plants absorb CO_2 through root respiration, so (D) is not the credited answer.

14. **B** Based on the information in the graph, this species of amoebas is more likely to thrive if cultured alone than if cultured in a mixed culture, since a population of amoebas cultured alone reaches much higher values than the population of the amoebas grown in a mixed culture. Therefore, you can eliminate (A). Choice (B) accurately describes the situation shown in the graph, and is the correct answer. Since the

population of amoebas grown alone seems to remain approximately constant after the population reaches 500, there is no evidence to support (C). The population of amoebas cultured in a mixed culture does dip slightly once it reaches approximately 175, but the graph does not tend toward the y-axis afterward, so there is no evidence to support (D).

15. **D** Since r, which represents the distance between the two objects, is in the denominator of the fraction, making r larger will make the fraction as a whole smaller. Therefore, you can eliminate both (A) and (B). Decreasing the value of M will make the fraction as a whole smaller, so (C) is incorrect. Increasing the value of M will make the fraction as a whole larger, since M is in the numerator, and decreasing the value of r will make the fraction as a whole larger, since r is in the denominator. Thus, (D) is the credited answer.

16. **9.5** To find the median of a list of numbers, write out the list of numbers and then look for the number in the middle of the list. In this case, the list is 2, 2, 4, 6, 8, 11, 13, 14, 15, 25. There are an even number of numbers, so the numbers 8 and 11 both fall in the middle of the list. Take the average of the two numbers to find the median: $8 + 11 = 19$, and $\frac{19}{2} = 9.5$ Therefore, the median is 9.5.

17. **A** Between March and April, the average rainfall increased from 50 mm to 100 mm, making the total increase between the two months equal to 50 mm. The average rainfall per month actually decreased between April and May and between May and June, so eliminate (B) and (C). The average rainfall per month remained the same between June and July, so you can eliminate (D).

18. **A** The mode of a list of numbers is the number that appears most frequently. Since both June and July experienced 40 mm of rainfall, and no two other months experienced the same rainfall as each other, the mode of the rainfall shown in the charts is 40, and the correct answer is (A).

19. **Oxygen (c), nitrogen (b), carbon (a).** According to the information presented, the atomic number of an element is the number of protons in one atom of that element, and the atomic weight is equal to the sum of the number of protons and the number of neutrons. The sum of the number of protons and the number of neutrons in oxygen is 16, so the atomic weight of oxygen is 16. Nitrogen has 7 protons, so the atomic number of nitrogen is 7. Finally, the sum of the number of protons and the number of neutrons in carbon is 12, so carbon has an atomic weight of 12.

20. **B** The passage indicates that the atomic number of an element is determined by the number of protons, not the number of electrons, in an element, so decreasing the number of electrons in an element would not change that element's atomic number. Eliminate (A). If fluorine has an atomic number of 9, then based on the information in the passage, it must have 8 protons. Since oxygen has 8 protons, then fluorine must have more protons than does oxygen, and (B) is the credited answer. If boron has an atomic weight of 10, then the sum of the number of protons and the number of electrons in boron is 10. If boron has an atomic number of 5, then it has 5 protons. Therefore, if boron has an atomic weight of 10, then it must have 5 neutrons. Carbon has 6 neutrons, so the statement in (C) is false. Finally, the passage indicates that the atomic weight of an element is determined by the sum of the number of protons and the number of electrons in an element, not by the number of electrons. Therefore, changing the number of electrons in oxygen would not change the atomic weight of oxygen. Eliminate (D).

21. **D** According to the information in the chart, a strong earthquake can cause damage in areas up to 100 miles distant from the epicenter of the quake. Since the house was located more than 100 miles from the

epicenter, the earthquake in question must have been more powerful than a strong earthquake. Therefore, you can eliminate (A), (B), and (C). The correct answer is (D).

22. **D** According to the information in the passage, an earthquake that measures 3.0 on the Richter scale has a shaking amplitude that is 100 times that of an earthquake that measures 2.0 on the Richter scale. Therefore, for every 1 point increase on the Richter scale, the shaking amplitude increases by 100. Thus, an earthquake that measures 5.0 on the Richter scale must have a shaking amplitude that is 100 times that of an earthquake with a shaking amplitude of 4.0, and an earthquake that measures 6.0 on the Richter scale must have a shaking amplitude that is 100 times that of the 5.0 earthquake. Since you must twice multiply the shaking amplitude of the 4.0 earthquake by 100 to find the shaking amplitude of the 6.0 earthquake, the ratio of the shaking amplitude of the 4.0 earthquake to the shaking amplitude of the 6.0 earthquake will be 1:100 × 100, or 1:10,000. The correct answer is therefore (D).

23. **C** According to the information given, autotrophs do not gain their nutrition from other creatures. Since elephant seals consume squids, elephant seals are not autotrophs, so you can eliminate (A). Primary consumers eat only autotrophs, so elephant seals are also not primary consumers. The passage indicates that primary consumers eat primary consumers, which in turn eat autotrophs. Since protists and algae are autotrophs, and squid eat both protists and algae, squid are primary consumers. Since elephant seals eat squid, elephant seals are therefore secondary consumers, and the correct answer is (C). Apex predators have no predators of their own. However, since killer whales eat elephant seals, elephant seals are not apex predators, and (D) is incorrect.

24. **C** According to the food web, cod eat only algae, and algae are autotrophs, and therefore do not feed on krill. Thus, the cod population would be unlikely to be affected were the population of krill depleted. Eliminate (A). Squid do not eat krill, and feed only on protists and algae, both of which are autotrophs and therefore do not eat krill. Thus, the squid population would be unlikely to be affected were the population of krill depleted, so (B) is incorrect. Leopard seals feed on cod and on penguins. Cod feed only on algae, but penguins feed on both algae and krill. Therefore, were the krill population depleted, the penguin population would likely also be affected, which in turn would mean that the leopard seal population would likely be affected. The correct answer is therefore (C). Elephant seals feed on squid, which feed on algae and protists, neither of which consume krill. Since the elephant seal food chain would not be disrupted were the population of krill depleted, elephant seals would be unlikely to be affected were the krill population depleted. Choice (D) is thus not the credited answer.

25. **1. Heat detected (c). 2. Spinal interneurons signaled (d). 3. Motor neurons excited (a). 4. Muscle cells signaled (e). 5. Muscle cells contract (b).** According to the passage, the first thing that happens when a person touches a dangerously hot object is that *sensory detectors detect dangerous heat levels*. Thus, the first box should contain *Heat detected*. Next, the passage indicates that sensory receptors *send signals... to spinal interneurons in the spinal cord*. Thus, the second box should contain *Spinal interneurons signaled*. The passage then says that *spinal interneurons excite the motor neurons that control arm muscles*. Therefore, the fourth box should contain *Motor neurons excited*. Finally, the passage says that *the muscle cells then contract*, so the fourth box should contain *Muscles contract*.

26. Answers may vary but should discuss the fact that the scientists should use a control group of individuals who are not exposed to the compound, and compare the results from these people to the results from the group that is exposed to the chemical. Additionally, the volunteers should be individuals who do not suffer from rashes due to allergies or similar rash-causing conditions. Finally, the two groups should experience similar conditions—that is, they should eat similar foods and be in similar environments—for the duration of the study.

27. **C** According to the information in the passage, Force = mass × acceleration. Therefore, if an aircraft has a mass of 1,800 kilograms, and has engines that provide a thrust force of 90,000 Newtons, then the 90,000 Newtons = 1,800 kilograms × acceleration. Divide both sides by 1,800 to find that 90,000 Newtons/1,800 kilograms = 50 meters/second^2. The passage indicates that the second aircraft experiences the same acceleration, so you know that Force = 1,500 kilograms × 50 meters/second^2 = 75,000 Newtons. Therefore, the correct answer is (C).

28. **A** According to the passage, scientists use index fossils to determine the time period at which other species may have existed. Therefore, the correct answer must include information about when a species existed. Choice (A) correctly describes this situation, since according to this choice, scientists are able to fix the era of *Mesolenellus hyperborea* because they find index fossils nearby. The passage does not indicate that two species that existed at the same time must have come from a similar habitat, so (B) is incorrect. Choice (C) does not include any mention of an index fossil, so (C) is also not the credited answer. Finally, (D) includes a discussion of habitat, rather than of time, so (D) is also incorrect.

29. **D** As pressure increases, the curve of the graph decreases quickly at first and then levels off slightly. If pressure and volume were directly proportional, then volume would increase as pressure increased. Since the graph shows the opposite to be true, you can eliminate (A). Choice (B) also suggests that volume increases as pressure increases, so (B) is also incorrect. As pressure rises from 1 atmosphere to 2 atmospheres, volume decreases from 8 liters to 3 liters, rather than 8 liters to 2 liters, so (C) is not the credited answer. When pressure is at 4 atmospheres, volume is at approximately 1 liter and is still decreasing. Therefore, if the trend shown in the graph continues, then when pressure reaches 5 atmospheres, volume should be near $\frac{1}{2}$ liter. Thus, (D) is the correct answer.

30. **Less, weight.** According to the information in the passage, mass is the amount of matter that an object contains, and weight is the mass of an object multiplied by the acceleration that the object feels due to gravity. Since the passage indicates that the acceleration that an object feels due to gravity is different on the moon than on the earth, but does not indicate that an object on the moon is actually composed of less matter on the moon than it would be on the earth, it is a person's weight, not his or her mass that changes. Additionally, the passage states that the acceleration due to gravity is less on the moon than it is on the earth, so a person's weight would be less on the moon than on the earth. Thus, the correct answer choices are *less* and *weight*.

31. **B** According to the information in the passage, creatures have analogous structures when they possess features that may appear different, but perform the same function. Since echolocation and sight are not the same function—they result from different senses—(A) is incorrect. Choice (B) gives an example of features that perform the same function—both types of wings provide flight capabilities—but that appear different, since bat wings are composed of membrane, while bird wings are not. Therefore, the correct answer is (B). Since (D) does not discuss physical features of either birds or bats, it is incorrect.

32. **C** The information given indicates that polyuria is excessive urine production, so those who suffer from the condition need to lower their urine production. Since the chart indicates that drinking caffeinated diet sodas raises, rather than lowers urine production, (A) is incorrect. The chart also indicates that during the week in which the subjects drank slightly salty water, their urine production was lower, so nothing in the chart indicates that drinking slightly salty water increases the risk of polyuria, so (B) is incorrect. The chart shows that drinking caffeinated diet sodas increases urine production, so those suffering from polyuria would want to avoid consuming too many caffeinated diet sodas. Therefore, the correct answer

is (C). Finally, nothing in the chart or in the passage suggests that those suffering from polyuria should vary the liquids that they consume, so you can eliminate (D).

33. **A** If the volunteers had eaten only watermelon one week, but had eaten only processed foods high in salt the second week, then the differences in urine production may have been due to changes in food diet, rather than changes in liquid diet. Therefore, the volunteers needed to follow the same diet throughout the study, and (A) is correct. The information in the passage indicates that all volunteers consumed the same amount of liquid per day, regardless of what they craved, so (B) is incorrect. The passage does not indicate whether the diet that the volunteers followed was nutritious, so (C) is incorrect. The information in the passage also states that the chart displays the average daily urine output for each volunteer. This suggests that the volunteers did not all produce the same amount of urine per day, so (D) is not the credited answer.

34. **D** According to the passage, cabbage juice turns blue when combined with a basic substance. The passage also indicates that basic substances have a pH above 7. Of the liquids in the chart, only ammonia has a pH above 7, so the correct answer is (D).

35. **C** According to the passage, igneous rocks either form below ground from magma or above ground from volcano lava. Metamorphic, rather than igneous, rock forms when rock undergoes profound chemical changes, so (A) is incorrect. Igneous rocks can form underground, but the passage does not discuss whether they can form underwater. Instead, the passage mentions that sedimentary rock can form underwater. Therefore, (B) is incorrect. Choice (C) indicates that the rock was found near a volcano, and since the passage indicates that igneous rocks can form from volcano lava, (C) supports the student's hypothesis, and is the correct answer. The passage indicates that sedimentary rock, rather than igneous rock forms from minerals, so (D) is also incorrect.

Cracking the GED® Test, 2019 Edition
Practice Test 1

The **Princeton Review**®

© 2018 by TPR Education IP Holdings, LLC.

YOUR NAME: _____
(Print)   Last   First   M.I.

SIGNATURE: _____   DATE: ___ / ___ / ___

HOME ADDRESS: _____
(Print)   Number and Street

_____
City   State   Zip Code

PHONE NO.: _____
(Print)

DATE OF BIRTH: ___ / ___ / ___
(Print)   Month / Day / Year

Section I — Reasoning Through Language Arts

1. Ⓐ Ⓑ Ⓒ Ⓓ
2. Ⓐ Ⓑ Ⓒ Ⓓ
3. Ⓐ Ⓑ Ⓒ Ⓓ
4. Ⓐ Ⓑ Ⓒ Ⓓ
5. Ⓐ Ⓑ Ⓒ Ⓓ
6. ☐ → ☐ → ☐ → ☐
7. _____   _____
   _____
8. Ⓐ Ⓑ Ⓒ Ⓓ
9. ┌────────────────────┐
   │   │
   └────────────────────┘
10. Ⓐ Ⓑ Ⓒ Ⓓ
11. Ⓐ Ⓑ Ⓒ Ⓓ
12. Ⓐ Ⓑ Ⓒ Ⓓ
13. Ⓐ Ⓑ Ⓒ Ⓓ
14. Ⓐ Ⓑ Ⓒ Ⓓ
15. Ⓐ Ⓑ Ⓒ Ⓓ
16. Ⓐ Ⓑ Ⓒ Ⓓ

Section I — Reasoning Through Language Arts

17. For each of the following four menus circle the option that correctly completes the sentence.

> neighborhood, just as I do.
> neighborhood. Just as I do.
> neighborhood just as I do too.
> neighborhood; you just as much as I do.

> The alarmingly increased burglary incidents, via news reports and social media posts, you must be aware of by now,
>
> By now, via news reports and social media posts, you must be aware of the alarming increase in burglary incidents
>
> Via news reports and social media posts you must be aware of by now, the alarming increase in burglary incidents
>
> The alarming increase in burglary incidents you must be aware of by now, via news reports and social media posts

> concerning our community, as we all do
>
> as we all were concerned about our community,
>
> as we are all concerned about our community,
>
> having concern about our community, as were we all,

> them
> it
> that
> one

Section II — Reasoning Through Language Arts

Write your Extended Response essay on a separate sheet of paper.

Section III — Reasoning Through Language Arts

18. Ⓐ Ⓑ Ⓒ Ⓓ
19. Ⓐ Ⓑ Ⓒ Ⓓ
20. Ⓐ Ⓑ Ⓒ Ⓓ
21. Ⓐ Ⓑ Ⓒ Ⓓ
22. Ⓐ Ⓑ Ⓒ Ⓓ
23. Ⓐ Ⓑ Ⓒ Ⓓ
24. Ⓐ Ⓑ Ⓒ Ⓓ
25. Ⓐ Ⓑ Ⓒ Ⓓ
26. ┌────────────────────┐
    │   │
    └────────────────────┘
27. Ⓐ Ⓑ Ⓒ Ⓓ
28. Ⓐ Ⓑ Ⓒ Ⓓ
29. Ⓐ Ⓑ Ⓒ Ⓓ
30. Ⓐ Ⓑ Ⓒ Ⓓ
31. Ⓐ Ⓑ Ⓒ Ⓓ
32. Ⓐ Ⓑ Ⓒ Ⓓ
33. Ⓐ Ⓑ Ⓒ Ⓓ
34. Ⓐ Ⓑ Ⓒ Ⓓ
35. Ⓐ Ⓑ Ⓒ Ⓓ
36. Ⓐ Ⓑ Ⓒ Ⓓ
37. Ⓐ Ⓑ Ⓒ Ⓓ
38. Ⓐ Ⓑ Ⓒ Ⓓ
39. Ⓐ Ⓑ Ⓒ Ⓓ
40. ┌──────────┬──────────┐
    │   │   │
    └──────────┴──────────┘

Section III Continued

41. Ⓐ Ⓑ Ⓒ Ⓓ
42. Ⓐ Ⓑ Ⓒ Ⓓ
43. Ⓐ Ⓑ Ⓒ Ⓓ
44. Ⓐ Ⓑ Ⓒ Ⓓ
45. Ⓐ Ⓑ Ⓒ Ⓓ
46. Ⓐ Ⓑ Ⓒ Ⓓ
47. _____

_____

48. Ⓐ Ⓑ Ⓒ Ⓓ
49. Ⓐ Ⓑ Ⓒ Ⓓ

50. For each of the following four menus circle the option that correctly completes the sentence.

During that period, it is with great pleasure that I see him developing
During that period, I had the great pleasure of seeing him develop
Seeing him develop during that period, I had great pleasure
As I saw him during that period, with great pleasure, he was developing

quickly and effectively, during
quickly, effectively, and during.
quickly and effectively. During
quick and effectively. During

worker, able to give guidance and step
worker. Just as able to give guidance and step
worker, just as able to give guidance and stepping
worker, just as able to give guidance as to step

Even a year after his resignation, still, he is remembered here fondly.
A year after his resignation, even he is still remembered fondly here.
He is remembered here still fondly, even a year after his resignation.
He is still remembered fondly here, even a year after his resignation.

Part I — Mathematical Reasoning

1. Ⓐ Ⓑ Ⓒ Ⓓ
2. Ⓐ Ⓑ Ⓒ Ⓓ
3. Ⓐ Ⓑ Ⓒ Ⓓ
4. Ⓐ Ⓑ Ⓒ Ⓓ
5. _____

Part II — Mathematical Reasoning

6. Ⓐ Ⓑ Ⓒ Ⓓ
7. Ⓐ Ⓑ Ⓒ Ⓓ

Questions 8 and 9

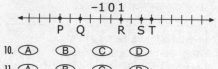

10. Ⓐ Ⓑ Ⓒ Ⓓ
11. Ⓐ Ⓑ Ⓒ Ⓓ
12. Ⓐ Ⓑ Ⓒ Ⓓ
13. Ⓐ Ⓑ Ⓒ Ⓓ
14. _____
15. _____ _____
16. _____
17. Ⓐ Ⓑ Ⓒ Ⓓ

18.

19. Ⓐ Ⓑ Ⓒ Ⓓ
20. Ⓐ Ⓑ Ⓒ Ⓓ
21. Ⓐ Ⓑ Ⓒ Ⓓ
22. Ⓐ Ⓑ Ⓒ Ⓓ
23. _____

Action-Adventure _____ Drama

24. Ⓐ Ⓑ Ⓒ Ⓓ
25. Ⓐ Ⓑ Ⓒ Ⓓ
26. _____
27. Ⓐ Ⓑ Ⓒ Ⓓ
28. Ⓐ Ⓑ Ⓒ Ⓓ

Part II Continued

29.

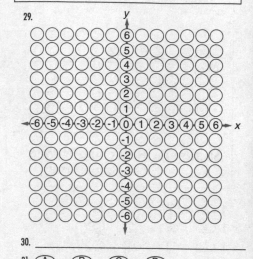

30. _____
31. Ⓐ Ⓑ Ⓒ Ⓓ
32. Ⓐ Ⓑ Ⓒ Ⓓ
33. Ⓐ Ⓑ Ⓒ Ⓓ
34. Ⓐ Ⓑ Ⓒ Ⓓ
35. Ⓐ Ⓑ Ⓒ Ⓓ
36. _____
37. Ⓐ Ⓑ Ⓒ Ⓓ
38. _____
39. Ⓐ Ⓑ Ⓒ Ⓓ
40. _____

Questions 41 and 42

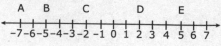

43.

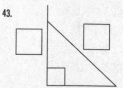

44. _____
45. Ⓐ Ⓑ Ⓒ Ⓓ
46. Ⓐ Ⓑ Ⓒ Ⓓ

Social Studies

1. Ⓐ Ⓑ Ⓒ Ⓓ
2. Ⓐ Ⓑ Ⓒ Ⓓ
3. Ⓐ Ⓑ Ⓒ Ⓓ
4. Ⓐ Ⓑ Ⓒ Ⓓ
5. Ⓐ Ⓑ Ⓒ Ⓓ
6. Ⓐ Ⓑ Ⓒ Ⓓ
7. Ⓐ Ⓑ Ⓒ Ⓓ
8. Ⓐ Ⓑ Ⓒ Ⓓ
9. Ⓐ Ⓑ Ⓒ Ⓓ
10. Ⓐ Ⓑ Ⓒ Ⓓ
11. Ⓐ Ⓑ Ⓒ Ⓓ
12. Ⓐ Ⓑ Ⓒ Ⓓ
13. Ⓐ Ⓑ Ⓒ Ⓓ
14. Ⓐ Ⓑ Ⓒ Ⓓ
15. Ⓐ Ⓑ Ⓒ Ⓓ
16. Ⓐ Ⓑ Ⓒ Ⓓ
17. Ⓐ Ⓑ Ⓒ Ⓓ
18. Ⓐ Ⓑ Ⓒ Ⓓ
19. Ⓐ Ⓑ Ⓒ Ⓓ
20. Ⓐ Ⓑ Ⓒ Ⓓ
21. Ⓐ Ⓑ Ⓒ Ⓓ
22. Ⓐ Ⓑ Ⓒ Ⓓ
23. Ⓐ Ⓑ Ⓒ Ⓓ
24. Ⓐ Ⓑ Ⓒ Ⓓ
25. Ⓐ Ⓑ Ⓒ Ⓓ
26. Ⓐ Ⓑ Ⓒ Ⓓ
27. Ⓐ Ⓑ Ⓒ Ⓓ
28. Ⓐ Ⓑ Ⓒ Ⓓ
29. Ⓐ Ⓑ Ⓒ Ⓓ
30. _____
31. Ⓐ Ⓑ Ⓒ Ⓓ
32. Ⓐ Ⓑ Ⓒ Ⓓ
33. Ⓐ Ⓑ Ⓒ Ⓓ
34. Ⓐ Ⓑ Ⓒ Ⓓ
35. Ⓐ Ⓑ Ⓒ Ⓓ

Science

1. Ⓐ Ⓑ Ⓒ Ⓓ
2. Ⓐ Ⓑ Ⓒ Ⓓ
3. _____
4. Ⓐ Ⓑ Ⓒ Ⓓ
5.

The type of coal most likely found closest to the surface of the earth:	The type of coal that contains the greatest amount of carbon per kilogram:

6. Ⓐ Ⓑ Ⓒ Ⓓ
7. Ⓐ Ⓑ Ⓒ Ⓓ
8. Ⓐ Ⓑ Ⓒ Ⓓ
9. Ⓐ Ⓑ Ⓒ Ⓓ
10.

The oldest rock layer:	The newest rock layer:

11. Ⓐ Ⓑ Ⓒ Ⓓ
12. Write your short-answer response on a separate sheet of paper.
13. Ⓐ Ⓑ Ⓒ Ⓓ
14. Write your short-answer response on a separate sheet of paper.
15. Write your answers in the blanks below:
   _____ _____
16. _____
17. Ⓐ Ⓑ Ⓒ Ⓓ
18. Ⓐ Ⓑ Ⓒ Ⓓ
19. Ⓐ Ⓑ Ⓒ Ⓓ
20. Ⓐ Ⓑ Ⓒ Ⓓ
21. Ⓐ Ⓑ Ⓒ Ⓓ

Science

22. **Waves That Foretell Tidal Waves**

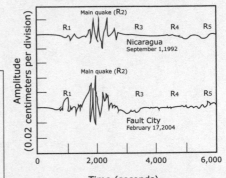

23. A Ⓑ Ⓒ Ⓓ
24. Ⓐ Ⓑ Ⓒ Ⓓ
25. Ⓐ Ⓑ Ⓒ Ⓓ
26. Ⓐ Ⓑ Ⓒ Ⓓ
27. Ⓐ Ⓑ Ⓒ Ⓓ
28. Ⓐ Ⓑ Ⓒ Ⓓ
29. Ⓐ Ⓑ Ⓒ Ⓓ
30. Ⓐ Ⓑ Ⓒ Ⓓ
31. Ⓐ Ⓑ Ⓒ Ⓓ
32. Ⓐ Ⓑ Ⓒ Ⓓ
33. Ⓐ Ⓑ Ⓒ Ⓓ

34. **Heat and Temperature of Water**

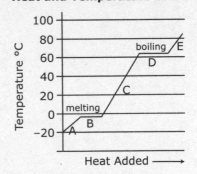

35. Ⓐ Ⓑ Ⓒ Ⓓ

Cracking the GED® Test, 2019 Edition
Practice Test 2

YOUR NAME: _____
(Print)   Last   First   M.I.

SIGNATURE: _____   DATE: ___/___/___

HOME ADDRESS: _____
(Print)   Number and Street

_____
City   State   Zip Code

PHONE NO.: _____
(Print)

DATE OF BIRTH: ___/___/___
(Print)   Month / Day / Year

Section I — Reasoning Through Language Arts

1. Ⓐ Ⓑ Ⓒ Ⓓ
2. Ⓐ Ⓑ Ⓒ Ⓓ
3. Ⓐ Ⓑ Ⓒ Ⓓ
4. Ⓐ Ⓑ Ⓒ Ⓓ
5. Ⓐ Ⓑ Ⓒ Ⓓ
6. Ⓐ Ⓑ Ⓒ Ⓓ
7. ☐ → ☐ → ☐ → ☐
8. Ⓐ Ⓑ Ⓒ Ⓓ

9.
Claim	Evidence	Evidence
The need for concentrating all power into a commission is evident.		
When one branch of the government dominates, checks and balances between the departments are lost.		

10. Ⓐ Ⓑ Ⓒ Ⓓ
11. Ⓐ Ⓑ Ⓒ Ⓓ
12. Ⓐ Ⓑ Ⓒ Ⓓ
13. Ⓐ Ⓑ Ⓒ Ⓓ
14. Ⓐ Ⓑ Ⓒ Ⓓ
15. Ⓐ Ⓑ Ⓒ Ⓓ
16. Ⓐ Ⓑ Ⓒ Ⓓ

Section I — Continued

17. For each of the following four menus circle the option that correctly completes the sentence.

---
are known nationwide, not only for their business success but also for

is known nationwide, not only for their business success but also for

is known nationwide, not only for its business success but also for

are known nationwide, not only for business success, but also for

---
to maintain a positive online reputation, for over 5 years

to maintain a positive online reputation for over 5 years

to maintain a positive online reputation. For over 5 years

to maintain for over 5 years a positive online reputation.

---
profiles, maintain a watch on major search engines for traffic to your site,

profiles, maintain a watch on major search engines for traffic to your site, and

profiles, maintaining a watch on major search engines for traffic to your site,

profiles, major search engines are maintained on watch for traffic to your site, and

---
it
they
to
we

Section II — Reasoning Through Language Arts

Write your Extended Response essay on a separate sheet of paper.

Section III — Reasoning Through Language Arts

18. Ⓐ Ⓑ Ⓒ Ⓓ
19. _____ _____
    _____
20. Ⓐ Ⓑ Ⓒ Ⓓ
21. Ⓐ Ⓑ Ⓒ Ⓓ
22. Ⓐ Ⓑ Ⓒ Ⓓ
23. Ⓐ Ⓑ Ⓒ Ⓓ
24. Ⓐ Ⓑ Ⓒ Ⓓ
25. Ⓐ Ⓑ Ⓒ Ⓓ
26.
27. Ⓐ Ⓑ Ⓒ Ⓓ
28. Ⓐ Ⓑ Ⓒ Ⓓ
29. Ⓐ Ⓑ Ⓒ Ⓓ

30.
The humorous story	The comic story

31. Ⓐ Ⓑ Ⓒ Ⓓ
32. Ⓐ Ⓑ Ⓒ Ⓓ

Section III Reasoning Through Language Arts

33. _____ _____

_____

34. ☐ → ☐ → ☐ → ☐

35. Ⓐ Ⓑ Ⓒ Ⓓ
36. Ⓐ Ⓑ Ⓒ Ⓓ
37. Ⓐ Ⓑ Ⓒ Ⓓ
38. Ⓐ Ⓑ Ⓒ Ⓓ
39. Ⓐ Ⓑ Ⓒ Ⓓ

40. _____

41. Ⓐ Ⓑ Ⓒ Ⓓ

42. For each of the following four menus circle the option that correctly completes the sentence.

earn him
earns him
earn them
earns them
party, ceremoniously, Ron will present the password for his workstation
party Ron's presentation of the password for his workstation will be ceremonious
party, Ron will ceremoniously present the password for his workstation
party, Ron's workstation will have its password ceremoniously presented
colleagues and project managers and his
colleagues and project managers. His
colleagues, his project managers, and, his
colleagues, his project managers, and his
Company,
company's
companies'
companies

Section III Reasoning Through Language Arts

43. Ⓐ Ⓑ Ⓒ Ⓓ
44. Ⓐ Ⓑ Ⓒ Ⓓ
45. Ⓐ Ⓑ Ⓒ Ⓓ

46. Write your answers in the blanks below.

President Taft's Address

_____

_____

E.T. Allen's Report

_____

_____

47. Ⓐ Ⓑ Ⓒ Ⓓ
48. Ⓐ Ⓑ Ⓒ Ⓓ
49. Ⓐ Ⓑ Ⓒ Ⓓ
50. Ⓐ Ⓑ Ⓒ Ⓓ

Part I Mathematical Reasoning

1. Ⓐ Ⓑ Ⓒ Ⓓ
2. Ⓐ Ⓑ Ⓒ Ⓓ
3. _____
4. Ⓐ Ⓑ Ⓒ Ⓓ
5. _____

Part II Mathematical Reasoning

6. Ⓐ Ⓑ Ⓒ Ⓓ
7. Ⓐ Ⓑ Ⓒ Ⓓ
8. _____
9. Ⓐ Ⓑ Ⓒ Ⓓ
10. Ⓐ Ⓑ Ⓒ Ⓓ
11. Ⓐ Ⓑ Ⓒ Ⓓ
12. Ⓐ Ⓑ Ⓒ Ⓓ
13. Ⓐ Ⓑ Ⓒ Ⓓ

Part II Continued

14. and 15.

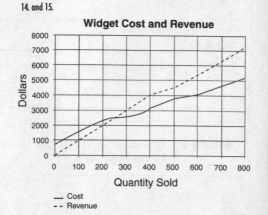

Widget Cost and Revenue

— Cost
-- Revenue

16. Write your answers in the blanks below.

_____

_____

17. Ⓐ Ⓑ Ⓒ Ⓓ
18. Ⓐ Ⓑ Ⓒ Ⓓ
19. Ⓐ Ⓑ Ⓒ Ⓓ
20. Ⓐ Ⓑ Ⓒ Ⓓ
21. Ⓐ Ⓑ Ⓒ Ⓓ
22. Ⓐ Ⓑ Ⓒ Ⓓ
23. Ⓐ Ⓑ Ⓒ Ⓓ
24. Ⓐ Ⓑ Ⓒ Ⓓ
25. _____

26. Write your answers in the blanks below.

_____

_____

_____

27. Ⓐ Ⓑ Ⓒ Ⓓ
28. Ⓐ Ⓑ Ⓒ Ⓓ
29. Ⓐ Ⓑ Ⓒ Ⓓ
30. Ⓐ Ⓑ Ⓒ Ⓓ

31.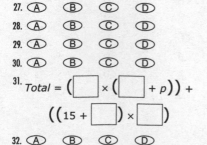

$$Total = (\boxed{} \times (\boxed{} + p)) + ((15 + \boxed{}) \times \boxed{})$$

32. Ⓐ Ⓑ Ⓒ Ⓓ

33. Write your answers in the blanks below.

_____

_____

_____

The Princeton Review®

© 2018 by TPR Education IP Holdings, LLC.

Part II   Continued

34. Ⓐ Ⓑ Ⓒ Ⓓ

35.

Migration Sightings			
Bird Type	2008	2009	2010
Cardinal	24	31	
Finch	40	37	
Grosbeak	19	23	
Harrier	31	38	
Sparrow	28	24	

36. Ⓐ Ⓑ Ⓒ Ⓓ
37. Ⓐ Ⓑ Ⓒ Ⓓ
38. Ⓐ Ⓑ Ⓒ Ⓓ
39. _____
40. Ⓐ Ⓑ Ⓒ Ⓓ
41. Ⓐ Ⓑ Ⓒ Ⓓ
42. Ⓐ Ⓑ Ⓒ Ⓓ
43. _____
44. _____
45. Ⓐ Ⓑ Ⓒ Ⓓ
46. Ⓐ Ⓑ Ⓒ Ⓓ

Social Studies

1. Ⓐ Ⓑ Ⓒ Ⓓ
2. Ⓐ Ⓑ Ⓒ Ⓓ
3. Ⓐ Ⓑ Ⓒ Ⓓ
4.

Yes	No

5. Ⓐ Ⓑ Ⓒ Ⓓ
6. Ⓐ Ⓑ Ⓒ Ⓓ
7. Ⓐ Ⓑ Ⓒ Ⓓ
8. Ⓐ Ⓑ Ⓒ Ⓓ
9. Ⓐ Ⓑ Ⓒ Ⓓ
10. Ⓐ Ⓑ Ⓒ Ⓓ
11. Ⓐ Ⓑ Ⓒ Ⓓ

Social Studies   Continued

12. Ⓐ Ⓑ Ⓒ Ⓓ
13. Ⓐ Ⓑ Ⓒ Ⓓ
14. Ⓐ Ⓑ Ⓒ Ⓓ
15. Ⓐ Ⓑ Ⓒ Ⓓ
16. Ⓐ Ⓑ Ⓒ Ⓓ
17. Ⓐ Ⓑ Ⓒ Ⓓ
18. Ⓐ Ⓑ Ⓒ Ⓓ
19. Ⓐ Ⓑ Ⓒ Ⓓ
20. Ⓐ Ⓑ Ⓒ Ⓓ
21. Ⓐ Ⓑ Ⓒ Ⓓ
22. Ⓐ Ⓑ Ⓒ Ⓓ
23. Ⓐ Ⓑ Ⓒ Ⓓ
24. Ⓐ Ⓑ Ⓒ Ⓓ
25. Ⓐ Ⓑ Ⓒ Ⓓ
26. Ⓐ Ⓑ Ⓒ Ⓓ
27. Ⓐ Ⓑ Ⓒ Ⓓ
28. Ⓐ Ⓑ Ⓒ Ⓓ
29. Ⓐ Ⓑ Ⓒ Ⓓ
30. Ⓐ Ⓑ Ⓒ Ⓓ
31. Ⓐ Ⓑ Ⓒ Ⓓ
32. Ⓐ Ⓑ Ⓒ Ⓓ
33. Ⓐ Ⓑ Ⓒ Ⓓ
34.

Yes	No

35. Ⓐ Ⓑ Ⓒ Ⓓ

Science

1. Ⓐ Ⓑ Ⓒ Ⓓ
2. Ⓐ Ⓑ Ⓒ Ⓓ
3. Ⓐ Ⓑ Ⓒ Ⓓ
4. Ⓐ Ⓑ Ⓒ Ⓓ
5. _____
6. Ⓐ Ⓑ Ⓒ Ⓓ
7. Write your short-answer response on a separate sheet of paper.
8. Ⓐ Ⓑ Ⓒ Ⓓ
9. Ⓐ Ⓑ Ⓒ Ⓓ
10. Ⓐ Ⓑ Ⓒ Ⓓ
11. _____
12. Ⓐ Ⓑ Ⓒ Ⓓ
13. Ⓐ Ⓑ Ⓒ Ⓓ
14. Ⓐ Ⓑ Ⓒ Ⓓ
15. Ⓐ Ⓑ Ⓒ Ⓓ
16. _____
17. Ⓐ Ⓑ Ⓒ Ⓓ
18. Ⓐ Ⓑ Ⓒ Ⓓ

19.

The element with an atomic weight of 16:	The element with an atomic number of 7:	The element with an atomic weight of 12:

20. Ⓐ Ⓑ Ⓒ Ⓓ
21. Ⓐ Ⓑ Ⓒ Ⓓ
22. Ⓐ Ⓑ Ⓒ Ⓓ
23. Ⓐ Ⓑ Ⓒ Ⓓ
24. Ⓐ Ⓑ Ⓒ Ⓓ
25. □ → □ → □ → □ → □
       1.   2.   3.   4.   5.
26. Write your short-answer response on a separate sheet of paper.
27. Ⓐ Ⓑ Ⓒ Ⓓ
28. Ⓐ Ⓑ Ⓒ Ⓓ
29. Ⓐ Ⓑ Ⓒ Ⓓ
30. Write your answers in the blanks below.

_____

_____

31. Ⓐ Ⓑ Ⓒ Ⓓ
32. Ⓐ Ⓑ Ⓒ Ⓓ
33. Ⓐ Ⓑ Ⓒ Ⓓ
34. Ⓐ Ⓑ Ⓒ Ⓓ
35. Ⓐ Ⓑ Ⓒ Ⓓ